International Handbook of Work and Health Psychology

'The timing of this Handbook could not be better. Now the World's economies appear to be starting to recover from Global Financial Crash, there will be a stronger need than ever for organizations to manage the health of their employees. Financial stringency, longer hours, demands for performance all contribute to stress and, unless managed appropriately, can result in negative health outcomes. What I really like about this book, therefore, is its increased emphasis on positive outcomes. It's not all doom and gloom. Based on the latest evidence-based research, the authors of the chapters in the Handbook provide a positive agenda for improving workplace health and well-being.'

Neal M. Ashkanasy, Professor of Management, The University of Queensland, Australia

'Health is a key driver of economic growth and an invaluable resource. This new edition of the Handbook of Work and Health Psychology is very timely in reflecting the important economic and social changes which have impacted on the nature of work, work organization and employee health and well-being in recent years.'

'In particular, the book highlights the key importance of an organizational strategy for health improvement build around intervention and prevention. The book is an excellent up-to-date resource for those interested or working in the area of occupational psychology and health.'

Professor Susan Cartwright, Centre for Organizational Health and Well Being, Lancaster University, UK

International Handbook of Work and Health Psychology

Third Edition

Edited by

Cary L. Cooper, James Campbell Quick and Marc J. Schabracq

WILEY Blackwell

This paperback edition first published 2015
© 2009 John Wiley & Sons, Ltd.

Edition history: John Wiley & Sons, Ltd. (hardback, 2009)

Registered Office
John Wiley & Sons Ltd, The Atrium, Southern Gate, Chichester, West Sussex, PO19 8SQ, UK

Editorial Offices
350 Main Street, Malden, MA 02148-5020, USA
9600 Garsington Road, Oxford, OX4 2DQ, UK
The Atrium, Southern Gate, Chichester, West Sussex, PO19 8SQ, UK

For details of our global editorial offices, for customer services, and for information about how to apply for permission to reuse the copyright material in this book please see our website at www.wiley.com/wiley-blackwell.

The right of Cary L. Cooper, James Campbell Quick and Marc J. Schabracq to be identified as the authors of the editorial material in this work has been asserted in accordance with the UK Copyright, Designs and Patents Act 1988.

Wiley also publishes its books in a variety of electronic formats. Some content that appears in print may not be available in electronic books.

100746621 5

Designations used by companies to distinguish their products are often claimed as trademarks. All brand names and product names used in this book are trade names, service marks, trademarks or registered trademarks of their respective owners. The publisher is not associated with any product or vendor mentioned in this book.

Library of Congress Cataloging-in-Publication Data

Cooper, Cary, L.
  International handbook of work and health psychology / edited by Cary L. Cooper, James Campbell Quick, Marc J. Schabracq. – 3rd ed.
    p. cm.
  Previous edition, published in 2003, has title: The handbook of work and health psychology.
  Includes index.
  ISBN 978-0-470-99806-9 (cloth) 978-1-119-05700-0 (paper)
1. Psychology, Industrial.   2. Job stress.   3. Employees–Mental health.   4. Stress management.
5. Employees–Counseling of.   I. Cooper, Cary L.   II. Quick, James C.   III. Schabracq, Marc.
IV. Handbook of work and health psychology.   V. Title.
  HF5548.8.H26313 2009
  158.7–dc22

                                              2009023914

A catalogue record for this book is available from the British Library.

Cover image: © Rob Melnychuk/Getty

Set in 11.5/13.5 Times by SPi Publisher Services, Pondicherry, India
Printed and bound in Malaysia by Vivar Printing Sdn Bhd

1   2015

Contents

About the Editors

Cary L. Cooper is Distinguished Professor of Organizational Psychology and Health at Lancaster University, UK. He is the author/editor of over 120 books (on occupational stress, women at work and industrial and organizational psychology), has written over 400 scholarly articles for academic journals, and is a frequent contributor to national newspapers, TV and radio. He is Founding Editor of the *Journal of Organizational Behavior* and Editor-in-Chief of the medical journal *Stress & Health*. Professor Cooper is President of the British Association of Counselling and Psychotherapy, the Chair of the Academy of Social Sciences and Chair of The Sunningdale Institute in the National School of Government. In 2001, Cary was awarded a CBE in the Queen's Birthday Honours List for his contribution to occupational safety and health. He holds Honorary Doctorates from Aston University (DSc), Heriot-Watt University (DLitt), Middlesex University (Doc. Univ) and Wolverhampton University (DBA); an Honorary Fellowship of the Faculty of Occupational Medicine in 2005, was awarded an Honorary Fellowship of the Royal College of Physicians (Hon FRCP) in 2006, a Lifetime Achievement Award from the Division of Occupational Psychology of the British Psychological Society in 2007 and an Honorary Fellow of the Royal College of Physicians of Ireland (occupational medicine) in 2008.

James Campbell Quick is John and Judy Goolsby Distinguished Professor, Goolsby Leadership Academy at The University of Texas at Arlington and Visiting Professor, Lancaster University Management School, UK. He is a Fellow of SIOP, APA and American Institute of Stress. He was honoured with a 2001 American Psychological Association Presidential Citation and the 2002 Harry and Miriam Levinson Award. He and his brother Jonathan originated preventive stress management, a term included in the 2007 APA Dictionary of Psychology. He has over 100 publications in 10 languages and holds a 2009 University Award for Distinguished Record of Research. Colonel (Ret) Quick was awarded The Legion of Merit and the Meritorious Service Award by United States Air Force. Dr. Quick was recognized with the Maroon Citation by Colgate University and the Edward J. Reifstack Character Award by the National Honor Society. He is married to the former

Sheri Grimes Schember; both are members of the Chancellor's Council of the University of Texas System; the Silver Society, American Psychological Foundation; and the President's Club of Colgate University.

Marc J. Schabracq (1949, Amsterdam, The Netherlands) is a work and health psychologist. As an independent organizational consultant, Marc Schabracq has acquired much experience with the human aspect of change in organizations (organizational culture change, personal transitions, stress management, leadership and ethics) in a great number of profit and non-profit organizations. In addition, he has worked at the University van Amsterdam from 1973 to 2008, subsequently at clinical psychology, social psychology and – since 1987 – work and organizational psychology. He has produced more than 20 scholarly and professional books about psychology, as well as more than 100 articles and book chapters. In addition, he wrote 3 novels and a bundle of short stories.

Cary L. Cooper
James Campbell Quick
Marc J. Schabracq

List of Contributors

Galit Armon, *Faculty of Management, Tel Aviv University, Ramat Aviv, PO Box 39010, Tel Aviv 69978, Israel*

Mark Attridge, *Attridge Studios, Minneapolis, USA*

Yehuda Baruch, *Group & Organization Management, Norwich Business School, UEA, UK*

Myrtle P. Bell, *Department of Management, The University of Texas at Arlington, Box 19467, Arlington, TX 76019-0467, USA*

Shlomo Berliner, *Tel-Aviv Sourasky Medical Center, Israel*

Caroline Biron, *Lancaster University Management School, Lancaster University, UK*

Ronald J. Burke, *York University, UK*

Neil Conway, *Birkbeck, University of London, UK*

Faye Cocchiara, *Department of Management and Marketing, Arkansas State University Jonesboro, PO Box 59, State University, AR 72467, USA*

Cary L. Cooper, *Lancaster University Management School, Lancaster University, Lancaster, LA1 4YW, UK*

Carla Dunahoo, *Dunahoo Psychological Associates LLC, USA*

Pamela A. Geller, *Drexel University, USA*

Siegfried Greif, *University of Osnabrück, Germany*

David Guest, *King's College London, UK*

Laura Guillén Ramo, *INSEAD, France*

Kai-Christoph Hamborg, *University of Osnabrück, Germany*

Stevan E. Hobfoll, *Rush Medical College, USA*

Manfred Kets de Vries, *INSEAD, France*

Rolf J. Kleber, *Utrecht University, The Netherlands*

Konstantin Korotov, *European School of Management and Technology, Germany*

Michael P. Leiter, *Centre for Organizational Research & Development, Acadia University, Wolfville, NS, B4P 2R6, Canada*

Rosemary Maellaro, *University of Dallas, Graduate School of Management, 7460 Warren Parkway, #100 Frisco, TX 75024, USA*

Laurenz L. Meier, *University of Bern, Department of Psychology Muesmattstr. 45, 3012 Bern, Switzerland*

Samuel Melamed, *Tel Aviv-Yaffo Academic College, and Department of Epidemiology and Preventive Medicine, Sackler Faculty of Medicine, Tel Aviv University, Israel*

Ben Moss, *Robertson Cooper Ltd, Williams House, Manchester Science Park, Lloyd Street North, Manchester M15 6SE, UK*

Stephen Palmer, *Centre for Stress Management, London, UK*

James Campbell Quick, *Goolsby Leadership Academy, The University of Texas at Arlington, PO Box 19377, Arlington, TX 76019-0377, USA*

Astrid M. Richardsen, *BI Norwegian School of Management, Norway*

Per Øystein Saksvik, *Norwegian University of Science and Technology (NTNU), Norway*

Marc J. Schabracq, *Human Factor Development, The Netherlands*

Norbert K. Semmer, *University of Bern, Department of Psychology Muesmattstr. 45, 3012 Bern, Switzerland*

Itzhak Shapira, *Tel-Aviv Sourasky Medical Center, Tel-Aviv, and Sackler Faculty of Medicine, Tel-Aviv University, Israel*

Arie Shirom, *Faculty of Management, Tel Aviv University, Ramat Aviv, PO Box 39010, Tel Aviv 69978, Israel*

Iva Smit, *E&E Consultants, Netterden, The Netherlands 7077*

Paul E. Spector, *Department of Psychology, University of South Florida, PCD 4118 Tampa, FL 33620, USA*

Naomi Stright, *Centre for Organizational Research & Development, Acadia University, Wolfville, NS, B4P 2R6, Canada*

Töres Theorell, *Karolinska Institute Stockholm, Sweden*

Gordon Tinline, *Robertson Cooper Ltd, Williams House, Manchester Science Park, Lloyd Street North, Manchester M15 6SE, UK*

Peter G. van der Velden, *Institute for Psychotrauma, The Netherlands*

J. Lee Whittington, *University of Dallas, Graduate School of Management, 7460 Warren Parkway, #100 Frisco, TX 75024, USA*

Helen Williams, *SHL People Solutions, UK*

CHAPTER 1

Introduction

Cary L. Cooper
Lancaster University, UK
James Campbell Quick
The University of Texas at Arlington, USA
and
Marc J. Schabracq
Human Factor Development, The Netherlands

1.1 THE THIRD EDITION

Since the publication of the first edition of this book in 1996 through 2003 when the revised edition was published, there were dramatic changes in the world as a context for business organizations. There have continued to be such changes since 2003. In Section 1.2 we explore the context of work and health psychology, with an eye to the past, attention to the present, and a focus on the future. Time is an increasingly necessary dimension in the world of work. Learning from the past while being anchored in the present is important for a positive, healthy dose of reality. However, the future is the stuff of imagination and dreams, which are every bit as vital to psychological health and the advancement of work activities. We believe that healthy, productive people and companies are ones that know where they have been, where they are, and where they are going. So much for the context of time for the moment!

As editors, we continue to be proud of and happy with this third edition of the *Handbook*, celebrating 13 years of life and vitality. The *Handbook* has changed yet again in this third edition, as well it should. It has been updated with the latest research findings by those on the cutting edge of the science, and yes the practice, of work and health psychology. We have authors who have been with us from the outset as well as a number of new authors who add their own perspectives and points of view to enrich the work. Through

International Handbook of Work and Health Psychology, Third Edition. Edited by Cary L. Cooper, James Campbell Quick, and Marc J. Schabracq.
© 2009 John Wiley & Sons, Ltd. Published 2015 by John Wiley & Sons, Ltd.

the revision process we have thus maintained continuity by being faithful to the past, invited new authors whose present work is enriching our field, and kept our focus on the future directions in which our discipline is unfolding.

In Section 1.3, we present a short overview of the book. This overview provides a preview of what is to unfold through the five parts and 20 chapters that are included in the third edition of the *Handbook*.

1.2   THE CONTEXT OF WORK AND HEALTH PSYCHOLOGY

Context is vitally important to the profession and practice of any discipline. For our purposes, we have chosen time as the dimension within which to place this third edition of the *Handbook*. As we learn in Ecclesiastes, for everything there is a season and a time for every matter. Therefore, let us explore the context of this third edition by looking first at the past, then at our attention to the present, and finally focusing our gaze on the future.

1.2.1   The Past

Since the first edition of this *Handbook* in 1996, the world of work has gone through enormous changes. We have moved from the entrepreneurial 1990s, where we lived and worked in boom times. During these years, jobs in the developed world at least were relatively secure or the opportunities of job mobility were good, as economies in Europe, North America and the Far East were growing. Although the stress levels were high, as there were fewer people doing more work to meet international competition to keep labour costs to a minimum, the opportunities to move from sector to sector or to create new businesses, given the availability of capital, was ever present.

Then at the beginning of the new millennium, we had the emergence of the BRIC economies of Brazil, Russia, India and China. Competition between these countries and other emerging economies, and the existing developed world of Western Europe and North America, grew even faster and more furious. This has meant in the West a more bottom-line management or micro managing of people at work, a higher use of technology and the consequent downsizing of staff and greater demands on employees to work longer and more unsocial hours to achieve the business objectives (why work–life balance issues began to emerge in employee surveys throughout the West). The demands on employees to be more fully committed, to 'allow' work to spill over into their personal and family life, to take on unmanageable workloads with difficult-to-achieve deadlines, have meant that 'real', consequential stress began to emerge among many workforces. In 2007, the Sainsbury

Centre for Mental Health (2007) estimated that the cost of stress and mental ill health at work costs employers in the UK alone £25.9 billion annually. Researchers found that absenteeism costs £8.5 billion, presenteeism £15.1 billion and turnover £2.4 billion. Presenteeism (that is people turning up to work with stress and mental health problems but not delivering to their products or services) began to increase as jobs became less secure and people felt that they needed to turn up to work even if they felt ill, both physically or psychologically (Biron, Brun & Cooper, 2008).

So the psychological contract between the employer and employee of reciprocity in terms of commitment was being seriously eroded and broken, as organizations began to demand more from employees but without guaranteeing secure employment or a reasonable quality of working life.

The past decade has seen the emergence of new demands and stressors in work environments, most notably a rise in bullying, violence and sexual harassment; the emergence of uncivil behaviour in the politics and political behaviour at work; and the adverse effects of organizational injustice and unfair treatment of people (Pandey *et al.*, in press). Within this same decade, globalization has continued to be a rampant force in the world economy with productivity pressures and health insurance trends becoming increasingly important factors in occupational health psychology (Macik-Frey *et al.*, in press).

1.2.2 The Present

And then came the 'credit crunch' and recession, which dramatically changed the nature of work after nearly two decades of constant economic growth. Jobs are now no longer for life, mobility between sectors, organizations and countries is constrained, fewer people are doing even more work and the issues of work–life balance, reasonable working hours, participative/transformational management are now part of a past era of prosperity. Although the intrinsic job insecurity is high, the hours of work even longer and the impact on the health and well-being of people more problematic than at any time in the recent past, there is an opportunity of reflecting on where we were, where we are and where we should be in the future (Weinberg & Cooper, 2007). It is during times of hardship that we can explore options for the future by learning lessons from the past. This third edition attempts to do that, to focus on issues like the psychological contract at work, the impact of new technology on our lives and stress, on flexible working, on how we can help people in difficult times with coaching, counselling and support systems, on our experiences of individualism v. communalism in our working relationships, and on how our careers will be changing given the new era of constraint and dwindling resources and opportunities.

1.2.3   The Future

It is safe to say that we have, at the start of this millennium, all the ingredients of workplace stress: an ever-increasing workload with a decreasing workforce in a climate of rapid change and with control over the financing increasingly being exercised by governments. During the recession as well we will have less stability and more job insecurity. The end result over the next few years is that there will be fewer people doing more work, working longer and in more job-insecure environments. The pressures on all of us therefore are likely to get worse not better. Stress is here to stay and cannot be dismissed as simply a bygone remnant of the entrepreneurial 80s and 90s. The challenge for all of us working in the field of work psychology and health in the future is to understand a basic truth about human behaviour that developing and maintaining a 'feel good' factor at work and in our economies generally is not just about bottom-line factors. It is, or should be, in a civilized society, about quality of life issues as well, such as hours of work, family time, manageable workloads, control over one's work and career and some sense of job security.

1.3   THE OUTLINE

In the two previous editions of this *Handbook* we tended to concentrate on understanding the psychosocial factors in the workplace or the sources of stress, with some work on stress management or organizational change approaches to enhancing well-being and reducing ill health. In this new volume, although we will highlight some new work and health psychology problems, we will devote more emphasis on individual and organizational interventions and prevention.

The book is divided into five parts. Part I is an introduction, 'the context of work and health psychology today', exploring the changing nature of work, the psychological contract at work, the social context of work life, burnout and engagement and the impact of job strain on health. In this section we are attempting to highlight the context within which workplace well-being is being adversely affected. It features work on the significance of the psychological contract and then illustrates how job strain can play a significant role in illness, particularly cardiovascular disease in many countries, and we finish with an exploration of 'presenteeism', which is likely to be more prevalent during economic downturn.

Part II focuses on the individual, 'individual differences and health', comprising several chapters examining the link between individual differences, work stress and health outcomes, as well as work experiences and stress on the health between the genders.

Part III, 'the role of workplace factors on health', looks at the recent work on job control in well-being and employee health, new technologies on stress, the impact of different career patterns and well-being, flexibility at work and its impact on health and acute stress in the workplace.

Part IV explores how we should enhance individual well-being at work and manage unhealthy stress, 'supporting individuals', by highlighting approaches to developing the whole person through management development, then we introduce the rapidly growing field of coaching in organizations and the potential benefits for employee well-being. We assess different approaches to helping women cope with their increasing work–home interface demands and, finally, the impact of employee assistance programmes at work.

Part V explores what we can do at the organizational level, 'organizational approaches to health and well-being', by looking at organizational culture, leadership and change, building interventions to improve staff well-being and an approach to changing organizational cultures.

In the concluding Epilogue, we explore where we have to go from here, the challenges and obstacles in these difficult economic times. We highlight the research opportunities available. We hope you will find these contributions useful both in terms of your research agenda for the future and in your work to help people cope better with the excessive demands of work. Terkel (1972), after interviewing hundreds of US workers, summarized his feelings of work in this rather negative way, 'work is by its very nature about violence—to the spirit as well as to the body. It is about ulcers as well as accidents, about shouting matches as well as kicking the dog around. It is, above all (or beneath all), about daily humiliations. To survive the day is triumph enough for the walking wounded among the great many of us'. After that gloomy account, he turned to what 'work' could be, 'work is about a search for daily meaning as well as daily bread, for recognition as well as cash, for astonishment rather than torpor, in short, for a sort of life rather than Monday through Friday sort of dying'. That is our challenge for the future.

REFERENCES

Biron, C., Brun, J.-P. & Cooper, C. (2008). At work but ill: psychosocial work environment and wellbeing determinants of presenteeism propensity. *Journal of Public Mental Health*, **5**(4), 26–37.

Macik-Frey, M., Quick, J.D., Quick, J.C. & Nelson, D.L. (2009). Occupational health psychology: from preventive medicine to psychologically healthy workplaces. In A. Antoniou *et al.* (Eds), *Handbook of Occupational Health Psychology and Medicine*. Cheltenham: Edward Elgar.

Pandey, A., Quick, J.C., Rossi, A.M., Nelson, D.L. & Martin, W. (in press). Stress and the workplace: ten years of science, 1997–2007. In A. Baum (Ed.), *Handbook of Stress Science*. Springer.

Sainsbury Centre for Mental Health (2007). *Mental Health at Work: Developing the Business Case*. London: Sainsbury Centre for Mental Health.

Terkel, S. (1972). *Working*. New York: Avon Books.

Weinberg, A. & Cooper, C.L. (2007). *Surviving the Workplace: A Guide to Emotional Well-being*. London: Thomson.

PART I

The Context of Work and Health Today

CHAPTER 2

Health and Well-Being: The Role of the Psychological Contract

David Guest

King's College London, UK

and

Neil Conway

Birkbeck, University of London, UK

2.1 INTRODUCTION

The psychological contract has become a widely used analytic construct that has proved useful in explaining certain employee attitudes and work behaviour. In this chapter we describe how it has been used to explore a range of employee outcomes including aspects of health and well-being. The early sections of this chapter outline what is meant by the psychological contract and explain how it is potentially relevant to the study of health and well-being at work. We then present an analytic framework within which to review evidence about the association between the psychological contract and a range of employee outcomes. That evidence is drawn from a wide range of sources but we give some emphasis to recent work that has focused in particular on the link between the psychological contract and employee well-being. Finally, we consider some of the policies and practices that might affect the psychological contract and, through this, work-related health and well-being.

International Handbook of Work and Health Psychology, Third Edition. Edited by Cary L. Cooper, James Campbell Quick, and Marc J. Schabracq.
© 2009 John Wiley & Sons, Ltd. Published 2015 by John Wiley & Sons, Ltd.

2.2   WHAT IS THE PSYCHOLOGICAL CONTRACT AND WHY IS IT RELEVANT TO THE STUDY OF EMPLOYEE HEALTH AND WELL-BEING?

The use of the term 'the psychological contract' first emerged in the 1960s. Argyris (1960), Levinson *et al.* (1962) and Schein (1965), among others, used it to describe the informal and implicit understanding that arose between a worker and the organization in which he or she worked. Schein, in his widely read book on organizational psychology, argued that a key to satisfaction and performance at work was a shared understanding between the worker and employer of what each expected from the other. He also accepted that the content of this exchange was important. Kotter (1973) tested and found some support for this proposition by showing that where a match existed, employees were more satisfied. In the present context, the work of Levinson *et al.* (1962) is particularly relevant. In their book, *Men, Management and Mental Health,* they provide a full elaboration of their view of the psychological contract, highlighting the often implicit and dynamic nature of mutual obligations that develop within the employment relationship. Central to their analysis is the assumption that mutual reciprocation of promises and expectations reinforces interdependencies and as long as these continue to be supported by fulfilment of this psychological contract, they will have a positive influence on the mental health of workers.

The more contemporary view of the psychological contract owes much to the work of Rousseau (1989, 1995) who offered a tighter set of general propositions about how it could usefully be defined. In contrast to earlier approaches that emphasized matching of mutual expectations, she argued that the psychological contract was best viewed only from the perspective of employees on the grounds that an organization cannot 'perceive', should not be anthropomorphized and therefore cannot have a psychological contract. Secondly, she emphasized promises, based on behaviour, rather than expectations that can arise from a variety of sources. Thirdly, she highlighted the importance of violation of the psychological contract as the mechanism whereby there is an influence on employee outcomes. She therefore defines the psychological contract as 'individual beliefs, shaped by the organization, regarding terms of an exchange agreement between the individual and their organization' (1995, p.9).

Rousseau's highly influential work has stimulated a considerable amount of research. However, each of the core elements is open to criticism (see, for example, Arnold, 1996; Guest, 1998; Meckler, Drake & Levinson, 2003; Conway & Briner, 2005; Cullinane & Dundon, 2006). Firstly, the argument that the psychological contract can only be viewed from the employee and not the employer perspective ignores the metaphor on which the concept is based and fails to recognize the role of managers as 'agents' of the organization as well as evidence that workers readily anthropomorphize their organization. The emphasis on promises provides a sharper focus but presents problems in drawing a boundary between promises, obligations and expectations and may fail fully to consider the importance of expectations and obligations that arise independently of any promise made by an organizational representative. Finally, while the emphasis on violation as the mechanism linking the psychological contract to attitudinal and behavioural outcomes again provides a distinctive focus for research, it presents both conceptual and operational problems. Conway and Briner (2002) have shown that breaches of the psychological contract are everyday events but are usually not in themselves sufficient to have any marked impact on attitudes and behaviour. Their research therefore supports the analysis by Morrison and Robinson (1997) in which they draw a distinction between breach and violation, the latter being more serious and entailing a significant emotional component. A further problem with a focus on violation of the psychological contract is that it presents difficulties in explaining the consequences of a positive fulfilment of the psychological contract. In the present context, it might help to explain reductions in well-being but is less able to explain improvements or to outline how organizations might enhance employee well-being.

The implication of this is that if the psychological contract is to prove useful in explaining both improvements as well as reductions in health and well-being, we need a conceptual framework that goes beyond that provided by Rousseau. European researchers have generally been less enthusiastic about following Rousseau's narrow view of the psychological contract. Instead, they have given more weight to an exchange-based model (Blau, 1964) that can incorporate what Gouldner (1960) has described as 'the norm of reciprocity'. Indeed some of Rousseau's more recent work (e.g. Dabos & Rousseau, 2004) has acknowledged the value of looking at both the individual and organizational perspective. We will therefore build on the definition of Herriot and Pemberton (1995) and define the psychological contract as 'the perceptions of both parties to the employment relationship, organisation and individual, of the reciprocal promises and obligations implied in that relationship' (Guest & Conway, 2004). We also need to develop a separate focus on fulfilment as well as violation of the psychological contract. However, having emphasized the importance of both parties to the psychological contract, much of what follows in this chapter will focus on the employees' perspective.

Why is the psychological contract likely to be useful in considering health and well-being at work? Firstly, it represents a potentially important mediator between managerial policy and practice and employee outcomes. Since it addresses the subjective perceptions of employees, it recognizes that it is not enough to link policy and practice to outcomes but that it is necessary to explore how they are perceived by employees as a first step in understanding their impact. Allied to this, it recognizes that it is not just a matter of whether management behaviour can be construed as more or less generous or benevolent; what is critical is how it stands up against the promises made, the obligations these entail and the expectation of what constitutes appropriate behaviour. A 20% pay rise may seem generous by some standards but it will not be perceived as such if a 50% rise had been promised.

A further feature of the psychological contract is that it is dynamic. It concerns a two-way exchange that can be modified by experience and by what Rousseau (2005) has described as I-Deals or individual and distinctive arrangements. In a context where greater emphasis is given to flexible work arrangements and to achieving work–life balance, the growth of individual and sometimes informal deals can become highly important for specific workers. At the same time, this can create a new set of problems because it raises issues of fairness and trust. Fairness can become an issue where one person arranges a specific deal that is not open to others; questions of trust can arise in the context of the dynamics of business life in which managers are frequently on the move within organizations. As a result, an implicit understanding with one manager may not carry over to her replacement, leading to the need for further negotiation and development of a new 'deal'. For this reason, it has been argued that it is useful for certain purposes to broaden the psychological contract to what can be termed 'the state of the psychological contract' (Guest, 2004). This incorporates an explicit analysis of fairness and trust alongside the fulfilment or violation of the psychological contract to provide a more complete understanding of the employment relationship. A broader perspective is particularly useful in a context where collective arrangements are declining, leaving a need for analytic frameworks within which to explore the emerging individualized employment relationship.

A further reason for utilizing the psychological contract is that it can be considered along a range of dimensions, thereby capturing some of the richness and complexity of the employment relationship. McLean Parks, Kidder and Gallagher (1998) identify several potentially relevant dimensions including its focus, time frame, stability, scope, tangibility and particularism, by which they mean the degree of what Rousseau (2005) terms idiosyncrasy. Although the logic behind this set of dimensions appears to be largely atheoretical, it does highlight both the flexibility and the potential complexity of psychological contracts. Two of the dimensions have been more extensively studied than the others. These are the breadth of the psychological contract, by which we mean the number of promises and commitments made and the focus, by which we mean the specific content. With reference to content, a conceptual distinction has been made between socio-emotional and more explicit transactional promises. Measures have been developed based on the assumption that this distinction is valid and important. However, they fail to take fully into account the idiosyncratic nature of psychological contracts. Although these dimensions have been widely studied (for a review see Conway & Briner, 2005), there is little understanding as to how they develop or what their consequences are. The dimensions may offer promising insight into understanding aspects of well-being, such as a lack of focus impacting role clarity, instability resulting in feelings of anxiety and insecurity, and so on. However, to date the main research interest has been directed to an assessment of the extent to which promises have been kept. While promises can be made from both sides, organization and employee, most of the research has focused on employee perceptions of organizational promises and commitments.

The final reason why the psychological contract is useful for understanding well-being is the breach concept. Dozens of studies support the basic finding that when employees report that their organization has breached their psychological contract (i.e., broken explicit or implicit promises), this results in negative outcomes for the employee and the organization. Researchers offer multiple explanations as to why breach affects outcomes and some of these are particularly relevant to well-being. For instance, breach by definition implies a discrepancy between promises and delivery, which mirrors similar discrepancy evaluations such as job dissatisfaction (Guest, 1998). Breach also involves depriving employees of some kind of rewards, which may thwart employee needs (e.g., Robinson & Rousseau, 1994). Breach is very likely to trigger feelings of inequity and feeling unsupported, which have both been found to affect well-being outcomes, such as job satisfaction (e.g., Cohen-Charash & Spector, 2001). Breach may also motivate employees to engage in certain types of behaviour, such as retaliation, bad-mouthing and cynicism, that may affect the well-being of others in the organization or disturb the affective climate (Bordia, Restubog & Tang, 2008). However, while breach offers a simple and intuitive explanation for negative well-being, it is less clear whether the opposite of breach, that is, psychological contract fulfilment, would account for positive well-being. At the least, we would expect that fulfilled psychological contracts avoid situations that can lead to negative well-being.

In summary, the psychological contract provides distinctive insights into the nature of the contemporary employment relationship, more particularly as that relationship becomes increasingly individualized. It serves as a useful mediating mechanism that can help to explain why and under what circumstances certain policies and practices have a greater or lesser impact on outcomes including work-related health and well-being. However, this claim needs to be supported by evidence. The following sections therefore review some relevant research findings.

2.3   RESEARCHING THE PSYCHOLOGICAL CONTRACT AND OUTCOMES

There are a range of potential outcomes from the psychological contract. In their meta-analysis of the consequences of breach of the psychological contract, Zhao *et al.* (2007) distinguish between attitudinal and behavioural outcomes. The dominant attitudinal outcomes that have been studied are job satisfaction, organizational commitment and intention to quit. Some studies have also used trust as an outcome (Bal, De Lange & Jansen, 2008). Behavioural outcomes include organizational citizenship behaviour, individual performance and actual quits. It is clear from these reviews that much of the research has focused on organizationally relevant outcomes and with the exception of job satisfaction have tended to ignore worker-related outcomes. Conway and Briner (2005) have provided a comprehensive review of these studies over the decade from the early 1990s when this type of study was flourishing. Most of them are cross-sectional and explore the relationship between a measure of the extent to which promises have been kept and the outcome under investigation. Breach or violation is therefore usually defined as the degree of non-fulfilment of promises. This has led to a neglect of psychological contract fulfilment and the potentially positive outcomes of this, except by reference to the negative outcomes of breach. There is a case for exploring the scope, the fulfilment and the violation of the psychological contract independently of each other to determine which has the greater impact.

Conway and Briner (2005) report the average correlations across the various, mainly North American studies. The association between psychological contract breach and organizational commitment is –0.32; with intention to quit it is 0.33; with actual quitting, where there are only a very few studies, it is 0.11; and with performance it is –0.19. As we noted, these studies are mostly cross-sectional. Perhaps encouragingly, the size of the association in the very few longitudinal studies is not markedly different from that in the cross-sectional research. There is also a large cluster of studies that explore the association with job satisfaction, a variable that comes closer to employee well-being, and the average correlation with breach is –0.46. This pattern of findings between breach and outcomes was confirmed by the two recent meta-analyses (Bal, De Lange & Jansen, 2008; Zhao *et al.*, 2007). Taken together, these studies confirm an association between the psychological contract and various outcomes. Too often, they fail to take account of other possible influences on these outcomes, potentially exaggerating the size of the psychological contract effect. They are also only tangentially relevant to employee well-being through their focus on job satisfaction.

2.4 STUDIES OF THE PSYCHOLOGICAL CONTRACT AND WELL-BEING

In a regular series of surveys of the UK working population, Guest and Conway have explored the state of the employment relationship through the lens of the psychological contract. Two of the surveys (Guest & Conway, 2002, 2004) paid some particular attention to aspects of health and well-being. In this section we present some of the relevant findings. In each case, the data are based on responses from a stratified random sample of employees in organizations employing 10 or more staff who were interviewed by telephone.

There are various ways in which work-related well-being can be defined (Warr, 2002; Guest, 2008). In this context, we build on the definition of Danna and Griffin (1999) who emphasize work-related satisfactions, non-work related satisfactions as affected by work, and general health. Warr (2002) argues that we need to go beyond satisfaction to a more positive concept of well-being reflecting what he sees as three dimensions, one of which relates to satisfaction while the others cover enthusiasm and contentment with their opposites of depression and anxiety. In other words, in the work context, we need to look at satisfaction plus these extra elements and to take account of the downsides such as stress.

Guest and Conway (2002) explored the association between the state of the psychological contract and stress. The state of the psychological contract was operationalized as the extent to which promises and commitments were fulfilled, the fairness of 'the deal' and the trust that management will continue to deliver it. Stress was measured through a standard global question used in the extensive Bristol surveys of stress (Smith, 2001) and a second related item. Of the sample, 25% reported that their jobs were very or extremely stressful compared with 39% who reported little or no work-related stress. A wide range of background, policy and job-related factors were taken into account and in a regression analysis they explained 18% of the variance in reported stress. The strongest beta weights were those associated with the amount of external control over the job (beta 0.18) and the state of the psychological contract (beta –0.17). The only other factors showing a highly significant association were gender (beta 0.13 for women) and working in the health service (beta 0.12). These results suggest that the psychological

Table 2.1 Perceptions of the impact of work experiences on health and well-being

	Very harmful	Somewhat harmful	No effect	Somewhat positive	Very positive
Your workload	7	30	48	12	3
The number of hours you work	7	27	54	9	4
Your job content – what you do on a day-to-day basis	4	22	55	15	4
Your work environment	6	23	46	18	8
The opportunities to use your skills	2	7	48	28	15
The amount of control you have over the work you do	1	12	43	27	16
The amount of support available at work	3	14	32	33	17
The amount of help available when you face a problem at work	3	14	25	37	21
The relationship you have with people at work	2	4	22	33	39

contract is a key factor associated with variations in reported levels of work-related stress, an important aspect of well-being at work.

The same survey also looked at features of work that workers perceived to have a harmful or a positive impact on health and well-being at work. The findings are presented in Table 2.1. The results show that the most typical response of workers is to claim that many features of work have no effect on their health or well-being. However, 37% believe their workload is harmful and 34% believe the hours they work are harmful. In contrast, 72% say relationships at work have a positive effect on their well-being and 58% cite the amount of help they get if they have a problem. While individual features of the experience at work may be harmful, it is likely to become more serious if there is a cumulative set of harmful experiences. We therefore examined the background factors associated with those who cited a higher number of factors as harmful rather than beneficial. In the regression analysis, three factors stood out as strong predictors. These were the state of the psychological contract (beta –0.25), organizational support (beta –0.16) and the level of external control (beta 0.10). This again confirms the key role of the state of the psychological contract in explaining perceptions of the damaging effect of aspects of work for health and well-being. By implication, it is not just the amount of workload or hours but whether the experience fits with what was promised in the job.

The same survey also explored wider aspects of well-being reflected in questions about work satisfaction, work–life balance and satisfaction with life as a whole. A range of background and work-related factors accounted for 41% of the variation in work satisfaction. The regressions showed that the main predictors were the state of the psychological contract (beta 0.26), the level of organizational support (beta 0.20) and the amount of external control over work (beta –0.17). The same background and work experience factors accounted for 20% of the variation in satisfaction with work–life balance with the strongest predictors being the state of the psychological contract (beta 0.18), the amount of external control (beta –0.18) and the hours worked (beta –0.17). The analysis showed that background and experience factors explained 15% of the variation in satisfaction with life as a whole. The main predictors were the amount of external control of their work (beta –0.16), whether the individual was single or divorced (beta –0.15) and the state of the psychological contract (beta 0.13).

These findings provide impressive support for the importance of the psychological contract since the analysis sets it in the context of a range of other possible influences on a number of indicators of well-being. It is notable that, in line with the Karasek (1979) model, external control over aspects of work has a negative effect on well-being. However, the psychological contract is consistently an important influence. The analysis confirms that as we move away from satisfaction with features central to work such as work satisfaction to life satisfaction the role of the psychological contract at work declines and the range of work-related factors can explain less of the variation in responses. Despite this, the psychological contract remains a key factor confirming again that it is the fulfilment or breach of promises rather than the policies and practices and other experiences at work that have a key influence. Finally, it is worth noting that very similar results were obtained when the questions were repeated in a subsequent survey (Guest & Conway, 2004).

A separate study reported by Guest and Clinton (2006) provides a much more in-depth analysis of the relationship between the psychological contract and work-related health and well-being. This research is the UK contribution to a wider seven-country European study of the relationship between employment contracts, the psychological contract and workers' well-being (Guest, Isaksson & De Witte, in press). In the context of health and well-being, it has two major advantages over many other studies. Firstly it explores various aspects of the psychological contract and secondly it explores a wide range of relevant outcomes. With respect to the psychological contract, the study obtained separate measures of the range or breadth of promises made, the fulfilment of promises, violation of promises and measures of fairness and trust that form part of the wider concept of the state of the psychological contract. Breadth and fulfilment were measured using a standard set of items and asking firstly whether a promise had been made by the organization and secondly whether it had been kept. Violation was explored using a new measure which asked about the extent to which the organization had or had not kept its promises recently and how this made people feel. They responded on a five-point strongly agree–strongly disagree scale about whether they felt happy, angry, pleased, violated, disappointed and grateful and an average score across these items was obtained. Fairness and trust were measured using items adapted from Guest and Conway (1998). This therefore provides some opportunity to establish which of these various elements has the strongest influence on outcomes. The outcomes included conventional issues such as job satisfaction and organizational commitment but also addressed several aspects of health and well-being at work including:

- Anxiety – contentment at work using a measure developed by Warr (1990).
- Depression – enthusiasm at work using another measure developed by Warr (1990).
- Irritation with work. A measure developed by Mohr *et al.* (2006).
- Physical health. A six-item measure developed by Ware (1999).
- Self-rated sickness absence.
- Self-rated sickness presence, a measure of the tendency to go to work even when not feeling well.

All the measures had satisfactory alpha scores.

The sample consisted of 642 workers drawn from three sectors: food manufacture, retail services and education. The aim in selecting this sample was to obtain a cross-section of different levels of employment from low skill to professional skills. The sample consisted of 62% women, had an average age of 37 and 20% belonged to a trade union. Given the focus of the study on employment contracts, 25% of the sample had temporary contracts although, contrary to expectations, temporary workers did not report poorer well-being. There were a large number of control variables covering organizational factors such as sector, size, trade union representation and individual factors ranging from standard biographical data to aspects of household income and household workload. The study also obtained measures of other possible work-related influences on health and well-being such as organizational support, features of the role such as autonomy and workload, job security, extent of choice of job, career and employment contract, and perception of career/job choices and alternatives.

The results confirm the importance of the psychological contract and in particular violation of the psychological contract. The strongest predictor of work-related anxiety was violation of the psychological contract (beta 0.41). Fulfilment of the psychological contract was not significant (beta –0.09) but a combined measure of fairness and trust was (beta –0.21). Results for the measure of depression–enthusiasm were very similar. Violation of the psychological contract was strongly associated with work-related depression (beta 0.41) as was the measure of fairness and trust (beta –0.20). There was again no association with the measure of fulfilment of the psychological contract (beta –0.08). The pattern of results for irritation at work was very similar but a little weaker (violation beta 0.31; fairness/trust beta –0.16; fulfilment beta –0.06).

This initial set of results confirms the strong association between violation of the psychological contract and some central measures of work-related well-being. This is not to deny the importance of other factors. For example organizational support, workload and more particularly greater experience of a set of human resource practices are also important. However, the psychological contract mediates the relationship between some of these and the measures of well-being.

Turning to the more health-related variables, on the measure of physical health, there is a significant association with violation of the psychological contract (beta –0.21) but not with any of the other psychological contract measures. Sickness absence is significantly associated with lower levels of fairness and trust (beta –0.13) and sickness presence is more strongly associated with the same measure (beta –0.23). None of the other measures associated with the psychological contract are significant. This suggests that we should not invariably assume that violation of the psychological contract is always the most important dimension of the construct. On the other hand, these data indicate that fulfilment of the psychological contract is less able to explain the various health and well-being outcomes. However, although we do not show it here, fulfilment of the psychological contract is associated with more central attitudinal variables such as organizational commitment and job satisfaction.

These two studies highlight the central role of the psychological contract in the analysis of work-related well-being. They appear to confirm a strong association, more particularly with violation of the psychological contract. As noted above, this does not deny the importance of other factors; but it does confirm that if promises are made and broken, then well-being can suffer. This raises the question of what kind of policies and practices are more likely to be associated with higher fulfilment and lower violation of the psychological contract.

2.5   POLICIES AND PRACTICES TO PROMOTE THE PSYCHOLOGICAL CONTRACT

If, as we have shown, the psychological contract is associated with work-related health and well-being, then it makes sense to develop policies and practices that are likely to promote fulfilment and more particularly prevent violation of the psychological contract. In the regular national surveys reported by Guest and Conway, we explored a range of organizational antecedents of the psychological contract. The findings were fairly consistent. Firstly, as we hinted above, those who report that they have experienced or have the opportunity to experience a wider range of human resource practices invariably report a more positive psychological contract. It appears that the presence of such practices creates some obligation on the part of the employer to keep their side of the exchange. Secondly, a friendly work climate with strong organizational support is consistently associated with a more fulfilled and less violated psychological contract. Thirdly, scope for direct involvement and participation in the work itself is consistently important.

In a separate study of the management of the psychological contract, Guest and Conway (2002) explored the employer's perspective based on a survey of over 1100 senior HR managers. They focused in particular on communication of the psychological contract and found that it was local communication of issues related to the work or to personal circumstances that were most likely to be associated with positive outcomes and that messages from senior levels such as exhortations from the chief executive and mission statements had much less impact. On the other hand, they did recognize the importance of messages communicated to those joining an organization and the implied promises and commitments that they contain. The key message in this context, familiar to all those who have explored the role of realistic job previews (Phillips, 1998), is 'don't make promises you can't keep'. It is worth bearing in mind that this is the assessment of managers but the evidence indicates that it is very likely to be strongly endorsed by the workforce. This suggests that a general context and climate can be created at senior levels, but it is the local 'agents' of the organization and the way they act to implement HR practices and to make and deliver promises that has the major bearing on a positive psychological contract and, through this, on employee well-being.

2.6 CONCLUSIONS

This chapter has outlined why the psychological contract is a useful analytic framework within which to explore aspects of work-related health and well-being. At the same time, most of the reported research has focused on outcomes that relate more to organizational concerns such as organizational commitment, intention to quit and organizational citizenship behaviour than to aspects of well-being. The exception is the extensive range of studies of the consequences of breach of the psychological contract for job satisfaction. The two meta-analyses and the more considered reviews of the evidence confirm that there is a strong association between breach of the psychological contract and lower job satisfaction.

The two studies described in more detail in this chapter expand the analysis to include data on well-being. They also confirm the powerful role of the psychological contract in general and the role of breach and more particularly violation of the psychological contract in affecting outcomes such as levels of anxiety and depression. There is also some survey evidence of a spillover into issues such as satisfaction with work–life balance and even with life as a whole.

Despite these promising findings, there are still areas of uncertainty in the theory and research on the psychological contract. The status of specific dimensions of the psychological and most notably the utility of any distinction between transactional and relational contracts and their link to outcomes has still not been convincingly established. The focus on breach and violation leaves a vacuum in relation to the role of psychological contract fulfilment in promoting well-being. Nevertheless, the relatively limited research on antecedents of fulfilment of the psychological contract and avoidance of breach point to the importance of the application of a range of human resource practices, of a supportive friendly organizational climate and of providing scope for a degree of personal control and participation at work. There is a need to extend this study of antecedents of the psychological contract as a further basis for developing policies and practices to promote well-being at work.

REFERENCES

Argyris, C. (1960). *Understanding Organizational Behavior*. Homewood, IL: Dorsey Press.

Arnold, J. (1996). The psychological contract: a concept in need of closer scrutiny. *European Journal of Work and Organizational Psychology*, 511–20.

Bal, P.M., De Lange, A.H. & Jansen, P.G.W. (2007). Psychological contract breach and job attitudes: a meta-analysis of age as a moderator. *Journal of Vocational Behavior*, **72**(1), 143–58.

Blau, P. (1964). *Exchange and Power in Social Life*. New York: John Wiley & Sons, Inc.

Bordia, P., Restubog, S. & Tang, R. (2008). When employees strike back: investigating mediating mechanisms between psychological contract breach and workplace deviance. *Journal of Applied Psychology*, **93**(5), 1104–17.

Cohen-Charash, Y. & Spector, P.E. (2001). The role of justice in organizations: a meta-analysis. *Organizational Behavior and Human Decision Processes*, **86**, 278–321.

Conway, N. & Briner, R. (2002). A daily diary study of affective responses to psychological contact breach and exceeded promises. *Journal of Organizational Behavior*, **23**, 287–302.

Conway, N. & Briner, R. (2005). *Understanding Psychological Contracts at Work: A Critical Evaluation of Theory and Research*. Oxford: Oxford University Press.

Cullinane, N. & Dundon, T. (2006). The psychological contract: a critical review. *International Journal of Management Reviews*, **8**(2), 113–29.

Dabos, G. & Rousseau, D. (2004). Mutuality and reciprocity in the psychological contracts of employees and employers. *Journal of Applied Psychology*, **89**, 52–72.

Danna, K. & Griffin, R. (1999). Health and well-being in the workplace: a review and synthesis of the literature. *Journal of Management*, **25**, 357–84.

Gouldner, A. (1960). The norm of reciprocity: a preliminary statement. *American Sociological Review*, **25**, 161–78.

Guest, D. (1998). Is the psychological contract worth taking seriously? *Journal of Organizational Behavior*, **19**, 649–64.

Guest, D. (2004). The psychology of the employment relationship: an analysis based on the psychological contract. *Applied Psychology: An International Review*, **53**, 541–55.

Guest, D. (2008). Worker well-being. In N. Bacon, P. Blyton, J. Fiorito & E. Heery (Eds), *Sage Handbook of Employment Relations*. Thousand Oaks, CA: Sage.

Guest, D. & Clinton, M. (2006). *Temporary employment contracts, workers' well-being and behaviour: evidence for the UK*. King's College, London. Working Paper.

Guest, D. & Conway, N. (1998). *Fairness at Work and the Psychological Contract*. London: CIPD.

Guest, D. & Conway, N. (2002). *Pressure at Work and the Psychological Contract*. London: CIPD.

Guest, D. & Conway, N. (2004). *Employee Well-being and the Psychological Contract*. London: CIPD.

Guest, D., Isaksson, K., & De Witte, H. (Eds), (in press). *Employment Contracts, Psychological Contracts and Worker Well-Being: An International Study*. Oxford: Oxford University Press.

Herriot, P. & Pemberton, C. (1995). *New Deals: The Revolution in Managerial Careers*. Chichester: John Wiley & Sons, Ltd.

Karasek, R. (1979). Job demands, job decision latitude and mental strain: implications for job design. *Administrative Science Quarterly*, **24**, 285–308.

Kotter, J. (1973). The psychological contract: managing the joining up process. *California Management Review*, **15**, 91–9.

Levinson, H., Price, C., Munden, K. & Solley, C. (1962). *Men, Management and Mental Health*. Cambridge, MA: Harvard University Press.

McLean Parks, J., Kidder, D. & Gallagher, D. (1998). Fitting square pegs into round holes: mapping the domain of contingent work arrangements onto the psychological contract. *Journal of Organizational Behavior*, **19**, 697–730.

Meckler, M., Drake, B. & Levinson, H. (2003). Putting psychology back into psychological contracts. *Journal of Management Inquiry*, **12**(3), 217–28.

Mohr, G., Muller, A., Rigotti, T., Aycan, Z. & Tschan, F. (2006). The assessment of psychological strain in work contexts: concerning the structural equivalency of nine language adaptations of the irritation scale. *European Journal of Psychological Assessment*, **22**, 198–206.

Morrison, E. & Robinson, S. (1997). When employees feel betrayed: a model of how psychological contract violation develops. *Academy of Management Review*, **22**, 226–56.

Phillips, J. (1998). Effects of realistic job previews on multiple organizational outcomes: a meta analysis. *Academy of Management Journal*, **41**, 673–90.

Robinson, S.L. & Rousseau, D.M. (1994). Violating the psychological contract: not the exception but the norm. *Journal of Organizational Behavior*, **15**, 245–59.

Rousseau, D. (1989). Psychological and implied contracts in organizations. *Employee Responsibilities and Rights Journal*, **2**, 121–39.

Rousseau, D. (1995). *Psychological Contracts in Organizations: Understanding Written and Unwritten Agreements*. Thousand Oaks, CA: Sage.

Rousseau, D. (2005). *I-Deals: Idiosyncratic Deals Employees Bargain for Themselves*. New York: M.E. Sharpe.

Schein, E. (1965). *Organizational Psychology*. Englewood Cliffs, NJ: Prentice-Hall.

Smith, A. (2001). Perceptions of stress at work. *Human Resource Management Journal*, **11**(4), 74–86.

Ware, J. (1999). SF-36 Health Survey. In M.E. Maruish (Ed.), *The Use of Psychological Testing for Treatment Planning and Outcomes Assessment* (2nd edn, pp. 1227–46). Mahwah, NJ: Lawrence Erlbaum.

Warr, P. (1990). The measurement of well-being and other aspects of mental health. *Journal of Occupational Psychology*, **63**, 193–210.

Warr, P. (2002). The study of well-being, behaviour and attitudes. In P. Warr, (Ed.), *Psychology at Work* (5th edn, pp. 1–25). London: Penguin.

Zhao, H., Wayne, S.J., Glibkowski, B.C. & Bravo, J. (2007). The impact of psychological contract breach on work-related outcomes: A meta-analysis. *Personnel Psychology*, **60**, 647–80.

CHAPTER 3

The Social Context of Work Life: Implications for Burnout and Work Engagement

Michael P. Leiter and Naomi Stright

Centre for Organizational Research & Development, Acadia University, Canada

The psychological connections of people with their work range from the drudgery of burnout to the vibrant experience of work engagement. Between these two extremes lies a continuum of experience that encompasses the more commonplace range of dull days and good days at work. A large body of research details a diverse set of environmental conditions that influence that experience. In this chapter we focus on social relationships at work. We consider research on employees' interactions with one another, with their organizational leaders, and with the larger organization. We consider the impact of unpleasant interactions on employees' emotional well-being and the benefit of social support at work. We conclude by reflecting on the potential of social relationships as targets for interventions designed to enhance the quality of work life.

3.1 DEFINITIONS AND BACKGROUND

Burnout is a chronic problem reflecting uneasy relationships between people and their work (Maslach & Leiter, 2005). It is a psychological syndrome involving three key dimensions: exhaustion–energy, cynicism–involvement, and inefficacy–efficacy (Maslach, Schaufeli & Leiter, 2001; Maslach & Leiter, 2008). Exhaustion captures feeling overextended, including depleted

International Handbook of Work and Health Psychology, Third Edition. Edited by Cary L. Cooper, James Campbell Quick, and Marc J. Schabracq.
© 2009 John Wiley & Sons, Ltd. Published 2015 by John Wiley & Sons, Ltd.

physical and emotional resources. Cynicism describes a detached response to various aspects of work. Finally, inefficacy describes feeling incompetent or nonproductive at work (Maslach, 2003). The opposite of burnout is work engagement: an energetic state of involvement with personally fulfilling activities that enhance a sense of personal efficacy (Leiter & Maslach, 1998). This chapter will reflect the second dimension of burnout, cynicism, which involves the interpersonal aspects of work.

3.2   PREDICTORS: DEMANDS, RESOURCES AND VALUES

Burnout relates to several organizational characteristics that we have organized under six key domains: workload, control, reward, community, fairness and values (Maslach & Leiter, 2008). This approach asserts that burnout occurs from a mismatch between the person and their workplace, in one or more of these six areas. The concept of a mismatch acknowledges that there is no single perfect work setting. Some people prefer specific direction in their work while others find close supervision to be oppressive. Some prefer busy workdays filled with client contact while others find those days chaotic and upsetting. Organizational surveys confirm this variety in preferences as they consistently demonstrate that workgroups include employees who are pleased with things as they are and employees who are highly dissatisfied or stressed with the current situation. Burnout is not a function solely of a person or of a work setting, but of a poor combination of a person with a specific work context. The six areas of work life are definitive in determining whether people will find matches or mismatches with their work.

Workload aggravates burnout through a mismatch of demands over resources. Employees judge that they lack the time, expertise, equipment or support staff necessary to address the requirements of the job. They feel especially burdened by demands that exceed legitimate expectations within their psychological contracts with work (Semmer *et al.*, 2007), but even legitimate demands become excessive in under-resourced situations. Employees may judge emotional labour as an illegitimate demand when it requires displaying emotions inconsistent with feelings (Brotheridge & Grandey, 2002). Exerting additional effort to address demands may deplete their physical, cognitive or emotional energy. Of the six areas of work life, workload has the closest relationship to exhaustion.

Control aggravates burnout when individuals lack the capacity to make decisions regarding resources or the authority to work in the most effective manner. A control mismatch is also evident when individuals have responsibilities that extend beyond their authority. The critical issue is whether

individuals or groups have authority and access to resources that are appropriate to their responsibilities.

Reward involves the lack of appropriate compensation or recognition for
the work that people do. The critical issues in reward vary with people
and with situations. A reward shortfall could be in terms of benefits, social
appreciation or intrinsic reward. Lack of reward is most closely related to the
dimension of inefficacy (Maslach, Schaufeli & Leiter, 2001).

Community exacerbates burnout when employees lack positive connections with others in the workplace. Connection with others serves as emotional support and instrumental assistance; it also makes the person feel a
part of a group with shared values. Some employees feel overwhelmed by too
much social contact while others may experience isolation. In this chapter
we will explore the community area extensively.

Fairness reflects employees' perception of organizational justice in their
work setting. Fairness involves questions of equity in workload or compensation or even-handed treatment on evaluations and promotions. Fairness
pertains to employees' evaluations about the outcomes of organizational
decisions – were they good or bad decisions? It also pertains to procedural justice or whether the process used in the decision reflects qualities of
openness and adherence to relevant criteria. Especially important in fairness
evaluations is relational justice or the consideration and respect shown during the decision-making process. Employees experience unfair treatment as
excluding them from the organizational community. They tend to recipro-
cate by distancing themselves away from the organization through a cynical
approach to work.

Value conflicts have a central role in the model. The primary issue is the
extent to which employees believe that their contribution to the organization
is furthering the employees' core values. This positive balance is more likely
when organization and employees share core values. Value congruence is
not simply a matter of good luck, but of a conscientious process of value
development and value clarification in organizational planning and in employees' integration into the workplace community. Values could involve
ethical or moral principles, aspirations or practices (Maslach, Schaufeli &
Leiter, 2001).

Leiter and Maslach (2004, 2005) integrated the six areas of work life
into a comprehensive model of burnout and work engagement. As displayed
in Figure 3.1, the model depicts the core elements underlying burnout as
measured by the Maslach Burnout Inventory – General Scale (MBI–GS;
Schaufeli et al., 1996) in positive terms: energy as the positive contrast to exhaustion; involvement as the positive contrast to cynicism; and efficacy as the
MBI–GS measures directly. Although other perspectives define work engagement as departing from the exact opposite of burnout, the qualities of vigour,

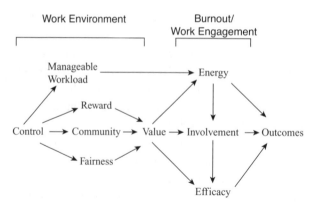

Figure 3.1   Model of burnout and work engagement.

dedication and absorption in the Utrecht Work Engagement Scale (UWES; Schaufeli & Bakker, 2004) have many similarities with these qualities.

The model includes two distinct pathways from the work environment to burnout/engagement. First, manageable workload arising from a sustainable balance of resources to demand has a direct and strong path to energy levels. Second, value incongruity has direct paths to energy, involvement and efficacy. This second route describes the proposition that value congruence with work has diverse implications. First, it builds energy by providing employees with the valuable resources inherent in doing work that reflects their values. Second, value congruence encourages employees to become deeply involved in their work activities. Third, doing work that furthers their core values builds confidence and assurance in themselves. In contrast, value conflicts undermine employees' psychological relationships with their work.

The model gives a pivotal position to control as shaping employees' capacity to manage their workloads or to pursue work they value. The intermediary constructs in these pathways include rewards systems, organizational justice as determining fairness, and community. Employees' interactions with their social environments regarding recognition, fairness or respect and values become integrated in their overall evaluation of value congruity or incongruity at work.

This chapter focuses primarily on the community area of work life: the overall quality of social interacting at work including issues of conflict, mutual support, closeness and the capacity to work as a team (Maslach & Leiter, 2008). When the community dimension is not working properly, problems arise and undermine the workplace climate. People are not happy; they are fighting with one another. Coworkers talk about other coworkers behind their back and blame each other for things that go wrong. A poorly functioning organizational community adds to employees' burdens at work without contributing anything positive. Poor collegial relationships constitute unnecessary workplace demands. Further, they actively block an essential workplace resource: the support of colleagues and immediate supervisors. In this chapter we will consider research on the social environments of work settings and consider approaches for improving that dimension of work life.

3.3 THE SOCIAL ENVIRONMENT OF WORK

3.3.1 Key People

The social environment of organizations comprises individuals in interaction with one another. As structured social environments, work settings include people who have equal levels of formal authority and people with unequal authority relationships. Work settings vary in intensity of collegial interaction with some embedded in closely knit teams and others working in relative isolation. Frontline supervisors guide the everyday tasks, while distant management oversees broader operations. In many organizations, the clientele makes up a crucial dimension of the work environment. For example, nurses, lawyers, receptionists, tellers, customer service representatives and teachers maintain ongoing interactions with service recipients throughout their work days.

3.3.2 Types of Interaction

Relationships with people at work have implications for demands, resources and values. On the positive side, people provide major work resources by contributing their time, expertise, effort and social support (Hobfoll, 2002). They assist one another in both organizational and personal objectives at work. The social environment of a workplace can provide one its most compelling attractions to employees (Casciaro & Lobo, 2005).

On the negative side, work relationships have their demanding characteristics. Regarding legitimate demands, supervisors impose tasks and deadlines while subordinates require direction and mentoring. Discussions with colleagues regarding work objectives consume project time. Illegitimate demands strain relationships more intensely. Aggression, abuse and incivility impose emotional pressures that exceed reasonable job requirements (Semmer *et al.*, 2007).

Both positive and negative relationships at work convey values. From an organizational culture perspective (Schein, 1988) employees evaluate values implicit in their interactions with the people, objects and activities at work. We propose that when colleagues persist in acting uncivilly, employees deduce that incivility serves as a condoned and effective way to contend with the demands within the work setting. Conformity to group norms provides one mechanism for incivility, as individuals blend into the accepted social discourse (Pinnington, 2002; Sechrist & Stangor, 2001). Reciprocity provides a second potential mechanism, as people mirror the tone of the interactions that they receive (Dabos & Rousseau, 2004). We propose that as employees encounter incivility from their colleagues, superiors and clients, they tend to respond in kind. Employees may give special considerations to their interactions with individuals in positions of authority when evaluating relationship norms at work. Observing or receiving incivility from supervisors or senior colleagues increases its legitimacy because of their status within the organization's hierarchies (Schein, 1988). Incivility may be inherent in an organization's power dynamics when people in authority or with seniority act uncivilly towards lower status people (Keashley, 1998; Vredenburgh & Brender, 1998). Through mechanisms of conformity and reciprocity, we expect employees to align their interpersonal behaviour to be consistent with their understanding of their organization's culture.

The social cultures of workplaces vary regarding civility, aggression and social support. Civility includes behaviour that preserves the norms of mutual respect at work; it comprises behaviours that are fundamental to connecting with others positively, building relationships and empathizing (Pearson, Andersson & Porath, 2000). Social support has a more active quality, including actions intended to help others (Deelstra et al., 2003). Aggression involves a clear intent for harm, including efforts by individuals to injure others (Baron & Neuman, 1996). Incivility has a less active quality than aggression. It includes rudeness and disregard towards others. It involves three main characteristics: norm violation; ambiguous intent to harm; and low intensity (Andersson & Pearson, 1999). As incivility becomes an accepted part of workplace culture, employees experience uncivil interactions as a value statement regarding their worth within the organizational community.

3.4   INCLUDING SOCIAL ENVIRONMENT INTO RESEARCH MODELS OF BURNOUT AND ENGAGEMENT

The social environment plays a vital role in a model of burnout and work engagement, in terms of its benefits such as social support (Harris, Winskowski & Engdahl, 2007; Kinnunen, Feldt & Mäkikangas, 2008; Baruch-Feldman et al., 2002; Elfering et al., 2002; Bakker et al., 2007; Etzion, 1984; Russell, Altmaier & Van Velzen, 1987), as well as its risks such as aggression of working within a social environment, (Mitchell & Ambrose, 2007; Kaukiainen *et al.*, 2001; Schat & Kelloway, 2000, 2003; Dupré & Barling, 2006; Baron & Neuman 1996), and incivility (Pearson, Andersson & Porath, 2000; Cortina *et al.*, 2001; Lim, Cortina & Magley, 2008; Cortina, 2008). As indicated by the wealth of literature on this question, social environments have received considerable attention within organizational research.

3.4.1   Research on Social Support

Social support provides a job resource with implications that span personal and organizational outcomes, such as job tenure or turnover intentions (Harris, Winskowski & Engdahl, 2007; Kinnunen, Feldt & Mäkikangas, 2008), productivity (Baruch-Feldman *et al.*, 2002), back pain (Elfering *et al.*, 2002) and most importantly for the purposes of this chapter, job burnout and work engagement (Bakker *et al.*, 2007; Etzion, 1984; Kinnunen, Feldt & Mäkikangas, 2008; Baruch-Feldman *et al.*, 2002; Russell, Altmaier & Van Velzen, 1987). These studies confirm that supervisor and coworker social support are crucial to a successful work environment, although there are various pathways to finding this effect.

3.4.2   Job Tenure/Turnover Intentions

Social support constitutes an important feature of the work environment with several pathways through which support may influence work-related outcomes. Harris, Winskowski and Engdahl (2007) investigated the impact of four types of social support on job tenure. Hill *et al.* (1989) defined these types as *task support* (the sharing and exchanging of work assignments and ideas), *career mentoring* (parent-like or adviser relationships with other individuals who have more experience), *coaching* (teaching organizational/professional rules and goals, including organizational politics), and *collegial social support* (sharing friendships, personal problems and confidences). They argued that each type provided valuable resources with implications for employees' success and well-being at work.

Harris *et al.* (2007) studied employees of two training hospitals in the USA to demonstrate that certain types of workplace social support predicted job tenure. Specifically, they found that coaching and task support predicted job tenure but career mentoring did not. Furthermore, they found that task support positively predicted job tenure whereas coaching negatively predicted job tenure. They explained the negative relationship between job tenure and coaching as arising from new employees seeking coaching to increase their familiarity with organizational rules and goals.

Kinnunen, Feldt and Mäkikangas (2008) considered three factors – perceived organizational support, effort–reward imbalance, and over-commitment – regarding their effect on turnover intentions and work engagement among Finnish managers. They found organizational support to be related negatively to turnover intentions and positively to work engagement. Overall, the study showed that organizational support was more important in determining the level of job attitudes and occupational well-being as compared to effort-reward imbalance or over-commitment. Together, these two studies provide consistent evidence that social support is an important resource which promotes work engagement and the decision to remain in the organization.

Thompson and Prottas (2005) focused on support for families as a specific organizational support for employees. They used data from the 2002 National Study of the Changing Workforce to investigate relationships between the availability of formal organizational family support (benefits and alternative schedules), job autonomy and informal organizational support (work–family culture, supervisor support and coworker support) on the dependent variables of perceived control, employee attitudes and well-being. Overall, formal organizational support, such as benefits and alternative schedules, had a minimal impact on the outcome variables, however, they found informal organizational support and job autonomy to have a large impact on the outcome variables. Specifically, informal social support and job autonomy related positively to job, family and life satisfaction as well as to positive spillover between job and home. They negatively related to stress, intentions to quit and work–family conflict. Further, perceived control was found to mediate the relationships between informal organizational support and job autonomy with the outcomes of turnover intentions, stress, job, family and life satisfaction, as well as work–family conflict. Employees with high informal organizational support and job autonomy had greater perceived control, which led to positive work and life outcomes. This study maintained the importance of social support at work to buffer negative work outcomes such as turnover intentions, stress and work–family conflict and to support satisfaction at home and at work.

3.4.3 Productivity

A recent trend in social support research is complementing its relevance to employees' well-being by considering its implications for productivity. Some research, (e.g., Baruch-Feldman *et al.*, 2002) supplemented self-reports of social support with other sources of information in a study of New York

City traffic enforcement agents. Overall, agents who felt well supported by all sources of support had moderate levels of burnout and job satisfaction. Results showed that family and unit supervisor support correlated negatively with burnout; the relationships between coworker support and immediate supervisor support with burnout were also negative, but non-significant. All forms of support were positively related to job satisfaction. Only immediate supervisor support was positively associated with productivity: immediate supervisor support accounted for almost 7% of the variance in productivity, after controlling for enforcement group and control variables.

Finally, average unit ratings of the supervisor did not predict burnout or job satisfaction. However, average unit ratings of immediate supervisor support were positively associated with productivity. This study strengthens the literature on social support by providing multi-source data supporting the contribution of social support to productivity, indicating the necessity of positive social support, specifically from the immediate supervisor, to the success of the organization.

3.4.4   Back Pain

Using an innovative perspective, Elfering *et al.* (2002) investigated constellations of social support from employees' closest colleagues and supervisors as predictors for back pain in 46 individuals with no previous back pain symptoms. Participants took part in a medical and psychological assessment at the onset including assessments on pain and disability, depression, biomechanical workload, social support and an MRI scan, and were retested after five years. Using this longitudinal design, they found supervisor support to be negatively related with the undesirable outcomes, and support from the closest colleague to be positively related with all of the outcome variables except one. The constellation involving high support from a close colleague and low support from the supervisor was found to predict the development of pain. The authors explained the discrepancy between supervisor and coworker social support by proposing that close colleagues may be more likely to empathize with the individual, showing sympathy and understanding that may inadvertently reinforce the complaint behaviour or create a dependency. This study maintained that support from supervisors is the most important predictor of positive work outcomes.

3.4.5   Work Engagement/Burnout

Social support has also been implicated in studies of work engagement and burnout. For example, Bakker *et al.* (2007) examined the relationship

between pupil misbehaviour and teacher job resources on job engage-
ment/burnout. Job resources included job control, supervisor support, information, organizational climate, innovativeness and appreciation. The study
demonstrated that supervisor support, innovativeness, information, appreciation and organizational climate buffered the relationship between negative
pupil behaviour and work engagement (and with job burnout). Specifically,
findings suggest that pupil misbehaviour was less damaging to teachers who
were receiving organizational or coworker support. The authors reasoned
that support serves as a coping resource for teachers. This study clearly indicates the need for offering teachers support when they are facing demanding
conditions such as pupil misbehaviour.

Similarly, Russell, Altmaier and Van Velzen (1987) investigated the relationship between job-related stressful events and various aspects (attachment, social integration, reassurance of worth, guidance, reliable alliance
and opportunity for nurturance) and sources of social support (supervisors,
coworkers, spouses and friends or relatives) among teachers at elementary
and secondary level. They found social support from supervisors to be the
only source of support that predicted burnout. Supervisor support also resulted in less exhaustion, more positive attitudes toward students and a greater
sense of personal accomplishment in teachers. In terms of aspects of social
support, assurance of worth and having a reliable alliance were found to be
important dimensions in predicting burnout.

Etzion (1984) examined the role of social support in buffering the relationship between stress (life and work) and burnout in men and women among
Israeli managers and social service professionals. Results showed a positive
relationship between stress (life and work) and burnout, and a negative relationship between social support (life and work) and burnout. Social support
moderated the effect of work stress (but not life stress) on burnout. Men
benefited from different sources of support than did women. Specifically,
supportive relationships in their work environment moderated men's work
stress, whereas non-work sources of support moderated women's stress. The
authors postulated that women talk more about their stress; therefore may
speak to others outside of their work. In contrast, men speak less about their
stress; therefore may speak to a support at work immediately, and not bring
it up again. This study shows further support of social support in buffering
burnout; and indicates a sex difference in the source of this support.

Together this research demonstrates the benefits of having positive social
support from supervisors at work. Such clear implications of the positive
outcomes of supervisor supports and the buffering of negative outcomes argues for targeting supervisor support in interventions aimed at decreasing
burnout and increasing engagement at work. The cost of non-intervention
may manifest itself through increased levels of burnout (Bakker *et al.*, 2007;

Etzion, 1984; Kinnunen, Feldt & Mäkikangas, 2008; Baruch-Feldman *et al.*, 2002; Russell, Altmaier & Van Velzen, 1987), decreased satisfaction at work and in life (Thompson & Prottas, 2005), increased turnover intention (Harris, Winskowski & Engdahl, 2007; Kinnunen, Feldt & Mäkikangas, 2008), decreased productivity (Baruch-Feldman *et al.*, 2002) and increased sick time due to back pain and other work problems (Elfering *et al.*, 2002).

3.4.6 Research on Aggression

Aggression is a serious type of workplace hazard with clear negative implications for the target of the behaviour, as well as the organization (i.e. Mitchell & Ambrose, 2007). Research has considered these negative outcomes (Mitchell & Ambrose, 2007; Kaukiainen *et al.*, 2001), factors that prevent or ameliorate aggression (Schat & Kelloway, 2000, 2003; Dupré & Barling, 2006), and its incidence in comparison to lesser forms of conflict, namely, incivility (Baron & Neuman 1996).

3.4.7 Negative Outcomes

Aggression in the workplace causes considerable problems for the target and the organizational environment. Mitchell and Ambrose (2007) investigated the relationship between aggression and three targets of deviance: deviance directed towards the supervisor, towards the organization, and towards coworkers among individuals called for jury duty by a circuit court in the Southeastern United States. They also factored in negative reciprocity beliefs (tendency to return negative treatment with negative treatment (Cropanzano & Mitchell, 2005), to examine its mediating role in the relationship. Although reported abusive supervision rates were found to be quite low among participants, it had powerful implications: abusive supervision was found to predict deviance at all three levels: supervisor-directed, organizational and interpersonal. Furthermore, negative reciprocity beliefs strengthened the relationship between supervisor abuse and supervisor-directed deviance. The results of this study indicated that abuse from a supervisor is extremely dangerous for an organization because it affects not only the target of this abuse, but undermines an organizational environment as well.

Kaukiainen *et al.* (2001) examined various types of aggression regarding their impact on employee well-being in mostly female, mostly male, or mixed work environments. Specifically, they investigated *direct overt aggression* (aggressor and perpetrator face to face; intention to harm is quite obvious); *indirect manipulative aggression* (perpetrator tries to cover his/her identity); *covert insinuative aggression* (perpetrator makes an effort to hide his/her intentions by applying strategies); and *rational-appearing aggression* (wrapping aggressive intentions into normal communication to disguise their harmful implications). They found direct aggression to be uncommon in everyday work settings and indirect manipulative and rational-appearing aggression to be the most common. They found being a target of aggression to be negatively related to well-being, especially among men. This result was evident regardless of the type of aggression: covert forms of aggression were found to have as great a negative impact as direct aggression. For male employees, but not female employees, rationale-appearing aggression had the strongest negative relationship to well-being. This study indicates the considerable negative effect of aggression on individuals as well as on the organization.

3.4.8   Preventing/Ameliorating Aggression

Knowing aggression's detrimental effects on employee well-being, the following research considered approaches to prevent or ameliorate the incidence of aggression in the workplace. Schat and Kelloway (2000) explored the role of employees' perceptions of control in ameliorating the negative outcomes associated with the experience of violence at work in a hospital setting. Results showed that perceived control did not offset the relationship of violence with fear, or the relationship of fear with emotional well-being, somatic health and neglect. However, they did find perceived control to be related directly with emotional well-being and indirectly to somatic heath and neglect (job withdrawal). Therefore, the authors recommended that training to enhance control would be effective in organizations where violence is known to be a problem. Unfortunately, they did not test this prediction with an intervention.

Schat and Kelloway (2003) investigated the role of *informational* (training) and *instrumental* organizational support (direct support following an incident) as buffers between workplace violence (physical violence, psychological aggression and vicarious violence) and outcomes for both the individual as well as the organization. They found instrumental support to moderate the effect of workplace violence on emotional well-being, somatic health and job-related affect, but not fear or job neglect. They also found informational support to moderate the effects of workplace violence on emotional well-being. Furthermore, results suggested that when employees experience workplace aggression or violence, the availability of both of these types of support were associated with fewer negative consequences. Importantly, neither type of support was able to moderate the relationship between workplace violence and fear or job neglect.

Dupré and Barling (2006) investigated factors related to the onset and prevention of workplace aggression towards supervisors using a sample of doctoral students and correctional service guards. The study found that employees' sense of interpersonal injustice towards their supervisor partially mediated the relationship between supervisory control over work performance and psychological workplace aggression. They also found that psychological workplace aggression partially mediated the relationship between interpersonal injustice and physical workplace aggression. Of considerable importance for organizations, the results indicated that perceived organizational sanctions moderated the relationship between interpersonal injustice and workplace aggression. Therefore, although perceived injustice predicted aggression, the relationship was minimized when policies were in place to punish people for their aggressive acts. These findings demonstrated that employees deduce organizational values concerning working relationships from the organization's reactions to aggressive events.

As can be seen by these studies, aggressive behaviour in organizations leads to a variety of negative outcomes for the target and organization alike. These studies propose a number of factors such as improving employees' sense of control, providing instrumental and informational support to employees, and implementing organizational sanctions as potential responses to aggressive behaviour. The actual impact of these strategies to prevent or ameliorate the negative effects of violence and aggression at work remain untested.

3.4.9   Aggression and Incivility

Although the outcomes of aggression are clearly detrimental to employees and the entire organization, studies assert that the incidences of such behaviours are fairly low among coworkers (i.e. Kaukianen et al., 2001) and supervisors (Mitchell & Ambrose; 2007). Baron and Neuman (1996) proposed that, although extremely distressing, physical acts of aggression and violence are a small component of a larger problem which is "verbal, passive and indirect rather than physical, active and direct" (p. 164). Furthermore, they predict that changes to organizations such as downsizing and increased workplace diversity may lead to conditions which contribute to incidences of workplace aggression. Results partially supported the first hypothesis; participants reported more verbal and passive forms of aggression than active and physical forms. Contrary to predictions, participants reported direct forms of aggression to be more frequent than indirect forms. Support for the second hypothesis was found: specifically, the study found more aggression when organizations had experienced recent disruptions.

Potentially disruptive changes included pay cuts, budget cuts, hiring freezes, increased use of part-time employees, changes in management, increased diversity, computer monitoring of performance and reengineering.

Verbal, passive and direct aggressive behaviours, such as failing to return a phone call or giving someone the silent treatment, are much more common than overt aggression in organizations (Baron & Neuman, 1996). They fall more under the category of incivility which includes rudeness and disregard towards others (Pearson, Andersson & Porath, 2000). In contrast, aggression includes efforts by individuals to harm others with whom they work or the organization itself (Baron & Neuman, 1996). The defining difference between the two behaviours is the intent to harm.

3.4.10   Research on Incivility/Civility

The everyday, rude, demeaning and neglecting behaviour of incivility seems to be a main culprit that causes people to dread and dislike their jobs. Violations of basic rules of kindness and respect are pervasive (Cortina *et al.*, 2001). Much of research into what Pearson, Andersson and Porath (2000) deem the basic rules of interpersonal demeanour and social intelligence pertains to its potential instigators and targets. More recently it has focused on incivility's consequences for organizational and individual functioning (Lim, Cortina & Magley, 2008; Cortina *et al.*, 2001) and its potential causes (Cortina, 2008).

3.4.11   Instigators and Targets of Incivility

Cortina *et al.* (2001) examined the incidence, targets, instigators and impact of incivility among employees of the US Eighth Circuit federal court system. Results of their study indicated that instances of incivility occurred at an extremely high rate in this study with 71% of employees in this sample reporting some experience with workplace incivility in the previous five years. Further, women experienced a higher rate of incivility than men. Employees in certain job positions experienced less incivility than others (secretaries and attorneys). Overall, those who experienced rude and disrespectful behaviour at work were less satisfied with their jobs, were more likely to consider quitting, and reported experiencing more psychological distress. This study provided clear evidence of the relationship between interpersonal mistreatment at work and psychological distress.

3.4.12 Impact

Lim, Cortina and Magley (2008) developed a theoretical model of incivility and its impact on occupational and psychological well-being. They also introduced the concept of *workgroup incivility*. They considered the impact of incivility occurring among members of the workgroup on individual employees' well-being. Results of this two-part study showed that experiences of incivility were associated with lower supervisor, coworker and overall work satisfaction. Supervisor and work satisfaction was associated with increased turnover intentions and decreased employee mental health. Incivility also related directly to turnover intentions. Personal incivility was found to be associated with decreased mental and physical health. Workgroup incivility had a negative impact on job satisfaction and mental health. Further, job satisfaction and mental health were found to mediate the relationship between workgroup incivility with turnover intentions and physical health. These findings emerged above and beyond the effect of job stress. In conclusion, the impact of incivility to a member of the workgroup extends beyond the target to other members of the workgroup.

Leiter *et al.* (November, 2008) investigated incivility among health care providers. Respondents reported coworker incivility to have more prevalence than supervisor incivility. Although all types of incivility were consistent with a more negative experience of work life, the less frequent supervisor incivility related more strongly with exhaustion, cynicism and turnover intention than did coworker incivility. The study found that the more serious events noted in the supervisor incidents and coworker incidents scales (including abuse, physical assault and sexual assault, as well as incivility) were similarly associated with burnout and turnover intention. Although these infractions violate norms more seriously, they occurred less frequently. The consistency among the various measures of incivility conveys that incivility from anyone at work, including oneself, reflected a negative experience of work life.

3.4.13 Causes

Cortina (2008) advanced a theory of incivility as an obscure form of sexism and racism among people at work. She drew from social psychological research on discrimination in order to create a model of selective incivility. She proposed that incivility, racism and sexism are one in the same representing "covert manifestations of gender and racial bias in the workplace" (p. 57). Cortina proposes that selective incivility could take place through personal and organizational discrimination including policies, leadership and local social norms, as well as affective and cognitive factors such as outgroup aversion, mild negative emotions towards members of the outgroup, differential esteem, social categorization and stereotyping. This position is consistent with Baron and Neuman's (1996) findings that increased diversity in the workplace relates positively with witnessed and experienced aggression. The proposed theory and evidence raise possibilities for future research on the intersections of incivility, sexism and racism.

Together, these studies highlighted some of the growing literature on incivility, including its negative impacts on workers (Cortina *et al.*, 2001) and organizations alike (Lim, Cortina & Magley, 2008). Although the expression and appearance of incivility seems to be less serious in its nature than aggression, the harm to the individual and organization remains considerable (Cortina *et al.*, 2001; Lim, Cortina & Magley, 2008) and its relatively mild appearance may even prevent the extent to which its instigators are reprimanded for their actions. As Kaukiainen *et al.* (2001) argued, perpetrators in work settings engage in aggressive acts that disguise their identity and motives as is the case with indirect manipulative and rational-appearing aggression. Therefore, the perpetrators avoid confrontation, the incivility continues, and harm to the individual and organization deepens.

3.5   PROPOSED MODEL AND RESEARCH QUESTIONS

Why do some people behave rudely when at work? How can people justify behaviours that have proven to be so detrimental to the people they work with and the organization? Several theories and biases may contribute to this unprecedented behaviour. Specifically, the attribution theory is a social psychological theory that describes how people assign responsibility for certain positive or negative behaviours and actions (e.g. Lagnado & Channon, 2008). The self-serving bias is a type of attribution that involves the tendency for people to evaluate reality in a manner that justifies their own actions while casting doubt on the motivations of others (Charness & Haruvy, 1999).

A need to make sense of the world and, specifically, to make sense of outcomes shape attributions about the self. People use attributions to understand the extent of their responsibility for events in their environment (Sheppard, Malone & Sweeny, 2008). Self-serving bias is a type of attribution with a tendency for people to evaluate reality in a manner that makes their actions seem competent if not admirable (Charness & Haruvy, 1999). This bias is implicated in organizational research on attribution of successes or failures (e.g. Giola & Sims, 1985; Campbell & Swift, 2006) and the relationship of rewards and effort (Charness & Haruvy, 2000). No research to date has investigated the role of attribution theory, and specifically self-serving bias, in the attribution of blame for uncivil behaviour at work.

This section begins with considering why people are self-serving in their attributions. This discussion introduces a new model of the attributions people use to assign responsibility when they have acted uncivilly towards others at work. It concludes with research questions concerning the role of attributions and biases in the relationship between incivility and negative workplace outcomes.

3.5.1   Bases for Self-Serving Bias

Sheppard, Malone and Sweeny (2008) reviewed two types of explanations for self-serving bias. They labelled the first type, motivational-driven, proposing that people strive to attribute responsibility in ways that are consistent with self-enhancement (Snyder, Stephen & Rosenfield, 1976) and self-presentation (e.g. Schlenker *et al.*, 1974). Self-enhancement (or egotism) is to present oneself in a positive light, preserving self-esteem (Snyder, Stephan & Rosenfield, 1976). Specifically, people tend to take credit for actions that make them look good and attribute blame to others for actions that make them look bad. Similarly, self-presentation (Schlenker *et al.*, 1974) is to present oneself as complying with social norms and attributing blame to others for behaviour that contravenes those norms.

The second type of explanation for self-serving bias is labelled cognitively-driven explanations. These types of explanations avoid the question of intention. The bias is not part of a strategy to deceive people. Instead, cognitively-driven explanations explain self-serving attributions as arising from implicit biases in cognitive processing of information (Sheppard, Malone & Sweeny, 2008). Reflections on one's behaviour filter out any information that is inconsistent with a positive self-image. Sheppard, Malone and Sweeny (2008) acknowledge that motivational and cognitive mechanisms only partially account for self-serving biases.

3.5.2   Social Rationales

From a perspective that emphasizes sense-making as an important motive (Weick, 1995), Leiter *et al.* (November, 2008) identified rationales that employees use to justify their rude and disrespectful behaviour to coworkers. These rudeness rationales attribute blame when they have acted rudely or uncivilly to another person. They allow the perpetrators of such uncivil acts such as ignoring someone, talking behind someone's back, or talking down to someone, to present themselves as behaving according to personal or shared social norms, despite exhibiting behaviour that is inconsistent with these norms. The rationales include pressure, toughness and sensitiveness.

Pressure rationales justify incivility by attributing one's behaviour to the situation: the perpetrator of the uncivil behaviour experienced strain that prompted uncharacteristic behaviour. Pressures may include pending deadlines, work overload or demanding clientele. A pressure rationale acknowledges behaving in a manner that contradicts personal or shared social norms. Attributing the cause of this behaviour to a transient situation permits one to maintain a positive self-image and public image. To the extent that members of one's social group accept this rationale, it perpetuates incivility within pressure situations.

The second rationale, toughness, justifies incivility by attributing one's behaviour to the recipients of incivility. A toughness rationale reflects a view that people, or at least some people, require harsh treatment. Perhaps they are lazy, inattentive or unmotivated. Tough rationales are consistent with a highly authoritarian leadership style. From this perspective, speaking rudely to subordinates, clients or colleagues reflects dedication to organizational goals and objectives. The behaviour is not actually inconsistent with social norms: when there is work to be done, it is necessary to put civility aside.

The third rationale, sensitive, denies that one's behaviour was uncivil. This perspective depicts one's behaviour as within accepted social norms. It characterizes the recipients who complain of the behaviour as excessively sensitive. Perhaps they lack a sense of humour or are simply too fragile to endure the reasonable demands of working relationships. Regardless of their specific shortcomings, the problem is not the behaviour about which they are complaining.

Health care providers acknowledged the presence of incivility, from supervisors, coworkers and themselves, showing that instances of incivility were very much present in their work environment (Leiter *et al.*, November, 2008). The frequency of incivility related positively to aspects of burnout, most strongly, exhaustion and cynicism and incivility at work was found to relate positively with turnover intention. Furthermore, respondents endorsed all three rationales, to varying extents. Importantly, the use of these rationales or attributions of blame was found to buffer the relationship of incivility with exhaustion and turnover intention.

Of the three types of rationales, respondents endorsed sensitive and tough rationales more strongly than they endorsed pressure rationales. The lower frequencies for pressure rationales may reflect the greater personal responsibility implied in that perspective. That is, pressure rationales accept that one acted in a manner contrary to one's ideals. In contrast, tough rationales argue that rudeness is an acceptable if not a preferred mode of interaction in some work situations and sensitive rationales deny that incivility ever occurred. Pressures rationales, however, do provide comfort to instigators by assigning blame to unreasonable demands in the workplace rather than to personal shortcomings.

An alternate explanation is that organizational cultures condone some rationales and discourage others. Tough rationales may fit the leadership style of organizations with a strong authoritarian culture while pressure rationales are better suited to an organization that cherishes self-sacrifice. Sampling across a variety of organizational cultures would help to explain the relative popularity of these three rationales and other ways of justifying incivility within workgroups.

Leiter *et al.* (November, 2008) presented evidence of rudeness rationales sustaining incivility at work. First, nurses' endorsement of all three rationales positively related to the frequency of their instigated incivility. That is, greater use of rationales was associated with more frequent incivility towards colleagues. Second, rationales moderated the relationship of social stressors with instigated incivility. Specifically, nurses who endorsed rudeness rationales were much more likely to instigate incivility towards colleagues when experiencing incivility from others. In contrast, nurses who did not endorse the rationales maintained a low level of instigated incivility regardless of whether they experienced incivility from others.

3.5.3 Incorporating Social Rationales into a Conceptual Model

The social environment of work provides a complex set of demands and resources with implications for employees' perceptions of organizational values. Qualities of social relationships contribute to their intensity. Social interactions have an inherent potential to be emotionally charged. At work, people interact about issues of considerable importance both professionally and personally. Some interactions have implications for identity as well as for one's potential to fulfil career aspirations. We propose that not only do employees experience social relationships at work as sources of support and of demands, but they interpret the quality of those relationships as indicative of personal and organizational values.

Our summary of existing research acknowledges the demanding and the supportive dimensions of working relationships. Research has identified positive contributions from both supervisor support and coworker support. It has also identified aggressive and abusive interactions from supervisors, coworkers or service recipients as major demands in work life. A distinctive quality of abuse or incivility at work is that employees challenge their legitimacy as a workplace demand. As noted by Semmer *et al.* (2007) the legitimacy of demands can be a crucial factor in employees' experience of stress or burnout. Incivility lacks legitimacy in that it constitutes a demand that makes no contribution to pursuing the organizational mission: rudeness among nurses does not help hospitals to provide better care. While nurses may consider incivility from patients to be part of the job, they consider incivility from colleagues to be an illegitimate burden (Leiter, 2005).

For employees, the prevalence of workplace incivility challenges the sincerity of management's commitment to organizational values. They perceive a tolerance of incivility as inconsistent with a valuing of supporting employees. Being aware that incivility diverts their time and energy away from providing services, they doubt management's commitment to productivity or customer service.

A potential focus for future research is contrasting processes with which people react to workplace incivility. Employees may perceive work life as having a distinct set of rules governing social relationships. The terms, 'business etiquette', 'collegiality' and 'professional relationship' imply that there are distinct ways of interacting within the workplace. When entering a setting with pervasive incivility, employees may fit into the predominant mode of discourse. For some, incivility is a matter of routine. For others, their instigated incivility prompts reflection that requires justification through a rationale that aligns their uncivil conduct with reasonable codes of conduct. It may be that for people with firm and clear personal values regarding social relationships, incivility at work poses a value conflict with their employer. Neither tolerating nor participating in incivility constitutes an acceptable option. Each of these positions has implications for employees' social behaviour, their well-being and their productivity.

REFERENCES

Andersson, L. & Pearson, C. (1999). Tit for Tat? The spiralling effect of incivility in the workplace. *Academy of Management Review*, **24**, 452–71.

Bakker, A., Hakanen, J., Demerouti, E. & Xanthopoulou, D. (2007). Job resources boost work engagement, particularly when job demands are high. *Journal of Educational Psychology*, **99**, 274–84.

Baron, R. & Neuman, J. (1996). Workplace violence and workplace aggression: evidence on their relative frequency and potential causes. *Aggressive Behavior*, **22**, 161–73.

Baruch-Feldman, C., Brondolo, E., Ben-Dayan, D. & Schwartz, J. (2002). Sources of social support and burnout, job satisfaction and productivity. *Journal of Occupational Health Psychology*, **7**, 84–93.

Brotheridge, C.A. & Grandey, A.A. (2002). Emotional labor and burnout: comparing two perspectives of 'people work'. *Journal of Vocational Behavior*, **60**, 17–39.

Campbell, C. & Swift, C. (2006). Attributional comparisons across biases and Leader-Member Exchange status. *Journal of Managerial Issues*, **18**, 393–408.

Casciaro, T. & Lobo, M.S. (2005) Competent jerks, lovable fools, and the formation of social networks. *Harvard Business Review*, **83**(6): 92–9.

Charness, G. & Haruvy, E. (2000). Self-serving biases: evidence from a simulated labour relationship. *Journal of Managerial Psychology*, **15**, 655–67.

Cortina, L. (2008). Unseen injustice: incivility as modern discrimination in organizations. *Academy of Management Review*, **33**, 55–75.

Cortina, L., Magley, C., Williams, J. & Langhout, R. (2001). Incivility in the workplace: incidence and impact. *Journal of Occupational Health Psychology*, **6**, 64–80.

Cropanzano, R. & Mitchell, M. (2005). Social exchange theory: an interdisciplinary review. *Journal of Management*, **31**, 874–900.

Dabos, G.E. & Rousseau, D.M. (2004). Mutuality and reciprocity in the psychological contracts of employees and employers. *Journal of Applied Psychology*, **89**, 52–72.

Deelstra, J., Peeters, M., Schaufeli, W., Stroebe, W., Zijlstra, F. & Doornen, L. (2003). Receiving instrumental support at work: when help is not welcome. *Journal of Applied Psychology*, **88**, 324–31.

Dupré, K. & Barling, J. (2006). Predicting and preventing supervisory workplace aggression. *Journal of Occupational Health Psychology*, **11**, 13–26.

Elfering, A., Semmer, N., Schade, V., Grund, S. & Boos, N. (2002). Supportive colleague, unsupportive supervisor: the role of provider-specific constellations of social support at work in the development of low back pain. *Journal of Occupational Psychology*, **7**, 130–40.

Etzion, D. (1984). Moderating effect of social support on the stress-burnout relationship. *Journal of Applied Psychology*, **69**, 615–22.

Giola, D. & Sims, H. (1985). Self-serving bias and actor–observer differences in organizations: an empirical analysis. *Journal of Applied Social Psychology*, **15**, 547–63.

Harris, J., Winskowski, A. & Engdahl, B. (2007). Types of workplace social support in the prediction of job satisfaction. *The Career Development Quarterly*, **56**, 150–6.

Hill, S., Bahniuk, M., Dobos, J. & Rouner, D. (1989). Mentoring and other communication support in the academic setting. *Group and Organization Management*, **14**, 355–68.

Hobfoll, S.E. (2002). Social and psychological resources and adaptation. *Review of General Psychology*, **6**, 307–24.

Kaukiainen, A., Salmivalli, C., Björkqvist, K., Österman, K., Labtinen, A. & Lagerspetz, K. (2001). Overt and covert aggression in work settings and relation the subjective well-being of employees. *Aggressive Behavior*, **27**, 360–71.

Keashley, L. (1998). Emotional abuse in the workplace: Conceptual and empirical issues. *Journal of Emotional Abuse*, **1**(1), 85–117.

Kinnunen, U., Feldt, T. & Mäkikangas, A. (2008). Testing the effort–reward imbalance model among Finnish managers: the role of perceived organizational support. *Journal of Occupational Health Psychology*, **13**, 114–27.

Lagnado, D. & Channon, S. (2008). Judgements of cause and blame: the effects of intentionality and foreseeability. *Cognition*, **108**, 754–770.

Leiter, M.P. (2005). Perception of risk: an organizational model of burnout, stress symptoms, and occupational risk. *Anxiety, Stress, and Coping*, **18**, 131–44.

Leiter, M.P., Laschinger, H.S., Day, A. & Gilin-Oor, D. (November, 2008). *Civility, respect, and engagement at work: improving collegial relationships among hospital employees*. Presentation at National Center for Organizational Development, Veterans Hospital System, Boston, MA.

Leiter, M.P. & Maslach, C. (1998). *Burnout*. In H. Freidman (Ed.), *Encyclopedia of Mental Health* (Vol. 1). San Diego, CA: Academic Press.

Leiter, M.P. & Maslach, C. (2004). Areas of work life: a structured approach to organizational predictors of job burnout. In P. Perrewé & D.C. Ganster (Eds), *Research in Occupational Stress and Well-being: Vol. 3. Emotional and Physiological Processes and Positive Intervention Strategies* (pp. 91–134). Oxford: JAI Press/Elsevier.

Leiter, M.P. & Maslach, C. (2005). A mediation model of job burnout. In A.S.G. Antoniou & C.L. Cooper (Eds), *Research Companion to Organizational Health Psychology* (pp. 544–64). Cheltenham: Edward Elgar.

Lim, S., Cortina, L. & Magley, V. (2008). Personal and workgroup incivility: impact on work and health outcomes. *Journal of Applied Psychology*, **93**, 95–107.

Maslach, C. (2003). Job burnout: new directions in research and innovation. *Current Directions in Psychological Science*, **12**, 189–92.

Maslach, C. & Leiter, M.P. (2005). Reversing burnout: how to rekindle your passion for work. *Stanford Social Innovation Review*, Winter, 43–9.

Maslach, C. & Leiter, M.P. (2008). Early predictors of job burnout and engagement. *Journal of Applied Psychology*, **93**, 498–512.

Maslach, C., Schaufeli, W. & Leiter, M.P. (2001). Job burnout. *Annual Review of Psychology*, **52**, 397–422.

Mitchell, M. & Ambrose, M. (2007). Abusive supervision and workplace deviance and the moderating effects of negative reciprocity beliefs. *Journal of Applied Psychology*, **92**, 1159–65.

Pearson, C., Andersson, L. & Porath, C. (2000). Assessing and attacking workplace incivility. *Organizational Dynamics*, **29**, 123–37.

Pinnington, A. (2002). Transformational leadership, corporate cultism and the spirituality paradigm: an unholy trinity in the workplace? *Human Relations*, **55**, 147–72.

Russell, D., Altmaier, E. & Van Velzen, D. (1987). Job-related stress, social support, and burnout among classroom teachers. *Journal of Applied Psychology*, **72**, 269–74.

Schat, A. & Kelloway, E. (2000). Effects of perceived control on the outcomes of workplace aggression and violence. *Journal of Occupational Health Psychology*, **5**, 386–402.

Schat, A. & Kelloway, E. (2003). Reducing the adverse consequences of workplace aggression and violence: the buffering effects of organizational support. *Journal of Occupational Health Psychology*, **8**, 116–22.

Schaufeli, W.B. & Bakker, A.B. (2004). Job demands, job resources and their relationship with burnout and engagement: a multi-sample study. *Journal of Organizational Behavior*, **25**, 293–315.

Schaufeli, W.B., Leiter, M.P., Maslach, C. & Jackson, S.E. (1996). Maslach Burnout Inventory – General Survey (MBI-GS). In C. Maslach, S.E. Jackson & M.P. Leiter (Eds), *Maslach Burnout Inventory Manual* (3rd edn.). Palo Alto, CA: Consulting Psychologists Press.

Schein, E. (1988). *Organizational Culture and Leadership*. San Francisco: Jossey-Bass.

Schlenker, B., Soraci, S., Schlenker, J. & Schlenker, P. (1974). Self-presentation as a function of performance expectations and performance anonymity. *Personality and Social Psychology Bulletin*, **1**, 152–4.

Sechrist, G. & Stangor, 2001. Perceived consensus influences intergroup behaviour and stereotype accessibility. *Journal of Personality and Social Psychology*, **80**, 645–54.

Semmer, N., Jacobshagen, N., Meier, L. & Elfering, A. (2007). Occupational stress research: the 'stress-as-offence-to-self' perspective. In J. Houdmont & S. McIntyre (Eds), *Occupational Health Psychology: European Perspectives on Research, Education and Practise*, Vol. 2 (pp. 43–60). Maia, Portugal: ISMAI.

Sheppard, J., Malone, W. & Sweeny, K. (2008). Exploring causes of the self-serving bias. *Social and Personality Compass*, **2**, 895–908.

Snyder, M., Stephan, W. & Rosenfield, D. (1976). Egotism and attribution. *Journal of Personality and Social Psychology*, **33**, 435–41.

Thompson, C. & Prottas, D. (2005). Relationships among organizational family support, job autonomy, perceived control and employee well-being. *Journal of Occupational Health Psychology*, **10**, 100–18.

Vredenburgh, D. & Brender, Y. (1998). The hierarchical abuse of power in work organizations. *Journal of Business Ethics*, **12**, 1337–47.

Weick, K. (1995). *Sensemaking in Organizations*. Thousand Oaks, CA: Sage.

CHAPTER 4

The Effects of Job Strain on Risk Factors for Cardiovascular Disease

Arie Shirom, Galit Armon
Faculty of Management, Tel Aviv University, Israel
Shlomo Berliner, Itzhak Shapira
Tel-Aviv Sourasky Medical Center, Israel
and
Samuel Melamed
Tel Aviv-Yaffo Academic College, Israel

4.1 THE OBJECTIVES AND SCOPE OF THE REVIEW

In our review, we focus on work-related psychological stress. Within this stress research domain, we exclude from our review event-based types of stress – including acute and critical job events such as being demoted or going on involuntary vacation (Eden, 1982, 1990). We also exclude work-related hassles, such as being caught in a traffic jam while commuting to work (cf. Gajendran & Harrison, 2007). It follows that we focus on chronic stress at work. Researchers may disagree on the conceptual definition of work-related chronic stress (Cooper, 1998; Monroe, 2008). There is basic agreement, however, about the notion that work-related chronic stress, hereafter referred to simply as stress, may be implicated in cardiovascular disease risk factors, specifically physiological ones, such as elevated cholesterol and blood pressure levels, and in certain maladaptive behavioural responses (Aboa-Eboule *et al.*, 2007; Chandola *et al.*, 2008; Chandola, Brunner & Marmot, 2006; Williams, 2008).

International Handbook of Work and Health Psychology, Third Edition. Edited by Cary L. Cooper, James Campbell Quick, and Marc J. Schabracq.

We decided to focus on the effects of work-related stress on risk factors for *cardiovascular disease* (CVD). We define CVD as a composite of coronary heart disease, stroke and cardiovascular mortality. This focus is due to the fact that CVD, including myocardial infarction (MI) and stroke, is a principal cause of death in most economically advanced countries; it is associated with multiple physiological, psychological and socio-demographic risk factors that often interact in complex causal paths (Brotman, Golden & Wittstein, 2007; Kiecolt-Glaser *et al.*, 2002; Williams, 2008). Chronic stress could be directly implicated in CVD by causing spasms of coronary blood vessels, electrical instability in the heart conduction system and abnormal heart rhythms (cf. Williams, 2008). Chronic stresses are thought to influence the pathogenesis of CVD by causing negative affective states such as burnout (Melamed *et al.*, 2006), and anxiety and depression (Suls & Bunde, 2005), which in turn exert direct effects on maladaptive behavioural and physiological responses. There are two major physiological mechanisms that are considered as the most likely mediators of the effects of chronic stress on CVD: the hypothalamic-pituitary-adrenocortical axis (HPA) and the sympathetic-adrenal-medullary (SAM) system (Miller, Chen & Zhou, 2007). Prolonged or repeated activation of the HPA and SAM axes can interfere with their control of other physiological systems, and could result in increased risk for a variety of physical and psychiatric disorders (McEwen, 2007). Cortisol, the primary endocrine response of the HPA axis, regulates a broad range of physiological processes, including the metabolism of fats and proteins represented in our review by blood lipids, and anti-inflammatory responses, represented in our review by biomarkers of micro-inflammation in the serum. SAM axis activation is associated with the secretion of catecholamines, which – interacting with the autonomic nervous system – exert regulatory effects on many organ systems in the body, including the cardiovascular system (Cohen, Janicki-Deverts & Miller, 2007). SAM axis activation is represented in our review by both elevated blood pressure and sleep disturbances.

The chapter begins by describing a general theoretical perspective within which our review is embedded. The general theoretical perspective provides a comprehensive, system-based view of the antecedents of stress– CVD risk factors linkages. We then briefly review three leading theoretical models that have been used to investigate stress–CVD risk factors associations: the person–environment fit model, the effort–reward model, and the job demand–control–support model (JDC-S) model, also referred to as the job strain model (hence the term *job strain* in the title). We explain why we chose to focus, in the following sections of our review, on the JDC-S model. We then use the JDC-S model to present what is known about the effects of work-related stress on four major risk factors for CVD: elevated levels of blood lipids; blood pressure; micro-inflammation biomarkers; and sleep disturbances. These risk factors represent only a subset of possible physio-logical and behavioural strains that may be impacted by work-related stress. For example, the effects of stress may include alterations in neuroendocrine factors, the autonomic nervous system and immune functions. The conclud-ing section discusses the limitations of this review and highlights promising avenues for future research in this field.

Above we explained several physiological considerations that guided the choice of the CVD risk factors covered here. There were additional con-siderations, related to the availability of empirical studies and the contents of other chapters in this volume. This review focuses on empirical studies; therefore, a body of such studies should exist. Additionally, an explicit at-tempt was made to avoid duplication with other chapters of this volume, including chapters that specifically cover the maladaptive health responses of psychological distress, drug abuse and alcoholism. The broad scope of this review necessarily limits the depth of the presentation. Readers should note that the range of the literature covered probably reflects the authors' personal viewpoints on several key issues.

4.2 A GENERAL FRAMEWORK FOR THE STUDY OF THE HEALTH CONSEQUENCES OF STRESS AT WORK

The theoretical model guiding this chapter is represented in Figure 4.1. Within the model, an individual's state of health is viewed as being deter-mined by multiple factors, including heredity, environment, early background and socioeconomic influences. This theoretical model draws on earlier con-ceptualizations (Macik-Frey, Quick & Nelson, 2007; Quick et al., 1997, pp. 65–89). Among the multiple causal chains leading to maladaptive health responses is the effect of work-related stress. This effect is depicted as be-ing moderated by individuals' coping resources and personality factors. To simplify the presentation of the main effects, several arrows indicating mod-erating effects were omitted from Figure 4.1. We focus on the hypothesized arrow that leads from work-related chronic stress to maladaptive physio-logical and behavioural responses, primarily because of the considerations detailed above. Stress is posited in Figure 4.1 as precipitating the develop-ment of maladaptive health responses, like when it is implicated in raising a person's blood pressure from normal to borderline. The following is a brief discussion of the theoretical model presented in Figure 4.1. It is introduced by a description of the conceptual approach followed by the definitions of stress and maladaptive health responses.

Early reviews of the vast area of work-related stress and physical health (Danna & Griffin, 1999; Ganster & Schaubroeck, 1991; Mackay & Cooper,

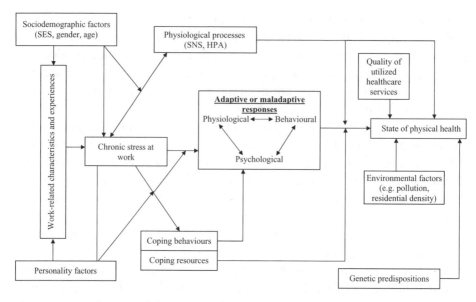

Figure 4.1 A theoretical framework depicting possible pathways for the effects of stress at work on physical health.

1987) mostly followed the theoretical framework depicted in Figure 4.1, defining health and well-being broadly to include psychological and physical health. By *maladaptive health responses*, we refer to a subclass of what has been labelled *strain* in the Michigan model, namely any deviation from the normal state of responses of the person (French, Caplan & Harrison, 1982). This definition of strain included psychological strain, such as job dissatisfaction and anxiety, physiological strain like high blood pressure, and behavioural symptoms of strain such as sleep disturbances. Continuing high levels of strain were postulated to affect morbidity and mortality levels (French *et al.*, 1982). In this review, we refer only to the latter two types of strain.

There are several reasons for introducing the model depicted in Figure 4.1 in this chapter. First, as argued by several researchers (Kasl, 1996; Marmot, Theorell & Siegrist, 2002), studies of the relationships between stress and maladaptive health responses need to maintain a broad conceptual perspective of the etiology of these responses. Specific etiological factors leading from the work environment to health responses are embedded in a complex matrix of additional psychosocial influences. There are several classes of variables that were included in Figure 4.1, but are not discussed or reviewed here because of space limitations. The potential usefulness of each of those panels needs to be considered by future researchers. Salient examples are socioeconomic indicators (cf. Gallo & Matthews, 2003), stable individual differences (cf. Smith *et al.*, 2004; Smith & MacKenzie, 2006), and work role and work environment characteristics that represent individuals' exposures to earlier work and job experiences (Theorell, 1998).

Figure 4.1 depicts several bi-directional arrows. These double-headed arrows represent interactions or non-recursive processes between panels of variables. To illustrate, the bi-directional arrow between psychological and physiological maladaptive responses represents reciprocal feedback loops that can occur, as when distress – such as depression or burnout – affects the immune system (cf. Melamed *et al.*, 2006). Again, given the confines of this review, it is not possible to discuss each double-headed arrow in detail.

The role of panels not discussed in our review could be illustrated by taking as an example the role of socioeconomic disadvantage, considered to have direct and indirect influences on maladaptive health responses. Decades of research have shown that socioeconomic status is a significant predictor of stress, strain and state of health (Banks *et al.*, 2006; Hemingway & Marmot, 1999; Marmot, 2006). Socioeconomic status differences are found for rates of morbidity and mortality for almost every disease and health condition (Adler *et al.*, 1994). Components of socioeconomic status, income, education and occupation shape individuals' early life experiences, including early-age health habits like diet and exercise, and significantly influence their work experiences, including access to coping resources such as social support at work (cf. Danna & Griffin, 1999).

Researchers have often posited a strong relationship between perceived stress – an individual's coping resources and coping mechanisms – and the etiology of stress-related maladaptive health responses (Lazarus, 1999; Taylor & Stanton, 2007). How an individual handles stress plays an important role in determining the health outcomes of the individual's encounter with stress. Coping may be loosely defined as things we think and actions we take to ameliorate or remove the negative aspects of stressful situations, including indirect coping like avoidance (Taylor & Stanton, 2007). The ability to cope with stress is represented in Figure 4.1 by the panel of work-related coping resources. These resources interact with individuals' subjective appraisal to determine their experienced stress. If a situation is not appraised as taxing or exceeding one's coping resources, it is not likely to be experienced as stress (Lazarus, 1999). Personality factors like hardiness represent additional coping resources. Because of space limitations, this chapter does not cover the issue of effective coping mechanisms, which may prevent psychosocial and physiological disequilibria that may in turn lead to stress-related illnesses.

Adaptive and maladaptive responses to stress represent a complex set of an organism's reactions intended to re-establish psychosocial and physiological equilibriums. As indicated, we focus only on a specific set of risk factors for CVD. The hypothesized effects of stress may appear in any combination of the physiological, behavioural and psychological domains of strain. To illustrate, high blood pressure, sleep disturbances and high levels of 'bad' serum cholesterol and obesity often co-occur. The synergic relationships among the panels of Figure 4.1 indicate that there is not any single consistent maladaptive health response applicable to most people in all work situations. This basic premise of inter-individual variability in stress response is related to the direct and indirect effects of coping resources and coping effectiveness considered above, and in addition to other individual difference variables depicted in other panels of Figure 4.1.

4.3   MODELS EXPLAINING THE EFFECTS OF WORK STRESS ON PHYSIOLOGICAL RISK FACTORS

In recent years, occupational health researchers have devoted considerable attention to possible paths of influence linking work and job characteristics with employees' physical health. They have been guided in their attempts to gain additional understanding of the pathways linking the world of work and employee physical health by several important and often used models. Each of these models represents a distinct way of reducing the complex reality into a comprehensive yet parsimonious model. Each of these models focuses on specific core elements in order to explain work-related physical health. One of the most important models is referred to as the job demand–control–support (JDC-S) model; for reasons explained below, we focus on this model in our review. However, we also briefly review in this section two additional models that have been used to explain the effects of chronic work-related stress on the risk factors for CVD considered in our review. We describe the two other models largely because they are based on similar theoretical principles and therefore could be combined with the JDC-S model in future research explaining the pathways linking work-related stress with risk factors for CVD.

4.3.1   The Person–Environment Fit Model

One of the earliest (French & Caplan, 1973) models focusing on stress and health outcomes is the person–environment fit model (P-E Fit). It has been widely applied to predict a variety of risk factors for disease (Edwards *et al.*, 2006; Edwards, Caplan & Van Harrison, 1998), including those that we focus on (cf. French, Caplan & Harrison, 1982). *Fit*, in this model, includes the relationships between environmental supplies and individuals' values and needs, referred to as the S-V (supplies–values) fit, and the relationships among environmental demands and individuals' abilities, skills and knowledge, referred to as the D-A (demands–abilities) fit. The model postulates that the more pronounced a misfit, either S-V or D-A, the higher the level of the resulting strains will be. An additional postulate of the model is that the major components of S-V, and in turn also D-A, interact to influence one's level of strain (Edwards *et al.*, 1998). Many additional types of person–environment fit that could conceptually exist were described in a major conceptual review of the area (Kristof, 1996). Kristof (1996) pointed out that the type of fit mainly investigated up until now has been the D-A rather than the S-V. Several other approaches to the study of stress–strain relationships have also incorporated elements of this model, such as cybernetic stress theory (Edwards, 1998).

A recent meta-analysis of the P-E fit literature at large, including studies that followed the specific P-E fit model described above (Kristof-Brown, Zimmerman & Johnson, 2005), concluded that fit was strongly associated with several attitudinal and behavioural outcomes. For example, person–job fit was found to be strongly linked with job satisfaction, job performance and turnover, while person–organization fit was closely associated with organizational commitment. However, the number of studies linking the model with physical health-related outcomes was found to be small (Schnall, Landsbergis & Baker, 1994), and therefore this was not the model chosen to guide our review.

4.3.2 Effort–Reward Imbalance at Work Model

The effort–reward imbalance (ERI) model (Siegrist, 1995) builds upon the notion of social reciprocity, a fundamental principle of interpersonal be- haviour which lies at the core of employment relationships. In the context of the ERI, social reciprocity is interpreted as representing the norm of return expectancy. *Return expectancy* refers to employees' expectations that the ef- fort they invest at work would be equal to the rewards they receive. *Efforts*, in the context of ERI, represent job demands and requirements that are imposed on the employee. *Rewards*, in turn, refer to money, job security, self-esteem and career opportunities, mostly distributed by the employer (but also by society at large). Reward in the ERI model is probably closely related to the notion of supplies in the P-E fit model, while efforts resemble the notion of demands in the P-E fit model. Therefore, it could be argued that the ERI model is embedded in the P-E fit model. A job situation characterized by high efforts and low rewards represents a reciprocity deficit. Perceived lack of reciprocity is hypothesized to lead to strong negative emotions. These negative emotions, in turn, lead to sustained autonomic and endocrine acti- vation and to negative health outcomes (Ursin & Eriksen, 2007). The wider the discrepancy between the costs incurred by employees, in terms of their efforts invested at work to face work-related demands; and their gains, in terms of the rewards they receive, the stronger the psychological strain reaction and the higher the likelihood that the employees concerned will develop maladaptive physiological responses.

The reciprocity norm is almost never fully explicated in employment contracts. Therefore, formal employment contracts are supplemented by mutual trust and informal understandings and commitments. Lack of trust reinforces and augments the effort–reward imbalance. Certain personality characteristics aggravate the imbalance once it exists. For example, intolerance of ambiguity may lead to exaggerated appraisals of uncertainties associated with rewards. Besides efforts and rewards, the model includes a third factor, referred to as *over-commitment* or *intrinsically-motivated investment of efforts at work*. The model predicts that over-committed employees are at high risk to experience efforts–rewards imbalance, relative to their under-committed colleagues. Additionally, highly over-committed employees experiencing imbalance will respond with more strain reactions to a reciprocity deficit, in comparison with less over-committed employees. This interactional hypothesis is often referred to as the 'intrinsic' ERI hypothesis (van Vegchel *et al.*, 2005).

In recent years, several qualitative reviews integrated and evaluated the many studies that had applied the ERI model to explain physical health outcomes (Tsutsumi & Kawakami, 2004; van Vegchel *et al.*, 2005). Generally, these qualitative reviews found that the 'extrinsic' ERI hypothesis – that is, the hypothesis that high efforts in combination with low rewards increase the risk of poor health – has gained considerable empirical support. However, support for the 'intrinsic' ERI remained inconclusive. The most recent review of the ERI model (van Vegchel *et al.*, 2005) found that 13 out of 17 studies supported the model in that employees reporting a high effort–low reward imbalance had higher levels of CVD risk factors, including blood lipids and blood pressure. However, less than half of the 17 studies used a prospective design. As argued by Tsutsumi and Kawakami (2004), the ERI model and the job demand-control-support (JDC-S) model, reviewed in the next section, are complementary. We decided to focus on the latter, rather than the former, primarily because of the fact that the preponderance of studies linking CVD risk factors with job characteristics used the JDC-S model (for an early review, see: Schnall, Landsbergis & Baker, 1994).

4.3.3   The Job Demand-Control-Support Model

Work-related stressors have been increasingly studied for their potential adverse effects on cardiovascular risk factors (Brotman, Golden & Wittstein,

2007). A leading theoretical model in studying the effects of job characteristics on physical health is the JDC-S model, developed by Karasek and Theorell (1990). In the initial formulation of the model, Karasek (1979) identified two crucial job aspects in the work situation which are expected to be associated with a number of health outcomes: job demands and job control. *Job demands* usually refers to psychological job demands, primarily defined as referring to perceived workload, while *job control* refers to the freedom permitted the worker in deciding how to meet demands or how to perform tasks (Karasek & Theorell, 1990). Based on empirical research, Johnson and his colleagues (Johnson & Hall, 1988; Johnson *et al.*, 1996) extended the initial model to include the dimension of 'workplace social support'; this extended model was termed the job demand–control–support (JDC-S) model (Karasek & Theorell, 1990). *Workplace social support* refers to 'overall levels of helpful social interaction available on the job from both co-workers and supervisors' (Karasek & Theorell, 1990, p. 69). Two major hypotheses were derived from the JDC-S model. The first, often referred to as the additive hypothesis, postulates that the model's components have additive effects on strain. The second hypothesis, dubbed as the interactional hypothesis, maintains that the most unfavourable and potentially stressful working environment, and the highest risk of poor psychological well-being and ill-health, occurs in the high *'iso-strain'* condition characterized by high job demands, low control and low social support (Karasek & Theorell, 1990). The first hypothesis is the simplest and has been supported by the most longitudinal studies testing the effects of the model's components on strain reactions (de Lange *et al.*, 2003). The second hypothesis received considerably less support and was often tested using inappropriate statistical procedures (Kasl, 1996; Sargent & Terry, 2000). Therefore, we focus below on the model's first hypothesis.

The JDC-S model, much like the ERI model, could be regarded as embedded in the PE-fit model. Previous reviews (Van Der Doef & Maes, 1998, 1999) found the JDC-S model to have predictive powers relative to both psychological and physiological strain. More recent qualitative reviews of the research on the JDC-S model (Belkic *et al.*, 2004; Steenland *et al.*, 2000) found that it predicted the prevalence and incidence of cardiovascular disease. A recent meta-analytic study summarized the results of 14 prospective cohort studies that quantitatively estimated the prediction of CVD by the JDC-S model (Kivimaki *et al.*, 2006). As reported by Kivimaki *et al.* (2006), they found that the highest incidence of cardiovascular morbidity and mortality in these studies occurred when individuals' jobs were characterized by high job demands, low amounts of employee control with which to cope with these demands and low levels of social support.

Researchers have suggested several specific pathways to explain the association between the JDC-S model and CVD. These mediating physiological mechanisms include excessive activation of the sympathetic nervous system and the hypothalamic-pituitary-adrenal (HPA) axis (Miller, Chen & Zhou, 2007), altered autonomic regulation of the heart (Belkic et al., 2004), and damaging health behaviours, including smoking, lack of physical activity and high calorie intake (Van der Doef & Maes, 1999). The precise biological mechanisms underlying the associations of the JDC-S model with CVD remain unclear (Belkic et al., 2004). Therefore, in the following sections we will present evidence linking the model with several CVD risk factors.

4.4 THE JDC-S MODEL AND BLOOD LIPIDS

We will first investigate the extent to which the model's components predict subsequent levels of blood lipids. We shall use the term *blood lipids* to refer to both lipids and lipoproteins. The physiological pathways linking exposure to chronic stress and elevated blood lipids have not yet been established, but they probably involve the mediation of the sympathetic nervous system and the HPA axis. Increased HPA activity during stress typically results in the secretion of catecholamines, cortisol and glucagon, which in turn cause lipolysis and the subsequent release of fatty acids into the circulation (Stoney, Bausserman et al., 1999; Stoney, Niaura et al., 1999). There is strong evidence linking work-related chronic stressors with atherogenic lipids, but there is less evidence that lipids are immediately responsive to elevations of chronic stressors (Niaura, Stoney & Herbert, 1992). The blood lipids investigated in this area of research were high-density lipoprotein cholesterol (HDL-C), high values of which are considered to be protective against CVD, and also low-density lipoprotein cholesterol (LDL-C) and triglycerides (TRI), high values of which are causally implicated in the etiology of CVD (Tirosh et al., 2007).

We conducted a search of English-language articles (i.e., excluding conference papers and doctoral dissertations) published between 1980 and 2007 that link the JDC-S model or its earlier variant, the JD-C model, with blood lipids at the individual level of analysis. We found 14 such studies (a table summarizing these studies is available from the first author upon request), all of which used a cross-sectional design, and therefore could not rule out the possibility that subclinical CVD – as indicated by high levels of LDL-C and TRI and low levels of HDL-C – influenced the components of the JDC-S model, rather than the reverse. The authors of nine studies (64%) reported that they found little or no support for the model's predictions. The remaining five studies provided only mixed and inconsistent support for the model's predictions.

Niaura *et al.* (1992), in their qualitative reviews of the literature on this subject, concluded that there was some evidence, albeit inconsistent, implicating objective or perceived stress as a source of elevated blood concentrations of lipids, particularly those lipid fractions that are most atherogenic. The qualitative review of 14 cross-sectional studies that we conducted provided mixed and inconsistent support for the expected link between the JDC-S model and blood lipids. Past research has been primarily concerned with episodic, or event-based, stress (Niaura *et al.*, 1992). Event-based and ongoing, chronic exposure-based conceptualizations of stress derive from differing theoretical approaches (Derogatis & Coons, 1993), and have often been found to be differently related to physiological risk factors in coronary heart disease (Kahn *et al.*, 1964). In their research report, Stoney *et al.* (1999) provided a summary of an unpublished meta-analytic study of the literature on stress and blood lipid concentrations. A total of 101 studies were included in this meta-analysis, and each study was separately analysed according to whether the stress was chronic (lasted more than 30 days), episodic (demands addressed during a period of 1 to 30 days) or acute (lasting no more than 24 hours). Acute and episodic stress relationships with lipids were both found to have positive effect sizes on several lipids' parameters. In comparison, chronic stress and total cholesterol associations resulted in a small positive effect size, but none of the other lipid parameters provided a significant effect size with chronic stress. Stoney *et al.* (1999) concluded that the evidence for a connection between acute and episodic stress on the one hand, and lipid reactivity on the other, is generally more consistent than the evidence for a connection between chronic stress and lipid reactivity. It should be noted, however, that these meta-analytic results might stem in part from the arbitrariness of the stress classification criteria, and from the small number of studies available on chronic stress and lipid parameters.

4.5   THE JDC-S MODEL AND BLOOD PRESSURE

Blood pressure and other biological parameters, such as catecholamines, continuously fluctuate in response to changes in the external or internal environment, to facilitate the adaptation of individuals to their environments (James & Brown, 1997). Researchers and clinicians label the maximal pressure of the pulse of blood expelled by the heart's left ventricle during contraction into the aorta as *systolic blood pressure*; the minimal pressure, exerted when the heart is at rest just before the next heartbeat, is labelled *diastolic blood pressure*. Arterial blood pressure may change substantially within seconds, in response to the physiological state and environmental conditions of the individual. Therefore, researchers tend to use non-invasive ambulatory monitors that can measure blood pressure response many times during daily life while the subjects go about their normal activities (Pickering, Shimbo & Haas, 2006); we refer to the results of these types of blood pressure measurements as *ambulatory blood pressure*. The other type of blood pressure measurement is referred to as *causal blood pressure*; it is usually undertaken while the examinee is sitting in the clinic and represents the average of several consecutive measurements of systolic and diastolic blood pressures.

The etiology of elevated blood pressure remains unknown, but it is well accepted that multiple factors are responsible for this CVD risk factor (Pickering *et al.*, 2006). Acute diastolic blood pressure reactivity to various stresses has been prospectively linked to increased incidence of cardiovascular disorders, including coronary heart disease, stroke and renal disease (e.g., Fredrikson & Matthews, 1990); however, the conceptual and empirical differences between acute and chronic stresses have already been discussed in the section on blood lipids. The growing interest in the effects of work-related stress on blood pressure is explained by the consistent finding that blood pressure measured at work is higher than all other measures of blood pressure taken during the day, independent of the time of day (James & Brown, 1997).

Chronic exposure to job-related demands may be associated with increased physical activity and changes in posture. These changes in activity level may in turn give rise to elevated levels of blood pressure. In a series of early longitudinal studies designed to test the effects of the JDC-S model on ambulatory blood pressure, the combination of low control (low decision latitude) and high demand (high workload) predicted elevated levels of blood pressure at work, at home and during sleep (for a review of the early studies, see Schwartz, Pickering & Landsbergis, 1996). This consistent finding has focused researchers' attention on the pivotal role of perceived job control as a powerful moderator of the effects of work-related stress on elevated blood pressure levels. Subsequent attempts to replicate this finding in longitudinal studies using ambulatory blood pressure yielded mixed results, with one study supporting the JDC-S model (Landsbergis *et al.*, 2003), and another study failing to find support for the model's expectations (Fauvel *et al.*, 2003). Considering only longitudinal studies that used the JDC-S model to predict future causal blood pressure, there is a relative preponderance of studies that found some support for the model's major hypotheses (Guimont *et al.*, 2006; Markovitz *et al.*, 2004; Ohlin *et al.*, 2007). The carefully conducted study of the effects of task (job) strain on ambulatory blood pressure (Kamarck *et al.*, 1998) did report a main effect of decisional control: situations rated in this study as high on control were associated with lower levels of diastolic blood pressure activity, suggesting that control may protect against acute sympathetic activation. In yet another carefully crafted study using ecological momentary assessment, Kamarck *et al.* (2002), found that the JDC-S model has predictive value with ambulatory blood pressure, again adding to the body of evidence that psychological demands are – independently of possible confounders – associated with ambulatory blood pressure fluctuations during daily work life.

4.6 THE JDC-S MODEL AND MICRO-INFLAMMATION BIOMARKERS

Several recent reviews of the literature have concluded that repeated episodes of acute psychological stress or chronic psychological stress can lead to a chronic inflammatory process (Black, 2002, 2003; Black & Garbutt, 2002). Accumulated evidence indicates that the inflammatory proteins fibrinogen and C-reactive protein, as well as the white blood cell count (WBC), were found to be independent predictors of CVD incidence (Madjid *et al.*, 2004; Mora *et al.*, 2006). Studies in healthy individuals exposed to chronic psychological stress have shown that they exhibited increased circulating concentrations of fibrinogen, CRP and WBC (Clays *et al.*, 2005). Based on past research, we evaluated the possibility that CRP, WBC and fibrinogen plasma concentrations could provide the mechanism linking the JDC-S model with CVD.

We were unable to find any past study that has related the JDC-S model to WBC. Three cross-sectional studies related the JDC-S model to CRP, reporting no association (Clays *et al.*, 2005; Hemingway *et al.*, 2003) and a significant positive association (Schnorpfeil *et al.*, 2003). The JDC-S model has been used to predict fibrinogen in several past studies. With one exception (Riese *et al.*, 2000), all other past studies relating the JDC-S model to fibrinogen were cross-sectional and most of them did not support the model (for a summary of the studies and references, see Shirom *et al.*, 2008) In our recent study (Shirom *et al.*, 2008) assessing the impact of the JDC-S model on the above inflammation biomarkers over a period of 18 months, we also failed to find support for the JDC-S model.

4.7 THE JDC-S MODEL AND SLEEP PROBLEMS

The modern era of sleep research began in the 1950s with the discovery that sleep is a highly active state, rather than a passive condition of non-response. The most prevalent type of sleep disturbance, insomnia, may occur in a transient, short-term or chronic form. Stress is probably the most frequent cause of transient insomnia (Gillin & Byerley, 1990). Chronic insomnia could result from an underlying medical or psychiatric disorder (cf. Gillin & Byerley, 1990).

Insomnia is defined as difficulties in initiating sleep or maintaining sleep, prolonged awakenings during the night, or waking up too early in the morning for more than a one-month period (Buysse *et al.*, 2006; Gillin & Byerley, 1990). Increasing evidence indicates that insomnia leads to fundamental impairments in quality of life and functional capacity, and represents a substantial economic burden (Roth & Ancoli-Israel, 1999; Walsh & Engelhardt, 1999; Zammit *et al.*, 1999). Insomnia has been linked to daytime fatigue, greater medical service utilization, self-medication with alcohol or over-the-counter medication, greater functional impairment, greater work absenteeism, impaired concentration and memory, decreased enjoyment of interpersonal relationships, and increased risk of serious medical illness and traffic and work accidents (Roth & Roehrs, 2003; Roth, Roehrs & Pies, 2007). Insomnia can be viewed as an inability to recover and replenish depleted resources after exposure to stress. This may result in a state of physiological and cognitive hyperarousal (Roth, Roehrs & Pies, 2007).

The association between the JDC-S model and insomnia may be maintained through a vicious circle where stress at work evokes physical and cognitive hyperarousal; this disturbs sleep, which in turn reduces the ability to renew coping resources (represented by perceived control and social support), and in turn increases the feeling of stress. Additionally, high levels of physiological tension, such as heart rate and muscle activity, may make it more difficult to relax. Psychosocial factors at work may also be a fundamental source for cognitive arousal, manifested by disturbing thoughts that become intrusive when a person attempts to sleep. Thus, while attempting to relax and fall asleep, thoughts about stressful situations at work may be a source of rumination, disrupt relaxation and create arousal which induces difficulties in falling asleep.

Akerstedt (2006) recently reviewed cross-sectional studies on the relationship between the JDC -S model and insomnia. This review (Akerstedt, 2006) concluded that most of these studies tend to support the model's predictions. Several cross-sectional studies that followed the above review (Akerstedt, Kecklund & Gillberg, in press; Knudsen, Ducharme & Roman, 2007) were also supportive of the JDC-S model's predictions. However, as noted above, in our review we focus on longitudinal studies. We found several studies that prospectively predicted insomnia by the JDC-S model. Linton (2004) found that only lack of social support predicted the development of new cases of insomnia one year later. Jansson and Linton (2006) found that only high work demand predicted the development of new cases of insomnia in a follow-up conducted approximately one year later. Subsequently, in a study based on a considerably larger national sample (Jansson-Frojmark *et al.*, 2007), it was found that among individuals with no insomnia at baseline, high work demands increased the risk of developing insomnia one year later. In the three prospective studies referred to above, the JDC-S components were found to reinforce the continuation of insomnia among individuals with insomnia at baseline. In summary, the evidence coming out of the three longitudinal studies provides support for the JDC-S model's prediction relative to sleep disturbances.

The study of the behavioural outcomes of the JDC-S model is complicated because these outcomes frequently appear in pairs or triads, analogous to the co-morbidity patterns of chronic illnesses. Different combinations of outcomes are the rule, rather than the exception. A well-known example is the very close associations of the JDC-S model's components with insomnia, smoking and burnout (Armon *et al.*, 2008). This has led to the construction of dual-diagnosis and triple-diagnosis schemes and to the development of comprehensive, multi-faceted treatment approaches. The pattern of appearance of several outcomes in an individual may vary, depending on background characteristics and genetic and environmental factors. Stress and sleep disturbances may reciprocally influence each other: stress may promote transient insomnia, which in turn causes stress and increases risk for episodes of depression and anxiety (Partinen, 1994).

4.8   SUMMARY AND CONCLUSIONS

In this concluding section, we discuss some of the theoretical and methodological issues reviewed in this chapter. Additionally, we present some of the limitations of the approach that we adopted and suggest promising avenues for future research on the model and CVD risk factors.

4.8.1   Major Conclusions

The maladaptive health responses covered in this chapter were all characterized as having multifactor etiology. For each of the maladaptive responses considered here, stress at work is but one of the possible culprits. For the great majority of the studies cited in this review, different additive and interactive combinations of the components of the JDC-S model were found to be the most powerful predictors. Still, one of the major conclusions that we could reach is that the JDC-S model was not found, in studies based upon longitudinal designs, to account for a significant proportion of the variance of blood lipids and of inflammation biomarkers. Therefore, we would like to suggest that blood lipids and inflammation biomarkers probably do not represent linking pins between the model's components and CVD.

The evidence on the effects of the JDC-S model on blood pressure tends to be equivocal. A recent review of the relationships between job-related stress and causal blood pressure that covered 48 studies, including studies that used the JDC-S model (Mann, 2006), concluded that the evidence for a relationship between chronic job stress and blood pressure is weak. However, there is a major difference between the three physiological risk factors for CVD reviewed in our chapter. While we could positively assert that the pathway leading from the components of the JDC-S model to blood lipids and inflammation biomarkers appears unpromising and dubitable, this is not the case for blood pressure. While the evidence is weak, some of the longitudinal studies that we reviewed above could be interpreted to mean that job demands, control and support – either additively or synergistically – could move individuals from the relatively benign category of 'borderline' to that of 'inflicted with hypertension and in need of medication'.

The JDC-S model is definitely a useful tool to investigate the etiology of insomnia, the only maladaptive behavioural outcome covered in our chapter. As we noted, insomnia is a prevalent condition in the general population worldwide, with conservative estimates ranging from 9% to 12% of all adults inflicted with this disorder (Ancoli-Israel & Roth, 1999). Therefore, the conclusion that the JDC-S model could profitably be used to predict future cases of insomnia is very important. Like all other risk factors included in our chapter, the pathogenesis of insomnia is both complex and multidimensional, with several mechanisms influencing the course of this condition's development (cf. Jansson & Linton, 2006). The JDC-S model is but one among many possible mechanisms.

4.8.2   Theoretical Issues in the Reviewed Field

A major theoretical postulate of this chapter has been that job demands have a positive influence, and that control and support have a negative influence on maladaptive health responses. Whenever possible, support for this underlying assumption was provided in the review of each of the specific maladaptive health responses using studies based on longitudinal designs because they provide more robust support for the unidirectional effects posited by the JDC-S model. However, the relationships between the JDC-S model and maladaptive health responses may be reciprocally related; the direction of influence may flow from the health response, such as sleep disturbance, to the appraisal of the job demands included in the model. In all the studies that we co-authored, referred to above, we also tested the reverse-causation hypothesis: only for insomnia did we find some support for it.

The reverse-causation hypothesis was investigated in a few recent studies; however, the criteria used in these studies were indicators of mental health. For example, a study conducted on a large sample of soldiers (Tucker *et al.*, 2008) used multilevel modelling to test the directionality of the relationships between the JDC-S model and mental health based on six waves of survey data collected at three-month time lags. Tucker *et al.* (2008) found strong support for the reverse causal effects such that higher initial strain was associated with higher subsequent work overload and lower control. Another recent study (de Lange *et al.*, 2004) investigated a large sample of Dutch employees, assessing psychological strain and the JDC-S model over four waves of data collection. The results provided support to the expectation that there are reciprocal effects between the model's components and strain over time. In the same vein, reciprocal relationships between the model's components and indicators of mental health were identified in another study (de Lange *et al.*, 2005). Therefore, we suggested that possible reciprocal relationships among the JDC-S model and risk factors for CVD should be systematically examined in future research, as well as the causal effects of physiological and behavioural strain on the JDC-S model.

An additional theoretical path of influence may stem from a third variable. That is, the empirical link between the JDC-S model and maladaptive health response might be spurious, arising from the relationship of both the model and maladaptive response to a third variable, such as a certain personality trait that may be genetically determined. For example, negative affectivity, or a person's predisposition to experience negative mood states such as depressive symptomatology, anger, guilt and fearfulness, may affect both stress appraisals and maladaptive health responses (Watson & Clark, 1984). Negative affectivity may lead to high job demands appraisals and low control and support appraisals because it is reflected in individuals being extremely vigilant in scanning their environment for stimuli that may threaten their well-being (Watson, Clark & Carey, 1988). Negative affectivity may be associated with reduced physical activity, obesity and elevated blood pressure (Burke, Brief & George, 1993), and acting through its influence on depressive symptomatology could influence most of the maladaptive health outcomes under consideration here (Suls & Bunde, 2005).

4.8.3   Methodological Issues in the Reviewed Field

A methodological limitation of the research literature covered in the review concerns the two approaches toward the conceptualization of stress referred to earlier, the one that focuses on chronic stress and the one that emphasizes critical or minor job events. These two approaches to stress measurement have seldom been combined in a single study designed to predict an outcome considered here (Frese & Zapf, 1988). For example, it is well established that episodic stressors cause transient elevations of blood pressure, but the relationships between transient elevations and persistent elevations of high blood pressure remain unclear (Mann, 2006). The same generalization is relevant to the combined use, in the same study, of family-related and work-related stress to predict either of the above outcomes. Seldom have antecedent variables, such as objectively measured job demands, been included in the research designs of the studies reviewed here. Finally, the longitudinal studies that we covered used diverse methodologies to assess the components of the JDC-S model.

Research on the JDC-S model has often been criticized for assessing the job characteristics included in the model subjectively, primarily by means of self-reports on questionnaires (Jones *et al.*, 1998; Kristensen, 1996). It was argued by these critics that self-reports do not necessarily represent 'true' job conditions due to distorted perceptions and other self-report biases. These claims were empirically examined in multi-methods studies that evaluated the JDC-S model using expert ratings and aggregated group evaluations (Griffin *et al.*, 2007; Theorell & Hasselhorn, 2005; Waldenstrom *et al.*, 2008) and in general did not provide any support for the subjectivity argument.

4.8.4   Limitations of the Current Review

Some limitations of the current review are common to any narrative review of a phenomenon. We have made an effort to cover meta-analytic studies for each of the maladaptive health responses discussed, but they were seldom available for the health outcomes that we focused on. When meta-analytic studies were not available, the most recent qualitative reviews were consulted. However, it was beyond the scope of our chapter to identify and discuss the major inconsistencies in the findings of the relevant longitudinal studies. Researchers used different follow-up times, different operationalizations of the JDC-S model's components, and different sets of control variables. Resolving such inconsistencies constitutes a major challenge for future meta-analytic investigations of the pertinent JDC-S model–maladaptive health response associations.

4.8.5   Suggestions for Future Research

We reviewed above three major theoretical perspectives that guided most of the research currently being carried out in the field of stress and physical health. After reviewing the P-E fit perspective, the ERI approach, and the JDC-S model, we decided to focus on the latter. Empirically, several studies systematically compared the predictive power of the ERI and the JDC-S models relative to different types of psychological strain (for references, see Dragano *et al.*, 2008; Griffin *et al.*, 2007; Rydstedt, Devereux & Sverke, 2007). These studies yielded inconsistent results, but generally provided support for the argument that each model probably explains a unique variance in strains and therefore combining them is the optimal strategy for increasing our understanding of the influence of work characteristics on people's health. These theoretical perspectives on stress–health relationships differ in their conceptualization of stress, strain and health, and place different emphases on some of the antecedent mediating and moderating variables depicted in Figure 4.1. However, as we noted, the three theoretical perspectives appear largely complementary. Therefore, we would like to suggest that one of the more promising avenues for research in this area is to systematically compare the predictive validity of these theoretical perspectives with regard to risk factors for CVD.

To illustrate the point made above, we would like to refer to a recent study (Bosma *et al.*, 1998), which compared the predictive validity of the effort-reward-imbalance perspective and the demand-control-support model with respect to coronary heart disease. Bosma *et al.* (1998), in a study of men and women (6895 and 3413, respectively) working in British government offices, found that low job control and high cost/low gain work conditions independently influenced the development of heart disease. This research exemplifies the advantages of combining several theoretical perspectives, in a longitudinal design, to predict maladaptive health responses.

Each of the maladaptive health responses may be conceptualized along several dimensions, including its level, variability or consistency, forms of appearance, temporal intensity and trajectory. For example, we noted above that inflammation biomarkers in the body include a group of indicators, and each could play a different role in the etiology of CVD. Future research on each of the maladaptive health responses covered in this review may consider including in the study design several important dimensions of the response investigated.

Another promising avenue for research concerns the interactive effects of the JDC-S model and socioeconomic disadvantages in predicting maladaptive health responses. Most epidemiological studies that assess the effects of the JDC-S model on the maladaptive health responses considered here statistically control for the effects of the subjects' age, sex, race-ethnicity, obesity, smoking behaviour, and a family history of hypertension or hyperlipidemia. Such a model assumes that the JDC-S model influences the maladaptive health response under consideration independently of the confounders that were controlled for. Often, this assumption is unwarranted.

It is well known that stress affects obesity and smoking behaviour as well as diet. In addition, it is plausible that some of the antecedent variables tapping socioeconomic disadvantage interact with stress to influence some of the maladaptive health responses. In future research, researchers should consider adopting theoretical models that allow for moderating or mediating influences of the above confounders on the relationships between the JDC-S model and the maladaptive health response under consideration.

REFERENCES

Aboa-Eboule, C., Brisson, C., Maunsell, E., Masse, B., Bourbonnais, R., Vezina, M. et al. (2007). Job strain and risk of acute recurrent coronary heart disease events. *Journal of the American Medical Association*, **298**(14), 1652–60.

Adler, N.E., Boyce, T., Chesney, M.A., Cohen, S., Folkman, S., Kahn, R.L. et al. (1994). Socioeconomic status and health: the challenge of the gradient. *American Psychologist*, **49**(1), 15–24.

Akerstedt, T. (2006). Psychosocial stress and impaired sleep. *Scandinavian Journal of Work Environment & Health*, **32**(6), 493–501.

Akerstedt, T., Kecklund, G. & Gillberg, M. (in press). Sleep and sleepiness in relation to stress and displaced work hours. *Physiology and Behavior*.

Armon, G., Shirom, A., Shapira, I. & Melamed, S. (2008). On the nature of burnout-insomnia relationships: a prospective study of employed adults. *Journal of Psychosomatic Research*, **65**(1), 5–12.

Banks, J., Marmot, M., Oldfield, Z. & Smith, J.P. (2006). Disease and disadvantage in the United States and in England. *Journal of the American Medical Association*, **295**(17), 2037–45.

Belkic, K.L., Landsbergis, P.A., Schnall, P.L. & Baker, D.B. (2004). Is job strain a major source of cardiovascular disease risk? *Scandinavian Journal of Work and Environment & Health*, **30**(2), 85–128.

Black, P.H. (2002). Stress and the inflammatory response: a review of neurogenic inflammation. *Brain, Behavior, and Immunity*, **16**(6), 622–53.

Black, P.H. (2003). The inflammatory response is an integral part of the stress response: implications for atherosclerosis, insulin resistance, type II diabetes and metabolic syndrome X. *Brain, Behavior, and Immunity*, **17**(5), 350–64.

Black, P.H. & Garbutt, L.D. (2002). Stress, inflammation and cardiovascular disease. *Journal of Psychosomatic Research*, **52**(1), 1–23.

Bosma, H., Peter, R., Siegrist, J. & Marmot, M. (1998). Two alternative job stress models and the risk of coronary heart disease. *American Journal of Public Health*, **88**(1), 68.

Brotman, D.J., Golden, S.H. & Wittstein, I.S. (2007). The cardiovascular toll of stress. *Lancet*, **370**(9592), 1089–100.

Burke, M.J., Brief, A.P. & George, J.M. (1993). The role of negative affectivity in understanding relations between self-reports of stressors and strains:

a comment on the applied psychology literature. *Journal of Applied Psychology*, **78**(3), 402–12.

Buysse, D.J., Ancoli-Israel, S., Edinger, J.D., Lichstein, K.L. & Morin, C.M. (2006). Recommendations for a standard research assessment of insomnia. *Sleep*, **29**(9), 1155–73.

Chandola, T., Britton, A., Brunner, E., Hemingway, H., Malik, M., Kumari, M. *et al.* (2008). Work stress and coronary heart disease: what are the mechanisms? *European Heart Journal*, **29**(5), 640–8.

Chandola, T., Brunner, E. & Marmot, M. (2006). Chronic stress at work and the metabolic syndrome: prospective study. *British Medical Journal*, **332**(7540), 521–5.

Clays, E., De Bacquer, D., Delanghe, J., Kittel, F., Van Renterghem, L. & De Backer, G. (2005). Associations between dimensions of job stress and biomarkers of inflammation and infection. *Journal of Occupational and Environmental Medicine*, **47**(4), 878–83.

Cohen, S., Janicki-Deverts, D. & Miller, G.E. (2007). Psychological stress and disease. *Journal of the American Medical Association*, **298**(14), 1685–7.

Cooper, C.L. (1998). *Theories of Organizational Stress*. New York: Oxford University Press.

Danna, K. & Griffin, R.W. (1999). Health and well-being in the workplace: a review and synthesis of the literature. *Journal of Management*, **25**(3), 357–84.

de Lange, A.H., Taris, T.W., Houtman, I.L. & Bongers, P.M. (2003). 'The very best of the millennium': Longitudinal research and the demand-control-(support) model. *Journal of Occupational Health Psychology*, **8**(4), 282–305.

de Lange, A.H., Taris, T., Kompier, M., Houtman, I.L.D. & Bongers, P.M. (2004). The relationships between work characteristics and mental health: examining normal, reversed, and reciprocal relationships in a 4-wave study. *Work and Stress*, **18**(2), 149–66.

de Lange, A.H., Taris, T.W., Kompier, M., Houtman, I.L.D. & Bongers, P.M. (2005). Different mechanisms to explain the reversed effects of mental health on work characteristics. *Scandinavian Journal of Work, Environment and Health*, **31**(1), 3–14.

Derogatis, L.R. & Coons, H.L. (1993). Self-report measures of stress. In L. Goldberger & S. Breznitz (Eds), *Handbook of Stress* (pp. 200–34). New York: Free Press.

Dragano, N., He, Y., Moebus, S., Jockel, K.H., Erbel, R. & Siegrist, J. (2008). Two models of job stress and depressive symptoms. *Social Psychiatry and Psychiatric Epidemiology*, **43**(1), 72–8.

Eden, D. (1982). Critical job events, acute stress, and strain: a multiple interrupted time series. *Organizational Behavior and Human Performance*, **30**, 312–29.

Eden, D. (1990). Acute and chronic job stress, strain, and vacation relief. *Organizational Behavior and Human Decision Processes*, **45**, 175–93.

Edwards, J.R. (1998). Cybernetic theory of stress, coping, and well-being. In C.L. Cooper (Ed.), *Theories of Organizational Stress* (pp. 122–53). New York: Oxford University Press.

Edwards, J.R., Cable, D.M., Williamson, I.O., Lambert, L.S. & Shipp, A.J. (2006). The phenomenology of fit: linking the person and environment to the subjective experience of person-environment fit. *Journal of Applied Psychology*, **91**(4), 802–27.

Edwards, J.R., Caplan, R.D. & Van Harrison, R. (1998). Person-environment fit theory: conceptual foundations, empirical evidence, and directions for future research. In C.L. Cooper (Ed.), *Theories of Organizational Stress* (pp. 28–68). New York: Oxford University Press.

Fauvel, J.P., M'Pio, I., Quelin, P., Rigaud, J.P., Laville, M. & Ducher, M. (2003). Neither perceived job stress nor individual cardiovascular reactivity predict high blood pressure. *Hypertension*, **42**(6), 1112–16.

Fredrikson, M. & Matthews, K.A. (1990). Cardiovascular responses to behavioral stress and hypertension: a meta-analytic review. *Annals of Behavioral Medicine*, **12**, 30–9.

French, J.R.P. & Caplan, R D. (1973). Organizational stress and individual strain. In A.J. Marrow (Ed.), *The Failure of Success* (pp. 30–66). New York: Amacom.

French, J.R.P., Caplan, R.D. & Harrison, R.V. (1982). *The Mechanisms of Job Stress and Strain*. Chichester: John Wiley & Sons, Ltd.

Frese, M. & Zapf, D. (1988). Methodological issues in the study of work stress: objective vs. subjective measurements of work stress and the question of longitudinal studies. In C.L. Cooper & R. Payne (Eds), *Causes, Coping and Consequences*. Chichester: John Wiley & Sons, Ltd.

Gajendran, R.S. & Harrison, D.A. (2007). The good, the bad, and the unknown about telecommuting: meta-analysis of psychological mediators and individual consequences. *Journal of Applied Psychology*, **92**(6), 1524–41.

Gallo, L.C. & Matthews, K.A. (2003). Understanding the association between socioeconomic status and physical health: do negative emotions play a role? *Psychological Bulletin*, **129**(1), 10–51.

Ganster, D.C. & Schaubroeck, J. (1991). Work stress and employee health. *Journal of Management*, **17**, 235–71.

Gillin, J.C. & Byerley, W.F. (1990). The diagnosis and management of insomnia. *New England Journal of Medicine*, **322**(4), 239–48.

Griffin, J.M., Greiner, B.A., Stansfeld, S.A. & Marmot, M. (2007). The effect of self-reported and observed job conditions on depression and anxiety symptoms: a comparison of theoretical models. *Journal of Occupational Health Psychology*, **12**(4), 334–49.

Guimont, C., Brisson, C., Dagenais, G.R., Milot, A., Vezina, M., Masse, B. *et al.* (2006). Effects of job strain on blood pressure: a prospective study of male and female white-collar workers. *American Journal of Public Health*, **96**(8), 1436–43.

Hemingway, H. & Marmot, M. (1999). Evidence based cardiology: psychosocial factors in the aetiology and prognosis of coronary heart disease: systematic review of prospective cohort studies. *British Medical Journal*, **318**(7196), 1460–7.

Hemingway, H., Shipley, M., Mullen, M.J., Kumari, M., Brunner, E., Taylor, M. *et al.* (2003). Social and psychosocial influences on inflammatory markers and vascular function in civil servants (the Whitehall II study). *The American Journal of Cardiology*, **92**(8), 984–7.

James, G.D. & Brown, D.E. (1997). The biological stress response and lifestyle: catecholamines and blood pressure. *Annual Review of Anthropology*, **26**(1), 313–35.

Jansson, M. & Linton, S.J. (2006). Psychosocial work stressors in the development and maintenance of insomnia: a prospective study. *Journal of Occupational Health Psychology*, **11**(3), 241–8.

Jansson-Frojmark, M., Lundqvist, D., Lundqvist, N. & Linton, S.J. (2007). Psychosocial work stressors for insomnia: a prospective study on 50-60-year-old adults in the working population. *International Journal of Behavioral Medicine*, **14**(4), 222–8.

Johnson, J.V. & Hall, E.M. (1988). Job strain, work place social support, and cardiovascular disease: a cross-sectional study of a random sample of Swedish working population. *American Journal of Public Health*, **78**(10), 1136–42.

Johnson, J.V., Stewart, W., Hall, E.M., Fredlund, P. & Theorell, T. (1996). Long-term psychosocial work environment and cardiovascular mortality among Swedish men. *American Journal of Public Health*, **86**(3), 324–31.

Jones, F., Bright, J.E.H., Searle, B. & Cooper, L. (1998). Modelling occupational stress and health: the impact of the demand-control model on academic research and on workplace practice. *Stress Medicine*, **14**(4), 231–6.

Kahn, R.L., Wolfe, D.M., Quinn, R.P., Snoek, J.D. & Rosenthal, R.A. (1964). *Organizational Stress*. New York: John Wiley & Sons, Inc.

Kamarck, T.W., Janicki, D.L., Shiffman, S., Polk, D.E., Muldoon, M.F., Liebenauer, L.L. *et al.* (2002). Psychosocial demands and ambulatory blood pressure: a field assessment approach. *Physiology and Behavior*, **77**(4–5), 699–704.

Kamarck, T.W., Shiffman, S.M., Smithline, L., Goodie, J.L., Paty, J.A., Gnys, M. *et al.* (1998). Effects of task strain, social conflict, and emotional activation on ambulatory cardiovascular activity: daily life consequences of recurring stress in a multiethnic adult sample. *Health Psychology*, **17**(1), 17–29.

Karasek, R. & Theorell, T. (1990). *Healthy Work: Stress, Productivity, and the Reconstruction of Working Life*. New York: Basic Books.

Kasl, S.V. (1996). The influence of the work environment on cardiovascular health: a historical, conceptual, and methodological perspective. *Journal of Occupational Health Psychology*, **1**(1), 42–56.

Kiecolt-Glaser, J.K., McGuire, L., Robles, T.F. & Glaser, R. (2002). Psychoneuroimmunology and psychosomatic medicine: back to the future. *Psychosomatic Medicine*, **64**(1), 15–28.

Kivimaki, M., Virtanen, M., Elovainio, M., Kouvonen, A., Vaananen, A. & Vahtera, J. (2006). Work stress in the etiology of coronary heart disease – a meta-analysis. *Scandinavian Journal of Work Environment and Health*, **32**(6), 431–42.

Knudsen, H.K., Ducharme, L.J. & Roman, P.M. (2007). Job stress and poor sleep quality: data from an American sample of full-time workers. *Social Science and Medicine*, **64**(10), 1997–2007.

Kristensen, T.S. (1996). Job stress and cardiovascular disease: a theoretic critical review. *Journal of Occupational Health Psychology*, **1**(3), 246–60.

Kristof, A.L. (1996). Person-organization fit: an integrative review of its con-
   ceptualizations, measurement, and implications. *Personnel Psychology*, **49**(1),
   1–49.
Kristof-Brown, A.L., Zimmerman, R.D. & Johnson, E.C. (2005). Consequences
   of individuals' fit at work: a meta-analysis of person-job, person-organization,
   person-group, and person-supervisor fit. *Personnel Psychology*, **58**(2),
   281–342.
Landsbergis, P.A., Schnall, P.L., Pickering, T.G., Warren, K. & Schwartz, J. E.
   (2003). Life-course exposure to job strain and ambulatory blood pressure in men.
   American Journal of Epidemiology, **157**(11), 998–1006.
Lazarus, R.S. (1999). *Stress and Emotion*. New York: Springer.
Linton, S.J. (2004). Does work stress predict insomnia? A prospective study. *British
   Journal of Health Psychology*, **9**(1), 127–36.
Macik-Frey, M., Quick, J.C. & Nelson, D.L. (2007). Advances in occupational
   health: from a stressful beginning to a positive future. *Journal of Management*,
   33(6), 809–40.
Mackay, C.J. & Cooper, C.L. (1987). Occupational stress and health: some current
   issues. *International Review of Industrial and Organizational Psychology*, **1**,
   167–99.
Madjid, M., Awan, I., Willerson, J.T. & Casscells, S. W. (2004). Leukocyte count and
   coronary heart disease: implications for risk assessment. *Journal of the American
   College of Cardiology*, **44**(10), 1945–56.
Mann, S.J. (2006). Job stress and blood pressure: a critical appraisal of reported
   studies. *Current Hypertension Reviews*, **2**, 127–38.
Markovitz, J.H., Matthews, K.A., Whooley, M., Lewis, C.E. & Greenlund, K.J.
   (2004). Increases in job strain are associated with incident hypertension in the
   CARDIA study. *Annals of Behavioral Medicine*, **28**(1), 4–9.
Marmot, M. (2006). Status syndrome: a challenge to medicine. *Journal of American
   Medical Association*, **295**(11), 1304–7.
Marmot, M., Theorell, T. & Siegrist, J. (2002). Work and coronary heart disease. In
   S.A. Stansfeld & M. Marmot (Eds), *Stress and the Heart* (pp. 51–71). London:
   BMJ Books.
McEwen, B.S. (2007). Physiology and neurobiology of stress and adaptation: central
   role of the brain. *Physiological Reviews*, **87**(3), 873–904.
Melamed, S., Shirom, A., Toker, S., Berliner, S. & Shapira, I. (2006). Burnout and
   risk of cardiovascular disease: evidence, possible causal paths, and promising
   research directions. *Psychological Bulletin*, **132**(3), 327–53.
Miller, G.E., Chen, E. & Zhou, E.S. (2007). If it goes up, must it come down?
   Chronic stress and the hypothalamic-pituitary-adrenocortical axis in humans.
   Psychological Bulletin, **133**(1), 25–45.
Monroe, S.M. (2008). Modern approaches to conceptualizing and measuring human
   life stress. *Annual Review of Clinical Psychology*, **4**(1), 33–52.
Mora, S., Rifai, N., Buring, J.E. & Ridker, P. M. (2006). Additive value of
   immunoassay-measured fibrinogen and high-sensitivity C-reactive protein levels
   for predicting incident cardiovascular events. *Circulation*, **114**(5), 381–7.

Niaura, R., Stoney, C.M. & Herbert, P.N. (1992). Lipids in psychological research: the last decade. *Biological Psychology*, **34**(1), 1–43.

Ohlin, B., Berglund, G., Rosvall, M. & Nilsson, P.M. (2007). Job strain in men, but not in women, predicts a significant rise in blood pressure after 6. 5 years of follow-up. *Journal of Hypertension*, **25**(3), 525–31.

Partinen, M. (1994). Sleep disorders and stress. *Journal of Psychosomatic Research*, **38**(Suppl 1), 89–91.

Pickering, T.G., Shimbo, D. & Haas, D. (2006). Ambulatory blood-pressure monitoring. *New England Journal of Medicine*, **354**(22), 2368–74.

Quick, J.C., Quick, J.D., Nelson, D.L. & Hurrell, J.J.J. (1997). *Preventive Stress Management in Organizations*. Washington, DC: American Psychological Association.

Riese, H., Van Doornen, L.J.P., Houtman, I.L.D. & De Geus, E.J.C. (2000). Job strain and risk indicators for cardiovascular disease in young female nurses. *Health Psychology*, **19**(5), 429–40.

Roth, T. & Ancoli-Israel, S. (1999). Daytime consequences and correlates of insomnia in the United States: results of the 1991 National Sleep Foundation Survey. *Sleep*, **22**(2), 354–8.

Roth, T. & Roehrs, T. (2003). Insomnia: epidemiology, characteristics, and consequences. *Clinical Cornerstone*, **5**(3), 5–15.

Roth, T., Roehrs, T. & Pies, R. (2007). Insomnia: pathophysiology and implications for treatment. *Sleep Medicine Reviews*, **11**(1), 71–9.

Rydstedt, L.W., Devereux, J. & Sverke, M. (2007). Comparing and combining the demand-control-support model and the effort reward imbalance model to predict long-term mental strain. *European Journal of Work and Organizational Psychology*, **16**(3), 261–78.

Sargent, L.D. & Terry, D.J. (2000). The moderating role of social support in Karasek's job strain model. *Work and Stress*, **14**(3), 245–61.

Schnall, P.L., Landsbergis, P.A. & Baker, D. (1994). Job strain and cardiovascular disease. *Annual Review of Public Health*, **15**(1), 381–411.

Schnorpfeil, P., Noll, A., Schulze, R., Ehlert, U., Frey, K. & Fischer, J. E. (2003). Allostatic load and work conditions. *Social Science and Medicine*, **57**(4), 647–56.

Schwartz, J.E., Pickering, T.G. & Landsbergis, P.A. (1996). Work-related stress and blood pressure: current theoretical models and considerations from a behavioral medicine perspective. *Journal of Occupational Health Psychology*, **1**(3), 287–310.

Shirom, A., Toker, S., Berliner, S. & Shapira, I. (2008). The job demand-control-support model and stress-related low-grade inflammatory responses among healthy employees: a longitudinal study. *Work and Stress*, **22**(2), 138–52.

Siegrist, J. (1995). Emotions and health in occupational life: new scientific findings and policy implications. *Patient Education and Counseling*, **25**(3), 227–36.

Smith, T.W., Glazer, K., Ruiz, J.M. & Gallo, L.C. (2004). Hostility, anger, aggressiveness, and coronary heart disease: an interpersonal perspective on personality, emotion, and health. *Journal of Personality*, **72**(6), 1217–70.

Smith, T.W. & MacKenzie, J. (2006). Personality and risk of physical illness. *Annual Review of Clinical Psychology*, **2**, 435–67.

Steenland, K., Fine, L., Belkic, K., Landsbergis, P., Schnall, P., Baker, D. *et al.* (2000). Research findings linking workplace factors to cardiovascular disease outcomes. *Occupational Medicine-State of the Art Reviews*, **15**(1), 7–68.

Stoney, C.M., Bausserman, L., Niaura, R., Marcus, B. & Flynn, M. (1999). Lipid reactivity to stress: II. Biological and behavioral influences. *Health Psychology*, **18**(3), 251–61.

Stoney, C.M., Niaura, R., Bausserman, L. & Matacin, M. (1999). Lipid reactivity to stress: I. Comparison of chronic and acute stress responses in middle-aged airline pilots. *Health Psychology*, **18**(3), 241–50.

Suls, J. & Bunde, J. (2005). Anger, anxiety, and depression as risk factors for cardiovascular disease: the problems and implications of overlapping affective dispositions. *Psychological Bulletin*, **131**(2), 260–300.

Taylor, S.E. & Stanton, A.L. (2007). Coping resources, coping processes, and mental health. *Annual Review of Clinical Psychology*, **3**(1), 377–401.

Theorell, T. (1998). Job characteristics in a theoretical and practical health context. In C.L. Cooper (Ed.), *Theories of Organizational Stress* (pp. 205–20). New York: Oxford University Press.

Theorell, T. & Hasselhorn, H.M. (2005). On cross-sectional questionnaire studies of relationships between psychosocial conditions at work and health – are they reliable? *International Archives of Occupational and Environmental Health*, **78**(7), 517–22.

Tirosh, A., Rudich, A., Shochat, T., Tekes-Manova, D., Israeli, E., Henkin, Y. *et al.* (2007). Changes in triglyceride levels and risk for coronary heart disease in young men. *Annals of Internal Medicine*, **147**(6), 377–85.

Tsutsumi, A. & Kawakami, N. (2004). A review of empirical studies on the model of effort–reward imbalance at work: reducing occupational stress by implementing a new theory. *Social Science and Medicine*, **59**(11), 2335–59.

Tucker, J.S., Sinclair, R.R., Mohr, C.D., Adler, A.B., Thomas, J.L. & Salvi, A. D. (2008). A temporal investigation of the direct, interactive, and reverse relations between demand and control and affective strain. *Work and Stress*, **22**(2), 81–95.

Ursin, H. & Eriksen, H.R. (2007). Cognitive activation theory of stress, sensitization, and common health complaints. *Annals of the New York Academy of Sciences*, **1113**(1), 304–10.

Van Der Doef, M. & Maes, S. (1998). The job demand-control (-support) model and physical health outcomes: a review of the strain and buffer hypotheses. *Psychology and Health*, **13**(4), 909–36.

Van der Doef, M. & Maes, S. (1999). The job demand-control (-support) model and psychological well-being: a review of 20 years of empirical research. *Work and Stress*, **13**(2), 87–114.

van Vegchel, N., de Jonge, J., Bosma, H. & Schaufeli, W.B. (2005). Reviewing the effort–reward imbalance model: drawing up the balance of 45 empirical studies. *Social Science and Medicine*, **60**(5), 1117–31.

Waldenstrom, K., Ahlberg, G., Bergman, P., Forsell, Y., Stoetzer, U., Waldenstrom, M. *et al.* (2008). Externally assessed psychosocial work characteristics and diagnoses of anxiety and depression. *Occupational and Environmental Medicine*, **65**(2), 90–6.

Walsh, J.K. & Engelhardt, C.L. (1999). The direct economic costs of insomnia in the United States for 1995. *Sleep*, **22**(2), 386–93.

Watson, D. & Clark, L.A. (1984). Negative affectivity: the disposition of the negative emotional states. *Psychological Bulletin*, **96**, 465–90.

Watson, D., Clark, L.A. & Carey, G. (1988). Positive and negative affectivity and their relation to anxiety and depressive disorders. *Journal of Abnormal Psychology*, **97**(3), 346–53.

Williams, R.B. (2008). Psychosocial and biobehavioral factors and their interplay in coronary heart disease. *Annual Review of Clinical Psychology*, **4**(1), 349–65.

Zammit, G.K., Weiner, J., Damato, N. *et al.* (1999). Quality of life in people with insomnia. *Sleep*, **22**, 379–85.

CHAPTER 5

Sickness Presenteeism and Attendance Pressure Factors: Implications for Practice

Caroline Biron
Lancaster University Management School, Lancaster University, UK
and
Per Øystein Saksvik
Norwegian University of Science and Technology (NTNU), Norway

Failure to report for work as scheduled, or absenteeism, has been a research topic since the 1920s (Johns, 2008b). Scholars from various fields have been interested in identifying the causes for this behaviour and its organizational and individual consequences. Absenteeism as a behavioural pattern has been studied by scholars from multiple disciplines such as sociology, economics, law, psychology, industrial relations and medicine (Johns, 2008a). More recently, sickness presenteeism has become an increasingly popular theme. The term was first coined by Cary Cooper in the 1990s to describe the growing propensity of workers who spent long hours in the workplace when they feared for their job (Chapman, 2005). Since then, many other definitions of sickness presenteeism have been developed and the term has been used inconsistently in the scientific literature. Although, the term seems to be increasingly popular, the concept is used in various ways and etiological knowledge is still scarce. In the present chapter, we review the literature to explore how the term has been used, its consequences, and the determinants which have been found to influence it. The implications for health promotion and occupational health programmes are discussed.

International Handbook of Work and Health Psychology, Third Edition. Edited by Cary L. Cooper, James Campbell Quick, and Marc J. Schabracq.
© 2009 John Wiley & Sons, Ltd. Published 2015 by John Wiley & Sons, Ltd.

5.1 DEFINING SICKNESS PRESENTEEISM

The definition given by Cooper describes the behaviour of workers who perceive their job to be in jeopardy. Although the association between job insecurity, absenteeism and presenteeism is quite complex and will be discussed
later, Cooper's conceptualization of presenteeism implied that presenteeism
was a behaviour determined by specific determinants (i.e. long-working hours
culture and a context of uncertainty). This tendency to stay at work longer
than required to display visible commitment is what Simpson (1998) calls
'competitive presenteeism', where people compete on who will stay in the
office the longest. Research has documented that organizational culture plays
an important role in shaping the decision as to whether or not a person will
come to work while ill (Nicolson & Johns, 1985). For example, McKevitt
et al. (1997) found that even though high levels of occupational stress can
lead to increased rates of absence, economic uncertainty and organizational
culture can foster presenteeism and induce artificially low absence rates.
Dew, Keefe and Small (2005), in a study based on focus groups and interviews, also illustrated how economic and social constraints as well as
workplace cultures influence how presenteeism is rationalized by workers
from different occupational groups. These studies are also conceptualizing
presenteeism as a behaviour which is influenced by a variety of factors. This
is in line with the definition given by Aronsson, Gustafsson and Dallner
(2000), for whom presenteeism refers to 'the phenomenon of people, who
despite complaints and ill health that should prompt rest and absence from
work, are still turning up at their jobs' (p. 503).

In much of the existing literature, presenteeism is not conceptualized as
behaviour but as the associated costs it represents in terms of productivity
losses. For example, the American College of Occupational and Environmental Medicine defines presenteeism as 'the measurable extent to which
health symptoms, conditions and diseases adversely affect the productivity
of individuals who choose to remain at work when ill' (Chapman, 2005,
p. 2). However, productivity loss and cutback days are in fact *consequences*
of people's decision to turn up to work despite their ill health. Given that
absenteeism is generally considered as behaviour, considering both absenteeism and presenteeism behaviours which lead to costly consequences is
conceptually more consistent. For the purpose of consistency with absenteeism research, the behavioural definition of presenteeism is here used to
refer to people who work through illness.

As far as measurement of the consequences of presenteeism, many different instruments of productivity loss engendered by it have been developed
and validated. They generally measure either the number of cutback days
(number of days where usual tasks were impaired by a health condition) (Lim,

Sanderson & Andrews, 2000), or the extent to which the quality or quantity of work was affected in general or in terms of specific tasks which cannot be performed due to the health impairment (Turpin *et al.*, 2004). For example, Loepkke (2006) mentions injury rates, product waste, unsatisfactory work culture as consequences of health-productivity losses. Reduced work output, errors, failure to meet company production standards are all measurable consequences of presenteeism. Sometimes, researchers have considered presenteeism as the absence of sick leave in persons with health conditions (Kivimäki *et al.*, 2005; McKevitt *et al.*, 1997). It is useful to distinguish between sickness presenteeism and people who are what may be called long-term healthy. Aronsson and Lindh (2004) have defined them as people who haven't been away from work for more than five days during a two-year period. Even though it is rare, there are people who are very rarely away from work. Most of us are present at work and require a few days of illness each year due to minor and temporary ailments. Existing instruments and their specific strengths and limitations have been reviewed (Lofland, Pizzi & Frick, 2004; Prasad *et al.*, 2004).

5.2 CONSEQUENCES OF PRESENTEEISM AND ABSENTEEISM

The vast majority of research on the consequences of presenteeism has been concentrated on the financial costs it represents for organizations. The costs of lost productivity can be measured by considering absenteeism (short and long term and workers' compensation), but this only provides a partial indication of the total costs (Burton *et al.*, 1999; Edington & Burton, 2003; Schultz, 2007). The costs resulting from absenteeism are diversified but include direct costs (e.g. insurance premiums so that the employees' wage is covered during the disability period) and indirect costs (e.g. overtime for colleagues, training the replacement worker including the lost productive time this involves) (Brun, 2008). Few studies have shown that productivity losses associated with workers whose health problems have not necessarily led to absenteeism are much higher than those associated with absenteeism. For example, the Sainsbury Centre for Mental Health in the UK estimates that the cost of presenteeism could be 1.8 times the cost of absenteeism (Cooper & Dewe, 2008). In the USA, Stewart *et al.* (2003) showed that the costs of lost productive time could be up to three times the costs of absence-related productivity loss. Sickness presenteeism also seems to be a prevalent phenomenon. Hansen and Anderson (2008) conducted a cross-sectional study with a sample of 12,935 people in Denmark's workforce and found that 70% of the workforce went to work whilst suffering from ill health at least once over the past 12 months. Other studies have also reported such high rates (Aronsson *et al.*, 2000; Biron, Brun & Ivers, 2006; Caverley, Cunningham & MacGregor, 2007).

Aronsson and Gustafsson (2005) highlight the gap in research on the relationship between sickness presenteeism and health. Other than research on the financial costs, there is a striking scarcity of studies evaluating the effects of presenteeism on workers' health and well-being (Johns, 2008b). Some evidence of negative consequences of working through illness is offered by Kivimäki *et al.* (2005). Their study showed 17% of unhealthy employees took no absence during the three-year duration of the follow-up period. Their incidence of serious coronary events was twice as high as unhealthy employees who showed moderate levels of sickness absenteeism. A recent research by Bergström *et al.* (2009) also suggests that the sickness presentees of today are the absentees of the future. This prospective research used public and private sector data (surveys and employers' register) with an overall sample of 6,242 employees. The results showed that employees who had more than five days of sickness presence during the baseline year had significantly higher risk of reporting more than 30 days of sick leave at follow-up measures (18-months and three years later). This risk was still significant after adjusting for several confounding variables. Hansen and Andersen (2008) reported that certain risks factors such as 'insufficient time and resources' not only lead to increased spells of presenteeism, but also to higher levels of musculoskeletal pain, spells of sickness absence and probability of suffering from chronic illness. Given the scarcity of research on presenteeism, it is difficult to say whether on a long-term basis, working despite illness bears certain negative health consequences. As Johns (2008b) points out, being ill, perceiving oneself as ill, and deciding to attend work or not are rather loosely coupled phenomena. Moreover, the impact of presenteeism on the workplace, colleagues and customers has not been studied yet. Since job performance and productivity are hindered by various types of illness, it is likely that presenteeism can be disruptive for colleagues who might have to compensate for the lost productive time.

Another area which has been left out in research is the possible positive effects of maintaining the employment relationship in cases where the health impairment is benign. For example, Sanderson *et al.* (2008) recently underlined the possibility that when the psychosocial work environment is healthy, maintaining the employment relationship could prove to be a healthy strategy, particularly in the case of people with mental illness. Indeed, in a prospective study in 10 call centres, adverse psychosocial work environments were associated with worse mental health and lower productivity from presenteeism. Presenteeism at baseline increased the risk for subsequent mental health problems, but there was some evidence that this association was only significant in the presence of an adverse work environment. In that sense, presenteeism could have either positive or negative consequences on workers and organizations. For example, employees with mental health problems who are exposed to a positive psychosocial work environment could find the routine provided by work and a supportive climate to be helpful even though their productivity is impaired while on the job with a mental illness.

As specified by Johns (2008b), although it seems surprising that presenteeism could be positive for well-being, working on less demanding tasks or with a lowered output still prevents the accumulation of work engendered by an absence, therefore making the return to work less abrupt. This notion of adjusting the tasks to help workers with minor ailments is in line with Johansson and Lundberg's (2004) concept of adjustment latitude. In a study of almost 5000 participants, they found that women with low adjustment latitude had higher rates of absenteeism. Adjustment latitude was defined as the 'opportunities people have to reduce or in other ways alter their work effort when feeling ill'. Johansson and Lundberg measured it with a single item and found some evidence (for women only) that not having the possibility to adjust one's work when ill increases the risk of absenteeism. Research should be conducted to explore how employers can offer flexible work arrangements to workers and on which health conditions these adjustments can be applied in order to promote health and not undermine it. Adapting the work environment and the work tasks in order to help the worker recover from certain minor illness without having to take sick leave could bear positive effects for both the worker and the employer. Not all health impairments would benefit from a maintained link with the workplace (e.g. not severe, acute or infectious health disorders) but this seems like a promising avenue which should be investigated further.

The amount of evidence showing the impacts that absenteeism can have is more substantial compared to presenteeism. It seems obvious that absenteeism helps in the recovery of workers with a severe illness. A common perception about absenteeism is that it helps workers to cope with high levels of work and non work-related stress. Since many studies have shown an association between psychological distress and absenteeism (e.g. Hardy, Woods & Wall, 2003; Johns & Xie, 1998), and between exposure to adverse psychosocial work environment and absenteeism (North *et al.*, 1996), it would seem plausible that a reversed causal relationship would exist. However, so far there is not that much support to show that being absent from work actually reduces distress levels. If this was to be the case, there would be important implications for organizations that use strict control measures to diminish absenteeism since it could unintentionally increase workers' distress and thus result in decreased performance (Hardy et al., 2003). Hacket and Bycio (1996) conducted a study with a small sample of nurses ($N = 20$) to evaluate if absenteeism can serve to restore high levels of emotional and physical fatigue. They collected self-reports of personal problems, tiredness, ill health, sleep disruption, stress and job dissatisfaction on a daily basis during four to five months, and then compared them before, during and after the absence. Their results demonstrate that a spell of absence might not serve as a coping mechanism which results in the reduction of strain, but as a maintenance function which helps employees regain some control over their doldrums and maintain stress-related symptoms at a manageable level. Kristensen (1991) also highlights the possibility that absence might serve as an individual coping strategy, in the sense that it might help workers cope with adverse work environments.

Although occasional and impromptu absenteeism possibly serves as a coping mechanism, it is unknown what the optimal level of absenteeism would be from a health perspective. On the other hand, however, there is evidence showing that absenteeism is not only costly for organizations but also for individuals. Indeed, evidence reviewed by Johns (2001) supports the notion of a withdrawal continuum where being late for work precedes absence, which in return precedes turnover. Moreover, absenteeism is often viewed as a negative and deviant behaviour, which can explain why most people tend to underreport absenteeism and overestimate their attendance record (Johns, 1994). Being absent from work with negative perceptions from the supervisor (Bycio, 1982) can be quite disruptive for teamwork (Grinyer & Singleton, 2000). Certified sickness absence has also been used as a measure of health status (Marmot et al., 1995), and as a predictor of mortality among male and female employees (Vahtera, Pentti & Kivimäki, 2004). This, however, quite possibly reflects the effects of outliers (people who are very sick and show high levels of absenteeism) (Johns, 2008b). Martocchio and Jimeno (2003) propose a model where absenteeism could have positive and negative effects depending on the affective experience associated with it. Depending on their personality, some people might be more likely to feel recharged and be less stressed and more productive upon returning to work. Other personality characteristics such as neuroticism might instead bring one to make the decision to take time off work hastily and impulsively, and then be stressed and fearful about work being piled up upon return. Although these propositions remain to be tested, Martocchio and Jimeno's model suggest absenteeism could be either functional or dysfunctional and have differential consequences on individuals. In sum, the decision to be absent or present at work when ill is a personal decision and it is possible that both positive and negative outcomes will result from that decision. There are many factors other than illness and disease which influence that judgement call.

5.3   PREDICTORS OF SICKNESS PRESENTEEISM

5.3.1   Attendance Pressure Factors

Attendance pressure factors are variables which pressurize people into work despite their health condition (Saksvik, 1996). They can be grouped into (at least) three main categories: (i) personal/family and situational circumstances; (ii) dispositional and attitudinal factors; and (iii) work-related factors. It seems important here to distinguish between positive factors that trigger workers to choose work because it truly is perceived as the best option, and factors that trigger attendance pressure. Attendance pressure factors are not salutogenic and exclude the notion of flexibility from the part of the employer in order to accommodate the worker to accomplish the job with lowered productivity given the illness or ailment. As the following theoretical review will show, there is a delicate balancing act between these factors in the workplace that stimulate to workers to come to work and yet don't result in negative health.

Personal and situational circumstances can influence sickness presenteeism. For example, workers with children or in situations where home is more taxing than work, employees with poorer health status, workers who had higher number of days of sickness absence in the past year, part-time and lower-wage workers tend to show higher rates of presenteeism (Aronsson & Gustafsson, 2005; Aronsson et al., 2000; Biron et al., 2006; Burton et al., 2006; Burton et al., 2005; Hansen & Andersen, 2008). Dispositional factors such as boundaryless people (who can't say no) or over-commited workers, or having a conservative attitude towards absenteeism can also increase people's tendency to work through illness (Aronsson & Gustafsson, 2005; Hansen & Andersen, 2008). Occupational status can also predict higher rates of presenteeism. Aronsson et al. (2000) found that workers in the education sector and in the care and welfare sector had the highest presenteeism rates. Members of these occupational sectors require the provision of care to other people and have a higher tendency to work through illness (Elstad & Vabo, 2008). In line with this, McKevitt et al. (1997) found that medical doctors and company fee earners had very low absenteeism rates but these were artificially induced since over 80% of all respondents had worked through illness. These occupations require that the worker is present in the workplace and that tasks cannot be performed from some other location. However, for knowledge workers, increased sophistication in information and communication technology reduces the need to work from a traditional office (O'Driscoll, Biron & Cooper, in press). Mobile technology means people can now be performing tasks from anywhere, including a train journey, home or an airport (Harrison, Wheeler & Whiteheard, 2004). This has considerable implications on how presenteeism is defined and measured, and on how it affects health and well-being.

The is growing evidence showing that characteristics of the psychosocial work environment are not only closely related to job stress and absenteeism, but are also significant attendance pressure factors. Insufficient time and resources, excessive workload, difficulties to be replaced and role conflict have been consistently related with increases in sickness presenteeism (Aronsson & Gustafsson, 2005; Biron et al., 2006; Elstad & Vabo, 2008; Hansen & Andersen, 2008). Thus, in organizational settings characterized by lean production and understaffing, presenteeism is quite likely to be high. Job control, in traditional stress models (Karasek, 1979; Karasek & Theorell, 1990), is considered a positive work characteristic, since it decreases the risk of physical and mental illness when job demands are high. Higher control is generally associated with lower risks of absenteeism (Bond, Flaxman & Loivette, 2006; Nielsen et al., 2004) but also with lower presenteeism rates (Aronsson & Gustafsson, 2005). Indeed, workers who have high job control are likely to be able to adjust the type of tasks and the working pace which can help them get through a day of illness at work. Skill discretion has also been found to be a significant determinant of presenteeism. This is in line with the possibility to be replaced. Indeed, it is likely that highly skilled people cannot find co-workers to accomplish their tasks if they are ill, and must therefore catch up on their workload on their return.

The way attendance pressure factors affect groups and individuals can also vary according to individual characteristics. Saksvik (1996) measured attendance pressure, job satisfaction, absenteeism and intentions to quit before and after a major restructuration in a large public organization ($N = 401$, $N = 301$). The results of a factor analysis showed there were four types of attendance pressure factors: importance pressure, censure pressure, moral pressure and security pressure. Importance pressure concerns issues like having a lot of responsibility at work, difficulties in obtaining temporary staff etc.; censure pressure is about 'hearing it' from the management or colleagues and being accused of shirking if away from work; moral pressure refers to one's own conscience while security pressure concerns fear of losing one's job unless present at work. Results suggest that low moral pressure and high censure pressure significantly predicted sickness absenteeism. The study indicated that employees who were absent during the reorganization period could be characterized as 'vulnerable', in the sense of having low job satisfaction, low personal work ethics with significant health problems. For practice, this suggests that adding more censure pressure, for example by implementing tighter control on absenteeism patterns, might worsen the situation.

Aronsson and Gustafsson (2005) formulated a model which can be tested in future studies. The model suggests that illness and loss of capacity are the strongest and most direct factors regarding both sickness presenteeism and sickness absenteeism. Sickness presenteeism and sickness absenteeism are mutual options when people are sick; and personal, work-related and dispositional factors will influence the individual's decision. The researchers further point out that there is a difference between positive and negative attendance factors. Negative attendance pressure factors can be conceptualized as 'double risk' since they constitute a risk for health (e.g. time pressure, overload, low job control), and influence people's decision to come to work while ill. Poorer health can lead to higher frequency of having to choose between being present and absent from work. Positive attendance factors, however, are salutogenic factors which influence people's decision to come to work regardless of their health condition. It is worth mentioning that Kristensen (1991) distinguishes between positive and negative attendance and absence factors, however, the distinction between the pressure factors and the stimulating, positive factors in relation to attendance is not so clear. Kristensen highlights interesting and stimulating work, high job satisfaction, rewards for low absence frequency and a good conscience. We believe that the last two factors are included in what we call attendance pressure factors. According to Kristensen, negative attendance factors include a high risk of getting fired and a strict control over absence from work, which, in our understanding, also constitutes attendance pressure factors. He also importantly points out that there are factors outside of work which can also contribute, and that interesting spare-time activities can be a positive absence factor.

5.3.2   Salutogenic Factors

Aronsson and Lindh (2004) highlight that research has been largely focused on bad health and how bad health occurs at the workplace. There has been far less focus on trying to define and operationalize health and to generate knowledge about health-promoting conditions in the workplace. Aronsson and Lindh have analysed both sickness presenteeism and long-term health, mainly derived from an analysis of the working conditions of the people ending up in these categories. Long-term health was defined as a combination of low sickness absenteeism and low sickness presenteeism over a period of two years. A total of 28% of the sample was hailed as long-term healthy. Regarding conditions in the workplace, the largest differences in percent (without controlling for other variables) between those who were long-term healthy and those who weren't, were found in the variable 'the possibility of receiving support from supervisor when the job feels difficult'. Among the workers who received support from their supervisor 42% belonged to the group long-term healthy. Large differences were also found regarding qualitative aspects of the work. Resources enabling people to a good job, being happy with the quality of their work, having the possibility to control their own work pace, and not being confronted with irreconcilable demands were also found to be important factors in long-term healthiness.

Managerial leadership has also been found to be a strong determinant of both illness and wellness. A study looking into the leader's significance with regards to good health has been conducted by Dellve, Skagert and Vilhelmsson (2007). This prospective study looked at how leadership qualities and strategies may act as key processes in the implementation of workplace health promotion. The study measured the effects of leaders on long-term presence at work. Long-term presence was defined as employees who had taken none or a maximum of seven days of sickness absence during the last year. The results showed that leaders who had clearly defined targets, and made use of rewards, recognition, and respect had higher prevalence of employee attendance. The leaders' attitudes towards and view of the employees' health was also important for implementation of interventions promoting health in the workplace. Multi-focused strategies had the greatest effect on workplace presence. Strategies that focus solely on either strengthening the individual or organizational resources were not related to an increase in long-term workplace presence. Along the same line, Nyberg et al. (2008), in a prospective study including just over 3000 Swedish males, showed that managers' consideration for employees, provision of clarity in roles and expectations, supplying information, promotion of employees' control and ability to carry out changes in a healthy way lowered the incidence of ischemic heart diseases. This is in line with other studies showing that the importance of managers' behaviours such as the capacity to manage changes in a healthy way (Saksvik et al., 2007) and treating employees fairly (Kivimäki et al., 2008; Vogli et al., 2007), are essential in order for the job to be a positive factor for employees' health and well-being.

High social support from colleagues was found to increase presenteeism (Hansen & Andersen, 2008). Similarly, Biron et al. (2006) found a significant interaction between the number of sick days, the quality of relationship with colleagues and presenteeism propensity. Workers with good relationships and who reported a small number of sick days had a higher tendency to work through illness compared to workers with a higher number of sick days.

Caverley *et al.* (2007) also found that trust in colleagues and supervisor's support was positively associated with presenteeism.

Along the same line, Lindberg *et al.* (2006) have conducted an epidemiological study ($N = 5638$) trying to identify factors promoting excellent work ability and factors preventing poor work ability (based on sick leave at 18-month follow-up). The results showed promoting excellent work ability seemed to be more dependent on factors such as not having a physically demanding job, having a good work position, having clarity of goals, expectations and responsibilities, and having a superior who appreciates work performance. Preventing poor work ability seemed to be more dependent on job security and psychosocial factors such as mastering the job and having a certain degree of decision making. The results also showed that lifestyle factors such as physical activity, even just once a week, being fully rested when starting work, and having energy throughout the working day was associated with excellent work ability. Although some factors predicted both poor and excellent ability to work, different patterns of factors predicting excellent and poor work ability were found and most of them were factors which can be influenced. This has important implications since it 'opens up the possibility of interventions for promoting excellent work ability and preventing poor work ability' (Lindberg *et al.*, 2006, p. 120). This is an important issue because traditionally occupational health and safety programmes focus on reducing the exposure to physical and psychosocial risks with a view to improving employees' health, whereas worksite health promotion programmes tend to address individual risk factors. In this sense, promoting wellness and preventing illness should not be viewed as mutually exclusive but as an integrated holistic approach (Gibbs & Burnett, forthcoming). Furthermore, evidence suggests that successful programmes are comprehensive and include both preventive and promotive factors (Giga *et al.*, 2003a; Giga *et al.*, 2003b; Lamontagne *et al.*, 2007). As summarized in Table 5.1, the evidence gathered so far illustrates some of the salutogenic and attendance factors which have been found to increase the tendency to work while ill. Salutogenic factors have a positive impact on health, whereas some of the attendance pressures (e.g. psychosocial risks at work) have been found to be a double risk and increase both sickness presenteeism and probability of ill health. Finding the right balance between optimal levels of presenteeism and absenteeism, from a well-being perspective, is a challenge.

5.4   IMPLICATIONS FOR PRACTICE

The following section will explore implications for organizational actions. A particular stance towards interventions implying stress and the psychosocial

Table 5.1 Determinants of presenteeism

	Work-related	Attitudinal/ Dispositional	Situational
Factors contributing to well-being	Job satisfaction Good leadership Group cohesiveness Quality of relationship with colleagues Flexibility in work arrangements The possibility to do less demanding work tasks for a period	Professionalism Training/educated for multiple work tasks Hardiness Interest derived from work Physical activity/training	High standard of the professional health and safety system
Attendance pressure factors	Workload Job (in)security (evidence for both) Censure pressure (fear of being perceived as shirking) Clientele awaiting Difficulty of replacement Role conflict Job control Low absenteeism reward system	Guilt and moral pressure factors Perceived seriousness of the ailment Conservative attitude Fear of negative repercussions at work Over-committed/ boundaryless traits	Financial insecurity Severe mental/physical illness Caring for sick family member Being self-employed Working in small firm

work environment is undertaken. This approach is favoured given that stress, depression and anxiety account for 46% of all reported illnesses according to a recent report by the Health & Safety Executive in the UK (Cooper and Dewe, 2008). In our understanding, the emphasis for organizations should be to focus on the prevention of working conditions which undermine the physical and mental health of employees (primary prevention), and the reduction of symptoms and illnesses (secondary and tertiary prevention). A recent systematic review by Lamontagne *et al.* (2007) has shown that intervention programmes which are more comprehensive (i.e. including primary, secondary and tertiary levels of prevention) are more effective and have stronger effects on the intended outcomes. Individual-focused interventions tended to favourably affect individual-level outcomes (such as somatic symptoms, physiological changes (e.g., blood pressure, cholesterol levels), skills (e.g., coping ability) and psychological outcomes (e.g., general mental health, anxiety). However, only more encompassing programmes (including more organizationally focused interventions) tended to be beneficial for both individual and organizational outcomes such as sickness absenteeism. Dame Carol Black, author of the *Working for a Healthier Tomorrow* report presented to the UK government in March 2008, states that

> Good health improves an individual's quality of life, and a focus on their well-being can also add value to organizations by promoting better health and increasing motivation and engagement of employees, in turn helping to drive increases in productivity and profitability. In other words the benefits of health and well-being extend far beyond avoiding or reducing the costs of absence or poor performance. But this requires a changed perception of health and well-being, and a willingness from both employers and employees to invest resources and change behaviour (Black, 2008, p. 51).

On the one hand, it would seem common sense that working while ill would not allow a chance of recovering to full health. Of course, the particular ailment which affects the individual (benign or severe, acute or chronic) must be taken into consideration. Studies have shown that productivity losses vary according to the specific type of ailment (Burton *et al.*, 2006; Burton *et al.*, 1999, Burton *et al.*, 2004). It is plausible that certain conditions necessitate rest and absenteeism from work until full recovery whereas other chronic conditions have a very slight probability of never being completely restored. In these cases where the ailment is benign and not sufficient to justify an absence from work, productivity losses could be reduced by adjusting certain aspects of the workplace. Although there is convincing evidence on the negative consequences of a pathogenic psychosocial work environment, there is also, however, compelling evidence that work is good for us. Indeed, work can have a beneficial impact on people's physical and mental health, development of identity and sense of self-worth. For example, the recent review, *Is Work Good for Your Health and Well-Being?* by Waddell and Burton (2006), concluded that good and safe work was generally beneficial for both physical and mental well-being and overweighed the negative effects of being without work or of prolonged sickness absence.

Caverley *et al.* (2007) investigated the relationship between sickness presenteeism, sickness absenteeism, and employee health. They particularly wanted to investigate to what extent the employees replaced sickness absenteeism with sickness presenteeism. The results indicated that the workforce was of average health, but that sickness absenteeism in the organization was less than half of the national average, and this difference could be explained by sickness presenteeism. The average number of days that employees were attending work when they were ill or injured was actually higher than the number of days of sick leave. This result supported the assumption that the employees substituted sickness absenteeism by sickness presenteeism also. The sickness presenteeism also correlated significantly with a reduction of work-related factors like job security, supervisor support and job satisfaction. This means that a reduction in these factors increased attendance pressure among employees. It may also be that high job security, supervisor support and job satisfaction are important factors concerning interventions in order to get sickness absentees back to work without worsening their health. According to Caverley *et al.* (2007) sickness presenteeism seems to be more strongly associated with health than sickness absenteeism, which indicates that the effort being done to improve workplace health may have a more immediate effect on sickness presenteeism than on sickness absenteeism.

A study by Burton *et al.* (2004) illustrates the significance of individual adjustments for sickness presentees. This study was done in order to compare patterns and severities of self-reported reduction of productivity with different medical conditions. It was assumed that each of the different medical conditions that were included would affect the four areas of workplace performance in different ways, and the results indicate that this was the case. Burton *et al.* (2004) point out that worksite interventions aimed at helping employees to handle their medical condition (disease management programmes) should be tailored to the specific medical condition. The study showed that the group that suffered from depression rate themselves as most impaired in the work domain of mental/interpersonal functioning (concentration and teamwork). The results from this study indicate that employees with different medical conditions could benefit from different individual interventions in order to function in their work.

Along with efforts in risk prevention, health promotion and disease management, organizations have to consider the importance of return to work programmes after prolonged sick leaves. According to St-Arnaud (2007), workers who indicate that work was the major cause of their absence have much less chance of a successful return to the workplace. Moreover, almost 44% of workers who had returned to their job considered that they still had a mental health problem which had not been resolved during the absence. This has important implications in terms of sickness presenteeism. Furthermore, the study showed that psychosocial risks, which contributed to the absence, are also contributing to the reintegration process and to the improvement of mental health problems and, thus, to job retention. This type of results calls for early detection of workers who develop ill health and supports comprehensive and holistic approaches to health and well-being. Table 5.2 illustrates some examples of interventions which can be applied for a whole

Table 5.2 Examples of interventions

	Primary prevention	Secondary/tertiary prevention (reduce the consequences of the stress factor)
Corporate actions (affecting all staff members or a particular job class)	Reorganize the line of authority to allow job control Fairer reward system which doesn't encourage undue sickness presenteeism Training to improve management skills and managerial leadership Improve physical and environmental constraints Work–family conciliation policy Flexitime Allowing telework	Promote a healthy lifestyle Offer exercise facilities on the workplace Employee assistance programme Comprehensive return to work programme/policy which takes into consideration work-related factors which contributed to the absence Clear guidelines to managers on how to manage absence/attendance Clear communication on what is expected from workers when ill (e.g. with contagious infections) High competence among doctors and psychologists to give the right advice on how/if beneficial to maintain work with temporary health impairment
Local actions (affecting staff in a particular sector / department or in a work team)	Changes in task organization Ensuring clear roles Constructive retrospective action concerning staff performance Co-development/team cohesion building programmes Staff training in various tasks/equipment to diminish disruption during absence and allow adjustment for sickness presentees Reorganizing a unit's working hours Task rotation Training with a view to improving the atmosphere in the work team	Allowing individuals to adjust their tasks and pace if ill Working hours adapted to particular cases Resolving interpersonal conflicts Taking into account the psychosocial work environment when planning return to work

Sources: Adapted from Brun *et al.*, 2008; Jordan *et al.*, 2003 and Kompier and Marcelissen, 1990.

organization or locally within teams and units, for each level of prevention (primary, secondary and tertiary).

In conclusion, sickness presenteeism is a frequent phenomenon, and low levels of absence can often imply higher levels of presenteeism. The two phenomena should therefore be studied together since they appear to be two sides of the same coin. Psychosocial risks in the workplace have been found to impair mental and physical health, increase absenteeism, and recent research has shown they are also determinants of higher presenteeism rates. Organizations should prioritize the reduction of psychosocial risks and other attendance pressure factors since they increase sickness attendance and impair health. On the other hand, there are aspects of work which can be salutogenic to health. Given the negative consequences of prolonged absence and the high costs of productivity losses engendered by workers with health impairments, employers should put resources into interventions which will help keeping people healthy and well. Promoting positive health must not, however, be strictly focused on improving individuals' health and thus exclude the prevention and reduction of all the work-related risk factors which are known to cause ill health. Health promotion and occupational health programmes should be comprehensive and include prevention of ill health, promotion of health, organization-, work- and worker-oriented strategies.

REFERENCES

Aronsson, G. & Gustafsson, K. (2005). Sickness presenteeism: prevalence, attendance-pressure factors, and an outline of a model for research. *Journal of Occupational and Environmental Medicine*, **47**(9), 958.

Aronsson, G., Gustafsson, K. & Dallner, M. (2000). Sick but yet at work. An empirical study of sickness presenteeism. *Journal of Epidemiology and Community Health*, **54**, 502–9.

Aronsson, G. & Lindh, T. (2004). Långtidsfriskas arbetsvillkor – en populationsstudie (work conditions of long time healthy workers – a population study). *Arbete och Hälsa. Vetenskaplig skriftserie*, **10**, 1–21.

Bergström, G., Bodin, L., Hagberg, J., Aronsson, G. & Josephson, M. (2009). Sickness presenteeism today, sickness absenteeism tomorrow? A prospective study on sickness presenteeism and future sickness absenteeism. *Journal of Occupational and Environmental Medicine*, **51**(6), 1–10.

Biron, C., Brun, J.-P. & Ivers, H. (2006). At work but ill: psychosocial work environment and wellbeing determinants of presenteeism propensity. *Journal of Public Mental Health*, **5**(4), 26–37.

Black, C. (2008). *Working for a Healthier Tomorrow*. London: The Stationery Office.

Bond, F.W., Flaxman, P.E. & Loivette, S. (2006). *A Business Case for the Management Standards for Stress* (No. RR 431). Norwich, UK: Health & Safety Executive.

Brun, J.-P. (2008). Links between mental wellbeing at work and productivity. In *Foresight – Mental Capital and Wellbeing*. London: Government Office for Science.

Brun, J.-P., Biron, C. & Ivers, H. (2008). *Strategic Approach to Preventing Occupational Stress* (Studies/Research No. R-577). Québec, Canada: Institut de recherche Robert-Sauvé en santé et en sécurité du travail.

Burton, W.N., Chen, C.Y., Conti, D.J., Schultz, A.B. & Edington, D.W. (2006). The association between health risk change and presenteeism change. *Journal of Occupational and Environmental Medicine*, **48**(3), 252–63.

Burton, W.N., Chin-Yu, C., Conti, D.J., Schultz, A.B., Pransky, G. & Edington, D.W. (2005). The association of health risks with on-the-job productivity. *Journal of Occupational and Environmental Medicine*, **47**(8), 769.

Burton, W.N., Conti, D.J., Chen, C.Y., Schultz, A.B. & Edington, D.W. (1999). The role of health risk factors and disease on worker productivity. *Journal of Occupational and Environmental Medicine*, **41**(10), 863–77.

Burton, W.N., Pransky, G., Conti, D.J., Chin-Yu, C. & Edington, D.W. (2004). The association of medical conditions and presenteeism. *Journal of Occupational and Environmental Medicine*, **46**, S38.

Bycio, P. (1982). Job performance and absenteeism: a review and meta-analysis. *Human Relations*, **45**, 193–220.

Caverley, N., Cunningham, J.B. & MacGregor, J.N. (2007). Sickness presenteeism, sickness absenteeism, and health following restructuring in a public service organization. *Journal of Management Studies*, **44**(2), 304.

Chapman, L.S. (2005). Presenteeism and its role in worksite health promotion. *American Journal of Health Promotion*, **19**(suppl 14), 1–8.

Cooper, C. & Dewe, P. (2008). Well-being – absenteeism, presenteeism, costs and challenges. *Occupational Medicine (London)*, **58**(8), 522–4.

Dellve, L., Skagert, K. & Vilhelmsson, R. (2007). Leadership in workplace health promotion projects: 1- and 2-year effects on long-term work attendance. *European Journal of Public Health*, **17**(5), 471–6.

Dew, K., Keefe, V. & Small, K. (2005). 'Choosing' to work when sick: workplace presenteeism. *Social Science Medicine*, **60**, 2273–82.

Edington, D.W. & Burton, W.N. (2003). Health and productivity. In R. J. McCunney (Ed.), *A Practical Approach to Occupational and Environmental Medicine* (3rd edn, pp. 140–52). Philadelphia: Lippincott, Williams & Wilkins.

Elstad, J.I. & Vabo, M. (2008). Job stress, sickness absence and sickness presenteeism in Nordic elderly care. *Scandinavian Journal of Public Health*, **36**(5), 467–74.

Gibbs, P. & Burnett, S. (forthcoming). Well-being at work, a new way of doing things? A journey through yesterday, today and tomorrow. In C.L. Cooper (Ed.), *Handbook of Occupational Health Psychology and Medicine*.

Giga, S., Faragher, B. & Cooper, C. L. (2003a). Identification of good practice in stress prevention/management. In J. Jordan et al. (Eds), *Beacons of Excellence in Stress Prevention* (Vol. HSE Research Report 133, pp. 1–45). Sudbury, England: HSE Books.

Giga, S.I., Cooper, C.L. & Faragher, B. (2003b). The development of a framework for a comprehensive approach to stress management interventions at work. *International Journal of Stress Management*, **10**(4), 280–96.

Grinyer, A. & Singleton, V. (2000). Sickness absence as risk-taking behaviour: a study of organisational and cultural factors in the public sector. *Health, Risk and Society*, **2**(1), 7.

Hackett, R.D. & Bycio, P. (1996). An evaluation of employee absenteeism as a coping mechanism among hospital nurses. *Journal of Occupational and Organizational Psychology*, **69**(4), 327.

Hansen, C.D. & Andersen, J.H. (2008). Going ill to work – what personal circumstances, attitudes and work-related factors are associated with sickness presenteeism? *Social Science and Medicine*, **67**, 956–64.

Hardy, G.E., Woods, D. & Wall, T.D. (2003). The impact of psychological distress on absence from work. *Journal of Applied Psychology*, **88**(2), 306–14.

Harrison, A., Wheeler, P. & Whiteheard, C. (2004). *The Distributed Workplace*. London: Spon Press.

Johansson, G. & Lundberg, I. (2004). Adjustment latitude and attendance requirements as determinants of sickness absence or attendance. Empirical tests of the illness flexibility model. *Social Science and Medicine*, **58**(10), 1857–68.

Johns, G. (1994). How often were you absent? A review of the use of self-reported absence data. *Journal of Applied Psychology*, **79**(4), 574.

Johns, G. (2001). The psychology of lateness, absenteeism, and turnover. In N. Anderson, D.S. Ones, J.K. Sinangil & C. Viswesvaran (Eds), *Handbook of Industrial, Work and Organizational Psychology* (Vol. 2). London: Sage.

Johns, G. (2008a). Absenteeism and presenteeism: not at work or not working well. In J. Barling & C.L. Cooper (Eds), *The Sage Handbook of Organizational Behavior* (Vol. 1). London: Sage.

Johns, G. (2008b). Absenteeism or presenteeism? Attendance dynamics and employee well-being. In S. Cartwright & C.L. Cooper (Eds), *Oxford Handbook of Organizational Well-Being* (pp. 7–30). Oxford: Oxford University Press.

Johns, G. & Xie, J.L. (1998). Perceptions of absence from work: People's Republic of China versus Canada. *Journal of Applied Psychology*, **83**, 515–30.

Jordan, J., Gurr, E., Tinline, G., Giga, S., Faragher, B. & Cooper, C. (2003). *Beacons of Excellence in Stress Prevention* (No. RR-133). Manchester: Health & Safety Executive.

Karasek, R. (1979). Job demand, job decision latitude, and mental strain: Implications for job redesign. *Administrative Science Quarterly*, **24**(2), 285–307.

Karasek, R. & Theorell, T. (1990). *Healthy Work: Stress, Productivity and the Reconstruction of Working Life*. New York: Basic Books.

Kivimäki, M., Ferrie, J.E., Shipley, M., Gimeno, D., Elovainio, M., de Vogli, R., *et al.* (2008). Effects on blood pressure do not explain the association between organizational justice and coronary heart disease in the Whitehall II study. *Psychosomatic Medicine*, **70**(1), 1.

Kivimäki, M., Head, J., Ferrie, J.E., Hemingway, H., Shipley, M.J. & Vahtera, J. (2005). Working while ill as a risk factor for serious coronary events: the Whitehall II study. *American Journal of Public Health*, **95**(1), 98–102.

Kompier, M.A.J. & Marcelissen, F.H.G. (1990). *Handboek werkstress*. Amsterdam: Nederlands Instituut voor Arbeidsomstandigheden.

Kristensen, T. (1991). Sickness absence and work strain among Danish slaughterhouse workers: an analysis of absence from work regarded as coping behaviour. *Social Science Medicine*, **32**, 15–27.

Lamontagne, A.D., Keegel, T., Louie, A.M., Ostry, A. & Landbergis, P.A. (2007). A systematic review of the job-stress intervention evaluation literature, 1990–2005. *International Journal of Occupational and Environmental Health*, **13**, 268–80.

Lim, D., Sanderson, K. & Andrews, G. (2000). Lost productivity among full-time workers with mental disorders. *Journal of Mental Health Policy and Economics*, **3**, 139–46.

Lindberg, P., Josephson, M., Alfredsson, L. & Vingard, E. (2006). Promoting excellent work ability and preventing poor work ability: The same determinants? Results from the Swedish Hakul study. *Occupational and Environmental Medicine*, **63**(2), 113–20.

Loepkke, R.R. (2006). Good health is good business. *Journal of Occupational and Environmental Medicine Occupational Medicine Forum*, **48**(5), 533–7.

Lofland, J.H., Pizzi, L. & Frick, K.D. (2004). A review of health-related workplace productivity loss instruments. *PharmacoEconomics*, **22**(3), 165.

Marmot, M., Feeney, A., Shipley, M., North, F. & Syme, S. L. (1995). Sickness absence as a measure of health status and functioning: from the UK Whitehall II study. *Journal of Epidemiology and Community Health*, **49**, 124–30.

Martocchio, J.J. & Jimeno, D.I. (2003). Employee absenteeism as an affective event. *Human Resource Management Review*, **13**(2), 227.

McKevitt, C., Morgan, M., Dundas, R. & Holland, W.W. (1997). Sickness absence and 'working through' illness: a comparison of two professional groups. *Journal of Public Health Medicine*, **19**(3), 295–300.

Nielsen, M.L., Rugulies, R., Christensen, K.B., Smith-Hansen, L., Bjorner, J.B. & Kristensen, T.S. (2004). Impact of psychosocial work environment on registered absence from work: a two-year longitudinal study using the IPAW cohort. *Work and Stress*, **18**(4), 323–35.

North, F.M., Syme, L., Feeney, A., Shipley, M. & Marmot, M. (1996). Psychosocial work environment and sickness absence among British civil servants: the Whitehall II study. *American Journal of Public Health*, **86**(3), 332–40.

Nyberg, A., Westerlund, H., Hanson, L.L.M. & Theorell, T. (2008). Managerial leadership is associated with self-reported sickness absence and sickness presenteeism among Swedish men and women. *Scandinavian Journal of Public Health*, **36**(8), 803.

O'Driscoll, M., Biron, C. & Cooper, C.L. (in press). Work-related technological change and psychological wellbeing. In Y. Amichai-Hamburger (Ed.), *Technology and Wellbeing*. New York: Cambridge University Press.

Prasad, M., Wahlqvist, P., Shikiar, R. & Shih, Y.-C.T. (2004). A review of self-report instruments measuring health-related work productivity: a patient-reported outcomes perspective. *PharmacoEconomics*, **22**(4), 225.

Saksvik, P.Ø. (1996). Attendance pressure during organizational change. *International Journal of Stress Management*, **3**(1), 47.

Saksvik, P.Ø. *et al.* (2007). Developing criteria for healthy organizational change. *Work and Stress*, **21**(3), 243– 263.

Sanderson, K., Hobart, J.N., Graves, N., Cocker, F. & Hobart, B.O. (2008). *Presenteeism and mental health: Can the problem be part of the solution?* Paper presented at the 7th APA-NIOSH-SOHP International Conference on Occupational Stress and Health, Washington, DC.

Schultz, A.B. (2007). Employee health and presenteeism: a systematic review. *Journal of Occupational Rehabilitation*, **17**(3), 547.

Simpson, R. (1998). Presenteeism, power and organizational change: long hours as a career barrier and the impact on the working lives of women managers. *British Journal of Management*, **9**, S37–S50.

St-Arnaud, L. (2007). Determinants of return-to-work among employees absent due to mental health problems. *Relations Industrielles [Industrial Relations]*, **62**(4), 690.

Stewart, W.F., Ricci, J.A., Chee, E., Hahn, S.R. & Morganstein, D. (2003). Cost of lost productive work time among US workers with depression. *Journal of American Medical Association*, **289**(23), 3135–44.

Turpin, R.S., Ozminkowski, R.J., Sharda, C.E., Collins, J.J., Berger, M.L., Billotti, G.M. *et al.* (2004). Reliability and validity of the Stanford presenteeism scale. *Journal of Occupational and Environmental Medicine*, **46**(11), 1123.

Vahtera, J., Pentti, J. & Kivimäki, M. (2004). Sickness absence as a predictor of mortality among male and female employees. *Journal of Epidemiology and Community Health*, **58**(4), 321–6.

Vogli, R.D., Ferrie, J.E., Chandola, T., Kivimäki, M. & Marmot, M. G. (2007). Unfairness and health: evidence from the Whitehall II study. *Journal of Epidemiology and Community Health*, **61**, 513–18.

Waddell, G. & Burton, A.K. (2006). *Is Work Good for Your Health and Well-Being?* London: The Stationery Office.

PART II

Individual Differences and Health

CHAPTER 6

Individual Differences, Work Stress and Health

Norbert K. Semmer and Laurenz L. Meier

University of Bern, Switzerland

6.1 INTRODUCTION

Despite many problems of individual studies, links between work stress and strain (i.e. physical and psychological health) are now quite well established (Sonnentag & Frese, 2003). With about 10% variance explained, the relationships found are typically not very strong, which is unsurprising, given the complex etiology of stress symptoms (Semmer, Zapf & Greif, 1996).

There can be no doubt that associations between stressors and strain do not hold for everyone in the same way (Spector, 2003). However, in current stress research there is a tendency to emphasize individual differences to the point where stress is being reduced to nothing but idiosyncratic appraisals and coping styles, rendering such concepts as 'environmentally induced stress' useless, as Lazarus and Folkman (1986, p. 75) asserted. This view tends to equate 'interpretation' with 'confined to the individual', and 'environment' with 'physical environment', and to neglect that the social environment is a powerful reality, where people in the same culture share 'rules of appraisal' (Averill, 1986) and ways of dealing with the world (Semmer, McGrath & Beehr, 2005; cf. Kahn & Byosiere, 1992). Thus, it should be kept in mind that not all individual differences found are only differences between individuals, but often differences between the (sub-) cultures they belong to.

This chapter will first discuss mechanisms that may be responsible for individual differences in stress reactions. It will then deal with the question of what makes stressors 'stressful', concentrating on goals people have. Individual differences in resources ('resourceful belief systems') will be covered next. Finally, we will deal with individual differences in coping.

International Handbook of Work and Health Psychology, Third Edition. Edited by Cary L. Cooper, James Campbell Quick, and Marc J. Schabracq.
© 2009 John Wiley & Sons, Ltd. Published 2015 by John Wiley & Sons, Ltd.

Rather than representing an exhaustive review of the literature, the chapter tries to tie together various 'literatures' under common themes. This will inevitably lead to oversimplifications. Yet, we are convinced that all too often we tend to dwell on differences and difficulties, and sometimes it seems worthwhile to see if there is some forest emerging behind the many trees.

Stress will be used as a rather general term in this chapter, denoting a state of tension that is experienced as aversive. Stress, therefore, involves negative emotional states such as anxiety, frustration, and the like (Lazarus, 1999). Stressors are characteristics of the environment that tend to elicit such emotional states in a given population (cf. Semmer *et al.*, 2005). Note that this does not require that each and every individual will experience stress vis à vis a stressor. All it requires is that in a given population certain characteristics tend to induce stress, on the basis of shared meaning in a given culture (Kahn & Byosiere, 1992; Semmer *et al.*, 2005).

6.2   INDIVIDUAL DIFFERENCES AND STRESS EXPERIENCES: BASIC MECHANISMS

If personality plays a role in the stress experience, it somehow must 'translate' into stressful experiences. We will discuss four mechanisms, which refer to (i) encountering stressors; (ii) appraising stressors; (iii) reacting to stressors; and (iv) coping tendencies. These mechanisms are not mutually exclusive, and may combine into a 'cascade' (Suls & Martin, 2005). Furthermore, we will briefly comment on personality profiles.

6.2.1   Encountering Stressful Situations

The most important factor determining the probability to encounter stressors is probably socioeconomic status (Adler *et al.*, 1999). However, personality also plays a role, which is reflected in the generally higher risk of encountering stress for people high in neuroticism (Suls & Martin, 2005), or the higher involvement in accidents of people low in agreeableness (Clarke, 2006). Furthermore, people may actively select or avoid situations associated with certain stressors, such as the risk of failure in the case of promotion vs. prevention orientation (Brockner & Higgins, 2001). Finally, they may involuntarily 'produce' stressors, as when hostile people induce conflict (Smith *et al.*, 2004). People's well-being may influence future working conditions (or the perception of these conditions), although these effects tend to be weaker than the effect of stressors on well-being (Zapf, Dormann & Frese, 1996). For instance, people high in negative affectivity are more likely to be in high stress jobs (Spector, Jex & Chen, 1995) and people high in self-esteem as well as those with an internal locus of control are more likely to end up in jobs they like (Brockner, 1988; Furnham, 1992).

6.2.2 Appraising Different Situations as Stressful

Many personality variables are linked to the way people appraise situations. Examples include the tendency of threatening appraisals when anxiety is high (Suls & Martin, 2005), of hostile attributions when hostility is high (Berkowitz, 1998), of interpreting failure as 'self-diagnostic' when self-esteem is low (Brockner, 1988).

6.2.3 Reacting Differently to Stressful Situations

Reacting more strongly to events that are appraised in a similar way constitutes another mechanism for the translation of personality variables into stress experiences. Even with appraisal held constant, people may display greater reactivity (see Suls & Martin, 2005, for anxiety; Grebner et al., 2004, for neuroticism). In fact, an important component of the very general traits of negative and positive affectivity (neuroticism, extraversion) can be seen in physiologically routed differential responsivity to negative and positive stimuli, respectively (Gray, 1987; Larsen & Ketelaar, 1991).

6.2.4 Dealing with Stressful Situations

Finally, there is some stability in the way people cope with stressful situations. This aspect will be discussed in more detail below (Section 6.5).

6.2.5 Personality Profiles

The general personality characteristic that seems most important for all mechanisms is neuroticism (Semmer, 2006). However, the few studies investigating *profiles* of personality traits show that the combination of high neuroticism and low conscientiousness is especially problematic (and the combination of low N and high C especially resilient) in terms of stress and coping (Vollrath & Torgersen, 2000).

6.3 WHAT MAKES STRESSORS STRESSFUL? THE ROLE OF GOALS AND ASPIRATIONS IN THE STRESS PROCESS

Basically, stress has to do with appraisals of threat and/or loss (Lazarus, 1999). Threat or loss are appraised with regard to goals (cf. the dimension of 'goal conduciveness' in appraisal theories; Ellsworth & Scherer, 2003). An event or condition therefore should be worse to the extent that the goal it threatens is important for the person. Such goals may refer to different levels of generality, such as general motives (McClelland, 1987), (professional) identities (Semmer, Jacobshagen, Meier & Elfering, 2009), personal projects (Emmons, 1996) or current task goals (cf. the concept of performance constraints – see Leitner & Resch, 2005; Spector & Jex, 1998; Semmer *et al.*, 1996). Since people differ with regard to the goals they pursue (Cropanzano, James & Citera, 1993), goals should be an important source of individual differences with regard to (occupational) stress (cf. Semmer, 2006).

The first aspect that seems important is simply *having* goals and being committed to them. Pursuing goals in general is associated with higher well-being (Emmons, 1996), and commitment to personal work goals is associated with higher job satisfaction (Roberson, 1990). However, not all goals are created equal. Thus, seeking positive goals is associated with better well-being than avoiding negative goals (Emmons, 1996), and the proportion of positive/negative work-related goals is associated with job satisfaction (Roberson, 1990). Furthermore, 'extrinsic' goals (e. g, money, good looks) are associated with well-being only to the extent that they are instrumental for achieving intrinsic goals (Diener & Fujita, 1995).

At the same time, however, being committed to a goal may increase vulnerability (Lavallee & Campbell, 1995). The two processes together may imply that people are better off on average when they are committed to a goal, yet suffer more when that goal is threatened. In line with this reasoning, Reilly (1994) reports that nurses who were more committed to their profession showed *lower mean levels* of emotional exhaustion (the core component of burnout). At the same time the *relationship* between the frequency of experienced stressors and emotional exhaustion was *stronger* for the more committed. Similarly, research by Brockner, Tyler and Cooper-Schneider (1992) shows that people who were highly committed to their organization reacted in an especially negative way to perceived unfair treatment. On the positive side, the importance placed on a given facet of one's work (e.g., opportunity for promotion, amount of decision making) moderated the relationship between the extent to which this facet is perceived to be present and overall job satisfaction in a study by Rice, Gentile and McFarlin (1991).

Motives represent rather general, and quite stable, goal strivings. There is some research on the implications of motives for stress, well-being and health. Thus, power strivings are associated with lower well-being (Emmons, 1991), and with stronger reactions to stressful events (Jemmott, 1987). Affiliation/intimacy strivings tend to be associated with positive indicators of well-being but with a stronger reaction to interpersonal stressors (Emmons, 1991, 1996). In line with such findings, women, who tend to be more committed to interpersonal goals than men, have been found to be more vulnerable to stress experienced by significant others (Kessler & McLeod, 1984). The main effect of need for achievement (nAch) is controversial (Veroff, 1982 vs. Emmons, 1991, 1996), which may be due to nAch having a 'toxic' and a 'non-toxic' component (Birks & Roger, 2000). Again, however, people high in nAch react more strongly to achievement-related events (Emmons, 1991). A high need for control (which is characteristic of people with the type A behaviour pattern) may induce people to set too high goals (Ward & Eisler, 1987) and to react strongly to control being threatened (Edwards, 1991).

A special case refers to multiple goals, which implies the possibility that these goals come into conflict with one another (Kahn & Byosiere, 1992). Multiple goals have often been studied in relation to the combination of work and family roles, in many cases referring to women participating in the labour force, in addition to their role as spouse and parent. As with goal pursuit *per se*, the main effect of multiple roles on well-being typically is positive rather than negative, provided that the attitude towards the multiplicity of roles is positive (Amstad & Semmer, 2009). At the same time, work–family conflict is a well-established predictor of strain (Amstad *et al.*, 2009).

The conclusion from these considerations is that differences in vulnerability to stressful experiences often are to be found in people's goals. It might be hypothesized that one way to reduce vulnerability is to reduce one's goals. And, indeed, being able to reduce or give up unrealistically high goals is important for a person's well-being (Wrosch *et al.*, 2003). At the same time, however, reducing one's aspirations is a double-edged sword (Hobfoll, 2001). Recall that the main effect of pursuing goals typically is positive. Giving up goals may therefore imply forgoing possible challenges that are experienced in a positive way and may entail positive consequences. Furthermore, giving up may have detrimental consequences. Especially if the goal in question is highly valued not only individually but also socially (e.g., achievement goals), giving up may have far-ranging negative social consequences. It is probably due to such negative consequences that people sometimes reduce goals in a resigned and resentful way, acquiescing themselves to the inevitable more than really giving up the goal. Wrosch *et al.*

(2003) characterize this mechanism as 'giving up effort, but remaining committed to the goal' (cf. the concept of 'resigned job satisfaction'; Büssing, 1992).

In line with these considerations, person-environment (P-E) fit research shows that 'fit' at low levels (e.g., having, and 'wanting' low complexity) is associated with more distress than fit at high levels (Edwards & Van Harrison, 1993). Frese (1992) reports similar results for people who reject, rather than aspire, control at work. The role of 'fit', therefore, cannot be assessed without considering absolute levels.

Thus, it seems that aspirations and expectations cannot be reduced *ad lib*. Rather, they may in many cases be indicators of a 'failed person–work interaction' (Büssing, 1992, p. 254). Note that this implies that employing 'stress-resistant' people may be counterproductive if their resilience is based not on high resources but on low commitment to certain goals (especially in the interpersonal domain; cf. Cobb, 1973).

6.4   VULNERABLE VS. RESILIENT PERSONS

6.4.1   Beliefs about the World and a Person's Relationship to it

People differ in their beliefs about the world and their relationship with it, especially possibilities to deal with it. Candidates for this kind of variables are hardiness (e.g. Kobasa, 1988) or sense of coherence (Antonovsky, 1991), locus of control (Rotter, 1966), self-efficacy (Bandura, 1989), optimism (Scheier & Carver, 1992), self-esteem (Brockner, 1988), or hostility (cf. Siegman, 1994a).

Popular concepts

Hardiness is conceived of as being composed of three components: commitment, challenge and control (see Maddi, 2002). 'Commitment is the ability to believe in the truth, importance, and interest value of who one is and what one is doing; and thereby, the tendency to involve oneself fully in the many situations of life... Control refers to the tendency to believe and act as if one can influence the course of events... Challenge is based on the belief that change, rather than stability, is the normative mode of life' (Kobasa, 1988, p. 101).

From this concept it follows that people high in hardiness should better be able to deal with stressful aspects of life. Research often shows the main effects of hardiness on physical and psychological health (Beehr & Bowling,

2005). Both stress appraisal and coping seem to be mediators of this relationship (Florian, Mikulincer & Taubman, 1995), as implied by the concept. However, evidence on moderator effects is mixed (Beehr & Bowling, 2005). Furthermore, recent longitudinal research also found a reverse relationship, showing that stress can have a negative effect on hardiness (Vogt *et al.*, 2008).

A basic problem with the hardiness construct is the confound with other constructs, such as neuroticism (or negative affectivity). Relations with such constructs are substantial, and associations with third variables usually drop considerably when controlling for these. In a number of studies, however, associations do remain even with these controls (Semmer, 2006).

Sense of coherence (SOC) also is quite a broad construct and overlaps with hardiness. Its three main features are that the environment is perceived as structured, predictable and explicable, and thus as *comprehensible*, that one perceives to have the resources necessary to deal with one's environment, thus perceiving *manageability*, and that the demands posed by one's environment are interpreted as challenges which are worthy to be taken up, leading to the perception of *meaningfulness* (Antonovsky, 1991).

Research on SOC shows relationships with a number of indicators of well-being and health (e.g. Antonovsky, 1993; Söderfeldt *et al.*, 2000). Main effects are predominant, but interactions with working conditions also are sometimes found (e.g. Feldt, 1997; Johansson Hanse & Engström, 1999; Söderfeldt *et al.*, 2000). Effects of SOC have also been demonstrated longitudinally for subjective health ratings (Suominen *et al.*, 2001), diabetes (Kouvonen *et al.*, 2008), and reduced mortality (Surtees *et al.*, 2006). Similar to hardiness, rather strong relationships with anxiety (Antonovsky, 1993), depression (Geyer, 1997), and other indicators of well-being (Eriksson & Lindström, 2005) have raised doubts about its distinctiveness from neuroticism, or negative affectivity (see Geyer, 1997).

Locus of control is one of the variables that has very often been shown to be related to well-being (Spector *et al.*, 2002). Locus of control may also be a moderator of the interaction proposed by Karasek (Karasek & Theorell, 1990). Thus, Meier *et al.* (2008) found that job control had a buffering effect only among individuals with an internal locus of control. Like locus of control, *self-efficacy* has consistently been shown to be related to well-being (cf. Bandura, 1992) and both are part of a chain of convictions regarding a person's possibility to cope. The two convictions are not the same, but they do overlap (cf. Ng, Sorensen & Eby, 2006). A number of studies have found self-efficacy to buffer the effects of stressors (e.g., Jex *et al.*, 2001; Jimmieson, Terry & Callan, 2004) or of resources like control (Jimmieson, 2000). Some recent findings suggest that the interaction between demands and control as specified in the Karasek model (Karasek & Theorell, 1990) might be valid only for people high in self-efficacy (e.g., Jimmieson, 2000;

Meier *et al.*, 2008; Schaubroeck & Merritt, 1997), resembling the pattern found for internal locus of control (see above). Self-efficacy not only has similarity with locus of control, but also with self-esteem. In its generalized form (general self-efficacy; Jerusalem & Schwarzer, 1992) it seems quite indistinguishable from self-esteem, at least from those parts of self-esteem that are related to a person's perceived competences (cf. Judge & Bono, 2001).

Both self-efficacy and *self-esteem* seem especially important for dealing with negative feedback and failure in terms of distress as well as persistence (Bandura, 1989; Brockner, 1988). However, Cohen and Edwards (1989) are very sceptical about the moderating effect of self-esteem, although some more recent studies do show such interactions (Ganster & Schaubroeck, 1991; Jex & Elaqua, 1999; Mäkikangas & Kinnunen, 2003). A number of studies indicate that it is not simply the level of self-esteem that is important but also its stability (Kernis, 2005). Unstable high self-esteem reflects a fragile feeling of self-worth which is associated with more hostility and anger (Kernis, Grannemann & Barclay, 1989) and a heightened responsiveness to self-threatening events, such as negative feedback, or unfair treatment (Greenier *et al.*, 1999). Maintaining self-esteem is an important goal (Lazarus & Folkman, 1984; Semmer *et al.*, 2007) and threats to self-esteem are perceived as stressful. In line with this, two studies of our group showed that individuals with a fragile self-esteem are especially reactive to ego-threatening job conditions like unfair treatment (Meier, Semmer & Hupfeld, 2009) and effort–reward imbalance (Meier & Semmer, 2008).

Optimism is distinct from control-related concepts because it does not require that the course of events is influenced by one's own actions. Rather, it includes the belief that things are likely to turn out reasonably well anyway (thus being related to a belief in a basically benign world). It has been shown to influence stress appraisals, well-being and coping strategies (Carver & Scheier, 1999). Optimists tend to employ more problem-solving strategies under controllable conditions, and more reinterpretation and acceptance under less controllable conditions (Nes & Segersstrom, 2006). Of special importance is the finding that optimists tend to accept failures better, which relates to the 'circumscribed' frustration as described by Hallsten (1993) and is indicative of the capability of putting things into perspective.

Hostility is often regarded as the major 'toxic' component of the type A behaviour pattern (Adler & Matthews, 1994), but some authors treat hostility and type A as related but independent constructs (Myrtek, 2007). Conceptually, we can distinguish between: (i) a cognitive component, involving hostile beliefs and attitudes about others (cynicism, mistrust, hostile attributions) – this aspect is dominant in the most frequently used Cook–Medley–Ho Scale (cf. Myrtek, 2007); (ii) an emotional component, involving anger; and (iii) a behavioural component, involving physical or verbal assault (Buss & Perry,

1992). The accumulated evidence suggests that hostility is predictive of ill health coronary heart disease (CHD), and all-cause mortality (Miller *et al.*, 1996), although a definitive conclusion cannot be drawn yet (Myrtek, 2007). Hostility is associated with vascular resistance during interpersonal stress (Davis, Matthews & McGrath, 2000) and stronger neuroendocrine, cardio-vascular and emotional responses to interpersonal harassment (Suarez *et al.*, 1998). Recent diary studies give interesting insight in the functioning of hostile people. Judge, Scott and Illies (2006) showed that among individuals high in trait hostility, perceived unfair behaviour by their supervisor was more strongly related to state hostility. State hostility, in turn, was negatively related to job satisfaction, and positively related to workplace deviance. However, hostile persons are not only particularly reactive to negative in-terpersonal but also to positive, supportive interactions: Vella, Kamarck and Shiffman (2008) showed that for people high in hostility (and only for them) instrumental social support increased diastolic blood pressure.

There has been quite some debate on the role of expressing anger as pre-dictor of CHD, with some authors (e.g., Steptoe, 1996) regarding anger-in, and others (e.g., Siegman, 1994b) anger-out as the important component. Ev-idence seems to be more supportive for anger-out as predictor of CHD (Miller *et al.*, 1996). Note, however, that the implication is not that components of hostility other than anger-out are irrelevant. They are weaker predictors only with regard to CHD, but they are good predictors of mortality from all causes (Miller *et al.*, 1996). Anger-in may be especially important for the develop-ment of cancer (Siegman, 1994b) and being low in anger expression may be involved in the development of high blood pressure (Steptoe, 2001).

Expressing or not expressing one's anger may, however, not be the most important aspect. Rather, it may be what expressing, or not expressing, one's anger does to the person in terms of ending vs. prolonging the anger. Express-ing anger can be constructive (e.g. explaining one's feelings to a partner) or antagonistic (offending, blaming the partner). Likewise, not expressing the anger may be antagonistic if associated with ruminating, self-pity, dreaming about revenge etc., but it may be non-antagonistic by putting things into perspective, trying to see them from a humorous side, trying to understand the other's perspective, etc. It may well be that it is the antagonistic vs. con-structive way of dealing with anger that is most important, not the question of whether it is expressed or not (Davidson *et al.*, 1999; cf. Semmer, 2006).

Convergences

Judging from one perspective, the different concepts and the findings re-lated to them are rather confusing. Although there is some overlap between different concepts, it is unclear how many different constructs are involved and how they are hierarchically ordered. Certainly, more studies are needed to investigate the communalities and differences involved.

From another perspective, however, the picture is not so gloomy. There do seem to be some common elements that appear in different studies, and if we look at the 'great lines', we might come to a conclusion like the following:

People who are resilient:

- tend to interpret their environment basically as benign, that is, they expect things to go well (optimism) and people to not intend harm (trust, agreeableness). All this does not apply unconditionally but it is the 'default' interpretation as long as there are no reasons to believe otherwise.
- tend to accept setbacks and failures (and, thus, stressful experiences) as normal, not necessarily indicative of their own incompetence and lack of worthiness (secure self-esteem) or indicative of a basically hostile world (low hostility). Negative experiences are, therefore, put into perspective, as having meaning beyond the present situation, for instance, as aversive but necessary and legitimate experiences on one's way to a more overarching goal. The comprehensibility and meaningfulness dimensions of the sense-of-coherence concept are relevant here, as is the commitment dimension of hardiness.
- tend to see life as something that can be influenced and acted upon (internal locus of control), and to see themselves as capable to do so (self-efficacy, manageability dimension of sense of coherence, competence elements of self-esteem). Related to this is the tendency to see stressful events as a challenge (challenge dimension of hardiness; challenge aspect of the meaningfulness dimension of sense of coherence).

All this implies also that people who are resilient do show emotional stability and do not have a tendency to experience negative emotions (neuroticism, negative affectivity).

Theoretically, the concepts mentioned should influence coping strategies which would imply that they should act as moderators in the relationship between stress and outcome variables. Such findings are obtained quite often (see above) but not nearly as consistently as would be expected theoretically.

One reason for this is certainly to be found in methodological difficulties, because moderated regression procedures tend to yield very conservative estimates of interaction effects (cf. Cohen & Edwards, 1989). A further reason for this might be that the resourceful belief system pictured here has an influence at a much earlier point, that is, changes the stress appraisal in the first place, as discussed in Section 6.2.2.

Is it only negative affectivity?

That resources in the sense of the belief systems discussed here are so often found to be directly related to symptoms points to another, very basic question. It is possible that all these measures are really indicators of NA (Watson, Pennebaker & Folger, 1987), or neuroticism (Dembroski & Costa, 1987). In fact, the measures discussed here are often found to correlate with one another, some have been combined to the larger meta-construct of 'core self-evaluations' (Judge & Bono, 2001), and controlling for NA often reduces associations between belief systems and symptoms (e.g., Schaubroeck & Ganster, 1991). Indeed, it would be quite strange if there were not a substantial relationship between the broad construct of NA and belief systems that have to do with an environment that is meaningful, basically benign and able to be influenced, and with a self-concept that involves the capability to actually influence this environment in accordance with one's goals. Also, the etiology for the aforementioned belief system involves experiences of mastery, as well as experiences of failure that can be dealt with; these are conditions that we would also assume to influence NA. And, indeed, chronic stress conditions are found to influence changes in NA over time (cf. Spector *et al.*, 2000).

Therefore, attributing an important role to NA in concepts of a disease (or health) prone personality does not imply that associations between stressors and health can be reduced to reflecting NA. Rather, NA would be seen as a factor that may influence the experience and perception of, as well as the reactions to, stress factors, but at the same time may be influenced by these factors (Spector *et al.*, 2000).

A related issue refers to common method variance. Since most studies on stress at work use self-report, common method variance may account for the associations found (and the common factor behind that may, again, be negative affectivity; cf. Spector, 2006). This has, however, not gone unrefuted (e.g., Chen & Spector, 1991; Spector, 2006; Spector *et al.*, 2000). Analyses with different indicators of job stressors (e.g., self-report and ratings by trained observers) in our research have consistently shown that correlations between stressors and symptoms are, indeed, inflated by common method variance but that substantive associations remain when this is controlled (e.g., Semmer, Zapf & Greif, 1996).

6.5   RESPONSE TENDENCIES AND COPING

Coping is one of the most important concepts in research on stress. It refers to all attempts to manage a stressful transaction, to make it less stressful (cf. Lazarus & Folkman, 1984). These attempts are based on an appraisal of the situation (primary appraisal) and a person's possibilities to deal with it (secondary appraisal) and are, therefore, specific to the characteristics of the situation. Nevertheless, it has become clear that people also have person-specific tendencies to use certain coping strategies (cf. Carver, Scheier & Weintraub, 1989). Stable individual differences in coping, however, do not require that certain people will always employ strategy A and others strategy B. There may also be differences on a 'meta-level' in that some people are habitually more flexible in their strategies. A recent meta-analysis shows that optimists are more likely to accept uncontrollable situations and more likely to use active coping strategies in controllable situations than are pessimists (Nes & Segersstrom, 2006). In other words: optimists show a tendency towards coping strategies that are adequate for the situation (Carver & Scheier, 1999).

6.5.1   Classifications of Coping

There are many classifications of coping, the most basic one being the dichotomy between problem-focused vs. emotion-focused coping (see Lazarus & Folkman, 1984). A somewhat different approach concentrates on the tendency to seek or avoid information concerning the stressful aspects of the situation. This is most clearly expressed in the coping styles called 'monitoring' and 'blunting' by Miller (e.g. 1990).

There are many expansions and blends of these approaches and there is by no means consensus over number and kind of the dimensions to be employed. This problem is further aggravated by the fact that the same labels do not necessarily imply the same concept. For example, items referring to alcohol consumption, eating or smoking are sometimes part of an avoidance or denial factor (e.g., Koeske, Kirk & Koeske, 1993; Endler & Parker, 1990; Carver, Scheier & Weintraub, 1989), but sometimes they belong to an emotion-focused factor (e.g., Billings & Moos, 1984).

In light of this confusion it is surprising that nevertheless there are some tendencies where research is converging. Thus, in general (and with many exceptions), the tendency to employ problem-focused coping is associated with better mental (and sometimes, physical) health while emotion-focused coping tends to show the opposite relationship (e.g., Carver et al., 1989). Problem-focused coping has also been found to moderate the relationship between control and demands according to the Karasek model (Karasek & Theorell, 1990), in that people who show 'active coping' profit most from control under conditions of high stress (e.g., Ippolito et al., 2005). Avoidance-oriented coping is often found to be beneficial in the short run but detrimental in the long run (Suls & Fletcher, 1985). Also, not surprisingly, avoidance is more beneficial if the problem is uncontrollable whereas approach is more instrumental when something can be done about the situation (Miller, 1990).

6.5.2 The Difficult Role of 'Emotion-Focused Coping'

Instrumental and detrimental aspects of emotion-focused coping

One aspect of this research that is somewhat difficult to interpret is the often-reported finding that 'emotional coping' tends to be associated with poorer mental health and poorer outcomes (Edwards, 1998). The reason why this is puzzling is that many authors postulate that emotional coping should not be detrimental *per se*. Rather, highly stressful experiences may require some management of intense emotions before a person is able to deal with the problem in a more active and direct way (e.g., Lazarus & Folkman, 1984; Reicherts & Perrez, 1992). Emotional coping in terms of trying to calm down has been found to predict calming down in a diary study by Elfering *et al.* (2005).

An especially interesting approach to this problem is presented by Reicherts and Perrez (1992). They formulate a 'behaviour rules approach' which specifies which coping strategies should work best under what conditions. In line with many others, they postulate that under conditions of greater controllability there should be more active and less avoidance coping. At the same time, however, they 'prescribe' more palliative coping under high stressfulness and more re-evaluation of standards when the probability of re-occurrence of the situation is judged to be high. In taking into account the 'fit' between characteristics of the situation and the coping strategies used, and by allowing analyses of how appraisals of and coping with a situation may change over time, this seems an especially interesting approach which can be expected to greatly enhance our understanding of coping effectiveness and of the role of individual differences in coping processes.

Coping or distress-intensity? Emotion-focused coping as 'inability to cope'

There is an additional problem, however, with the conceptualization and, especially, the operationalization of 'emotion-focused' coping. As an example, Carver *et al.* (1989) report a scale they call 'focus on and venting of emotions', with items such as 'I get upset and let my emotions out'; Endler and Parker (1990) report an emotion-focused scale that taps 'self-blame'. These scales correlate with several scales indicative of NA, such as anxiety, depression or neuroticism. If we define coping as 'efforts to manage specific external and/or internal demands' (Lazarus & Folkman, 1984, p. 141), then it is doubtful whether what is being measured here can really be called coping. Rather, items like these seem to measure how strongly a person feels distressed and the inability to concentrate on anything than the distressing thoughts. Based on these considerations, Kälin and Semmer (2008) developed an instrument that aims at assessing 'true' emotional, or palliative, coping. Unlike traditional measures of emotional coping, such as the respective subscale of the CISS (Endler & Parker, 1990), it correlates negatively with measures of strain (cf. Elfering *et al.*, 2005).

6.5.3   Summary

In general, people who have a tendency to cope by dealing actively with problems tend to be better off. However, where the situation is taken into account, is becomes clear that palliative modes of coping may be beneficial in highly stressful situations where palliation may be instrumental in building up the resources needed for other forms of coping, and in situations that cannot be controlled. The latter also call for a re-evaluation of one's goals. Such coping strategies do seem to have a habitual component, as does the tendency to adjust one's strategy to the characteristics of the situation and its changes over time. These strategies, in turn, depend, at least in part, on personality characteristics such as hostility, neuroticism and on resourceful belief systems.

6.6   FINAL COMMENTS

It becomes increasingly clear that resilient people have a certain way of dealing with reality. Coping actively under all circumstances, nourishing illusions over one's capabilities that are far from reality, or having a naive optimism, are not characteristics of this effectiveness. While individual differences with regard to coping with and suffering from stressors are pervasive, they should not seduce us to reduce everything to idiosyncratic, exclusively subjective, phenomena (see Hobfoll, 2001). In many cases, it is not the objective situation *per se* but the way people deal with it that decides about outcomes. It should be kept in mind, however, that resiliency itself is, albeit only partly, a product of such circumstances. If one examines the effects of stress on health on the one hand and on the development of resiliency vs. vulnerability on the other, the parallels are striking. Apart from traumatic single experiences, it is chronically stressful conditions that overtax people's resources, impairing not only their health but also their coping resources. This often leads to the perception of the person being 'the cause' of the problems, because he or she seems unable to deal with problems that other people do deal with effectively. This supports an attribution error – for lay people and scientists alike – that induces people to overemphasize individual differences and to underemphasize reality and not to see the vicious circle in which one is reinforcing the other. The picture worsens when some of these cumulative effects refer to characteristics of the person that tend to irritate others (e.g. excessive complaints – Silver, Wortman & Crofton, 1990) or even antagonize them (e.g., uncivil behaviour – Blau & Anderson, 2005). In such a case, the person does, indeed, create new stressors for him- or herself as well as for others, and it becomes very difficult for others to see how much this 'actor' is also a 'victim' of stressful life circumstances during his or her life.

REFERENCES

Adler, N. & Matthews, K. (1994). Health psychology: why do some people get sick and some stay well? *Annual Review of Psychology*, **45**, 229–59.

Adler, N.E., Marmot, M., McEwen, B.S. & Stewart, J. (1999). Socioeconomic status and health in industrial nations: social, psychological, and biological pathways. *Annals of the New York Academy of Sciences*, **896**.

Amstad, F.T. & Semmer, N.K. (2009). Recovery and the work–family interface. *Research in Occupational Stress and Well-being*, **7**, 125–66.

Amstad, F.T., Elfering, A., Fasel, U. & Semmer, N.K. (2009). *Do work-to-family conflicts impact different life domains than family-to-work conflicts? A meta-analysis.* Manuscript submitted for publication, Department of Psychology, University of Bern.

Antonovsky, A. (1991). The structural sources of salutogenic strengths. In C.L. Cooper & R. Payne, (Eds), *Personality and Stress: Individual Differences in the Stress Process* (pp. 67–104). Chichester: John Wiley & Sons, Ltd.

Antonovsky, A. (1993). The structure and properties of the Sense of Coherence Scale. *Social Science and Medicine*, **36**, 725–33.

Averill, J.R. (1986). The acquisition of emotions during adulthood. In R. Harré (Ed.), *The Social Construction of Emotions* (pp. 98–118). Oxford: Basil Blackwell.

Bandura, A. (1989). Self-regulation of motivation and action through internal standards and goal systems. In L.A. Pervin (Ed.), *Goal Concepts in Personality and Social Psychology* (pp. 19–85). Hillsdale, NJ: Lawrence Erlbaum.

Bandura, A. (1992). Exercise of personal agency through the self-efficacy mechanism. In R. Schwarzer (Ed.), *Self-Efficacy: Thought Control of Action* (pp. 3–38). Washington, DC: Hemisphere.

Beehr, T.A. & Bowling, N.A. (2005). Hardy personality, stress, and health. In C.L. Cooper (Ed.), *Handbook of Stress and Health* (2nd edn, pp. 193–211). New York: CRC Press.

Berkowitz, L. (1998). Aggressive personalities. In D.F. Barone, M. Hersen, & V.B. van Hasselt (Eds), *Advanced personality* (pp. 263–285). New York: Plenum.

Billings, A.G. & Moos, R.H. (1984). Coping, stress, and social resources among adults with unipolar depression. *Journal of Personality and Social Psychology*, **46**, 877–91.

Birks, Y. & Roger, D. (2000). Identifying components of type-A behaviour: 'toxic' and 'non-toxic' achieving. *Personality and Individual Differences*, **28**, 1093–105.

Blau, G. & Anderson, L. (2005). Testing a measure of instigated workplace incivility. *Journal of Occupational and Organizational Psychology*, **78**, 595–614.

Brockner, J. (1988). *Self-esteem at work*. Lexington, MA: Lexington Books.

Brockner, J. & Higgins, E. T. (2001). Regulatory focus theory: implications for the study of emotions at work. *Organizational Behavior and Human Decision Processes*, **86**, 35–66.

Brockner, J., Tyler, T.R. & Cooper-Schneider, R. (1992). The influence of prior commitment to an institution on reactions to perceived unfairness: the higher they are, the harder they fall. *Administrative Science Quarterly*, **37**, 241–61.

Buss, A.H. & Perry, M. (1992). The aggression questionnaire. *Journal of Personality and Social Psychology*, **63**, 452–9.

Büssing, A. (1992). A dynamic view of job satisfaction in psychiatric nurses in Germany. *Work and Stress*, **6**, 239–59.

Carver, C.S. & Scheier, M.F. (1999). Optimism. In C.R. Snyder (ed.), *Coping: The Psychology of What Works* (pp. 182–204). New York: Oxford University Press.

Carver, C.S., Scheier, M.F. & Weintraub, J.K. (1989). Assessing coping strategies: a theoretically based approach. *Journal of Personality and Social Psychology*, **56**, 267–83.

Chen, P.Y. & Spector, P.E. (1991). Negative affectivity as the underlying cause of correlations between stressors and strains. *Journal of Applied Psychology*, **76**, 398–407.

Clarke, S. (2006). Contrasting perceptual, attitudinal and dispositional approaches to accident involvement in the workplace. *Safety Science*, **44**, 537–50.

Cobb, S. (1973). Role responsibility. The differentiation of a concept. *Occupational Mental Health*, **3**, 10–14.

Cohen, S. & Edwards, J.R. (1989). Personality characteristics as moderators of the relationship between stress and disorder. In R.W.J. Neufeld (Ed.), *Advances in the Investigation of Psychological Stress* (pp. 235–83). New York: John Wiley & Sons, Inc.

Cropanzano, R., James, K. & Citera, M. (1993). A goal hierarchy model of personality, motivation, and leadership. *Research in Organizational Behavior*, **15**, 267–322.

Davidson, K., MacGregor, M.W., Stuhr, J. & Gidron, Y. (1999). Increasing constructive anger verbal behavior decreases resting blood pressure: a secondary analysis of a randomized controlled hostility intervention. *International Journal of Behavioral Medicine*, **6**, 268–78.

Davis, M.C., Matthews, K.A. & McGrath, C.E. (2000). Hostile attitudes predict vascular resistance during interpersonal stress in men and women. *Psychosomatic Medicine*, **62**, 17–25.

Dembroski, T.M. & Costa, P. (1987). Coronary prone behavior: components of the Type A pattern and hostility. *Journal of Personality*, **55**, 211–35.

Diener, E. & Fujita, F. (1995). Resources, personal strivings, and subjective well-being: a nomothetic and ideographic approach. *Journal of Personality and Social Psychology*, **68**, 926–35.

Edwards, J.R. (1991). The measurement of Type A behavior pattern: an assessment of criterion-oriented validity, content validity, and construct validity. In C.L. Cooper & R. Payne, (Eds), *Personality and Stress: Individual Differences in the Stress Process* (pp. 151–80). Chichester: John Wiley & Sons, Ltd.

Edwards, J.R. (1998). A cybernetic theory of organizational stress. In C.L. Cooper (Ed.), *Theories of Organizational Stress* (pp. 122–52). Oxford: Oxford University Press.

Edwards, J.R. & van Harrison, R. (1993). Job demands and worker health: three-dimensional reexamination of the relationship between person–environment fit and strain. *Journal of Applied Psychology*, **78**, 628–48.

Elfering, A., Grebner, S., Semmer, N.K., Kaiser-Freiburghaus, D., Lauper-Del Ponte, S. & Witschi, I. (2005). Chronic job stressors and job control: effects on event-related coping success and well-being. *Journal of Occupational and Organizational Psychology*, **78**, 237–52.

Ellsworth, P.C. & Scherer, K.R. (2003). Appraisal processes in emotion. In R.J. Davidson, K.R. Scherer & H.H. Goldsmith (Eds), *Handbook of Affective Sciences* (pp. 572–95). New York: Oxford University Press.

Emmons, R.A. (1991). Personal strivings, daily life events, and psychological and physical well-being. *Journal of Personality*, **59**, 453–72.

Emmons, R.A. (1996). Striving and feeling: personal goals and subjective well-being. In J. Bargh & P. Gollwitzer (Eds), *The Psychology of Action* (pp. 314–37). New York: Guilford.

Endler, N.S. & Parker, J.D.A. (1990). Multidimensional assessment of coping: a critical evaluation. *Journal of Personality and Social Psychology*, **58**, 844–54.

Eriksson, M. & Lindström, B. (2005). Validity of Antonovsky's sense of coherence scale: a systematic review. *Journal of Epidemiology and Community Health*, **59**, 460–6.

Feldt, T. (1997). The role of sense of coherence in well-being at work: analysis of main and moderator effects. *Work and Stress*, **11**, 134–47.

Florian, V., Mikulincer, M. & Taubman, O. (1995). Does hardiness contribute to mental health during a stressful real-life situation? The roles of appraisal and coping. *Journal of Personality and Social Psychology*, **68**, 687–95.

Frese, M. (1992). A plea for realistic pessimism: on objective reality, coping with stress, and psychological dysfunction. In L. Montada, S.-H. Filipp & M.J. Lerner

(Eds), *Life Crises and Experiences of Loss in Adulthood* (pp. 81–94). Hillsdale, NJ: Lawrence Erlbaum.

Furnham, A. (1992). *Personality at Work. The Role of Individual Differences in the Workplace*. London: Routledge.

Ganster, D.C. & Schaubroeck, J. (1991). Role stress and worker health: an extension of the plasticity hypothesis of self-esteem. *Journal of Social Behavior and Personality*, **6**, 349–60.

Geyer, S. (1997) Some conceptual considerations on the sense of coherence. *Social Science and Medicine*, **44**, 1771–80.

Gray, J.A. (1987). *The Psychology of Fear and Stress* (2nd edn). Cambridge: Cambridge University Press.

Grebner, S., Elfering, A. Semmer, N.K., Kaiser-Probst, C. & Schlapbach, M.-L. (2004). Stressful situations at work and in private life among young workers: an event sampling approach. *Social Indicators Research*, **67**, 11–49.

Greenier, K.D., Kernis, M.H., McNamara, C.W., Waschull, S.B., Berry, A.J., Herlocker, C.E. *et al.* (1999). Individual differences in reactivity to daily events: examining the roles of stability and level of self-esteem. *Journal of Personality*, **67**, 185–208.

Hallsten, L. (1993). Burning out: a framework. In W.B. Schaufeli, C. Maslach & T. Marek (Eds), *Professional Burnout. Recent Developments in Theory and Research*. (pp. 95–113). London: Taylor & Francis.

Hobfoll, S.E. (2001). The influence of culture, community, and the nested-self in the stress process: advancing conservation of resources theory. *Applied Psychology: An International Review*, **50**, 337–421.

Ippolito, J., Adler, A.B., Thomas, J.L., Litz, B.T. & Holzl, R. (2005). Extending and applying the Demand-Control Model: the role of soldiers coping on a peacekeeping deployment. *Journal of Occupational Health Psychology*, **10**, 452–64.

Jemmott, J.B. III (1987). Social motives and susceptibility to disease: stalking individual differences in health risks. *Journal of Personality*, **55**, 267–98.

Jerusalem, M. & Schwarzer, R. (1992). Self-efficacy as a resource factor in stress appraisal. In R. Schwarzer (Ed.), *Self-Efficacy: Thought Control of Action* (pp. 195–213). Washington, DC: Hemisphere.

Jex, S.M., Bliese, P.D., Buzzell, S. & Primeau, J. (2001). The impact of self-efficacy on stressor-stain relations: coping style as an explanatory mechanism. *Journal of Applied Psychology*, **86**, 401–9.

Jex, S.M. & Elacqua, T.C. (1999). Self-esteem as a moderator: a comparison of global and organization-based measures. *Journal of Occupational and Organizational Psychology*, **72**, 71–81.

Jimmieson, N.L. (2000). Employee reactions to behavioural control under conditions of stress: the moderating role of self-efficacy. *Work and Stress*, **14**, 262–80.

Jimmieson, N.L., Terry, D.J. & Callan, V.J. (2004). A longitudinal study of employee adaptation to organizational change: the role of change-related information and change-related self-efficacy. *Journal of Occupational Health Psychology*, **9**, 11–27.

Johansson Hanse, J. & Engström, T. (1999). Sense of coherence and ill health among the unemployed and re-employed after closure of an assembly plant. *Work and Stress*, **13**, 204–22.

Judge, T.A. & Bono, J.E. (2001). Relationship of core self-evaluations traits – self-esteem, generalized self efficacy, locus of control, and emotional stability – with job satisfaction and job performance: a meta–analysis. *Journal of Applied Psychology*, **86**, 80–92.

Judge, T.A., Scott, B.A. & Ilies, R. (2006). Hostility, job attitudes, and workplace deviance: test of a multilevel model. *Journal of Applied Psychology*, **91**, 26–38.

Kahn, R.L. & Byosiere, P. (1992). Stress in organizations. In M.D. Dunnette & L.M. Hough (Eds), *Handbook of Industrial and Organizational Psychology*, vol. **3** (pp. 571–650). Palo Alto, CA: Consulting Psychologists Press.

Kälin, W. & Semmer, N.K. (2008). *'True' emotional coping*. Unpublished manuscript, University of Bern, Switzerland.

Karasek, R.A. & Theorell, T. (1990). *Healthy work: Stress, productivity and the reconstruction of working life*. New York: Basic Books.

Kernis, M.H. (2005). Measuring self-esteem in context: the importance of stability of self-esteem in psychological functioning. *Journal of Personality*, **73**, 1–37.

Kernis, M.H., Grannemann, B.D. & Barclay, L.C. (1989). Stability and level of self-esteem as predictors of anger arousal and hostility. *Journal of Personality and Social Psychology*, **56**, 1013–22.

Kessler, R.D. & McLeod, J. (1984). Sex differences in vulnerability to undesirable events. *American Sociological Review*, **47**, 217–27.

Kobasa, S.C.Q. (1988). Conceptualization and measurement of personality in job stress research. In J.J. Hurrell, Jr., L.R. Murphy, S.L. Sauter & C.L. Cooper (Eds), *Occupational Stress: Issues and Developments in Research* (pp. 100–9). New York: Taylor & Francis.

Koeske, G.F., Kirk, S.A. & Koeske, R.D. (1993). Coping with job stress: which strategies work best? *Journal of Occupational and Organizational Psychology*, **66**, 319–35.

Kouvonen, A.M., Väänänen, A., Woods, S.A., Heponiemi, T., Koskinen, A. & Toppinen-Tanner, S. (2008). Sense of coherence and diabetes: a prospective occupational cohort study. *BMC Public Health*, **8**, 46.

Larsen, R.J. & Ketelaar, T. (1991). Personality and susceptibility to positive and negative emotional states. *Journal of Personality and Social Psychology*, **61**, 132–40.

Lavallee, L.F. & Campbell, J.D. (1995). Impact of personal goals on self-regulation processes elicited by daily negative events. *Journal of Personality and Social Psychology*, **69**, 341–52.

Lazarus, R.S. (1999). *Stress and Emotion*. London: Free Association Books.

Lazarus, R.S. & Folkman, S. (1984). *Stress, Appraisal, and Coping*. New York: Springer.

Lazarus, R.S. & Folkman, S. (1986). Cognitive theories of stress and the issue of circularity. In M. Appley & R. Trumbull (Eds), *Dynamics of Stress* (pp. 63–80). New York: Plenum.

Leitner, K. & Resch, M.G. (2005). Do the effects of job stressors on health persist over time? A longitudinal study with observational stressor measures. *Journal of Occupational Health Psychology*, **10**, 18–30.

Maddi, S.R. (2002). The story of hardiness: twenty years of theorizing, research, and practice. *Consulting Psychology Journal: Practice and Research*, **54**, 173–85.

Mäkikangas, A. & Kinnunen, U. (2003). Psychosocial work stressors and well-being: Self-esteem and optimism as moderators in a one-year longitudinal sample. *Personality and Individual Differences*, **35**, 537–57.

McClelland, D.C. (1987). *Human Motivation*. Cambridge: Cambridge University Press.

Meier, L.L. & Semmer, N.K. (2008). *When narcissists get stressed: the role of an imbalance between effort and reward*. Manuscript submitted for publication, University of Bern, Switzerland.

Meier, L.L., Semmer, N.K., Elfering, A. & Jacobshagen, N. (2008). The double meaning of control: three-way interactions between internal resources, job control, and stressors at work. *Journal of Occupational Health Psychology*, **13**, 244–58.

Meier, L.M., Semmer, N.K. & Hupfeld, J. (2009). The impact of unfair treatment on depressive mood: the moderating role of self-esteem level and self-esteem instability. *Personality and Social Psychology Bulletin*, **35**, 643–55.

Miller, S.M. (1990). To see or not to see: cognitive informational styles in the coping process. In M. Rosenbaum (Ed.), *Learned Resourcefulness: On Coping Skills, Self-Control, and Adaptive Behavior* (pp. 95–126). New York: Springer.

Miller, T.Q., Smith, T.W., Turner, C.W., Guijarro, M.L. & Hallet, A.J. (1996). A meta-analytic review of research on hostility and physical health. *Psychological Bulletin*, **119**, 322–48.

Myrtek, M. (2007). Type A behavior and hostility as independent risk factors for coronary heart disease. In A.M. Zeiher, J. Jordan & B. Barde (Eds), *Contributions toward Evidence-Based Psychocardiology: A Systematic Review of the Literature* (pp. 159–83). Washington, DC: American Psychological Association.

Nes, L. & Segersstrom, S.C. (2006). Dispositional optimism and coping: a meta-analytic review. *Personality and Social Psychology Review*, **10**, 235–51.

Ng, T.W.H., Sorensen, K.L. & Eby, L.T. (2006). Locus of control at work: a meta-analysis. *Journal of Organizational Behavior*, **27**, 1057–87.

Reicherts, M. & Perrez, M. (1992). Adequate coping behavior: the behavior rules approach. In M. Perrez & M. Reicherts (Eds), *Stress, Coping, and Health* (pp. 161–82). Seattle: Hogrefe & Huber.

Reilly, N.P. (1994). Exploring a paradox: commitment as a moderator of the stressor-burnout relationship. *Journal of Applied Social Psychology*, **24**, 397–414.

Rice, R.W., Gentile, D.A. & McFarlin, D.B. (1991). Facet importance and job satisfaction. *Journal of Applied Psychology*, **76**, 31–9.

Roberson, L. (1990). Prediction of job satisfaction from the characteristics of personal work goals. *Journal of Organizational Behavior*, **11**, 29–41.

Rotter, J.B. (1966). Generalized expectancies for internal versus external control of reinforcement. *Psychological Monographs: General and Applied*, **80**, 1 (Whole No. 609).

Schaubroeck, J. & Ganster, D.C. (1991). Associations among stress-related individual differences. In C.L. Cooper & R. Payne, (Eds), *Personality and Stress: Individual Differences in the Stress Process* (pp. 33–66). Chichester: John Wiley & Sons, Ltd.

Schaubroeck, J. & Merritt, D.E. (1997). Divergent effects of job control on coping with work stressors: the key role of self-efficacy. *Academy of Management Journal*, **40**, 738–54.

Scheier, M.F. & Carver, C.S. (1992). Effects of optimism on psychological and physical well-being: theoretical overview and empirical update. *Cognitive Therapy and Research*, **16**, 201–28.

Semmer, N.K. (2006). Stress, personality, and coping. In M.E. Vollrath (Ed.), *Handbook of Personality and Health* (pp. 73–113). Chichester: John Wiley & Sons, Ltd.

Semmer, N.K., Jacobshagen, N., Meier, L.L. & Elfering, A. (2009). *Illegitimate tasks as a source of stress*. Manuscript submitted for publication, University of Bern, Switzerland.

Semmer, N.K., Jacobshagen, N., Meier, L.L. & Elfering, A. (2007). Occupational stress research: the 'Stress-as-Offense-to-Self' perspective. In J. Houdmont & S. McIntyre, (Eds), *Occupational Health Psychology: European Perspectives on Research, Education and Practice* (Vol. **2**, pp. 43–60). Castelo da Maia, Portugal: ISMAI Publishing.

Semmer, N.K., McGrath, J.E. & Beehr, T.A. (2005). Conceptual issues in research on stress and health. In C.L. Cooper (Ed.), *Handbook of Stress Medicine and Health* (pp. 1–43). Washington, DC: CRC Press.

Semmer, N., Zapf, D. & Greif, S. (1996). 'Shared job strain': a new approach for assessing the validity of job stress measurements. *Journal of Occupational and Organizational Psychology*, **69**, 293–310.

Siegman, A.W. (1994a). From Type A to hostility to anger: reflections on the history of coronary-prone behavior. In A.W. Siegman & T.W. Smith (Eds), *Anger, Hostility, and the Heart* (pp. 1–21). Hillsdale, NJ: Lawrence Erlbaum.

Siegman, A.W. (1994b). Cardiovascular consequences of expressing and repressing anger. In A.W. Siegman & T.W. Smith (Eds), *Anger, Hostility, and the Heart* (pp. 173–97). Hillsdale, NJ: Lawrence Erlbaum.

Silver, R.C., Wortman, C.B. & Crofton, C. (1990). The role of coping in support provision: the self-presentational dilemma of victims of life crises. In B.R. Sarason, I.G. Sarason & G.R. Pierce (Eds), *Social Support: An Interactional View* (pp. 397–426). New York: John Wiley & Sons, Inc.

Smith, T.W., Glazer, K., Ruiz, J.M. & Gallo, L.C. (2004). Hostility, anger, aggressiveness, and coronary heart disease: an interpersonal perspective on personality, emotion, and health. *Journal of Personality*, **72**, 1217–70.

Söderfeldt, M., Söderfeldt, B., Ohlson, C.-G., Theorell, T. & Jones, J. (2000). The impact of sense of coherence and high demand/low-control job environment on self-reported health, burnout and psychophysiological stress indicators. *Work and Stress*, **14**, 1–15.

Sonnentag, S. & Frese, M. (2003). Stress in organizations. In W.C. Borman, D.R. Ilgen & J.R. Kimoski (Eds), *Handbook of Psychology, Vol., 12: Industrial and Organizational Psychology* (pp. 453–91). New York: John Wiley & Sons, Inc.

Spector, P.E. (2003). Individual differences in health and well-being in organizations. In D.A. Hoffman & L.E. Tetrick (Eds), *Health and Safety in Organizations: A Multilevel Perspective* (pp. 29–55). San Francisco: Jossey-Bass.

Spector, P.E. (2006). Method variance in organizational research: truth or urban legend? *Organizational Research Methods*, **9**, 221–32.

Spector, P.E., Cooper, C.L., Sanchez, J.I., O'Driscoll, M., Sparks, K., Bernin, P. *et al.* (2002). Locus of control and well-being at work: how generalizable are Western findings? *Academy of Management Journal*, **45**, 453–66.

Spector, P.E. & Jex, S.M. (1998) Development of four self-report measures of job stressors and strain: Interpersonal Conflict at Work Scale, Organizational Constraints Scale, Quantitative Workload Inventory, and Physical Symptoms Inventory. *Journal of Occupational Health Psychology*, **3**, 356–67.

Spector, P.E., Jex, S.M. & Chen, P.Y. (1995). Personality traits as predictors of objective job characteristics. *Journal of Organizational Behavior*, **16**, 59–65.

Spector, P.E., Zapf, D., Chen, P.Y. & Frese, M. (2000). Why negative affectivity should not be controlled in job stress research: don't throw out the baby with the bath water. *Journal of Organizational Behavior*, **21**, 79–95.

Steptoe, A. (1996). Psychophysiological processes in the prevention of cardiovascular disease. In K. Orth-Gomér & N. Schneiderman (Eds), *Behavioral Medicine Approaches to Cardiovascular Disease Prevention* (pp. 135–48). Mahwah, NJ: Lawrence Erlbaum.

Steptoe, A. (2001). Psychophysiological bases of disease. In D.W. Johnston & M. Jonston (Eds), *Health Psychology. Vol. 8: Comprehensive Clinical Psychology* (pp. 39–78). Amsterdam: Elsevier.

Suarez, E.D., Kuhn, C.M., Schanberg, S.M., Williams, R.B. & Zimmermann, E.A. (1998). Neuroendocrine, cardiovascular, and emotional responses of hostile men: the role of interpersonal challenge. *Psychosomatic Medicine*, **60**, 78–88.

Suls, J. & Fletcher, B. (1985). The relative efficacy of avoidant and non-avoidant coping strategies: a meta-analysis. *Health Psychology*, **4**, 247–88.

Suls, J. & Martin, R. (2005). The daily life of the garden-variety neurotic: reactivity, stressors exposure, mood spillover, and maladaptive coping. *Journal of Personality*, **73**, 1–25.

Surtees, P.G., Wainwright, N.W.J., Luben, R., Khaw, K.-T. & Day, N.E. (2006). Mastery, sense of coherence, and mortality: evidence of independent associations from the EPIC-Norfolk prospective cohort study. *Health Psychology*, **25**, 102–10.

Suominen, S., Helenius, H., Blomberg, H., Uutela, A. & Koskenvuo, M. (2001). Sense of coherence as a predictor of subjective state of health: results of 4 years of follow-up of adults. *Journal of Psychosomatic Research*, **50**, 77–86.

Vella, E.J., Kamarck, T.W. & Shiffman, S. (2008). Hostility moderates the effects of social support and intimacy on blood pressure in daily social interactions. *Health Psychology*, **27**, 155–62.

Veroff, J.B. (1982). Assertive motivations: achievement vs. power. In D.G. Winter & A.J. Stewart (Eds), *Motivation and Society*. San Francisco: Jossey-Bass.

Vogt, D.S., Rizvi, S.L., Shipherd, J.C. & Resick, P.A. (2008). Longitudinal investigation of reciprocal relationship between stress reactions and hardiness. *Personality and Social Psychology Bulletin*, **34**, 61–73.

Vollrath, M. & Torgersen, S. (2000). Personality types and coping. *Personality and Individual Differences*, **29**, 367–78.

Ward, C.H. & Eisler, R.M. (1987). Type A behavior, achievement striving, and a dysfunctional self-evaluation system. *Journal of Personality and Social Psychology*, **53**, 318–26.

Watson, D., Pennebaker, J.W. & Folger, R. (1987). Beyond negative affectivity: Measuring stress and satisfaction in the work place. In J.M. Ivancevich & D.C. Ganster (Eds), *Job stress: From Theory to Suggestion* (pp. 141–57). New York: Haworth Press.

Wrosch, C., Scheier, M.F., Carver, C.S. & Schulz, R. (2003). The importance of goal disengagement in adaptive self-regulation: when giving up is beneficial. *Self and Identity*, **2**, 1–20.

Zapf, D., Dormann, C. & Frese, M. (1996). Longitudinal studies in organizational research: a review of the literature with reference to methodological issues. *Journal of Occupational Health Psychology*, **1**, 145–69.

CHAPTER 7

Gender and Work Stress: Unique Stressors, Unique Responses

Faye K. Cocchiara

Arkansas State University, USA

and

Myrtle P. Bell

The University of Texas at Arlington

Managing stress is a major problem in organizations for both employers and employees (Gyllensten & Palmer, 2005). Around 30% to 40% of workforces in the USA and Europe are exposed to workplace stress, and those levels appear to have risen over the past 20 years (Melchoir *et al.*, 2007). As a result, considerable research has been devoted to investigating the causes and consequences of workplace stress, particularly the role that gender plays in the relationship between stress and its dysfunctional effects. The bulk of this research has found that gender moderates (or changes) the relationship between stress and strain in the workplace. While stress is an inevitable component of most any workplace, both men and women must learn to manage it in order to be successful.

It is important that we clarify the differences between healthy stress that serves to stimulate and unhealthy stress that often has harmful effects. Stress that tends to arouse or motivate individuals to meet certain challenges, for example, is referred to as 'eustress', a term with origins from the ancient Greek word, *euphoria*. For all intents and purposes, this is viewed as 'positive' stress. On the other hand, unmanaged stress often leads to 'distress' or 'strain' (Nelson & Quick, 2008). Whether the response to strain is to 'fight

International Handbook of Work and Health Psychology, Third Edition. Edited by Cary L. Cooper, James Campbell Quick, and Marc J. Schabracq.

or flee' or 'tend and befriend' (e.g., Taylor *et al.*, 2000), what we've gleaned
from research in a variety of fields is that women face similar, yet unique
stressors when compared with men (Gyllensten & Palmer, 2005; Nelson &
Quick, 1985; Swanson, 2000); and that women tend to respond differently
(Swanson, 2000). The ways in which women manage job stress have been
a topic of much discussion within the past 30 years, in part because women
have entered the labour force in record numbers over that same period. In
addition, the issue of women's health has been the focus of increased government interest and private advocacy (Parker-Pope, 2007), also resulting in
increased attention to women's stress responses.

The literature documents three unique stressors to which working women
are exposed: multiple conflicting roles; lack of career progress; and discrimination and stereotyping. This chapter discusses these unique stressors for
women in the workplace and the ways in which they tend to cope. While
our primary emphasis is on unique stressors for women, we will call attention to stressors that affect men and women. The first part of the chapter
describes the unique stressors that plague many women in organizations.
Following is a discussion of the most documented reactions that working
women have to these stressors. We conclude the chapter with a discussion of
within-gender-group differences in the potential causes and consequences of
job stress.

7.1   UNIQUE STRESSORS FOR WORKING WOMEN

7.1.1   Multiple Conflicting Roles

> Balance is hard. It's one of the biggest issues for women. They get the majority
> of home responsibilities put on their shoulders, and understandably single moms
> in particular are torn between what they owe to family and what [they owe] to
> work (Bettye Martin Musham, Former CEO Gear Holdings, Inc).

Indeed, balance *is* hard. Achieving some level of balance between work and
family, work and leisure time, and work and any number of non-work activities is an important goal for both women and men in organizations worldwide
(Hall, 2003; Lockwood, 2003). Sixty percent of Hoechst Celanese employees
surveyed reported that the ability to balance their work and family responsibilities was an important factor in their decision to stay with the company
(Lockwood, 2003). A survey conducted by the UK Department of Trade
and Industry found that 69% of employees reported that work–life balance
was an important consideration when evaluating potential job opportunities

(Hall, 2003). A major reason why so many working women seek balance in their lives is due to inter-role conflict.

Inter-role conflict is defined as 'conflicting expectations related to two separate roles' (Nelson & Quick, 2008, p. 223). A sick child presents the mother who works outside the home with a conflict between her role as a mother and that of an employee. The first-grade teacher who is also planning a wedding and house-hunting with her future husband experiences conflicts between her roles as teacher, spouse and homeowner (*WebMD*, 2005). According to one researcher (Langan-Fox, 1998), the more roles one takes on, the higher the potential for stress. That women experience more role conflict than men is well documented (e.g., Cleveland *et al.*, 2006; Davidson & Cooper, 1984; Frone, Russell & Cooper, 1992; Noor, 2004). An early study of managers in the UK (e.g., Davidson & Cooper, 1984) found that the female managers in their sample reported significantly higher occupational stress levels than their male counterparts, including those who dealt with the conflicting responsibilities associated with juggling a home and career. Interestingly, whether working women have spouses/partners who also work tends to have little or no effect on women's experiences with role conflict. Spousal employment played no role in reducing the perceptions of role conflict experienced by women faculty (Cleveland *et al.*, 2006); suggesting family responses are borne more by women. 'For too many women, being sick or having an ill family member presents an untenable choice: stay at work when you shouldn't, or lose pay (and perhaps a job) by staying home' (Institute for Women's Policy Research, 2007, p. 1).

Role conflict has been identified as a common stressor for both men and women (Nelson & Burke, 2000), so why do we pay so much attention to studying inter-role conflict for working women? An important reason is the significant change in labour force demographics, particularly in the United States. Women comprise 59.4% of the US labour force (US Bureau of Labor Statistics, 2007). The labour force participation rate of mothers with dependent children (under the age of 18 years) rose substantially from 1975 through 2006, from 47% to 71% respectively (ibid., 2007). This change in workforce demographics has led to an overwhelming need by many workers, both women and men, to understand and find ways to strike a balance between expectations at work and those at home. Because women tend to bear the majority of home and childcare responsibilities (Chafetz, 1997), adding paid work to their responsibilities creates additional conflicts and stress.

A number of researchers have found negotiating multiple roles to be a unique source of stress for many working women (Gyllensten & Palmer, 2005; Nelson & Quick, 1985; Smith, 2000). The influx of women into the labour force makes them susceptible to the same occupational stressors (prolonged exposure to stressful working conditions) as men. While men's work consists primarily of paid employment, women's work tends to be diffused between paid work, childcare and housework (e.g., Krantz, Berntsson & Lundberg, 2005). This diffusion has had a detrimental effect on women's health in the form of increased exhaustion, heart disease, depression, anxiety, increased and sustained stress. Sixty percent of women in a US Department of Labor survey reported that job stress was their number one problem (cf. Swanson, 2000).

Though the issue of work–family balance is not exclusive to women, working women remain by far, our families' primary caregivers and are still responsible for the majority of household duties despite the increasing numbers of stay-at-home dads (Institute for Women's Policy Research, 2007; Shelton, 1992; Smith, 2000). According to Gyllensten and Palmer (2005, p. 278), 'Although there have been big changes in family structure and labour force participation, there have been only minor changes in responsibility for domestic chores' (see also Chafetz, 1997; Hochschild, 1989; Shelton, 1992). In addition to regular care-giving, for nearly half of all working mothers, it is still their responsibility to take time off work to care for a sick child or take their child(ren) to doctors' appointments. This is compared to 30% of working fathers. As a result, the challenge of balancing work and family remains a major stressor for many working women (e.g., Davidson & Cooper, 1984).

Although increasing numbers of jobs are becoming more flexible with regard to work hours, there generally remains a lack of flexible benefit programmes available to women who work outside the home. The Institute for Women's Policy Research (2007) reports that 40% of working women have no paid sick days and in the industries that employ the majority of women (retail and food service), that number rises to 55% and 78%, respectively. The lack of paid organizational leave programmes and policies in these industries exacerbates this issue. Unfortunately this situation has not improved much over the years. A recent study conducted by the Families and Work Institute (Galinsky *et al.*, 2008) found no change in the length of time employers offered parents and caregivers and that only 16% of employers provided full maternity benefits, down from 27% in 1998.

7.1.2   Lack of Career Progress

We find more and more that women 'drop out' of the corporate pipeline when they reach middle management, some because of lifestyle decisions, but many out of frustration (Gretchen Tibbits, President, National Association for Female Executives (NAFE)).

A second unique source of stress and strain for many working women is the lack of progress towards achieving their career goals (Gyllensten & Palmer, 2005; Nelson *et al.*, 1990). Despite having similar credentials, women managers fail to move up corporate hierarchies as quickly as men managers (Stroh, Brett & Reilly, 1992). How does failing to achieve one's career goals translate into negative stress? A look to the field of medicine can help explain how the process works. It begins with one's appraisal of a demand. When a worker is presented with a particular demand (career mobility in this instance) and she perceives that giving in to the demand outweighs the rewards, stress is often the result (cf. Nelson & Quick, 1985). Our bodies are remarkably resilient instruments that, under normal circumstances, have natural defences that help us withstand certain demands and retain the body's normal steady state balance (homeostasis). However, certain demands have the capability of throwing our bodies out of their normal balance and setting off an alarm response in the form of increased heart rate, elevated blood pressure and a weakening of the immune system among other manifestations (Cannon, 1935). For many working women, doing what they believe are all the 'right' things to achieve higher organizational levels yet failing to achieve a level representative of their efforts can result in frustration and distress.

The literature points to certain aspects of the organizational culture as major contributors to a lack of career progress for women. We discuss two of the most commonly cited ones in the next sections, glass ceilings and social isolation.

Glass ceilings

The 'glass ceiling' is a metaphor used to describe the largely invisible barriers that limit the career advancement of women, particularly in large organizations and in male-dominated professions such as engineering and medicine. Some have described the glass ceiling for women in corporations as having the executive suite within their grasps but not being able to break through to the top, calling attention to just 'how far women haven't come in corporate America' (Hymowitz & Schellhardt, 1986, p.1). The issue transcends the notion that fewer women are represented at all levels of management; the term, 'glass ceilings', suggests that women face increasingly more difficulty gaining access to the highest rungs of organizational hierarchies, those that represent 'real' power (Wright & Baxter, 2000).

Though invisible, glass ceilings are very apparent to women who experience them and have bona fide effects on their career mobility. Ninety percent of women managers surveyed responded that the glass ceiling was the most significant problem that they faced (cf. Smith, 2000). One need only look at

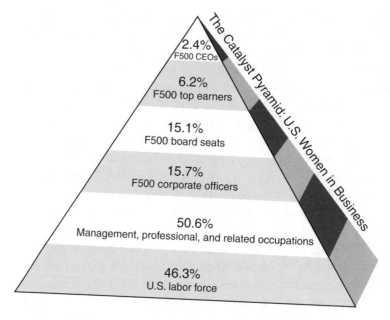

Figure 7.1   US women in business pyramids
Source: © Catalyst, December 2008.
Catalyst Research
Catalyst, *2008 Catalyst Census of Women Corporate Officers and Top Earners of the Fortune 500*
Catalyst, *2008 Catalyst Census of Women Board Directors of the Fortune 500*
Current Population Survey, Annual Averages, 2007

the small proportion of women who hold leadership positions in business as an example. Catalyst (2008a) published a very revealing pyramid depicting the diminishing proportions of women leaders in US business, from a large proportion of women in the labour force (46.3%) to only 2.4% of women CEOs in *Fortune 500* companies during the same reporting period (See Figure 7.1). Only one woman headed a *Fortune 500* company in 1985; she acknowledged that it was due to the fact that her family owned a controlling share of the firm (Hymowitz & Schellhardt, 1986, p. 1).

The situation is similar for working women in other countries. In Canada, women comprise 47.1% of the labour force. Yet they hold 35.3% of all management positions and 30.5% of senior level management positions. Their presence in higher positions is considerably smaller. Canadian women held 15.1% of corporate officer positions in 2006 and 12% of FP500 board seats in 2005 (Catalyst, 2008b). Women in the UK are 34.7% of the country's managers and senior level officials. Of the 100 FTSE companies, women hold 10.4% of board of director positions. Only 2% of FTSE 100 companies have

CEOs who are women (Catalyst, 2007). 'The virtual absence of women at the top of the organization is thus the result of discrimination that is intensified and concentrated in the middle of the organization, not simply the cumulative effect of discrimination at all levels' (Wright & Baxter, 2000, p. 816).

The motives of women themselves have been advanced to explain the persistence of the glass ceiling. Two studies conducted by van Vianen and Fischer (2002) indicated that some women examine the cultural preferences (whether masculine or feminine) of organizations to determine whether they were attracted to one cultural dimension or the other. These researchers speculated that it was this acceptance of the organizational culture that had the most impact on whether women achieved management positions. Nevertheless, many women seem to have a defeatist attitude when asked about their chances of achieving the highest levels of management in organizations. Some of them suggest that 'Even women who seem very close to the top concede that they don't have a shot at sitting in the chief executive's chair' (Hymowitz & Schellhardt, 1986, p. 1).

Social isolation

It seems lonely at the top – especially for women leaders. Evidence indicates that when women achieve higher organizational levels, they are often the first (and only) ones in their positions. The result is often a type of exclusion in the workplace with limited opportunities to form interpersonal relationships or receive other subtle communication and informational cues required to achieve high levels of performance. The loneliness and isolation that women leaders suffer reduces their overall well-being (Nelson & Quick, 1985). This is especially the case when women either lead or are members of male-dominated work groups (McDonald, Toussaint & Schweiger, 2004). In essence, this situation sets up these women as tokens in their organizations. Kanter's (1977) seminal work established 'tokens' according to numerical representations of demographic groups within organizations; organizational members are tokens if they represent 15% or less of an organization and, as a result, are disadvantaged as a result of discrimination by the dominant group. The argument is that 'tokens', simply by being less numerically represented, will receive increased attention, their actions in the workplace will be scrutinized more, and their personal characteristics will be contrasted more carefully than those in the majority.

Being a 'token' in a workforce has been found to have more negative consequences for women compared to men in the same situation. Some evidence has shown that men may actually benefit from their token status as a result of the status ascribed to men relative to women. Even men who work in traditionally 'female' professions are tracked to higher positions deemed more suitable (e.g., male school teachers guided towards administrator positions) – a phenomenon referred to as the 'glass escalator' (Maume, 1999; Williams, 1992). McDonald *et al.* (2004) found that it was social status rather than gender that accounted for the differential outcomes for women in token situations. In contrast to women, men receive favourable outcomes in part because of their social identification with other men who generally hold higher status positions in organizations (Budig, 2002).

Researchers have found a persistent link between social isolation and psychological health. A recent study (Hitlan, Cliffton & DeSoto, 2006) examining the effect of workplace exclusion on work attitudes and psychological health found that the effect differed according to the gender of the worker. Results indicated that at high levels of social exclusion, men were affected more negatively than women. This finding would seem to contradict what we know about women and their desire for affiliation and social support particularly under conditions of stress (e.g., Taylor *et al.*, 2000). Hitlan *et al.* (2006) offer two explanations for this contradictory finding. First, women as a whole do not identify with their work as much as men do; and second, women may be accustomed to receiving limited support in organizations and thus have become adept at coping.

7.1.3   Discrimination and Stereotyping

> The failure of women to have reached positions of leadership has been due in large part to social and professional discrimination (Rosalyn Sussman Yalow, 1977 Nobel Laureate in Medicine).

Related to the lack of career progress for working women is the issue of discrimination and gender stereotyping. Perceived discrimination has been linked to a variety of outcomes, including psychological distress (e.g., Fischer & Holz, 2007). Being the object of discrimination (perceived or actual) is harmful in many ways. When women perceive they are the object of sex discrimination, they tend to have more negative views of themselves as individuals and as a member of the group (Fischer & Holz, 2007). Such negative views can lead to increased psychological distress and feelings of worthlessness which can lead to reduced performance (e.g., Kaiser, Major & McCoy, 2004).

A different, more subtle form of discrimination for women leaders is the 'glass cliff' (Ryan & Haslam, 2006). Whereas glass ceilings describe boundaries for many women managers, glass cliffs describe the precarious nature of the organizational roles in which women leaders are placed in what some believe is a deliberate attempt to highlight their deficiencies. Ryan and Haslam (2006) sought to investigate claims that women board members in the UK had been reducing the effectiveness of corporations in the country, specifically comparing the share price of the companies in question before and after the leader was put in place. They found evidence to the contrary. Appointments of women to the corporations' boards actually had a positive effect on share price. What was more interesting during this examination of share prices was the pattern of corporate performance prior to the appointments of women board members. The researchers found that women were appointed to the boards of companies that had experienced consistently poor performance compared to men board members whose appointments occurred during relatively stable performance. Based on this pattern of appointment, the researchers surmised that women were differentially selected for leadership positions in times of crisis where failure is an almost certain outcome (e.g., Ryan & Haslam, 2006). The researchers argue that men are placed in safer, more secure jobs while women are put in positions where they feel they have been set up for failure because the assignment comes with such a high risk of failure.

Another form of discrimination against women with negative effects is gender stereotyping. Women in leadership positions often find themselves in a bit of quandary in terms of how they should behave in the workplace. The case of Ann Hopkins, a highly successful business manager with Price Waterhouse, is a prime example. Hopkins amassed more billable hours than any other prospective partner and was successful in bringing in $25 million in new business, yet she was denied partnership on the basis that she wasn't feminine enough (cf. Ryan & Haslam, 2007). She was told to wear makeup and carry a purse instead of a briefcase to increase her (unsuccessful) chances of making partner the next year (Babcock & Laschever, 2003; Gentile, 1996). This outcome for Hopkins is consistent with other research that has found less favourable evaluations for women leaders than their male counterparts even when they behave in exactly the same manner (e.g., Eagly, Makhijani & Klonsky, 1992). However, a woman who is caring, cries, or otherwise shows her 'feminine' side is deemed as not possessing the traits associated with being an effective leader. Rosener (1995) believes that many women who aspire to higher positions of power will support the dominant culture and behave as the dominant culture does. Men are often uncomfortable with differences in the ways that women lead (e.g., building consensus, sharing power and information, multi-tasking). This difference equates to a perceived deficiency in leadership with the result being discrimination, although sometimes at the subconscious level. Women are painfully aware of this view; and in an effort to defend against this kind of treatment, women may consciously minimize displaying aspects of their femininity and succumb to the 'one best model', thinking and acting not as themselves but as the men who maintain the dominant culture (Rosener, 1995).

Experiencing discrimination and being the object of gender stereotypes are common stressors for many working women. However, it should be pointed out that unhealthy job stress is not an inevitable outcome of pressures in the workplace. As we stated earlier, some stress is helpful and provides many benefits for working women. Women who work generally experience fewer health-related illnesses such as cardiovascular disease and enjoy increased emotional well-being through challenging jobs, emotional support and encouragement (Nelson & Burke, 2000). Perhaps the most obvious benefit of work for women is the increase in financial resources (Swanson, 2000). Characteristics of the jobs are also important. Jobs with limited control are inherently more stressful than those with increased amounts of latitude for conducting job tasks (Nelson & Quick, 2005). For example, one study found that women clerical workers experienced higher rates of coronary heart disease (CHD) than their counterparts in professional jobs (Haynes & Feinleib, 1980). Although there may be other potential correlates of higher rates of CHD for women who perform clerical work (e.g., economic stress, a non-supportive boss, family responsibilities), evidence suggests that jobs with decreased autonomy combined with increased demand are important predictors of job strain and employee well-being (cf. Beatty, 1996; Karasek & Theorell, 1990). It would seem reasonable to believe then that leadership positions, given their wide autonomy and control over how work is to be accomplished, would be beneficial rather than detrimental to the overall well-being of these leaders. Unlike challenges that are inherent with especially higher level organizational roles, having to downplay important attributes of one's self (e.g., femininity) and 'glass cliff' positions can create stress levels over and above that which is reasonably expected by having a leadership role.

The link between increased risk of failure and increased stress is established by a process called 'gender-stress-disidentification' (Ryan & Haslam, 2006, p. 46) which can have damaging effects for the individual and the organization. According to the model, women leaders who are placed in positions where they are destined to fail will experience large amounts of unhealthy stress. This stress results in a distancing from the organization in the form of poor communication, reduced productivity and decreased organizational citizenship behaviour. The effect of this reduction in organizational identification is often physical withdrawal. Having had enough, women workers will simply walk away from their jobs. In sum, being placed in highly stressful leadership situations can lead to increased occupational stress in the form of increased burnout, depression, sick leave and ultimately withdrawal. It may be that 'as they [women] advance up the corporate ladder women are exposed to greater stress than their male counterparts' (Ryan & Haslam, 2006, p. 46).

7.2 RESPONSES TO WORKPLACE STRESSORS

Experts place the human stress response into three major categories: physio-logical (medical); psychological; and behavioural (Nelson & Quick, 2005). Many pressures that individuals face in the workplace can be stressors. New research that followed 1000 Dunedin-born people from their birth to age 32 found that almost half of all the cases of depression and anxiety disorders diagnosed among study participants were directly related to workplace stress and the demands of high pressure jobs (cf. Management, 2007). Schedules, supervision, job characteristics, overload, interpersonal relations – all of these represent stressors that need to be managed. These stressors can result in chronic distress if left unchecked.

Our focus in the next section of this chapter is on the ways in which individuals, particularly working women, cope. Responses to workplace stressors range from positive activities such as using social support, eating healthy diets and exercising (Nelson & Burke, 2000) to engaging in unhealthy practices such as smoking and alcohol abuse – all in an attempt to deal with organizational pressures. In the same way that working women are susceptible to the same organizational stressors as men, they tend to have the same general reactions and coping mechanisms, but with some important differences. In some cases, workplace stress is becoming the great equalizer for men and women with its consequences (e.g., cardiovascular disease, stroke) causing as much damage for women as previously identified for men. First, we highlight an important category of stress responses that reflects the uniqueness of the stress experienced by many working women, specifically, physiological.

7.2.1 Physiological

Both men and women experience physical symptoms when faced with stress and strain. If we look closely at the medical illnesses suffered by workers, we are likely to find that each illness has a stress-related component (Nelson & Quick, 2005). This is a reasonable outcome given Cannon's (1935) recognition of the sympathetic nervous system as a key component in stressful conditions. As we noted earlier, the human body is wired in such a way that it is capable of protecting itself from any pressures that threaten homeostasis (Cannon, 1935). We can think of this approach to stress as the body preparing itself to fight any potential stressors that threaten to harm it. Blood is redirected to the brain and large muscle groups; visual and auditory senses are sharpened; important sugars are released into the bloodstream to help the body sustain itself during 'battle'. In times of chronic stress, however, the ability to do so is made more difficult and often manifests in decreased physical health.

We are somewhat limited in our knowledge of gender differences in terms of health-related outcomes of chronic stress. Two reasons account for this disparity. First, a disproportionate amount of the early research linking job stress to health was conducted using working men as subjects (Swanson, 2000). Next, many medical professionals fail to investigate and attribute health complaints of men and women to work-related causes – further limiting what we know about the causes and consequences of work-related stress. Therefore the evidence that exists for working women is comparatively smaller. Though that is the case, the evidence exists nevertheless; in the following we present some of the most documented medical effects of stress for women.

Although many working women find work stimulating, challenging and financially beneficial, the stress of handling multiple roles can have a damaging effect on their health. The damaging physical health effects of workplace stress are well documented in the literature. But why do women react differently to workplace stress than men? It depends on whom you ask. One study of high-ranking employees found that the responsibilities of work and home combined with increased workloads led to elevated levels of norepinephrine (a stress hormone) in women both during and after work (Lundberg & Frankenhaeuser, 1999). The release of 'stress' hormones has been noted by medical professionals as one of the most important reasons why men and women react differently to stress. Dr Robert Sapolsky, a professor of neurobiology at Stanford University, suggests that it is the amounts of a particular hormone called oxytocin that make all the difference. When women face stressful situations, oxytocin is secreted at higher levels, countering the production of harmful stress hormones like cortisol and epinephrine and instead promoting relaxation and nurturing. Men also secrete oxytocin under conditions of stress, but the difference, according to Sapolsky, is that the nurturing hormone is released at much lower levels (*Web*MD, 2005).

Organizational behaviour experts emphasize factors such as role conflicts, structural characteristics of organizations and societal expectations of the genders. Nelson and Quick (1985) indicate that women executives experience health ailments more commonly associated with men and suggest that these women are more likely to fall victims to such medical conditions as ulcers and high blood pressure. In fact, a study of more than 1300 Swedish white-collar professionals found that twice as many women than men surveyed suffered from frequent and severe health symptoms in the form of stomach pain, headaches, lower back pain, loss of appetite and shoulder and neck pain (Krantz *et al.*, 2005). The researchers attributed the severity and frequency of symptoms to the double exposure to paid work and household responsibility experienced by the women in the study. A more recent study (Tytherleigh *et al.*, 2007) studied the interactive effects of age and gender on workplace stressors that lead to ill health using, as their sample, academics in two types of university settings. The researchers found a significant interaction of age and gender on the ill health of the study participants. Aside from men in the youngest age group, ill health stemming from stress decreased for men as they got older. However, women reported consistently poorer health as a result of stress across all age groups. This study shed light on additional factors that could potentially explain differential outcomes of workplace stress. It also supports the contention that women tend to live longer but suffer more (e.g., Quick *et al.*, 2008).

Indeed, women are different from men. And although both genders are exposed to the same stressors in the workplace, women react differently to those stressors than men. Their different reaction has an often ill effect on their physical well-being, manifested by increased fatigue, tension headaches, muscle pain and increased work-related injuries. Gaumer, Shah and Ashley-Cotleur (2005) suggest that working women's dual roles have a great dealt to do with the difference in physiological reactions. How is it that men seem better able to unwind after a challenging day at work more quickly than women? Gaumer and colleagues (2005) suggest that the reason is fairly clear. The reason women have difficulty unwinding is that they may be anticipating the 'second leg' of their day when they get home, giving credence to the old adage, 'A woman's work is never done'.

7.2.2 Psychological

According to the World Health Organization (2008), depression is the leading cause of disability and is on course to become the world's second-highest burden of disease by the year 2020. The connection between depression and work stress has come under investigation recently as a result of changes in the structure and demographic makeup of the workplace. Work stress has been found to precipitate the onset of depression and anxiety disorders in otherwise healthy individuals regardless of socioeconomic position (e.g., Melchoir *et al.*, 2007). A better understanding of the symptoms and causes of depression and other psychological diseases is needed if organizations are to remain productive and healthy places to work – a goal of many – if not all, organizations.

There are stark differences between men and women in the presentation of work-related stress outcomes, particularly depression. Depression reportedly affects nearly five million working women in the United States each year. Some estimate that one in five people will suffer depression or some form of mental illness during their lifetime (Lunn, 2008). A major research study commissioned by the National Mental Health and American Women's Health Associations found from their interviews with 751 working women that depression was the number one barrier to their success, greater than care-giving responsibilities, sexual harassment, the glass ceiling and sexism (National Mental Health Association, 2003). Interestingly, the women who failed to seek professional treatment but suffered major symptoms of depression were younger, included more minorities, and worked in more blue-collar jobs. Could it be that their depression was a consequence of sexual harassment, glass ceilings or sexism? While these questions were not a part of the research design, we believe it to be a reasonable assumption. For example, it is estimated that 75% of women have experienced or will experience sexual harassment, which is associated with a host of physical and psychological problems (Shaffer *et al.*, 2000).

Instances of depression have also been associated with job strain. The most widely validated model of the link between job stress and health is Karasek and Theorell's (1990) job-strain model. According to the model, job strain is the result of high job demands and decreased worker latitude. A recent longitudinal study of over 36,000 Canadian working men and women aged 15 to 75 found that a significant proportion of those studied experienced major episodes of depression in the 12 months preceding the study, with the causes of depression differing along lines of gender (Blackmore *et al.*, 2007). While both men and women were negatively impacted (reported instances of depression) as a result of increased job strain, the effect for men was more severe than it was for women. That the researchers did not find a more significant link between increased job strain and instances of depression among women in the study is surprising and conflicts with other studies that suggest women may be more vulnerable to higher amounts of work-related stress and strain than men. Perhaps, as the researchers speculated, the type of job and associated task demands were important predictors of the stress–strain relationship. Women in the latter study were more likely employed in part-time jobs where high task demands and consequently high job strain were unlikely.

Supportive of this view that type of occupation may be the key to understanding job stress for working women are findings from a recent study of 1100 workers in Victoria, Australia to assess the role of job strain on inequalities in mental health (LaMontagne *et al.*, 2008). The researchers were interested in the effects of stressful working conditions defined as high job demands and low control over how to perform the job. They found that more working women experienced job stress than the men perhaps because the women were in lower skilled occupations, representing a high strain condition. Risk of depression increased progressively as the skill level of workers declined. When it came to depression, 17% of women who suffered from depression attributed their mental state to job stress. This is compared to 13% of men who reported depression as a result of job-related stress. Since women were more likely to experience greater levels of job-related stress, it is likely that women will also bear a greater share of job-related stress depression. While gender differences were found, the study called attention to the prevalence of mental health diseases among both working women and men including those cases of depression in men that may go unreported or unnoticed.

While depression is perhaps one of the most highly popularized psychological stress outcomes, it is not the only outcome of unhealthy workplace stress. Nearly three-quarters of women in Davidson and Cooper's (1984) study attributed psychological problems such as tension, increased anxiety, sleeplessness, frustration and dissatisfaction with life and work (as well as depression) to high levels of work-related stress. The Whitehall II Study measured psychiatric disorders of 10,308 male and female civil servants in a variety of different occupations using the General Health Questionnaire and found gender differences in the relationships between work characteristics (decision latitude, job demands, social support, effort-rewards) and a number of mental health outcomes (Stansfield, Head & Marmot, 2000). Women had higher levels of psychiatric disorders than men in five of six of the occupational groups in the investigation. Although the Whitehall Study II used self-reports of ill health, the study is important as it further established the correlation between work-related factors and the onset of ill mental health outcomes. Findings from these studies imply and are consistent with others that suggest that a wide range of psychological health symptoms are associated with stressors found in the workplace (Swanson, 2000).

7.2.3 Behavioural

Behavioural responses to workplace stress and job strain can fall into two categories, individual and organizational. The effects of chronic workplace stress and strain can be seen almost everywhere. News reports document instances where workers have 'gone postal', often accompanied by tremendous shock and disbelief by the public (e.g., Lenz, 2008). Although they are rare, extreme actions such as these represent the aggression that can come as a result of high stress levels. In the same way that gender differences have been found for medical and psychological outcomes, researchers have also found that men and women differ in their susceptibility to certain behavioural outcomes of job stress.

The literature documents both positive and negative ways that women use to cope with the pressures of work and increasingly, work and home. The use of social networks is one of those coping mechanisms. Nelson and Burke (2000) suggest that women's use of social support systems and exercise has been successful in deterring the negative effects of job-related stress. However, they note that women seem to be particularly vulnerable to tobacco and emotion-based coping strategies such as venting. However, women are less likely to engage in alcohol consumption than men are. There is evidence that women may be mimicking historically 'male' behaviours to deal with the pressures they face in the workplace. For each male alcoholic in the United States in 1962, there were five female alcoholics. By the late 1970s, however, there were two female alcoholics for every male alcoholic (Nelson & Quick, 1985). It took less than a decade for women to go from 20% to 50% of reported alcoholics. How can we explain this change in behaviour on the part of women? Perhaps the most comprehensive study of factors that influence workers' ability to engage in health-enhancing behaviours was conducted by Hellerstedt and Jeffery (1997). The researchers extended prior studies that linked job demands and job strain to cardiovascular disease (CVD) by investigating the effect of body weight in addition to factors previously associated with increased risk of CVD, smoking and lack of physical activity. As they predicted, women who experienced increased demands on the job smoked more, exercised less and had higher average BMI (body mass indicator) numbers, increasing their risk of CVD.

Characteristics of the workplace can result in responses to workplace stress that not only harm the individual but can also have a negative effect on organizational competitiveness (e.g., Gaumer, Shah & Ashley-Cotleur, 2005). In response to work–family conflict, low opportunities, discrimination and career frustrations, many women have chosen to become entrepreneurs. In 2006, 30.4% of all US privately held firms were majority (51% or more) owned by women. The number of majority (51% or more) women-owned firms grew 42.3% between the years of 1997 and 2006, nearly two times the rate for all privately held firms in the United States (Center for Women's Business Research, 2006). Why are so many women leaving their corporate careers? Having been 'pushed out' of the organization, many women believe their talents could be best put to use somewhere else. Consider Lois Silverman, who founded CRA Managed Care (now Concentra Managed Care, a company posting more than $1 billion a year). Silverman chose to leave her insurance company job to pursue other opportunities where she would feel less isolated and left out. In her own words, 'I was working in a male-dominated environment, and I no longer felt as if I was a part of the company. I began to feel that there was something here I could do better' (cf. Swersky, Gorman & Reardon, 2007).

Another reason that has been cited is the lack of control that many women hold in traditional corporate positions. Sharon Hadary, the executive director of the Center for Women's Business Research suggests, 'They [women] don't want fewer hours, but control over what they do' (McLaughlin, 2006). Consider also the woman manager who, after several years, reached her goals of a position in the executive office. As a result of her hard work and commitment, she finally makes it. Now she's in a position that not only tests her physical stamina but also her continued commitment to the organization. As discussed earlier, placing women in 'glass cliff' positions has been cited as a primary reason for organizational withdrawal for women (MacRae, 2005). This mass exodus of women from the workplace not only disrupts women's careers but when organizations lose large portions of their talent, they stand to suffer tremendously (Hymowitz & Schellhardt, 1986). In sum, withdrawing from the organization is one of the responses to workplace stress for many working women. Having put up with more than they can, some women believe that walking away is their only viable alternative.

7.3   *WITHIN*-GROUP GENDER STRESSORS?

We know more about differences between gender groups on the causes and consequences of job stress than we do about differences *within* gender groups. Focusing on what we don't know about these gender differences may be equally important for understanding the variability of workplace stressors and individual outcomes (Quick *et al.*, 2008). Are there organizational factors that affect minority women differently or in a more harmful way than for non-minority women? For instance, does the 'double-bind' that black women experience lead to higher levels of job stress? There is a lack of research that has explicitly investigated this topic so we must extrapolate from research on minorities in general.

Some researchers suggest that the unique experiences of minorities, especially being the object of stereotypes and experiencing discrimination, may present psychological stressors and lead to increased ill health among the victims which include increased risk of heart disease and alcohol dependence (Cocchiara & Quick, 2004). Women, in general, have difficulty being accepted as managers and in establishing informal networks in corporate environments. Women of colour may experience even more difficulty. In one survey, five out of every 10 black women reported that they felt accepted as a member of their respective organizations, while eight out of 10 white women felt the same way (Bell & Nkomo, 2001). Gender stereotypes that negatively affect the perceived suitability of women as leaders combine with cultural stereotypes that plague minority women. The perception that black women will miss work more often because they are single parents or that Hispanic women have lower levels of commitment to the organization because of their family responsibilities, though inaccurate, represents barriers to their acceptance (Cocchiara, Bell & Berry, 2006). When gender or cultural behaviours are at odds with those expected by organizations, and the expected behaviours stem from stereotypes, the result can be undue stress for the individual at the centre of the conflict.

7.4 SUMMARY

Work pressures are more strongly associated with more health complaints than any other life stressor (DiversityInc.com). Both men and women fall victims but there are certain stressors that are more common for working women than men. Although common, are the unique stressors that women face in the workplace linked to specific outcomes? For instance, can we say that women who experience role conflict are the most likely candidates to become heavy smokers? Are women who experience 'glass ceilings' or who see men take the 'glass escalator' to the top destined to exit the organization or to a life of job-related illness or depression if they remain? As shown in Figure 7.2, three workplace stressors are unique to working women. The responsibilities of raising children, caring for elderly parents, and providing for families present a challenge for women, and more increasingly men, to negotiate and prioritize among these multiple conflicting roles. Though women have been a large part of the labour force for several decades, they have yet to reach organizational levels that are commensurate with their investments in education and experience. Women continue to face inaccurate

Figure 7.2 Unique stressors and responses for working women.

stereotypes that dictate how women should behave in the workplace in addition to discriminatory organizational practices. Undue stress accompanied by a wide range of medical, psychological and behavioural health outcomes often follows.

REFERENCES

Babcock, L. & Laschever, S. (2003). *Women Don't Ask*. Princeton, NJ: Princeton University Press.

Beatty, C.A. (1996). The stress of managerial and professional women: is the price too high? *Journal of Organizational Behavior*, **17**, 233–51.

Bell, E.L.J.E. & Nkomo, S.M. (2001). *Our Separate Ways: Black and White Women and the Struggle for Professional Identity*. Boston, MA: Harvard Business School Press.

Blackmore, E.R., Stansfeld, S.A., Weller, I., Munce, S., Zagorski, B.M. & Stewart, D.E. (2007). Major depressive episodes and work stress: results from a national population survey. *American Journal of Public Health*, **97**(November), 2088–93.

Budig, M.J. (2002). Male advantage and the gender composition of jobs: who rides the glass escalator? *Social Problems*, **49**(2), 258–77.

Cannon, W.B. (1935). Stresses and strains of homeostasis. *American Journal of the Medical Sciences*, **189**, 1–14.

Catalyst (2007). Women in the Labour Force in the U.K. Quick Takes. Retrieved on 13 June 2008 at http://www.catalyst.org/file/191/qt_women_in_the_labour_force_in_the_uk.pdf.

Catalyst (2008a). U.S. Women in Business. Retrieved on 5 January 2009 at http://www.catalyst.org/publication/132/us-women-in-business.

Catalyst (2008b). Canadian Women Quick Takes. Retrieved on 12 June 2008 at http://www.catalyst.org/file/158/qt_canadian_women.pdf.

Center for Women's Business Research. (2006). Women-Owned Businesses in the United States, 2006: a fact sheet. Retrieved on 25 June 2008 at http://www.cfwbr.org/assets/344_statesoverviewwebcolorfac.pdf.

Chafetz, J.S. (1997). I need a 'traditional' wife. In D. Dunn (Ed.), *Workplace/Women's Place* (pp. 116–24). Los Angeles: Roxbury.

Cleveland, J.N., Cordeiro, B., Fisk, G. & Mulvaney, R.H. (2006). The role of person, spouse and organizational climate on work–family perceptions. *The Irish Journal of Management*, **27**(2), 229–53.

Cocchiara, F., Bell, M.P. & Berry, D.P. (2006). Latinas and Black women: key factors for a growing proportion of the U.S. workforce. *Equal Opportunities International*, **25**, 272–84.

Cocchiara, F.K. & Quick, J.C. (2004). The negative effects of positive stereotypes: ethnicity-related stressors and implications on organizational health. *Journal of Organizational Behavior*, **25**, 781–5.

Davidson, M.J. & Cooper, C.L. (1984). Occupational stress in female managers: a comparative study. *Journal of Management Studies*, **21**, 185–205.

DiversityInc.com. http://www.diversity.com.

Eagly, A.H., Makhijani, M.G. & Klonsky, B.G. (1992). Gender and the evaluation of leaders: a meta-analysis. *Psychological Bulletin*, **111**, 3–22.

Fischer, A.R. & Holz, K.B. (2007). Perceived discrimination and women's psychological distress: the roles of collective and personal self-esteem. *Journal of Counseling Psychology*, **54**, 154–64.

Frone, M., Russell, M. & Cooper, M. (1992). Antecedents and outcomes of work–family conflict: testing a model of the work–family interface. *Journal of Applied Psychology*, **77**, 65–78.

Galinsky, E., Bond, J.T., Sakai, K., Kim, S.S. & Giuntoli, N. (2008). National Study of Employers. *Families and Work Institute*.

Gaumer, C.J., Shah, A.J. & Ashley-Cotleur, C. (2005). Enhancing organizational competitiveness: causes and effects of stress on women, *Journal of Workplace Behavioral Health*, **21**, 31–43.

Gentile, M.C. (1996). *Managerial Excellence through Diversity*. Prospect Heights, IL: Waveland Press.

Gyllensten, K. & Palmer, S. (2005). The role of gender in workplace stress: a critical literature review. *Health Education Journal*, **64**(3), 271–88.

Hall, M. (2003). Government survey shows strong employee preference for flexible working. *EIROnline* (January). Retrieved on 3 June 2008 from http://www.eiro.eurofound.ie/2003/01/inbrief/uk0301102n.html.

Haynes, S.G. & Feinleib, M. (1980). Women, work and coronary heart disease: prospective findings from the Framingham Heart Study. *American Journal of Public Health*, **70**(2), 133–41.

Hellerstedt, W.L. & Jeffery, R.W. (1997). The association of job strain and health behaviours in men and women. *International Journal of Epidemiology*, **26**(3), 575–83.

Hitlan, R.T., Cliffton, R.J. & DeSoto, M. (2006). Perceived exclusion in the workplace: the moderating effects of gender on work-related attitudes and psychological health. *North American Journal of Psychology*, **8**(2), 217–36.

Hochschild, A. (1989). *The Second Shift*. New York: Avon Books.

Hymowitz, C. & Schellhardt, T.D. (1986). The glass ceiling: why women can't seem to break the invisible barrier that blocks them from the top jobs. *The Wall Street Journal* (Eastern edition), p. 1.

Institute for Women's Policy Research. (2007). Women and paid sick days: crucial for family well-being. IWPR #B254a (February), 1–4.

Kaiser, C.R., Major, B. & McCoy, S.K. (2004). Expectations about the future and the emotional consequences of perceiving prejudice. *Personality and Social Psychology Bulletin*, **30**(2), 173–84.

Kanter, R.M. (1977). *Men and Women of the Corporation*. New York: Basic Books.

Karasek, R.A. & Theorell, T. (1990). *Health Work: Stress, Productivity and the Reconstruction of Working Life*. New York: Basic Books.

Krantz, G., Berntsson, L. & Lundberg, U. (2005). Total workload, work stress and perceived symptoms in Swedish male and female white-collar employees. *European Journal of Public Health*, **15**(2), 209–14.

LaMontagne, A.D., Keegel, T., Vallance, D., Ostry, A. & Wolfe, R. (2008). Job strain – attributable depression in a sample of working Australians: assessing the contribution to health inequalities. *BMC Public Health*, **8**, 181–9. Available online at http://www.biomedcentral.com/1471-2458/8/181.

Langan-Fox, J. (1998). Women's careers and occupational stress. *International Review of Industrial and Organizational Psychology*, **13**, 273–302.

Lenz, R. (2008). Police: 6 dead in Kentucky shooting. *Time* (25 June). Available online at http://www.time.com/time/nation/article/0,8599,1817724,00.html.

Lockwood, N.R. (2003). Work/life balance: challenges and solutions. *Society for Human Resource Management (SHRM) Research Quarterly*. Retrieved on 3 June 2008 from http://www.ispi.org/pdf/suggestedReading/11_Lockwood_Work LifeBalance.pdf.

Lunn, S. (2008). Women prone to job-stress blues. *The Australian*, 2 June, **1**, 3.

Lundberg, U. & Frankenhaeuser, M. (1999). Stress and workload of men and women in high-ranking positions. *Journal of Occupational Health Psychology*, **4**, 142–51.

MacRae, N. (2005). Women and work: a ten year retrospective. *Work*, **24**, 331–9.

Management (2007, September). High pressure jobs linked to depression and anxiety. Retrieved on 8 July 2008 at http://www.archivesearch.co.nz/default.aspx?webid=MGT&articleid=26692.

Maume, D.J., Jr. (1999, November). Glass ceilings and glass escalators: occupational segregation and race and sex differences in managerial promotions. *Work and Occupations*, **26**(4), 483–509.

Melchoir, M., Caspi, A., Milne, B.J., Danese, A., Poulton, R. & Moffitt, T.E. (2007). Work stress precipitates depression and anxiety in young, working women and men. *Psychological Medicine*, **37**, 1119–29.

McDonald, T.W., Toussaint, L.L. & Schweiger, J.A. (2004). The influence of social status on token women leaders' expectations about leading male-dominated groups. *Sex Roles*, **50**(5/6), 401–9.

McLaughlin, T. (2006). Top Wall Street jobs still elude women, minorities. *Boston.com*. Retrieved 25 June 2008 at http://www.boston.com/business/articles/2006/12/27/top_wall_street_jobs_still_elude_women_minorities/.

National Mental Health Association. (2003). Depression among women in the workplace. Retrieved on 24 June 2008 at http://www1.nmha.org/newsroom/womenWorkplaceDepression.pdf.

Nelson, D.L. & Burke, R.J. (2000). Women executives: health, stress, and success. *Academy of Management Executive*, **14**, 107–21.

Nelson, D.L. & Quick, J.C. (1985). Professional women: are distress and disease inevitable? *Academy of Management Review*, **10**, 206–18.

Nelson, D.L. & Quick, J.C. (2008). *Organizational Behavior: Science, the Real World, and You*. Mason, OH: South-Western Cengage Learning.

Nelson, D.L., Quick, J.C., Hitt, M.A. & Moesel, D. (1990). Politics, lack of career progress, and work/home conflict: stress and strain for working women. *Sex Roles*, **23**, 169–83.

Noor, N. (2004). Work–family conflict, work- and family-role salience, and women's well-being. *Journal of Social Psychology*, **144**, 389–405.

Parker-Pope, T. (2007). The man problem. *The Wall Street Journal*, 24 April.

Quick, J.C., Cooper, C.L., Gavin, J.H. & Quick, J.D. (2008). *Managing Executive Health: Personal and Corporate Strategies for Sustained Success* (pp. 99–116). New York: Cambridge University Press.

Rosener, J.B. (1995). *America's Competitive Secret: Women Managers*. New York: Oxford University Press.

Ryan, M. & Haslam, A. (2006). The glass cliff: the stress of working on the edge. *European Business Forum*, **27**(Winter), 42–7.

Ryan, M.R. & Haslam, S.A. (2007). The glass cliff: exploring the dynamics surrounding the appointment of women to precarious leadership positions. *Academy of Management Review*, **32**, 549–72.

Shaffer, M.A., Joplin, J.R.W., Bell, M.P., Oguz, C. & Lau, T. (2000). Disruptions to women's social identity: a comparative study of workplace stress experienced by women in three geographic regions. *Journal of Occupational Health Psychology*, **5**, 441–56.

Shelton, B.A. (1992). *Women, Men, and Time: Gender Differences in Paid Work, Housework, and Leisure*. Westport, CT: Greenwood Press.

Smith, D.M. (2000). *Women at Work: Leadership for the Next Century*. Upper Saddle River, NJ: Prentice-Hall.

Stansfield, S., Head, J. & Marmot, M. (2000). Work related factors and ill health: the Whitehall II Study, Contract Research Report 266/2000. *Health & Safety Executive*: 1-61. Retrieved on 24 June 2008 at http://www.hse.gov.uk/research/crr_pdf/2000/crr00266.pdf.

Stroh, L.K., Brett, J.J. & Reilly, A.H. (1992). All the right stuff: a comparison of female and male managers' career progression. *Journal of Applied Psychology*, **77**, 251–60.

Swanson, N.G. (2000). Working women and stress. *Journal of the American Medical Women's Association (JAMWA)*, **55**(2), 76–9.

Swersky, P., Gorman, A. & Reardon, J. (2007). We've got the power: the rise of women entrepreneurs. *New England Journal of Public Policy*, **22**(1/2), 73–80.

Taylor, S.E., Klein, L.C., Lewis, B.P., Gruenewald, T.L., Gurung, R.A.R. & Updegraff, J.A. (2000). Biobehavioral responses to stress in females: tend-and-befriend, not fight-or-flight. *Psychological Review*, **107**, 411–29.

Tytherleigh, M.Y., Jacobs, P.A., Ricketts, C. & Cooper, C. (2007). Gender, health and stress in English university staff – exposure or vulnerability? *Applied Psychology: An International Review*, **56**(2), 267–87.

U.S. Bureau of Labor Statistics (2007). Women in the labor force: A databook, Report 1002 (September 2007). Retrieved on 22 May 2008 from http://www.bls.gov/cps/wlf-databook-2007.pdf.

Van Vianen, A.E.M. & Fischer, A.H. (2002). Illuminating the glass ceiling: the role of organizational culture preferences. *Journal of Occupational and Organizational Psychology*, **75**, 315–37.

*Web*MD (2005). Why men and women handle stress differently. Reviewed by B. Nazario, MD. Retrieved on 10 June 2008 at http://women.wedmd.com/features/stress-women-men-cope.

Williams, C.L. (1992). The glass escalator: hidden advantages for men in the 'female' professions. *Social Problems*, **39**(3), 253–67.

World Health Organization. (2008). Information on mental health disorders management: depression. Retrieved on 24 June 2008 at http://www.who.int/mental_health/management/depression/definition/en.

Wright, E.O. & Baxter, J. (2000). The glass ceiling hypothesis: a reply to critics. *Gender and Society*, **14**, 814–21.

CHAPTER 8

Work Experiences, Stress and Health among Managerial Women: Research and Practice

Ronald J. Burke

York University, UK

and

Astrid M. Richardsen

BI Norwegian School of Management, Norway

8.1 INTRODUCTION

This chapter reviews research on work experiences, stress and health among managerial women. The chapter is more relevant today than when it was originally written for the first edition of this *Handbook*. Over the past decade, there is evidence that the percentage of women who hold managerial positions has increased (Russell, 2006; Stroh, Langlands & Simpson, 2004) However, there is still a great disparity when comparing the number of women in the labour force with the number of women in top management. In an increasingly global business environment, organizations need high levels of talent to be successful, and it may be more difficult now to attract and retain such talent (Davidson & Burke, 2004). As more women enter the workforce with appropriate levels of education, experience, training and skill, they comprise a large percentage of the talent pool. Organizations historically have done a relatively poor job of managing their talent, but ignoring or misusing the talents of half the population is a luxury that organizations cannot afford today. Thus, further understanding of the work experiences, satisfactions and stressors, and well-being of these women should become an urgent

International Handbook of Work and Health Psychology, Third Edition. Edited by Cary L. Cooper, James Campbell Quick, and Marc J. Schabracq.

priority. Too many women opt out of large organizations, and those wanting to re-enter the workforce have difficulties doing so (Hewlett & Luce, 2005). Fortunately the women in management area continues to attract research attention (Burke & Mattis, 2005; Eagly & Carli, 2007; Vinnicombe & Banks, 2003).

The focus on managerial women, a highly educated, motivated and well-paid group, is taken in this chapter because this group is growing in size and importance, serves both as an important model for younger women and as an indicator of women's progress towards equality, and may be frustrated with their relative lack of progress and increased stress (Davidson & Burke, 2004; Fielden & Davidson, 2001; Lyness & Terrazas, 2006). It goes without saying that other groups of women not included in this review may experience as much or even more work stress.

There are several reasons why this chapter makes an important contribution. Firstly, the costs to organizations, women and men resulting from stress-related illnesses are both large and growing (Campbell Quick *et al.*, 1997). Secondly, there is evidence that the managerial job itself is a demanding one (Burke, 1988). Thirdly, there is a growing consensus that work stressors are associated with a range of short-term quality of life and health outcomes (Repetti, 1993).

The chapter builds on established occupational stress research frameworks (Jex & Beehr, 1991); it extends them to incorporate work stressors and experiences unique to women. Such frameworks commonly include a number of work stressors (e.g., overload, role conflict, work–family conflict), stress responses (physiological, psychological, behavioural), moderating factors (e.g., individual variables, coping efforts), and long-term consequences for individual health and work performance. This review focuses primarily on various stressors, individual differences and coping; while the strains and long-term consequences encompass a variety of emotional and physical health outcomes considered in one or more specific research studies. The chapter emphasizes the breadth and variety of research in this area rather than depth. A second purpose of this chapter is to spur organizational initiatives to reduce work and family stress and improve health. The field offers opportunities for both research and practice, which, if well conceived and undertaken, should improve the quality of life and health of managerial women (Ilgen, 1990; Nelson & Burke, 2001).

The following content areas are addressed:

- Work experiences of female and male managers
  - the glass ceiling
  - barriers to women's advancement
  - cross-cultural research

- Occupational stress and health
  - role conflict
  - work and family
  - dual-career couples
  - sexual harassment
  - organizational downsizing
- Research and practice
  - workplace flexibility
  - intervention and policy implications
  - future research and action directions

8.2   WORK EXPERIENCES OF MANAGERIAL WOMEN AND MEN

8.2.1   The Glass Ceiling

There is considerable evidence that managerial women face a 'glass ceiling' that limits their advancement to top management in large organizations (Lyness & Terrazas, 2006; Morrison & von Glinow, 1990; Morrison, White & van Velsor, 1987; Stroh *et al.*, 2004). The glass ceiling refers to a subtle and almost invisible, but strong barrier that prevents women from moving up to senior management levels. There is an emerging belief that the glass ceiling exists worldwide, based on labour statistics which show that although women represent close to half the labour force in most industrialized countries, their representation in managerial jobs is much lower (Davidson & Burke, 2004; Lyness & Terrazas, 2006). Such gender segregation of management jobs exists in many countries and refers to both the fact that women are usually found at the low and middle management levels, while the majority of senior level management positions are held by men; and the fact that at the same managerial level, women are usually found in staff or support positions, and are not as highly represented as men in positions that offer promotion opportunities (Lyness & Terrazas, 2006). For example, a study of gender differences in job moves found that among managers in staff positions, women were less likely than were men to move to line positions or different organizational functions in the company (Lyness & Schrader, 2006).

Recent reviews of the research literature and of international labour statistics indicate that despite some increase of women in top management positions over the past decade, the glass ceiling still persists (Lyness & Terrazas, 2006; Stroh *et al.*, 2004). Three hypotheses have been suggested to explain why this ceiling has remained impenetrable. The first builds on individual differences in attributes and ways in which women are different from men. This hypothesis suggests that women's education, training, attitudes, behaviours, traits and socialization handicap them in particular ways. Almost all research evidence shows little or no difference in the traits, abilities, education and motivations of managerial and professional women and men (Powell, 1999).

A second hypothesis builds on notions of bias and discrimination by the majority towards the minority. It suggests that managerial and professional women are held back as a result of bias and stereotypes of women, particularly in organizational selection and promotion decisions (Heilman, 1995). Such bias or discrimination is either sanctioned by the labour market or rewarded by organizations, despite the level of job performance of women (Lyness & Heilman, 2006). In addition, there is widespread agreement that the good manager is seen as male or masculine (Heilman *et al.*, 1989), although recent studies have found that ratings of good leadership attributes reflect less emphasis on masculine characteristics than they did 15 to 30 years ago (Duehr & Bono, 2006; Powell, Butterfield & Parent, 2002; Sczesny *et al.*, 2004). Thus, there is some research support for this hypothesis.

The third hypothesis emphasizes structural and systemic discrimination as revealed in organizational policies and practices, which affects the treatment of women and limits their advancement (Kanter, 1977). These policies and practices include women's lack of opportunity and power in organizations, the existing sex ratio of groups in organizations, tokenism, lack of mentors and sponsors, and denial of access to challenging assignments. This hypothesis has also received empirical support (Burke & McKeen, 1992; Lyness & Thompson, 2000). The glass ceiling is the result of barriers to women's career advancement.

8.2.2   Barriers to Women's Advancement

There is considerable agreement on the barriers faced by managerial women. Morrison (1992) listed six as most important: (i) prejudice, treating differences as weaknesses; (ii) poor career planning and development (lack of opportunities for women); (iii) a lonely, hostile, unsupportive working environment; (iv) lack of organizational savvy on the part of women; (v) the old boys' network (greater comfort men have in dealing with other men); and (vi) difficulty in balancing career and family (overload, conflict, stress). Lyness and Thompson (2000) identified the following: lack of fit with the male-dominated culture at senior management levels; exclusion from informal networks with male peers; lack of effective mentoring and difficulty obtaining mentors; more dependence on merits and consideration of objective qualifications for women's advancement in comparison to men's; stereotyping and preconceptions about women's abilities and suitability for

leadership positions; difficulties in obtaining challenging developmental assignments needed for advancement; managers' aversion to placing women
in line positions; and difficulties in obtaining opportunities for geographical mobility. In a review of persistent barriers and career counselling for
women in management, Russell (2006) outlined the following; discriminatory attitudes and sex-role stereotypes, discrimination in the workplace (e.g.,
compensation discrimination, limited access to training and development opportunities, biased performance evaluations, sexual harassment), and social
isolation (e.g., tokenism, few female role models, limited access to mentoring, limited access to informal networks and communication channels). Yet
others have included difficulties combining work and family responsibilities
(Lyness & Terrazas, 2006).

Morrison (1992) proposed a model of leadership development in which
she suggested three critical components: challenge; recognition; and support.
She observed that in many organizations, the barriers to advancement faced
by women provided them with inordinate levels of challenge, without similar increases in recognition and support. Ohlott, Ruderman and McCauley
(1994) provided empirical evidence that suggests this may in fact be the
case. They surveyed male and female managers about developmental components in their current jobs. Their results suggested that men experienced
some greater task-related developmental challenges, but women experienced
greater developmental challenges resulting from obstacles that they faced in
their jobs. A study comparing matched samples of male and female executives on perceived barriers and facilitators of advancement, also found that
women experienced greater barriers, especially lack of culture fit and being
excluded from informal networks, even if career success for both genders was
positively related to breadth of experience and developmental assignments
(Lyness & Thompson, 2000).

8.2.3   Cross-Cultural Research

An increasing number of studies have examined managerial women's work
experiences, stress and health across countries (see Davidson & Burke, 2004).
The evidence from these studies show remarkable similarity across countries
when it comes to the number of women in the workforce, the number of
women in management, and the number of women in executive positions
(in pressBurke, in press). However, there are few large-scale studies that
have provided cross-cultural comparisons. One large-scale study of cul-
tural/societal values and work (Hofstede, 1980) did not include measures at
the level of specificity to illustrate managerial women's work experiences,
or permit comparisons with those of men.

Bajdo and Dickson (2002) conducted a study of 3544 individuals from 114 organizations in 32 countries based on the GLOBE Research Program (House *et al.*, 1999). They found that organization members reported high percentages of women in management in organizations with high shared *values* of humane orientation and high gender equity. Also, high percentages of women in management were reported in organizations that had organizational cultural *practices* which emphasized high humane orientation, high gender equity, high performance orientation, and low power distance. The authors concluded that organizational cultural practices related to gender equity were the most important predictor of women in management.

Burke (in press) reviews some of the writing on cultural values and women's work and career experiences. Two aspects of his review are illustrative of the cross-cultural work conducted to date. First, he reports that relationships of particular work experiences (e.g., training and development, support and encouragement) were related to work and well-being outcomes (job and career satisfaction, exhaustion) in the same way in some various countries (e.g., Canada, Bulgaria, Norway). Second, he notes that measures of career priority, the extent to which women place their careers above or at the same level of importance as family, were generally similarly related to work and well-being outcomes in several countries (e.g., Bulgaria, Canada, Norway, Singapore, Turkey). This similar relationship of work experiences and work and health outcomes was observed in different samples in the various countries.

These studies have identified the barriers to women's advancement that commonly exist in organizations. In addition, women report greater obstacles to advancement than do men. One consequence of these additional barriers is heightened work and family stress.

8.3 OCCUPATIONAL STRESS AND HEALTH

There is considerable evidence that the experience of work stress among managers is associated with undesirable consequences (Cooper & Payne, 1988). Most of this research has involved male managers since men have traditionally filled managerial roles (Burke, 1988). As more women have entered managerial jobs, they have increasingly become subjects of stress research (Davidson & Fielden, 1999). With the appearance of this body of work, some researchers have begun asking whether women or men experience more work stress, exhibit more negative consequences, or have different coping or social support responses (Fielden & Cooper, 2002; Portello & Long, 2001). Recent studies have revealed that managerial women experience unique sources of stress related their minority status and gender (Fielden & Davidson, 2001).

Offerman and Armitage (1993), Davidson and Fielden (1999) and Langan-Fox (1998) reviewed the literature on stress and health outcomes among women managers. They noted that some stressors were shared by women and men (e.g., role conflict, overload, ambiguity), but that women experienced additional work stressors unique to them, as well as exhibiting different ways of interpreting and coping with the uniquely female and the common stressors. These researchers categorized stressors experienced by women managers into three groups: (i) from society at large (work–family interface, off-the-job support, attitudes towards women in management, discrimination); (ii) from organizations (e.g., on-the-job support, sexual harassment, tokenism, sex discrimination, old boys' network); and (iii) from women themselves (type A behaviour, personal control, self-esteem). The stress experienced by managerial women results from a combination of sources from all three groups, with health outcomes affected as a result. In addition, in keeping with previous work stress frameworks, individual differences operated at several places to influence the stress–health process.

Davidson and Cooper (1992) have contributed much to our understanding of the effects of work and extra-work stressors on managerial women. In addition, some of their research has compared the experiences of women and men. They proposed a research framework in which demands (stressors) in three arenas (work, home and social, and the individual) serve as precursors of a wide range of stress outcomes. They reviewed differences and similarities between female and male managers in relation to work stressors in the three arenas as well as stress outcomes, and reported that female managers scored higher on both stressors and stress outcomes compared to their male counterparts. Women managers also reported significantly greater type A behaviour.

Several studies have found differences in the sources and amounts of stress experienced by men and women. Iwasaki, MacKay and Ristock (2004) used a series of focus groups to explore the stress experiences among female and male managers and found that women managers reported more emotional stress than men related to relationships and perceived responsibilities for caretaking both at work and at home, and more stress related to the challenge of balancing home and work aspects; whereas men reported more physical health problems and stress related to technology.

In a study of stress and workload among female and male managers, Lundberg and Fankenhaeuser (1999) found that both women and men reported positive attitudes towards their work situation. However, women reported significantly more stress because of lack of communication, lack of support from superiors and having to perform better than men to have the same chance of promotion. In addition, women spent twice as much time on unpaid and household work than men, despite no differences in time spent in paid work, and women managers also showed higher physiological stress responses after work than did men. Thus, despite the fact that both women and men experience their jobs as challenging and stimulating, the data indicate a more favourable situation for men than for women (Lundberg & Fankenhaeuser, 1999).

Davidson, Cooper and Baldini (1995) studied occupational stress in 126 female and 220 male undergraduate business majors. Their results indicated that female middle and junior-level managers reported being under greater pressure than their male counterparts. Women, not surprisingly, reported greater stress on gender issues, such as discrimination, prejudice and home–work conflict. Females also indicated more mental and physical ill health symptoms than men. Similarly, Hochwarter, Perrewe and Dawkins (1995) found that women managers perceived more job demands and less job control than their male counterparts in both male-dominated and female-dominated occupations.

This limited review of the occupational stress literature suggests that although women and men share some common work stressors, women also experience unique sources of stress. These emanate from discrimination and bias, role conflict and work–family demands, resulting in overload.

8.3.1   Role Conflict

One of the most common occupational stressors is role conflict – that is, the simultaneous occurrence of two (or more) sets of pressures, such that compliance with one would make compliance with the other more difficult. Another type of role conflict is inter-role conflict with pressures from other group memberships. For example, pressures to spend long hours at the office may conflict with demands or expectations from family members to spend time at home. Role conflict can occur at work, within the family and between work and family roles.

Greenglass, Pantony and Burke (1988) examined relationships between role conflict, work stress and social support in women and men, and the psychological consequences of role conflict. Their results indicated that role conflict was higher in women than in men. Significant correlations between role conflict and work stress and social support, primarily in women, suggested a greater interdependence between work and family spheres in women.

In a study examining the relationships between work characteristics, job pressures, organizational supports and health indicators among 191 managerial women, Richardsen, Burke and Mikkelsen (1999) found that women who experienced high work conflict and work–family pressures also reported poor health outcomes and little life satisfaction. Organizational initiatives to support and develop women's careers were associated with low exhaustion and psychosomatic complaints, and high life satisfaction.

8.3.2 Work and Family

Work and family are the major life roles for most employed adults. Work–family conflict is experienced when pressures from work and family roles are incompatible, such that participation in one role makes it more difficult to participate in the other (Friedman & Greenhaus, 2000). Research evidence has shown that work–family conflict has negative effects on well-being in both work and family (Burke & Greenglass, 1987). Building on their earlier work, Greenhaus and Parasuraman (1994) proposed two dominant forms of work–family conflict: time-based conflict and strain-based conflict. Time-based conflict is experienced when the time devoted to one role makes it difficult to fill the requirements of the other role. Strain-based conflict is experienced when the strain produced in one role spills over or intrudes into the other role. In addition, work interference with family may have different antecedents and consequences than family interference with work. Work–family conflict is more likely to occur than family–work conflict (Greenhaus & Parasuraman, 1999), perhaps because the organization's demands on an individual's time are more important since the employer provides the salary needed to provide for one's family.

Extensive work–family conflict can lead to dissatisfaction and distress within the work and family domains (Frone, Yardley & Markel, 1997; Netermeyer, Boles & McMurrian, 1996; Parasuraman et al., 1996). In a cross-national study of managers in England, the United States and Hong Kong, Wharton and Blair-Loy (2006) found that job and workload characteristics were related to higher worries about the effect of long hours on the family. For every additional hour worked, the odds that respondents would worry about the effect on family increased by 7%. In addition, in all three countries, women managers experienced higher work–family conflict than men, and women with young children were most likely to experience work–family conflict. Similar results were obtained by Blair-Loy and Wharton (2004) in a study of 500 finance managers. While mothers and fathers did not differ in terms of the average number of hours worked per week, women managers reported greater work–family conflict. Parents who experienced more scheduling flexibility and who took advantage of corporate flexibility policies were less likely to experience work–family conflict. There is also evidence that such conflicts can have negative impacts on parenting (Stewart & Barling, 1996).

Interviews with senior female international managers have revealed that women experienced extra strain and guilt feelings about balancing an international career with family responsibilities, and therefore work–family conflicts are a major threat to females partaking in international management (Linehan & Walsh, 2000). The majority of female managers also perceived organizational inflexibility, gender role expectations and ignorance of non-work arenas by the company as obstacles to their career success. These studies indicate that organizations can no longer treat the arenas of work and non-work as separate spheres (Kirchmeyer, 1993).

8.3.3   Dual-Career Couples

Most managerial women develop relationships with partners who are likely to be career-oriented, hence creating the dual-career couple (Gilbert, 1993). Experts have predicted that the number of dual-career couples will continue to increase (Hertz, 1986). This trend has obvious implications for managerial and professional women, who historically have been predominantly single (never married, separated, divorced) and childless (Brett, Stroh & Reilly, 1992). The effects on women of being in a dual-career situation are more pervasive since relatively more married managerial women than men are in such relationships. In addition, the impact of dual-career couple status is greater for women than for men (Lewis, 1994; White, Cox & Cooper, 1992). For example, in a study of married couples, women reported significantly greater effect of marital and family stress, and less perceived spousal support for their careers than did their male partners (Phillips-Miller, Campbell & Morrison, 2000).

Research has also shown that there are cross-over effects (the process by which a stressor or strain experienced by one person affects the level of stress or strain in another person) of work–family conflict from one spouse to the other (Hammer, Bauer & Grandey, 2003; Westman & Etzion, 2005). In a study of military women and their spouses, both job and family stressors predicted work–family conflicts for women, but not for men (Westman & Etzion, 2005). When number of children, job stress and family stress were controlled for, spouses' work–family conflict contributed significantly to wives' work–family conflict and vice versa. Hammer *et al.* (2003) studied effects of couples' work–family and family–work conflict on withdrawal behaviours at work, defined as interruptions, lateness and absence. They found that spouses' family–work conflict was positively related to wives' absence from work, whereas wives' family–work conflict was positively related to spouses' interruptions at work and absence. These studies clearly indicate some of the pressures of dual-career couples.

8.3.4 Sexual Harassment

Sexual harassment is a widespread problem in the workplace with estimates ranging from 28% to 90% for females and 14% to 18% for males (Fitzgerald, Gelfand & Drasgow, 1995; Schneider, Swan & Fitzgerald, 1997). Sexual harassment is 'any behavior of a sexual nature that an individual perceives to be offensive and unwelcome (whether or not it is legally or conceptually defined as such)' (Bowes-Sperry & Tata, 1999, p. 265). It has been proposed that sexual harassment has three components: gender harassment (hostile or insulting attitudes or behaviours); unwanted sexual attention; and sexual coercion (sexual cooperation linked to job outcomes) (Gelfand, Fitzgerald & Drasgow, 1995).

Consequences of sexual harassment can be viewed as job related, psychological/somatic and organizational. Fitzgerald and his coworkers (Fitzgerald *et al.*, 1997) reported a relationship between self-reported sexual harassment and headaches, sleep disturbances and psychosomatic symptoms (reduced self-esteem, increased stress, anger, fear, depression and anxiety). The dynamics and consequences of sexual harassment of women managers in non-traditional professions have also been outlined by Collinson and Collinson (1996). Such consequences have both individual and organizational costs.

The research programme headed by Gutek (1985) has contributed much to our understanding of the impact of social sexual behaviour and harassment on women, men and organizations. In the area of sexual harassment, she found that women reported more sexual harassment than men, that male harassers were not demographically different from other men at work, that women who were harassed were usually afraid that they would be blamed for the incident, and did not lodge formal complaints because they did not want to ruin the harasser's career and believed that their organization would not do anything anyway. In contrast to women, who felt insulted, men were generally flattered by sexual overtures from women. It is clear that sexual harassment creates significant problems for both individuals and can impact negatively on work settings.

8.3.5 Organizational Downsizing

Significant reorganization or downsizing of firms has been common-place throughout the past decade and will continue during the next. The accumulating evidence indicates these changes typically have profound effects on both survivors and victims of job loss, almost always negative (Noer, 1999). It is also clear that women and men are likely to be affected in similar ways.

Women, however, may experience some unique issues associated with corporate restructuring. Interviews with senior women managers who voluntarily left a public sector organization in the midst of restructuring found that the most cited reasons were the lack of opportunities for career advancement and stress (Karambayya, 1998, 2001). In addition, these women commonly reported that they believed the restructuring process had exacerbated existing gender issues, and created a backlash against women that would hinder their career prospects. Senior management appeared to close ranks, increasingly appearing to be an old boys' club. Women were often over-represented in support functions, common targets of cost cutting. Women were also likely to be the most recent entrants to senior management ranks and did not have the personal and professional networks to protect them. The lean and mean values of the organization became increasingly antithetical to their personal values. These preliminary findings suggest that managerial and professional women may be particularly vulnerable to the effects of organizational restructuring.

8.4   RESEARCH AND PRACTICE

8.4.1   Workplace Flexibility

The findings related to unique workplace stressors experienced by managerial and professional women indicate that rigid work schedules and work overload interfered with women's satisfaction and family life (Burke & Greenglass, 1987). As a consequence, more organizations are currently experimenting with a variety of programmes to provide employees with greater flexibility in work schedules (Rodgers & Rodgers, 1989).

Mattis (1990) investigated various types of flexible work arrangements for managers and professionals in major US corporations: part-time work, job sharing and telecommuting. She reported that most employees select flexible work arrangements to balance work and family responsibilities. Although part-time work was the most common flexible work option for managers in the companies studied, both job sharing and telecommuting showed increasing acceptance. Despite these findings, the number of employees on flexible work arrangements constitutes a small percentage of the total company workforce.

Organizational resources (e.g., flexible working hours, a mentor or role model) were associated with fewer symptoms of strain and greater job satisfaction in a sample of 195 female personnel professionals (Nelson *et al.*, 1990). Burke and McKeen (1994), in a study of 792 managerial and professional women, built on the stress literature and extended it to include work and career experiences associated with career advancement of women. The dependent variables were aspects of emotional well-being, which have long been a staple in stress research. Specific work experiences (e.g., support and encouragement, challenging jobs, the absence of strain from conflict, overload and ambiguity) and work outcomes (considered as short-term responses to work conditions) were fairly consistently and significantly related to self-reported emotional well-being in this large sample of managerial women. These studies show that organizational support for balancing work and non-work can increase health and ultimately work performance.

8.4.2   Intervention and Policy Implications

It is important to target interventions relating to work stress and health since women have unique needs and experiences (Nelson & Burke, 2000a, 2000b). Because executive women have more resources at their disposal than other workers, it is tempting to argue that they should not be targets for organizational interventions. They may be healthier than women at lower levels of the organization, but it is especially important that they are healthy. As decision makers and policy setters, they hold the keys to the well-being of the organization. They also serve as models for the health-related behaviors of the people they lead. An awareness of the needs of different managerial groups can reshape the culture of the organization in healthy ways by broadening and enriching the majority culture. For example, changing an inflexible, long-working-hours culture benefits not only women, but men as well.

For male and female executives alike, preventive management involves enhancing strengths and managing risks. Preventive management provides a three-part framework that can be used to develop interventions to improve the health of executive women. There are three levels of interventions: primary, secondary and tertiary. Primary preventive efforts are directed at eliminating or reducing the sources of stress or the risk factors. Secondary preventive efforts focus on helping executive women manage their responses to the inevitable demands of work and home. Tertiary prevention involves healing executive women and organizations through appropriate professional care.

Primary prevention efforts should focus on the stressors of politics, overload, barriers to achievement, sexual harassment and other social-sexual behaviours, and work–home conflict (Burke, 1996). Research findings suggest that one of the issues that must be addressed by organizations is how to alter employment demands so that they mesh more easily with family responsibilities. Unfortunately, most employers do not consider their employees' concerns as family members to be organizational concerns (Friedman, 1990). Policies and practices are designed as if responsibilities outside the job were subordinate to work demands. If, rather than ignoring these, companies were to acknowledge them and assist their employees, a great deal of employment–family conflict could be alleviated (Friedman, DeGroot & Christensen, 1998). By offering flexible work schedules, alternative work arrangements like telecommuting, and company assistance with childcare and eldercare, such interventions can help women deal with overload and work/home issues (Mattis, 1994). Childcare is a demand on the family that poses conflict between work and family interests, particularly in the single-parent family. While childcare and eldercare are offered more frequently by large corporations, most medium-sized and small organizations have yet to adopt these benefits.

Politics, barriers to achievement and sexual harassment can be effectively diminished by aggressive organizational efforts in terms of corporate policy, and a system of rewards that reinforces equitable treatment of all organizational members (Schwartz, 1992). To address the issue of wage differential, reward systems that promote equitable pay for women are necessary (Stroh *et al.*, 2004). In addition, audits of development programmes should be conducted to see whether women are unfairly disadvantaged in terms of development opportunities. It is also important to develop zero-tolerance policies for social-sexual behaviours and sexual harassment.

Efforts to build social support, such as mentoring and networking programmes, can be of special benefit to executive women (Kram, 1996). The phrase 'lonely at the top' certainly applies in this case, and programmes that foster connections with other executives can help female executives gain social support and build important networks. Mentoring programmes allow women to be either mentors or protégés, or both, and being a provider of social support to others also has beneficial health effects. In addition, mentoring and networking efforts benefit the organization by developing a diverse talent pool of future executives.

Executive women also have a responsibility for preventively managing their health. At the primary level, the most important action is to identify sources of stress and work towards managing or mitigating them. Part of primary prevention is changing the stressor. Alternatively, executive women can develop personal resilience through changing their perceptions of stressors. All executives suffer from stress of some form, and often do not take the time to do a careful self-analysis to pinpoint exactly the causes of stress. A personal stress management plan, developed through careful introspection, may be the best insurance against burnout.

It is also important to recognize the inevitability of work–home conflict and work to manage it. Women executives need to ask for programmes like flexible work arrangements and for assistance from other family members such as spouses. They need to recognize that asking for help is a sign of strength, and that they can overcome their own limitations by asking for help from others.

Secondary prevention efforts focus on helping women manage their own responses to stress, and usually come in the form of exercise or ways to emotionally release tension. Organizations can assist women in several ways, including making exercise facilities available. Interventions that educate women about the stress management benefits of exercise and encourage them to engage in exercise are also warranted. Research has found that women are less likely to utilize exercise as a coping technique than are men. This may be so because women have less discretionary time to pursue options like health club memberships, and often must find childcare to be able to exercise. Organizations can provide convenient on-site exercise facilities with babysitting services, along with flexitime, to help remedy this problem. Referrals to appropriate exercise facilities offer another alternative. Companies may also encourage training in yoga and meditation, which has been found to be powerful antidotes to the stress of executive life.

Secondary prevention efforts may include encouraging networking groups to facilitate emotional release. Support groups to facilitate emotional release and training in relaxation methods can help women managers deal more effectively with the transition from work to home environment with less stress spill-over. Talking with trusted colleagues can provide emotional ventilation, allow executive women to work through their experiences and benefit from input from others, and thereby increase problem solving.

The suggestions for women to take responsibility for secondary prevention parallel those for the organization, e.g., making exercise a daily ritual, learning a meditation technique, and talking to others. It must be noted, however, that secondary prevention alone is a palliative technique. Without accompanying primary interventions that focus on changing the stressors, little headway can be gained by executive women or organizations.

Tertiary prevention efforts are directed at symptom management or at healing the wounds of executive life. It is essential that employee assistance programmes recognize the special needs of women in provision of services and/or referral to appropriate professional care. Certain behavioural distress symptoms, such as eating disorders, alcohol abuse and smoking, may be more effectively treated with gender-specific interventions. Organizations have a major role to play in this level of prevention.

Executive women must also take responsibility for tertiary prevention. This can be accomplished by developing a network of qualified professionals to rely on. This means establishing relationships with physicians, psychologists and other trained professionals in advance of the need so that they will be available in times of crisis.

The three-level prevention framework provides ways of understanding what both executives and organizations can do to manage risks and enhance health. Care must be taken in these efforts to recognize that women at different life stages may have different needs. Childcare assistance, for example, may not be a high priority for mid-life women. This raises the importance of dialogue between executive women and others in the organization. To develop interventions that improve the health and well-being of executive women, decision makers must listen to women's concerns and ascertain what they need. The perceptions of others concerning what might benefit executive women may not be accurate.

The health and well-being of the organization is dependent on the health and well-being of all of its members. Women at the top of the organization are no exception. In a study mentioned earlier, company initiatives in general areas likely to address some of the demands experienced by managerial and professional women, included work and family programmes, flexible work arrangements, leadership and career development, mentoring programmes, and total cultural change (Mattis, 1994). The most proactive approach organizations can take is to change the source of stress; that is, find out what is causing executive women's stress and modify the cause. The three-part preventive management framework proposes that interventions should mainly focus on the primary level, supplemented by secondary and tertiary prevention. This framework provides an effective means for enhancing executive women's strengths and managing their health risks.

8.4.3   Future Research and Action Directions

There have been some pleasantly encouraging signs that research interest in the content examined in this chapter has increased. This is shown particularly in studies of work and family, and occupational stress experienced by managerial women. On the other hand, several other areas are still underresearched (Repetti, Mathews & Waldron, 1989), including the effects of employment gaps on career satisfaction, consequences of the more varied patterns that women's careers reveal, gender proportions, and the effects of various work experiences on both career aspirations and emotional well-being.

Considerably more work needs to be done on the potential benefits of efforts of organizations to support the career aspirations of managerial and professional women through cultural change efforts and policy implementation

(Morrison, 1992). There is an urgent need to document best practice in this area (Kraut, 1992). It is important to develop case studies of successful and less than successful change efforts to further our understanding of how best to bring about positive change. In addition, more research attention needs to address the effectiveness of a variety of specific policies for creating a women-friendly environment (Galinsky & Stein, 1990; Kraut, 1990). These include policies in the areas of sexual harassment, flexible working hours, part-time work and working at home.

Organizations have an important role to play, in cooperating with government agencies, in achieving a balance of childcare and careers through flexible work policies and childcare support, as well as through changes in organizational culture that come to place greater value on families. The formal policy changes required to ease work–family conflict include initiatives to assist with childcare and elder care, alternative patterns of work, part-time work with career opportunities and benefits, career breaks, enhanced maternity, parental and family leave, and changes in both relocation and anti-nepotism policies. Without the active support by the top of the organizations, training in their understanding and use, and consistent and intelligent applications, well-conceived policies often fall considerably short. This seems particularly important because there has been recent speculation that companies may be less family-friendly in an increasingly competitive marketplace (Fierman, 1994).

ACKNOWLEDGEMENTS

Preparation of this chapter was supported in part by the School of Business, York University and BI Norwegian School of Management.

REFERENCES

Bajdo, L.M. & Dickson, M.W. (2002). Perceptions of organizational culture and women's advancement in organizations: a cross-cultural examination. *Sex Roles*, **45**(5–6), 399–414.

Blair-Loy, M. & Wharton, A. S. (2004). Mothers in finance: surviving and thriving. *The Annals of The American Academy*, **596**, 151–71.

Bowes-Sperry, L. & Tata, J. (1999). A multi-perspective framework of sexual harassment. Reviewing two decades of research. In G.N. Powell (Ed.), *Handbook of Gender and Work* (pp. 263–80). Thousand Oaks, CA: Sage.

Brett, J.M., Stroh, L.K. & Reilly, A.H. (1992). What is it like being a dual-career manager in the 1990s? In S. Zedeck (Ed.), *Work, Families and Organizations* (pp. 138–67). San Francisco: Jossey-Bass.

Burke, R.J. (1988). Sources of managerial and professional stress in large organizations. In C.L. Cooper & R. Payne (Eds), *Causes, Coping and Consequences of Stress at Work* (pp. 77–114). New York: John Wiley & Sons, Inc.

Burke, R. J. (1996). Workaholism among women managers: work and life satisfactions and psychological well-being. *Equal Opportunities International*, **18**, 25–35.

Burke, R.J. (in press). Cultural values of women's work and career experiences. In R.S. Bhagat & R.M. Steers (Eds), *Handbook of Cultures, Organizations, and Work*. Cambridge, MA: Cambridge University Press.

Burke, R.J. & Greenglass, E.R. (1987). Work and family. In C.L. Cooper & I.T. Robertson (Eds), *International Review of Industrial and Organizational Psychology: 1987* (pp. 245–83). New York: John Wiley & Sons, Inc.

Burke, R.J. & Mattis, M.C. (2005). *Supporting Women's Career Advancement: Challenges and Opportunities*. Cheltenham: Edward Elgar.

Burke, R.J. & McKeen, C.A. (1992). Women in management. In C.L. Cooper & I.T. Robertson (Eds), *International Review of Industrial and Organizational Psychology* (pp. 245–83). New York: John Wiley & Sons, Inc.

Campbell Quick, J., Quick, J.D., Nelson, D. L. & Hurrell Jr., J.J. (1997). *Preventive Stress Management in Organizations*. Washington, DC: American Psychological Association.

Collinson, M. & Collinson, D. (1996). 'It's only Dick': the sexual harassment of women managers in insurance sales. *Work, Employment & Society*, **10**(1), 29–56.

Cooper, C.L. & Payne, R. (Eds) (1988). *Causes, Coping and Consequences of Stress at Work*. New York: John Wiley & Sons, Inc.

Davidson, M.J. & Burke, R.J. (2004). Women in management worldwide: facts, figures and analysis – an overview. In M.J. Davidson & R.J. Burke (Eds), *Women in Management Worldwide: Facts, Figures and Analysis* (pp. 1–15). London: Ashgate.

Davidson, M.J. & Cooper, C.L. (1992). *Shattering the Glass Ceiling: The Woman Manager*. London: Paul Chapman.

Davidson, M.J., Cooper, C.L. & Baldini, V. (1995). Occupational stress in female and male graduate managers. *Stress Medicine*, **11**, 157–75.

Davidson, M.J. & Fielden, S.L. (1999). Stress and the working woman. In G.N. Powell. (Ed.), *Handbook of Gender and Work* (pp. 413–26). Thousand Oaks, CA: Sage.

Duehr, E.E. & Bono, J.E. (2006). Men, women, and managers: are stereotypes finally changing? *Personnel Psychology*, **59**(4), 815–46.

Eagly, A.H. & Carli, L.L. (2007). *Through the Labyrinth*. Cambridge, MA: Harvard Business School Press.

Fielden, S.L. & Cooper, C. (2002). Managerial stress: are women more at risk? In D.L. Nelson & R.J. Burke (Eds), *Gender, Work Stress, and Health* (pp. 19–34). Washington, DC: American Psychological Association.

Fielden, S.L. & Davidson, M.J. (2001). Stress and the woman manager. In J. Dunham (Ed.), *Stress in the Workplace: Past, Present and Future* (pp. 109–29). Philadelphia, PA: Whurr Publishers.

Fierman, J. (1994). Are companies less family-friendly? *Fortune*, **21**(March), 64–7.

Fitzgerald, L.E., Drasgow, F., Hulin, C.L., Gelfand, M.J. & Magley, V.J. (1997). Antecedents and consequences of sexual harassment in organizations: a test of an integrated model. *Journal of Applied Psychology*, **82**, 578–89.

Fitzgerald, L.E., Gelfand, M.J. & Drasgow, F. (1995). Measuring sexual harassment: theoretical and psychometric advances. *Basic and Applied Social Psychology*, **17**, 425–45.

Friedman, D.E. (1990). Work and family: the new strategic plan. *Human Resource Planning*, **13**, 79–89.

Friedman, S.D., DeGroot, J. & Christensen, P. (Eds) (1998). *Integrating Work and Life: The Wharton Resource Guide*. San Francisco: Jossey-Bass.

Friedman, S.D. & Greenhaus, J.H. (2000). *Allies or Enemies? How Choices About Work and Family Affect the Quality of Men's and Women's Lives*. New York: Oxford University Press.

Frone, M.R., Yardley, J.K. & Markel, K. S. (1997). Developing and testing an integrative model of the work–family interface. *Journal of Vocational Behavior*, **50**, 145–67.

Galinsky, E. & Stein, P. J. (1990). The impact of human resource policies on employees: balancing work and family life. *Journal of Family Issues*, **11**, 368–83.

Gelfand, M. J., Fitzgerald, L.F. & Drasgow, F. (1995). The structure of sexual harassment: a confirmatory analysis across cultures and settings. *Journal of Vocational Behavior*, **47**, 164–77.

Gilbert, L.A. (1993). *Two Careers/One Family*. Newbury Park, CA: Sage.

Greenglass, E.R., Pantony, K.L. & Burke, R. J. (1988). A gender-role perspective on role conflict, work stress and social support. *Journal of Social Behavior and Personality*, **3**, 317–28.

Greenhaus, J.H. & Parasuraman, S. (1994). Work–family conflict, social support and well-being. In M.J. Davidson & R.J. Burke (Eds), *Women in Management: Current Research Issues* (pp. 213–29). London: Paul Chapman.

Greenhaus, J.H. & Parasuraman, S. (1999). Research on work, family and gender: current status and future directions. In G.N. Powell (Ed.), *Handbook of Gender and Work* (pp. 391–412). Thousand Oaks, CA: Sage.

Gutek, B.A. (1985). *Sex and the Workplace: The Impact of Sexual Behavior and Harassment on Women, Men and the Organization*. San Francisco: Jossey-Bass.

Hammer, L.B., Bauer, T.N. & Grandey, A.A. (2003). Work–family conflict and work-related withdrawal behaviors. *Journal of Business and Psychology*, **17**(3), 419–36.

Heilman, M.E. (1995). Sex stereotypes and their effect in the workplace: what we know and what we don't know. *Journal of Social Behavior and Personality*, **10**, 3–26.

Heilman, M.E., Block, C J., Martell, R.F. & Simon, M.C. (1989). Has anything changed? Current characterizations of men, women and managers. *Journal of Applied Psychology*, **74**, 935–42.

Hertz, R. (1986). *More Equal than Others: Women and Men in Dual-Career Marriages*. Berkeley, CA: University of California Press.

Hewlett, S.A. & Luce, C.B. (2005). Off-ramps and on-ramps: keeping talented women on the road to success. *Harvard Business Review*, March, 43–54.

Hochwarter, W.A., Perrewe, P.L. & Dawkins, M.C. (1995). Gender differences in perceptions of stress-related variables: do the people make the place or does the place make the people? *Journal of Managerial Issues*, **7**(1), 62–74.

Hofstede, G.H. (1980). *Culture's Consequences: International Differences in Work-Related Values*. Thousand Oaks, CA: Sage.

House, R.J., Hanges, P.J., Ruiz-Quintanilla, S.A., Dorfman, P.W., Javidan, M., Dickson, M.W., *et al.* (1999). Cultural influences on leadership: Project GLOBE. In W. Mobley, J. Gessner & V. Arnold (Eds), *Advances in Global Leadership* (Vol. **1**, pp. 171–233). Stamford, CT: JAI Press.

Ilgen, D.R. (1990). Health issues at work: opportunities for industrial/organizational psychology. *American Psychologist*, **45**, 273–83.

Iwasaki, Y., MacKay, K.J. & Ristock, J. (2004). Gender-based analyses of stress among professional managers: an exploratory qualitative study. *International Journal of Stress Management*, **11**(1), 56–79.

Jex, S. & Beehr, T.A. (1991). Emerging theoretical and methodological issues in the study of work-related stress. *Research in Personnel and Human Resources Management*, **9**, 311–65.

Kanter, R.M. (1977). *Men and Women of the Organization*. New York: Basic Books.

Karambayya, R. (1998). Caught in the cross-fire: women and corporate restructuring. *Canadian Journal of Administrative Sciences*, **15**, 333–8.

Karambayya, R. (2001). Women and corporate restructuring: sources and consequences of stress. In D.L. Nelson & R.J. Burke (Eds), *Gender, Work Stress and Health*. Washington, DC: American Psychological Association.

Kirchmeyer, C. (1993). *Managing the boundary between work and non-work: an assessment of organizational practices*. Paper presented at the Annual Meeting of the Academy of Management.

Kram, K.E. (1996). A relational approach to career development. In D.T. Hall (Ed.), *The Career is Dead - Long Live the Career*. San Francisco: Jossey-Bass.

Kraut, A.I. (1990). Some lessons on organizational research concerning work and family issues. *Human Resource Planning*, **13**, 109–18.

Kraut, A.I. (1992). Organizational research on work and family issues. In S. Zedeck (Ed.), *Work, Families and Organization* (pp. 208–35). San Francisco: Jossey-Bass.

Langan-Fox, J. (1998). Women's careers and occupational stress. In C.L. Cooper & I.T. Robertson (Eds), *International Review of Industrial and Organizational Psychology* (pp. 273–304). New York: John Wiley & Sons, Inc.

Lewis, S. (1994). Role tensions and dual career families. In M.J. Davidson & R.J. Burke (Eds), *Women in Management: Current Research Issues*. London: Paul Chapman.

Linehan, M. & Walsh, J.S. (2000). Work–family conflict and the senior female international manager. *British Journal of Management*, **11**, S49–S58.

Lundberg, U. & Fankenhaeuser, M. (1999). Stress and workload of men and women in high-ranking positions. *Journal of Occupational Health Psychology*, **4**(2), 142–51.

Lyness, K.S. & Heilman, M.E. (2006). When fit is fundamental: performance evaluations and promotions of upper-level female and male managers. *Journal of
Applied Psychology*, **91**(4), 777–85.

Lyness, K.S. & Schrader, C.A. (2006). Moving ahead or just moving? An examination of gender differences in senior corporate management appointments. *Group
& Organization Management*, **31**(6), 651–76.

Lyness, K.S. & Terrazas, J.M.B. (2006). Women in management: an update on
their progress and persistent challenges. In G.P. Hodgkinson & J.K. Ford (Eds),
International Review of Industrial and Organizational Psychology 2006 (Vol. **21**,
pp. 267–94). Hoboken, NJ: John Wiley & Sons, Inc.

Lyness, K.S. & Thompson, D.E. (2000). Climbing the corporate ladder: do female
and male executives follow the same route? *Journal of Applied Psychology*, **85**(1),
86–101.

Mattis, M.C. (1990). *Flexible Work Arrangements for Managers and Profession-
als: New Approaches to Work in US Corporations*. London, Ontario: National
Centre for Management Research and Development, University of Western
Ontario.

Mattis, M.C. (1994). Organizational initiatives in the USA for advancing managerial
women. In M.J. Davidson & R.J. Burke (Eds), *Women in Management: Current
Research Issues* (pp. 241–76). London: Paul Chapman.

Morrison, A.M. (1992). *The New Leaders*. San Francisco: Jossey-Bass.

Morrison, A.M. & von Glinow, M.A. (1990). Women and minorities in management.
American Psychologist, **45**, 200–8.

Morrison, A.M., White, R.P. & van Velsor, E. (1987). *Breaking the Glass Ceiling*.
Reading, MA: Addison-Wesley.

Nelson, D.L. & Burke, R.J. (2000a). Women executives: health, stress and success.
Academy of Management Executive, **14**, 107–121.

Nelson, D.L. & Burke, R.J. (2000b). Women, work stress and health. In M.J. Davidson & R.J. Burke (Eds), *Women in Management* (Vol. II, pp. 177–91). London:
Sage.

Nelson, D.L. & Burke, R.J. (2001). *Gender, Work Stress and Health*. Washington,
DC: American Psychological Association.

Nelson, D.L., Quick, J.C., Hitt, M.A. & Moesel, D. (1990). Politics, lack of career
progress and work/home conflict: stress and strain for working women. *Sex Roles:
A Journal of Research*, **23**, 169–85.

Netermeyer, R.G., Boles, J.S. & McMurrian, R. (1996). Development and validation
of work–family conflict and family–work conflict scales. *Journal of Applied
Psychology*, **81**, 400–10.

Noer, D. (1999). Layoff survivor sickness: what it is and what to do about it. In M.K.
Gowing, J.D. Kraft & J. Campbell Quick (Eds), *The New Organizational Real-
ity: Downsizing, Restructuring, and Revitalization*. Washington, DC: American
Psychological Association.

Offermann, L.R. & Armitage, M.A. (1993). Stress and the woman manager: sources,
health outcomes and interventions. In E.A. Fagenson (Ed.), *Women in Management: Trends, Issues and Challenges in Managerial Diversity* (pp. 131–61).
Newbury Park, CA: Sage.

Ohlott, P.J., Ruderman, M.N. & McCauley, C.D. (1994). Gender differences in managers' developmental job experiences. *Academy of Management Journal*, **37**, 46–67.

Parasuraman, S., Purohit, Y.S., Godshalk, V.M. & Beitell, N. (1996). Work and family variables, entrepreneurial career success and psychological well-being. *Journal of Vocational Behavior*, **48**, 275–300.

Phillips-Miller, D.L., Campbell, N.J. & Morrison, C.R. (2000). Work and family: satisfaction, stress, and spousal support. *Journal of Employment Counseling*, **37**(1), 16–30.

Portello, J.Y. & Long, B.C. (2001). Appraisals and coping with workplace interpersonal stress: a model for women managers. *Journal of Counselling Psychology*, **48**(2), 144–56.

Powell, G.N. (1999). *Reflections on the Glass Ceiling: Recent Trends and Future Prospects*. Thousand Oaks, CA: Sage.

Powell, G.N., Butterfield, D.A. & Parent, J.D. (2002). Gender and managerial stereotypes: have the times changed? *Journal of Management*, **28**(2), 177–93.

Repetti, R.L. (1993). The effects of workload and the social environment at work on health. In L. Goldberger & S. Breznitz (Eds), *Handbook of Stress*, 2nd edn. New York: Free Press.

Repetti, R.L., Mathews, K.A. & Waldron, I. (1989). Employment and women's health: effects of paid employment on women's mental and physical health. *American Psychologist*, **44**, 1394–401.

Richardsen, A.M., Burke, R.J. & Mikkelsen, A. (1999). Job pressures, organizational support, and health among Norwegian women managers. *International Journal of Stress Management*, **6**(3), 167–77.

Rodgers, F.S. & Rodgers, C. (1989). Business and the facts of family life. *Harvard Business Review*, **67**, 121–9.

Russell, J.E.A. (2006). Career counseling for women in management. In J.S. Walsh & M.J. Heppner (Eds), *Handbook of Career Counseling for Women* (2nd edn) (pp. 453–512). Mahwah, NJ: Lawrence Erlbaum.

Schneider, K.T., Swan, S. & Fitzgerald, L.F. (1997). Job-related and psychological effects of sexual harassment in the workplace: empirical evidence from two organizations. *Journal of Applied Psychology*, **82**, 401–15.

Schwartz, F.N. (1992). *Breaking with Tradition*. New York: Warner Books.

Sczesny, S., Bosak, J., Neff, D. & Schyns, B. (2004). Gender stereotypes and the attribution of leadership traits: a cross-cultural comparison. *Sex Roles*, **51**(11–12), 631–45.

Stewart, W. & Barling, J. (1996). Father's work experiences affect children's behaviors via job-related effect and parenting behaviors. *Journal of Organizational Behavior*, **17**, 221–32.

Stroh, L.K., Langlands, C.L. & Simpson, P.A. (2004). Shattering the glass ceiling in the new millennium. In M.S. Stockdale & F.J. Crosby (Eds), *The Psychology and Management of Workplace Diversity* (pp. 147–67). Malden, MA: Blackwell Publishing.

Vinnicombe, S. & Banks, J. (2003). *Women with Attitude*. London: Routledge.

Westman, M. & Etzion, D.L. (2005). The crossover of work–family conflict from one spouse to the other. *Journal of Applied Social Psychology*, **35**(9), 1936–57.

Wharton, A.S. & Blair-Loy, M. (2006). Long work hours and family life – a cross-national study of employees' concerns. *Journal of Family Issues*, **27**(3), 415–36.

White, B., Cox, T.C. & Cooper, C.L. (1992). *Women's Career Development*. Oxford: Blackwell.

PART III

The Role of Workplace Factors on Health

CHAPTER 9

The Role of Job Control in Employee Health and Well-Being

Paul E. Spector

Department of Psychology, University of South Florida, USA

Research over the past few decades has established a clear link between control in its various forms at work and health, both physical and psychological. Much of the work on control has viewed it as a major component in the job stress process in which exposure to stressful conditions at work can adversely affect employee physical health and emotional well-being. Control variables play a prominent role in the job stress process. Control affects how people view their work environment, and it may serve to buffer the emotional impact of that environment. Furthermore, control can affect people's behavioural coping responses to workplace stressors. Less attention has been paid to other effects of control that may have little to do with stressful job conditions. Specifically, control might play a role in accidents and injuries in the workplace, perhaps by having an influence on people's exposure to unhealthy work conditions, or their safety-related behaviour.

Control is the extent to which individuals are able to influence their environment. In the workplace an employee can have control over many different aspects of the job, such as when and where to work, and how to perform job tasks. Other forms of control have to do with being able to influence how others will do their jobs. Although there are objective features of the work environment that allow or prevent control, it is the perception of control that has perhaps the most important impact on health and well-being. Objective control is certainly an important element in the job stress process, but likely much of its effect is mediated by perceptions of control, as will be discussed at greater length below.

International Handbook of Work and Health Psychology, Third Edition. Edited by Cary L. Cooper, James Campbell Quick, and Marc J. Schabracq.
© 2009 John Wiley & Sons, Ltd. Published 2015 by John Wiley & Sons, Ltd.

Control can be viewed from the perspective of the environment, and as noted, we can distinguish among different aspects of control, such as control over work schedule or control over work tasks. We can also distinguish objective (characteristics of the work environment) from perceived (people's idiosyncratic view of the environment) control. However, there are a number of control-related personality constructs that reside in the individual, as well. Locus of control is the tendency to believe one does or does not have control, and self-efficacy is the belief one can effectively perform tasks.

This chapter will provide an overview of the literature relating control to health and well-being. It will discuss research on the role control plays in the job stress process, and how individual differences in control-related variables relate to health and well-being. Not all of the control-related constructs have received much research attention in the organizational literature, so more emphasis will be placed on some topics than others. The chapter will begin with a theoretical framework whereby control influences the job stress process. It will then summarize the existing evidence that relates control to health and well-being, and discuss three models of how control affects the stress process. Finally, the two personality variables of locus of control and self-efficacy will be reviewed.

9.1 CONTROL AND STRESS IN THE WORKPLACE

Most theories of stress in general and job stress in particular have adopted some form of an environment-reaction or stressor-strain approach (Beehr & Newman, 1978; Lazarus, 1991). Figure 9.1 presents a general model of stress linking the environment to the individual's reactions. The individual is seen as monitoring his or her environment, perceiving and evaluating or appraising (Lazarus, 1991) that environment. Conditions or events seen as overly challenging or threatening are perceived as job stressors that lead to physical and psychological strains, both in the short and long term. Short-term strains include immediate negative emotional responses, most likely anger or anxiety (Keenan & Newton, 1985; Liu, Spector & Shi, 2007; Narayanan, Menon & Spector, 1999), and associated physiological responses, such as increased

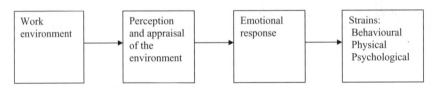

Figure 9.1   A general model of job stress

heart rate and blood pressure (Bishop *et al.*, 2003), and catecholamine and cortisol secretion into the bloodstream (Frankenhaeuser, 1978). The immediate emotional response can contribute to a variety of behavioural, physical and psychological strains. Behavioural strains are actions taken by the individual to cope with the stressful event or condition, and might include alcohol or drug (e.g., tranquilizer) consumption, or withdrawal from the situation (e.g., absence from work). Physical strains include immediate physiological reactions as well as headache or stomach distress. Psychological strains might be job dissatisfaction as the byproduct of being in a disagreeable situation. Longer-term strains are the cumulative effect of short-term strains, and could include post-traumatic stress disorder in response to continued exposure to stressors (Del Ben *et al.*, 2006), or heart disease from the continued exposure to elevated cortisol (Frankenhaeuser & Johansson, 1986). Individuals will engage in a number of coping strategies designed to eliminate or escape the stressor, or reduce the strain response.

Evidence exists to support the linkages in the Figure 9.1 model. First, studies have shown that measures of the work environment relate to perceived stressors in both experimental and nonexperimental research (Spector, 1992). A large body of literature has established connections between perceived job stressors and both emotions and strains. Results of many such cross sectional studies have been summarized in a variety of meta-analyses showing links of various strains to stressors such as role ambiguity and conflict (Jackson & Schuler, 1985; Örtqvist & Wincent, 2006), injustice (Cohen-Charash & Spector, 2001), working hours (Sparks *et al.*, 1997), interpersonal conflict, organizational constraints and workload (Spector & Jex, 1998). Two Scandinavian studies found that high job control was significantly associated with low work–family conflict in Finland (Heponiemi *et al.*, 2008) and Sweden (Grönlund, 2007). Interestingly, both studies found the same −.11 correlation between the two variables.

Figure 9.2 incorporates the likely role that control plays in the job stress process. Perceived control arises from an interaction between the person and the environment. Although there is not a perfect correspondence, perceived control reflects the amount of control an individual believes he or she has in the workplace. It is a reflection of experiences in which control attempts were successful or unsuccessful. Beyond actual experience are individual factors that predispose people to believe they have control over situations or that they are capable of being effective in accomplishing goals. Individual differences in control beliefs are the personality variable of locus of control (Rotter, 1966), which has been adapted to workplace settings as work locus of control (Spector, 1988). Individuals who believe they have control over rewards and success at work are said to be internals, whereas individuals who believe luck, fate or powerful others control such things are said to be

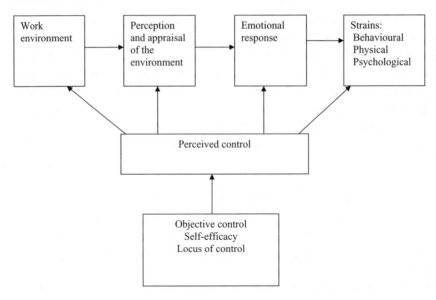

Figure 9.2 The many roles of control in the job stress process

externals. Individual differences in the extent to which a person believes he
or she is effective in conducting job tasks is self-efficacy within the work
setting (Jex & Bliese, 1999).

Perceived control influences the actual work environment, as individuals
who perceive control are likely to be proactive in dealing with workplace
challenges. Thus a high control individual will show initiative to solve problems that might otherwise become stressors. For example, the individual
might seek the help of others to handle a heavy workload, or might call
the appropriate technician to fix a piece of equipment that was malfunctioning. To the extent that such efforts are successful, the individual's perceived
control would be enhanced, as well as self-efficacy and perhaps locus of
control.

Beyond affecting direct action, control is also a factor in appraisal and
perception. Conditions and events that are perceived as controllable are less
likely to be perceived as stressors than conditions and events seen as uncontrollable. The belief in control over a stressor, particularly the belief in
being able to escape or terminate that stressor, will reduce the extent to
which it is perceived as threatening, and thereby the impact of that stressor
on strains. Empirical support for the connection between control perceptions
and stressors are easy to find in the literature. Spector's (1986) meta-analysis
showed significant correlations between perceived control and both role
ambiguity and role conflict of −.33 and −.32, respectively. In another meta-
analysis, Spector and Jex (1998) found correlations of perceived autonomy

of −.21 with organizational constraints, −.20 with interpersonal conflict, but only −.04 with workload. Spell and Arnold (2007) found that perceived control related to distributive, procedural and interactive justice, with individuals perceiving high control perceiving more justice.

Studies have compared relationships between perceived stressors and control with correlations between objectively assessed stressors (or at least stressors assessed with methods unaffected by the subject's perceptions) and control. Ganster, Fox and Dwyer (2001) assessed the workloads of nurses via either patient loads or a self-report scale. Perceived control was related to the perceived measure but not the objective. Spector, Dwyer and Jex (1988) compared self with supervisor reports of stressors in their correlations with perceived control. For self-reports, correlations were significant for organizational constraints ($r = -.21$) and role ambiguity ($r = -.30$), but for supervisor reports of the same stressors, correlations were not significant ($r = -.16$ and −.12, respectively), although for constraints the corresponding correlations were not much different. Interestingly, the number of working hours, which is more of a factual measure of workload, was significant regardless of whether it was reported by the subject (.18) or the supervisor (.25). Taken together these two studies suggest that it is in fact perceptions of stressors that most relate to perceived control.

Control is also related to both emotions and other strains. Spector's (1986) control meta-analysis found relationships between control and emotional distress ($r = -.25$), job satisfaction ($r = .30$), physical symptoms ($r = -.25$) and absenteeism ($r = -.19$). Other studies have found an association between low control and high burnout (Akerboom & Maes, 2006; McClenahan, Giles & Mallett, 2007), anxiety and depression (Griffin et al., 2007). Mausner-Dorsch and Eaton (2000) linked control to not only depressed mood, but clinical depressive episodes, as well.

Of perhaps even more concern is that a number of studies have linked control to physical illness. Ganster et al. (2001) found that high control predicted lower use of medical services over the five-year span of their study. This study does not indicate what sorts of illnesses were associated with control, but there is evidence linking control to a variety of physical conditions and disease. For example, Schaubroeck, Jones and Xie (2001) showed that perceived workplace control correlated −.20 with upper respiratory illness, suggesting a link between control and the immune system. A more extensive body of research links both stress and control to physical symptoms that can contribute to cardiovascular disease, as well as indicators of cardiovascular symptoms themselves. Examples include markers of inflammation (Clays et al., 2005), glycolipid allostatic load (Li et al., 2007), and subclinical arteriosclerosis in men but not women (Kamarck et al., 2007). Although gender differences have been found in other studies, they might be attributable to the greater frequencies of men than women in blue collar jobs (Landsbergis *et al.*, 2001) where the impact of control on cardiovascular symptoms is higher (Gallo *et al.*, 2004). In a prospective study, Bosma, Stansfeld and Marmot (1998) tracked 9000 British civil servants over a five-year span. Control assessed from both subjects and their supervisors predicted subsequent coronary heart disease. Furthermore, control at work has been linked to mortality due to cardiovascular disease (Kivimäki *et al.*, 2002).

Beyond physical illness, control has also been shown to relate to the incidence of workplace injuries and accidents. Goldenhar, Williams and Swanson (2003) in a survey study showed that perceived control related to not only psychological strain and physical symptoms, but workplace injuries as well, although the latter relationship was quite small ($r = -.10$). An even stronger correlation of $-.21$ was found between control and injury when the measure of control consisted of items concerning safety (Huang *et al.*, 2006).

Although the aforementioned studies suggest that high control is uniformly preventative when it comes to both minor and serious illness, at least one study suggests that the situation can be more complex. Johnson and Hall (1988) found that under some conditions high control was associated with cardiovascular disease. They speculated that at times the responsibility associated with high control can serve as an additional demand that can have negative effects. Nevertheless, the bulk of the research shows a clear link between control at work and strains, and that control can be an important factor in even serious illness.

9.2   MODELS OF CONTROL AND STRESS

Additional environmental and individual factors can serve as moderators of the connection between stressors and strains. Karasek's (1979) control-demand model posits that control serves as a buffer, so that strain occurs in response to stressors primarily under conditions of low control. This idea was expanded into the control-demand-support model that included an additional buffer of social support (Karasek & Theorell, 1990). According to this model, the effects of stressors on strain occur most strongly under the conditions of low control and low social support. Spector (1998) presented a control-emotion model that distinguishes dispositional, environmental and perceived control, and explains how it fits into the job stress process.

9.2.1   The Control-Demand Model

Perhaps the most influential control theory of stress is Karasek's (1979) control-demand model. This model suggests that the negative effects of being exposed to stressors can be buffered by having high control. The model distinguishes demands (stressors) from decision latitude (control) which consists of having discretion over how the job is done as well as ability to do the job. Karasek (1979) argues that demands (stressors) induce an energized or motivated state within the individual. Control allows that energy to be directed outward towards meeting those demands. Constraints produced by a lack of control leave the energy unreleased within the individual, thus resulting in strain. Thus, strain is seen as a byproduct of the combination of high demands and high control. This could be due to the impact of control on the appraisal of demands. Terry and Jimmieson (1999) suggest that Miller's (1979) mimimax hypothesis might better serve as the mechanism. Specifically, control reduces negative responses to demands because the individual believes he or she can minimize the maximum aversiveness of those demands. In other words, one can control his or her own exposure by reducing or even eliminating the demand if it begins to induce too much strain. That knowledge alone of being able to terminate an aversive stimulus can reduce the strain response has been well researched in the general stress literature (Thompson, 1981).

Whereas the minimax hypothesis concerns the effect of perceived control on appraisal and responses, other mechanisms concern the actual behaviour of individuals to better manage and cope with stressors. Individuals who believe they have control are more likely to engage in direct control behaviour that can be effective in accomplishing job tasks. This could occur by finding better and more effective ways to accomplish tasks, seeking assistance of others, managing time more effectively and overcoming obstacles. Of course, actual control in these circumstances is important, as attempts to exert perceived control one does not have can result in additional demands as time and effort are expended in failed control attempts that could have been used to address the demands themselves. For example, if one has a heavy workload, time spent in vain to seek assistance or restructure the tasks, leaves less time and energy to accomplish the workload that has not been reduced.

Terry and Jimmieson (1999) thoroughly reviewed tests of the control-demand model. This review concluded that support for control as a general buffer of demands has been mixed. Many studies that reported tests of control as a moderator of the demand-strain or stressor-strain relationship have not been statistically significant. They caution, however, that it may be premature to discard this model, as a more precise conceptualization might prove to be better supported. The specific nature of the control, type of strain and additional moderating factors such as social support may be key factors to consider in refinements of the model. They point to the distinction between control over tasks versus being allowed input into broader organizational decisions, with the former but not the latter form having a moderator effect.

De Jonge *et al.* (2000) provided evidence that the specific form of control must match the stressors experienced for buffering to occur. Spector (1998) suggested that one must have control over the stressor itself for buffering to occur. Thus having control over workload will be unhelpful if the stressor is role conflict or some social aspects of the job. This suggests that one cannot easily identify a specific type of control to serve as a buffer, but must link control to the specific demands experienced by the individual.

There are additional factors that should be considered before discarding the control-demand model as being unsupported, including the nature of the stressor, statistical power to detect moderator effects in studies and level of analysis. Although there is insufficient research to fully evaluate each of these possible factors, likely they contribute to the lack of consistent support for the model.

A wide variety of demands and stressor variables can be found throughout the various tests of the control-demand model. Some studies have used Karasek's Job Content Questionnaire (JCQ) (Karasek, 1979; Karasek *et al.*, 1998), which is a general measure that focuses on the content of job tasks, including workload, conflicting demands and interruptions. Other studies have looked at specific stressors, some of which overlap in content with the JCQ, such as workload. Some studies have also looked at stressors that go beyond job content into the social domain, such as interpersonal conflict (Spector, 1987). The inclusion of a wide variety of disparate demands and stressors across studies likely introduced variance into the outcomes of model tests. Although one might be tempted to hypothesize that all forms of demands/stressors should be affected in the same way by control, such might not be the case. In part it might be that some stressors by their nature are more controllable than others, thus the link between control and demand varies. Assuming that control must match the stressor, this would be an important factor. In part it might also be the fact that some stressors by their nature are more serious, and thus for them control is more important. Finally, perhaps some stressors require control to best cope, whereas others do not. Control would not be particularly effective in cases where stressors are not controllable, and might actually be counterproductive.

Another issue that likely contributes to inconsistency in moderator tests is that such tests tend to have low statistical power due to high multicolinearity between the additive and product terms in multiple regression analyses, and effect sizes for moderators generally found in the literature tend to be quite small (Aguinis *et al.*, 2005). Indeed it has been noted that the size of the control buffering effect is likely modest (Payne & Fletcher, 1983). Most tests of the control-demand model have had samples of less than optimal size, with sample sizes below 200 not being uncommon. Given a combination of small effect sizes and low power due to high multicolinearity and small samples, it should be no surprise that results are inconsistent across studies.

Another issue that deserves mention concerns the level of analysis. Some studies have investigated the model's predictions at the level of the individual employee, testing for the moderating effects of an employee's own perceptions of control on the relationship between perceptions of demands (or stressors) and strains. Others have focused on the job classification as the unit of analysis. Such studies test hypotheses about the possible effects of control and demands at the job level on the incidence rates for various illnesses and other outcomes. It would seem that the model itself is concerned with the impact that control has on reactions to demands/stressors by individuals, and thus this would be the most appropriate level of analysis for testing. Indeed Morrison, Payne and Wall (2003) conducted a large multi-level study of more than 6700 employees from 81 different jobs, finding support for the model at the individual but not the job level.

An additional issue with the level of analysis has to do with whether the study investigates general job conditions for an individual or specific events. Most studies ask employees to report on the general level of stressors and control at work. It is presumed that individuals who tend to have high levels of stressors and low control are more subject to strains. However, this approach fails to recognize variability in stressors and strains over time, and fails to link specific stressor to specific control. An alternative to this approach is event sampling, in which multiple measurements are taken for individuals so that strains can be linked in time to specific instances of stressors and control. Bishop *et al.* (2003) conducted just such a study, finding support for the control buffering effect on heart rate and blood pressure.

Taken all together, there are a variety of reasons that would explain the lack of strong support for the control-demand model. These issues hold for the more complex models that add additional moderators, such as control-demand-support to be discussed next. Clearly additional research studies are needed using large samples, more precise measures of control and a variety of specific demand/stressor measures. Ideally, multi-level studies would be conducted, including both the individual employee and the job classification level. Such large-scale studies would have the statistical power to fully explore differences among types of control and stressors, and to better show the interplay between person-level and job-level relationships. Far more definitive conclusions would then be possible concerning the control-demand model. An example of a larger-scale study that allowed for a comparison of the JCQ measure of discretion (control) with a more specific measure of control was conducted by Wall *et al.* (1996) who showed that the latter but not the former yielded the hypothesized moderator effects of control on job anxiety, depression and job (dis)satisfaction.

9.2.2   Control-Demand-Support Model

The control-demand model has been expanded to include the additional buffer of social support (Karasek & Theorell, 1990). The combination of high control and high support would jointly buffer the effects of job stressors on strain. Conversely, high stressor jobs with low control and low support will be the most stressful. Some studies have found additive effects of the three components, that is, high stressors, low control and low social support tend to be associated with high levels of a variety of strains, such as job dissatisfaction, psychological distress, burnout (Akerboom & Maes, 2006; McClenahan *et al.*, 2007), and somatic symptoms (Akerboom & Maes, 2006), although not all components were significantly associated with all strains in some studies (Parkes, Mendham & von Rabenau, 1994). As with the control-demand model, tests of the multiplicative or joint buffering effects in the control-demand-support model have been inconsistent. De Lange *et al.* (2003) reviewed what they termed 'the very best' longitudinal studies of the control-demand and control-demand-support. For both models the majority of multiplicative tests were nonsignificant. Furthermore, most studies include more than one strain, and in such studies it is not uncommon to find a significant joint product term for only some of them. For example, Parkes *et al.* (1994) found a significant joint buffering effect for somatic symptoms but not job dissatisfaction.

In addition to reasons discussed with the control-demand model, some of the inconsistencies in results for the control-demand-support model might be due to variations in operationalizations of key measures. On the support side, measures differ in the sources and types of support assessed. Some measures tapped instrumental support, that is, the extent to which others offered assistance is getting things done (Sargent & Terry, 2000), whereas other studies included scales that focused more on emotion-focused support (e.g., Akerboom & Maes, 2006). In some studies the source of support mattered, for example, Sargent and Terry (2000) found a joint buffering effect with supervisor support but not coworker support. Thus it is possible that the control-demand-support model is correct, but only under certain combinations of control, demands and support.

De Jonge and Kompier (1997) critically reviewed work on the control-demand-support model, noting a number of methodological issues that might have contributed to the lack of consistent support for the buffering effects. They point out that there is ambiguity in the nature of the relationships proposed, confounding among stressors and control in many of the instruments used, confounding of stressors and control with additional variables, such as socioeconomic status and individual differences, and the possible moderating effect of personality. Finally, they note that the model suggests that characteristics of jobs are related to strain. However, almost all studies assess stressors and control through self-reports, thus making it difficult to disentangle the effects of the objective environment from people's perceptions of it.

As with the control-demand model, it might be premature to conclude that the control-demand-support model cannot be supported. Likely the joint buffering effect is rather modest in size, requiring large samples to provide conclusive tests. Furthermore, closer attention needs to be paid to the matching of control and support to stressors. As with control, support should be something that helps the individual cope with the stressor. Instrumental support to deal with heavy workloads might serve as a buffer for the effects of workload on strain, but it is unlikely to buffer the effects of social stressors. Furthermore, instrumental support is likely most beneficial for stressors that are in fact controllable. Uncontrollable stressors would best be buffered by emotional support. What the existing research has demonstrated is that the connections among control, demands and support are likely to be complex, and are in need of additional work that can help disentangle how they might interact.

9.2.3   Control-Emotion Model of Stress

Spector (1998) has proposed a control-emotion transactional model of stress that links the objective environment to perceptions of both control and stressors. As illustrated in Figure 9.3, the core of the model suggests a causal flow from the environment, through perceptions of the environment to strains. Negative emotion is the immediate response to stressors, and mediates the relationship with other forms of strain. On the physical side, negative emotion is associated with immediate physiological responses, such as increased blood pressure and secretion of cortisol into the bloodstream. Long-term exposure to such physiological responses can lead to more chronic and serious physical illness.

Control plays an important role in the model, especially perceived control. As Figure 9.3 shows, perceived control is determined by both the objective environment and personality. Individual perception is affected to a great extent by personality, as individuals who have an internal locus of control and individuals who have high self-efficacy (both of which will be discussed in detail later) are predisposed to perceive control, especially when there is ambiguity in the situation. However, perceptions are not divorced from reality, and certainly the degree to which the environment allows control affects perceptions.

The action of control in the job stress model is largely in moderating the relationship between the environment and perception of stressors. It is

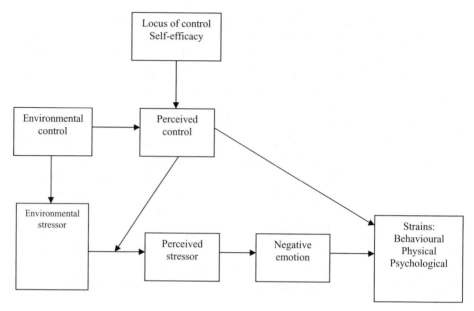

Figure 9.3 Spector's (1998) control-emotion model of stress
Source: Reprinted with permission from Paul Spector, "A control theory of the job stress procedures" in C.L. Cooper (ed.), *Theories of Organizational Stress*, Oxford University Press, New York © 1998.

situations that are seen as uncontrollable that are most likely to be seen as stressors that lead to negative emotional responses. Situations that are seen as controllable are likely to be perceived more as challenges that can be associated with more positive responses. For example, if an individual is given a job assignment, he or she will be more likely to perceive it as a stressor if he or she has no control over whether or not to accept the assignment, and if he or she perceives an inability to successfully complete the assignment. If the person perceives control over accepting the assignment and believes it is feasible to accomplish it, the perception will be quite different. If he or she sees the assignment as a chance to enhance his or her career or to develop important skills, the emotional response is likely to be positive excitement over the opportunity.

Spector (1998) discusses evidence in support of many of the links in the model. The one critical link for which evidence is limited is the potential moderating effect of perceived control on the environment-perceived stressor relationship. Few studies exist that have explored this connection, and those that have looked at the moderating effect of control on stressor measures that do not rely on employee perceptions (e.g., supervisor ratings) have not linked specific control to specific stressors. As with the control-demand and control-demand-support models, the moderating role of control is not clear.

9.3   CONTROL PREDISPOSITIONS

Most of the work linking control to stressors and strains, either as direct or moderating effects, has assumed that control affects everyone similarly (de Jonge & Kompier, 1997). However, people differ in their predisposition to perceive control, and it is indeed possible that people's personality might affect the tendency for control to relate to other variables. It is also possible that many of the findings linking perceived control to other variables are attributable in whole or part to personality, in that certain personality traits might underlie people's reports of stressors, control and strains (de Jonge & Kompier, 1997). Thus a complete treatment of control must also consider individual differences. Two personality variables are of particular concern in the study of control: locus of control (the tendency to perceive control in situations) and self-efficacy (belief in one's ability to accomplish something).

9.3.1   Locus of Control

Locus of control (Rotter, 1966) is the predisposition to believe one has control over rewards in life (internality) or that control of rewards is due to the action of luck, fate or powerful others (externality). Indeed locus of control has been shown to relate to perceived control, but the magnitude of relationship between locus of control and perceived control was surprisingly modest in a recent meta-analysis (mean $r = .16$ in Ng et al., 2007). It should be kept in mind that Ng et al. included studies that assessed autonomy which is the extent to which individuals have discretion in completing their job tasks. This is quite different from the general tendency to believe one controls rewards reflected in locus of control. An individual might easily perceive autonomy in doing tasks, but not see the link between that autonomy and rewards. For example, an employee can have a great deal of autonomy at work, but might feel relatively powerless to control raises and other rewards, or to have significant impact on the organization itself. Thus locus of control might be more relevant to some aspects of control than others. Furthermore, it might well be that the existence of autonomy is fairly obvious, leaving little room for the action of locus of control. Regardless of one's locus of control, one recognizes the existence or lack of autonomy on the immediate job. On the other hand, the rather modest convergence between incumbent and other sources on autonomy (e.g., Spector & Fox, 2003) suggests that perhaps there is a great deal of room for individual differences in perceptions. It seems that locus of control is not the major reason for such perceptual differences.

Despite the rather modest relationship between locus of control and autonomy at work, it has been linked to health and well-being at work, as well as to job stressors. Ng *et al.*'s (2007) meta-analysis showed that internality had mean correlations with mental well-being ($r = .30$), physical health whether self-reported ($r = .22$) or objectively measured ($r = .13$), job satisfaction ($r = .26$), turnover intentions ($r = -.14$) and burnout ($r = -.23$). They also reported correlations showing high levels of internality were associated with job stressors of role ambiguity (mean $r = -.15$), role conflict (mean $r = -.21$) and overall job stress (mean $r = -.19$).

Most of the studies meta-analysed by Ng *et al.* (2007) used general measures of locus of control. Spector (1988) developed a work-specific locus of control scale that assesses predispositions to perceive control over rewards (e.g., promotions and raises) at work. Some studies have shown that work locus of control relates perhaps even more strongly than indicated in the Ng *et al.* (2007) meta-analysis. For example, Spector (1988) reported relationships in five samples between work locus of control (high scores are externality) and job satisfaction (mean $r = -.54$) and turnover intentions (mean $r = .23$). These are higher in magnitude than in Ng *et al.* who scored locus of control in the opposite direction.

As suggested for perceived control, locus of control has been explored as a potential buffer of the stressor-strain relationship with inconsistent results (e.g., Lu *et al.*, 2000; Moyle & Parkes, 1999). Many of the same methodological issues arise in testing for the buffering effects of locus of control as with perceived control, such as low statistical power, and the lack of matching between control and stressor. One intriguing possibility is that the buffering effect occurs for women and not men, as was found for health symptoms by Muhonen and Torkelson (2004). Unfortunately, their study did not shed much light on the reasons for gender differences which they concluded are in need of further study.

Most of the studies that have investigated locus of control used cross-sectional designs that leave open many possible alternative explanations for results. At least two prospective studies assessed locus of control at pre test and stressors and/or strains at post test, allowing more confident conclusions about the role of personality. Moyle and Parkes (1999) surveyed supermarket employees one month prior and six months following a job transfer. They found that locus of control predicted both job satisfaction and psychological distress over time. Likewise, Spector and O'Connell (1994) assessed locus of control in a sample of college seniors during their final semester in school, and assessed job stressors and strains approximately one year after graduation. Locus of control was significantly related to job satisfaction and work anxiety, as well as autonomy, role ambiguity, role conflict and interpersonal conflict. These two studies lend more confidence to the conclusion that there is something inherent in the individual that leads to perceptions of stressors and strains. Both help rule out the possibility of occasion factors such as mood, that might have affected reports of all variables. The Spector and O'Connell study rules out the possibility that exposure to the job might have affected personality because none of the subjects in their study had begun the job prior to completing the pre-test survey.

9.3.2 Self-Efficacy

Self-efficacy is the belief an individual has that he or she can successfully accomplish an objective or outcome (Bandura, 1977). Such beliefs can be narrowly construed to a particular task of a specific difficulty level, or they can cover a broad class of situations (Bandura, 1977). Self-efficacy can be considered a personality variable in that individuals differ in their level of self-efficacy in a given context. It can also be considered a form of perceived (or believed) control, in that it reflects the extent to which a person believes he or she can turn effort into success (Bandura, 1989). As a form of control, self-efficacy is expected to be relevant to stress and well-being (Bandura, 1989; Bandura et al., 1988).

Although not entirely consistent in their findings, a number of work-place studies have found that high self-efficacy is associated with low levels of strains, including burnout (Xanthopoulou et al., 2007), emotional distress (Fillion et al., 2007; Jex & Bliese, 1999; Jex et al., 2001; Lubbers, Loughlin & Zweig, 2005; Siu, Lu & Spector, 2007), job satisfaction (Jex & Bliese, 1999) and physical health (Schaubroeck et al., 2001). An exception is Jimmieson (2000), who failed to find a significant correlation of self-efficacy with emotional strain, job satisfaction and somatic symptoms. Furthermore, self-efficacy has been shown to act as a buffer of the relationship of both demands and control with strain. For example, Jex and Bliese (1999) found that workload related to psychological and physical strain only for individuals who were low in self-efficacy. Those who were highly self-efficacious showed little to no increase in strain with increasing demands at work.

Self-efficacy has also been shown to moderate the effect of control on strain, in that individuals who are high in self-efficacy may prefer and respond well to high control, whereas their low self-efficacy counterparts may find high control to be stressful. Evidence for this possibility comes from two studies. Jimmieson (2000) found in a sample of customer service representatives that the job satisfaction of high self-efficacy individuals was lower than low self-efficacy individuals under conditions of low perceived control, and higher under conditions of high perceived control. Furthermore, the somatic health of high self-efficacious employees increased and the low self-efficacious decreased with increasing control.

A more complex three-way interaction between demands, control and self-efficacy was found by Schaubroeck, Lam and Xie (2000). Their results showed an opposite interaction between demands and control for high and low self-efficacy employees. The pattern of results supported the control-demand model for individuals high in self-efficacy in that high control buffered the impact of demands. However, for individuals low in self-efficacy, it was low control that acted as a buffer. For them, having control seemed to be counterproductive, and led to an increase in anxiety as demands increased. It seems likely that when individuals have control, but do not believe they can be effective, the control acts as an additional demand that compounds their strain. Thus control can only have a positive effect when the individual believes he or she is able to successfully use it to accomplish work goals and tasks.

9.4   MOVING FORWARD

The area of research on control has been vibrant, showing a clear connection between control and both psychological strains and physical health. As in many active research areas, we are left with perhaps more questions than answers, particularly in figuring out the extent to which control can act as a buffer of stressful job conditions. Throughout the chapter a number of methodological issues with tests of the control-demand and control-demand-support models were noted. Despite these limitations, the literature has provided some strong hints about how complex the relationships can be among control, stressors and other variables in potentially leading to strain.

One issue that is of concern in this literature is that the vast majority of studies have been cross-sectional, and usually with single-source self-report surveys. Such designs are quite useful at early stages of research to show that variables of interest are in fact related. There are some studies that have used more complex designs, such as multi-source that included both incumbents and their coworkers or supervisors. Yet others have been longitudinal, although limitations to such designs when they use arbitrary time periods need to be kept in mind (Spector, 2002). Clearly, more work is needed to rule out feasible alternative explanations for observed relationships among variables, and to better establish causal connections. The control-demand model itself is clearly implying that control plays a causal role, yet most tests involve designs that do not allow for confident causal conclusions.

In addition to design limitations, there are measurement issues that need to be considered in this area. At least some of the variability in results across studies might be attributable to the use of different measures that are not completely comparable. Furthermore, many of the tests of the control-demand model used the discretion measure from the Job Content Questionnaire (Karasek *et al.*, 1998). A number of critics have noted that this scale confounds control with task characteristics such as skill utilization (Ganster & Fusilier, 1989), so the effects of control might well be obscured.

Measures of perceived control often have rather general items that may leave themselves open to subjective biases, thus potentially confounding the measure of control with other variables. In an attempt to reduce such bias, Spector and Fox (2003) devised the Factual Autonomy Scale (FAS) that asked specific questions about the respondent's control, such as whether or not they needed a supervisor's permission to take a lunch break. In two studies they compared results with this new scale to the popular autonomy subscale of the Job Diagnostic Survey (JDS; Hackman & Oldham, 1975). Both studies were multi-source with both self-reports of autonomy by incumbents plus either supervisor (Study 1) or coworker (Study 2). Convergence of sources for both Study 1 and 2 on the FAS was considerably higher ($r =$ significant .53 and .38, respectively) than for the JDS ($r =$ nonsignificant .15 and .16, respectively). Furthermore, the relationship of job satisfaction was weaker with the FAS ($r = .09$ and .22, respectively) than with the JDS ($r = .21$ and .45, respectively). Finally, corresponding correlations of autonomy and criteria between the employees and the other two sources were closer in magnitude for the FAS than the JDS. For example, the correlations between autonomy and job performance for employees versus supervisors were .22 versus .27, respectively for the FAS, but were .04 versus .45 for the JDS. Taken together these results suggest that the FAS is assessing something that comes closer to reflecting the objective environment that is less influenced by employee attitudes (i.e., job satisfaction) and feelings about work.

Since much of the control-health literature is concerned with establishing a connection between exposure to job conditions and subsequent illness, such as heart disease, it makes sense to focus attention on general workplace conditions. However, many of the models and studies have been concerned with the underlying process by which control might operate. Such processes often occur at the moment-by-moment level, and would be best studied episodically. Event sampling methods would be particularly instructive in showing if in fact control over potentially stressful incidents affects appraisal and perception, and if it serves as a buffer alone or in combination with other factors. These methods have the potential to shed a great deal of light on the control process.

Control as it occurs in the objective environment, as it is perceived, and as an inherent part of one's personality are all important elements in stress and health. Although much of the evidence is merely suggestive, perhaps the most reasonable conclusion is that control plays an important role in health and well-being. While it might be tempting to assume that the higher the level of control the better, some studies have suggested caution in that at times control can be a detriment to people (e.g., Schaubroeck *et al.*, 2000). Thus there may well be an optimal level of control, depending upon characteristics of job environments and people. Further work is needed to better clarify exactly what those environmental and individual characteristics are, and how they interact in influencing health and well-being of employees.

REFERENCES

Aguinis, H., Beaty, J.C., Boik, R.J. & Pierce, C.A. (2005). Effect size and power in assessing moderating effects of categorical variables using multiple regression: a 30-year review. *Journal of Applied Psychology*, **90**, 94–107.

Akerboom, S. & Maes, S. (2006). Beyond demand and control: the contribution of organizational risk factors in assessing the psychological well-being of health care employees. *Work and Stress*, **20**, 21–36.

Bandura, A. (1977). Self-efficacy: toward a unifying theory of behavioral change. *Psychological Review*, **84**, 191–215.

Bandura, A. (1989). Human agency in social cognitive theory. *American Psychologist*, **44**, 1175–84.

Bandura, A., Cioffi, D., Taylor, C. & Brouillard, M.E. (1988). Perceived self-efficacy in coping with cognitive stressors and opioid activation. *Journal of Personality and Social Psychology*, **55**, 479–88.

Beehr, T.A. & Newman, J. E. (1978). Job stress, employee health, and organizational effectiveness: a facet analysis, model, and literature review. *Personnel Psychology*, **31**, 665–99.

Bishop, G.D., Enkelmann, H.C., Tong, E.M., Why, Y.P., Diong, S.M., Ang, J. *et al.* (2003). Job demands, decisional control, and cardiovascular responses. *Journal of Occupational Health Psychology*, **8**, 146–56.

Bosma, H., Stansfeld, S.A. & Marmot, M.G. (1998). Job control, personal characteristics, and heart disease. *Journal of Occupational Health Psychology*, **3**, 402–9.

Clays, E., De Bacquer, D., Delanghe, J., Kittel, F., Van Renterghem, L. & De Backer, G. (2005). Associations between dimensions of job stress and biomarkers of inflammation and infection. *Journal of Occupational & Environmental Medicine*, **47**, 878–83.

Cohen-Charash, Y. & Spector, P.E. (2001). The role of justice in organizations: a meta-analysis. *Organizational Behavior and Human Decision Processes*, **86**, 278–321.

de Jonge, J., Dollard, M.F., Dormann, C., Le Blanc, P.M. & Houtman, I.L. (2000). The demand-control model: specific demands, specific control, and well-defined groups. *International Journal of Stress Management*, **7**, 269–87.

de Jonge, J. & Kompier, M.A. (1997). A critical examination of the demand-control-support model from a work psychological perspective. *International Journal of Stress Management*, **4**, 235–58.

de Lange, A.H., Taris, T.W., Kompier, M.A., Houtman, I.L. & Bongers, P.M. (2003). 'The very best of the millennium': longitudinal research and the demand-control (support) model. *Journal of Occupational Health Psychology*, **8**, 282–305.

Del Ben, K.S., Scotti, J.R., Chen, Y.-C. & Fortson, B.L. (2006). Prevalence of post-traumatic stress disorder symptoms in firefighters. *Work and Stress*, **20**, 37–48.

Fillion, L., Tremblay, I., Truchon, M., Cote, D., Struthers, C. & Dupuis, R. (2007). Job satisfaction and emotional distress among nurses providing palliative care: empirical evidence for an integrative occupational stress-model. *International Journal of Stress Management*, **14**, 1–25.

Frankenhaeuser, M. (1978). *Psychoneuroendocrine approaches to the study of emotion as related to stress and coping:* Nebraska Symposium on Motivation Vol. 26, 123–61.

Frankenhaeuser, M. & Johansson, G. (1986). Stress at work: psychobiological and psychosocial aspects. *International Review of Applied Psychology*, **35**, 287–99.

Gallo, L.C., Bogart, L.M., Vranceanu, A.-M. & Walt, L.C. (2004). Job charac-teristics, occupational status, and ambulatory cardiovascular activity in women. *Annals of Behavioral Medicine*, **28**, 62–73.

Ganster, D.C., Fox, M.L. & Dwyer, D.J. (2001). Explaining employees' health care costs: a prospective examination of stressful job demands, personal control, and physiological reactivity. *Journal of Applied Psychology*, **86**, 954–64.

Ganster, D.C. & Fusilier, M.R. (1989). Control in the workplace. In C.L. Cooper & I.T. Robertson (Eds), *International Review of Industrial and Organizational Psychology: 1989* (pp. 1235–80). Chichester: John Wiley & Sons, Ltd.

Goldenhar, L.M., Williams, L.J. & Swanson, N.G. (2003). Modelling relationships between job stressors and injury and near-miss outcomes for construction labour-ers. *Work & Stress*, **17**, 218–40.

Griffin, J.M., Greiner, B.A., Stansfeld, S.A. & Marmot, M. (2007). The effect of self-reported and observed job conditions on depression and anxiety symptoms: a comparison of theoretical models. *Journal of Occupational Health Psychology*, **12**, 334–49.

Grönlund, A. (2007). More control, less conflict? Job demand-control, gender and work-family conflict. *Gender, Work and Organization*, **14**, 476–97.

Hackman, J. & Oldham, G.R. (1975). Development of the Job Diagnostic Survey. *Journal of Applied Psychology*, **60**, 159–70.

Heponiemi, T., Elovainio, M., Pekkarinen, L., Sinervo, T. & Kouvonen, A. (2008). The effects of job demands and low job control on work-family conflict: the role of fairness in decision making and management. *Journal of Community Psychology*, **36**, 387–98.

Huang, Y.H., Ho, M., Smith, G.S., Chen, P.Y. & Mith, S. (2006). Safety climate and self-reported injury: assessing the mediating role of employee safety control. *Accident Analysis and Prevention*, **38**, 425–33.

Jackson, S.E. & Schuler, R.S. (1985). A meta-analysis and conceptual critique of research on role ambiguity and role conflict in work settings. *Organizational Behavior and Human Decision Processes*, **36**, 16–78.

Jex, S.M. & Bliese, P.D. (1999). Efficacy beliefs as a moderator of the impact of work-related stressors: a multilevel study. *Journal of Applied Psychology*, **84**, 349–61.

Jex, S.M., Bliese, P.D., Buzzell, S. & Primeau, J. (2001). The impact of self-efficacy on stressor-strain relations: coping style as an explanatory mechanism. *Journal of Applied Psychology*, **86**, 401–9.

Jimmieson, N.L. (2000). Employee reactions to behavioural control under conditions of stress: the moderating role of self-efficacy. *Work and Stress*, **14**, 262–80.

Johnson, J.V. & Hall, E.M. (1988). Job strain, work place social support, and cardiovascular disease – A cross-sectional study of a random sample of the Swedish working population. *American Journal of Public Health*, **78**, 1336–42.

Kamarck, T.W., Muldoon, M.F., Shiffman, S.S. & Sutton-Tyrrell, K. (2007). Experiences of demand and control during daily life are predictors of carotid atherosclerotic progression among healthy men. *Health Psychology*, **26**, 324–32.

Karasek, R.A. (1979). Job demands, job decision latitude, and mental strain-implications for job redesign. *Administrative Science Quarterly*, **24**, 285–308.

Karasek, R.A., Brisson, C., Kawakami, N., Houtman, I., Bongers, P. & Amick, B. (1998). The Job Content Questionnaire (JCQ): an instrument for internationally comparative assessments of psychosocial job characteristics. *Journal of Occupational Health Psychology*, **3**, 322–55.

Karasek, R.A. & Theorell, T. (1990). *Healthy Work: Stress, Productivity and the Reconstruction of Work Life*. New York: Basic Books.

Keenan, A. & Newton, T. (1985). Stressful events, stressors and psychological strains in young professional engineers. *Journal of Occupational Behaviour*, **6**, 151–6.

Kivimäki, M., Leino-Arjas, P., Luukkonen, R., Riihimaki, H., Vahtera, J. & Kirjonen, J. (2002). Work stress and risk of cardiovascular mortality: prospective cohort study of industrial employees. *British Medical Journal*, **325**, 857.

Landsbergis, P.A., Schnall, P.L., Belkic, K.L., Schwartz, J., Pickering, T.G. & Baker, D. (2001). Work stressors and cardiovascular disease. *Work: Journal of Prevention, Assessment and Rehabilitation*, **17**, 191–208.

Lazarus, R.S. (1991). Psychological stress in the workplace. *Journal of Social Behavior and Personality*, **6**, 1–13.

Li, W., Zhang, J.-Q., Sun, J., Ke, J.-H., Dong, Z.-Y. & Wang, S. (2007). Job stress related to glyco-lipid allostatic load, adiponectin and visfatin. *Stress and Health: Journal of the International Society for the Investigation of Stress*, **23**, 257–66.

Liu, C., Spector, P.E. & Shi, L. (2007). Cross-national job stress: a quantitative and qualitative study. *Journal of Organizational Behavior*, **28**, 209–39.

Lu, L., Kao, S.-F., Cooper, C.L. & Spector, P.E. (2000). Managerial stress, locus of control, and job strain in Taiwan and UK: a comparative study. *International Journal of Stress Management*, **7**, 209–26.

Lubbers, R., Loughlin, C. & Zweig, D. (2005). Young workers' job self-efficacy and affect: pathways to health and performance. *Journal of Vocational Behavior*, **67**, 199–214.

Mausner-Dorsch, H. & Eaton, W.W. (2000). Psychosocial work environment and depression: epidemiologic assessment of the demand-control model. *American Journal of Public Health*, **90**, 1765–70.

McClenahan, C.A., Giles, M.L. & Mallett, J. (2007). The importance of context specificity in work stress research: a test of the demand-control-support model in academics. *Work and Stress*, **21**, 85–95.

Miller, S.M. (1979). Controllability and human stress: method, evidence and theory. *Behaviour Research and Therapy*, **17**, 287–304.

Morrison, D., Payne, R.L. & Wall, T.D. (2003). Is job a viable unit of analysis? A multilevel analysis of demand-control-support models. *Journal of Occupational Health Psychology*, **8**, 209–19.

Moyle, P. & Parkes, K. (1999). The effects of transition stress: a relocation study. *Journal of Organizational Behavior*, **20**, 625–46.

Muhonen, T. & Torkelson, E. (2004). Work locus of control and its relationship to health and job satisfaction from a gender perspective. *Stress and Health: Journal of the International Society for the Investigation of Stress*, **20**, 21–8.

Narayanan, L., Menon, S. & Spector, P.E. (1999). Stress in the workplace: a comparison of gender and occupations. *Journal of Organizational Behavior*, **20**, 63–73.

Ng, T.W., Sorensen, K.L., Eby, L.T. & Feldman, D.C. (2007). Determinants of job mobility: a theoretical integration and extension. *Journal of Occupational and Organizational Psychology*, **80**, 363–86.

Örtqvist, D. & Wincent, J. (2006). Prominent consequences of role stress: a meta-analytic review. *International Journal of Stress Management*, **13**, 399–422.

Parkes, K.R., Mendham, C.A. & von Rabenau, C. (1994). Social support and the demand-discretion model of job stress: tests of additive and interactive effects in two samples. *Journal of Vocational Behavior*, **44**, 91–113.

Payne, R. & Fletcher, B.C. (1983). Job demands, supports, and constraints as predictors of psychological strain among schoolteachers. *Journal of Vocational Behavior*, **22**, 136–47.

Rotter, J.B. (1966). Generalized expectancies for internal versus external control of reinforcement. *Psychological Monographs: General and Applied*, **80**(1), 1–28.

Sargent, L.D. & Terry, D.J. (2000). The moderating role of social support in Karasek's job strain model. *Work and Stress*, **14**, 245–61.

Schaubroeck, J., Jones, J.R. & Xie, J.L. (2001). Individual differences in utilizing control to cope with job demands: effects on susceptibility to infectious disease. *Journal of Applied Psychology*, **86**, 265–78.

Schaubroeck, J., Lam, S.S. & Xie, J.L. (2000). Collective efficacy versus self-efficacy in coping responses to stressors and control: a cross-cultural study. *Journal of Applied Psychology*, **85**, 512–25.

Siu, O.-l., Lu, C.-Q. & Spector, P.E. (2007). Employees' well-being in greater China: the direct and moderating effects of general self-efficacy. *Applied Psychology: An International Review*, **56**, 288–301.

Sparks, K., Cooper, C., Fried, Y. & Shirom, A. (1997). The effects of hours of work on health: a meta-analytic review. *Journal of Occupational and Organizational Psychology*, **70**, 391–408.

Spector, P.E. (1986). Perceived control by employees: a meta-analysis of studies concerning autonomy and participation at work. *Human Relations*, **39**, 1005–16.

Spector, P.E. (1987). Interactive effects of perceived control and job stressors on affective reactions and health outcomes for clerical workers. *Work and Stress*, **1**, 155–62.

Spector, P.E. (1988). Development of the Work Locus of Control Scale. *Journal of Occupational Psychology*, **61**, 335–40.

Spector, P.E. (1992). A consideration of the validity and meaning of self-report measures of job conditions. In C.L. Cooper & I.T. Robertson (Eds), *International Review of Industrial and Organizational Psychology: 1992* (pp. 123–51). Chichester: John Wiley & Sons, Ltd.

Spector, P.E. (1998). A control model of the job stress process. In C.L. Cooper (Ed.), *Theories of Organizational Stress* (pp. 153–69). Oxford: Oxford University Press.

Spector, P.E. (2002). Research methods in industrial and organizational psychology: data collection and data analysis with special consideration to professional issues. In N. Anderson, D.S. Ones, H.K. Sinangil & C. Viswesvaran (Eds), *Handbook of industrial, work and organizational psychology, Volume 1: Personnel psychology* (pp. 10–26). Thousand Oaks, CA: Sage.

Spector, P.E., Dwyer, D.J. & Jex, S.M. (1988). Relation of job stressors to affective, health, and performance outcomes: a comparison of multiple data sources. *Journal of Applied Psychology*, **73**, 11–19.

Spector, P.E. & Fox, S. (2003). Reducing subjectivity in the assessment of the job environment: development of the factual autonomy scale (FAS). *Journal of Organizational Behavior*, **24**, 417–32.

Spector, P.E. & Jex, S.M. (1998). Development of four self-report measures of job stressors and strain: Interpersonal Conflict at Work Scale, Organizational Constraints Scale, Quantitative Workload Inventory, and Physical Symptoms Inventory. *Journal of Occupational Health Psychology*, **3**, 356–67.

Spector, P.E. & O'Connell, B.J. (1994). The contribution of personality traits, negative affectivity, locus of control and Type A to the subsequent reports of job stressors and job strains. *Journal of Occupational and Organizational Psychology*, **67**, 1–12.

Spell, C.S. & Arnold, T. (2007). An appraisal perspective of justice, structure, and job control as antecedents of psychological distress. *Journal of Organizational Behavior*, **28**, 729–51.

Terry, D.J. & Jimmieson, N.L. (1999). Work control and employee well-being: a decade review. In C.L. Cooper & I.T. Robertson (Eds), *International Review of Industrial and Organizational Psychology: 1999* (pp. 95–148). Chichester: John Wiley & Sons, Ltd.

Thompson, S.C. (1981). Will it hurt less if I can control it? A complex answer to a simple question. *Psychological Bulletin*, **90**, 89–101.

Wall, T.D., Jackson, P.J., Mullarkey, S. & Parker, S.K. (1996). The demands-control model of job strain: a more specific test. *Journal of Occupational and Organizational Psychology*, **69**, 153–66.

Xanthopoulou, D., Bakker, A.B., Demerouti, E. & Schaufeli, W.B. (2007). The role of personal resources in the job demands-resources model. *International Journal of Stress Management*, **14**, 121–41.

CHAPTER 10

Stress and Careers

Yehuda Baruch

Norwich Business School, University of East Anglia, UK

Motto

Stress is sometimes the price many people are happy to pay for a successful career. It is also a factor that sends successful careers to their downfall.

Stress is a major factor in human life, and can influence people in many ways, either positively or negatively. The management of stress is crucial for both individual and organizational processes. Within the work realm, stress can come in the form of occupational stress, job stress, organizational stress and other types of stress-related issues. A number of studies have examined the impact of stress on work attitudes and outcomes, but there is less knowledge and understanding about the specific impact of work-related stress on people's careers (Clarke & Cooper, 2004, p. 23). In this chapter I will investigate the association in terms of career choice, commitment and success at the individual level, and explore the relevance of organizational interventions like career planning and management for work stress.

Much of the literature on stress and its impact focuses on the negative aspects of high-stress environments. There are two principal reasons for this tendency. First, the phenomenon of people suffering from high levels of stress and its negative outcomes (e.g. anxiety, burnout) reflects a reality in many contemporary workplaces. The second reason is concerned with political correctness. It is easier for academic scholars to take the high-moral ground view and preach to managers and executives about the need to be positive, supportive and accommodating towards employees, whereas business needs and fierce competition might mean that many professions and roles are highly demanding. This is particularly true for managerial roles. To compete effectively and motivate employees, managers may need to put a certain level of pressure on their employees. At the same time, effective

International Handbook of Work and Health Psychology, Third Edition. Edited by Cary L. Cooper, James Campbell Quick, and Marc J. Schabracq.

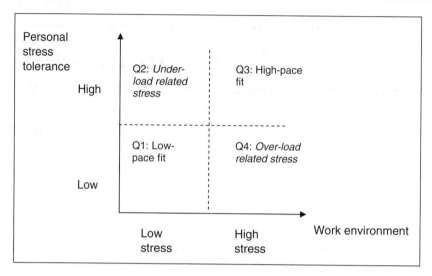

Figure 10.1 Fit between personal stress tolerance and work environment characteristics

management would require high ability to manage and cope with stress. In
this chapter I will reflect on both perspectives. First, why stress is an essential
part of the modern work environment – required for effective performance;
and second, why stress should be kept at a manageable level.

Figure 10.1 presents the four quadrants of fit along two dimensions. These
two dimensions are the individual level of stress tolerance and the work environment characteristics, which reflect vocational, professional and occupational characteristics. It is a schematic framework, and there are a number of
other inputs and factors that determine prospects of fit and either negative or
positive impacts of stress at work. These factors include a range of personal
sensitivities and a variety of possible stressors.

The framework presented in Figure 10.1 relates to the theory of person–job
fit (Cable & Judge, 1996; Edwards, 1991) and career choice (Holland, 1959).
Holland claims that high fit between personal attributes and the characteristics
of the work environment would lead to both high job performance and job
satisfaction. Vast empirical evidence supports this assertion (Assouline &
Meir, 1987). Conversely, discrepancy between the two would lead to poor
performance and low satisfaction.

The four quadrants are:

- *Q1: Low-pace fit.* This quadrant represents cases where people have low
  stress tolerance, prefer to avoid a high-stress, high-demanding work atmosphere, and where the work environment provides them with such needs.
  One may think of a person who wishes to have a quiet place, with relatively

low intellectual demands and minimal surprises. For such a person, the role of allocating returned books into the correct shelves in a library might be an ideal job.

- *Q2: Under-load related stress.* In this quadrant, people with a high need for stimulation, who look for challenges and possibly high rewards, are placed in a non-demanding work environment. Take an ambitious law graduate who aspires to be a top barrister finding herself in a back-office of a solicitor's practice, having to draft conventional lease contracts for property transactions.
- *Q3: High-pace fit.* Some people enjoy the rough and tumble of business life. Stock-market traders flourish when they are constantly put under pressure, given high (but manageable) targets, immerse themselves in the job, and gain high personal and financial benefits. For such people this quadrant represents a best-fit model.
- *Q4: Over-load related stress.* The contemporary business environment is very dynamic and competitive. It puts high demands on people, and for many it is more than they can cope with. The pressure may be to reach unattainable performance targets, stay for long hours, or work in hazardous and risky environments, to name a few factors (Cooper & Baglioni, 1988). Examples can be overwork, long working hours (Peiperl & Jones, 2001) and extreme workaholism (Burke, 1999).

People need to work for a number of reasons, not merely to gain income. Work gives purpose in life, helps to shape identity development (Ibarra, 2003) and satisfies a wide range of human needs (Baruch, 2004). People need work, and as adults, they find identity and are identified by the work they do (Gini, 1998). Work offers challenges, which is a great thing – but challenges are associated with stress. Stress is part of life, and thus part of work. Management of stress is a key factor to appropriate functioning.

As a sense-making rule of thumb, people should aim to avoid both Q2 and Q4, because operating under such conditions is very likely to generate negative stress, possibly leading to distress and burnout (Maslach, 2006), and subsequently ending with negative career outcomes such as poor performance, withdrawal and career frustration or crisis. Q2 environments lead to boredom (Game, 2007) and feeling of being undervalued and underperforming, whereas Q4 environments lead to both psychological (e.g. anxiety) and physiological or medical setbacks (Kivimäki *et al.*, 2002). People who have effective boredom-coping strategies reported significantly better job-related affective well-being (lower depression and anxiety) compared with those who do not cope well (Game, 2007).

Much of the literature on work-related stress focuses on the over-load related stress. This is mainly due to negative outcomes, in particular burnout.

Job burnout is a psychological syndrome that involves a prolonged response to chronic interpersonal stressors on the job (Maslach, 2006). It has a significant negative impact on work and health-related outcomes (Melamed *et al.*, 2006). In extreme cases, overwork can lead to the ultimate outcome – death due to hard work – known as *karoshi* in Japan, where it became an unfortunate phenomenon in a culture of high-stress work environments (Kawakami & Haratani, 1999; Nishiyama & Johnson, 1997).

10.1 PERSONAL DIFFERENCES

Different people have different 'stress triggers'. A person can cope very well and enjoy a highly demanding business environment working with sophisticated computer systems dealing with future commodities. Put that same person in front of kindergarten children, and the stress level can become unbearable. Take the same library worker from the Q1 example, and ask her to deal with anxious students needing a limited number of books before exams and arrogant academics demanding books required for their research but are not on the shelf where they are supposed to be, and the same person will suffer considerable stress. Dealing with people, dealing with information technology, dealing with numbers – each task requires different faculties and qualities, and can put certain people under severe stress, whereas for others it would be a preferred situation to manage.

Individual personality is then a major factor. Cattell's 16PF (Cattell & Kline, 1977) is an example of a validated tool that can help to identify right or wrong fit.

Let us look at the following five of the 16 factors:

- emotional vs. emotionally stable;
- shy, restrained vs. venturesome, bold;
- tough minded vs. tender minded;
- confident, complacent vs. worrying, insecure; and in particular
- relaxed, tranquil vs. tense, frustrated.

These factors are crucial in figuring out which type of person might be inclined to high stress if allocated a role in the Q2 or Q4 quadrants. Someone who is 'venturesome, bold', who finds himself positioned in a quiet, monotonous role, would suffer stress due to under-load, whereas someone who is 'tender minded' and perhaps also 'worrying, insecure' would be under the danger of a nervous breakdown if positioned in a role within the Q4 environment.

Many other factors can influence people's careers and priorities. Some are demographics, though most are related to individual differences associated with personality, values and competences. Gender impact is relevant, as are many other areas of individual differences and managerial practices. Working women have to endure the dual stress of work and being the major child carer and thus are more inclined to suffer stress (Hobfoll *et al.*, 1994). Differences related to occupational level and/or gender were found for autonomy and social support at work, competitiveness, gender role and reported conflict between demands from paid work and other responsibilities (Frankenhaeuser *et al.*, 1989). The stress profile of female managers was considered in terms of possible long-term health risks.

Mainiero and Sullivan (2006), in their *Kaleidoscope Careers*, identified three 'mirrors' through which people examine their career priorities. These are:

- *Authenticity*: a striving to be genuine, to be one's true self, to create a healthy alignment between one's values and outward behaviours.
- *Balance*: finding a healthy congruence between work and non-work.
- *Challenge*: the need to continuously learn and find stimulating, exciting work.

They argue that two factors are instrumental in setting career priorities across the three 'mirrors' – career stage and gender. Alpha and Beta are identified as two 'archetypes':

- Alpha – mostly characterizing males:
  - early life into midlife: focus on challenge;
  - latter part of midlife: focus on authenticity;
  - later life: focus on balance.
- Beta – mostly characterizing females:
  - early life: focus on challenge;
  - midlife: focus on balance;
  - later life: focus on authenticity.

Intuitively, high challenge may cause certain stress levels, which can be energizing for further career investment, but less so when people find they cannot manage the stress. The need for balance emerges from levels of stress in ones career.

A different factor influencing feelings of stress is the ability to control a situation. Less ambiguity reduces stress (Cooper, 1983, 1998, 2002). Studies showed that being in control, even when the situation is apparently highly stressful, enables executives to feel less stressed (Baruch & Woodward, 1998).

More generally, looking at an integrated model of career stages (Baruch, 2004, p. 54), different sources for stress, which might arise in different stages of a person's career, can be identified (Table 10.1).

As can be seen, stress-inducing issues vary across the career stages. One in particular, which spans over the whole career cycle, is the need for money. While positive thinking and philosophical writing suggest that money is not a strong motivator, lack of money is certainly a major stressor. The use of money will vary – from getting on the housing ladder, to purchasing basics and luxuries, through to enabling dignified retirement (see Feldman, 2007, p. 163). People need money, people need purpose, and people need fulfilment. Maslow's hierarchy of needs is not dead, but for different people the priorities vary, and they certainly vary throughout the different career stages. People make mistakes along the way – and while we can learn best from mistakes, studies about career mistakes are rarely reported in the literature. A typical mistake can be a mismatch between expectations and reality, which may arise because expectations are based on individual experience rather than on information provided by the organization (Blenkinsopp & Zdunczyk, 2005).

As I mentioned in my book (Baruch, 2004), a major difference between the early models on career stages and the integrated model is the ability and availability of re-running stages (b)–(e) (see Table 10.1) for another round or more of the career cycle. This is a significant contribution to stress release for people. In the past people were stuck in a career, having no real choice to move on. In contemporary labour markets, people are more free to chose and change their careers (Hall, 1996, 2002). Contemporary labour markets are dynamic and career changes are frequent, many times initiated and led by individuals (Hall, 1996; Peiperl & Baruch, 1997). Not everyone can move easily, though. People may find they are stuck in a certain career, not progressing, and yet do not have the ability or will to change, they are at a plateau, which can be another factor causing stress (Elsass & Ralston, 1989).

Career-related stressors may come in the shape of too fast success, too low success, plateau in success, or the 'wrong' type of success (Derr, 1986). Derr pointed out five individual career success indicators or dimensions:

(a) Getting ahead: motivation derives from the need to advance both in professional standing and up the organizational ladder.
(b) Getting secure: having a solid position within the organization.
(c) Getting high: being inspired by the nature and content of the work performed.

Table 10.1 Career stage and sources of career stress

Stage	Description	Sources of stress – individual quest
(a) Foundation	Childhood and adolescence experience and education help in planting the seeds of career aspiration	What do I want to do when I grow up? What do I need to do to gain it? How do I deal with uncertainty?
(b) Career entry	Usually through attainment of profession. Can be done via being an apprentice, training on the job, attending college, university or other professional training. Usually even for qualified people, the first stage of work will include further professional establishment	Will I get a job? Will I keep it? Is it the right place to start? Where it may lead me? Is the money enough?
(c) Advancement	Both professional and hierarchical development within organization(s) or expanding own business. This stage can be characterized with either continuous advancement or reaching a plateau. In today's career environment and concepts, this stage will typically be associated with several changes of employer	Am I advancing? Is it a good pace of advancement? How do I do against my reference group? Do I do too much? How can I manage multiple commitments – what price do I pay in terms of my other life interests? Is the money enough?
(d) Re-evaluation	Checking match between aspiration and fulfilment; rethinking job/role/career. Can emerge from internal feeling or need (e.g., bored due to lack of challenge, life crisis), or external force (redundancy, professional obsolescence). May end with decision to keep in the same path or change career direction, returning to stage (b)	Shall I change? To What? What will it cost me vs. what I may gain from it? Can I deal with risk taking? Will the money still be enough?

(continued)

Table 10.1   *(Continued)*

Stage	Description	Sources of stress – individual quest
(e) Reinforcement	After making the decision a reinforcement of present career or returning to the learning stage (b) for re-establishment of a new career cycle	Am I adjusting well? Am I still worth it? Do I gain self-actualization?
(f) Decline	Most but the few (who have full life of advancement until the latest moment) will start at a certain stage to envisage a withdrawal from working life, which can be swift or long term, spreading over a few years	When shall I retire? Shall I do something else? Will the money be enough?
(g) Retirement	Leaving the labour market (not necessarily at age 65)	What should I do? Will it be satisfying? Will I manage with the money?

(d) Getting free: being motivated by a need for autonomy and the ability to create your own work environment.

(e) Getting balanced: attaching equal or greater value to non-work interests.

People with different career aims are inclined to suffer stress for different reasons. For example, if someone's aim is to reach the top of the ladder at any cost, this is a case of extreme careerism, which may mean that certain people are too eager and ambitious, leading to manipulative behaviour on their side (Bratton & Kacmar, 2004). Such a rat-race career is very stressing, and if a person does not reach their aim it leads to frustration, inevitable when many aim to reach the top, where positions are few and contenders are many. Others who look for autonomy may benefit from an entrepreneurship career (Fuller & Tian, 2006). Having one's own business puts high risk on the entrepreneur, again a possible source of stress.

Thus, the role of management, as I will elaborate on later, is to realize the various sources for stress, and to treat different people in different ways. This is not to say by discrimination – all should have equal opportunity. Yet, sense-making means realization and acceptance of differences.

10.2 WHAT IS THE 'RIGHT' LEVEL OF STRESS?

Figure 10.2 shows the inverse U curve relationship between stress and performance. Basically it builds on the activation theory, which anticipates behaviour related to variations in task design (Scott, 1966). Too low level of stress might lead to withdrawal, lack of interest and stimuli. Too high level of stress might lead to lack of ability to cope, and withdrawal due to over-load.

The cognitive activation theory of stress (CATS), suggested by Ursin and Eriksen (2004), used the term 'stress' for four aspects: stress stimuli; stress experience; the non-specific, general stress response; and experience of the stress response. Activation theory (Berlyne, 1960, 1963; Fiske & Maddi, 1961) argues that people, employees in the context of work and careers, try to alter their stimulus field so as to attain an optimal level of the potential to create personal stimulation. When the actual stimulation is below the optimal level, discomfort in the form of boredom results. When the stimulation is above that optimal level, it produces discomfort in the form of stress. Both boredom and stress are negative affective states.

The stress response is a general alarm in a homeostatic system, producing general and unspecific neurophysiological activation from one level of stimulation to another. Stress response is an essential and necessary response (Ursin & Eriksen, 2004). The unpleasantness of the alarm is no health threat. However, if sustained, the response may lead to negative results – in

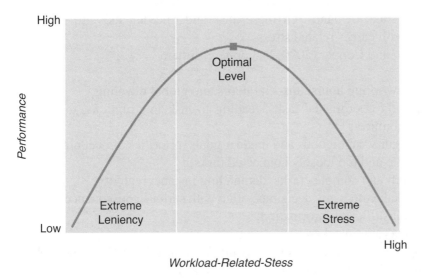

Figure 10.2 Assumed association between work-related stress and work performance

terms of work attitudes, behaviours, as well as physiological results such as illness. Much research was conducted following Beehr and Newman's (1978) call for further study on the impact of job stress on employees' health.

Stressors can operate at individual and organizational level. Up to this point my emphasis has been at the individual level of analysis.

10.3 STRESS MANAGEMENT – ORGANIZATIONAL PERSPECTIVE

Moving to the organizational level, there are major factors contributing to a level of stress for individual employees (at all levels, including managerial). The prominent ones are general change, in particular changes involving restructuring and downsizing – not only for those made redundant, but for the survivors too (Brokner *et al.*, 1992). Mergers and acquisitions (Cartwright & Cooper, 1996; Larsson & Finkelstein, 1999) and overall anxiety (Baruch & Lambert, 2007) are catalysts for increased stress levels across organizations.

Again, it must be remembered that while change might cause stress, having no change is not an option in the current dynamic business and social environment. Steadiness in time of environmental dynamism means lack of ability to respond. This too can generate stress.

The following list of stress-related organizational causes was suggested by Quick and Quick (1984): task demands; physical demands; role demands; and interpersonal demands. Of these, task and role demands are strongly associated with career-related stress.

Schabracq and Cooper (2000) elaborated further:

- too many working hours, unsocial hours and global traveling;
- inadequately coordinated tasks, leading to task interruptions, territorial and role conflicts;
- role ambiguity, ambiguous and unclear goals, priorities, procedures;
- too variable and too loosely connected tasks;
- too difficult and complex tasks, demanding instant creativity;
- having to take too many decisions, often with serious consequences, often based on insufficient information;
- risks of making mistakes;
- working in different and changing configurations of very diverse people;
- exposure to 'contagiously' stressful colleagues;
- exposure to frequent changes in tasks, equipment, managers, colleagues, working arrangements, production processes and jobs;

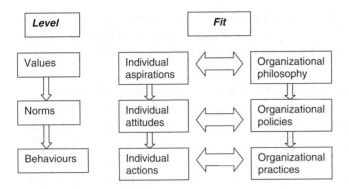

Figure 10.3 The career active system triad.
Adapted from Baruch, Y. (2004). *Managing Careers: Theory and Practice*. Harlow: FT-Prentice Hall/Pearson

- spill-over to other life domains;
- organizational changes such as acquisitions*, outsourcing, lay-off and job mobility between organizations.

The CAST – Career Active System Triad (see Figure 10.3) – manifests how individuals and organizations plan and manage careers at three different levels. At the individual level, relating to career-related stress, people may take various actions, as described in the early section of this chapter. At the organizational level, the organization needs to develop a set of policies, derived from its strategy and leading philosophy of management. Employing 'best practice' would help to control and reduce high levels of stress and ensure people have enough stimuli to avoid under-load stress induced reactions.

The challenges for the organization are to maintain a fit between individual needs, competences and career aims and the organizational operational and future goals.

Gaining both procedural and distributive justice is of high relevance in generating acceptable psychological contracts (Herriot & Pemberton, 1996). Matching individual career plans and organizational career management is a real test for managing the new psychological contract. The concept is not new (see Granrose & Portwood, 1987).

Rousseau argues that people gain specific employment arrangements that, on the positive side, enable flexibility, but may also lead to injustice

---

* Note that in their original list, Schabracq and Cooper refer to mergers, but there is rarely, if ever real merging of two firms into one new coherent blend of the two – it is almost always that one firm is taking over the other. I thus prefer the term acquisition. The stressors would be different for each part of the new firm – those taking over and those being taken over.

(Rousseau, 2004, p. 265). A number of career management practices exists (see Baruch 1999, 2004), many of these can help in maintaining career-related stress at a manageable level. Later in this chapter I will focus on such cases.

However, there are also negative practices. An example of problematic practices is forcing employees and managers to work overtime (Peiperl & Jones, 2001). Long hour culture is a clear factor that causes spill-over from work to family life, generating inevitable conflicts (Bellavia & Frone, 2005). Lee and Ashforth's (1996) meta-analysis examined how demand and resource correlates and behavioural and attitudinal correlates were related to three different dimensions of job burnout. They found that emotional exhaustion is more strongly related to the demand correlates than to the resource correlates, suggesting that workers might have been sensitive to the possibility of resource loss.

Job strain (job dissatisfaction, depression, psychosomatic symptoms) and burnout were found to be higher in jobs that combine high workload demands with low decision latitude (Landsbergis, 1988). Indeed, being in control is a factor that reduces stress even in highly demanding positions and roles (Baruch & Woodward, 1998).

While Clarke and Cooper (2004, p. 23) lamented the apparent lack of studies on the specific impact of work-related stress on people's careers, some issues such as burnout have been intensively studied. There is clear evidence based on empirical research that supports the assumptions that high levels of work stress lead to negative work outcomes (Harpaz & Snir, 2003; Porter, 2004; Spence & Robbins, 1992), and non-work outcomes (Bonebright, Clay & Ankenmann, 2000; Gini, 1998). The mechanism by which stress leads to such outcomes is typically via burnout, and the results of burnout are detrimental to people's career and well-being (Westman & Eden, 1997). Another direction of the relationship is that career stressors like lack of promotion opportunities lead to negative outcomes, such as involuntary turnover (Jones et al., 2007; 2008McCabe et al., 2008; Reisenberg, 2005) and even accidents (Clarke & Cooper, 2004, p. 144). Short-term fix-it solutions would not necessarily work in the long run. For example, providing a vacation is not a long-term solution, as stress levels are fast to return within a short time (Westman & Eden, 1997).

It is hard, probably impossible to 'win' the delicate balance of maintaining career-related stress. There are a number of stressors, many of them that are not under the control of a single person or organization. And as indicated, it is not about simply minimizing stress, but finding the right measure, the optimal level, a moving target which depends on individual characteristics, and changes as time goes by.

10.3.1   Organizational Interventions and Practices to Identify and Tackle Career-Related Stress

The so-called 'best practice' offers a number of organizational interventions, policies and practices, and it is assumed that appropriate application of these would help in many ways, including in the management of career-related stress. First I wish to point out that the expression 'best practice' is contradictory to both contingency theory and common sense. Contingency means that under different circumstances, different actions should be taken. Thus a given set of 'best practice' cannot serve as a 'one-size-fits-all' option.

There is a further contradiction inherent in the label 'best practice': let us assume that there is such a thing as a well-known, valid and reliable set of practices that enhance individual and organizational performance. If that is the case, each organization will employ these 'best practices' and all will be successful, above their competition. But the competition would also employ it, meaning that all will be 'best'. In fact, to have a competitive advantage over others means doing things differently – contradicting the basic concept of 'best practice'.

Yet, some caveats for the above arguments are valid too. It is not only the 'what', but also the 'how' of these practices. Having a 'mentoring' system is great HR practice in general (Kram, 1985), but even this practice can become dysfunctional (Scandura, 1998; Scandura & Pellegrini, 2007) and cause more harm than good. Generally, though, mentoring is a type of career practice that could help in stress management, not necessarily directly, by helping individuals set themselves attainable career goals. Similar impact can be made from the availability of career counselling. Some of the impact of these practices derives from having social support within the organizational boundaries. Social support was found to buffer the impact on physical aspects of stress such as anxiety, depression and somatic symptoms, but not for job attitudes like job satisfaction and boredom (LaRocco, House & French, 1980).

10.4   A PORTFOLIO OF STRESS-RELATED CAREER MANAGEMENT PRACTICES

Below is listed the wide portfolio of career management practices that may be associated with stress management (for the full list see Baruch, 1999, 2004). Clear practices can help in controlling and reducing negative stress, even in a 'lean production' environment (Conti et al., 2006).

Posting (advertising) internal job openings

Ambiguity increases stress, thus when organizations openly publish new vacancies within, and let current employees have a first go at applying for these positions, that is a best practice which reduces ambiguity, hence, indirectly, helps in stress prevention.

Formal education as part of career development

Some organizations select people of managerial or technical potential and send them on a programme of formal study as part of their development path. This may take the shape of short training courses, and span up to a full university degree sponsorship. This practice manifests that the employer is happy to make investment in human capital and value its people. Not directly aimed at stress reduction, but improves well-being in general.

Lateral moves to create cross-functional experience

Lateral moves to create cross-functional experience are on the increase, and may be seen as elementary career planning and management practices which most organizations with HRM systems need to apply. The flattening of organization means fewer hierarchy levels, and thus fewer opportunities for upward mobility. If that was the case, lateral moves would be seen as a failure indicator, and thus generate stress. When this is done widely and accepted as a slow burn to the top, such moves will be accepted and not inflict stress and negative feeling on the employees.

Retirement preparation programs

This practice is directed at a target population of employees approaching retirement and about to leave the organization. In these programs the employee is prepared to face the retirement in several ways. Attention is devoted to financial considerations such as understanding the pension conditions and learning tax regulations as well as to psychological issues surrounding an individual's need to re-adjust to life without work. This practice certainly helps to reduce stress which will otherwise be induced due to the approaching major life change for retiring people (and can be relevant to people facing early retirement as a replacement of redundancy).

Booklets and/or pamphlets on career issues

Booklets, pamphlets or leaflets on career issues represent a formal presentation by an organization regarding all kinds of career-related information. Such information is useful to reduce ambiguity, and similarly to the job posting practice, indirectly reduces stress.

Dual ladder

The dual ladder provides an organizational hierarchy for non-managerial staff, such as professional or technical employees, that is parallel to the managerial hierarchy. The major role of such a ladder is to enable 'upward mobility' and recognition for those employees who cannot or do not wish to pursue a managerial role in the organization. Without such an option, stress levels can be high if people cannot see a route for promotion.

Induction or socialization

The process of introducing people to their new organization is the first CPM practice which the employee experiences. This is a process whereby all newcomers learn the behaviours and attitudes deemed necessary for assuming roles in the organization as well as reinforcing organizational identity. Part of this process is formal, led by organizational officials, whereas other aspects may be acquired more effectively via informal routes. Smooth induction helps people to be more relaxed in the first stages of their employment.

Assessment and development centers

Assessment centers have been found as a reliable and valid tool for identifying managerial potential and for developmental processes. They are used to increase and manifest procedural justice, crucial in developing a stress-free culture in terms of equality, though their existence may imply a culture of promotion to those deemed worthy of progress. Such a culture is inevitably one that generates stress – which can be the right level for encouraging people to target managerial roles, even though these roles tend to be stressful.

Mentoring

The principal aim of mentoring is to bring together a person with managerial potential and an experienced manager, who is not necessarily the direct manager. Such a senior manager can provide advice and tutoring, serving as metaphorical 'uncle/aunt' in the workplace. This practice helps to reduce stress by the availability of support and consulting options. Yet, mentoring might also be dysfunctional, due, for example, to a negative relationship between mentor and protégé, a possible collision of interests between the individual's mentor and his or her direct manager, and the challenges of managing a cross-gender relationship.

Career workshops

Career workshops are short-term workshops focusing on specific aspects of career management that aim to provide managers with relevant knowledge, skills and experience. These can help to reduce career ambiguity and prepare people for progress and development, again, reducing unwarranted stress.

Performance appraisal as a basis for career planning

In the vast majority of organizations, and certainly when organizational size passes the threshold of a few hundred, a formal system of performance appraisal (PA) is often introduced. It serves both evaluation needs and de-velopmental purposes. PA is perhaps the most fundamental system to be utilized by HR to provide information regarding internal human capital. The appraised member of the organization is put under pressure, which may be the right level of push they need to invest in their future in the organiza-tion in order to become best performers. It is not the opportunity to inflict harsh derogatory feedback on the employee (unless, of course, the employee 'deserves' to be told, for example, if they were not performing, or harass-ing colleagues). The appraiser running the process is also under pressure and possible stress – it is not the easiest task to tell people that they are under-performers. A different method is providing a 360-degree feedback, a relatively new system introduced in the 1990s, and adopted by a number of organizations, utilizing sources such as self-appraisal, peer appraisal, upward appraisal and a combination of several sources in addition to that given by the direct manager. This practice is very demanding in terms of the time that needs to be invested and the analysis that needs to be conducted.

Career counselling

Career counselling represents a two-way communication between the em-ployer and the employee for formal or informal discussion about the future of the employee, within or outside the organizational boundaries. Two main sources are available to conduct the counselling: the direct manager (or another higher manager) and the HRM manager. Depending on the complexity and the financial resources of the organization, external counselling can also be provided. Such counselling, when done appropriately, will eliminate possible sources of stress (and when done inappropriately might induce unnecessary stress too).

Succession planning

Succession planning determines the possible replacement of every manager within the organizational ranks, and evaluates the promotional potential of each manager. It is primarily directed towards the managerial workforce. Careful analysis of the succession planning should be concerned with its implications for other CPM practices. The availability of succession planning means people can learn the prospects for their future, and thus reduces stress, in particular if they are perceived as high potential. Knowing that others compete for the same future role, though, might generate competition-related stress.

Programmes for special populations of employees

With an increasing level of employee diversity, new work arrangements and globalization, career practices need to address the needs of specific populations, such as ethnic minorities, women, physically disabled, expatriation/repatriation and dual-career couples. Under the banner of equal opportunities and with increased litigation brought against companies, organizations realize the need to go beyond paying lip service to equality and to make sure that all members are given fair promotional opportunities. This is certainly a stress reduction practice. Yet, some might suspect positive discrimination in a way that achieving balance is challenging to the HR manager.

Building psychological contracts

The establishment of new psychological contracts can be counted among the new career planning management practices. I have already introduced in the early part of the chapter the concept of psychological contract as a crucial aspect of the employment relationship and thus a stress-mitigating factor. Breaking or breaching these psychological contracts is a stress-generating event, in particular redundancies. Organizations should be able to set the 'unwritten rules' in a sensible way, without generating apparent conflicts with the formal, legal contract.

Secondments

Another new career planning management practice is the secondment – a temporary assignment to another area within the organization, and sometimes even to another associated organization (such as a customer or supplier). A person from the managerial or professional echelons of one organization is transferred to another organization for a specific time period (usually 1–3 years). Experience is shared to benefit both the organizations and the individual involved. When this is done as an alternative to redundancy, it helps to prevent the redundancy-related stress.

Written personal career planning for employees

The CPM practice of having written personal career planning for employees represents long-term commitment, but such a promise for life-time employment has become virtually an extinct feature of organizational life. Written personal career plans are also problematic in the sense of creating employee expectations that the organization may not be capable of fulfilling, inducing long-term stress. This practice is rarely applied in the contemporary workplace.

Common career paths

A career path is the most preferred and recommended route for the career advancement of a manager in an organization. Such career paths may be based on the way former executives progressed to top positions ('historic path') or on a thorough analysis of the requirements from certain top positions ('logic path'). The use of career paths spread rapidly in the 1970s and 1980s and led people through various departments and units within the organization. It can make sense in very complex organizations. With traditional hierarchical structures flattening and diminishing and with the creation of boundaryless careers, it has become the norm, rather than the exception, for organizations to have no fixed career paths and for individuals to see no further than one or two years ahead.

To these specific HR practices I would add the existence of clear leadership. Leadership is another factor within the organization that can help people manage their career and cope with career-related stress, but poor leadership can harm, for example, poorly led reward systems (Kelloway *et al.*, 2005.

p. 98) and instead of reassuring employees about the future, can create anxiety and fear (Baruch & Lambert, 2007).

10.5   INDIVIDUAL IMPLICATIONS

People need to be aware of their own level of stress compared with their own 'optimal' level of stress. They can then learn how to manage stress, and 'live in peace' with it.

After setting awareness, people should identify the various sources of stress (there are rarely single causes of stress), and then develop suitable coping strategies and practices. It is more difficult to identify unconscious sources of stress, though they do exist.

Macik-Frey, Quick and Nelson, (2007) have pointed out the burden of health-related suffering due to stress and consider both the economic and humanitarian results of poor occupational health. For employees with high job strain, a combination of high demands at work and low job control had a 2.2-fold cardiovascular mortality risk compared with their colleagues with low job strain (Kivimäki *et al.*, 2002). The reader can find more on individual responses and approaches to stress in other chapters of this *Handbook*, as the present chapter is more focused on the organizational perspective.

10.6   MANAGERIAL IMPLICATIONS

Employees need a push. Sometimes they will have an inner push, a strong urge to work, an ambition that energizes them to invest in achieving work-desirable outcomes. Sometimes the drive needs to come from the system, typically from managers. Managers should be aware that this should be a push forward, not a push over the cliff.

It is the role of 'management' to identify how much people can do and wish to do, and find out how to motivate them. Stress management is not a creation of tranquillity in the workplace. Yet, if people are pushed too hard, they can reach the stage of burnout, and this will be too late and will require double the amount of managerial effort to regain their trust and get them back to work. Thus it is much better to focus on prevention and identification of initial signs of high stress. Treatment might mean having to move an employee to a less demanding role, or losing him or her entirely.

10.7   WHOSE JOB IT IS?

People management should be undertaken by *all* managers. And the responsibility for it should rest also at the individual level. Human resource management should be the guide, the facilitator and the policy maker. Direct managers should apply the policies.

Management should not take overall responsibility – this should be shared with all employees. Much of the feeling of stress is self-imposed. The way people perceive pressure determines whether they are stressed by it. There is a certain level of inner choice between seeing it as positive in terms of providing challenges and opportunities or as negative, taking it as a threat, which might result in anxiety and burnout. Managers can help employees realize that they have a choice in controlling stress.

New careerists may mean many things and HR managers need to be able to realize the variance and how to deal with it. Such is Derr's (1986) differentiation of career success characteristics for different people. Similarly the Kaleidoscope careerists need HR policies that allow them to make changes in their careers given their needs for authenticity, balance and challenge (Mainiero & Sullivan, 2006). But, even if individuals have aims of progress and high investment, managers may need to step in and make sure that workaholism does not lead to a wide variety of life and work-related problems (Burke, 1999; Porter, 2004).

Psychological contracts should be established (Rousseau, 1996). They reduce ambiguity, clarify mutual expectations and lead to appropriate work relationships. When these are breached, the results are high levels of stress. Managers should stick to what was agreed – for example, changing the work load without consent could lead to burnout (van Emmerik & Sanders, 2005).

Keeping career-related stress at the right level is a managerial responsibility of HR managers, as stress is an unavoidable part of working life (as well as life in general).

Stress is an inevitable companion of motivational efforts, of challenging goal setting, of high need for achievement. It is a predictable side effect of any competitive arena. Conversely, having no stress is probably a reflection of a boring job, eventless tasks, that could lead to stress due to lack of challenge.

REFERENCES

Assouline, M. & Meir, E.I. (1987). Meta-analysis of the relationships between congruence and well-being measures. *Journal of Vocational Behavior*, **31**(3), 319–32.

Baruch, Y. (1999). Integrated career systems for the 2000s. *International Journal of Manpower*, **20**(7), 432–57.

Baruch, Y. (2004). *Managing Careers: Theory and Practice*. Harlow: FT-Prentice Hall/Pearson.

Baruch Y. & Lambert R. (2007). Organizational anxiety: applying psychological concepts into organizational theory. *Journal of Managerial Psychology*, **22**(1), 84–99.

Baruch, Y. & Woodward, S. (1998). Stressful situation? The case of management buyout/buyins. *Management Decisions*, **36**(10), 641–8.

Bellavia, G.M. & Frone, M.R. (2005). Work–family conflict. In J. Barling, E.K. Kelloway & M.R. Frone, (Eds), *Handbook of Work* Stress (pp. 113–47). Thousand Oaks: Sage.

Beehr, T.A. & Newman, J.E. (1978). Job stress, employee health, and organizational effectiveness: a facet analysis, model, and literature review. *Personnel Psychology*, **31**(4), 665–99.

Berlyne, D.E. (1960). *Conflict, Arousal, and Curiosity*. New York: McGraw-Hill.

Berlyne, D.E. (1963). Motivational problems raised by exploratory and epistemic behavior. In S. Koch (Ed.), *Psychology: A Study of a Science*, Vol. 5 (pp. 284–364). New York: McGraw-Hill.

Blenkinsopp, J. & Zdunczyk, K. (2005). Making sense of mistakes in managerial careers. *Career Development International*, **10**(5), 359–74.

Bonebright, C.A., Clay, D.L., & Ankenmann, R.D. (2000). The relationship of workaholism with work–life conflict, life satisfaction, and purpose in life. *Journal of Counseling Psychology*, **47**, 469–77.

Bratton, V.K. & Kacmar, K.M. (2004). Extreme careerism: the dark size of impression management. In R.W. Griffin & A.M. O'Leary-Kelly (Eds), *The Dark Side of Organizational Behavior* (pp. 291–308). San Francisco: Jossey-Bass.

Brockner, J., Tyler, T.R. & Cooper-Schneider, R. (1992). The influence of prior commitment to an institution on reactions to perceived unfairness: the higher they are, the harder they fall. *Administrative Science Quarterly*, **37**, 241–61.

Burke, R.J. (1999). It's not how hard you work but how you work hard: evaluating workaholism components. *International Journal of Stress Management*, **6**(4), 225–39.

Cable, D.M. & Judge, T.A. (1996). Person–organization fit, job choice decisions, and organizational entry. *Organizational Behavior and Human Decision Processes*, **67**, 294–311.

Cartwright, S. & Cooper, C.L. (1996). *Managing Mergers, Acquisitions and Strategic Alliances: Integrating People and Cultures*. Oxford: Butterworth Heinemann.

Cattell, R.B. & Kline, P. (1977). *The Scientific Analysis of Personality and Motivation*. New York: Academic Press.

Clarke, S. & Cooper, C. L. (2004). *Managing the Risk of Workplace Stress*. London: Routledge.

Conti, R., Angelis, J., Cooper, C.L., Faragher, B. & Gill, C. (2006). The effects of lean production on worker job stress. *International Journal of Operations & Production Management*, **26**, 1013–38.

Cooper, C.L. (1983). Identifying stressors at work: recent research developments. *Journal of Psychosomatic Research*, **27**(5), 369–76.

Cooper, C.L. (1998). *Theories of Organizational Stress*. Oxford: Oxford University Press.

Cooper, C.L. (2002). The changing psychological contract at work. *Occupational and Environmental Medicine*, **59**(6), 355.

Cooper, C.L. & A.J. Baglioni (1988). A structural model approach toward the development of a theory of the link between stress and mental health. *British Journal of Medical Psychology*, **61**(1), 87–102.

Cooper, C.L. & Cartwright, S. (1994). Healthy mind, healthy organization. *Human Relations*, **47**(4), 455–71.

Derr, B.C. (1986). *Managing the New Careerists: The Diverse Career Success Orientation of Today's Workers*. San Francisco: Jossey-Bass.

Edwards, J.R. (1991). Person–job fit: a conceptual integration, literature review and methodological critique. In C.L. Cooper & I.T. Robertson (Eds), *International Review of Industrial and Organizational Psychology*, **6**, 283-357.

Elsass, P. M. & Ralston, D.A. (1989). Individual responses to the stress of career plateauing. *Journal of Management*, **15**, 35–47.

Feldman, D.C. (2007). Late career and retirement issues. In H. Gunz & M.A. Peiperl, (Eds), *Handbook of Career Studies* (pp. 153–68). Thousand Oaks: Sage.

Fiske, D.W. & Maddi, S.R. (1961). *Functions of Varied Experience*. Homewood, IL: Dorsey Press.

Frankenhaeuser, M., Lundberg, U., Fredrickson, M. *et al.* (1989). stress on and off the job as related to sex and occupational status in white-collar workers. *Journal of Organizational Behavior*, **10**, 321–46.

Fuller, T. & Tian, Y. (2006). Social and symbolic capital and responsible entrepreneurship: an empirical investigation of SME narratives. *Journal of Business Ethics*, **67**, 287–304.

Game, A. (2007). Workplace boredom coping: health, safety and HR implications. *Personnel Review*, **36**, 701–21.

Gini, A. (1998). Work, identity and self: how we are formed by the work we do. *Journal of Business Ethics*, **17**(7), 707–14.

Granrose, C. & Portwood, J. (1987). Matching individual career plans and organizational career management. *Academy of Management Journal*, **30**, 699–720.

Hall, D.T. (1996). Long live the career. In D.T. Hall (Ed.), *The Career is Dead – Long Live the Career* (pp. 1–12). San Francisco: Jossey-Bass.

Hall, D.T. (2002). *Careers In and Out of Organizations*, Thousand Oaks: Sage.

Harpaz, I. & Snir, R. (2003). Workaholism: its definition and nature. *Human Relations*, **56**(3), 291–319.

Herriot, P. & Pemberton, C. (1996). Contracting careers. *Human Relations*, **49**, 757–90.

Hobfoll, S.E., Dunahoo, C.L., Ben-Porath, Y. & Monnier, J. (1994). Gender and coping: the dual axis model of coping. *American Journal of Community Psychology*, **22**, 49–82.

Holland, J.L. (1959). A theory of vocational choice. *Journal of Counseling Psychology*, **6**, 35–45.

Ibarra, H. (2003). *Working Identity: Unconventional Strategies for Reinventing Your Career*. Cambridge, MA: Harvard Business School Press.

Jones, E., Chonko, L., Rangarajan, D. & Roberts, J. (2007). The role of overload on job attitudes, turnover intentions, and salesperson performance. *Journal of Business Research*, **60**, 663–71.

Kawakami, N. & Haratani, T. (1999). Epidemiology of job stress and health in Japan: review of current evidence and future directions. *Individual Health*, **37**, 174–86.

Kelloway, E.K., Sivanthan, N., Francis, L. & Barling, J. (2005). Poor leadership. In J. Barling, E.K. Kelloway & M.R. Frone (Eds), *Handbook of Work Stress* (pp. 89–112). Thousand Oaks: Sage.

Kivimäki, M., Leino-Arjas, P., Luukkonen, R., Riihimäki, H., Vahtera, J. & Kirjonen, J. (2002). Work stress and risk of cardiovascular mortality: prospective cohort study of industrial employees. *British Medical Journal*, **325**, 857–60.

Kram, K.E. (1985). *Mentoring at Work: Developmental Relationships in Organizational Life*. Glenview, IL: Scott, Foresman.

Landsbergis, P.A. (1988). Occupational stress among health care workers: a test of the job demands–control model. *Journal of Organizational Behavior*, **9**, 217–39.

LaRocco, J.M., House, J.S. & French, J.R.P. Jr. (1980). Social support, occupational stress, and health. *Journal of Health and Social Behavior*, **21**(3), 202–18.

Larsson, R. & Finkelstein, S. (1999). Integrating strategic, organizational and human resource perspective on mergers and acquisitions: a case survey of synergy realization. *Organization Science*, **10**, 1–26.

Lee, R.T. & Ashforth, B.E. (1996). A meta-analytic examination of the correlates of the three dimensions of job burnout. *Journal of Applied Psychology*, **81**(2) 123–33.

Macik-Frey, M., Quick, J.C. & Nelson, D.L. (2007). Advances in occupational health: from a stressful beginning to a positive future. *Journal of Management*, **33**(6), 809–40.

Mainiero, L. & Sullivan, S. (2006). *The Opt Out Revolt: Why People are Leaving Companies to Create Kaleidoscope Careers*. Davies-Black

Maslach, C. (2006). Understanding job burnout. In A.M. Rossi, P.L. Perrewe, & S.L. Sauter (Eds), *Stress and Quality of Working Life: Current Perspectives in Occupational Work* (pp. 37–51).

McCabe, B.C., Feiock, R.C., Clingermayer, J.C. & Stream, C. (2008). Turnover among city managers: the role of political and economic change. *Public Administration Review*, **68**, 380–6.

Melamed, S., Shirom, A., Toker, S., Berliner, S. & Shapira, I. (2006). Burnout and risk of cardiovascular disease: evidence, possible causal paths, and promising research directions. *Psychological Bulletin*, **32**, 327–53.

Nishiyama, K. & Johnson, J.V. (1997). *Karoshi* – death from overwork: occupational health consequences of Japanese production management. *International Journal of Health Services*, **27**, 625–41.

Peiperl, M. & Baruch, Y. (1997). Back to square zero: the post-corporate career *Organizational Dynamics*, **25**(4), 7–22.

Peiperl, M. & Jones, B. (2001). Workaholics and overworkers. *Group and Organisation Management*, **26**(3), 369–93.

Porter, G. (2004). Work, work ethic, work excess. *Journal of Organizational Change Management*, **17**(5), 424–39.

Quick, J.C. & Quick, J.D. (1984). *Organizational Stress and Preventive Management*. New York: McGraw-Hill.

Scandura, T.A. (1998). Dysfunctional mentoring relationships and outcomes. *Journal of Management*, **24**, 449–67.

Scandura, T.A. & Pellegrini, E.K. (2007). Workplace mentoring: Theoretical approaches and methodological issues. In T.D. Allen & L.T. Eby (Eds), *The Blackwell Handbook of Mentoring: A Multiple Perspectives Approach* (pp. 71–91). Malden, MA: Blackwell.

Scott, Jr. W.E. (1966). Activation theory and task design. *Organizational Behavior and Human Performance*, **1**, 3–30.

Spence, J.T. & Robbins, A.S. (1992). Workaholism: definition, measurement, and preliminary results. *Journal of Personality Assessment*, **58**, 160–78.

Reisenberg, K. (2005). The trouble with CFOs. *Harvard Business Review*, **83**(11), 19.

Rousseau, D.M. (2004). Under-the-table deals: preferential, unauthorized, or idiosyncratic? In R.W. Griffin & A.M. O'Leary-Kelly (Eds), *The Dark Side of Organizational Behavior* (pp. 262–90). San Francisco: Jossey-Bass.

Schabracq, M.J. & Cooper C.L. (2000). The changing nature of work and stress. *Journal of Managerial Psychology*, **15**, 227–41.

Ursin, H. & Eriksen, H.R. (2004). The cognitive activation theory of stress. *Psychoneuroendocrinology*, **29**, 567–92.

Van Emmerik, I.J.H. & Sanders, K. (2005). Mismatch in working hours and effective commitment. *Journal of Managerial Psychology*, **20**, 712–26.

Westman, M. & Eden, D. (1997). Effects of a respite from work on burnout: vacation relief and fade-out. *Journal of Applied Psychology*, **82**, 516–27.

CHAPTER 11

New Technologies and Stress

Kai-Christoph Hamborg and Siegfried Greif

University of Osnabrück, Germany

11.1 INTRODUCTION

Technological innovation is important for industrial organizations trying to survive in competitive markets. However, innovation is never a simple or smooth process. Faced with major technological changes, people react differently; although some seem to relish the challenge, many show symptoms of stress. In the 1970s, new computer technologies started to change nearly every workplace, and also influenced private life. Since then the pace of computer hardware and software innovation has accelerated and the scope of technical change has increased (Clegg *et al.*, 1997). Computer systems have become standard, at least in modern industries and administration, for some time now.

Ever since the beginning of this development, many people feared that stress and unemployment would be the future consequences of the technological revolution. Scientists conducted empirical research to either support or contradict these expectations. In the meantime, it has become evident that innovation and new technologies are not a source of unemployment or low qualification requirements *per se* (Welsch, 1989). The question is how people react to such permanent innovation, whether it results in stress and which practical psychological consequences should be drawn to help them cope with the consequences.

This chapter provides a summary of research into new technologies and stress. Initial basic concepts and research findings into the impact of new technologies on stress are presented. Following this, practical consequences

International Handbook of Work and Health Psychology, Third Edition. Edited by Cary L. Cooper, James Campbell Quick, and Marc J. Schabracq.

concerning implementation strategies, job and software (re)design and employee training programmes are discussed.

11.2   THE IMPACT OF NEW TECHNOLOGIES ON STRESS

11.2.1   Basic Stress Model

Faced with technological changes, not all people show stress reactions. According to the transactional stress model (Lazarus, 1976), an individual's appraisal of the stressor, its resources and coping competences have to be considered in this context. Some people clearly seem to appreciate the challenge of technological novelty. Only subjects who expect a long-lasting aversive experience after the appraisal of the whole situation and its consequences will react with stress. Research into the impact of new technologies on stress, therefore, has to take into account many different factors and conditions of work systems that might affect the appraisal process and the stress reaction. In order to develop a systematic research overview we have to consider types of stressors, different resources, short- and long-term consequences of stress and the means to measure these consequences.

11.2.2   A Definition of Stress in the Context of New Technologies

We define stress as a state of intense and aversive tension, which the subject strongly wants to avoid. The sensation of stress depends on the expected persistence, closeness and lack of control of the situation (Greif, 1991a). The application of this definition implies several seemingly trivial, but often neglected, consequences. Stress is not suffered by people who neither show nor expect persistent aversive tension nor want to avoid the change before or after the implementation of new technologies. Most people, apparently, do not worry about technological changes that may or may not emerge in the long run. At least people who are able to control technological problems, either by avoiding them or learning to manage them, will show no stress reactions.

Stressors can be defined simply as factors that are assumed with a high probability to lead to stress reactions (Semmer, 1984). Technology itself, as well as the expected direct or mediated consequences of its implementation, may be a source of stress. Following the transactional stress model and action theory, Semmer (1984; see also Leitner *et al.*, 1993; Frese & Zapf, 1994; Fay, Sonnentag & Frese, 2001) makes a distinction between three major groups of hypothetical stressors at work:

1. *Overtaxing regulations* are characterized by an overload of mental demands, such as high speed and intensity of regulation or high concentration, required to achieve goals. For example, time pressure due to long and unpredictable system response times or poor system handling may result in overtaxing regulations because it calls for working at high speed or intensity (Fay, Sonnentag & Frese, 2001).

2. *Regulatory uncertainty* means that the individual does not know how to achieve a goal due to a lack of knowledge or ambiguous feedback. Instances of regulatory uncertainty are qualitative overload, role conflict and role ambiguity (Fay, Sonnentag & Frese, 2001). In the field of new technology it may be caused, for example, by complex hardware and software systems, unclear wording and insufficient, delayed feedback, unclear error messages or incomprehensible manuals, as well as by the high complexity of tasks or the whole job, due to the implementation of new technology.

3. *Regulation obstacles* are events or conditions that impede or make it harder to pursue and achieve a goal. Regulation obstacles demand additional effort, such as repeated actions, detours or even starting anew to ensure task completion. Typical obstacles are interruptions due to computer breakdown or regulation difficulties caused by inadequate tools or a lack of information (Frese & Zapf, 1994).

A differentiation can be made between the short-term and long-term consequences of stress. Examples of short-term consequences include biochemical and psycho-physiological reactions, such as increased blood pressure, pulse rate and catecholamine excretion. Moreover, consequences such as eye or musculo-skeletal strain symptoms and lower performance efficiency (especially a higher rate of errors) are also short-term indicators that are found to be related to stress in some studies. Typical long-term consequences that have been examined within the scope of new technology and stress include reduced well-being, psychosomatic complaints and diseases. In the next section an overview of research results on sources of stress associated with new technologies is given. Studies on the overall consequences of both technology and the implementation process are summarized in Section 11.3.

11.2.3   Research into Different Factors and Sources of Stress

Several basic sources of organizational stress can be distinguished. Most of these sources have also been investigated in conjunction with work and new technologies: e.g. job demands, job control, job content, as well as human factor constraints and career/future concerns (Briner & Hockey, 1988; Carayon, 1993; Carayon *et al.*, 1995; Frese, 1991a).

Human factor constraints are related to hardware and software properties of computing environments. Important hardware components that have been studied in experiments and field studies include workstation layout, input devices (keyboards, mice, etc.) and visual display units (VDUs). In the case of VDUs, results vary. Whereas Çakir (1981) and Zeier *et al.* (1987) found no properties directly related to physiological reactions and musculo-skeletal discomfort, Sauter *et al.* (1991) reported an association between work with VDUs and musculo-skeletal complaints.

Furthermore, empirical evidence has been found on the impact of delayed or unpredictable system response times on stress (Johansson & Aronsson, 1984). In a summary of experimental research applying psycho-physiological measures, Boucsein (1988) infers that system response times that are either too long or too short may induce stress.

Additionally, there is also evidence of the impact of software design and of hardware reliability and performance on stress. Problems such as system failures, especially crashes, definitely appear to cause stress. In an investigation by Johansson and Aronsson (1984), white-collar workers showed significantly different adrenalin excretion and diastolic blood pressure during a breakdown compared to ordinary conditions. Carayon (1997, p. 330f) points out that the cumulative effect of so-called acute stressors, such as slow computer performance and computer breakdowns, can result in chronic symptoms of stress.

Another source of stress related to the software itself are human errors due to design flaws, software complexity or, more generally, to a lack of usability. Corresponding experimental results show that computer novices, unlike experts, make significantly more errors in higher level, consciously processed actions and inefficiencies (see Frese & Zapf, 1994) when working with highly complex software in contrast to working with low complexity software (Hamborg, 1996). Especially errors located at the intellectual level of action regulation give rise to emotional reactions such as anger or even helplessness (Krone *et al.*, 2002). A field study conducted by Brodbeck *et al.* (1993) revealed that both novices and experts using standard software systems make mistakes or action slips every few minutes, and spend about 10% of computer working time handling errors. Since errors are strong 'barriers to task fulfilment' (cf. Semmer and Meier, this volume), they principally have to be considered as stressful events.

Regarding the increasing complexity of software systems in office work, errors will become even more likely in the future. This effect is probably strengthened by short update and implementation cycles, especially in conjunction with new releases, the quality and reliability of which often remain insufficient.

Stress may not only be caused by errors but by regulation obstacles, such as the frequent occurrence of minor malfunctions and hindrances due to bad design users have to deal with in their daily work with computers.

Even though technology may not cause any difficulties, the anticipation of errors due to a lack of knowledge can, according to the above definition of stress, be enough to cause stress.

The designs of workstations, hardware and software components, the furnishings, and interior equipment are important factors related to stress. However, research shows that it is insufficient to consider human factors constraints and the ergonomic design of equipment as the only sources of stress. Several authors emphasize that the type of work carried out at VDUs, and the embedding organizational conditions, seem to be the main cause of health complaints and stress reactions (Agervold, 1987; Briner & Hockey, 1988; Çakir, 1981; Frese, 1991a). New technology may lead to changes in work structure and human–machine redivision of labour (Buchanan & Boddy, 1982; Levi, 1994; Turner & Karasek, 1984). This in turn may result in changes to work demands, e.g. work overload or underload, time pressure (Saupe & Frese, 1981; Schulz & Höfert, 1981), task interruptions (Johansson & Aronsson, 1984; Leitner et al., 1993) as well as anxiety (Mohr, 1991), uncertainty (Saupe & Frese, 1981; Turner & Karasek, 1984), lack of job control (Buchanan & Boddy, 1982, Sauter et al., 1983) and career concerns, such as uncertainty of job future and career advancement (Carayon, 1993). The following section briefly describes the role of intervening or moderating variables. Field studies on the overall consequences of new technologies and their implementation are addressed in Section 11.3.

11.2.4 Resources

Resources can be thought of as characteristics of the person, the job and/or the organization that mediate or moderate the impact of the implementation of new technologies on the individual and that may help to compensate or balance out possible negative effects (Korunka et al., 2003). Control, technological knowledge and competence as well as social support are the major resources that have been studied in this field.

Job control

Job control, defined as the subjective probability of reducing stress reactions, is often mentioned as an important buffering resource (cf. Frese & Brodbeck,

1989; Greif, 1991a; Johansson, 1989). Control at work implies the possibility of successfully changing environmental conditions or one's own activities (cf. Frese, 1989). Job control (Spector, 1998) ranges from autonomy (control over immediate scheduling and tasks) to participation in decision-making processes (control over the organizational decision-making process). Low decision latitude and little control over the scheduling of tasks may follow from the inadequate (re)design of jobs after the implementation of new technologies (Buchanan & Boddy, 1982; Frese & Zapf, 1987). Carayon (1993), however, ascertained that, while job demands and career/future concerns are related to stress outcomes in office work, job control is not. According to Jones and Fletcher (2003), the latter point does not seem to be a clear-cut issue.

Technological knowledge and competencies

Technological knowledge and coping competencies are very powerful resources in meeting the challenge of technological change. Such changes require intensive, adaptive effort. Briner and Hockey (1988) supposed that, in the short term, differences between old and new work demands and the lack of competencies are likely to be the main sources of stress. Training and development of the necessary technological knowledge and skills provide security and self-confidence. Expert knowledge and competencies reduce the probability of errors. Furthermore, the development of special error management competencies appears to be an important resource that prevents stress (Frese et al., 1991). For this reason, the implementation of new technologies should be accompanied by extensive training efforts. Methods of learning and error management training are considered in Section 11.4.

Social support and help

Social support and help by colleagues and experts is a well-known resource that moderates stress reactions (Frese & Semmer, 1991; Udris, 1989; Humphrey, Nahrgang & Morgeson, 2007). Accompanying the implementation of new technology, hardware and software retailers are expected to provide training programmes and user support. Beyond this support, the development of a social support network within the work environment seems to facilitate individual learning, problem solving and error management (Briner & Hockey, 1988; Dutke & Schönpflug, 1987; Greif, 1986).

Moreover several findings show that the implementation of new technologies may reduce social interaction (Buchanan & Boddy, 1982; Turner &

Karasek, 1984; Stellman *et al.*, 1987). For this reason, special investments in the development of personal help networks and a positive social team and organizational climate may be necessary to compensate for an impairment of such resources.

Finally, resources related to the organizational change process have been considered recently. Besides passive and active participation, which is related to job control (see above), and the perceived quality of training, they include the organization of the implementation process (Korunka *et al.*, 2003).

11.3 RESEARCH INTO THE IMPLEMENTATION OF NEW TECHNOLOGIES

11.3.1 Cross-Sectional Studies

Studies on the overall influence of the implementation of new technologies show controversial results on strain and stress reactions. Some studies report an increase, others a decrease and several no differences in stress-related reactions linked to the introduction of new technologies.

The implementation strategy plays an important role in this context. Often a technology-led strategy is pursued and the impact on work characteristics is largely ignored (Clegg *et al.*, 1997). In many cases, dealing with the associated problems of work design and organizational change follows the principle of 'muddling through' (von Benda, 1990; Greif, 1991b). As a consequence, the likelihood of unintended and negative outcomes increases and employees' fear of negative job changes, unemployment, social isolation, role change and increasing supervision may arise (von Benda, 1990; Frese, 1991a; Frese & Brodbeck, 1989).

An increase in strain due to VDU usage, especially in connection with high workload and repetitive tasks, is reported by Stellman *et al.* (1987). The authors investigated more than 1000 female office clerical workers subdivided into five groups: part-time typists, full-time typists, clerical workers, part-time VDU operators and full-time VDU operators. Full-time terminal users reported higher levels of job and physical environment stressors than part-time VDU users, typists and other clerical workers. Musculoskeletal strain, symptoms such as eye strain and dissatisfaction were also highest among full-time terminal users. With regard to psychological symptoms (depression, anxiety, hopelessness, irritation), no consistent or significant differences were observed between the groups. Typists and clerical workers who also held supervisory positions reported fewer stressors and greater job satisfaction than workers with no supervisory tasks. However, there were no such differences between supervisors and non-supervisors engaged in full-time VDU work with terminals.

The authors suppose that the potential advantage of increased supervisory responsibilities may be annihilated when full-time VDU operators are involved in highly demanding, repetitive work. This group reported the highest levels of workload demands and repetitiousness, and also the lowest levels of decision-making latitude, ability to learn new things on the job and understanding of the overall work process. Furthermore, full-time users of terminals reported the highest level of ergonomic sources of stress, although they had a greater ability to adjust the height and back of their chairs compared to other groups.

The results of Stellmann *et al.* (1987) correspond with a study on insurance staff by Johansson and Aronsson (1984), which showed that the highest level of stress was found among those doing repetitive tasks and constant work with VDUs.

Differing from these results, in an investigation of a representative sample of 907 white-collar workers, Agervold (1987) found that the incidence of mental fatigue, stress and psychosomatic complaints was the same in the sub-groups working with or without new technology. The results of a close comparison indicated that there was no correlation between the impairment of the psychological work environment and new technologies. On the contrary, there seemed to be some improvement in the quality of work, although this was combined with an increase in workload (pressure of work and mental strain). With regard to psychological strain, the only effect of working with new technology was a tendency of higher levels of mental fatigue. Stress and psychosomatic reactions, however, seemed to remain unaffected.

Agervold (1987, p. 149) concludes that new technologies seem to only have negative consequences in terms of stress if they are associated with changes in important psychological aspects of work (e.g. less personal influence, fewer cognitive demands, greater isolation, more pressure at work, higher mental and physical workload). The results of this study indicate that the consequences of the introduction of new technology concerning job content, quality of work, influence, satisfaction and stress are determined by the kind of job and the degree of change in the organization of work, combined with changes in work pressure.

In a study investigating the impact of computer technology on work content, feedback, job control and mental strain in text preparation in printing shops, Kalimo and Leppänen (1985) found that subjects working with the most advanced technology assessed their mental activity and self-determination at work more positively than subjects whose tasks involved less advanced technology. The former subjects were more satisfied with their work than the others. Their tasks demanded more decision making and were more complex.

Even for subjects with minimal initial task variety and challenge, however, Kalimo and Leppänen found that computer technology and the application of VDUs may increase performance feedback and quality control. Therefore, this kind of work was associated with a positive impact on the whole work setting and positive changes in the daily workload, too. The results of this investigation show that new technologies may diminish stress even when combined with simple tasks.

The reported findings demonstrate that the impact of new technologies on stress and its consequences can be extremely varied. We should be careful not to attribute observed increases of stress reactions to new technologies *per se*. Rather, issues such as task demands, performance feedback and other mediating organizational factors seem to be more important factors, which have to be considered carefully in work design and the implementation process (Briner & Hockey, 1988; Frese & Brodbeck, 1989; Greif, 1986).

Cross-sectional field research has often been criticized in that it can be misleading when it comes to causal inferences. Correlations between hypothetical stressors and stress reactions may result from hidden factors or even from a reversed causal relation (for example, a stress reaction may increase time pressure). The same is true for observed mean differences between groups. It is impossible to control all relevant conditions and factors that may influence the results of field studies. Controversial results should therefore be of no surprise.

In contrast, longitudinal studies are advantageous because they, at least partly, allow the chronological order of hypothetical causes and effects to be controlled. Although longitudinal studies demand higher and longer research investments, several studies of this kind have been conducted, especially in the past decade. The following section summarizes the results of several longitudinal studies on the consequences of implementing new technologies.

11.3.2   Longitudinal Studies

Frese and Zapf (1987) investigated the impact of new technologies on qualification demands, decision latitude and stress within a longitudinal design. The study used two measurement points, before and after the technological changes. In 1979, before the changes, 218 blue-collar workers in the German car and steel industry participated in a comprehensive survey. At that time, hardly any computer-aided machines or robots were used in the workplaces. Six years later, in 1985, 166 subjects of the first sample were studied again.

In the study the changes between five groups of technological demands were compared:

1. Traditional jobs that have not experienced technological changes.
2. Computer-supported work without programming tasks.
3. Computer-supported work with some influence on programming (but not practised by the employees themselves).
4. Computer-supported work with programming tasks.
5. Operators of industrial robots.

The authors found only minor changes and differences in job demands, stressors and hypothetical resources that may mediate stress reactions. One result was a low but significant increase in job decision latitude for all groups, from 1979 to 1985, and also a minor but significant general decrease in time pressure and concentration demands, with the exception of group 4. Job satisfaction increased significantly for groups 3 and 4 after the changes.

The results of the study show that job demands, stressors and resources have remained stable over time for the different groups, i.e. workers who had a high level of job discretion or complexity before the implementation of the new technology also had jobs with similar attributes after the change. The authors conclude that new technology has only a very low – if any – impact on stress and resources, although they concede that this finding may have been due to selection effects.

Comparing individual changes, Marjchrzak and Cotton (1988) have shown in a longitudinal study that stress reactions can be found only for subjects with unfavourable starting conditions who face major technological changes. In his longitudinal study, Kühlmann (1988) assessed individual attitudes of employees faced with the implementation of new technologies and their expectations of negative changes. Immediately before the change, most employees developed an optimistic attitude and seemed to underestimate potential negative job changes compared to their later observations. This tendency to simplify and belittle unpredictable future difficulties could be interpreted as a way of coping with future uncertainty and new, unpredictable situations. Kühlmann (1988) recommends that employees who are very concerned and worried about whether they will be able to master the changes before they occur should receive special psychological support.

While Frese and Zapf (1987), Marjchrzak and Cotton (1988) and Kühlmann (1988) investigated the impact of the change before and after implementation of new technologies, Korunka et al. (1993) also included a comparison of different styles of the initial implementation of new technology in a longitudinal study with three measurement points: (i) prior to implementation; (ii) during implementation; and (iii) one year after implementation. Strain reactions and satisfaction were assessed for all three times. In particular, stress induced by job content, organizational aspects and physical conditions of the environment were considered. The sample consisted of 279 employees either using computer-aided design (CAD) software, doing clerical work or carrying out telephone information tasks. To assess the style of the implementation process, the authors used three criteria: (i) organization of the project; (ii) participation of employees; and (iii) training and supervision.

The results of the study show a significant overall increase in subjectively experienced stress and physical complaints (presumably due to an insufficient provision of ergonomic furnishings) across all measurements. Paired comparisons between the measurement points revealed a significant increase in stress and physical complaints, as well as a significant increase in dissatisfaction between the first two measurement points (*prior to implementation* and *during implementation*). Additionally, physical complaints significantly increased between the first and the third measurements (*prior to implementation* and *one year after implementation*).

Results concerning the style of implementation revealed that stress after the implementation decreased significantly in those companies that practised more active employee participation in the change process but not in companies with lower participation. Participation generally resulted in higher ratings of satisfaction with the technological changes, while the overall extent of physical complaints was attenuated by participation. Moreover, high participation led to a decrease, while low participation was associated with an increase in dissatisfaction. Furthermore, the authors differentiated between four job clusters with regard to qualification demands. Employees in highly ranked job clusters had more opportunities to participate in the implementation process than personnel from the less qualified clusters (Korunka et al., 1993, 1995). In the cluster with the lowest qualification ('Extremely monotonous work'), most psychosomatic complaints and decreased job satisfaction were observed. This result corresponds to a similar outcome of the cross-sectional study by Agervold (1987), cited above. On the other hand, employees in the highly technological qualified cluster showed an increase in job satisfaction and only slightly increased psychosomatic complaints after the introduction of new technologies (Korunka et al., 1995).

Korunka et al. underline that their results match Karasek's demand-control model (Karasek & Theorell, 1990), which postulates that the most strain is associated with high demands and low decision latitude. High employee participation in the implementation process appears to generate a higher level of acceptance and leads to a high degree of attenuation of subjectively experienced stress and dissatisfaction, while low participation results in an increase of these variables: 'It seems to be that a participatory managerial style may counteract any negative effects of the new technologies' (Korunka *et al.*, 1995, p. 138).

In a follow-up study, Korunka, Zauchner and Weiss (1997) investigated the effects of continuous implementation (implementation in workplaces already equipped with computers) of new technologies on strain and dissatisfaction in 10 companies ($N = 466$). In contrast to a control sample consisting of five subsamples with pending implementation, employees in the implementation sample, including six projects, showed a significant increase in subjectively experienced stress but not in dissatisfaction two weeks after implementation, in contrast to pre-implementation data. Regarding the different implementation projects, changes in stress and dissatisfaction varied notably. Further analysis of job-related decision latitude and external workload shows that subjectively experienced stress seems to increase after implementation, especially in workplaces with low decision latitude and high external workload. This marked statistical trend corresponds with the results of the first longitudinal study (Korunka *et al.*, 1993, 1995). However, it seems worth mentioning that, contrary to the conclusions of the above-mentioned study by Korunka *et al.* (1993), subjectively experienced stress in general was higher and dissatisfaction was lower for participants with high decision latitude in contrast to participants with low decision latitude. Concluding, the study suggests that not only the initial introduction of new technologies but also the continuous change of information technologies affect employees' strain and satisfaction.

An advanced analysis of the follow-up study by Korunka and Vitouch (1999) investigated the impact of personal (individual differences, external workload) and situational factors like job design (e.g. job complexity, decision latitude) as well as implementation content factors on strain (psychosomatic complaints, subjectively experienced stress) and satisfaction. Implementation content factors were: (i) adaptational demands placed on employees due to the new technology (qualification, duration of training and changes in program functionality); (ii) 'software-ergonomic changes'; and (iii) participation. Data were collected over a period of one-and-a-half to five-and-a-half months before implementation and three to six months after implementation of information technology. As expected, a significant influence of personal dimensions on strain and satisfaction was found: internal locus of control, higher self-esteem and positive attitudes towards information technologies were associated with job satisfaction and less strain.

Implementation content factors revealed significant effects on the changes in users' strain and satisfaction at the second measurement point. Furthermore, results show that participation, adaptational demands and the ergonomic quality of the software are relevant factors explaining employees' reactions to technological change. While adaptational demands, such as changes in users' qualification, duration of training and changes to the software's functionality, are inversely related to strain measures. The opposite is true for the usability of software systems: it was found that software implementations retaining a character-based interface showed strong negative effects on strain and satisfaction compared to implementations changing graphical user interfaces.

The authors state that the study provides additional support for the positive effects of user participation in the case of the continuous implementation of new technologies and that during the implementation process increased attention should be paid to current developments of user interfaces.

Slightly positive effects of the implementation of new technologies are reported in some longitudinal Scandinavian studies investigating the implementation process of new technologies. In his review of several longitudinal studies carried out in the field of the public service, a bank, a library and an insurance company, Huuhtanen (1997) summarizes a positive overall impact of new technology on work content experienced by employees in all occupation and age groups. He states that new technologies seem to have more often increased than decreased those characteristics that are important for mental well-being at work. 'Compared with the expectations before the change, the work has become more interesting and the employees felt that they could use their abilities better' (p. 397), although office tasks have become somewhat more difficult, and the work pace has increased.

Mixed results are presented by Järvenpää (1997), who conducted a longitudinal study over a four−year period on the implementation of office automation at a district court. After the implementation, office workers perceived their jobs as slightly more interesting than before the implementation. Short-term mental strain was also slightly lower after the implementation, but this positive effect seemed to decrease over time. On the other hand, a slight increase in office workers' long-term strain (e.g. stomach symptoms, chest pain, restlessness, fatigue and eye symptoms) was observed, although no effect relating to job satisfaction was found.

An important aspect regarding the results of longitudinal studies on job design and stress was given by Carayon et al. (1995). The results of their three-year longitudinal study investigating the relationship between job design variables and strain of office workers from a public service organization indicate that the relationship between job design and strain changes over time. At the first point of measurement, quantitative workload, work pressure and supervisor support were related to most measures of worker strain. At the second point, supervisor support was related to all of the strain measures as well as task clarity except for one, while job future ambiguity, quantitative workload and job control were related respectively to more than half or to half of the eight measures of worker strain. Eventually, at the last point of measurement, task clarity was related to seven, attention and job future ambiguity to five and job control to four measures of strain. The authors suggest that the lack of stability of the correlations between work stressors and worker strain may be due to changes in management or, more generally, that work environments and people may change over time. Following this assumption, they conclude that in theories of job design and worker strain we have to take into account the flexibility of working environments.

To summarize the results of the cross-sectional and longitudinal field studies on the implementation of new technologies, there is no definite support for the simple assumption that computer technologies themselves may exert stress. A lack of usability of software, including malfunctions and usability problems, as well as the poor ergonomic design of hardware and ergonomic furnishings are problems, which in most cases can be reduced to a tolerable level by professional experts or by means of usability engineering. Where stress reactions are found, they seem to result from negative interactions between technology and job design (especially monotony and time pressure: Carayon, 1997, p. 325) or an inadequate technology-led implementation process. Most experts recommend the following as remedies: user participation during the implementation process (Briner & Hockey, 1988; Huuhtanen, 1997; Karasek & Theorell, 1990; Korunka & Vitouch, 1999), and task and job (re)design, as well as training of employees to manage the complex technological changes (Korunka & Vitouch, 1999). Possible practical implications are presented in the following section.

11.4 PRACTICAL IMPLICATIONS

With respect to the reported findings, it seems to be reasonable to apply an integrated approach that addresses the prevention of major problems and risk factors, including: (i) an integrative and participative implementation process; (ii) participative task and job design; (iii) user-oriented hardware and software design; and (iv) an adequate training programme as well as the establishment of personal help networks. The ideal vision is a learning organization whose members actively participate in current and future technological and job changes. In the following subsections, we will outline important aspects of the four components of our holistic approach.

11.4.1 Integrative and Participative Implementation Process

Field surveys and practical observations show that systematic implementation strategies of new computer technologies are rare (Bjørn-Andersen, 1985; Dzida *et al.*, 1984; Hirschheim *et al.*, 1985). Organizations often follow technology-led implementation strategies or simply buy and apply the 'best' technological system and 'muddle through' the resulting organizational problems.

We advocate the following strategy for implementation:

1. detailed information in advance;
2. active participation;
3. learning to master the changes.

Detailed information in advance

Planned technological changes put many people into a state of uncertainty, which can be accompanied by strong emotional reactions (Kanter, 1985). Many questions arise concerning the consequences of the changes. Typical concrete questions are:

- Is my job still safe after the change or will technological rationalization render it obsolete?
- Will I be able to master or learn the new technology?
- Who will help me if I need help?
- What will happen if I am unable to adapt to these changes or less able than my colleagues?
- Which of my basic tasks and responsibilities will change?
- How about stress at work? How can I cope with problems whilst learning the new technology and doing my work at the same time?
- Will time pressure increase?
- Will the firm buy good ergonomic and usable systems?

Information received about the need for change and the changes themselves are predictive of higher levels of employee openness to the changes (Coch & French, 1948; Wanberg & Banas, 2000). Therefore these questions should be answered by credible and concrete information, which shows how the demands can be successfully mastered, step by step. The management should ensure clear and satisfactory answers to such questions at the start of the change process. Change anxiety and stress will not be reduced by information which is subjectively rated as unreliable. To attempt to hush up existing high risks is itself a risky strategy. People do not forget lip services or false promises in such situations and it is easy to lose long-term credibility. It would be better to give reliable information about possible risks in combination with an optimistic and encouraging personal statement that risks can be managed.

Hofmann and Bungard (1995) have demonstrated the advantages of giving concrete information in advance regarding car model changes in the automobile industry. Before the changes, workers were invited to inspect the new model and plans (after signing an obligation of secrecy). The results were very convincing. Nearly all workers turned up and were willing to participate in the change processes. Many were even very enthusiastic about the future changes. The whole process was less stressful, with fewer conflicts, and was substantially shorter than any previous technological change in the companies. This example demonstrates that investing in concrete information in advance pays off, reducing typical insecurities and negative attitudes of the people involved.

Active participation of employees

Active participation refers to the active involvement of organizational members who will ultimately use the new technology (Symon & Clegg, 2005). The benefit of involving future users is – among other things – that it helps to create better systems, increase user ownership and commitment to change, it provides an opportunity for users to influence the design of their own work processes and gives them an opportunity to gain control over the design process (Clegg et al., 1997; Symon & Clegg, 2005). Hence active participation in job and task redesign is a strategy that helps to avoid insecurity and resistance that may result from unknown future changes (Kanter, 1985).

Participation is rarely an easy process, especially where the expected technological and organizational changes are large and where people see a risk of losing their achieved status. It is therefore recommended that change managers guide and monitor the change process (Bennebroek Gravenhorst, Werkman & Boonstra, 2003). They should try to help the participants to cope with stressful situations that are typical to many change processes: extreme complexity, high time urgency and role conflicts. A further task of change managers is to solve communication problems and to create a team atmosphere that supports mutual information, trust, constructive communication and common problem solving. An open attitude of change managers towards employees' ideas and experiences is supposed to stimulate active support (Bennebroek Gravenhorst et al., 2003).

Learning to master the changes

Research results on success and failure of change management projects show that the risk of failure is very high. Evidence on the introduction of new technologies and the consequences thereof point to low levels of success (Clegg *et al.*, 1997; Waterson *et al.*, 1999; Boonstra, 2000). An interview study with leading UK experts concerning the performance of IT investments found that 80% to 90% of IT investments do not meet their objectives (Clegg *et al.*, 1997). The authors argue that the reasons for this are rarely purely technical in origin but are, among other things, due to the context of technical change, the ways in which the new technologies are developed and implemented, and a range of human and organizational factors.

Failure can result in existential crisis situations and is always an extremely stressful threat to all those involved. Nevertheless, technological changes cannot be ignored. Therefore, learning to master urgent and complex periodical or continuous changes becomes a core competence of organizations and their members. Where possible, the organization should start with small, manageable pilot projects that serve as learning encounters for future changes to reduce stress reactions.

Even if concrete information is given in advance and active participation is realized, individuals may still remain anxious and may doubt whether they will be able to master the changes. Although there are no clear research results indicating substantial anxiety due to technological innovations (Kühlmann, 1988), people may be concerned about losing their jobs and may therefore hesitate to admit fears of making errors or of failure and avoid necessary training as long as possible. In Section 11.4.4 we describe learning approaches that have been successfully applied in training complex software systems and error management.

11.4.2 Participative Task and Job Design

The introduction of new technologies into work organizations usually affects task and work design and may – but need not – have unfortunate and unplanned implications that put people under stress. However, as pointed out above, the resulting effects are not merely due to the technology itself. Rather the versatility of new technologies often creates new options for the design and management of organizations (Blackler & Brown, 1986). Whether and how these options are tapped depends to a large extent on the way in which the technology is implemented and whether the consequences of technology on job design are systematically considered during the process of implementation.

Industrial and organizational psychology provides elaborate and well-validated (e.g. Humphrey, Nahrgang & Morgeson, 2007) theoretical approaches to job and work design (for an overview, see Kompier, 2003), such as the Job Characteristics Model (Hackman & Lawler, 1971), Warr's Vitamin Model (Warr, 1987) or German Action Theory (Frese & Zapf, 1994), which have partly been integrated in expanded frameworks for work design recently (Parker & Wall, 2001; Morgeson & Campion, 2003).

Essential claims concerning task design in consideration of VDT-based information processing systems are condensed in ISO 9241-2, Guidance on task design (ISO 9241, 1992). The objective of this international standard concerning task design for users of 'VDT-based information systems' is to provide for 'optimal working conditions with regard to human well-being, safety and health, taking into account technological and economic efficiency' (ISO 9241-2, 1992, p. 1). Overload or underload, undue repetitiveness, time pressure and a lack of social contact should be avoided.

In terms of ISO 9241-2 tasks should (ISO 9241-2, 1992, p. 2):

- Recognise the experience and capabilities of user populations;
- Provide for the application of an appropriate variety of skills, capabilities, and activities;
- Ensure that the tasks performed are identifiable as whole units of work rather than fragments;
- Ensure that the tasks performed make a significant contribution to the total function of the system, which can be understood by the user;
- Provide an appropriate degree of autonomy to the user in deciding priority, pace and procedure;
- Provide sufficient feedback on task performance in terms meaningful to the user;
- Provide opportunities for the development of existing skills and the acquisition of new skills with respect to the tasks concerned.

While job design theories and guidelines for task design formulate characteristics and criteria that promote meaningful work and well-being, they do not directly address 'how' the work design should be and the processes involved in successfully designing or redesigning work (Parker & Wall, 2001).

For this reason, methods are needed to support participative and integrative systems development in order for organizational requirements and options and critical work characteristics to be considered alongside technical opportunities (Eason, Harker & Olphert, 1996, p. 418).

Besides existing approaches of stress-oriented job analysis (Zapf, 1993) and comprehensive preventive health strategies (Bamberg et al., 1998; Winnubst & Diekstra, 1998), special methods supporting the integrated design of work systems have been developed and empirically evaluated in the recent past (e.g. Blyth, 1995; Carroll, 1995; Beyer & Holtzblatt, 1998; Nadin, Waterson & Parker, 2001; Waterson, Older-Gray & Clegg, 2002; Hamborg, Schulze & Sendfeld, 2007). These methods focus on the question of task and function allocation between humans and between humans and the new technologies. They share the following characteristics.

In the first step, the actual state of a given work system is evaluated by means of task, job and requirements analysis. Analysis mainly focuses on the identification of tasks, workflows and stakeholders. Second, a vision is generated representing the future work system in consideration of the technology to be implemented. The vision specifies how the system will work after the implementation of the new technology, the related job design implications and the associated organizational structure and the roles that exist within that structure and the organizational arrangements to be adopted (Waterson, Older-Gray & Clegg, 2002). The design methods outlined differ concerning the way in which the design vision is represented. While some of the methods use graphical representations (Blyth, 1995; Beyer & Holtzblatt, 1998; Waterson, Older-Gray & Clegg, 2002; Hamborg, Schulze & Sendfeld, 2007), others make use of narrative representations, especially scenarios (Carroll, 1995; Nadin, Waterson & Parker, 2001), or tabular representations (Waterson, Older-Gray & Clegg, 2002). The representation of the future work system is used to support problem-solving tasks associated with the design of a new work system (e.g. identify and decide on allocation options or job demands) as well as to communicate design ideas to the employees involved and to provide a means to evaluate the design ideas.

Most of the methods include participatory evaluation guided by work design criteria (Nadin, Waterson & Parker, 2001; Waterson, Older-Gray & Clegg, 2002; Hamborg, Schulze & Sendfeld, 2007). With regard to the theoretical background, some of the methods follow the socio-technical systems approach (Nadin, Waterson & Parker, 2001; Waterson, Older-Gray & Clegg, 2002) or action theory (Hamborg, Schulze & Sendfeld, 2007), while others are rather pragmatic approaches (Beyer & Holtzblatt, 1998).

11.4.3   User-Oriented Hardware and Software Design

Inappropriate hardware and software design may be considered an important instance of 'barriers to task fulfilment' (Semmer and Meier, this volume), causing 'regulation obstacles' and especially regulation difficulties (Frese & Zapf, 1994), as well as human errors, and consequentially stress reactions. Therefore the design of usable software represents a means of stress prevention. The design of usable software is the topic of usability engineering (Nielsen, 1993).

Usability engineering is concerned with the systematic integration of methods and techniques of building usable software in the system development process. It can be characterized as a process that covers the definition and the measurement of product usability in general (Wixon & Wilson, 1997, p. 654). Usability engineering requires a software engineering model, which allows revisions and feedback loops. These models include prototyping approaches, iterative system design and user participation (Gould, 1988; Mayhew, 1999; Wixon & Wilson, 1997). Models of usability engineering are often subdivided into three phases (Gould, 1988; Mayhew, 1999; Nielsen, 1993).

Phase 1: analysis and specification

The first step – the 'Gearing-Up Phase' – starts with preparatory activities, such as choosing general principles for the design, for example, relevant standards, development models and tools. In the next step, the 'requirements analysis' focuses on the characterization of users and the set-up of user profiles; additionally, tasks and workflows have to be analysed. The information obtained is used to plan the activities of 'work re-engineering' and for the design of the user interface. Analysis and design activities for job and software design have some overlap here (see previous section).

Phase 2: iterative development

The results of the preceding phase are used to design the organizational and work flow part of the system. In this phase, it should be remembered that the design and introduction of computer systems are considered part of the job design and should therefore be seen in an organizational context (Zapf, 1995, p. 72; see above 'participative job and task design'). Conceptual models of the software are developed which can be used to produce early prototypes, for instance, paper and pencil prototypes or mock-ups. Using an iterative and participative design approach, the prototypes are evaluated and changed continuously by means of user testing (Rubin, 1994) or inspection methods (Nielsen & Mack, 1994). This helps to identify and remove major usability problems. The evaluation (re)design cycle is repeated until the goals of the user-centred design are met. It is recommended to utilize user participation in all phases of the design process (see ISO 13407, 1999). The product can be evaluated to ascertain whether it fulfils the user-oriented requirements and/or whether it is in accordance with other international standards, such as ISO 9241 (for an overview of software evaluation, see Gediga *et al.*, 2002).

Phase 3: system installation

The final phase concerns the system installation and user training. Furthermore, acceptance of the system has to be assured, and system support and maintenance must be organized. Software evaluation procedures in the application phase have to be planned in order to obtain feedback about the usability of the system. This information can be used to design new releases. It may be neccserary to revise the system after a certain period of application. In such a case, a new version of the software should be designed corresponding to the principles of the phases of usability engineering.

Furthermore, the design of software and especially the human–computer interface should consider knowledge from the research field of human–computer interaction (Helander *et al.*, 1997; Shneidermann & Plaisant, 2005). We cannot give a detailed overview at this time, but some important design aspects should be mentioned. The design – or redesign – of software systems should avoid too much complexity (Shneidermann & Plaisant, 2005). A reduction of complexity, while maintaining sufficient features of the system, may be achieved by the modularization of the system, for example, into task-related components. Complexity, moreover, may be decreased if software systems are adaptable to task and user requirements (Greif, 1994; Haaks, 1992). To anticipate and minimize errors, a consistent system structure and design, unambiguous and clearly available feedback about the state of the system, and the reversibility of actions should be realized (Brodbeck & Rupietta, 1994; Norman, 1983, 1988; Rasmussen & Vicente, 1989). Zapf (1995) emphasizes that tools supporting error handling can contribute towards coping with stress. In particular, he mentions backup files, undo functions and context-sensitive help.

11.4.4   Adequate Training Programmes and Personal Help Networks

After implementing new technology, most organizations offer professional training programmes for their employees. Participants are expected to acquire computer knowledge and skills through these training programmes. Often the main principle of these training programmes is to provide detailed instructions on correct task solutions and to prevent participants from making errors (cf. Keith & Frese, 2008). However, since human errors occur frequently in human–computer interaction (see above section 11.2.3), it is vitally important to train employees in the detection and management of errors (Frese, 1991b). Users should not always fall back on support hotlines or their team when they face a problem that they can try to manage themselves. However, if the problem is too complex or if the consequences of errors cannot be eliminated, novices in particular should seek personal help. Like Carroll and Mack (1983), we tried to activate self-organized exploratory behaviour in the learning process using minimal guidelines for self-instruction instead of handbooks and teacher-centred instruction methods. Since we concentrated especially on the exploration of error situations, we call our learning concept 'exploratory error training' (Greif, 1986, 1994). A similar approach called 'error management training' has been introduced by Frese and his co-workers (see Irmer et al., 1991).

The main characteristics of 'exploratory error training' are that participants are not only encouraged to choose learning tasks themselves and to explore software systems actively, but also to explicitly make errors. Heuristics for diagnosing and coping with errors are integrated systematically into the training programme. Moreover, the concept intends to cultivate social support and establish personal help networks by encouraging trainees to ask colleagues for help in error situations.

In addition, we recommend the design of learning environments, which support active and successful self-organizing learning activities when interacting with new and often continuously changing technologies. For practical use, the initial design of exploratory learning environments that are well suited for different learners is a rather difficult task. Our solution is to combine the design of minimal guidelines for self-instruction and exploratory learning tasks. We allow for individual differences. Individuals can choose between learning resources and can determine the level of system and task complexity, as well as the individual speed of learning. According to theory (Greif & Keller, 1990), exploration should facilitate the development of skills and self-efficacy. This could encourage future exploratory learning, creativity and role innovation (Farr & Ford, 1990; Englehardt & Simmons, 2002).

Exploratory error training and self-organized learning approaches have been evaluated in several experimental studies, as well as in practice (Greif, 1994). The results show clearly that most computer novices, after exploratory error training, are able to perform complex tasks successfully. Evidence from a follow-up study demonstrates that, after training, most subjects were able to learn new complex software systems quickly on their own (Greif, 1994). One strength of self-organized learning is that it initiates personal help networks and social support between colleagues.

Error management training involving active exploration has also shown better effects on performance, and seems to be better suited for promoting the transfer to novel tasks in contrast to error avoidance training (Keith & Frese, 2008). There seems to be evidence that performance differences are mediated by emotion control and metacognitive activities (Keith & Frese, 2005).

11.5 CONCLUSION

In summary, the results of both experimental and field research show that new technology is not a source of stress *per se*. There are no studies that are able to prove such a simple assumption. On the contrary, in many studies on different factors and on the overall impact of new technologies, we find groups of employees where stress remains constant or even declines following the implementation of new computer systems at work. However, stress may result from many concrete problems, such as malfunction and the lack of usability of software systems, as well as the poor ergonomic design of hardware equipment and furnishings, insufficient training and especially from poor task and job design.

Cross-sectional and longitudinal studies dealing with the overall impact of technological changes on stress and well-being show that a basic problem of the introduction of new technology is an inadequate implementation process.

In this chapter, approaches and methods have been presented that should help to manage these problems by active employee participation in the implementation process as well as in the (re)design of technological and organizational systems with respect to psychosocial work characteristics.

Learning how to manage technological and other changes in the organization is a very important investment for innovative organizations. Today, computer systems are standard technologies in modern industries and administrations, but technological innovation does not stop. On the contrary, the pace of innovation in computer hardware and software has accelerated. For this reason, 'stress by permanent changes' is an emerging problem that should be observed carefully. Nonetheless, new technologies and stress will remain a major challenge for organizations in the future.

REFERENCES

Agervold, M. (1987). New technology in the office: attitudes and consequences. *Work and Stress*, **2**, 143–53.

Bamberg, E., Ducki, A. & Metz, A.-M. (Eds) (1998). *Handbuch betriebliche Gesundheitsförderung*. Göttingen: Verlag für Angewandte Psychologie.

Benda, H. von (1990). Information und Kommunikation im Büro. In C. Graf Hoyos & B. Zimolong (Eds), *Enzyklopädie der Psychologie D III/2. Ingenieurpsychologie* (pp. 479–510). Göttingen: Hogrefe.

Bennebroek Gravenhorst, K.M., Werkman, R.A. & Boonstra, J.J. (2003). The change capacity of organisations: general assessment and five configurations. *Applied Psychology: An International Review*, **52**(1), 83–105.

Beyer, H. & Holtzblatt, K. (1998). *Contextual Design*. San Francisco: Morgan Kaufmann.

Bjørn-Andersen, N. (1985). Training for subjection or participation. In B. Shackel (Ed.), *Human-Computer Interaction - Interact '84* (pp. 839–46). Amsterdam: North Holland.

Blackler, F., & Brown, C. (1986). Alternative models to guide the design and introduction of the new information technologies into work organizations. *Journal of Occupational Psychology*, **59**(4), 287-313.

Blyth, A. (1995). Modelling the business process to derive organisational requirements for information technology. *SIGOIS Bulletin*, **16**(1), 25–33.

Boonstra, J. (2000). De zinloosheid van HRM bij organisatieverendering. *Tijdschrift voor HRM*, **3**, 25–51.

Boucsein, W. (1988). Wartezeiten am Rechner - Erholung oder Streß? *Zeitschrift für Arbeitswissenschaft*, **4**, 222–225.

Briner, R. & Hockey, R.J. (1988). Operator stress and computer-based work. In C.L. Cooper & R. Payne (Eds), *Causes, Coping and Consequences of Stress at Work* (pp. 115–40). Chichester: John Wiley & Sons, Ltd.

Brodbeck, F.C. & Rupietta, W. (1994). Fehlermanagement und Hilfesysteme. In E. Eberleh, H. Oberquelle & R. Oppermann (Eds), *Einführung in die Software-Ergonomie* (pp. 197–234). Berlin: De Gruyter.

Brodbeck, F. C., Zapf, D., Prümper, J. & Frese, M. (1993). Error handling in office work with computers: a field study. *Journal of Occupational and Organizational Psychology*, **66**(4), 303–17.

Buchanan, D.A. & Boddy, D. (1982). Advanced technology and the quality of working life: the effects of word processing on video typists. *Journal of Occupational Psychology*, **55**, 1–11.

Çakir, A. (1981). Belastung und Beanspruchung bei Bildschirmtätigkeiten. In M. Frese (Ed.), *Streß im Büro* (pp. 46–71). Bern: Huber.

Coch, L. & French, J. (1948). Overcoming resistance to change. *Human Relations*, **1**, 512–32.

Carayon, P. (1993). Job design and job stress in office workers. *Ergonomics*, **36**(5), 463–77.

Carayon, P. (1997). Temporal issues of quality of working life and stress in human-computer interaction. *International Journal of Human-Computer Interaction*, **9**, 325–42.

Carayon, P., Yang, C.-L. & Lim, S.-Y. (1995). Examining the relationship between job design and worker strain over time in a sample of office workers. *Ergonomics*, **38**, 1199–211.

Carroll, J.M. (Ed.) (1995). *Scenario-Based Design. Envisioning Work and Technology in System Development.* New York: John Wiley & Sons, Inc.

Carroll, J.N. & Mack, R.L. (1983). Active learning to use a word processor. In: W.E. Cooper (Ed.), *Cognitive Aspects of Skilled Typewriting* (pp. 259–82). Berlin: Springer.

Clegg, C., Axtell, C., Damodaran, L., Farbey, B., Hull, R., Lloyd-Jones, R. *et al.* (1997). Information technology: a study of performance and the role of human and organizational factors. *Ergonomics*, **40**(9), 851–71.

Dutke, S. & Schönpflug, W. (1987). When the introductory period is over: learning while doing one's job. In M. Frese, E. Ulich & W. Dzida (Eds), *Psychological Issues of Human-Computer Interaction* (pp. 295–310). Amsterdam: North-Holland.

Dzida, M., Langenheder, W., Cornelius, D. & Schardt, L.P. (1984). *Auswirkungen des EDV-Einsatzes auf die Arbeitssituation und Möglichkeiten einer arbeitsorientierten Gestaltung.* St. Augustin: GMD-Studie, No. 82.

Eason, K., Harker, S. & Olphert, W. (1996). Representing socio-technical systems options in the development of new forms of work organization. *European Journal of Work and Organizational Psychology*, **5**(3), 399–420.

Englehardt, C.S. & Simmons, P.R. (2002). Creating an organizational space for learning. *Learning Organization*, **9**, 39–47.

Farr, J. & Ford, C.M. (1990). Individual innovation. In M. West & J Farr (Eds), *Innovation and Creativity at Work: Psychological Approaches* (pp. 63–80). New York: John Wiley & Sons, Inc.

Fay, D., Sonnentag, S. & Frese, M. (2001). Stressors, innovation, and personal initiative: are stressors always detrimental? In C.L. Cooper (Ed.), *Theories of Organizational Stress* (pp. 170–89). New York: Oxford University Press.

Frese, M. (1989). Human computer interaction within an industrial psychology framework. *Applied Psychology: An International Review*, **38**, 29–44.

Frese, M. (1991a). Streß und neue Techniken. Was ändert sich? In S. Greif, E. Bamberg & N. Semmer (Eds), *Psychischer Streß am Arbeitsplatz.* (pp. 120–34). Göttingen: Hogrefe.

Frese, M. (1991b). Fehlermanagement: Konzeptionelle Überlegungen. In M. Frese & D. Zapf (Eds), *Fehler bei der Arbeit mit dem Computer* (pp. 139–50). Bern: Huber.

Frese, M. & Brodbeck, F.C. (1989). *Computer in Büro und Verwaltung.* Heidelberg: Springer.

Frese, M., Brodbeck, F., Heinbokel, T., Mooser, C., Schleiffenbaum, E. & Thiemann, P. (1991). Errors in training computer skills: on the positive function of errors. *Human-Computer Interaction*, **6**(1), 77–93.

Frese, M. & Semmer, N. (1991). Streßfolgen in Abhängigkeit von Moderatorvariablen: Der Einfluß von Kontrolle und sozialer Unterstützung. In S. Greif, E. Bamberg & N. Semmer (Eds), *Psychischer Streß am Arbeitsplatz* (pp. 135–53). Göttingen: Hogrefe.

Frese, M. & Zapf, D. (1987). Die Einführung von neuen Techniken verändert Qualifikationsanforderungen, Handlungsspielraum und Stressoren kaum. *Zeitschrift für Arbeitswissenschaft*, **41**(13 NF), 7–14.

Frese, M. & Zapf, D. (1994). Action as the core of work psychology: a German approach. In H.C. Triandis, M.D. Dunnette & L.M. Hough (Eds), *Handbook of Industrial and Organizational Psychology* (Vol. **4**, pp. 271–340). Palo Alto, CA: Consulting Psychologists Press.

Gediga, G., Hamborg, K.-C. & Düntsch, I. (2002). Evaluation of software systems. In A. Kent & J.G. Williams (Eds), *Encyclopedia of Computer Science and Technology* (Vol. **45**, pp. 127–53). New York: Marcel Dekker.

Gould, J.D. (1988). How to design usable systems. In M. Helander (Ed.), *Handbook of Human Computer Interaction* (pp. 757–89). Amsterdam: Elsevier.

Greif, S. (1986). Neue Kommunikationstechnologien -Entlastung oder mehr Streß? In K.-K. Pullig, U. Schäkel & J. Scholz (Eds), *Streß im Unternehmen* (pp. 178–99). Hamburg: Windmühle GmbH Verlag.

Greif, S. (1991a). Streß in der Arbeit -Einführung und Grundbegriffe-. In S. Greif, E. Bamberg & N. Semmer (Eds), *Psychischer Streß am Arbeitsplatz* (pp. 1–28). Göttingen: Hogrefe.

Greif, S. (1991b). Organisational issues and task analysis. In B. Shackel & S Richardson (Eds), *Human Factors for Informatics Usability* (pp. 247–67). Cambridge: Cambridge University Press.

Greif, S. (1994). Fehlertraining und Komplexität beim Softwaredesign. *Zeitschrift für Arbeitswissenschaft*, **48**(20NF), 44–53.

Greif, S. & Keller, H. (1990). Exploratory behavior in human-computer interaction. In M. West & J. Farr (Eds), *Innovation and Creativity at Work: Psychological Approaches* (pp. 231–50). New York: John Wiley & Sons, Inc.

Haaks, D. (1992). *Anpaßbare Informationssysteme*. Göttingen: Verlag für Angewandte Psychologie.

Hamborg, K.-C. (1996). Zum Einfluß der Komplexität von Software-Systemen auf Fehler bei Computernovizen und Experten. *Zeitschrift für Arbeits- und Organisationspsychologie*, **40**, 3–11.

Hamborg, K.-C., Schulze, L. & Sendfeld, M. (2007). Mensch-Computer Interaktion: Von der Arbeitsmittel- zur Arbeits- und Organisationsgestaltung. In T. Gross (Ed.), *Mensch & Computer 2007. Interaktion im Plural* (pp. 199–208). München: Oldenbourg.

Hirschheim, R.A., Land, F.F. & Smithson, S. (1985). Implementing computer-based information systems in organisations: issues and strategies. In B. Shackel (Ed.), *Human-Computer Interaction - Interact '84* (pp. 855–62). Amsterdam: North Holland.

Hofmann, K. & Bungard, W. (1995). Modellwechsel in der Automobilindustrie. In H.J. Warnecke (Ed.), *Aufbruch in fraktalen Unternehmen – Praxisbeispiele für Denken und Handeln*. Heidelberg: Springer.

Humphrey, S.E., Nahrgang, J.D. & Morgeson, F.P. (2007). Integrating motivational, social, and contextual work design features: a meta-analytic summary and theoretical extension of the work design literature. *Journal of Applied Psychology*, **92**(5), 1332–56.

Huuhtanen, P. (1997). Toward a multilevel model in longitudinal studies on computerization in offices. *International Journal of Human-Computer Interaction*, **9**, 383–405.

Hackman, J.R. & Lawler, E.E. (1971). Employee reactions to job characteristics. *Journal of Applied Psychology*, **55**(3), 259–86.

Helander, M., Landauer, T.K. & Prabhu, P. (Eds) (1997). *Handbook of Human-Computer Interaction*. Amsterdam: Elsevier Science.

Irmer, C., Pfeffer, S. & Frese, M. (1991). Konsequenzen von Fehleranalysen für das Training: Das Fehlertraining. In M. Frese & D. Zapf (Eds), (*Fehler bei der Arbeit mit dem Computer* (pp. 151–65). Bern: Huber.

ISO 9241-2 (1992). *Ergonomic requirements for office work with visual display terminals (VDT's)*. Part 2: Guidance on task requirements. Genf: ISO.

ISO 9241-11 (1998). *Ergonomic requirements for office work with visual display terminals (VDT's)*. Part 11: Guidance on usability. Genf: ISO.

ISO 13407 (1999). *Human-centred design processes for interactive systems*. Genf: ISO.

Järvenpää, E. (1997). Implementation of office automation and its effects on job characteristics and strain in a district court. *International Journal of Human-Computer Interaction*, **9**, 425–42.

Johansson, G. (1989). Stress, autonomy, and the maintenance of skill in supervisory control of automated systems. *Applied Psychology: An International Review*, **38**, 45–56.

Johansson, G. & Aronsson, G. (1984). Stress reactions in computerized administrative work. *Journal of occupational Psychology*, **5**, 159–81.

Jones, F. & Fletcher, B.C. (2003). Job Control, Physical Health and Psychological Well-Being. In M.J. Schabracq, J.A.M. Winnubst & C.L. Cooper (Eds.), *The Handbook of Work & Health Psychology* (2nd edition, pp. 121–142). New York: John Wiley & Sons, Inc.

Kalimo, R. & Leppänen, A. (1985). Feedback from video display terminals, performance control and stress in text preparation in the printing industry. *Journal of Occupational Psychology*, **58**, 27–38.

Kanter, R.M. (1985). Managing the human side of change. *Management Review*, **74**(4), 52–7.

Karasek, R. & Theorell, T. (1990). *Healthy Work: Stress, Productivity and the Reconstruction of Working Life*. New York: Basic Books.

Keith, N. & Frese, M. (2005). Self-regulation in error management training: emotional control and metacognition as mediators of performance effects. *Journal of Applied Psychology*, **90**(4), 677–91.

Keith, N. & Frese, M. (2008). Effectiveness of error management training: a meta-analysis. *Journal of Applied Psychology*, **93**(1), 59–69.

Kompier, M. (2003). Job Design and Well-Being. In M.J. Schabracq, J.A.M. Winnubst & C.L. Cooper (Eds.), *The Handbook of Work & Health Psychology* (2nd edition, pp. 429–454). New York: John Wiley & Sons, Inc.

Korunka, C. & Vitouch, O. (1999). Effects of the implementation of information technology on employees' strain and job satisfaction: a context dependent approach. *Work and Stress*, **34**, 341–63.

Korunka, C., Weiss, A., Huemer, K.-H. & Karetta, B. (1995). The effect of new technologies on job satisfaction and psychosomatics complaints. *Applied Psychology: An International Review*, **44**, 123–42.

Korunka, C., Weiss, A. & Karetta, B. (1993). Effects of new technologies with special regard for the implementation process per se. *Journal of Organizational Behavior*, **14**, 331–48.

Korunka, C., Zauchner, S. & Weiss, A. (1997). New technologies, job profiles, and external workload as predictors of subjectively experienced stress and dissatisfaction at work. *International Journal of Human-Computer Interaction*, **9**, 407–24.

Krone, A., Hamborg, K.-C. & Gediga, G. (2002). Zur emotionalen Reaktion bei Fehlern in der Mensch-Computer Interaktion. *Zeitschrift für Arbeits- und Organisationspsychologie*, **46**, 185–200.

Kühlmann, T.M. (1988). *Technische und organisatorische Neuerungen im Erleben betroffener Arbeitnehmer*. Stuttgart: Enke.

Lazarus, R.S. (1976). *Patterns of Adjustment*. New York: McGraw-Hill.

Leitner, K., Lüders, E., Greiner, B., Ducki, A., Nierdermeier, R. & Volpert, W. (1993). *Analyse psychischer Anforderungen und Belastungen in der Büroarbeit*. Göttingen: Hogrefe.

Levi, L. (1994). Work, worker and wellbeing: an overview. *Work and Stress*, **8**, 79–83.

Marjchrzak, A. & Cotton, J. (1988). A longitudinal study of adjustment to technological change: from mass to computer-automated batch production. *Journal of Occupational Psychology*, **61**, 43–66.

Mayhew, D. (1999). *The Usability Engineering Lifecycle. A Practitioner's Handbook for User Interface Design*. San Francisco: Morgan Kaufmann.

Mohr, G. (1991). Fünf Subkonstrukte psychischer Befindensbeeinträchtigung bei Industriearbeitern: Auswahl und Entwicklung. In S. Greif, E. Bamberg & N. Semmer (Eds), *Psychischer Streß am Arbeitsplatz*. Göttingen: Hogrefe, pp. 91–119.

Morgeson, F.P. & Campion, M.A. (2003). Work design. In W.C. Borman, D.R. Ilgen & R.J. Klimoski (Eds), *Handbook of Psychology: Industrial and Organizational Psychology* (Vol. **12**, pp. 423–52). New York: John Wiley & Sons, Inc.

Nadin, S.J., Waterson, P.E. & Parker, S.K. (2001). Participation in job redesign: an evaluation of the use of a sociotechnical tool and its impact. *Human Factors and Ergonomics in Manufacturing*, **11**(1), 53–69.

Nielsen, J. (1993). *Usability Engineering*. Boston, MA: AP Professional.

Nielsen, J. & Mack, R.L. (Eds) (1994). *Usability Inspection Methods*. New York: John Wiley & Sons, Inc.

Norman, D.A. (1983). Design rules based on analyses of human error. *Communications of the ACM*, **26**, 254–8.

Norman, D.A. (1988). *The Psychology of Everyday Things*. New York: Basic Books.

Parker, S. & Wall, L. (2001). Work design: learning from the past and mapping a new terrain. In N. Anderson, D.S. Ones, H.K. Sinangil & C. Viswesvaran (Eds), *Handbook of Industrial, Work and Organizational Psychology* (Vol. **1**, pp. 91–109). Thousand Oaks, CA: Sage.

Rasmussen, J. & Vicente, K.J. (1989). Coping with human errors through system design: implications for ecological interface design. *International Journal of Man-Machine Studies*, **31**, 517–34.

Rubin, J. (1994). *Handbook of Usability Testing*. New York: John Wiley & Sons, Inc.

Saupe, R. & Frese, M. (1981). Faktoren für das Erleben und die Bewältigung von Streß im Schreibdienst. In M. Frese (Ed.), *Streß im Büro* (pp. 199–224). Bern: Huber.

Sauter, S.L., Gottlieb, M.S., Jones, K.C., Dodsen, V. & Rohrer, K.M. (1983). Job and health implications of VDT use: initial results of the Wisconsin NIOSH study. *Communications of the ACM*, **26**, 284–94.

Sauter, S.L., Schleifer, L.M. & Knutson, S.J. (1991). Work posture, workstation design and muscoskeletal discomfort in a VDT data entry task. *Human Factors*, **33**, 151–67.

Schulz, P. & Höfert, W. (1981). Wirkungsmechanismen und Effekte von Zeitdruck bei Angestelltentätigkeiten. In M. Frese (Ed.), *Streß im Büro* (pp. 72–95). Bern: Huber.

Semmer, N. (1984). *Streßbezogene Tätigkeitsanalyse: Psychologische Untersuchungen zur Analyse von Streß am Arbeitsplatz*. Weinheim: Beltz.

Shneidermann, B. & Plaisant, C. (2005). *Designing the User Interface. Strategies for Effective Human-Computer Interaction* (4th edn). Boston, MA: Addison Wesley.

Spector, P.E. (1998). A control theory of the job stress process. In C.L. Cooper (Ed.), *Theories of Organizational Stress* (pp. 153–69). New York: Oxford University Press

Stellman, J.M., Klitzman, S., Gordon, G.C. & Snow, B.R. (1987). Work environment and the well-being of clerical and VDT workers. *Journal of Occupational Behaviour*, **8**, 95–114.

Symon, G. & Clegg, C. (2005). Constructing identity and participation during technological change. *Human Relations*, **58**, 1141–66.

Turner, J.A. & Karasek, R.A. (1984). Software ergonomics: effects of computer application design parameters on operator task performance and health. *Ergonomics*, **27**, 663–90.

Udris, I. (1989). Soziale Unterstützung. In S. Greif, H. Holling & N. Nicholson (Eds), *Arbeits- und Organisationspsychologie. Internationales Handbuch in Schlüsselbegriffen* (pp. 421–5). München: PVU.

Wanberg, C.R. & Banas, J.T. (2000). Predictors and outcomes of openness to changes in a reorganizing workplace. *Journal of Applied Psychology*, **85**(1), 132–42.

Warr, P. (1987). *Work, Unemployment and Mental Health*. Oxford: Clarendon Press.

Waterson, P.E., Clegg, C.W., Bolden, R., Pepper, K., Warr, P.B. & Wall, T.D. (1999). The use and effectiveness of modern manufacturing practices: a survey of UK industry. *International Journal of Production Research*, **37**(10), 2271–92.

Waterson, P.E., Older-Gray, M.T. & Clegg, C.W. (2002). A sociotechnical method for designing work systems. *Human Factors*, **44**(3), 376–91.

Welsch, J. (1989). Technischer Wandel und Arbeitsmarkt -Ausgewählte Ergebnisse der META-Studie des Bundesforschungsministeriums. *WSI Mitteilungen*, **42**, 503–16.

Winnubst, J.A.M. & Diekstra, R.F.W. (1998). Work and health psychology: Methods of intervention. In P. J. D. Drenth & H. Thierry. (Eds.), *Handbook of work and organizational psychology* (2nd edition), vol. **3**: Personnel psychology (pp. 395–408). Hove: Psychology Press/Erlbaum.

Wixon, D. & Wilson, C. (1997). The usability engineering framework for product design and evaluation. In M. Helander, T. Landauer & P. Prabhu (Eds), *Handbook of Human-Computer Interaction* (pp. 653–88). Amsterdam: Elsevier.

Zapf, D. (1991). Fehler, Streß und organisationaler Kontext. In M. Frese & D. Zapf (Eds), *Fehler bei der Arbeit mit dem Computer* (pp. 106–17). Bern: Huber.

Zapf, D. (1993). Stress-oriented analysis of computerized office work. *The European Work and Organizational Psychologist*, **3**, 85–100.

Zapf, D. (1995). Stress oriented analysis of computerized office work. In J.M. Peiró, F. Prieto, J.L. Meliá & O. Luque (Eds), *Work and Organizational Psychology: European Contributions of the Nineties. Proceedings of the Sixth European Congress of Work and Organizational Psychology* (pp. 61–760. London: Taylor & Francis.

Zeier, H., Mion, H., Läubli, Th., Thomas, C. & Senn, E. (1987). Augen- und Rückenbeschwerden bei Bildschirmarbeit in Abhängigkeit von ergonomischen und biopsychosozialen Faktoren. *Zeitschrift für experimentelle und angewandte Psychologie*, **XXXIV**, 155–79.

CHAPTER 12

Flexibility at Work in Relation to Employee Health

Töres Theorell

Karolinska Institute Stockholm, Sweden

12.1 PHYSIOLOGICAL FLEXIBILITY

From a medical perspective it is important to begin discussions about flexibility at work with the individual physiological mechanisms underlying reaction patterns. A recent development in physiology is the formulation of 'chaos theory' (Cotton, 1991; Goldberger, 1991), which can be regarded as the biological basis of flexible coping. It is, accordingly, of fundamental importance to the analysis of flexibility at work in relation to employee health. It postulates that the reactions in the healthy organism are unpredictable by means of conventional 'linear' models because there are a large number of possible responses to demanding situations. This is mirrored in the fact, for example, that the healthy human being has a large number of cycles in its variation in heart rate. The most well-known cycle is the one that is associated with breathing: when we take in air the heart rate accelerates and vice versa. As we grow old or develop certain kinds of heart disorders this respiratory 'sinus arrhythmia' disappears and so do several of the heart rate variability cycles. Most of our biological functions show variability that follows several cycles at the same time, and it seems to be true that ageing and sickness – for instance, heart disease – are associated with extinction of several of these cycles.

The unpredictable biological variability is also associated with the number of possible biological responses to demands in the environment. The larger the number of biological cycles, the larger the number of 'ways out' from difficult situations. Perhaps this biological principle is also applicable in psychosocial processes.

International Handbook of Work and Health Psychology, Third Edition. Edited by Cary L. Cooper, James Campbell Quick, and Marc J. Schabracq.

12.2 PSYCHOLOGICAL FLEXIBILITY

Biological chaos theory has its counterpart in psychological coping theory. One way of summarizing this is to say that individuals who report that they have many different ways of responding to demands – coping strategies – at their disposal will do better in demanding situations. Shalit (1978) developed his 'coping wheel' in order to predict which young men and women would be more able than others to stand the horrors of the Arab–Israeli wars during the 1960s and 1970s. His ideas were simple and straightforward. Those who report that they have many interests and areas of activity in life would do better than others. Furthermore, those who feel that they are in control of and have positive feelings about most of these activities – particularly those that are rated to have high priority – would be more likely to do better than others. According to these ideas, Shalit constructed a measurement technique that consists of a wheel with 12 segments. The subjects are asked to describe what activities they have in life. They only use one or two of their own words to describe the activity and they may use as many segments as they please. Afterwards they are asked to order the activities with regard to magnitude of importance (if they feel they are able to), and to rate them with regard to emotional feelings that they are associated with (from negative through neutral to positive) and with regard to the degree to which they feel they are in control. A recent study from our group has shown, for instance, that a programme for mental stimulation by means of pictures of pieces of art and discussion about the thoughts that these pictures evoke (exercises that take place for an hour once a week during four months) can increase the number of coping strategies and improve the pattern of coping in old people (Wikström *et al.*, 1994). The effects of this programme were compared to the effects of ordinary conversations of the same frequency and amount. Improved emotional state and health were observed along with the improved coping patterns in the experimental group, but not in the control group.

In parallel with the observations on coping patterns in general, it might be speculated that flexible coping patterns could protect workers from poor health, and also that a work situation that enforces the development of such coping patterns stimulates the development of health in the workplace.

Another way of categorizing coping patterns is to group them into open and covert strategies. In a series of studies we have used a Swedish short version of a questionnaire measuring coping patterns (Harburg *et al.*, 1973; Knox *et al.*, 1985; Theorell *et al.*, 1993). The person is asked what he or she would typically do if exposed to unfair treatment by the boss. Parallel questions are made about unfair treatment from a workmate. A number of fixed response categories are used, and the degree to which the person uses different strategies is rated on a four-graded scale. Factor analyses have shown that the responses can be grouped into open ('I would say immediately what I think' etc.) and covert ('I would not do anything', 'I would brood about it at home' etc.) patterns. Covert coping is associated with sleep disturbance in both men and women (Theorell *et al.*, 1993). This reaches statistical significance only for women in the study presented in Table 12.1. In a more recent study of 6000 employed women and men, however, a low decision latitude was statistically significantly related to a less open and a more covert coping pattern in both men and women although the relationship was stronger in women than in men (Theorell *et al.*, 2000). In this later study we also found that a covert coping pattern – at least in men – was associated with high blood pressure. This may indicate that there is a psychophysiological cost (long-lasting energy mobilization) in covert coping.

The meaning and social context of flexibility may be markedly different for different groups. For instance, there are marked gender differences in the way in which psychosocial work organization correlates with individual coping patterns. Both intellectual discretion and authority over decisions increase significantly with age in men but not in women. This is consistent with findings in other countries. There are strong inverse correlations between social support, on the one hand, and psychological demands and the less covert coping, on the other, for women: the more support, the fewer demands and covert coping. In men, on the other hand, no relationship is found between covert coping and social support, whereas a weaker inverse relationship is found between social support and psychological demands. Social support at work stands out as a more significant buffer against stressful experiences for women than it does for men in this study.

But how do we stimulate flexible coping patterns in the work environment? In the following section I use Karasek's demand-control model (Karasek, 1979) to clarify my points.

12.3   ORGANIZATIONAL FLEXIBILITY

The organization – for example, of a workplace – can be regarded in the same way as that of a human being. According to most of the management literature, flexibility is an important ingredient in prosperous organizations (Anderson & King, 1993). There may, unfortunately, be a conflict between organizational flexibility and the individual's flexibility. This is one of the important themes in this review.

Table 12.1 Correlations between self-reported coping patterns and self-reported work environment in randomly selected working men and women in Stockholm ($n = 80$–90 for both groups)

	Open coping	Covert coping	Psychological demands	Intellectual discretion	Authority over decisions	Social support
Men						
Covert coping	−0.16					
Psychological demands	0.07	−0.01				
Intellectual discretion	0.08	0.16	0.28*			
Authority over decisions	0.15	0.07	0.16	0.62*		
Social support	−0.10	−0.13	−0.22*	0.08	0.15	
Age	−0.03	0.13	0.01	0.23*	0.23*	0.07
Women						
Covert coping	−0.26*					
Psychological demands	−0.01	0.22*				
Intellectual discretion	0.15	0.17	0.07			
Authority over decisions	0.20*	−0.07	0.01	0.45*		
Social support	−0.04	−0.29*	−0.61*	0.06	0.04	
Age	−0.13	0.16	−0.05	−0.03	0.00	0.05

*Significant at least on the 5% level.

12.3.1   Flexibility from the Individual's Point of View in Relation to Health Risk

One of the most widely applied theoretical models for studying work organization in relation to individual health risks is the demand-control model. When Karasek introduced this model, it was an architect's synthesis of the stress research/psychology and the sociology research traditions (Karasek, 1979). Generating the concept 'lack of control', or 'lack of decision latitude', as Karasek labelled it, goes back to the old sociologists' question: 'is the worker alienated from the work process?'. It was assumed that the possibility to utilize and develop skills (*skill utilization*), a concept developed in work psychology, was closely related to *authority over decisions*. In factor analysis of responses to questions about work content these two factors are mostly positively related, and, accordingly, they have been summated to constitute *decision latitude* (Karasek & Theorell, 1990). The other dimension, psychological demands, included qualitative as well as quantitative demands.

It should be emphasized that the demand-control model was never intended to explain all work environment related illness. Thus, there was no element of individual variation introduced into its original construction. On the contrary, the model dealt with the way in which work is organized, and the way in which this relates to illness. This simplicity has made the model useful in organizational work. A model that tries to explain 'all of the variance' would have to be more complicated and would be scientifically more, but educationally less, successful than the simple model that was introduced.

According to the model, there is interaction between high psychological demands and low decision latitude. If demands are regarded as the *x*-axis, and decision latitude as the *y*-axis in a two-dimensional system and the different combinations of high–low demands and high–low decisions are regarded, four combinations are recognized. The high demand/low decision latitude combination is regarded as the most relevant to illness development. Karasek uses a drastic analogy to describe this combination: if a person is crossing a street and he sees a truck approaching he may speculate that he will be able to cross the street without being hit by the truck – if he regulates his speed appropriately. However, if his foot gets stuck in the street his decision latitude diminishes dramatically and he is now in an extremely stressful situation. According to the theory, this kind of situation (not necessarily so dramatic), if prolonged and repeated for a long time, increases sympathoadrenal arousal and at the same time decreases anabolism, the body's ability to restore and repair tissues. The combination of high psychological demands and high decision latitude is defined as the active situation. In this situation the worker has more possibility to cope with high psychological demands because he or she can choose to plan working hours according to his or her own biological rhythm, and also has good possibilities for developing good coping strategies, facilitating feelings of mastery and control in unforeseen situations. The low demand/high decision latitude situation (relaxed) is theoretically associated with the smallest illness risks for the majority of subjects, whereas the low demand/low decision latitude situation, which is labelled 'passive', may be associated to some extent with the development of psychological atrophy: skills that the worker had when he was employed may be lost (Karasek & Theorell, 1990).

The most important component in Karasek's demand-control model is perhaps *decision latitude*, since it is directly translatable into work redesign. Using our reasoning above regarding coping strategies, it can be stated that the two components of decision latitude both have major importance for the development of flexible coping strategies. A work site with a high degree of intellectual discretion will *stimulate* the development of such strategies in the employees and a high degree of authority over decisions will *allow* this to occur.

12.3.2　Introduction of Social Support to the Model

There have been two recent developments aimed at introducing social support to the demand-control model.

Iso-Strain

Firstly, Johnson has included social support in the theoretical model. A study of cardiovascular disease prevalence in a large random sample of Swedish men and women indicated that the joint action of high demands and lack of control (decision latitude) is of particular importance to blue-collar men, whereas the joint action of lack of control and lack of support is more important for women and white-collar men (Johnson & Hall, 1988). The multiplicative interaction between all the three aspects (iso-strain; demands × lack of control × lack of support) was tested in a nine-year prospective study of 7000 randomly selected Swedish working men. Interestingly, for the most favoured 20% of men (low demands, good suport, good decision latitude) the progression of cardiovascular mortality with increasing age was slow, and equally so in the three social classes. In blue-collar workers, however, the age progression was much steeper in the worst iso-strain group than it was in the corresponding iso-strain group in white-collar workers (Johnson *et al.*, 1989).

Working life career

Secondly, attempts are now being made to use the occupational classification systems in order to describe the 'psychosocial work career'. Researchers have pointed out that an estimate of work conditions at only one point in time may provide a very imprecise estimation of the total exposure to adverse conditions (House *et al.*, 1986). Therefore, in order to explore the effects of the total working career, a large group of randomly selected working men and women in Sweden were interviewed about occupations that they had had throughout their whole career. For each year the job description was translated to the Nordic classification of occupations. Occupational scores were subsequently used for a calculation of the 'total lifetime exposure'. These scores had been derived from the average scores (demands, control and support) calculated separately for a number of subgroups within each occupation. Thus, they were calculated separately for men and women, for those below and above 45 years of age, and for those with less than 5 years of employment, between 5 and 20 years and finally above 20 years of employment. The 'total job control exposure' in relation to nine-year age-adjusted cardiovascular mortality in working Swedes was studied. It was observed for both men and women that the cardiovascular mortality differences between the lowest and highest quartiles were two-fold, even after adjustment for age, smoking habits and physical exercise. Furthermore, if the individual had had several large fluctuations in job control over the years, the risk of cardiovascular death during follow-up increased even more, up to almost three-fold compared to the high control group (Johnson *et al.*, 1993). The index of psychological demands recorded in this study did not predict risk of cardiovascular death in the way that was expected. (The index consisted of two questions: 'Is your work hectic?' and 'Is your work psychologically demanding?') For men it had no predictive value at all, and for women it predicted significantly in the reversed direction: the higher the psychological demands during the career, the lower the risk. These latter findings may indicate either that the index is not capturing psychological demands or that demands are associated with risk in different ways in the short term (according to previous studies) compared to the long term. They also illustrate differences between men and women in the patterns of correlations between psychosocial factors and cardiovascular disease risk (Hall, 1990).

A recent study has shown that the level of control inferred from the job title – after taking age, gender and time of exposure to the occupation into account – has a different development in working men who have developed a first myocardial infarction during the 10 preceding years than in a control group of age matched men without this experience (Theorell *et al.*, 1998). The 25% of the employed men who had had the least favourable development with regard to decision latitude during the preceding 10 years had a significantly elevated risk of developing a myocardial infarction. This was particularly true in the 45–54-year-old men, among whom the excess risk was 80% after adjustment for accepted biomedical risk factors and social class. This observation may illustrate that the timing of a first myocardial infarction in a working man may be related to falls in control level at work. In the near future there will be increasing numbers of lay-offs and changes in jobs. Due to the increasing pressures in the labour markets, individuals will have to accept jobs with much lower levels of decision latitude than they have been accustomed to. Thus, it is to be expected that the number of myocardial infarctions will show a further increase.

12.4 PHYSIOLOGICAL COUNTERPARTS OF THE DEMAND-CONTROL-SUPPORT MODEL

It has been hypothesized that working in an active situation stimulates the anabolic restoring and protective processes in the body (Karasek & Theorell, 1990), whereas working under job strain inhibits anabolism. In both active jobs and job strain, psychological demands are high. This means that mobilization of energy has a high priority. Long-lasting energy mobilization may lead to catabolism, the breakdown of protein for the provision of energy 'at any cost'. Due to the high level of anabolism taking place in the active jobs, the body will be able to stand these periods of energy mobilization well. In flexibility terms, this means that the active jobs enhance the body's capacity to stand periods of energy mobilization. This could be one way of describing flexibility in physiological terms. However, in the job strain situation, anabolism is inhibited and the body's capacity to stand periods of energy mobilization is therefore limited.

Anabolic processes correspond predominantly to certain hormones such as testosterone, growth hormone and insulin, which stimulate restoration and repair of worn-out tissue material in the body. The activity of this type of hormone typically peaks during deep sleep, when restoration and reparation activities are at maximum levels, whereas typical endocrine counterparts of energy mobilization are cate-cholamines and thyroid hormones.

Few studies have been published that have explored empirically the relationship between psychosocial job factors, on the one hand, and the balance between energy mobilization and anabolism, on the other. In a study performed by our group, working men and women were followed longitudinally during one year at three-month intervals, and spontaneous variations in job strain were recorded by means of questionnaires. It was shown that spontaneously occurring periods of job strain (according to the person's own standards) were associated with elevated blood pressure levels during working hours, increased sleep disturbance and lower testosterone concentration levels in plasma, findings compatible with increased energy mobilization and decreased anabolism (Theorell *et al.*, 1988). These results illustrate that there may be physiological mechanisms linking an increased rigidity (from the employee's point of view) under demanding conditions to changes in health.

12.5 COMBINING THE INDIVIDUAL'S NEED FOR FLEXIBILITY WITH THAT OF THE WORK ORGANIZATION

The above review indicates that hard health outcome criteria, as well as mortality, covary with factors that are relevant to flexibility for the individual, and can be summarized under the heading of decision latitude with the two components:

1 Opportunity to develop and use one's own skills.
2 Opportunity to issue control over one's own situation.

Some of our empirical findings give a hint that long-term exposure to low decision latitude jobs creates even more pronounced health risks than does short exposure and, furthermore, that a sudden deterioration in decision latitude may be followed by increased health risks within a couple of years.

Although slightly less well established, good social support at work, which may be associated with flexible solutions from the individual's point of view (good social interactions may increase the number of options in difficult working situations), may protect the individual from the adverse effects of a rigid work environment. In at least two of our studies of personnel in adverse job conditions – prison personnel and airport freight handlers (Härenstam *et al.*, 1988, Theorell *et al.*, 1990) – it became evident that personnel working under bad conditions can stand low decision latitude more easily if they derive support from colleagues.

The central question in this contribution is how flexibility in the biological and psychological sense and from the perspective of the individual – in the long term, in particular – can be obtained in work organization. It is likely that organizational changes favouring the development of increased intellectual discretion and authority over decisions in individuals may stimulate flexibility in coping patterns.

Flexibility for the individual may not always be the same as flexibility for the organization. It is important to make this distinction. Organizational flexibility may mean, for instance, that employees should be able to change workplace and work hours at short notice. This may, of course, imply a lack of decision latitude for employees and their families. Such a development has been studied very recently by our research group in a large, prosperous international corporation with rapid technological development. In this company, expansion has made it impossible for the company to build sufficient office space for all employees. This has stimulated the development of alternative strategies for constructing offices. These alternative strategies are intertwined with changes in work organization. Employees do not work in jobs, but instead in projects, which last for only three months on average. As a consequence of their moves between projects, employees also make many geographical moves. Accordingly, it is meaningless for them to have offices of their own. In this situation, employees have a very stimulating work situation with good opportunities to develop and use their skills. They also feel that they have good opportunities to exercise control in their work situation. However, a basic sense of belonging and social support may be lost, and this may be a threat to the individual's possibility of exercising flexibility. Furthermore, we may be facing an era that goes too far in emphasizing the benefits of active work (see above). Our evidence does, indeed, indicate that active work is associated with good health. However, if demands are pushed excessively, with extreme working hours, for example, social support from the family may be lost; if this is combined with loss of continuous support from workmates, we may face serious problems.

In a pilot study of the consequences of the first version of these sociotechnical changes, two different departments were studied. The same change was perceived very differently by the staff in the two departments. In one case, the work contents suited the proposed organization; the staff had asked for the change and they felt mentally prepared for it. In the other case the management had decided that the change should take place, the staff had no mental preparation for it and the change did not suit the work contents. Obviously, the change was perceived as good in the first department and as bad in the second. This enforces the importance of good preparation and democratic processes preceding any change. However, the long-term consequences of these new ways of organizing work are largely unknown.

A large study of work sites in Sweden based upon line managers and personnel managers has shown that a number of changes have taken place in the management of Swedish working life during recent years (Edling & Sandberg, 1994). The analysis of the effects of decentralization in this study showed that the correlation between decentralization and skill utilization is highly complex. In Sweden, in general, the perceived skill utilization among employees has, contrary to expectations, become lower in work sites in which a flat hierarchy had been introduced than in those with a pyramidical hierarchy. This may reflect differences in management changes in different sectors of society. It may also illustrate that management interventions aiming at increased decision latitude for the employees cannot be achieved by one and the same solution in different sectors. This important result may also be due to too short a time perspective in the follow-up. It may take many years before the introduction of a flat hierarchy becomes functional, and in the Swedish case most of the work organizational changes have lasted for shorter periods. Furthermore, if the organizational changes are not paralleled by corresponding changes in the financial framework, the organizational changes may not function in an optimal way and complications may arise. Perhaps the disappointing results based upon randomly selected working Swedes may be explained on such grounds.

12.5.1 Work Organization Changes that Induce Flexibility

What characterizes work organization changes that induce flexibility, both for the company and for the individuals, and how does this relate to health? There are a few examples of work organization changes that have been evaluated in relation to changes in health or physiology of the employees. Some of these are described here, with the goal of exploring what characterizes changes that are successful for both the employees and the company.

One of the first controlled evaluations using a pre- and post-test design with two randomly selected groups of work sites was Jackson's (1983) study. The work change offered in the experimental group was aimed at improving both decision latitude and social support. No systematic changes were instituted in the control group. The groups studied were outclinic departments. Regular staff meetings every second week were instituted, with the specific aim of examining work organization and trying to improve it. These meetings may have affected both the employees' authority over decisions and the social climate in the ward. The other component of the evaluation was a teaching programme for solving interpersonal conflicts – a social support orientated measure. The results showed that the experimental outclinic wards had diminished sick-leave rates as well as decreased personnel turnover rates after the institution of these changes. There were also indications of improved quality of care. No similar changes took place in the comparison wards.

Another controlled evaluation was performed in a service institution for the elderly in Stockholm, by Arnetz *et al.* (1982). The basic idea underlying the intervention programme focused on one aspect of the quality of care given: it was felt that the elderly tenants were excessively passive and isolated from one another. The service institution was relatively new – only two years old – and the tenants, who had not known one another in advance, had been recruited from a large area, frequently with the implicit understanding that they would receive all kinds of service and 'would have to do nothing' themselves. The first component in the method for changing this pattern was exploration of hobbies and interests among the tenants, with subsequent formation of activity groups. One activity group, for example, studied the history of the region; a second one grew plants during the summer and studied this topic during the winter; a third group jointly constructed a work of art; and a fourth went to theatre performances together. The other component was teaching the staff about various aspects of the importance of social activity among the elderly. The members of staff were also activated in the data collection for the evaluation of this programme. A longitudinal study was performed, with measurements of social activity, psychological states, and endocrinological and metabolic conditions in the tenants before, during and after the programme. Parallel measurements were performed in a comparable ward, which served as a control group.

The results indicated that the tenants in the experimental ward improved with regard to endocrinological and metabolic conditions (improved carbohydrate metabolism and anabolic/catabolic balance), social activity (more contacts with other tenants and more social activities for the elderly outside the home) and psychological state (less feelings of restlessness and more evidence of activity rather than passiveness, according to observations) (Arnetz, 1983; Karasek & Theorell, 1990). During the first year of follow-up an unfavourable trend with regard to sick-leave rates was broken in the staff in the experimental ward but not in the control ward. Personnel turnover was reported to decrease in the experimental ward but, again, not in the control ward. The experience in this case seemed to indicate that a more variable work content with increased mental stimulation and increased attention to the social activities of the tenants – which required more imagination and creativity on the part of the personnel – is associated with improved health among the employees.

A number of other examples have been described. Karasek has summarized several recent efforts and analysed the characteristics of successful and unsuccessful programmes (Karasek, 1992).

12.6   PUBLIC HEALTH PERSPECTIVES

An observation of a more general nature was made by Karasek (1990) in a group of Swedish employees who had participated in a national longitudinal survey of living conditions in Sweden, with questionnaire measurements in 1968 and 1974. This particular study was focused on employed men and women who had gone through major changes in their job situation. As a group, these individuals had developed more health problems at the time of the second observation than at the time of the first one. However, when the group was divided according to reported changes in work organization leading to changes in decision latitude, it was shown that those employees who had had increased decision latitude did not report increased health problems. Deteriorating health was reported mainly among those employees who had recorded decreased decision latitude at work to have been a consequence of the changes they had gone through. This observation indicates that spontaneously occurring, decreased decision latitude in working life may result in marked deterioration in public health. The Swedish nationwide longitudinal study of health and working life (Szulkin & Tåhlin, 1994) has indicated that job strain became an increasingly frequent problem from the 1970s to the end of the 1980s in working women – but not in men – in Sweden. During the same period sick-leave rates increased markedly in Swedish women but not in men. Multivariate analyses indicated that these findings could not be explained by increasing total work hours in women, and pointed at the interpretation that they were due to changes in work contents. The most pronounced changes were found in the health care and service sectors. Sweden underwent dramatic changes during the study period, with increasing emphasis on effectiveness and productivity in these sectors. Cardiovascular symptoms increased particularly in these groups of female employees.

Marked and frequent fluctuations in financial climates are an increasing worldwide problem for enterprises. As pointed out by Brenner (1983), recessions create problems, not only because enterprises may have to decrease the number of employees, but also because a period of marked financial activity may follow shortly after the recession, which means that the remaining employees in the enterprise will have to work very hard to meet the demands from the customers. These unpredictable short-cycle swings may be one of the more important mechanisms behind the relationship between rising unemployment in a country and subsequent rise in cardiovascular and other mortality. This relationship has been discussed extensively (see Janlert, 1991), and most authors claim that it exists, although the time lag between recession and mortality has been a point of debate. The important argument for the flexibility discussion in this chapter is that rising unemployment is a multifaceted problem, which affects not only those who become unemployed but also those who remain employed. It is one of the most important tasks for governments and management to find flexible solutions to this problem.

Unfortunately, a common belief in management is that during financial crisis there is a need to take more control – and hence to decrease the decision latitude of employees – and at the same time increase psychological demands in order to increase the company's ability to compete. The arguments that have been formulated in this chapter clearly speak against this common wisdom – in the long run, the ultimate result will be increasing health problems, and productivity will not increase.

The demand-control-support model has proved educationally useful. In an interactive process involving managers, unions and employees, it is a tool that can be used to initiate a dialogue. In this chapter I have given some examples indicating that it is the *balance* between the three components that is important. For instance, if demands are increased excessively, with extreme working hours, this may have secondary effects on the individual's total social support system. If the long working hours are combined with work outside the office, social support from workmates may be lost. This may jeopardize flexibility and may also be a threat to health. An excessive number of projects and activities will also decrease the individual's ability to experience control in his or her own situation, since the likelihood that complications will arise increases with the number of projects. When complications arise in one of the projects, this takes time and energy and the individual will have gross difficulties in managing all of the other activities. Thus, lack of flexibility is an inevitable consequence of an excessive number of activities (as well as of any form of task overload).

If biological chaos theory is correct, the human organism needs to play with as many possibilities as possible. Although highly speculative, if we limit the possibilities to respond by restricting the number of options, the number of spontaneous variations may decrease and health may deteriorate.

Finally, analyses of the national surveys in Sweden indicate that simplistic solutions aiming at increased authority over decisions for the employees– such as a flattened hierarchy – may not always be a good way of achieving increased flexibility.

Since the chapter was written this group of researchers have published several reports that seem to confirm the points raised in the text:

For an updated summary of the physiological aspects of "positive coping", see Theorell (2009).

Several prospective studies of the demand control model in relation to risk of developing coronary heart disease have been published and the results are summarised in Eller *et al.* (2009). The results of this systematic review are mixed. The model is predictive for men especially before age 55 but for women the findings are less consistent. During the recent past ten year period, the factor psychological job demands has gained in predictive importance.

During later years, the demand control support model has been increasingly utilised in prospective predictions of mental health; see, for instance, Magnusson Hanson *et al.* (2008). The findings related to covert coping have been extended to short- and long-term sick leave. According to

Theorell *et al.* (2005) a high degree of covert coping in men is related to increased risk of long-term sick leave prospectively.

The importance of leadership styles to employee health has been explored in more recent research. Results from our research show that dictatorial and laissez faire leadership styles (as reported by the employees) are related to sick leave patterns in both men and women (Nyberg *et al.* 2008). In addition, a prospective study of the risk of developing myocardial infarction in employed men showed that those who reported that they had psychosocially competent managers had a lower risk than others and that this risk decreased with duration of employment in such a work site (Nyberg *et al.* 2009).

REFERENCES

Anderson, N. & King, N. (1993). Innovation in organizations. In C.L. Cooper & I.T. Robertson (Eds), *International Review of Industrial and Organizational Psychology* (vol. 8, pp. 1–34). Chichester: John Wiley & Sons, Ltd.

Arnetz, B.B. (1983). *Psychophysiological effects of understimulation in old age.* Thesis, Medical Faculty, Karolinska Institute, Stockholm.

Arnetz, B.B., Eyre, M. & Theorell, T. (1982). Social activation of the elderly, a social experiment. *Social Science and Medicine*, **16**, 1685–90.

Brenner, M.H. (1983). Unemployment and health in the context of economic change. *Social Science and Medicine*, **17**, 1125–38.

Cotton, P. (1991) Chaos, other nonlinear dynamics research may have answers: applications for clinical medicine. *Journal of the American Medical Association*, **266**(1), 12–18.

Edling, C. & Sandberg, A, (1994). Är Taylor död och pyramiderna rivna? Nya former för företagsledning och arbetsorganisation [Is Taylor dead and are the pyramids torn down? New forms of management and work organization]. In C. Le Grand, R. Szulkin & M. Tåhlin (Eds), Sveriges arbetsplatser – organisation, personalutveckling, styrning [Swedish Work Sites – Work Organization, Personnel Development and Management]. Stockholm: Prisma.

Eller, N.H., Netterstrøm, B., Gyntelberg, F., Kristensen, T.S., Nielsen, F., Steptoe, A. & Theorell, T. (2009). Work-related psychosocial factors and the development of ischemic heart disease: a systematic review. *Cardiology in Review*, **17**(2), 83–97.

Goldberger, A.L. (1991). Is the normal heartbeat chaotic or homeostatic? *NIPS*, **6**, 87–91.

Hall, E.M. (1990). *Women's work: an inquiry into the health effects of invisible and visible labor.* Thesis, Karolinska Institute, Stockholm.

Harburg, E., Erfurt, J., Havenstein, L.S., Chape, C., Schull, W.J. & Schork, M.A. (1973). Socioecological stress, suppressed hostility, skin color and black–white blood pressure. *Psychosomatic Medicine*, **35**, 276–86.

Härenstam, A., Plam, U.-B. & Theorell, T. (1988). Stress, health and the working environment of Swedish prison staff. *Work and Stress*, **2**, 281–90.

House, J.S., Strecher, V., Metzner, H.L. & Robbins, C. (1986). Occupational stress and health among men and women in the Tecumseh Community Health Study. *Journal of Health and Social Behavior*, **27**, 62–77.

Jackson, S. (1983). Participation in decision making as a strategy for reducing job related strain. *Journal of Applied Psychology*, **68**, 3–19.

Janlert, U. (1991). *Work deprivation and health, consequences of job loss and unemployment*. Thesis. Medical Faculty, Karolinska Institute, Stockholm.

Johnson, J.V. & Hall, E.M. (1988). Job strain, workplace social support and cardiovascular disease: a cross-sectional study of a random sample of the Swedish working population. American Journal of Public Health, **78**, 1336–42.

Johnson, J.V., Hall, E.M., Stewart, W. & Theorell, T. (1993). Work stress over the life course, project report. Stockholm: Swedish Work Environment Fund.

Johnson, J.V., Hall, E.M. & Theorell, T. (1989). Combined effects of job strain and social isolation on cardiovascular disease morbidity and mortality in a random sample of the Swedish male working population. *Scandinavian Journal of Work and Environmental Health*, **15**, 271–9.

Karasek, R.A. (1979). Job demands, job decision latitude and mental strain: implications for job redesign. *Administrative Science Quarterly*, **24**, 285–307.

Karasek, R.A. (1990). Lower health risk with increased job control among white-collar workers. *Journal of Occupational Behavior*, **11**, 171–85.

Karasek, R.A. (1992). Stress prevention through work reorganization: a summary of 19 international case studies. Conditions of Work Digest, **11**, 23–41.

Karasek, R.A. & Theorell, T. (1990). Healthy Work. New York: Basic Books.

Knox, S., Theorell, T., Svensson, J. and Waller, D. (1985). The relation of social support and working environment to medical variables associated with elevated blood pressure in young males: a structural model. *Social Science and Medicine*, **21**, 525–31.

Magnusson Hanson, L.L., Theorell, T., Oxenstierna, G., Hyde, M. & Westerlund, H. (2008). Demand, control and social climate as predictors of emotional exhaustion symptoms in working Swedish men and women. *Scandinavian Journal of Public Health*, **36**(7), 737–43.

Nyberg, A., Alfredsson, L., Theorell, T., Westerlund, H., Vahtera, J. & Kivimäki, M. (2009). Managerial leadership and ischaemic heart disease among employees: the Swedish WOLF study. *Occupational and Environmental Medicine*, **66**(1), 51–5.

Nyberg, A., Westerlund, H., Magnusson Hanson, L. & Theorell, T. (2008). Managerial leadership is associated with self-reported sickness absence and sickness presenteism among Swedish men and women. *Scandinavian Journal of Public Health*, **36**(8), 803–11.

Shalit, B. (1978). *The instrument, design, administration and scoring, report no. 1.* FOA-rapporter. Försvarets forskningsanstalt, Huvudavdelning 2, Stockholm.

Szulkin, R. & Tåhlin, M. (1994). Arbetets utveckling [The development of work]. In J. Fritzell & O. Lundberg (Eds), Vardagens villkor [Conditions of Everyday Life]. Stockholm: Brombergs.

Theorell, T. (2009). Anabolism and catabolism at work. In S. Sonnentag, P. Perrewé & D. Ganster (Eds), *Current perspectives on job-stress recovery*. (vol. 7, of the book series: Research in Occupational Stress and Well-being (pp. 249–76). Emerald.

Theorell, T., Ahlberg-Hultén, G., Sigala, F., Perski, A., Söderholm, M., Kallner, A. & Eneroth, P. (1990). A biomedical and psychosocial comparison between men in six service occupations. Work and Stress, **4**, 51–63.

Theorell, T., Alfredsson, L., Westerholm, P. & Falck, B. (2000). Coping with unfair treatment at work – what is the relationship between coping and hypertension in middle-age men and women? *Psychotherapy and Psychosomatics*, **69**(2), 86–94.

Theorell, T., Michélsen, H., Nordemar, R. & Stockholm MUSIC Study 1 Group (1993). Validitetsprövning av psykosociala indexbildningar. In M. Haberg & C. Hogstedt (eds) *Stockholmsundersöknoningen*, vol. 1. Stockholm: MUSIC Books.

Theorell, T., Perski, A., Åkerstedt, T., Sigala, F., Ahlberg-Hultén, G., Svensson, J. & Eneroth, P. (1988). Changes in job strain in relation to changes in physiological state – a longitudinal study. *Scandinavian Journal of Work and Environmental Health*, **14**, 189–96.

Theorell, T., Perski, A., Orth-Gomér, K., Hamsten, A. & de Faire, U. (1991). The effects of the strain of returning to work on the risk of cardiac death after a first myocardial infarction before age 45. *International Journal of Cardiology*, **30**, 61–7.

Theorell, T., Reuterwall, C., Hallquist, J., Emlund, N., Ahlbom, A. & Hogstedt, C. (1994). Metodstudier kring psykosociala faktorer i SHEEP. [Studies in methods used for measuring psychosocial factors in SHEEP]. *ONYX (Karolinska Hospital)*, (1), 11–13.

Theorell, T., Tsutsumi, A., Hallqvist, J.J., Reuterwall, C., Hogstedt, C., Fredlund, P., Emlund, N., Johnson, J. & the Stockholm Heart Epidemiology Program (SHEEP). (1998). Decision latitude, job strain, and myocardial infarction: a study of working men in Stockholm. The SHEEP Study Group. Stockholm Heart Epidemiology Program. *American Journal of Public Health*, **88**(3), 382–8.

Theorell, T., Westerlund, H., Alfredsson, L. & Oxenstierna, G. (2005). Coping with critical life events and lack of control – the exertion of control. *Psychoneuroendocrinology*, **30**(10), 1027–32.

Wikström, B.-M., Sandström, S. & Theorell, T. (1994). Emotional and medical health effects of mental stimulation of pictures of art. *Psychotherapy and psychosomatics*, **60**, 195–206.

CHAPTER 13

Acute Stress at Work

Rolf J. Kleber
Utrecht University, The Netherlands
and
Peter G. van der Velden
Institute for Psychotrauma, The Netherlands

13.1   INTRODUCTION

A bank employee becomes a victim of a hold-up. A large company is suddenly confronted with the suicide of one of its workers. A moment of inattentiveness and suddenly a school teacher has to deal with a serious accident affecting a pupil. Fire-fighters discover in a burned house the corpse of one of their colleagues. These are all forms of acute stress in work situations. Unsuspectedly, an employee has to cope with an overwhelming experience at work which he or she can hardly handle.

The consequences of acute stress at work can be serious and sometimes long lasting for those involved. One can discern direct emotional reactions, like dismay, shock and disbelief. These are followed by reactions like fear, anger, depression and tiredness. The employee concerned will be angry for some time because such an experience happened to him or her, or will fear that it might happen again. Sometimes victims blame themselves for not having done enough. All of these reactions influence work performance and functioning at home. The employee finds it difficult to concentrate, suffers from forgetfulness and has difficulties in communicating with others. After some time tensions at work may develop, which become apparent through deterioration of work performance, irritations, fatigue, burnout and absenteeism.

The interest of scientists in the consequences of acute and extreme stress has a long history. Already in the second half of the nineteenth century scientists and clinicians dealt with the psychological reactions from train accidents (for example, Erichsen, 1866; see for an overview Trimble, 1981).

International Handbook of Work and Health Psychology, Third Edition. Edited by Cary L. Cooper, James Campbell Quick, and Marc J. Schabracq.
© 2009 John Wiley & Sons, Ltd. Published 2015 by John Wiley & Sons, Ltd.

The studies into the consequences of war stress in and after the Second World War (Grinker & Spiegel, 1945) and into the effects of brief, taxing circumstances (Basowitz *et al.*, 1955) are also examples of this interest. However, in the domain of work and health the attention of researchers has been directed mainly to chronic stress, as is shown by the many studies on work overload and role insecurity. Only since the 1990s have scientists as well as practitioners turned their attention to the impact of acute stressors at the workplace.

In this chapter we will deal with the characteristics and consequences of acute stress in the work situation – especially confrontations with violence – and with aspects of victim assistance and organizational health care. Acute stress phenomena will be analysed from a trauma perspective. Many painful and extraordinary experiences have been associated with traumatic stress: rape, criminal violence, sexual abuse of children, torture, combat, natural disasters, technological disasters and traffic accidents (Keane, Marshall & Taft, 2006; Van der Kolk, McFarlane & Weisaeth, 1996). Findings and concepts concerning various consequences of traumatic stress and disturbances in the process of adaptation with traumatic experiences will be used in this chapter, as well as insights on mental health care with regard to traumatic events, in particular trauma counselling.

13.2   WHAT IS ACUTE STRESS?

Whenever persons are required to do something which they cannot or do not want to do, they may experience stress. Using the well-known transactional definition of stress (Lazarus, 1981), the concept refers to a discrepancy between the demands of the environment and the resources of the individual. This discrepancy generally takes the form of the demands taxing or exceeding the resources.

'Acute' means that this discrepancy occurs suddenly. The term does not imply that the stressor should necessarily be an extreme event. However, this is usually the case. A short argument at work does not get attention, unless it leads to intense emotions or is part of a long slumbering conflict.

The following forms of acute stress at work can be discerned:

- Extreme experiences during work, such as confrontations with violence or with accidents. Examples of persons who experience work-related violence are employees of banks, money transport companies, supermarkets and shops, but also prison guards and police officers. Examples of people who experience accidents are fire-fighters (Wagner, Heinrichs & Ehlert, 1998), ambulance service workers (Van der Ploeg & Kleber, 2003; Van der

Velden, Kleber & Koenen, 2008) and railway employees who have to deal with traffic accidents and suicide attempts, and employees of industrial plants confronted with explosions, fires and other calamities.

- Radical changes in company structure – reorganization, collective discharge, bankruptcy – resulting in a situation in which people suddenly lose their security with regard to work and have to deal with a completely changed situation.
- Extreme experiences in social networks. For example the suicide of a coworker in a situation in which it may be supposed that the reasons for the suicide are related to problems in the work setting.
- Extreme experiences from outside, like technical, natural and environmental catastrophes. For instance, rescue workers have been sent to catastrophes, such as the sinking of the ferry, *The Herald of Free Enterprise*, a disaster on a drilling platform (Hull, Alexander & Klein, 2002), the explosion of a fireworks storage facility in a city (Van der Velden *et al.*, 2006), airplane crashes and terrorist acts, such as the attack on the Twin Towers in New York. These workers are confronted with diverse stress reactions during and after their work (Paton & Violanti, 1996).

In this chapter we will focus especially on the category of extreme experiences during work, in particular the confrontation with acts of violence in the work situation. Bank robberies or hold-ups (Leymann, 1988) may serve as the prototypical examples here, but it should be kept in mind that hold-ups also occur in other settings, for instance gas stations, hotels, catering industries and shops. Other examples of the confrontation with violence are sexual assault at the workplace and aggressive clients who attack paramedics, doctors or the nursing staff of psychiatric institutions (Haller & Deluty, 1988; Merecz *et al.*, 2006). Violence is inherent to our society, and there are many situations, also at work, in which we are confronted with it (Spector *et al.* 2007). It is remarkable to notice that, nevertheless, not many studies on the impact of work-related violence have been conducted.

13.3 THEORETICAL BACKGROUND

Well-known scientific approaches to job stress can hardly be used for the analysis of acute stress. The Michigan approach to organizational stress (French & Caplan, 1973) or the job demand-control model (Karasek & Theorell, 1990) approach are mostly directed on long existing sources of problems and their consequences. That is why we start from a comprehensive perspective on coping with extreme stress which is based on cognitive perspectives on trauma combined with concepts from social and cognitive psychology (Brewin & Holmes, 2003; Kleber & Brom, 1992).

An extreme event characteristically causes an intense powerlessness. During a violent crime a person is reduced to a thing, an object used by the perpetrator to attain something. This experience disrupts the normal certainties of existence. It contrasts with our functioning as an independent individual, which is based partly on obvious and mostly implicit expectations and suppositions. For instance, everybody implicitly assumes invulnerability: 'something like this will not happen to me' (Perloff, 1983). Daily life generally seems to be predictable and secure. There is an expectation of being treated honestly. These implicit ideas are useful and meaningful. They prevent continuous vigilance for all possible hazards, which would constitute high levels of enduring distress.

Then suddenly an actual threat takes place, against which one is almost powerless. The normal control over one's life is disrupted and feelings of security are superseded by feelings of (death) anxiety. At once the victim realizes that he or she can be confronted with a violent crime again and again. Certainties and suppositions which constitute basic trust and stability vanish after traumatic events. The core beliefs or basic assumptions – which could also be called illusions – are shattered (Janoff-Bulman, 1992).

Incidents like violent crimes and disasters are followed by a variety of psychological processes that are labelled as 'coping with traumatic stress' (Kleber & Brom, 1992). This is a form of coping that is typical for these kinds of events, during which mainly intra-psychic ways of dealing with the stressor are important. After all, the incident has already taken place. Nothing can change that. The person has to learn to live with what has happened to him or her. He or she has to regain or restore feelings of security, control and trust in one way or another.

13.4   THE PROCESS OF COPING

The process of coping with acute stress develops in the following way. During an extreme situation the person concerned will first react with disbelief and bewilderment, although usually acting reasonably adequately at the same time. Panic and aggressive resistance, for instance, do not often occur. It is as if victimized employees automatically respond in such a way that possible escalations are minimized. In a few cases a total blocking of emotions is reported, that is, the overwhelming emotions are directly inhibited and the person responds with derealization, depersonalization and disorientation. This phenomenon is called peritraumatic dissociation (Shalev et al., 1996).

When the event is over and the person concerned begins to realize what has happened, various kinds of emotions emerge, predominantly emotions of fear, anger, despair and self-blame. These emotions are often accompanied by physical reactions, such as headache, trembling or the inclination to vomit. In some cases these reactions occur a few days after the event when there are no special commands any more. This is seen especially in victims who have to deal with all kinds of matters directly after the event, like the management of a bank confronted with a robbery.

The alternation between two central psychological processes – intrusion and denial – is characteristic for the psychological coping process after extreme events (Creamer, 1995; Horowitz, 2001). Intrusion refers to reexperiencing the traumatic event. It takes a number of forms, the most common being the involuntary recollection of the stressor. A person continuously deals with what has happened. Memories and emotions come up again and again. Nightmares and repetitive dreams are also a common way in which thoughts, feelings and images related to the event are re-experienced. At night the person sleeps restlessly and has bad dreams about the event. Finally, there are startle reactions in situations that resemble the original situation. For instance, employees victimized by an industrial disaster report distress triggered by the smell of gasoline or by loud noises. The psychological process of denial has to do with a general numbing of psychic responsiveness. It is expressed by not wanting to talk about it, by avoiding the location of the event and other avoidance behaviours, by diminished interest in significant activities, and by emotional numbness.

In itself, this alternation between denial and intrusion can be regarded as a normal and necessary process. After all, old certainties and expectations which have been overthrown by the event need to be restored or replaced by new ones. This cannot be done at once: the victim would be overwhelmed by emotions. The person lets, as it were, the experience permeate bit by bit. That is why intrusion – being preoccupied by the event – is alternated by denial – avoiding memories about the event.

An important element in the coping process is the search for a meaning, that is, the victim looks for a way to understand the situation by means of interpretations of what has happened to him (Janoff-Bulman & Frantz, 1997). For instance, victims ask themselves: 'why has this happened to me?' or 'how could this happen?'. They may also blame themselves for having made mistakes. In these ways, they try to regain control over their own life (Thompson, Armstrong & Thomas, 1998). Especially in cognitive-oriented approaches of coping with traumatic stress, much attention has been paid to this process of attributing meaning and replacing old ideas by new ones (Schok et al., 2008).

The coping process furthermore affects the energy level of a person. He or she becomes tired and exhausted after even small activities at work or at home. The normal interest in significant others or activities decreases, and minor problems with the spouse or the children easily evoke impatience and aggression. Irritation about the unsafe work situation is vented off on colleagues and relatives.

Hypervigilance and jumpiness after violent events are other prominent reactions. These are often of a specific nature – that is, they are connected with the characteristics of the violent situation. For a prison guard who has been beaten up, a screaming prisoner again evokes the fear for aggression. A bank employee who has been involved in a hold-up approaches every client suspiciously and feels continuously on his or her guard. Intrusive thoughts are provoked in the same way. Looking at a television programme about a hostage induces painful memories of the colleague who was used as a hostage. The smell of burned food provokes images of the dead child who was found by a fire-fighter.

Adaptation takes time. After a few weeks to a few months the symptoms of intrusion and denial as well as the various emotional, behavioural and somatic reactions decrease in frequency and intensity. Sometimes it takes longer, much longer even, as research on the aftermath of war and violence has shown (Keane *et al.*, 2006). The coping process is completed when the person only suffers occasionally or not at all from intrusion and avoidance as well as other symptoms related to the event. The person can think of the event without being overwhelmed by emotions and the memory of what has happened does not have to be avoided any more.

13.5   LONG-TERM DISTURBANCES

Some persons who are struck by an extreme incident suffer from permanent psychological problems. Overviews of empirical studies into the consequences of extreme events (Breslau, 1998; Kleber & Brom, 1992) have shown that about 10 to 30% of all victims suffer from serious malfunctioning. These disturbances may take the form of a mood disorder (which is manifested in – among others – major depression), a posttraumatic stress disorder, substance abuse, burnout or other mental disturbances. Prevalence rates for posttraumatic stress difficulties among rescue workers are generally lower (Van der Velden *et al.*, 2006).

Posttraumatic stress disorder (PTSD) is the well-known and well-established diagnostic term for mental problems after extreme experiences. The lingering and painful effects of the Vietnam war in the United States led to the introduction of this concept in the *Diagnostic and Statistical Manual of Mental Disorders* of the American Psychiatric Association. The distinctive criteria of the disorder are: (i) an extreme stressor; (ii) persistent intrusive and reexperiencing symptoms; (iii) permanent avoidance of stimuli associated with the traumatic experience and numbing symptoms; (iv) symptoms of persistent hyperarousal; (v) a duration of the symptoms of at least one month; and (vi) significant impairment in social, occupational, or other important areas of functioning, such as problems with work and relationships (APA, 2000). Since its introduction in 1980, a vast amount of articles and books has been published on the aetiology and diagnostics of PTSD as well as on the various forms of counselling and psychotherapy. There is also a growing stream of publications indicating that posttraumatic stress disorder is associated with abnormalities in psychobiological processes, in particular mechanisms in neurotransmitter and neurohormonal systems (Olff, Langeland & Gersons, 2005).

PTSD can be assessed by standardized questionnaires, such as the Self-Rating Scale for Posttraumatic Stress Disorder (SRS-PTSD; Carlier *et al.*, 1998), the PTSD Symptom Scale (PSS; Foa *et al.*, 1993) and the Impact of Event Scale (IES; Horowitz, Wilner & Alvarez, 1979; Van der Ploeg *et al.*, 2004). The assessment of a structured interview conducted by a professional (such as the Clinician Administered PTSD Scale – CAPS; Weathers, Keane & Davidson, 2001) is considered as the golden standard. It has been found that PTSD rates from diagnostic interviews are considerably lower than estimates from standardized questionnaires (Engelhard *et al.*, 2007). PTSD is the most widely recognized posttraumatic disorder (although not without dispute; Rosen, Spitzer & McHugh, 2008), but also depression, anxiety disorders, substance misuse and adjustment disorders may develop. These, along with non-psychiatric issues causing distress (e.g., finances, lack of information and relationship breakdown), should be considered in addition to PTSD in patients with mental health problems after violence and disaster. Damage to the victim's health also becomes manifest in an increase of sick leave, in enduring stress at work, in fatigue and in burnout. For instance, in a Dutch study of ambulance workers (Van der Ploeg & Kleber, 2003) it was found that more than a tenth suffered from a clinical level of posttraumatic distress, that a tenth reported a fatigue level that put them at high risk for sick leave and work disability, and that nearly a tenth suffered from burnout. In the same way that chronic stress may be associated with financial costs and with decreases of production and identification with the organization, acute stress may be followed by similar negative consequences.

Finally, the absence of a disorder such as PTSD does not imply the absence of difficulties in the adaptation with acute stress. Although, the majority of people struck by these experiences will show a form of resilience, a large part of the victimized persons will suffer from specific symptoms which interfere with work, such as irritations, sleeping disturbances, fatigue at the workplace and concentration difficulties. Nevertheless, in most cases these problems disappear after some time and the person's functioning will return to an adequate level.

13.6   RISK FACTORS

In acute stress the nature of the stressor plays a dominant role. However, the nature and seriousness of the consequences of an acute stressor are moderated or mediated by several social and psychological variables. A distinction could be made here between risk factors present before, during and after the event. One should realize that none of these factors is by itself capable of producing chronic disturbances (Kleber & Brom, 1992; Ozer *et al.*, 2003).

Earlier stressful life events or recently experienced critical events are a major risk factor for long-lasting coping disturbances (Breslau, 1998). It was found that some bank employees became victims to several hold-ups in a period of a few months (Van der Velden *et al.*, 1991). This accumulation of violence causes permanent damage to the feeling of security of the persons concerned. Repeated violence enhances the feeling of powerlessness and fear (Rothbaum *et al.*, 1992). Furthermore, pre-existing psychological problems can augment mental health problems after critical incidents (Breslau, 1998; McFarlane, 1989).

Risk factors during the event are the severity of the stressor itself as well as so-called peritraumatic factors, such as sustained physical harm, vehement negative emotions and the already mentioned dissociative responses. It has been shown that injuries as well as immense powerlessness and anxiety can be important risk factors (Kilpatrick *et al.*, 1989). The victims' perception of the seriousness of the threat may even be of more significance that the objective circumstances (Brewin & Holmes, 2003; Lazarus, 1981). Furthermore, peritraumatic dissociation had been found to be a determinant of later disturbances (Marmar *et al.*, 1996), but recent studies have shown that this factor is not as important as assumed. Results indicate that initial mental health problems, among other factors, might be better predictors of PTSD symptomatology (Van der Velden & Wittmann, 2008).

Besides personal factors and the seriousness of the incident, social factors after the event play an important part in the coping process. On the one hand the support from the social network (family, relatives, friends, colleagues) may have a positive influence on the coping process (Ullman, 1995). On the other hand, negative interventions of others (like police, media, insurance companies, medical authorities) can aggravate the consequences (Figley & Kleber, 1995), a process that is called 'secondary victimization' (Symonds, 1980). Victims of violence are often not adequately informed about police and legal procedures. When employees of banks and money transport companies are questioned, they often get the impression they are under suspicion themselves. Most people regard this as a serious breach of confidence. In addition, chronic and re-occurring organizational stressors may influence mental health problems. They can even be better predictors for consequent mental health problems than confrontations with violence and death, as was found in a New Zealand study of police officers (Huddleston, Stephens & Paton, 2007).

13.7   INTERVENTION

Those who are confronted with acute stress show various symptoms, such as sleeplessness, irritability, absenteeism, feelings of insecurity and lower work performance. Undoubtedly, personality characteristics play a part, but it should be remembered that most victims have hardly any responsibility for what has happened. Banks and supermarkets happen to get robbed and employees of social welfare services are sometimes confronted with clients who threaten them (or members of their family) physically. Because the incident has to do with the nature of the work setting itself, intervention at the work level is appropriate.

Intervention programmes for victimized employees are a development of the 1980s and 1990s. They can take different forms. Firstly, there is primary intervention. This ensures that situations of acute stress occur as infrequently as possible. Such an approach is, of course, justified, but many unpleasant and extreme incidents can hardly be prevented. Accidents and violent crimes do take place, however adequate the prevention policy of the company.

It is also possible to make sure that the employees are optimally prepared for the event and its consequences. This is the aim of trainings in the field of 'stress management' and 'aggression regulation' (Mitchell & Dyregrov, 1993; Parks & Steelman, 2008). Bank employees are prepared for hold-ups, police officers for shooting incidents and railway employees for suicide attempts or accidents involving trains. However, one should not overestimate the efficacy of this preparedness: anticipation is only useful when the stressor is reasonably expectable and not too complex (Sarason *et al.*, 1979). For instance, if a hold-up takes place two years after the training, the content of the whole training programme may have faded away.

This is the reason why secondary prevention is important. The organization should explicitly pay attention to the consequences of acute stress at work and to the possibilities of direct assistance afterwards, so that employees will feel supported and will be better prepared to deal with the aftermath of the overwhelming experience.

13.7.1   Intervention Elements

Based on the theoretical approach of coping with extreme experiences described above, a number of intervention elements can be discerned. Firstly, stress reactions should not be interpreted as symptoms of mental disorders in intervention programmes after extreme incidents. Instead, the normal character of the reactions to an acute stress situation is emphasized (Kleber & Brom, 1992). Going through an experience of violence can be seen as a job risk. One should avoid the medicalization of reactions to such an event and the resulting danger of stigmatizing the person(s) concerned. Employees should be taken seriously. People should be supported in such a way that they will not get stuck in their problems, but will be able to function again at work and in their personal lives as before.

Secondly, the person needs *recognition and (practical) support* after the extreme experience. Recognition is a highly relevant element in the support of victims. Often this is what victims are looking for: recognition that they have gone through a very unpleasant situation. Support from the organization and especially from superiors is often limited. In several investigations (Day & Livingstone, 2001; Van der Ploeg & Kleber, 2003) it has been found how much victimized employees appreciated support and recognition, and how little of this support was often received. It has also been established that the social atmosphere in many police departments deteriorated because of inadequate support after shooting incidents (Anshel, 2000; Gersons, 1989). The reason why colleagues and superiors pay little attention is often due to misunderstandings about the coping process and social support. They often assume that attention and questions about what happened will increase the psychological problems of the victims concerned or, instead of serious attention, they make jokes about the event with the intention to distract the victim. Supplying *information* is also important. The person concerned wants to know what can be expected. People who fall victim to violence while performing their work have to deal with all kinds of judiciary and business consequences afterwards. Information is crucial. However, information not only concerns practical matters and juridical affairs, but also psychological aspects, that is, the characteristics of the coping process and stress reactions. Rendering this information while stressing the normality of the psychological reactions provides rest and assurance. It prevents victims (and their family) from getting upset about unexpected stress reactions.

Another goal is to create an opportunity to *express the thoughts and feelings* which accompanied the critical event. The person may vent personal thoughts with regard to the event and emotions like fear, anger and sorrow. In individual or group meetings he or she gets the chance to talk about the experience of the hold-up, the related thoughts and feelings, and the influence on work and personal life. Experimental studies in social psychology have shown that disclosure about traumatic experiences (e.g. talking or writing about one's experience) has a strong positive effect on various indicators of physical and mental health (Pennebaker, 1997). However, disclosure has to do with all aspects of the experience, not only the emotional aspects. In the last decade many authors on early interventions after trauma (e.g. Solomon, 1999) have emphasized that one should be very careful with the ventilation of emotions and that this element is not as important as originally assumed. The focus on emotions negatively affected psychological recovery in some trauma victims, as was found in a randomized controlled study in the Netherlands (Sijbrandij *et al.*, 2006). Too much emphasis can be harmful.

This brings us to another goal of the intervention programme: *confrontation with what has happened*. It may be important to recollect the event in a detailed way, because of the person's need to recognize what he or she has been through. Such a confrontation may enhance the coping process and the integration of the experience in his or her personal life. However, some victims do not show this need and prefer to refrain from such a detailed recollection.

13.7.2 An Illustration of an Intervention Programme for Victimized Employees

Many organizations are confronted with employees victimized by some kind of violence, such as robberies, hijackings, hold-ups and physical abuse. Intervention programmes for banks, transport companies and rescue workers have been developed in the Netherlands by representatives of the Institute for Psychotrauma (Brom & Kleber, 1989; Brom, Kleber & Hofman, 1993; Van der Velden, Hazen & Kleber, 1999; Van Loon, 2008). Manton and Talbot (1990) developed a somewhat similar approach to victims in Australia in which the bank permanently hires specialists.

An intervention programme can only be successful if one starts with explicit principles. Such concepts have been formulated (Dunning, 1988; Mitchell & Dyregrov, 1993; Van der Velden *et al.*, 1999) during the development and implementation of various intervention programmes in organizations. The aim is twofold: to reduce sources of new stress (called psychosocial crisis management) and to enhance self-efficacy, normal coping and recognition of problems (called victim assistance). These principles are as follows:

1. Violence and disaster are accompanied by crisis. Primary task is, therefore, psychosocial crisis management aimed at reducing sources of stress and chaos. Those responsible and in charge – mostly superiors or management – must develop a general idea of problems and needs of those involved. Based on this assessment, plans for the coming days and week should be formulated. Vital questions are: what are the direct

consequences of the event, which problems might be expected on the longer term, which measures are best suited to diminish these negative consequences, and which persons will conduct necessary interventions? Dependent on the impact and nature of the event, it is also necessary to develop plans for dealing with the media.

2. Concrete and practical assistance is offered directly after the event. Directly after a hold-up police and management have to deal with other matters, which usually is not in accordance with the employees' interest. Support of the employees during contact with the police is useful to protect the victim. For instance, an employee of a money transport company immediately becomes a suspect when his van has been robbed.

3. The fact that victims are sometimes very emotional directly after the event, does not necessarily indicate that they are at risk for posttraumatic stress disturbances. As mentioned before, these are normal reactions after abnormal events. However, it may be necessary to have several contacts during a longer period with affected persons. It is important to follow these employees in this process, also because the concern from the near environment soon tends to ebb away. Dependent on the needs and the intensity of the posttraumatic reactions, an intervention programme consists of several contacts over a period of four to six or eight weeks. The differences between the meetings are described below. However, when employees are involved in a legal process or formal investigation, they ought to be supported over a longer period, such as to prepare them for possible stressful developments.

4. All employees who have been involved in some way with the acute stressor should be offered support and recognition. Those at risk for ongoing posttraumatic stress reactions should be invited to take part in a specific intervention programme (however, participation is not mandatory). In other cases, 'watchful waiting' is a recommended approach since the probability that they will develop event-related mental health disturbances is low.

5. Intervention programmes can be offered by people from within the company, like superiors, social workers and personnel officers, after the required specialized training. Such support programmes find themselves on the intersection of volunteer assistance and professional assistance. The organization appoints an employee who is explicitly responsible for the intervention programme. This employee may be a professional, but this is not necessarily the case. Sometimes, a close colleague or direct supervisor is better suited for the task. Preferably, the person receives training crisis management as well as in the field of social skills and assistance to victimized persons. It is important to notice that this person should be accepted by the other employees and should be available at any moment.

6. During the aftermath of the event interventions and currents needs should be regularly evaluated, in order to be able to formulate additional plans or measures. It is evident that the duration of the aftermath is dependent on the nature of the event and the specific problems.
7. The intervention programme is introduced formally as a programme within the organization. This also means that all procedures should be laid down in an explicit plan or intervention strategy. Explicit rules make clear who in the organization is responsible for the intervention programme and which rules exist within the organization for it.
8. The organization allows certain changes in the work situation, for instance special rules if an employee needs extraordinary leave after an extreme incident.
9. When, after the introduction of an intervention programme in an organization, everything is going as it is supposed to, professionals from outside the company are only called in during or after large-scale disasters and, of course, in case of serious disorders that necessitate specialized assistance. The organization should be able to refer the employees concerned to specialized assistance, such as a psychotherapist.

Before describing more details of the intervention programme, it must be realized that a concrete assistance programme is never a direct copy of the model described above. Any model for company-directed assistance has to be specified in an actual programme, depending on the specific problems raised by the incident and the specific characteristics of the organization and the work setting (see Section 13.7.5 for a differentiation in approach). Thus, in some case the above mentioned crisis intervention or victim assistance may be dominant, while in other cases crisis management will be sufficient to reduce sources of stress.

Furthermore, self-coping efficacy of affected employees as well as social support from their unaffected colleagues should not be underestimated. In addition, in trying to solve the adverse effects of critical incidents and prevent further sources of stress, one might be confronted with existing problems, such as organizational problems and conflicts. In these cases, the critical incident reveals what was going on for a longer period. In these circumstances one needs to be careful to attribute mental health problems solely to the event. This may imply other interventions than described here.

With respect to individual care, these interventions most often consist of meetings lasting about one or two hours. The aims of the various contacts differ. During the first contact mainly providing structure and social support should be offered. In addition, needs of the participants are assessed and discussed. Dependent on their needs, attention is given towards their own experiences of the incident. The aim is to reduce arousal levels and enhance coping efficacy. For some persons concise information about possible stress reactions (for instance about nightmares and sleeping problems that may appear during the first nights) is helpful: it decreases fear about their own stress reactions.

If needed, a couple of days or weeks after the first contact the second meeting can be scheduled. Again attention is given towards their experiences, thoughts and feelings, and remaining needs of the participants are assessed and discussed. General education about stress symptoms and the coping process after critical incidents is usually provided while the victims talk about their own stress reactions.

Possible further contacts are especially aimed at monitoring the development of the coping process and enhancing self-coping efficacy. Attention towards the coping process prevents dominant avoidance tendencies. Furthermore, positive and negative reactions are discussed and ways to counteract sceptical and obnoxious responses from colleagues and significant others are explored. About 4–6 weeks after the incident the process is evaluated, that is: the presence of the aforementioned avoidance reactions, intrusive thoughts and other stress reactions is systematically assessed. The period of 4–6 weeks (in some cases 8 weeks) is chosen – note that the diagnosis of PTSD can be made after one month – because it gives a better insight in presence or absence of lasting coping disturbances. When most stress reactions have dissipated, possible changes in personal values and attitudes towards work and family life are investigated and discussed. If various stress reactions are still very intense and normal functioning has not returned yet, psychotherapy is proposed to the victim. This offer should be made carefully because victims often associate therapy with personal weakness or 'being mad'. These ideas are often accompanied with feelings of shame and fear that it will jeopardize their career.

13.7.3 Psychological Debriefing

Rescue workers have to do their work under high pressure and in difficult circumstances. Acute stress is part of their job. Moreover, they sometimes do not work in a permanent organization and soon disperse after the event. For assistance to various categories of rescue workers after calamities Mitchell developed a group-directed assistance programme called 'Critical Incident Stress Debriefing' in the early 1980s (Mitchell, 1983; Mitchell & Everly, 1995).

Maximally three days after an extreme situation a team of rescue workers comes together in a debriefing session, headed by a specialized helper, for 'emotional ventilation' and 'stress education'. The event as well as the resulting thoughts, reactions and emotions it has evoked are discussed in the peer group. The specialized helper emphasizes that such emotions and stress reactions are normal after extreme events and informs the participants about the various consequences. Usually there is only one such a group meeting, although it preferably should be followed by a follow-up meeting some time after the event.

The method of debriefing, as developed by Mitchell, as well as the term debriefing itself became immensely popular in the 1990s. However, in the second half of the decade strong criticisms were directed at this method. The central point of this disapproval was that the effects of debriefing are rather poor or even non-existing. Debriefed rescue workers may not suffer from posttraumatic stress symptoms to a lesser extent than comparable non-debriefed groups. This criticism has proven to be justifiable. Controlled studies on one-session forms of counselling have shown that this kind of help does not have any effect or has only very minor effects (Bisson, 2003). Indeed, some evidence even indicated that these debriefings are harmful. As a result, crisis debriefing was placed on a list of treatments that have the potential to cause harm in clients (Lilienfeld, 2007).

However, the debate on debriefing also showed that the term itself was used in an improper way. Nearly all kinds of early intervention were called debriefing and the specific criticisms on debriefing were therefore also generalized to these other types of assistance. This generalization is not justifiable. First of all, research has shown that early and brief forms of psychotherapy are quite successful (Foa & Meadows, 1998). Furthermore, expectations with regard to debriefing have been quite exaggerated. One can hardly expect that people will recover from a horrible experience in just one session. Next, it is also questionable whether all forms of early interventions focus so much on emotion ventilation and on PTSD prevention. Research findings in experimental social psychology (Rimé et al., 1998) indicate that people show positive improvements with regard to job satisfaction, social support, general outlook on life, physical health, but not so much on emotional recovery. 'Sharing an emotion cannot change the emotional memory' (Rimé, 1999, p. 177).

The debate on early interventions after acute stress is still going on (Devilly, Gist & Cotton, 2006), but it is by now clear that one-session forms of trauma counselling should be avoided. It has also become clear that proper counselling is not the same as just talking about one's emotions and finally that it is important to pay proper attention to the social context of the people involved.

13.7.4   Brief Psychotherapy

An intervention programme is essentially different from psychotherapy. It is focused on stimulating normal coping with extreme stress, not on

disturbances in these coping processes. Such a programme of crisis counselling consists of a broad range of basic intervention tools. It is concerned
with information supply, practical advice and assistance from the management of the company as well as psychological support.

Nevertheless, psychotherapy may be necessary, namely in case of employees who suffer from serious disorders, for instance after a very dangerous
incident or after repeated violence. Such treatments usually are of short duration (usually 5 to 15 sessions of therapy). Various effective short-term psychotherapies for the treatment of PTSD, in particular cognitive behavioural
therapy (e.g. exposure) and EMDR (eye movement desensitization and re-
processing), are available (Bisson et al., 2007b; Brom, Kleber & Defares,
1989; Foa & Meadows, 1998).

Relatively new developments are early psychotherapies focused on acute
disturbances after traumatic experiences. These therapies are somewhere between multiple-session standardized intervention programmes and normal
psychotherapy. They focus solely on individuals with clear and serious disturbances after acts of violence and other calamities, but in contrast to normal
psychotherapy they are rather brief: 3–5 sessions. They mostly follow a pro-
tocol based on cognitive behavioural therapy (Bryant et al., 2008; Creamer,
2008). Randomised controlled studies have shown that this trauma-focused
cognitive-behavioural therapy within three months of a traumatic event are
effective for individuals with traumatic stress symptoms, especially those
who meet the threshold for a clinical diagnosis. They have been found to
be more effective than waiting lists or supportive counselling conditions
(Roberts et al., 2009).

13.7.5   Variation in Individual Care

Originally, many intervention programmes for victimized employees were
directed at all people involved in the violent event. Such a standardized approach has an 'outreaching' nature. Studies into victim support (for example,
Maguire & Corbett, 1987; Van der Ploeg & Kleijn, 1989) had shown that
this kind of health care was usually more appropriate than a more passive
approach. Risk groups were also reached better in this way. Indeed, stress
reactions and disorders have been found to appear especially with victims
who would rather avoid (professional) assistance (Weisaeth, 1989). The goal
of such a standardized outreaching approach is also to avoid an association
between victim assistance and personal weakness.

Nevertheless, most people affected by violence are able to recover by
themselves and with a little help. They need support and information, but
not specialized help. Shortly after a traumatic event, it is important that

those affected be provided with practical support and information about reactions, coping strategies and help from those around them. We should not underestimate the resilience of people (Bonanno, 2004). The perspective in this approach is called watchful waiting (Driffield & Smith, 2007). At the same time some people (e.g. individuals who show hyper arousal responses) get overwhelmed by a straightforward approach and need specialized help. As mentioned above, brief psychotherapy has proven to be quite effective for subgroups of victims. Therefore, one should make a distinction in groups of affected victims and in time. Most people will receive a low level of support (Bisson *et al.*, 2007a). Those who show serious indications of disturbances will receive an offer for treatment. The issue in this kind of stepped care model is, of course, the question of how to make a distinction between the two groups. As we showed earlier, there are many risk factors, but none of these factors is decisive.

13.8 CONCLUSIONS

Acute stress at work can take different forms, one of which is confrontation with violence during work. One of the direct consequences is crisis and chaos. Victimized employees experience a shattering of their personal autonomy and their confidence in others. The diversity of reactions is usually large: bewilderment, anger, fear, listlessness, absenteeism. Employees experience a general feeling of insecurity; often people in the near environment who were not victimized themselves suffer from this as well (Figley & Kleber, 1995). In general, adjusting to these experiences takes longer than assumed beforehand.

Fighting the causes of violence in the company is, of course, necessary, as is preparation for the possible occurrence of these extreme events, but acute stress cannot always be prevented. Intervention after the event is useful, in order to reduce sources of stress and chaos, to enable employees to realize the meaning of what they have been through, to provide recognition of their thoughts and emotions, and to prevent, as far as possible, undesired stress reactions.

In many organizations a structured assistance approach exists for victims of acts of violence and other calamities. The experiences with it are positive and employees are mostly quite satisfied with it. The target groups of these approaches have been broadened in the last decade: first the banking business, then the police, later supermarkets, fire-fighters and rescue workers. The introduction of the assistance mostly takes place in an ad hoc fashion, usually in response to a violent incident that has drawn attention to the problem. Regrettably robust studies on the efficacy and effectiveness of these intervention programmes are still rather scarce.

An integral approach of acute stress is essential. An approach that is only directed at the individual side has little use if crisis management is not addressed and the care is not accepted by the management of the organization. The fact that employees are emotional during the first hours or days, does not necessarily imply that individual care for affected employees should be provided by an 'expert'. Adequate psychosocial crisis management may be important to effectively reduce sources of stress: in several cases 'talking about their experiences' with the affected employees is only part of the solution. Before any interventions are undertaken, first an adequate taxation of raised and possible future problems need to be made.

REFERENCES

APA (2000). *Diagnostic And Statistical Manual of Mental Disorders, Fourth Edition (Text Revision)-DSM-IV TR*. Washington, DC: American Psychiatric Association.

Anshel, M.H. (2000). A conceptual model and implications for coping with stressful events in police work. *Criminal Justice and Behavior*, **27**, 375–401.

Basowitz, H., Korchin, S.J., Persky, H. & Grinker, R.R. (1955). *Anxiety and Stress*. New York: McGraw-Hill.

Bisson, J.I. (2003). Single-session early psychological interventions following traumatic events. *Clinical Psychology Review*, **23**, 481–99.

Bisson, J.I., Brayne, M., Ochberg, F.M. & Everly Jr., G.S. (2007a). Early psychosocial intervention following traumatic events. *American Journal of Psychiatry*, **164**, 1016–19.

Bisson, J.I., Ehlers, A., Matthews, R., Pilling, S., Richards, D. & Turner, S. (2007b). Psychological treatments for chronic post-traumatic stress disorder. Systematic review and meta-analysis. *British Journal of Psychiatry*, **190**, 97–104.

Bisson, J.I., Shepherd, J.P., Joy, D. *et al.* (2004). Early cognitive-behavioural therapy for post-traumatic stress symptoms after physical injury. Randomised controlled trial. *British Journal of Psychiatry*, **184**, 63–9.

Bonanno, G.A. (2004). Loss, trauma, and human resilience: have we underestimated the human capacity to thrive after extremely aversive events? *American Psychologist*, **59**, 20–8.

Breslau, N. (1998). Epidemiology of trauma and posttraumatic stress disorder. In R. Yehuda (Ed.), *Psychological Trauma* (pp. 1–30). Washington, DC: American Psychiatric Press.

Brewin, C.R. & Holmes, E.A. (2003). Psychological theories of posttraumatic stress disorder. *Clinical Psychology Review*, **23**(3), 339–76.

Brom, D. & Kleber, R.J. (1989). Prevention of posttraumatic stress disorders. *Journal of Traumatic Stress Studies*, **2**, 335–51.

Brom, D., Kleber, R.J. & Defares, P.B. (1989). Brief psychotherapy for posttraumatic stress disorders. *Journal of Consulting and Clinical Psychology*, **57**(5), 607–12.

Brom, D., Kleber, R.J. & Hofman, M.C. (1993). Victims of traffic accidents: incidence and prevention of posttraumatic stress disorder. *Journal of Clinical Psychology*, **49**, 131–40.

Bryant, R.A., Mastrodomenico, J., Felmingham, K.L., *et al.* (1998). Clinical utility of a brief diagnostic test for posttraumatic stress disorder. *Psychosomatic Medicine*, **60**, 42–7.

Carlier, I.V.E., Uchelen, J.J. van, Lamberts, R.D. & Gersons, B.P.R. (1998). Clinical utility of a brief diagnostic test for posttraumatic stress disorder. *Psychosomatic Medicine*, **60**, 42–7.

Creamer, M. (1995). A cognitive processing formulation of posttrauma reactions. In R.J. Kleber, Ch.R. Figley & B.P.R. Gersons (Eds), *Beyond Trauma: Societal and Cultural Dimensions* (pp. 55–74). New York: Plenum.

Creamer, M. (2008). Treatment of acute stress disorder: a randomized controlled trial. *Archives of General Psychiatry*, **65**, 659–67.

Day, A.L. & Livingstone, H.A. (2001). Chronic and acute stress among military personnel: do coping styles buffer their negative impact on health? *Journal of Occupational Health Psychology*, **6**, 348–60.

Devilly, G.J., Gist, R. & Cotton, P. (2006). Ready! Fire! Arm! The status of psychological debriefing and therapeutic interventions: in the work place and after disasters. *Review of General Psychology*, **10**, 318–45.

Driffield, T. & Smith, P.C. (2007). A real options approach to watchful waiting: theory and an illustration. *Medical Decision Making*, **27**, 178–88.

Dunning, C. (1988). Intervention strategies for emergency workers. In M.L. Lystad (Ed.), *Mental Health Response to Mass Emergencies: Theory and Practice* (pp. 284–307). New York: Brunner/Mazel.

Engelhard, I., Hout, M.A. van Den, Weerts, J., Arntz, A., Hox, J.J.C.M. & McNally, R.J. (2007). Deployment-related stress and trauma in Dutch soldiers returning from Iraq: a prospective study. *British Journal of Psychiatry*, **91**, 140–5.

Erichsen, J.E. (1866). *On Railway and Other Injuries of the Nervous System*. London: Walton & Maberly.

Figley, Ch.R. & Kleber, R.J. (1995). Beyond the 'victim': secondary traumatic stress. In R.J. Kleber, Ch.R. Figley & B.P.R. Gersons (Eds), *Beyond Trauma: Cultural and Societal Dimensions* (pp. 75–98). New York: Plenum.

Foa, E.B. & Meadows, E.A. (1998). Psychosocial treatments for posttraumatic stress disorder. In R. Yehuda (Ed.), *Psychological Trauma* (pp. 179–204). Washington, DC: American Psychiatric Press.

Foa, E.B., Riggs, D.S., Dancu, C.V. & Rothbaum, B.O. (1993). Reliability and validity of a brief instrument for assessing post-traumatic stress disorder. *Journal of Traumatic Stress*, **6**, 459–73.

French, J.R.P. & Caplan, R.D. (1973). Organizational stress and individual strain. In A.J. Marrow (Ed.), *The Failure of Success*. New York: Amacom.

Gersons, B.P.R. (1989). Patterns of PTSD among police officers following shooting incidents: a two-dimensional model and treatment implications. *Journal of Traumatic Stress*, **2**, 247–58.

Grinker, R.R. & Spiegel, J.P. (1945). *Men under Stress*. Philadelphia: Blakiston.

Haller, R.M. & Deluty, R.H. (1988). Assaults on staff by psychiatric in-patients. *British Journal of Psychiatry*, **152**, 174–9.

Horowitz, M.J. (2001). *Stress Response Syndromes, Fourth Edition*. New York: J. Aronson (First Edition 1976).

Horowitz, M.J., Wilner, N. & Alvarez, W. (1979). Impact of Event Scale: a measure of subjective stress. *Psychosomatic Medicine*, **41**, 209–18.

Huddleston, L., Stephens, C. & Paton, D. (2007). An evaluation of traumatic and organizational experiences on the psychological health of New Zealand police recruits. *Work*, **28**, 199–207.

Hull, A.M., Alexander, D.A. & Klein, S. (2002). Survivors of the Piper Alpha oil platform disaster: long-term follow-up study. *British Journal of Psychiatry*, **181**, 433–8.

Janoff-Bulman, R. (1992). *Shattered Assumptions: Towards a New Psychology of Trauma*. New York: Free Press.

Janoff-Bulman, R. & Frantz, C.M. (1997). The impact of trauma on meaning: from meaningless world to meaningful live. In M. Power & C.R. Brewin (Eds), *The Transformation of Meaning in Psychological Therapies* (pp. 91–106). Chichester: John Wiley & Sons, Ltd.

Karasek, R.A. & Theorell, T. (1990). *Healthy Work: Stress, Productivity and the Reconstruction of Working Life*. New York: Basic Books.

Keane, T.M., Marshall, A.D. & Taft, C.T. (2006). Posttraumatic stress disorder: etiology, epidemiology and treatment outcome. *Annual Review of Clinical Psychology*, **2**, 161–97.

Kilpatrick, D.G., Veronen, L.J., Amick, A.E., Villeponteaux, L.A. & Ruff, G.A. (1985). Mental health correlates of criminal victimization: a random community survey. *Journal of Consulting and Clinical Psychology*, **53**, 866–73.

Kleber, R.J. & Brom, D. in collaboration with Defares, P.B. (1992). *Coping with Trauma: Theory, Prevention and Treatment* (Seventh imprint 2003). Amsterdam: Swets & Zeitlinger.

Lazarus, R.S. (1981). The stress and coping paradigm In C. Eisdorfer, D. Cohen, A. Kleinman & P. Maxim (Eds), *Models for Clinical Psychopathology* (pp. 177–214). New York: Spectrum.

Leyman, H. (1988). Stress reactions after bank robberies: psychological and psychosomatic reaction patterns. *Work and Stress*, **2**, 123–32.

Lilienfeld, S.O. (2007). Psychological treatments that cause harm. *Perspectives on Psychological Science*, **2**, 53–70.

Maguire, M. & Corbett, C. (1987). *The Effects of Crime and the Work of Victim Support Schemes*. Aldershot: Gower.

Manton, M. & Talbot, A. (1990). Crisis intervention after an armed hold-up: guidelines for counsellors. *Journal of Traumatic Stress*, **3**, 507–22.

Marmar, C.R., Weiss, D.S., Metzler, T.J. & Delucchi, K. (1996). Characteristics of emergency services personnel related to peritraumatic dissociation during critical incident exposure. *American Journal of Psychiatry*, **153**, 94–102.

McFarlane, A.C. (1989). The aetiology of posttraumatic morbidity: predisposing, precipitating and perpetuating factors. *British Journal of Psychiatry*, **154**, 221–8.

Merecz, D., Rymaszewska, J., Mościcka, A., Kiejna, A. & Jarosz-Nowak J. (2006). Violence at the workplace – a questionnaire survey of nurses. *European Psychiatry*, **21**(7), 442–50.

Mitchell, J.T. (1983). When disaster strikes . . .: the critical incident stress debriefing process. *Journal of Emergency Medical Services*, **8**, 36–9.

Mitchell, J.T. & Dyregrov, A. (1993). Traumatic stress in disaster workers and emergency personnel: prevention and intervention. In J.P. Wilson & B. Raphael (Eds), *International Handbook of Traumatic Stress* (pp. 905–14). New York: Plenum.

Mitchell, J.T. & Everly, G.S. (1995). Critical Incident Stress Debriefing (CISD) and the prevention of work-related traumatic stress among high risk occupational groups. In G.S. Everly & J.M. Lating (Eds), *Psychotraumatology: Key Papers and Core Concepts in Post-Traumatic Stress* (pp. 267–80). New York: Plenum.

Olff, M., Langeland, W. & Gersons, B.P.G. (2005). The psychobiology of PTSD: coping with trauma. *Psychoneuroendocrinology*, **30**, 974–82.

Ozer, E.J., Best, S.R., Lipsey, T.L. & Weiss, D.S. (2003). Predictors of posttraumatic stress disorder and symptoms in adults: a meta-analysis. *Psychological Bulletin*, **129**, 52–73.

Parks, K.M. & Steelman, L.A. (2008). Organizational wellness programs: a meta-analysis. *Journal of Occupational Health Psychology*, **13**, 58–68.

Paton, D. & Violanti, J.M. (1996). *Traumatic Stress in Critical Occupations: Recognition, Consequences and Treatment*. Springfield, IL: Charles. C. Thomas.

Pennebaker, J.W. (1997). *Opening Up: The Healing Powers of Expressing Emotions*. New York: Guilford.

Perloff, L.S. (1983). Perceptions of vulnerability to victimization. *Journal of Social Studies*, **39**, 193–210.

Rimé, B. (1999). Expressing emotion, physical health, and emotional relief: a cognitive-social perspective. *Advances in Mind-Body Medicine*, **15**, 175–9.

Rimé, B., Finkenhauer, C., Luminet, O., Zech, E. & Philippot, P. (1998). Social sharing of emotion: new evidence and new questions. In W. Stroebe & M. Hewstone (Eds), *European Review of Social Psychology, Volume 9* (pp. 225–58. Chichester: John Wiley & Sons, Ltd.

Roberts, N.P., Kitchiner, N.J., Kenardy, J. & Bisson, J.I. (2009). Systematic review and meta-analysis of multiple-session early interventions following traumatic events. *American Journal of Psychiatry*, Feb 2. [Epub ahead of print]

Rosen, G.M., Spitzer, R.L. & McHugh, P.R. (2008). Problems with the posttraumatic stress disorder and its future in DSM-V. *British Journal of Psychiatry*, **192**, 3–4.

Rothbaum, B.O., Foa, E.B., Murdock, T. *et al.* (1992). A prospective examination of posttraumatic stress disorder in rape victims. *Journal of Traumatic Stress*, **5**, 455–75.

Sarason, I.G., Johnson, J.H., Berberich, J.P. & Siegel, J.M. (1979). Helping police officers to cope with stress: a cognitive-behavioral approach. *American Journal of Community Psychiatry*, **7**, 593–603.

Schok, M.L., Kleber, R.J., Elands, M.E. & Weerts, J.M.P. (2008). Meaning as a mission: review of empirical studies on appraisals of war and peacekeeping experiences. *Clinical Psychology Review*, **28**, 357–65.

Shalev, A.Y., Peri, T., Canetti, L. & Schreiber, S. (1996). Predictors of PTSD in injured trauma survivors: a prospective study. *American Journal of Psychiatry*, **153**, 219–25.

Sijbrandij, M., Olff, M., Reitsma, J.B., Carlier, I.V., de Vries, M.H. & Gersons, B.P.R. (2007). Treatment of acute posttraumatic stress disorder with brief cognitive behavioral therapy: a randomized controlled trial. *American Journal of Psychiatry*, **164** (1), 82–90.

Solomon, S. (1999). Interventions for acute trauma response. *Current Opinion in Psychiatry*, **12**, 175–80.

Spector, P.E., Coulter, M.L., Stockwell, H.G. & Matz, M.W. (2007). Relationships of workplace physical violence and verbal aggression with perceived safety, perceived violence climate, and strains in a healthcare setting. *Work & Stress*, **21**, 117–30.

Symonds, M. (1980). The second injury to victims/acute responses of victims to terror. *Evaluation and Change*, special issue, 36–41.

Thompson, S.C., Armstrong, W. & Thomas, C. (1998). Illusions of control, underestimations and accuracy: a control heuristic explanation. *Psychological Bulletin*, **123**, 143–61.

Trimble, M.R. (1981). *Post-Traumatic Neurosis: From Railway Spine to the Whiplash*. Chichester: John Wiley & Sons, Ltd.

Ullman, S.E. (1995). Adult trauma survivors and posttraumatic stress sequelae: an analysis of reexperiencing, avoidance and arousal criteria. *Journal of Traumatic Stress*, **8**, 179–88.

van der Kolk, B., McFarlane, A.C. & Weisaeth, L. (1996) (Eds.). *Traumatic Stress: The Overwhelming Experience on Mind, Body and Society*. New York: Guilford.

Van der Ploeg, E. & Kleber, R.J. (2003). Acute and chronic job stressors among ambulance personnel: predictors of health symptoms. *Occupational and Environmental Medicine*, **60** (Supplement 1), i40–6.

Van der Ploeg, E., Mooren, T.T.M., Kleber, R.J., Velden, P.G. van der & Brom, D. (2004). Internal validation of the Dutch version of the Impact of Event Scale. *Psychological Assessment*, **16**, 16–26.

Van der Ploeg, H.M. & Kleijn, W.C. (1989). Being held hostage in The Netherlands: a study of long-term after effects. *Journal of Traumatic Stress*, **2**, 153–71.

Van der Velden, P.G., Burg, S. van der, Bout, J. van den & Steinmetz, C.H.D. (1991). *Risk factors for health problems after a bank robbery*. Paper presented on the annual meeting of the International Society for Traumatic Stress Studies, Washington, DC.

Van der Velden, P.G., Christiaanse, B., Kleber, R.J. *et al.* (2006). The effects of disaster exposure and post-disaster critical incidents on intrusions, avoidance and health problems among firefighters: a comparative study. *Stress, Trauma, and Crisis: An International Journal*, **9**, 73–93.

Van der Velden, P.G., Hazen, K. & Kleber, R.J. (1999). Traumazorg in organisaties [Trauma care in organizations]. *Gedrag & Organisatie*, **12**, 397–412.

Van der Velden, P.G., Kleber, R.J. & Koenen, K.C. (2008). Smoking predicts post-traumatic stress symptoms among rescue workers: A prospective disaster study of ambulance personnel. *Drug and Alcohol Dependence*, **94**, 267–71.

Van der Velden, P.G. & Wittmann, L. (2008). The independent predictive value of peritraumatic dissociation for PTSD symptomatology after type I trauma: a systematic review of prospective studies. *Clinical Psychology Review*, **28**, 1009–20.

Van Loon, P. (2008). Psychosociaal crisis management after calamities: casussen and interventies [Psychosocial crisis management after calamities: cases and interventions]. *Psychologie & Gezondheid*, **36**, 111–16.

Wagner, D., Heinrichs, M. & Ehlert, U. (1998). Prevalence of posttraumatic stress disorder in German professional firefighters. *American Journal of Psychiatry*, **155**, 1727–32.

Weathers, F.W., Keane, T.M. & Davidson, J.R. (2001). Clinician-Administered PTSD Scale: a review of the first ten years of research. *Depression and Anxiety*, **13**, 132–56.

Weisaeth, L. (1989). Importance of high response rates in traumatic stress research. Special Issue. Traumatic stress: empirical studies from Norway. *Acta Psychiatrica Scandinavica*, **80**, 131–7.

PART IV

Supporting Individuals at Work

CHAPTER 14

Management Development for Well-Being and Survival: Developing the Whole Person

Rosemary Maellaro and J. Lee Whittington
University of Dallas, USA

14.1 INTRODUCTION

The very competitive global environment and attendant economic pressures experienced by organizations today make managing especially challenging (Whetten & Cameron, 2002). Lawler's (2000) new millennium prediction that the business environment would become increasingly complex has materialized in the form of a boundaryless economy, worldwide labour markets, instantly linked information and agile new organizations. Accordingly, increasing amounts of competitive pressure has shifted to the management ranks in organizations. Hence, the creation of healthy work environments that flourish in these challenging, stressful times is a priority because the one competitive advantage that remains and becomes even more important in the current business environment is an organization's employees.

One way an organization can protect the significant investment in the *human* resources that provide a competitive edge is to be intentional about improving the overall well-being of their managers. Increased well-being allows managers to strike a healthier balance between their work and personal lives and thus better allocate their time, focus and energy to myriad demands made on them by all of the things that have to be done (Mariotti, 1998). Overall well-being has both physical and mental components and 'it's about feeling positive and having enough energy to be productive at work and to enjoy non-working life' (O'Reilly, 2006, p. 22).

International Handbook of Work and Health Psychology, Third Edition. Edited by Cary L. Cooper, James Campbell Quick, and Marc J. Schabracq.

As the line between work and home has become blurred by our ability to communicate and share information 24/7, the work day has expanded and now often intrudes into the home lives of managers (Mariotti, 1998). Therefore, it is important that organizations help managers develop the skills that are necessary to manage their personal lives as well as their work lives. While this approach may initially appear to be altruistic on the part of the organization, it is, in fact, imperative for the organization's success. Lack of balance between work life and personal life can cause burnout, low productivity, dissatisfaction and stress-related illnesses at all levels of the organization (Wiley, 2006). Developing the whole person by addressing all aspects of managers' lives can yield positive outcomes for both organizations and individuals.

This chapter focuses on management development for the purpose of increasing the overall well-being of leaders, using the manager's whole-life model as a framework. The manager's whole-life model implies a broader perspective for management development in contrast to a narrower perspective. Rather than emphasizing career and work development to the exclusion of a manager's family, personal, spiritual and community life, the model places career and work in the context of overall life development. The underlying dynamic for the model is a cooperative, win-win strategy as opposed to a competitive, win-lose strategy.

What follows in Section 14.2 is an examination of management development within the context of today's organizations as complex, open systems. Section 14.3 provides a general overview of the manager's whole-life model, a brief description of its components and the rationale for using it to frame management development for well-being. Section 14.4 focuses on developing managers in the personal arena and addresses the importance of self-awareness for managers, how emotional intelligence can enhance personal development and preventative stress management techniques for managerial well-being. Section 14.5 proposes an agenda for management development programmes that can effectively cultivate a person. It also addresses the topics of interpersonal skill development, career development, learning to lead from strengths and servant-leadership as a redefinition of what it means to be a leader today. Section 14.6 discusses the need for managers to 'stay alive' amidst the chaos that is organizational life in the twenty-first century and addresses the final three components of the whole-life model: family, spiritual and community.

14.2 MANAGEMENT DEVELOPMENT WITHIN ORGANIZATIONS AS COMPLEX OPEN SYSTEMS

The dominant organizational paradigm remains wedded to scientific management theories which reflect a philosophy that remains committed to a need for control and prediction. This need for control reflects our need for safety and our fear of the unknown and being at the mercy of someone or something (Keene, 2000).

Rapid changes over the last several decades have brought us a global economy, increased competition, quantum improvements in our ability to share information instantaneously and the growing diversity of the population and the workforce. Because we cannot fully understand a system without constantly considering the forces that impinge upon it (Katz & Kahn, 1966), we must leave behind our conceptualization of organizations as closed, rational systems. Open systems theory provides a much more dynamic and adequate framework for understanding and managing organizations because it acknowledges that environmental influences have a major impact on the effective functioning of the organization as a complex social system. An organization must find and obtain needed resources, interpret and act on environmental changes, dispose of outputs, and control and coordinate internal activities in the face of environmental disturbances and uncertainty. This embodies the definition of an open system, one that must interact with its environment to survive and therefore continually change to adapt to its environment if it is to remain a viable entity (Daft, 2001).

Managers are typically trained to equate equilibrium and harmony with success, while, in reality, organizations are capable of spontaneous change. Managers may participate in these changes, but have little or no control over such changes, so it is imperative for their success that they develop a capacity to adapt and live creatively with those changes (Stacey, Griffin & Shaw, 2000). Accordingly, the notions of nonlinearity, randomness, complexity and chaos that are natural, legitimate, necessary and inescapable aspects of reality (Goldstein, 1994; Merry, 1995; Stacey, Griffin & Shaw, 2000; Wheatley, 1999) must be integrated with the old command and control methods for managing organizations – that is, the order, certainty, predictability and regularity that managers are taught they should attempt to impose in organizations.

The environment facing today's organizations has become increasingly dynamic and more complex. This has implications for the organizational structures – they must become more organic to adapt to these challenges. But these changes also have implications for the nature of managerial work. Adaptive problems are contrasted with technical problems in the work of Heifetz (1994; Heifetz & Linsky, 2002). Technical problems are familiar, they have been dealt with before. Thus a solution is known and can be applied. Alternatively, adaptive problems present a challenge that has not been encountered before. Understanding the problem requires learning and the solution must be learned as those who are facing the problem work through it. In a stable and certain environment, the manager is the locus of control who has the answer and instructs the organization to apply known solutions. In complex and dynamic environments, the leader must facilitate adaptive work as the organization learns its way to a solution. Therefore, as the environment continues to become more complex and turbulent, managers will find themselves confronting adaptive problems more frequently and will be able to succeed only if they can learn quickly and apply that learning to unpredictable, rapidly occurring new situations (Daudelin & Hall, 1997; Heifetz & Linksy, 2002).

14.2.1 Management Development Programmes

Management development is an ongoing process of learning, growing and changing to enhance people's skills and/or knowledge. In the United States alone there are more than five million managers and management development is provided to qualify managers for their jobs and/or to upgrade their positions (Pace, Smith & Mills, 1991). Management development is one way to design and build healthy, vital work environments. Management development may be undertaken by an individual manager or by the organization, or it may be a shared responsibility.

Management development has been defined in many ways and is used by different organizations for various reasons. Some of the most commonly cited reasons by organizations for implementing management development programmes include: building managerial interpersonal skills; developing individuals for increased responsibility; increasing management productivity; augmenting the pool of promotable management employees; and providing increased opportunities for women and minorities (Rothwell & Kazanas, 1993).

The core of our discussion of management development as a means of increasing well-being in the organization is based on its definition simply as 'an attempt to improve managerial effectiveness through a planned and deliberate learning process' (Rothwell & Kazanas, 1993, p. 5). Our general focus will be on management development not only as a way to enhance the well-being of managers, but also as a means of improving the organization's ability to effectively respond to environmental change. In other words, our position is that management development need not be viewed as a zero-sum game. We believe that management development can be a win-win proposition – one that balances the economic goals of the organization with social goals that address the needs of individual managers as well (Friedman, Christensen & DeGroot, 1998).

The historically predominant view of organizations as static and closed systems led to management development programmes that typically are organization-specific. Such programmes have been rooted in functional rationality and have the conscious intention of equipping managers with explicit knowledge, skills and abilities to fulfill roles and attain goals that have been predetermined (Garavan, Barnicle & O'Suilleabhain, 1999; Kuchinke, 1999). As such, this approach is deterministic and uses universal, linear notions of cause and effect to provide managers with the tools they believe they need to predict the future, choose strategies and control activities. The goal has been to create a state of equilibrium, consensus and conformity that were associated with organizational success (Stacey, Griffin & Shaw, 2000).

The problem with this approach to management development, however, is that today's organizations do not behave as mechanistic systems and are more accurately viewed as open systems that continuously interact with the external environment (Buhler, 2000). As such, they are complex, adaptive systems in which 'work life is more complex, uncertain and anxiety-provoking. Under these conditions information is incomplete, ambiguous and the consequences of actions are highly unpredictable' (Aram & Noble, 1999, p. 321). The long-held belief that managers are able to control organizational outcomes is no longer viable. These factors all contribute to managers' stress levels, making well-being at work more difficult to achieve.

To be more effective, new management development programmes must be based on principles that do not leave managers with the illusion that they are in charge and in control when, in fact, they are not (Stacey, Griffin & Shaw, 2000). Given the permanent white water of contemporary organizational reality, the critical element in managerial development may no longer be the acquisition and mastery of specific skill sets; rather, effective management development programmes will be aimed at developing managers who are capable of delivering successful organizational adaptation and renewal (Garavan, Barnicle & O'Suilleabhain, 1999). This is not to imply, however, that individual managers should sacrifice their personal growth and engage in development activities solely for the benefit of the organization. The goal is to develop the whole person, one that is better equipped to succeed in personal arenas as well as the workplace.

Inherent in this approach to management development is the notion that the organization and individual managers both play key roles in the process. For its part, the organization must create a culture that is characterized by clear and consistent openness to experience, encouragement of responsible risk taking and willingness to acknowledge failures and learn from them. It must become a learning organization.

A learning organization is one that embodies the following traits (Senge, 1990):

- Personal mastery – individuals within the organization are committed to their own life-long learning and continually strive to increase their personal levels of proficiency in areas that they value and are able to see reality objectively.

- Mental models – the deeply held assumptions or generalizations that influence how people view the world and prepare to take action.
- A shared vision – a set of guiding principles and practices that unite people in pursuing lofty goals for the organization.
- Team learning – individuals are learning more rapidly as members of teams that develop extraordinary capacity for coordinated action.
- Systems thinking – the ability to see the connection between issues, events and diverse data points to integrate them into a whole greater than the sum of its parts.

Learning organizations are healthy organizations that are characterized by generative learning, also called double-loop learning, as opposed to the adaptive, or single-loop learning that characterizes most organizations (Argyris, 1991; Argyris & Schön, 1974). Adaptive learning results in self-sealing behaviour that discourages the generation and expression of alternative views or negative feelings. This is based on the beliefs that we live in a win-lose world, rational behaviour is most effective and the public testing of assumptions is intolerably risky.

Generative learning, on the other hand, emphasizes continuous experimentation and feedback in an ongoing examination of the very way in which organizations go about defining and solving problems. It promotes learning and growth by relying on valid information, free and informed choice, internal commitment to the choice and constant monitoring of its implementation. Noteworthy properties of this type of organizational learning are its ability *not* to be self-sealing and its tendency to permit progressively more effective testing of assumptions and progressively greater learning about a person's effectiveness rather than attempting to protect people in the organization by covering up difficult issues.

14.3 THE MANAGER'S WHOLE-LIFE MODEL: FIVE ARENAS OF LIFE

When managers go to work each day, they do not bring with them only that part of themselves that is needed to perform their job. They bring a whole person. Even though all facets of the person are not engaged in the workplace, other aspects of a person's life have an impact on an individual while at work. This notion of *partial inclusion* stems from the fact that the entire individual is not required for the individual's designated role in the organization. Roles at work stipulate behaviours, which imply that only a psychological slice of

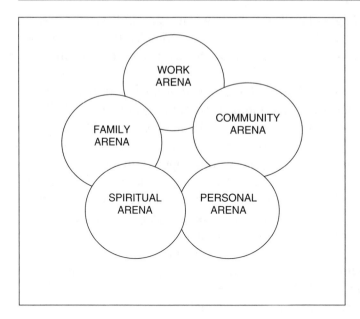

Figure 14.1 The manager's whole-life model: five arenas of life.

the person is needed to perform his/her duties, yet the organization brings within its boundaries the entire person (Katz & Kahn, 1966). Each individual member of any given organization is also part of many other systems (family, church, social organizations, schools, etc.), however. The significance of this is that their behaviour in one organization most likely will be impacted by the many other segmental commitments they bring with them from participating as members of these other organizations.

There is a growing trend to recognize managers and employees as whole beings, not mere factors of production. The concept of well-being extends beyond the organization and the non-work arenas of life may well affect occupational well-being. Borrowing from Sherman and Hendricks (1989), our view of well-being transcends the work arena and also includes the four non-work arenas of life shown in Figure 14.1. This whole-life model emphasizes each of life's five arenas. Well-being is a function of balance of time, commitment and the investment of emotional energy in these five areas of life.

Managers who define themselves in terms of these five arenas have greater self-complexity (Linville, 1985). Linville's (1987) self-complexity buffering hypothesis suggests that individuals with high levels of self-complexity are buffered from distress and strain when a stressful life event occurs in one life arena. According to Linville, when an individual's self-worth is based on their total self-concept, stressful events in one life arena are not as devastating. Individuals whose self-worth is dominated by only one role or arena are more likely to experience higher levels of distress when a stressful event occurs in that arena. While Linville's (1985) notion of self-complexity argues for the relative independence of the areas in life, we have argued for recognition of the interdependence.

More recent views on leadership development also support this concept. Friedman (2006) believes that development programmes should not be limited to improving skills that are needed only in the workplace. He suggests that organizations develop the whole person to create what he calls total leadership. He proposes that management development models emphasize performance in all domains of life and that synergies across work, family, community and self be leveraged to produce more meaningful overall results. He contends that the work and personal lives of managers can be aligned rather than being viewed as in conflict with each other.

Occupational health psychology (OHP) focuses on the design and construction of healthy work environments (Murphy & Cooper, 2000; Quick, 1999a, 1999b; Quick & Tetrick, 2003). OHP is concerned with both the physical and the psychosocial, interpersonal design features of the work environment in order to manage the health risks that these design features may present. OHP is, therefore, a science of design aimed at creating opportunities for employees to grow, develop and strive to maximize their intellectual and physical potential free from unreasonable and/or unnecessary psychological risks.

OHP has three design dimensions: the work environment; the person; and the work environment–family system interface. First, the work environment dimension devotes attention to psychosocial aspects of work. This dimension addresses the issues of work design, organizational culture, corporate policies and procedures related to personal actions, families and due process. Control, uncertainty and conflict are parameters of particular interest within this design dimension (Landy, Quick & Kasl, 1994). Second, the person dimension requires attention to cognitive, moral and human development, as well as to skills and abilities required for the demands of a competitive or stressful work environment (Whetten & Cameron, 2002). Third, the work–family interface dimension addresses the manager's non-work life arenas shown in Figure 14.1. While the family is of particular concern in this regard (Piotrkowski, 1979; Quick et al., 1994), the community, spiritual and personal arenas are important as well (Seta, Paulus & Baron, 2000).

A relatively new concept known as work–family enrichment theory suggests that participation in roles at work and at home can have positive additive effects on physical and psychological well-being. Individuals who participate in satisfying work and family roles have been known to experience greater well-being than those who participate in only one of the roles or who are dissatisfied with one or more of their roles. In much the same way that a diverse financial portfolio protects an individual's financial well-being from poor performance in a particular type of investment, participation in multiple social roles can buffer managers from distress that may originate from one particular role (Greenhaus & Powell, 2006).

The manager's whole-life model in Figure 14.1 provides a useful framework for implementing management development programmes that address the OHP's dimensions of healthy work environments and encourages active engagement in multiple life roles. The whole-life model suggests interdependence, not complete independence, of the personal, work, family, spiritual and community arenas that comprise an individual's life. It advocates well-being and balanced investment in all five arenas.

Development in the personal arena is increasingly viewed as critical to a manager's overall success. Unless and until an individual has developed a keen sense of self-awareness, has increased his or her emotional intelligence and gained the ability to effectively manage his or her own stress, it will be more difficult to successfully supervise and lead others to high levels of business achievement.

Development in the work arena focuses on honing skills that will enable managers to operate more effectively in complex organizations, better serve their employees in guiding them to attain organizational objectives and effectively manage their own careers.

The spiritual arena includes the cultivation of a relationship with God or a higher power, as enhanced by personal efforts in prayer, meditation and study. The community arena suggests the need to be involved in the community, with the intent to serve others. The family arena emphasizes a manager's responsibilities to spouse and children. It also addresses obligations to siblings and parents, which is becoming a more prevalent issue as the parents of many workforce members are ageing and require more care.

The size and relative importance of each arena varies by individual manager. For example, problems in the work arena may spill over into the family arena, or the reverse may also occur, which can be problematic (Kabanoff, 1980; Quick *et al.*, 1994). Therefore, as we focus primarily on management development in the personal and work arenas, sensitivity to the interdependence of a manager's five life arenas is important.

14.4 DEVELOPMENT IN THE PERSONAL ARENA

The personal arena includes a person's emotional and innermost life; that is, the private world of the self (MacDonald, 1985). This private world can be viewed as our essence and the ordering of this arena in life provides an anchoring stability around which the other life arenas may be structured. Management development in the personal arena provides the foundation for development in the other four arenas. Organizations that facilitate development in this arena find that their managers are more personally engaged in their work, exhibit a greater commitment to helping others succeed and are better prepared to contribute to achieving the overall goals of the organization (Lash, 2002). Additionally, managers who are more engaged in their work are better able to cope with job stress (O'Reilly, 2006), which further contributes to their overall well-being.

Finding the point of balance between all things that managers want to accomplish with their career, family, friends, community and other outside interests is as much an issue of choice as it is of time. Balancing work and life for greater overall well-being is not simply a matter of where and how managers spend their time; it involves making choices about what is important to them and aligning their actions with those values (Gurvis & Patterson, 2005). The process of aligning life choices with core values naturally begins with self-awareness.

14.4.1 Self-Awareness

Management development is much more than simply learning the latest leadership theories or management skills. Leaders must experience self-growth first in order to achieve outstanding results for themselves and their organizations (Lash, 2002). Self-awareness is a broad concept that concentrates on the image that an individual has of him/herself, how well that is aligned with their personal values and whether or not that image is accurate in comparison with how others perceive that individual (McCarthy & Garavan, 1999). Whetten and Cameron (2002) contend that the knowledge managers possess about themselves is a critical component of management capability. 'We cannot improve ourselves or develop new capabilities unless and until we know what level of capability we currently possess'. They go on to note that, 'Considerable empirical evidence exists that individuals who are more self-aware are more healthy, perform better in managerial and leadership roles and are more productive at work' (p. 57). Others have claimed that effective leaders are those that have a congruent sense of self (Nichols, 2008) and who exhibit integrity, people acumen and trust-building behaviour (Stein & Book, 2001). Because these traits all stem from high levels of self-awareness, we believe that increasing managers' self-awareness must be the first step in management development programmes. Self-awareness provides the cornerstone for building personal success, while a deficit in self-awareness can be debilitating both to a person's personal relationships and career (Goleman, 1995).

The goal of self-awareness for managers is to gain an understanding of what is important to them, how they experience things, what they want, what they feel and how they come across to others – essentially to understand what makes them do what they do (Weisinger, 1998). The process of increasing self-awareness therefore is essentially an inner journey (Lash, 2002) that can be accomplished through careful introspection, or with the help of assessments by others. Various standardized inventories are also available to assist with self-analysis (Roe & Lunneborg, 1990).

Weisinger (1998) suggests that increasing self-awareness does not necessarily require long hours of psychotherapy; what is needed is 'some serious thoughtfulness and the courage to explore how you react to the people and events in your life' (p. 6). He recommends the following steps for managers who wish to work on increasing their self-awareness:

- *Examine how you make appraisals.* These are the various impressions, interpretations and expectations that people have about themselves and others. By tuning into this inner dialogue, managers can become more aware of how their thoughts influence their feelings and actions. Additionally, by seeking information about how others make appraisals, managers will then be able to compare their appraisals and alter their actions if necessary.
- *Tune into your senses.* It is through the five senses of sight, sound, smell, taste and touch that people receive information about their worlds. It is critical, however, to clearly distinguish between sensory data and appraisals, as our judgements about ourselves, others and any given situation can act as a filter to the senses.
- *Get in touch with your feelings.* Feelings are the spontaneous emotional responses people have about their interpretations and expectations. Feelings are often denied or ignored because getting in touch with them can be difficult. While acknowledging feelings can cause discomfort or distress for some people, doing so is a key to understanding why people behave the way they do. It is important to deal with feelings as they occur and then move on so negative feelings do not fester. Additionally, it is impossible to effectively manage feelings that are not acknowledged.
- *Learn what your intentions are.* Determining what their desires are, particularly in the short term, can help managers become more strategic in their actions. Once again, this may be a difficult task because apparent intentions are often confused with hidden agendas. True intentions are more readily identified when people use their behaviours as clues, trust their feelings and are honest with themselves.
- *Pay attention to your actions.* While the preceding suggestions deal with internal processes, this one addresses people's overt actions. This is an

important distinction in that others can also observe behaviours, yet may interpret them in any number of ways. In this case, it is the nuances or the unconscious actions (for example, speech patterns, body language and nonverbal behaviour) that can provide valuable clues to underlying attitudes and behaviours rather than broad, obvious actions (such as walking, speaking, etc.).

Lack of self-awareness is often the reason that some really intelligent people sometimes fail miserably in organizations (Noel & Dotlich, 2008). When managers do not understand who they are and the impact they have on others they will find it more difficult to gain the respect and trust of the people they must work with and through to achieve organizational goals. Once managers attain increased self-awareness, however, they also can realize several other benefits that contribute to their overall physical and emotional well-being. They will act in ways that are more congruent with their real selves, their behaviour will become more flexible because they are acting in the here and now rather than in response to old feelings and they will be able to more directly pursue their goals as they gain greater clarity about what they want – out of life in general and out of work more specifically (Segal, 1997).

14.4.2   Developing Emotional Intelligence

It would be remiss to address self-awareness without recognizing that it is a foundational component of emotional intelligence (EI), which has played a considerable role in management development programmes of late. EI has been defined in numerous ways, but its essence lies in the notion that 'rational thinking involves emotions and that the two cannot be separated' (Caruso & Salovy, 2004, p. 195). It is the ability to be aware of one's emotions and *intentionally* use them to guide behaviour and thinking in ways that enhance outcomes (Weisinger, 1998).

Many scholars and practitioners have come to believe that increased EI can provide managers with a critical edge in the work and family arenas (McCarthy & Garavan, 1999). Daniel Goleman (1995), who is largely responsible for introducing the concept to the business world, argues that IQ accounts for only about 20% of a person's success in life and that the rest can be accounted for by EI. Caruso and Salovey (2004) believe that EI can provide managers an edge in building loyalty and commitment among employees. As they point out, 'If you examine current theories of leadership or descriptions of trusted leaders, it is clear that emotional competencies . . . may play at least as important a role as technical competencies and industry knowledge, perhaps even more so' (p. 196). They also describe how higher levels of EI can contribute to a manager's ability to adapt and survive in today's complex organizations: 'A person functioning in amorphous situations marked by rapid change needs to be able to form strong teams quickly and efficiently, interact effectively with people, communicate goals and obtain buy-in from these self-directed, autonomous groups' (Caruso & Salovy, 2004, p. xvii).

As noted above, self-awareness can help leaders better understand the implications of their own thoughts, feelings and intentions, as well as the feelings of others. This is a central aspect of the motivational mechanism of transformational leadership (Sosik & Magerian, 1999). Yet self-awareness is only one of four domains of EI, which also includes self-management, social awareness and relationship management (Goleman, Boyatzis & McKee, 2002).

Self-management

> What you don't recognize, you can't manage. If you aren't aware of what you're doing, why you're doing it and the way it is affecting others, you can't change (Stein & Book, 2000, p. 55).

Once managers gain sufficient self-awareness, they can progress to the self-management domain of EI. Contrary to what some may believe, self-management does not involve stifling one's feelings; rather it is about understanding them in an effort to make situations more favourable and taking charge of one's thoughts and visceral reactions to behave intentionally (Weisinger, 1998). Managers with strong self-management competencies are able to establish an environment of mutual respect as they consider the needs of others while calmly asserting their own needs (Segal, 1997; Sosik & Magerian, 1999). They are transparent, optimistic, flexible in adapting to changing situations or overcoming obstacles, have high personal standards that they strive to achieve, recognize and eagerly seize opportunities and effectively manage their disturbing emotions and impulses (Goleman, Boyatzis & McKee, 2002).

The ability to effectively manage stress is an integral aspect of self-management and will be addressed in a separate section later in the chapter.

Social awareness and empathy

The primary competency within the social awareness domain is empathy, which is the ability to tune into and read the thoughts and feelings of other people – that is, to see the world from their perspective – while not losing sight of one's own separate emotional experience (Stein & Book, 2000;

Segal, 1997). Goleman, Boyatzis and McKee (2002) describe empathy as a type of 'social radar' that allows individuals to sense and understand the felt, yet unspoken, emotions of others. The goal of empathy is to convey understanding of what other people are going through without taking on their feelings, agreeing with their point of view, or attempting to fix things (Segal, 1997; Switankowsky, 2000).

Some managers who confuse empathy with sympathy are reluctant to show empathy because they fear it will make them appear weak and vulnerable. Empathy, however, is not sympathy. Whereas empathy is about truly listening to another person in an effort to see the world from their perspective and understand their feelings without getting involved in them, sympathy is more reactionary and often involves personal identification with another person's feelings and the assumption of their pain (Norris, 2004; West, 2006). Another important distinction between the two concepts is that in showing empathy the self is merely a vehicle for understanding and does not lose its own identity. On the other hand, sympathy reduces rather than enhances self-awareness because it is concerned more with communion than accuracy (Switankowsky, 2000).

The ability to show empathy can be a decided advantage for managers. Empathy requires a person to make an effort and actively engage with others, which can help managers get to know their employees and understand what motivates them. This forms the basis for trusting relationships that, in the long run, contribute to the well-being of both parties. Goleman (1995) referred to empathy as 'the fundamental people skill' and says that 'people with empathy are natural leaders who can express the unspoken collective sentiment and articulate it so as to guide a group toward its goals' (p. 97).

Showing empathy is similar to Lundin and Lundin's (1994) notion of healing managers. They suggest that organizations need to build trust by directly confronting feelings and emotions in the workplace. Healing managers help others grow emotionally and intellectually by evoking the spirit and values of an organization committed to creating a caring, humane and compassionate work environment. Healing managers forge the emotional pathway to healthy relationships.

Relationship management

An organization exists as a result of the relationships of its members (Stacey, Griffin & Shaw, 2000); therefore positive interpersonal interactions are critical for organizational as well as individual well-being. The ultimate objective for developing EI competence in managers is to enhance their ability to establish and maintain effective interpersonal relationships. Technical skills remain as core job requirements, but a lack of good interpersonal skills negatively impacts job performance and personal well-being (Centko, 1998).

Managers with high EI are more likely to be successful in managing relationships because they possess awareness that allows them to accurately analyse relationships and adjust their behaviours accordingly, they manage their emotions effectively to make interpersonal interactions more productive and they are able to connect meaningfully with others with their empathy skills (Weisinger, 1998).

14.4.3 Preventive Stress Management and Health Psychology

Work-related psychological disorders and distress have been among the 10 leading occupational health risks in the United States for more than a decade (Sauter, Murphy & Hurrell, 1990). There are a variety of contributing factors for such health risks, including the corporate warfare manifested in mergers, acquisitions, downsizing and bankruptcies, which has come with increasing competition (Nelson, Quick & Quick, 1989; Thurow, 1993). Based on the translation of the epidemiological and public health notions of prevention into a stress-process framework, *preventive stress management* was developed as an organizational philosophy for leading and managing organizations to enhance health while averting distress in the workplace (Quick *et al.*, 1997). Two of the guiding principles of preventive stress management are especially relevant to managers interested in creating healthy work environments.

- Principle 1: Individual and organizational health are interdependent.
- Principle 2: Leaders have a responsibility for individual and organizational health.

The first principle calls for managers to enhance their own health and well-being because they make important contributions to the health and well-being of the organization as a whole and are important role models for their employees. Organizations cannot maintain vitality and productivity when the individuals throughout them are distressed and in varying degrees dysfunctional. Hence, management has a responsibility for individual and organizational health (Principle 2). As managers develop their own health, they should do so considering the personal, family, spiritual and community arenas of their lives, because parenting, community involvement and recreation have positive benefits for their functioning in the work area (Kirchmeyer, 1992).

Within the preventive stress management model, Quick, Nelson and Quick (1990) found that chief executives who managed stress in a healthy manner varied substantially in the prevention methods each found personally most effective. However, all were found to be self-reliant in the way they formed and maintained a social support network of professional and personal (e.g. family, spiritual and community) relationships (Quick, Nelson & Quick, 1987). Furthermore, a study of the US Navy's top 140 major weapon system managers found that such social support constituted an effective prevention method for reducing burnout associated with perceived environmental uncertainty (Bodensteiner, Gerloff & Quick, 1989).

Goodness of fit

The person–environment fit theory of stress concerns the interaction between person and environment dimensions, thus offering a point of departure for understanding the flexible fit dynamics required in OHP (Edwards & Cooper, 1990). The three design elements of OHP operate interdependently, not independently. Goodness of fit is an important element in a design process. Hence, blaming distressed victims or workplaces for health problems is of little value when design modifications in one of the other design dimensions may solve the problem. The principles of preventive stress management imply a shared responsibility for health at work and imply joint problem solving to enhance healthy human potential in organizations. The notion of goodness of fit between the person and the work environment suggests the potential for no-fault problems and the need to mould each. The work environment, the person and the family all must have degrees of flexibility. Hence, the need for a flexible fit among the three design dimensions. Quick et al. (2001) recently used dynamic effect spirals in proposing an isomorphic theory of stress that extends person–environment fit theory and the goodness-of-fit concept. An isomorphic theory refers to a dimension-specific extension of person–environment fit theory and focuses attention on corresponding characteristics in the person and the environment. The isomorphic theory proposed by Quick et al. (2001) brings attention to the dimensions of control, uncertainty and interpersonal relationships. Further, the theory suggests that through mutual, dynamic accommodations along each dimension, goodness of fit and healthy levels of stress can be achieved.

14.5   DEVELOPMENT IN THE WORK ARENA

As the very nature of organizations has changed dramatically, so too have the competencies that are necessary for effective management of those organizations. Human and social systems can no longer be understood by reducing them to the sum of their ever-changing parts (Merry, 1995); therefore, the knowledge and skill bases that have defined functional managers over recent decades are no longer complete. To meet the challenges of global competition and chaos in the world of work, more critical to management success are the capacities of adaptability, flexibility, open-mindedness and self-reliance (Quick, Nelson & Quick, 1990; Weir & Smallman, 1998). Thus, the topics addressed in management development programmes aimed at increasing managerial competence must be modified accordingly.

Merry (1995) notes that humans are social animals who need to interrelate with others to work, produce and ensure the necessities of life. 'To ensure these relationships, there must be a measure of certainty, order, regularity, predictability and some degree of stability and steadiness in the way people behave toward each other' (p. 19). While many organizations and individuals try to ensure this through control and domination, the New Sciences suggest that chaos and order are fused in such a way that they cannot be disentangled (Merry, 1995). The paradoxical view of organizations as complex systems, however, has not been widely adopted by managers in organizations today. Stacey, Griffin and Shaw (2000) deem this to be the source of stress and anxiety for many managers, in that they believe that life should not be paradoxical and that they should be able to find solutions to the problems that paradox creates and experience another thing, which is the reality of chaos.

The central role of managers in organizations is changing from one of attempting to reduce and control uncertainty to one of being able to live creatively with it (Stacey, Griffin & Shaw, 2000). One way managers will be able to make this transition will be to learn how to operate within a systems thinking mindset, one that requires them to think in terms of the whole system, realizing that this whole is greater than the sum of its parts and understanding the nonlinear nature of those systems while also being able to discern underlying patterns.

It is also crucial that management development programmes focus on developing managerial capabilities needed to function effectively at the edge of chaos, tolerate ambiguity, produce business results under unpredictable circumstances and deal productively with constant change.

14.5.1   Managerial Interpersonal Skills

One competency that remains constant as a source of employee well-being is the need for managers to develop and maintain healthy relationships within the organization (Quick, Nelson & Quick, 1990). A surprising number of otherwise intelligent and technically qualified individuals unnecessarily fail in management positions because of limited interpersonal competence. Many have not succeeded in management positions because they were unable to establish and maintain the type and quality of relationships with others that would have enabled them to achieve both personal and organizational goals. This can have a decidedly negative impact on the well-being of these managers, in addition to the well-being of their employees and ultimately on the success of their companies.

While the ability to establish and maintain mutually beneficial, productive interpersonal relationships with coworkers and employees can be enhanced as managers work on increasing their emotional intelligence as discussed above, management development programmes must also offer opportunities that are dedicated specifically to developing interpersonal skills. Professor and consultant John Hayes has had experience working with managers who are considered to be technically and professionally competent, but who are not as successful when it comes to achieving organizational goals and efficiently accomplishing tasks with a minimum of unnecessary disruption. He notes,

> The distinguishing factor between these and more successful managers appears to be their level of interpersonal competence. Those who pay attention to interpersonal relationships and who, when necessary, are able to consciously manage the way they relate with others seem to be much more successful in terms of achieving their goals (Hayes, 1994, p. vii).

Simply helping managers gain knowledge about interpersonal competence is not enough, however. As Boyatzis (1982) contends, 'It is usually not the lack of knowledge but the inability to *use* knowledge that limits effective managerial behavior' (p. 4). Therefore, organizational management development programmes must address the acquisition of knowledge *and* skills in the area of interpersonal competence; knowledge is a necessary first step, but by itself it is not sufficient for changing leadership behaviour (Georges, 1988; Whetten, 1983). New knowledge must be put into action (McDonald-Mann, 1998).

As an initial step in this process, organizations must determine the particular skills that differentiate individuals who establish and maintain successful interpersonal relationships within their own organizations from those who do not. This is because this concept is often unique to an organization's culture and because it is difficult, if not impossible, to find a consistent meaning of interpersonal competence. It has been defined variably by scholars and practitioners as interpersonal skills, people skills, soft skills, communication skills and relationship skills in very general terms. Although specific interpersonal skills are rarely delineated, one study (Maellaro, 2008) determined that there were 11 specific interpersonal skills that were most preferred by those who hire managers. These were: empathy, assertiveness, collaborative bargaining, political acumen, giving feedback, asking probing questions, reflecting on what others say, diagnostic skills (to identify problems in groups that may be hindering productivity), intervention skills (to effectively resolve performance issues), preparing information for employees and presenting it in a credible manner.

14.5.2   Career Development

Career development enhances management development while encouraging individual and organizational health. This process constitutes an important part of the individual–organization exchange relationship. Individuals look to the organization to provide a series of meaningful, satisfying work experiences and organizations expect high levels of performance and commitment from individuals to whom they provide opportunities. Career development consists of the actions individuals take, alone or with the aid of others, to manage their careers in specific ways (Quick *et al.*, 1997).

Successful career development efforts can encourage the health of both managers and organizations, although a demanding career may also have adverse effects on a manager's family investment (Kirchmeyer, 1992). For individuals, career development serves several functions. It increases self-efficacy by building in opportunities for growth and success. In addition, sound career choices can decrease strain. For the organization, inattention to career development can have dysfunctional consequences. Poor performance, low commitment, low job satisfaction and high turnover rates can result from the frustration that employees experience in conjunction with poorly managed careers. Career development can best be considered a joint responsibility for individuals and organizations.

Key components of career development

There are two key components of effective career development (Greenhaus, 1987). One is the process of self-analysis that provides information about individual strengths, weaknesses, interests and abilities. The insights gained by managers in the inner journey taken for development in the personal arena can readily be used for purposes of career development as well.

The other key component is environmental exploration, which includes an analysis of opportunities available to the individual. This activity has become increasingly challenging in today's organizations because of the flattening of organizations, downsizing and the elimination of many middle management jobs. Career paths in organizations are no longer feasible because of the increasing pace of change (Dalton, 1989). Nevertheless, individuals must develop information about the role requirements of particular jobs that they envision filling.

Good self-analysis and opportunity analysis lead a manager to form a strategic career plan, which should be placed in the context of an overall balanced life. The concept of a career as a series of upward moves may no longer be realistic in light of the radical organizational changes afoot (Thurow, 1993; Waterman, Waterman & Collard, 1994). Careers may need to be reconceptualized as a series of lateral moves with attendant breadth in skill acquisition, a perspective very consistent with a developmental view for management. Organizations should not relinquish their roles in opportunity analysis in the face of such challenges. Instead, they should be as honest and forthright as possible with individuals about their futures. Self-analysis and opportunity analysis are reciprocally related and are both essential to forming a strategic career plan. Extensively relying on one process without sufficient attention to the other will produce incomplete career development.

Alternative sources of career development support

Career development support may come in the form of self-help, counsellor assistance, organizational programmes and career planning courses (Gray *et al.*, 1990). Organizations can take some initiatives and can provide opportunities for managers to undertake others.

Self-help Individuals can engage in career development pursuits on their own. The self-exploration that they undertake as part of the development in their personal arena can be a part of such activities, whereby they assess their values, interests, skills, work preferences, strengths and weaknesses. By learning as much as possible about themselves, individuals can begin to develop meaningful career goals and strategies for achieving the goals. In addition to self-exploration, individuals can conduct library research on careers of interest or contact organizations of interest and ask for published materials. Another alternative is the informational interview, which has the advantage of learning the perspectives of others who have insights about potential career strategies. While self-help avenues of career development have the advantage of low cost, they require significant investments of the individual's time.

Counsellor assistance A second career development source is engaging the assistance of a career counsellor or consultant. While universities provide such services at relatively low cost to students, counsellors in private practice provide these services for substantially higher fees. Most counsellors take a comprehensive approach to career development, combining individual assessment with opportunity analyses. A typical approach uses both standardized instruments that focus on job interests, career maturity and abilities, along with in-depth interviews. The advantages of using counsellors or consultants include the interactive feedback provided to the individual and the expertise provided by the counsellor. Two potential disadvantages of this approach are its cost and the danger of the employee forming an unhealthy dependency reliance on the counsellor.

Organizational programmes Many organizations have their own programmes for career development that integrate individual career planning with human resource planning and the development of succession plans. By creating career paths that encourage individual growth and development, organizations ensure a supply of talent to meet their future staffing needs. Career development programmes in organizations may include newcomer orientation, job rotation, goal setting, mentoring, assessment centre evaluations and management training. These efforts all work to strengthen the individual–organizational relationship.

Career-planning courses Universities or professional associations often offer career-planning courses. One advantage of such courses is the information exchange between individuals and their fellow students and instructors. This exchange provides several points of independent feedback and provides opportunities for considerable interaction. Typical courses include readings, lectures, standardized tests, cases, individual and group experiential activities and guest speakers. In summary, there are several sources of career development support and a variety can be used to achieve maximum benefits.

Value added to the workplace

Career development encourages individual health by providing individuals with opportunities to learn new skills, acquire more knowledge and work toward achieving their full potential. By providing and developing goals and direction, it can reduce the anxiety and frustration that individuals may experience without a guiding force behind their careers.

For organizations, the value of career development is that it helps identify training needs, staffing opportunities and undiscovered potential talent in the workforce. It forces an organization to look ahead in terms of its human resource needs and to proactively develop individuals who can meet those needs. Career development also serves an important communicative function within organizations. It conveys a message to employees that management believes individual well-being and organizational well-being are linked and that investing in the long-term developmental activities of employees ultimately pays off in organizational health.

14.5.3   Learning to Lead from Strengths

Many leaders find themselves burned out because they spend an inordinate amount of time on activities that are outside their zone of competence. Leaders who are able to sustain effective leadership have discovered the importance of channelling their energy into those arenas that are closely aligned with their giftedness and passion. This is difficult because leaders have a natural desire to prove themselves in everything they do. This is often rooted in a need for achievement. While this is certainly an important trait for leaders, this orientation may in fact be detrimental to leaders and their organizations if it is not disciplined by a focus on the leader's core competencies. Many leaders allow their time and emotional energy to be consumed by tasks that are outside their zone of competence. This drains leaders' physical and emotional energy and detracts from their ability to make the greatest contribution possible to the organization. According to Stanley (2003, p. 21), 'the moment a leader steps away from his core competence, his effectiveness as a leader diminishes. Worse, the effectiveness of every other leader in the organization suffers too'. According to Stanley, the solution is for leaders to lead from their strengths and to 'only do what only you can do'.

Overcoming this tendency to spend time and energy on activities outside the zone of competence requires a leader to identify and lead from his or her strengths. The most effective leaders are able to do this and then delegate those activities that are not core competencies to others. While this principle seems obvious, resistance to implementing this is reinforced by factors within the leader and within the organization. Many leaders are insecure and uncomfortable relinquishing control to others. Therefore, the thought of handing over any activities, even those they do not enjoy, is difficult for some. Often a leader's insecurity or ego prevents them from admitting a lack of competence.

Even when a leader is willing to admit this vulnerability, the members of the organization may resist such a delegation because of their implicit leadership theory (Lord & Maher, 1991) and expectations of the leader. For many, the leader is expected to be the person who always has the answers and solution to the problems faced by the organization. Yet, as the operating environment becomes increasingly dynamic and complex, the nature of the task facing the members of the organization moves from technical to adaptive (Heifetz, 1994; Heifetz & Linkskey, 2002). Adaptive problems require the leader to facilitate adaptive work and give the work back to the people who actually have the problem.

Stanley (2003) identifies five obstacles that keep leaders from being able to reframe their role and to lead from their strengths. First, leaders often strive for balance. While we strongly endorse leading a balanced life, within the work arena the most effective leaders should strive for a focused approach by leading from their zone of strength and competence and delegating other activities. The goal should be to have a focused leader and a balanced organization.

The second obstacle is the leader's inability to distinguish between authority and competence. All leaders have authority over areas in which they have little or no competence. This obstacle is reinforced by the leader's own self-perceptions and the followers' expectations as we discussed earlier. However, leaders must realize that exercising authority and becoming involved in areas outside their competency will hinder and may even derail projects. This over involvement may also demotivate those employees who are competent in that area (Stanley, 2003). This may also be complicated by a leader's inability to distinguish between competencies and noncompetencies. Many leaders suffer from a halo effect and assume that their competencies in one area spill over into areas in which they are not competent. Overcoming this obstacle will require leaders to engage in honest self-assessment to discover their strengths and their weaknesses. But discovery of weaknesses is only the first step. The leaders must then be willing to be vulnerably transparent and admit the weaknesses and delegate to others.

The ability to admit weaknesses and delegate to others may be a difficult step because of personal insecurity. The difficulty of doing this may be exacerbated by feelings of guilt. Leaders may resist delegating tasks they don't enjoy or in which they lack competence because they assume the task would be equally unpleasant for others. Yet, a leader's weakness is often a strength for others and delegation allows that person to develop and make a more significant contribution.

The final obstacle is the leader's unwillingness to invest in the development of others. According to the servant-leadership philosophy (Greenleaf, 1977), one of the primary tasks of the leader is to develop others. When a leader refuses to delegate, they are denying prime developmental opportunities for their followers. This limits the capacity of the follower (and over time the entire organization) and fuels the misallocation of the leader's strengths and focus. Thus, failure to use delegation as a developmental tool reinforces a cycle of depletion and burnout.

14.5.4   Redefining the Leader's Role: Servant-Leadership

The willingness of a leader to view his or her primary task as a developer of others may require a transformation of the manager's mindset. We believe that the philosophy of servant-leadership provides a useful framework for this transformation. In this section we will describe the philosophy and practice of servant-leadership. In doing so we emphasize the fact that this is a philosophy, a mindset, not another set of traits or behaviours. While behaviours certainly flow from the philosophy, authentic servant-leadership flows from a deep, internalized set of beliefs and values. Any attempt to merely behave as servant-leader will be perceived an inauthentic and result in the loss of trust and credibility associated with pseudo-transformational leadership.

The recent growth in the interest of this perspective on leadership can be traced to the work of Robert Greenleaf (1977). Greenleaf, in turn, identifies Herman Hesse's (1956) *A Journey to the East* as the source of his idea of the servant as leader. In his book, Hesse tells a somewhat autobiographical story of a journey taken by a band of men. The story centres on Leo, who accompanies the group. Leo performs a variety of menial chores and sustains the group with his spirit and songs. When Leo disappears, the group falls apart and the journey is abandoned. Years later, Leo is discovered to be the leader of the Order that had sponsored the journey. Greenleaf offers Leo as the prototypical servant-leader. Leo was the leader of the journey throughout, yet was servant first. This servant-first attitude was rooted in Leo's deepest convictions. Leadership was bestowed externally by others upon a man who was first a servant by nature. According to Greenleaf (1977), the servant nature of Leo was the real man and because this servant nature had not been granted or assumed, it could not be taken away.

For Greenleaf (1977, 1998), the servant-leader is servant first – an attitude that flows from a deep-rooted, natural inclination to serve. The conscious choice to lead comes after the desire to serve. Greenleaf distinguishes between those who would be 'leader-first' and those who are 'servant-first'. In fact, for him, these two are extreme types that form the anchors of a leadership continuum. The defining difference between the two is the concern taken by the servant-first to make sure that others' highest priority needs are being served. This distinction is captured in Greenleaf's (1977, pp. 13–14) 'test' for those who would be identified as servant-leaders:

> The best test and most difficult to administer, is this: Do those served grow as persons? Do they, while being served, become healthier, wiser, freer, more autonomous, more likely themselves to become servants? And what is the effect on the least privileged in society; will they benefit, or, at least, not be further deprived?'

Greenleaf's legacy has been perpetuated by the work of The Greenleaf Center for Servant-Leadership. Spears (1998, p. 3) summarizes servant-leadership as a leadership that 'emphasizes increased service to others, a holistic approach to work, promoting a sense of community and the sharing of power in decision making. At its core, servant-leadership is a long-term, transformational approach to life and work – in essence, a way of being – that has the potential for creating positive change throughout our society'. According to Spears, servant-leadership is manifested through 10 characteristics: listening, empathy, healing, awareness, persuasion, conceptualization, foresight, stewardship, commitment to the growth of people and building community.

Servant-leaders demonstrate a deep commitment to listening intently to others. Through listening, the servant-leader identifies and clarifies the will of his or her followers. This commitment to listening helps the servant-leader to understand and empathize with others. While perhaps rejecting behaviour or performance, the servant-leader accepts people for their inherent goodness and unique design. The acceptance that flows from empathy and a commitment to listening provides the potential for the servant-leader to 'help make whole' those with broken spirits and emotional hurts.

Awareness refers to the discernment that servant-leaders possess that enables them to evaluate the ethical dimensions of a situation from an integrated, holistic and value-based position. This principle-centred (Covey, 1990) awareness allows servant-leaders to operate from an inner serenity that does not require reliance on positional authority to influence others. Thus, servant-leaders use persuasion rather than coercion to make decisions and exert influence. Servant-leaders also demonstrate an ability to conceptualize and to use foresight.

Conceptualization and foresight are closely related. Conceptualization refers to the servant-leader's capacity to look beyond the day-to-day details in an effort to encompass a broader perspective. Foresight refers to the ability to foresee the likely outcome of a situation using lessons from the past and the realities of the present. Former TDIndustries CEO, Jack Lowe, Jr, believes that a failure of foresight is an ethical failure (Whittington & Maellaro, 2006). The leader must anticipate the future and prepare the organization and its employees to adapt to the challenges presented by the ever evolving environment.

The final three characteristics are rooted in the servant-leader's other-centred orientation. Stewardship refers to the fact that the servant-leader is holding his or her organization in trust for someone else and serving the institution for a greater good that transcends any agenda centred on the personal advancement of the leader. This other-centred orientation also manifests itself in the servant-leader's commitment to the development of

others. Because they view others as having intrinsic, as opposed to instrumental, value, servant-leaders use the power of their positions to nurture the
personal, professional and spiritual growth of their followers.

Finally, servant-leaders seek to build a sense of community among the
members of the organizations they serve. Given the guidelines provided by
Greenleaf's 'test' and Spears' view of servant-leadership as one that promotes
a sense of community by emphasizing service to others and the sharing of
power in decision making, we expect that servant-leaders will demonstrate
behaviours that facilitate the growth of others while respecting their dignity
and autonomy. The focus on others will manifest itself in listening, showing empathy, providing support through resources and encouragement and
creating an environment where people are free to develop their full potential.

14.6 STAYING ALIVE

The complexity of contemporary organizational life creates a great deal of
stress on those who lead those organizations. In this section we discuss
several aspects of a plan for personal well-being that can help the leader
'stay alive' (Heifetz & Linskey, 2002). According to Heifetz and Linskey,
leaders sometimes bring themselves down by forgetting to pay attention to
themselves. The leaders become consumed by the cause and 'forget that
exercising leadership is, at heart, a personal activity' (p. 163). In the midst
of the challenge, the adrenaline is flowing and leaders forget that they are
vulnerable to the limits of physical and emotional capacity.

In order to stay alive in a leadership role, a leader must learn to be aware
of and manage his or her own hungers. Recovery programmes have long
advocated the HALT principle: never get too hungry, too angry, too lonely,
or too tired because these situations create a heightened vulnerability that can
diminish a leader's ability to act wisely. Managing these hungers requires
self-awareness and personal discipline.

While self-awareness and personal discipline are important, too often
leaders are blind to the toll the role and its expectations are having on
them. Every leader needs to cultivate an inner circle of people who are
willing to help the leader maintain balance and proper boundaries. Heifetz
and Linskey (2002) refer to these people as confidants. Confidants provide
a safe place where a leader can say everything that is in his or her heart
without the need to script or edit the raw feelings and emotions. These are
people who can put a leader 'back together again' when they have just lived
through a Humpty Dumpty-like falling off the wall (Heifetz & Linskey,
2002). Confidants provide a unique perspective because they care about
the leader as individual and may or may not be devoted to the leader's

cause. They can listen intently and objectively. Confidants are people who tell the leader what he or she needs to hear. They provide information and insight that a leader may not want to hear and will not be able to hear from anybody else. Reciprocally, confidants can be confided in without concern that the leader's revelations will spill back into the organization. Leaders must cultivate confidants and allow them into their lives if they are to run the leadership race with endurance.

In addition to managing hungers and cultivating confidants, a leader must also create a readily available sanctuary (Heifetz & Linskey, 2002). A sanctuary is a designated place where the leader can withdraw for reflection and renewal. A sanctuary is a place that provides emotional and physical security and allows the leader to suspend the stress of the workplace. Creation of sanctuary requires the discipline to structure schedules and routines so that the benefit of the sanctuary is not lost in the busyness of the leader's life. The form of the sanctuary may vary. It could be a jogging trail, a garden, or a special room that provides the quiet and solace needed to have a quiet time for reflection and renewal.

14.6.1   The Family Arena

The family arena emphasizes a manager's responsibilities to spouse and children, yet also includes obligations to siblings and to parents. Planning and budgeting for household management requirements, spending significant time with children and continuously cultivating one's spousal relationship are all activities associated with the family arena. Family demands appear to be related more strongly to psychological distress for women than men because women may take more responsibility in the family arena than do men (Baruch, Biener & Barnett, 1987). The reverse appears to occur for men, with work demands related more strongly to psychological distress (Seta, Paulus & Baron, 2000).

14.6.2   The Spiritual Arena

The spiritual arena includes the cultivation of a relationship with God, as enhanced by personal efforts in prayer, meditation and study, as well as involvement in a community of like believers. Internalized, intrinsic and individually active religion has been associated with less illness and better physical health (McIntosh & Spilka, 1990).

14.6.3   The Community Arena

The community arena suggests the need to be involved in the community, with the intent to serve others. A manager's spiritual and secular communities may or may not overlap. Community suggests the need for healthy interpersonal attachments for the purpose of social support. Secure interpersonal attachments may exist in the work, family and community arenas, while a secure transcendent attachment to God exists within the spiritual arena (Quick *et al.*, 1995).

14.7   CONCLUSION

Even though the nature of organizations has changed dramatically in recent years and the nature of managerial work has had to change to remain aligned with modern organizations, leaders and managers are still viewed as central to an organization's success and as the key to overall employee well-being (Hernez-Broome & Hughes, 2004). It is imperative that organizations and individuals work as partners to maintain the physical, mental and emotional health of managers so they will be able to effectively guide and develop the efforts of their employees in the attainment of business goals and objectives.

Management development programmes have evolved as well and the goal of the new conceptualization is to develop 'whole leaders'. A whole leader is one who is more fully developed in all of life's arenas – personal, work, family, spiritual and community. A whole leader possesses intellectual ability and technical expertise, self-awareness, interpersonal proficiency and leadership know-how to balance the needs of employees with the requirements of the business and has the ability to take care of him/herself well enough to stay alive amidst the chaos they continually encounter. If organizational management development programmes can facilitate the development of whole leaders, the overall well-being of their entire workforce will be more likely.

ACKNOWLEDGEMENTS

The authors wish to express their appreciation to the original authors of this chapter, Paul B. Paulus and James Campbell Quick, from The University of Texas at Arlington. We are grateful for their research and insights on management development and well-being, which provided a substantial foundation upon which to build and share our views.

REFERENCES

Aram, E. & Noble, D. (1999). Educating prospective managers in the complexity of organizational life. *Management Learning*, **3**(30), 321–43.

Argyris, C. (1991). Teaching smart people how to learn. *Harvard Business Review*, May–June.

Argyris, C. & Schön, D.A. (1974). *Theory in Practice: Increasing Professional Effectiveness*. San Francisco: Jossey-Bass.

Baruch, G.K., Biener, L. & Barnett, R.C. (1987). Women and gender in research on work and family stress. *American Psychologist*, **42**, 130–6.

Bodensteiner, W.D., Gerloff, E.A. & Quick, J.C. (1989). Uncertainty and stress in an R&D project environment. *R&D Management*, **19**, 309–23.

Boyatzis, R.E. (1982). *The Competent Manager: A Model for Effective Performance*. New York: John Wiley & Sons, Inc.

Buhler, P.M. (2000). Changing organizational structures and their impact on managers. *Supervision*, **10**(6), 15–17.

Caruso, D.R. & Salovey, P. (2004). *The Emotionally Intelligent Manager: How to Develop and Use the Four Key Emotional Skills of Leadership*. San Francisco: Jossey-Bass.

Centko, J. (1998). Addressing the humanistic side of workforce education. *Journal of Industrial Teacher Education*, **2**(35), 74–8.

Covey, S. (1990). *Principle-Centered Leadership*. New York: Simon & Schuster.

Daft, R.L. (2001). *Organization Theory and Design* (7th edn). Cincinnati, OH: South-Western College Publishing.

Dalton, G.W. (1989). Developmental views of careers in organizations. In M.B. Arthur, D.T. Hall & B.S. Lawrence (Eds) *Handbook of Career Theory* pp. 89–109). New York: Cambridge University Press.

Daudelin, M.W. & Hall, D.T. (1997). Using reflection to leverage learning. *Training and Development*, **12**(51), 13–14.

Edwards, J.R. & Cooper, C.L. (1990). The person-environment fit approach to stress: recurring problems and some suggested solutions. *Journal of Organizational Behavior*, **11**, 293–307.

Friedman, S.D. (2006). Learning to lead in all domains of life. *The American Behavioral Scientist*, **9**(49), 1270.

Friedman, S.D., Christensen, P. & DeGroot, J. (1998). Work and life: the end of the zero-sum game. *Harvard Business Review*, November/December.

Garavan, T.N., Barnicle, B. & O'Suilleabhain, F. (1999). Management development: contemporary trends, issues and strategies. *Journal of European Industrial Training*, **4/5**(32) 702–191.

Georges, J.C. (1988). Why soft skills training doesn't take. *Training*, **25**, 42–7.

Goldstein, J. (1994). *The Unshackled Organization: Facing the Challenge of Unpredictability through Spontaneous Reorganization*. Portland, OR: Productivity Press.

Goleman, D. (1995). *Emotional Intelligence: Why it can Matter more than IQ*. New York: Bantam Books.

Goleman, D., Boyatzis, R. & McKee, A. (2002). *Primal Leadership: Realizing the Power of Emotional Intelligence.* Boston, MA: Harvard Business School Press.

Gray, D.A., Gault, F.M., Meyers, H.H. & Walther, J.E. (1990). Career planning. In J.C. Quick, R.E. Hess, J. Hermalin & J.D. Quick (Eds), *Career Stress In Changing Times* (pp. 43–59). New York: Haworth Press.

Greenhaus, J.H. (1987). *Career Management.* New York: CBS College Publishing.

Greenhaus, J.H. & Powell, G.N. (2006). When work and family are allies: A theory of work–family enrichment. *The Academy of Management Executive*, **1**(31), 72.

Greenleaf, R. (1977). *Servant-Leadership.* New York: Paulist Press.

Greenleaf, R. (1998). *The Power of Servant-Leadership: Selected Essays.* L. Spears (Ed.), San Francisco: Berrett-Koehler.

Gurvis, J. & Patterson, G. (2005). Balancing act: finding equilibrium between work and life. *Learning in Action*, **6**(24), 4–9.

Hayes, J. (1994). *Interpersonal Skills: Goal-Directed Behavior at Work.* London: Routledge.

Heifetz, R. (1994). *Leadership without Easy Answers.* Cambridge, MA: Belknap Press.

Heifetz, R. & Linsky, M. (2002). *Leadership on the Line: Staying Alive through the Dangers of Leading.* Boston, MA: Harvard Business School.

Hernez-Broome, G. & Hughes, R.L. (2004). Leadership development: Past, present and future. *Human Resource Planning*, **1**(27), 24–33.

Hesse, H. (1956). *A Journey to the East.* New York: Noonday Press.

Kabanoff, B. (1980). Work and nonwork: a review of models, methods and findings. *Psychological Bulletin*, **88**, 60–77.

Katz, D. & Kahn, R.L. (1966). *The Social Psychology of Organizations.* New York: John Wiley & Sons, Inc.

Keene, A. (2000). Complexity theory: the changing role of leadership. *Industrial and Commercial Training*, **32**(1), 15–18.

Kirchmeyer, C. (1992). Perceptions of nonwork-to-work spillover: Challenging the common view of conflict-ridden domain relationships. *Basic and Applied Social Psychology*, **13**, 231–49.

Kuchinke, K.P. (1999). Adult development towards what end? A philosophical analysis of the concept as reflected in the research, theory and practice of human resource development. *Adult Education Quarterly*, **4**(49), 148.

Landy, F., Quick, J.C. & Kasl, S. (1994) Work, stress and well-being. *International Journal of Stress Management*, **1**, 33–73.

Lash, R. (2002). Top leadership taking the inner journey. *Ivy Business Review*, **5**(6), 44–8.

Lawler, E.A. (2000). *From the Ground Up: Six Principles for Building the New Logic Corporation.* San Francisco: Jossey-Bass.

Linville, P.A. (1985). Self-complexity and affective extreme: don't put all your eggs in one cognitive basket. *Social Cognition*, **3**, 94–120.

Linville, P.A. (1987). Self-complexity as a cognitive buffer against stress-related illness and depression. *Journal of Personality and Social Psychology*, **52**, 663–76.

Lord, R. & Maher, K. (1991). *Leadership and Information Processing: Linking Perceptions and Performance*. Boston, MA: Routledge.

Lundin, W. & Lundin, K. (1994). *The Healing Manager*. New York: Berret-Kohler.

MacDonald, G. (1985.) *Ordering Your Private World*. Nashville, TN: Oliver Nelson.

Maellaro, R. (2008). Determining the ideal combination of interpersonal skills for MBA graduates: a conjoint analysis study of hiring manager preferences. Unpublished dissertation. Fielding Graduate University, Santa Barbara, CA.

Mariotti, J. (1998). Management's search for meaning. *Industry Week*, **19**(247), 154.

McCarthy, A. & Garavan, T.N. (1999). Developing self-awareness in the managerial career development process: the value of 360-degree feedback and the MBTI. *Journal of European Industrial Training*, **9**(2), 437–45.

McDonald-Mann, D.G. (1998). Skill-based training. In C.D. McCauley, R.S. Moxley & E. Van Velsor (Eds), *The Center for Creative Leadership Handbook of Leadership Development*. San Francisco: Jossey-Bass.

McIntosh, D. & Spilka, B. (1990). Religion and physical health: the role of personal faith and control beliefs. *Social Science of Religion*, **2**, 167–94.

Merry, U. (1995). *Coping with Uncertainty: Insights from the New Sciences of Chaos, Self-Organization and Complexity*. Westport, CT: Praeger.

Murphy. L.R. & Cooper, C.L. (2000). *Healthy and Productive Work: An International Perspective*. New York: Taylor & Francis.

Nelson, D.L., Quick, J.C. & Quick, J.D. (1989). Corporate warfare: preventing combat stress and battle fatigue. *Organizational Dynamics*, **18**, 65–79.

Nichols, S. (2008). Somatics and leadership. In J. Noel & D. Dotlich (Eds), *The 2008 Pfeiffer Annual: Leadership Development* (pp. 393–403). New York: John Wiley & Sons, Inc.

Noel, J. & Dotlich, D. (2008). The future of leadership development. In J. Noel & D. Dotlich (Eds), *The 2008 Pfeiffer Annual: Leadership Development* (pp. 325–333). New York: John Wiley & Sons, Inc.

Norris, W.C. (2004). *Sympathy versus empathy* [Article]. Federation of Fire Chaplains. Retrieved 10 September 2007, from http://firechaplains.org/articles2.html.

O'Reilly, S. (2006). Are you making your staff ill? *Personnel Today*, 20 June, 22.

Pace, R.W., Smith, P.C. & Mills, G.E. (1991). *Human Resource Development: The Field*. Englewood Cliffs, NJ: Prentice-Hall.

Piotrkowski, C.A. (1979) *Work and the Family System*. New York: Free Press.

Quick, J.C. (1999a). Occupational health psychology: historical roots and future directions. *Health Psychology*, **18**(1), 82–8.

Quick, J.C. (1999b). Occupational health psychology: the convergence of health and clinical psychology with public health and preventive medicine in an organizational context. *Professional Psychology: Research and Practice*, **30**(2), 123–8.

Quick, J.C., Joplin, J.R., Gray, D.A. & Cooley, C.E. (1994). Occupational life cycle and the family. In L.L. Abate (Ed.), *Handbook of Developmental Family*

Psychology and Psychopathology (pp. 157–75). New York: John Wiley & Sons, Inc.

Quick, J.C., Nelson, D.L. & Quick, J.D. (1987). Successful executives: how independent? *Academy of Management Executive*, **1**(2), 139–45.

Quick, J.C. Nelson, D.L. & Quick, J.D. (1990). *Stress and Challenge at the Top: The Paradox of the Successful Executive*. Chichester: John Wiley & Sons, Ltd.

Quick, J.C., Nelson, D.L., Quick, J.D. & Orman, D.K. (2001). An isomorphic theory of stress: the dynamics of person-environment fit. *Stress and Health*, **17**, 147–57.

Quick, J.C., Quick, J.D., Nelson, D.L. & Hurrell, J.J. Jr. (1997). *Preventive Stress Management in Organizations*. Washington, DC: American Psychological Association.

Quick, J.D., Nelson, D.L., Matuszek, P.A.C, Whittington, J.L. & Quick, J.C. (1995). Social support, secure attachments and health. In C.L. Cooper (Ed.), *The Handbook of Stress Medicine* (pp. 269–87). Boca Raton, FL: CRC Press.

Roe, A. & Lunneborg, P. (1990). Personality development and career choice. In D. Brown & L. Brooks (Eds), *Career Choice and Development* (2nd edn, pp. 68–101). San Francisco: Jossey-Bass.

Rothwell, W.J. & Kazanas, H.C. (1993). *The Complete AMA Guide to Management Development: Training, Education, Development*. New York: AMACOM.

Sauter, S.L., Murphy, L.R. & Hurrell, L.L. (1990). Prevention of work related psychological distress: a national strategy proposed by the National Institute for Occupational Safety and Health. *American Psychologist*, **45**, 1145–58.

Segal, J. (1997). *Raising Your Emotional Intelligence, a Practical Guide: A Hands-On Program for Harnessing the Power of Your Instincts and Emotions*. New York: Henry Holt & Co.

Senge, P.M. (1990). *The Fifth Discipline: The Art and Practice of the Learning Organization*. New York: Currency Doubleday.

Seta, C.E, Paulus, P.B. & Baron, R.A. (2000). *Effective Human Relations: A Guide to People at Work*. Needham Heights, NJ: Allyn & Bacon.

Sherman, D. & Hendricks, W. (1989) *How to Balance Competing Time Demands*. Colorado Springs, CO: NAV Press.

Spears, L. (1998). *Insights on Leadership: Service, Stewardship, Spirit and Servant-Leadership*. New York: John Wiley & Sons, Inc.

Stacey, R.D., Griffin, D. & Shaw, P. (2000). *Complexity and Management: Fad or Radical Challenge to Systems Thinking?* New York: Routledge.

Sosik, J.J. & Magerian, L.E. (1999). Understanding leader emotional intelligence and performance: the role of self-other agreement on transformational leadership perceptions. *Group and Organizational Management*, **24**(3), 367–90.

Stanley, A. (2003). *The Next Generation Leader*. Sisters, OR: Multnomah.

Stein, S.J. & Book, H.E. (2001). *The EQ Edge: Emotional Intelligence and Your Success*. Niagara Falls, NY: Stoddart.

Switankowsky, I. (2000). Sympathy and empathy. *Philosophy Today*, **44**(1), 86–93.

Thurow, L. (1993). *Head to Head: The Coming Economic Battle among Japan, Europe and America*. New York: Warner Books.

Waterman, R.H., Waterman, J.A. & Collard, B.A. (1994). Toward a career-resilient workforce. *Harvard Business Review*, **72**(4), 87–95.

Weir, D. & Smallman, C. (1998). Managers in the year 2000 and after: a strategy for development. *Management Decision*, **1**(36), 43.

Weisinger, H. (1998). *Emotional Intelligence at Work: The Untapped Edge for Success*. San Francisco: Jossey-Bass.

West, M. (2006). Business relationships: opportunities waiting to happen. *The British Journal of Administrative Management*, February/March, 17.

Wheatley, M.J. (1999). *Leadership and the New Science: Discovering Order in a Chaotic World*. San Francisco: Berrett-Koehler.

Whetten, D.A. (1983). Management skills training: a needed addition to the management curriculum. *Exchange: The Organizational Behavior Teaching Journal*, **8**(2).

Whetten, D.A. & Cameron, K.S. (2002). *Developing Management Skills* (5th edn). New York: HarperCollins.

Whittington, J.L. & Maellaro, R. (2006). Servant-Leadership at TDIndustries: principles and practice. *The John Ben Shepperd Journal of Practical Leadership*, **1**, 130–44.

Wiley, S.L. (2006). Creating work/life balance within your organization. *Catalyst*, September/October, 26.

CHAPTER 15

Coaching in Organizations

Helen Williams
SHL People Solutions, UK
and
Stephen Palmer
Centre for Stress Management, London, UK

15.1 INTRODUCTION

This chapter focuses on the history and definition of coaching in organizations, its purpose and recommendations on process, from positioning of coaching within organizations, identification of need and coaching objectives to selection of coaches, accreditation, training and supervision, the contracting process and evaluation of coaching effectiveness. Consideration is given to its varied applications, a selection of theories and models and what the future might hold for coaching in organizations.

15.1.1 The History of Coaching in Organizations

The formal systematic study of the psychology of coaching may be tracked back to the work of Coleman R. Griffith whom in the 1920s set up the Laboratory for Research in Athletics. His seminal work was *The Psychology of Coaching* (1926), which focused on sports coaching. Grant (2005) noted that one of the earliest scholarly papers on workplace coaching was by Gorby (1937), who described how experienced employees coached newer employees in how to reduce waste and thereby increase company profits. This had an additional advantage of maximizing their profit-sharing bonuses. Later, humanistic psychologists such as Maslow focused on motivational influences in the well-known 'hierarchy of needs' (Maslow, 1968; Grant, 2007). The

International Handbook of Work and Health Psychology, Third Edition. Edited by Cary L. Cooper, James Campbell Quick, and Marc J. Schabracq.

humanistic psychology movement influenced the early development of 'positive psychology' and the 'human potential movement', and the establishment of both scientific and eclectic pragmatic utilitarianism coaching practices (Grant, 2007), the latter having the most influence on the early development of the contemporary commercial coaching industry (Grant, 2006).

Coaching now represents a significant component of organizational learning and development offerings aimed at enhancing performance and executive development (Grant, 2006), with 63% of organizations surveyed reporting use of coaching in 2007, increasing to 71% of organizations in 2008 (CIPD, 2007, 2008). It is fast becoming an established development tool in organizations in the UK and increasingly worldwide (CIPD, 2007). Whilst coaching is not the most prevalent leadership development activity, it has been found to be among the most effective (Jarvis, 2005), with an estimated global market value of $2 billion annually (Fillery-Travis & Lane, 2006). Given the rapid growth of the industry, the focus in recent years has been on establishment of standards of practice and related guidelines for buyers, recipients and providers of coaching services (Knights & Poppleton, 2007).

15.1.2   Definitions of Coaching in Organizations

A number and variety of definitions of coaching are available (Palmer & Whybrow, 2007), a selection of which are listed here. Coaching is:

> Unlocking a person's potential to maximize their own performance. It is helping them to learn rather than teaching them (Whitmore, 2002, p. 8).

> The art of facilitating the performance, learning and development of another (Downey, 1999, p. 15).

> Collaborative, individualised, solution-focused, results-oriented, systematic and stretching; it fosters self-directed learning, it should be evidence based and incorporate ethical professional practice (Grant, 2007, p. 25).

The CIPD definition of coaching focuses on personal development for performance improvement linked to organizational objectives (CIPD, 2007), whilst the Association for Coaching, in its guidelines for coaching in organizations, emphasizes enabling clients by supporting their development to accelerate progress in achieving their goals (AC, 2004a).

Distinction needs to be drawn between coaching and two related activities of mentoring and counselling. Whilst coaching is typically for a set duration of time, with structured meetings focused on development and performance and on achieving specific, immediate goals (Jarvis, 2004), mentoring in contrast may see working relationships as established more informally and over a longer period of time, and be focused on career and professional development through the sharing of knowledge, advice and opportunities (Jarvis, 2004). Counselling typically takes a broader focus on longer term, historical psycho-social issues as well as performance (Jarvis, 2004). Whilst coaching is present, future and solution focused, and concentrates on the growth and development of psychologically well individuals, counselling is focused on the past, and involves reflective listening and the resolution of pathological conditions (Peltier, 2001). However, counselling and psychotherapy include a range of different approaches and some of the more recently developed approaches such as solution focused and cognitive behavioural devote much less time, if any in some clinical cases, to the past.

15.2   THE PURPOSE OF COACHING IN ORGANIZATIONS

The purpose of coaching in organizations has been previously stated as skills acquisition, performance improvement, personal and career development, leadership and executive development and facilitation of organizational change (Jarvis, 2005; CIPD 2004, 2008; AC, 2004b; Peltier, 2001).

When facilitating coaching in organizations it is important to understand the market context, strategy and key business objectives that provide the context for the coaching. From this we can define the results expected from the leadership or future leadership team, articulate the behaviours and attributes that will drive these results, and assess and develop talented individuals against this clear framework (SHL People Solutions, 2007).

Executive coaching can play a significant role in achieving core business objectives. Macro-level goals may be set to provide the context for the coaching engagements, for example on driving key areas of business performance, organizational change or leadership, therefore maximizing return on investment for the organization. Discussion of personal goals may be linked back directly to how they contribute to the organization achieving its overarching business goals or facilitating the organization's cultural transition through role modelling of effective values and behaviours.

There are a number of purpose clusters for coaching in organizations. Three of them include: talent management and leadership development; organizational development and change management; and specific applications (e.g. individual development, well-being and stress management, team development). Whilst the first two are organizationally driven, the third is more likely driven by line management and HR in response to a specific business function or employee need. This section will consider each purpose cluster in turn.

15.2.1   Talent Management and Leadership Development

The concept of talent management has gained in popularity and importance over the last decade, in essence bringing together all HR practices to enable organizations to define, measure and realize the talent needed to meet their business objectives (SHL People Solutions, 2007). Indeed, with the changing business context and labour market due to globalization, an ageing workforce and declining birth rates particularly in Japan and Europe (*The Economist*, 2006) and changing expectations of employees towards continuous learning and enhanced employability, talent management has been identified as a key strategic HR priority for organizations globally. As the baby boomer generation nears retirement, emphasis is being placed on knowledge transfer, building sufficient future leadership capability and succession planning through leadership development, coaching and mentoring.

In the UK, improving leadership development has been identified as a top HR challenge (Strack *et al.*, 2007), recognizing that people performance is fundamental to the continued success of the business. Coaching is increasingly positioned as an integral part of an organization's leadership development offering, enhancing an organization's attraction and retention strategy and employee value proposition, and being an effective tool through which to align, develop and engage key leadership and high potential talent to drive achievement of business goals.

15.2.2   Organizational Development and Change Management

Continuous change in business and organizations places increasing demands on talent to lead and manage an organization to success. For these reasons strategic HR initiatives include continuous improvement, creation of learning organizations and development of coaching cultures (Clutterbuck & Megginson, 2005):

- Embedding an openness to learning and different ways of working through coaching programmes where a pool of trained internal coaches work with operational management levels to drive focus on continuous improvement to encourage a learning organization.
- Establishing coaching as a management and leadership style to increase in-house coaching capability and create a coaching culture.

15.2.3   Specific Applications

There may be specific cases whereby coaching is deemed an appropriate intervention to drive the desired development outcomes. Rather than being driven by HR strategy, these instances of coaching are more likely driven through discussion with HR, line management and the individual employee, identifying their needs and the appropriate development intervention.

Examples include individual personal and career development, well-being and stress management or team development. In the USA employee health coaching has also been used to minimize health insurance claims within companies (see Duke Prospective Health, 2008). Whilst these specific coaching interventions have been implemented for both reward and remedial purposes, caution is given against use of coaching for the latter, since this may limit acceptance of coaching and its potential application elsewhere in the organization. Research in to what makes coaching programmes successful identified the importance of coaching being perceived as developmental and not as a remedial intervention (Knights & Poppleton, 2007).

15.3   THE COACHING PROCESS

There are a number of critical elements to the coaching process typically governed by HR (Knights & Poppleton, 2007), including structuring coaching within the organization, identification of need, selection of coaches, accreditation, training and supervision, the contracting process and evaluation of coaching. In this section each of these elements shall be considered in turn.

15.3.1   Positioning of Coaching within Organizations

Organizations set different levels of strategy, policy and process for coaching, depending on the purpose of coaching and the existing culture and climate determining the approach most likely to be accepted (Knights & Poppleton, 2007). Research has identified three broad levels of structure: centralized and structured; organic and emergent; and tailored middle ground (Knights & Poppleton, 2007).

Knights and Poppleton (2007) found the centralized and structured approach involved the setting of a formal strategy, an executive-sponsored launch of coaching within the organization and centrally managed coaching programmes to ensure consistent service and standards, supporting the development of a coaching culture. The organic and emergent structure referred to a more informal emergence of coaching where reputation is built through referral and coaching requirements identified on a case-by-case basis to meet local requirements. The tailored middle ground structure sees coaching managed through established learning and development relationships across the organization whilst providing a certain level of standards and thereby ensuring a consistency of service.

15.3.2   Identification of Need

The process for identifying need for coaching may differ according to the level of structure for coaching within the organization. Where there is a centralized and structured approach to coaching, it is likely that coaching requirements will be identified through talent management reviews driven by HR learning and development. It is important in these instances for there to be an objective nomination process, with clear criteria, a transparent process and full communications of what may be expected from the coaching programme and similarly what will be expected of participants. Where the coaching structure is more organic and emergent, it is likely that specific cases will be brought to the attention of HR through discussions with line managers and the employee.

15.3.3   Selection of Coaches

Coaching is cross-disciplinary, with coaches from a variety of professional backgrounds, including consulting, management, corporate, teaching, sales and psychology (Grant, 2007). Coaching in organizations may be delivered by external or internal coaches, line managers or members of the HR department (CIPD, 2007). Once a need for coaching has been identified, and the broad individual and organizational objectives understood, then the next step is to decide whether an internal or external coach will be most appropriate to achieve these goals (Trapp, 2005).

Internal coaches are most effective when the organization is looking to develop a coaching culture, when cost-efficiency is a driving factor or when knowledge of the company culture and politics is important for the success of the coaching engagement (Trapp, 2005). It is important that these coaches are effectively selected, trained and developed with access to a coaching network, continual professional development and supervision (Knights & Poppleton, 2007). The management population may take on differing levels of involvement in the coaching process, either supporting the coaching process, developing coaching skills to allow a coaching management style with team members or acting as an internal coach for others within the organization (Knights & Poppleton, 2007).

External coaches are most often engaged where there is a lack of internal resources, there is conflict of interest impacting upon confidentiality, specialized expertise or business background is required, or the coaching is for senior executives or part of a wider leadership development programme (Jarvis, 2004; Trapp, 2005; Knights & Poppleton, 2007).

Whether the coach is internal or external, there are a number of factors that should be considered, such as coach background (coaching experience, wider business or industry experience, qualifications and training, membership of professional bodies, references, case studies and testimonials), coaching methods (contracting process, tools and techniques, supervision, process for and evaluation) and fit of the coach's interpersonal style to both the individual and the organizational culture (Jarvis, 2004; Chapman, 2006).

Consideration must also be given to the best format for the coaching engagement, whether this will be individual coaching, group coaching or facilitated peer coaching.

15.3.4   Accreditation, Training and Supervision

There are a number of recognized professional bodies relating to coaching and coaching psychology in the UK. Some of these are also international bodies. The not-for-profit bodies include:

- AC – Association for Coaching
- APECS – Association for Professional Executive Coaching and Supervision
- BPS, SGCP – British Psychological Society' Special Group in Coaching Psychology
- CIPD – Chartered Institute of Personnel and Development
- EMCC – The European Mentoring and Coaching Council
- ICF (UK) – International Coaching Federation, UK
- SCP – Society for Coaching Psychology

The fact that there is no one leading industry body has been highlighted as creating a particular challenge for HR practitioners trying to ascertain an appropriate standard of coaching for their organization (Jarvis, 2005). However, many of these professional bodies have now produced standards frameworks, coach competency frameworks, codes of practice, guidelines for supervision, course recognition and accreditation processes (Jarvis, 2005; Wilson, 2006). In addition, National Occupational Standards do exist in the

UK for workplace in-house coaching by managers and these can provide a guide for the basic competencies required. In addition, the BPS Special Group in Coaching Psychology has produced benchmark psychological standards for those practising as coaching psychologists (BPS, 2008).

Supervision may be taken in a variety of forms – individual (supervisor or peer), group supervision (led by supervisor or leaderless peer group), telephone or email/postal supervision (AC, 2005). The Association for Coaching conducted a survey of its members in 2008 to ascertain the prevalence and type of supervision taking place within the industry. Supervision was found to be more prevalent than in 2005, increasing from 48% to 72% of respondents (McDougall, 2008). The main benefits reported from supervision by coaching professionals were provision of a basis to learn and develop and a place to discuss ethical issues/concerns, whilst the main barriers were being able to find the right supervisor at the right cost (McDougall, 2008).

The top 10 competencies identified as important for the coach supervisor included ability to support and challenge, upholding ethical standards of a membership organization, taking a holistic approach, sharing knowledge of a range of coaching models and flexibility in the way support is provided, i.e. face to face or by telephone, through individual or group supervision (McDougall, 2008). Qualities included being professionally and personally mature, encouraging exploration of new ideas and techniques, maintaining consistent and appropriate boundaries, accepting and celebrating difference and clarifying the style and expectations of supervision (McDougall, 2008).

15.3.5   Contracting

Contracting with the coaching client and line manager or sponsor is an essential stage of the coaching process to ensure clearly defined expectations and measurable outcomes for evaluating return on investment at both the individual and organizational level. The majority of organizations set business as well as individual objectives for a coaching engagement, utilizing a 'three- or four-cornered contract' with coaching client, line manager, HR representative and coach (Knights & Poppleton, 2007), established through face-to-face meetings with the relevant parties in attendance. A typical agreement is for between four and seven sessions, most often face to face with telephone and email support (AC, 2004a).

A robust coaching contract is likely to include discussion and agreement of organization and individual objectives for the coaching, measurable outcomes, the coaching process to be followed, confidentiality and feedback to the organization (McMahon, 2005). Before undertaking a coaching engagement it is critical to agree issues relating to confidentiality and internal follow-up. For example, it may be agreed that the content of the coaching sessions is to be kept confidential in order to build and maintain trust. Participants may be encouraged or requested to share key aspects of their insights and development plans with their manager and/or HR representative. This provides accountability back to the organization, whilst maintaining the trust and confidentiality that is essential for coaching to be effective.

15.3.6 Evaluation

Evaluating coaching interventions effectively and carefully has been identified as one of the key factors for successfully embedding coaching in organizations (Bresser, 2006), yet there is doubt as to how frequently this actually takes place. A survey conducted by the Association for Coaching, found few organizations were measuring the benefits of coaching, with over 75% of respondents relying on feedback from the coaching client and line manager (AC, 2004a). Sherman and Freas (2005) observed that the interpersonal nature of coaching, which makes it so effective, is also what makes it so difficult to evaluate in quantifiable, financial measures. In practice most organizations rely on informal, immediate feedback from coaches and line managers, with only 8% of organizations following more formal and structured evaluation options (CIPD, 2008).

KirkPatrick's model of training evaluation provides a useful framework for the evaluation of coaching, measuring immediate satisfaction through coaching client feedback, learning outcomes through self and manager report, behaviour change through pre- and post-coaching 180 or 360 questionnaires and business results through review of organizational outcome measures (KirkPatrick, 1994). Well-structured practitioner case studies can also provide an excellent evidence base for the efficacy of coaching in organizations (Lowman, 2001; Passmore & Gibbes, 2007).

In more recent years coaching psychology research has increased (Grant, 2007), both in supply and demand. The first scholarly paper was published in 1955, with a noticeable increase in both articles and research chapters from 1996 onwards (Grant, 2006). Kampa-Kokesch and Anderson (2001) found that just seven articles focusing on the evaluation of executive coaching were published prior to 2001, whilst Passmore and Gibbes (2007) found a further 13 papers were published between 2001 and 2007. Grant identified 78 empirical studies relating to coaching since 1955 (67 of which have been published since 2001) and 314 articles (Grant, 2006).

Although the industry is relatively young, there is now a growing body of empirical research in support of its efficacy (Grant, 2006; Passmore & Gibbes, 2007), and an increasing collaboration amongst coaching academics and practitioners of varying backgrounds (Grant, 2007) with the shared aim of advancing a *'vibrant and diverse professional coaching industry'* (Grant, 2007, p. 25).

Coaching is reported to have significant and widespread positive effects across surveys conducted by professional bodies and both academic and practitioner research. The AC survey indicated that managers identified better people management skills and increased levels of motivation, whilst coaching clients reported improved work–life balance and increased levels of motivation (AC, 2004a). Academic research papers report benefits of increased leadership behaviours (Kampa-Kokesch & Anderson, 2001; Cortvriend *et al.*, 2008), improved performance (Smither & London, 2003; Cortvriend *et al.*, 2008), increased collaborative work behaviours (Gonzalez, 2004), increased self-efficacy (Evers *et al.*, 2006) reduction of workplace stress (Gyllensten & Palmer, 2005) and significant return on investment (McGovern *et al.*, 2001). The reader is referred to Kampa-Kokesch and Anderson (2001) and Passmore and Gibbes (2007) for comprehensive reviews of this research.

From an organization perspective, coaching has again been reviewed positively. A group survey conducted through structured interviews of 17 HR practitioners reported moderate to good success of previous coaching programmes, and an indicated intention to use coaching in the future (Dagley, 2006). The two most common barriers to coaching were executives making time for coaching sessions, and the cost, although benefits were reported to exceed costs (Dagley, 2006).

15.4 APPLICATIONS

15.4.1 Performance Coaching, Transitional Coaching and Transformational Coaching

Performance coaching focuses on improving performance against current objectives, building on behavioural strengths and actioning development opportunities or acquiring new skills or capabilities.

Transitional coaching focuses on equipping individuals and teams to move through the 'transition' curve more skilfully. Example topics might be determining a career move or change of direction, supporting a new executive during their first 100 days in a new organization, a senior manager taking on a very different role, location, project, or leading a strategically important change.

Transformational coaching is designed to help individuals achieve breakthrough performance by fundamentally changing how they are behaving and how they see and think about themselves. A breakthrough would be something that currently appears impossible. However, unlike other forms of coaching, transformational coaching is often about 'being' and not just about 'doing' so goes beyond the usual focus on enhancing productivity.

15.4.2   Leadership Pipeline

Each type of coaching will have its place and application at different levels within the organization as employees progress through the 'leadership pipeline' (Charan, Drotter & Noel, 2001).

The 'leadership pipeline' is a concept popularized by Charan and associates (2001), and gives recognition to a number of key transition points for individuals to work their way up to the most senior role in an organization. These can be summarized against three broad levels:

- Managing self.
- Managing others – managing others and managing managers.
- Managing the business – functional manager, business manager, group manager and enterprise manager.

At each transition point a different set of role objectives, key result areas, expected behaviours and management and leadership styles are expected and required for success in the role. Openness to learning and learning agility is crucial, as what has made individuals successful in the past may not be what will make them successful in the future (Eichinger & Lombardo, 2004). Performance is evaluated differently requiring a shift in both behaviour and mindset on the part of the individual. Coaching may be instrumental in helping the individual to focus on optimizing performance in role, preparing for promotion or evolving through the transition period, with different types of coaching and coaching programmes being relevant at each level in the pipeline, for example:

- Managing self – performance coaching for graduates and high potentials.
- Managing others – middle management and leadership development.
- Managing the business – executive coaching, business coaching and mentoring.

15.4.3   Coaching Models and Tools

A wide variety of coaching models and tools are available, derived from a number of well-respected theoretical traditions including solution focused, person-centred, psychodynamic, cognitive behavioural, sports psychology, systems thinking, positive psychology and strengths, Gestalt, neurolinguistic programming and existential coaching (Peltier, 2001; Palmer & Whybrow, 2008). The most appropriate approach may be determined based on consideration of the business context and organizational objectives, individual coaching client's needs and skills of the coach.

Whybrow and Palmer (2006) conducted two surveys 23 months apart looking at the types of coaching methodologies used by coaching psychologists and found the most common coaching psychology practices across both surveys were business, executive, leadership and performance, followed by career and personal life coaching. Both surveys showed popular psychological frameworks and approaches to be facilitation, cognitive, behavioural, goal-focused and solution-focused approaches (Whybrow & Palmer, 2006).

15.4.4   Leadership Models

A number of leadership models are available stemming from both academic and applied research. Leadership models may provide the basis for organizational goals and a language with which to communicate objectives and desired outcomes at the contracting stage of coaching, providing the link between an individual's personal development and an organization's needs and expectations of its management and leadership population. It may also be contracted that feedback from the organization will be collected for the coaching client against this model of leadership, to feed in to the coaching engagement, through tools such as 360-degree feedback questionnaires. Many organizations have developed their own leadership models in the form of competency-based and values-based frameworks.

One example is the SHL corporate leadership model (Bartram, 2002, 2005) (see Table 15.1), which combines both transactional and transformational leadership dimensions with four functions of the leadership cycle, and the associated behaviours with each, forming the SHL great eight competency factors (Kurz & Bartram, 2002). The competency framework that sits behind the leadership model is known as the SHL universal competency framework (UCF). Translated into 11 different languages, the great eight factors of the UCF divide into 20 dimensions of competency comprising 112 components (Bartram, 2002, 2005).

The SHL UCF was developed through a five-year, in-depth study of research on job performance and employee and leadership behaviour. Validation of the great eight factors included a meta-analysis of 29 validation studies comparing measures of potential (ability, personality) of 4861 managers and leaders to the line managers' rating of performance against the

Table 15.1 The SHL corporate leadership model

Functions	Competencies	
	Transactional focus	Transformational focus
1 *Developing the vision: the strategy domain*	Analysing and interpreting	Creating and conceptualizing
2 *Sharing the goals: the communication domain*	Interacting and presenting	Leading and deciding
3 *Gaining support: the people domain*	Supporting and cooperating	Adapting and coping
4 *Delivering success: the operational domain*	Organizing and executing	Enterprising and performing

Source: Bartram, 2002. Reprinted with permission © Bartram, 2002.

great eight factors, finding moderate to good relationships between both personality and ability and the great eight, and even stronger predictive power through a combination of the two (Bartram, 2004).

15.4.5 The GROW Model

The GROW model, developed by Graham Alexander and promoted by Sir John Whitmore (Whitmore, 1992, 2004; Alexander & Renshaw, 2005), is well established and used internationally, particularly in a performance coaching context. In essence, the GROW model is used to structure the coaching conversation exploring the goal for the session, the current reality, options available and the will of the coaching client to commit to action.

The following summarizes key facilitative questions at each step:

- **Goal** – What is your overall goal, and your goal for the coaching session?
- **Reality** – What has happened so far?
- **Options** – What choices are there to help move towards achievement of the goal?
- **Will** – What will you commit to, specified through SMART objectives and a written action plan?

The GROW model, with its simplicity and accessibility, is instrumental in equipping line managers as coaches, building internal coaching capability and developing a coaching culture within the organization.

15.4.6   The PRACTICE Model

PRACTICE is an acronym for a problem solving and solution focused model that has been used within coaching, counselling, psychotherapy and stress management (Palmer, 2007, 2008). The model may be used by the coach to facilitate the coaching client to identify the **P**roblem or issue concerned, develop **R**ealistic goals, generate **A**lternative solutions and **C**onsider, **T**arget and **I**mplement the **C**hosen solutions and **E**valuate outcomes. Table 15.2 provides details of each sequential step.

15.4.7   The ABCDEF Model

The ABCDEF psychological model of coaching (Ellis *et al.*, 1997; Neenan & Dryden, 2002; Palmer, 2002) taken from the rational emotive behaviour (REB) approach, focuses on the identification of **A**ctivating events or a general **A**wareness of a problem or issue, then elicitation of the associated unhelpful, performance-interfering **B**eliefs and the subsequent **C**onsequences/responses to the issue concerned, before **D**iscussion/ **D**isputing/challenging those beliefs. Then an alternative, more **E**ffective response is chosen. Finally there is a discussion about what has been learnt that will be helpful to the coachee in the **F**uture (see Palmer & Szymanska, 2007). It is worth noting that in the UK, the REB approach and the PRACTICE model have been integrated within a general cognitive behavioural coaching approach (Palmer, 2009).

The coach facilitates discussion flexibly around the model according to the need of the individual and the appropriateness to the coaching conversation, emphasizing the importance of how unhelpful beliefs can impact upon behaviour, performance and feelings. Through discussion these beliefs can be modified to enhance performance and reduce stress.

15.4.8   Assessment Tools and Psychometrics in Coaching

Assessment has an important role to play in coaching and executive coaching (Peltier, 2001) to allow individual and organizational goals to be established (McLeod, 2003) and to ensure structured, constructive feedback is provided to compliment the individual's own self-awareness and insights (Peltier, 2001).

A clear measure of current performance and potential may be obtained through use of a range of diagnostic tools and simulation exercises, psychometric tests and questionnaires, simulation exercises and 360-degree

Table 15.2 PRACTICE model of coaching, counselling, psychotherapy and stress management

Steps	Questions/Actions
1. **P**roblem identification	What's the problem or issue or concern or topic you would like to discuss?
	What would you like to change?
	Any exceptions when it is not a problem, issue or concern?
	How will we know if the situation has improved?
	On a scale of 0 to 10 where '0' is nowhere and '10' is resolved, how near are you now today, to resolving the problem or issue?
	Any distortions or can the problem or issue be viewed differently?
	Can you imagine waking up tomorrow morning and this problem (or issue or concern) no longer existed, what would you notice that was different? (An alternative would be to use the standard Solution Focused Miracle Question – see Palmer, Grant & O'Connell, 2007)
2. **R**ealistic, relevant goals developed (e.g. SMART goals)	What do you want to achieve?
	Let's develop SMART goals
3. **A**lternative solutions generated	What are your options?
	Let's note them down.
4. **C**onsideration of consequences	What could happen?
	How useful is each possible solution?
	Let's use a rating 'usefulness' scale for each solution where '0' is not useful at all, and '10' is extremely useful.
5. **T**arget most feasible solution(s)	Now we have considered the possible solutions, what is the most feasible or practical solution(s)?
6. **I**mplementation of **C**hosen solution(s)	Let's implement the chosen solution by breaking it down into manageable steps.
	Now go and do it.
7. **E**valuation	How successful was it?
	Rating scale 0 to 10
	What can be learnt?
	Can we finish coaching now or do you want to address or discuss another issue or concern?

feedback. Potential measures include personality (fit of preferred style to the role requirements or competencies), motivation, cognitive ability, values and attitudes (Bartram, 2004). Performance measures tend to focus on assessment of behaviours and competencies through measures such as assessment/development centre simulations (group exercises, analysis presentations and role-plays), interviews or 360-degree feedback questionnaires (Bartram, 2004).

Psychometric measures come in two forms: those measuring ability and those measuring personality (Rust, 2004). There are four underlying psychometric principles that govern the quality of the psychometric instrument – reliability, validity, freedom from bias and standardization (Peltier, 2001; Rust, 2004). Whilst the instrument must first meet these four principles, the true value of the assessment will come through a validation interview or discussion with the individual (McDowall & Kurz, 2007). In the UK the British Psychological Society requires a minimum standard of training to be able to administer, evaluate and feedback psychometric instruments (BPS, 2006; McDowall & Kurz, 2007).

A range of personality questionnaires are available, including both 'type' and 'trait' questionnaires, for example the Myers Briggs Type Indicator (MBTI), 16PF and the Occupational Personality Questionnaire (OPQ) (see Passmore, 2008 for details of a full range of psychometrics in coaching).

The SHL Occupational Personality Questionnaire (OPQ) was specifically designed for the world of work, and provides insight into 32 dimensions of personality across three domains of relationships with people, thinking styles and feelings and emotions (Burke, 2008). The OPQ can be used to inform coaching conversations around the individual's preferred style of working, and how this preferred style acts as an enabler or barrier to higher levels of performance. As such it is an indicator of competency potential (Burke, 2008).

The Myers Briggs Type Indicator is a frequently used psychometric tool within coaching, developed by Katharine Briggs and her daughter Isabel Briggs Myers based on Carl Jung's theory of psychological type (Carr et al., 2008). The MBTI emphasizes the benefits of diversity by providing positive descriptions of personality through four pairs of opposites: extraversion and introversion; sensing and intuition; thinking and feeling; and judging and perceiving (Carr et al., 2008). The theoretical assumption is that an individual is predisposed to use one side of each pair of opposites more naturally, and in receiving feedback on their preferred style may make informed choices about their own behaviour, and also understand how others prefer to operate (Carr et al., 2008).

Motivation is 'the driving force behind job success. It determines how much energy will be channelled into job performance, for how long, and under what circumstances effort will be maintained' (Bartram, Fradera &

Marsh, 2008, p. 116). The SHL Motivation Questionnaire (MQ) 'is concerned with assessment of individual differences in the factors that energise, direct and sustain behaviour in the workplace' (Bartram *et al.*, 2008, p. 119). The MQ provides insight into 18 dimensions of motivation and de-motivation, clustered into four domains of energy and dynamism, synergy, intrinsic, and extrinsic.

360-degree feedback questionnaires are typically competency based and provide a valuable measure of performance and an insight for individuals on how they are perceived to behave in their current role. 360-degree feedback is a widely accepted practice within organizations (Peltier, 2001; Knights & Poppleton, 2007) and typically involves collection of feedback for development purposes from self, colleagues, line managers and others, often against a 1–5 rating scale ranging from 'outstanding' to 'clear development', or from 'consistently demonstrated' to 'rarely demonstrated'.

15.4.9   Recurrent Coaching Themes in Organizations

Across the literature there are a number of recurring themes that form popular coaching topics within organizations, such as presentation skills (see Palmer & Szymanska, 2007), interpersonal and social skills (see Palmer & Cooper, 2007), assertiveness coaching (see Neenan & Dryden, 2002), time management and delegation (see Neenan & Dryden, 2002), self-confidence (see Wilding & Palmer, 2006) and stress management (see Palmer & Cooper, 2007). These topics may be effectively coached through individual or group coaching.

15.5   CASE EXAMPLES

15.5.1   Specific Application: Performance Coaching

The coaching client came to the contracting session with the goal of finishing a research paper for an impending presentation. She had been procrastinating, putting off completing the paper for fear of not doing a good job, and feeling increasingly nervous and fearful at the prospect of presenting her work. This, she realized, linked to her increasingly frequent and severe tension headaches. She explained that past presentations had not gone well and so she worried she would fail at this one too.

Cognitive behavioural coaching methods were used to explore a past presentation that had not gone to plan. Having captured the essence of the situation, the coaching client identified the elements of the situation, her behaviours, cognitions and emotions that had caused her the most difficulty at the time. Through the iterative process she was able to challenge unhelpful beliefs and assumptions, take a new perspective and generate alternative ways of thinking, feeling and behaving.

The client felt renewed energy to complete her research paper and enjoyment at the prospect of giving the presentation. Keeping a reflective journal to track her progress, she described how the cognitive behavioural tools helped raise her self-awareness, meaning that where she was previously stuck, she had now propelled herself forward with a great sense of empowerment and confidence to achieve her goals.

15.5.2   Organizational Change and Change Management

SHL was invited to complete an executive coaching programme at a leading telecommunications company. The coaching was delivered to sales directors to help facilitate a major strategic change in direction.

The organization was striving for a fundamental shift in the way its sales force operated. It needed to move away from a simple transactional sell, to a much more consultative approach. This in turn required a different set of skills and a new approach from the sales people.

Following clarification of the sales competencies and objective assessments of the sales directors, a programme of executive coaching was proposed. Focused on the individual's needs, career development and aspirations, these sessions provided necessary time away from the day to day, creating opportunities for self-examination and personal development planning (SHL, 2004a).

15.5.3   Talent Management and Leadership Development

The organization, a leader in the fast-moving consumer goods sector, was seeking to accelerate its business performance within its market sector and understood that investment in the personal development of those at the top of the business, developing their ability to drive success, was critical in achieving this. The senior leaders were each offered six individual coaching sessions with an executive coach from SHL.

The coaching engagements started with initial assessment and feedback of motivations, preferences and competency-based behavioural strengths and development needs. An example outcome of coaching for one individual was the ability to redefine his role within the organization in order to incorporate the objectives he wanted to achieve, whilst enhancing the value he provided to the organization and its business goals (SHL, 2004b).

15.6   FUTURE OF COACHING IN ORGANIZATIONS

Coaching in organizations is an increasingly sophisticated, mature market (Grant, 2007), and as a result procurers of coaching within companies are clarifying their expectations and demanding more from coaching providers in terms of standards, models of practice, accreditation, supervision and experience. As a consequence there is an increasing demand and supply of university-recognized or supported, theoretically based coaching programmes to degree and post-graduate degree level, and accreditation programmes from professional coaching bodies (Grant, 2007). In addition, in the UK coaching training courses for organizations and their managers may incorporate the National Occupational Standards for coaching and mentoring.

The area of positive psychology and strengths psychology is increasingly gaining recognition and application in learning and development initiatives within organizations, and particularly in people management, leadership development and coaching (Woolston & Linley, 2008). Strengths coaching 'supports the identification, use and development of strengths to enable optimal functioning, performance and development' (Woolston & Linley, 2008, p. 8). In a time when organizations are focusing on enhancement of engagement and well-being, positive and strengths psychology, and its application through coaching, has a valuable part to play.

Coaching psychologists have an important role to play in providing continued evidence-based practice and research, having the potential to offer collaborative and client-centred approaches and models (Grant, 2007). Therefore 'coaching psychology needs to be theoretically inclusive and . . . the professional coaching psychologist should be able to draw on a range of theoretical frameworks, using client-congruent, theoretically grounded techniques to best help the client reach their coaching goals' (Grant, 2007, p. 32).

With continued globalization of business and organizations managers and leaders are increasingly working in an internationalized environment requiring heightened cultural awareness and integration. This will be reflected in the need for coaches to be both diversity aware and aware of their own diversity competence (Law, 2008), as well as being able to coach on cultural diversity awareness and performance (Law, 2008). At the time of writing it is very likely that the world will be going into a recession and financial constraints may restrict what organizations spend their money on. Traditionally during recessions, training budgets get cut back. It is debatable whether or not organizations will reduce their spending on coaching. However, financial restraints are likely to lead to more coaching being undertaken in-house and by managers.

REFERENCES

Alexander, G. & Renshaw, B. (2005). *Super Coaching: The Missing Ingredient for High Performance*. London: Random House Business Books.

AC (2004a). *Summary Report: ROI from Corporate Coaching*. Downloaded on 24 October 2008 from http://www.associationforcoaching.com/memb/ACSumROI.pdf.

AC (2004b). *Guidelines to Coaching in Organizations*. Downloaded on 24 October 2008 from http://www.associationforcoaching.com/pub/pub07.htm.

AC (2005). *Association for Coaching: Supervision Report*. Downloaded on 13 October 2008 from http://www.associationforcoaching.com/pub/ACsr0405.pdf.

AC (2008). *Association for Coaching: Supervision Report*. Downloaded on 19 October 2008 from http://www.associationforcoaching.com/pub/ACSurveyAnalsys CoachMentorSupervisionJUN08.pdf.

Bartram, D. (2002). The SHL Corporate Leadership Model. SHL White Paper (2002). Downloaded on 24 October 2008 from http://www.shl.com/SHL/en-int/Thought_Leadership/White_Papers/WhitePapers.aspx.

Bartram, D. (2004). Assessment in organisations. *Journal of Applied Psychology*, **53**, 237–59.

Bartram, D. (2005). The great eight competencies: a criterion-centric approach to validation. *Journal of Applied Psychology*, **90**(6), 1185–203.

Bartram, D., Fradera, A. & Marsh, H. (2008). Coaching with the motivation questionnaire. In J. Passmore (Ed.), *Psychometrics in Coaching: Using Psychological and Psychometric Tools for Development*. London: Kogan-Page.

Bartram D., Robertson, I.T. & Callinan, M. (2002). A framework for examining organizational effectiveness. In I.T. Robertson, M. Callinan & D. Bartram (Eds), *Organizational Effectiveness: The Role of Psychology*. Chichester: John Wiley & Sons, Ltd.

BPS (2006). *Psychological Testing: A User's Guide*. Leicester: BPS Psychological Testing Centre.

BPS (2008). *BPS Special Group in Coaching Psychology Standards Framework for Coaching Psychology, May 2008*. Downloaded on 13 October 2008 from http://www.bps.org.uk/document-download-area/document-download$.cfm?file_uuid=C6E622E6-1143-DFD0-7EB2-CFB9EA9E1174&ext=pdf.

Bresser, F. (2006). Coaching in business: 10 key factors for success. *The Bulletin of the Association for Coaching*, **7**, 5–7. Downloaded on 12 October 2008 from http://www.associationforcoaching.com/pub/ACB0602.pdf.

Burke, E. (2008). Coaching with OPQ. In J. Passmore (Ed.), *Psychometrics in Coaching: Using Psychological and Psychometric Tools for Development*. London: Kogan-Page.

Carr, S., Cooke, B., Harris, L. & Kendall, B. (2008). Coaching with MBTI. In J. Passmore (Ed.), *Psychometrics in Coaching: Using Psychological and Psychometric Tools for Development*. London: Kogan-Page.

Chapman, H. (2006). *Top 10 Tips for Selecting the Right Executive Coach*. Association for Coaching, downloaded on 13 October 2008 from http://www.associationforcoaching.com/pub/ACSelectingTheRightCoach.pdf.

Charan, R., Drotter, S.J. & Noel, J.L. (2001). *The Leadership Pipeline: How to Build the Leadership Powered Company.* San Francisco: Jossey-Bass.

CIPD (2004). *Coaching Fact Sheet.* Downloaded on 24 October 2008 from http://www.cipd.co.uk/subjects/lrnanddev/coachmntor/coaching.htm.

CIPD (2007). *Annual Learning and Development Survey.* Downloaded on19 October 2008 from http://www.cipd.co.uk/surveys.

CIPD (2008). *Annual Learning and Development Survey.* Downloaded on19 October 2008 from http://www.cipd.co.uk/subjects/lrnanddev/general/_lrngdevsvy.htm?IsSrchRes=1.

Cortvriend, P., Harris, C. & Alexander, E. (2008). Evaluating the links between leadership development coaching and performance. *International Coaching Psychology Review,* **3**(2), 164–78.

Clutterbuck, D. & Megginson, D. (2005). *Making Coaching Work.* London: Chartered Institute of Personnel and Development.

Dagley, G. (2006). Human resources professionals' perceptions of executive coaching: efficacy, benefits and return on investment. *International Coaching Psychology Review,* **1**(2), 34–45.

Downey, M. (1999). Effective coaching. In M. Neenan & W. Dryden (Eds), *Life Coaching: A Cognitive Behavioural Approach.* London: Orion Business Books.

Duke Prospective Health (2008). *Duke Prospective Health.* Downloaded on 22 May, 2008 from www.dukeprospectivehealth.org.

Eichinger, R.W & Lombardo, M.M. (2004). *The 6Qs of Leadership: A Blueprint for Enduring Success at the Top.* Downloaded on 24 October 2008 from http://www.lominger.com/pdf/The6QsOfLdrshp.pdf.

Ellis, A., Gordon, J., Neenan, M. & Palmer, S. (1997). *Stress Counseling: A Rational Emotive Behavior Approach.* New York: Springer.

Evers, W.J.G., Brouwers, A. & Tomic, W. (2006). A quasi-experimental study of management coaching effectiveness. *Consulting Psychology Journal: Practice and Research,* **58**(3), 174–82.

Fillery-Travis, A. & Lane, D. (2006). Does coaching work or are we asking the wrong questions? *International Coaching Psychology Review,* **1**(1), 23–36.

Gonzalez, A.L. (2004). Transforming conversations: executive coaches and business leaders in dialogical collaboration for growth. *Dissertation Abstract International Section A: Humanities and Social Science, Vol. 65 (3-A) 1023.* Ann Arbor, MI: Proquest, International Microfilms International.

Gorby, C.B. (1937). Everyone gets a share of the profits. *Factory Management and Maintenance,* **95**, 82–3.

Grant, A.M. (2001) *Towards a Psychology of Coaching.* Downloaded on 19 October 2008 from http://www.cipd.co.uk/subjects/lrnanddev/coachmntor/coachbuyservs.htm.

Grant, A.M. (2005) *Workplace, Executive and Life Coaching: An Annotated Bibliography from the Behavioural Science Literature (March 2005).* Unpublished paper, Coaching Psychology Unit, University of Sydney, Australia.

Grant, A.M. (2006). Workplace and executive coaching: a bibliography from the scholarly business literature. In D.R. Stober & A.M. Grant (Eds), *Evidence Based Coaching Handbook* (pp. 367–88).

Grant, A.M. (2007). Past, present and future: the evolution of professional coaching and coaching psychology. In S. Palmer & A. Whybrow (Eds), *Handbook of Coaching Psychology: A Guide for Practitioners* (pp. 23–39). London: Routledge.

Gyllensten, K. & Palmer, S. (2005). The relationship between coaching and workplace stress. *International Journal of Health Promotion and Education*, **43**(3), 97–103.

Jarvis, J. (2004). *CIPD Coaching and Buying Coaching Services: A Guide*. Downloaded on 19 October 2008 from http://www.cipd.co.uk/subjects/lrnanddev/coachmntor/coachbuyservs.htm.

Jarvis, J. (2005). *The Rise and Rise of Coaching: An Insight into the Increase in Coaching, and how it can Make a Significant Contribution to Business and Play a Major Part in Leadership Development*. Downloaded on 24 October 2008 from http://www.cipd.co.uk/coachingatwork/presales/The+rise+and+rise+of+coaching.htm.

Kampa-Kokesch, S. (2002). Executive coaching as an individually tailored consultation intervention: does it increase leadership? *Dissertation Abstracts International: Section B: The Sciences & Engineering, Vol. 62 (7-B). 3408.* Ann Arbor, MI: Proquest, International Microfilms International.

Kampa-Kokesch, S. & Anderson, M. (2001). Executive coaching: a comprehensive review of the literature. *Consulting Psychology Journal: Practice and Research*, **53**(4), 205–27.

KirkPatrick, D.L. (1994). *Evaluating Training Programs: The Four Levels*. San Francisco: Berrett-Koehler.

Knights, A. & Poppleton, A. (2007). *CIPD Research Insight: Coaching in Organisations*. Downloaded on 24 October 2008 from http://www.cipd.co.uk/subjects/lrnanddev/coachmntor/_cchngorgs.htm.

Kurz, R. & Bartram, D. (2002). Competency and individual performance: modelling the world of work. In I.T. Robertson, M. Callinan & D. Bartram (Eds), *Organizational Effectiveness: The Role of Psychology*. Chichester: John Wiley & Sons, Ltd.

Law, H. (2008). Diversity coaching. *People and Organisations at Work*, **8**, 6–7.

Lowman, R.L. (2001). Constructing a literature from case studies: promises and limitations of the method. *Consulting Psychology Journal: Practice and Research*, **53**(2), 119–23.

Maslow, A.H. (1968). *Toward a Psychology of Being*. New York: Van Nostrand Reinhold.

McDougall, M. (2008). *Association for Coaching: Coaching Supervision: Analysis of Survey Findings*. Downloaded on 19 October 2008 from http://www.associationforcoaching.com/pub/ACSurveyAnalsysCoachMentorSupervisionJUN08.pdf.

McDowall, A. & Kurz, R. (2007). Making the most of psychometric profiles – effective integration into the coaching process. *International Coaching Psychology Review*, **2**(3), 299–309.

McGovern, J., Lindeman, M., Vergara, M., Murphy, S., Baker, L. & Warrenfeltz, R. (2001). Maximising the impact of executive coaching: behavioural change, organisational outcomes and return on investment. *The Manchester Review*, **6**(1), 1–9.

McLeod, A. (2003). *Performance Coaching: The Handbook for Managers, HR Professionals and Coaches*. Carmarthen: Crown House Publishing.

McMahon, G. (2005). Behavioural contracting and confidentiality in organisational coaching. *Counselling at Work*, Spring, 1–3.

Neenan, M. & Dryden, W. (2002). *Life Coaching: A Cognitive Behavioural Approach*. London: Routledge.

Palmer, S. (2002). Cognitive and organisational models of stress that are suitable for use within workplace stress management/prevention coaching, training and counselling settings. *The Rational Emotive Behaviour Therapist*, **10**(1), 15–21.

Palmer, S. (2007). PRACTICE: a model suitable for coaching, counselling, psychotherapy and stress management. *The Coaching Psychologist*, **3**(2), 71–7.

Palmer, S. (2008). The PRACTICE model of coaching: towards a solution-focused approach. *Coaching Psychology International*, **1**(1), 4–8.

Palmer, S. (2009). Rational coaching: a cognitive behavioural approach. *The Coaching Psychologist*, **5**(1), 12–18.

Palmer, S. & Cooper, C. (2007). *How to Deal with Stress*. London: Kogan-Page.

Palmer, S., Grant, A. & O'Connell, B. (2007). Solution-focused coaching: lost and found. *Coaching at Work*, **2**(4), 22–9.

Palmer, S. & Szymanska, K. (2007). *Cognitive Behavioural Coaching: An Integrative Approach*. In S. Palmer & A. Whybrow (Eds). *Handbook of Coaching Psychology: A Guide for Practitioners*. Hove: Routledge.

Palmer, S. & Whybrow, A. (Eds) (2007). *Handbook of Coaching Psychology: A Guide for Practitioners*. London: Routledge.

Passmore, J. (Ed.) (2008). *Psychometrics in Coaching: Using Psychological and Psychometric Tools for Development*. London: Kogan-Page.

Passmore, J. & Gibbes, C. (2007). The state of executive coaching research: what does the current literature tell us and what's next for coaching research? *International Coaching Psychology Review*, **2**(2), 116–28.

Peltier, B. (2001). *The Psychology of Executive Coaching: Theory and Application*. London: Routledge.

Rust, J. (2004). *People Who Need People. Does Psychometrics have a Place in Staff Selection? City Insights Lecture*. Downloaded on 19 October 2008 from http://www.psychometrics.sps.cam.ac.uk/page/111/people-who-need-people.htm.

Sherman, S. & Freas, A. (2005). The wild west of executive coaching. *Harvard Business Review*, **82**(11), 82–90.

SHL People Solutions (2004a). *Achieving Life Balance through SHL Executive Coaching*. SHL client case study downloaded on 31 October 2008 from http://www.shl.com/SHL/en-int/Company/Clients/Case_Studies/Case_Study_List/anon-telecoms-company.htm.

SHL People Solutions (2004b). *Honing your Personal Brand through Executive Coaching*. SHL client case study downloaded on 31 October 2008 from http://www.shl.com/SHL/en-int/Company/Clients/Case_Studies/Case_Study_List/anon-executive-coaching.htm.

SHL People Solutions (2007). *Talent Management: Issues and Observations. SHL People Solutions White Paper 2007*. Downloaded on 4 November 2008 from http://www.shl.com/SHL/en-int/Thought_Leadership/White_Papers/White-Papers.aspx.

Smither, J. & London, M. (2003). Can working with an executive coach improve multi-source feedback ratings over time? A quasi-experimental field study. *Personnel Psychology*, **56**, 23–44.

Strack, R., Caye, J.-M., Leicht, M., Villis, U., Bohm, H. & McDonnel, M. (2007). *The Future of HR in Europe: Key Challenges through 2015. The Boston Consulting Group and European Association for Personnel Management Survey 2007*. Downloaded on 24 October 2008 from http://www.eapm.org/.

The Economist (2006). The battle for brainpower. Downloaded on 24 October 2008 from http://www.economist.com/surveys/displaystory.cfm?story_id=7961894.

Trapp, R. (2005). How to select a coach: advice on how a finance manager might use a coach to ensure his successful next step to board level. *CIPD Coaching at Work*. Downloaded on 13 October 2008 from http://www.cipd.co.uk/coachingatwork/presales/How+to+select+a+coach.htm.

Whitmore, J. (1992). *Coaching for Performance*. London: Nicholas Brealey

Whitmore, J. (2002). *Coaching for Performance*. London: Nicholas Brearley.

Whybrow, A. & Palmer, S. (2006). Taking stock: a survey of coaching psychologists' practice and perspectives. *International Coaching Psychology Review*, **1**(1), 56–70.

Wilding, C. & Palmer, S. (2006). *Zero to Hero: From Cringing to Confident in 100 Steps*. London: Hodder Arnold.

Wilson, C. (2006). The history of coaching and the need for accreditation. *The Bulletin of the Association for Coaching*, Summer (8), 7–10. Downloaded on 13 October 2008 from http://www.associationforcoaching.com/pub/ACB0607.pdf.

Woolston, L. & Linley, A. (2008). Strengths coaching at work. *People and Organisations at Work*, Autumn, 8–10.

CHAPTER 16

Women's Coping: Communal Versus Individualistic Orientation

Pamela A. Geller
Drexel University, USA

Stevan E. Hobfoll
Rush Medical College, USA

and

Carla Dunahoo
Dunahoo Psychological Associates LLC, USA

16.1 STRESSORS IN THE WORKPLACE

Although women have been entering the workplace in steadily increasing numbers since the beginning of the twentieth century, even in this twenty-first century, the examination of how work affects people has continued to be conducted from a gender-segregated perspective. Studies of men at work have tended to focus on the influence of work itself on men. In contrast, studies of women at work have tended to focus on role strain that women experience from being torn between work and home (Barnett & Baruch, 1987; Simon, 1992; Thoits, 1992). This segregation was more reasonable when most working men had women at home shoring up the non-work related aspects of their lives. Hence, their stress may have been more clearly based on work itself. However, when the vast majority of couples (at least in the USA) have both partners working in the paid workforce, this distinction is no longer valid.

More recent research has attempted to compare men's and women's work experiences (Barnett *et al.*, 1993), and there is much to be said for this approach. By comparing men and women who perform similar jobs and who

International Handbook of Work and Health Psychology, Third Edition. Edited by Cary L. Cooper, James Campbell Quick, and Marc J. Schabracq.

have similar home lives, we might better understand the influence of work *per se*. In such tests, the limited number of studies conducted to date suggest that there are few differences in the stress experienced by men and women at work or in its influence on them (Barnett *et al.*, 1993; Rodin & Ickovics, 1990; Wethington & Kessler, 1989).

Nevertheless, this picture is also unsatisfying because although the effects of work on men and women who are directly comparable is one key focus for research, it does not represent the current picture of men's and women's experiences with work. Men tend to be in more senior positions, have greater autonomy, spend fewer hours on household labour, receive more pay and hold more supervisory positions (Blumberg, 1991; Grossman & Chester, 1990; Powell, 1988). Even when they hold the same job, men tend to be given greater autonomy and are more likely to be given leadership roles, rather than maintenance tasks (Powell, 1988). Women are more likely to have to move to accommodate their partner's career opportunities, be subjected to sexual harassment, and have to accommodate special demands when reproductive health issues appear to interfere with company policy (i.e., pregnancy considered a problem, whereas men's greater incidence of alcoholism and heart disease is not considered a gender relevant concern). In addition, women are more likely to be expected to take time off work for care of an ill child or parent (even her spouse's parent), and are more likely to be expected to take time away from their careers for child rearing.

Psychology has further blurred the study of how women are affected by work through applying individualistic models of stress and coping to the study of women's workplace experiences. This chapter focuses on this theme and discusses the literature on women's stress and coping by introducing a communal perspective to our evaluation. In particular, there has been an almost exclusive emphasis on the study of the individual's perceived control in the workplace, to the point that few other psychological dimensions of either the work environment or people's response to it have been studied (Karasek *et al.*, 1981, 1987). This is not to say that the lack of control influences men, but not women. LaCroix and Haynes (1984) found that the situation of high demand and low control in the workplace increased women's risk of coronary heart disease (CHD), compared to women in job situations of low demand and high control. Men's CHD in these studies was not found to be differentially affected by levels of demand and control. Moreover, women employed in jobs with high demand, low control and low social support have been found to experience the largest deterioration in health status and health outcomes across the board, and these specific work environments contributed to declines in health functioning over time (Cheng *et al.*, 2000). High-demand/low-control work environments have similarly been associated with women's reports of greater cigarette smoking and chest pain (Biener *et al.*, 1986; Haynes *et al.*, 1987). These studies, however, tend to focus on clerical workers, a category in which women are overrepresented and which may provide particularly low levels of autonomy and compensation. Hence, the studies may actually represent the risk of a given occupational category, and not of the general lack of control. Furthermore, studies have equated role ambiguity or clarity of supervisors as indicators of control, whereas many low-control situations are neither ambiguous nor unclear.

The primary question that we raise is whether control and individual action are the central variables to study in order to understand women's experience of stress in the workplace.

Miller (1980) found that control was more a concern for men than for women. For men, job satisfaction was associated with positional authority, having decision-making power, and not having close supervision. For women, high job satisfaction was associated with the use of thought and independent judgement, and the opportunity to utilize skills and ability.

Another way to look at the influence of work experiences on men's and women's lives is to take a cultural perspective. The workplace is traditionally dominated by a male culture, which is based not on the team model that is marketed by personnel departments, but on an individualistic, dominance-based model. Power and authority are the main themes in this culture. Even when people work together, status and hierarchical relationships predominate. To the extent that there exists a distinguishable women's culture, it does not seem to differ from the current workplace culture on the need for esteem or the value of success. Rather, women tend to both offer and receive support more often and more effectively than men (Hobfoll & Vaux, 1993; Kessler *et al.*, 1985). They tend to be more willing to work with a team, rather than dominate the team (Powell, 1988; Radecki & Jennings, 1980), and they are more likely to consider others' needs, as well as their own. This is not to say that there is not appreciable overlap between men's and women's cultures. Even when collectivistic and individualistic cultures that characterize Eastern versus Western cultures are compared, considerable overlap exists, at the same time that they are distinctive (Triandis *et al.*, 1990).

In this chapter we examine how stress affects women and how coping may moderate the effects of that stress. We also explore the underlying assumptions of the individualistic model of stress and coping, and contrast them with a model that incorporates both individualism and communalism. Our own multiaxial model of coping is presented as an alternative structure that provides a different perspective on the experience of stress and how coping strategies may operate in response to stress.

16.2 EXAMINING THE MODEL OF RUGGED INDIVIDUALISM

Coping behaviours play an important role in people's response to stress (Endler & Parker, 1990; Lazarus & Folkman, 1984; McCrae & Costa, 1986). However, the influence of coping is still not well understood, and research regarding its influence has tended to be atheoretical (Carver *et al.*, 1989; Schwarzer & Schwarzer, 1996). In particular, we criticize current methods as being tuned to an individualistic perspective that sociologically has been termed 'rugged individualism'. Rugged individualism pits man against the elements in his fight for survival. This perspective esteems control and action and ignores social and communal aspects of coping (Riger, 1993). Important gender and ethnic differences in coping are missed by adopting this *Lone Ranger*, 'man against the elements' perspective. Esteeming individualism asserts two underlying assumptions. As Riger (1993, p. 280) writes:

> A great deal of research in psychology rests on the assumption that the healthy individual is one who is self-contained, independent and self-reliant, capable of asserting himself and influencing his environment.

Coping research, particularly that conducted on stress in the workplace, has promoted this perspective, with an emphasis on active, problem-focused coping. That problem-focused efforts may even be antisocial and affect others negatively or sabotage potential support has been ignored (Lane & Hobfoll, 1992). Some coping scales even categorize such behaviours as 'Visit a friend' and 'Spend time with a special person' as types of avoidant coping (Endler & Parker, 1990). It is instructive that avoidant coping, as measured by this scale, was related to negative outcomes for men, but unrelated to negative outcomes for women.

Secondly, individualism denies the influence of the environment. Sampson (1993, p. 12) writes:

> Effort is expended in developing precise ways to measure and assess individual psychological states and perceptions and to evaluate individual behavior outcomes. The social context within which these individual perceptions and activities take place is put off to the side, occasionally alluded to, but rarely if ever systematically addressed.

Coping research suggests that when action is not chosen, the alternatives are either avoidance or 'passive' attempts to reduce discomforting emotions (Lazarus & Folkman, 1984). These alternative strategies are the most strongly related to psychological outcomes, with more avoidance and emotion-focused coping producing greater psychological distress (Endler &

Parker, 1990; Freedy *et al.*, 1992). Research has suggested that men are more likely to adopt actions designed to alter the problem, whereas women are more likely to cope by managing their emotional responses to stress or by using avoidance (Billings & Moos, 1984; Endler & Parker, 1990; Stone & Neale, 1984). Some have suggested that these gender differences result from the action demands that men experience versus the emotional demands that women encounter because of the different role settings they typically occupy (Folkman & Lazarus, 1980; Roth & Cohen, 1986). However, we argue that, because the underlying models are based on individualism, the positive things that women are more likely to do are never measured.

16.3   THE STRESS OF WORK AND ITS INFLUENCE ON WOMEN

With more women entering the labour force, women are being confronted with workplace stressors that are shared with men, as well as stressors unique to their gender. Although they may share particular work-related stressors, men and women may perceive and react to these stressors differently according to their social support resources and coping orientation.

Both male and female employees experience stressors related to such variables as: (i) role ambiguity, involving a lack of clarity about job roles, expectations or criteria in order to perform adequately; (ii) role conflict, where directives are incompatible and conflicting, or when available resources are insufficient to meet job demands; (iii) role overload, which involves having too many demands, and may include time pressure; and (iv) lack of autonomy, resulting from significant supervisor control combined with limited opportunity to participate in decision making (Billings & Moos, 1982).

Although the specific ways in which men and women react to and choose to cope with these shared stressors may differ, in general, all can contribute to a sense of job dissatisfaction, and may have a variety of additional implications. For example, chronic job-related stress can result in job tedium, burnout and reduced efficiency, motivation and productivity (Akabas, 1988; Maslach, 1982; Pines & Aronson, 1981). The working environment itself plays a role in creating demands and restraints that cause the depletion of resources (Gorgievski & Hobfoll, in press), and research has shown that high demands and a lack of resources at the workplace also are contributing factors to employee burnout (Schaufeli & Bakker, 2004). Physical health problems and somatic complaints, as well as various mental health problems (e.g. anxiety, depression, marital discord) also have been linked to workplace stressors (House & Wells, 1978; Jackson & Maslach, 1982; LaRocco & Jones, 1978; LaRocco *et al.*, 1980; Repetti *et al.*, 1989).

When studies began to address the impact of employment specifically for women, research focused less on the specific workplace stressors mentioned above, and more on the addition of the employee role to those of wife and mother. Conceptualizations of multiple roles for women included the *scarcity hypothesis* (Goode, 1960), where a greater number of roles is likely to deplete limited resources, with negative consequences for women's health and well-being, and the *enhancement hypothesis* (Marks, 1977; Sieber, 1974), where an increased number of roles provides greater potential to access resources (e.g., self-esteem, social status, financial gains), and the ability to delegate obligations required by the various roles. More roles, therefore, provide expanded opportunities that are likely to result in greater health benefits (Gove & Zeiss, 1987; Thoits, 1983; Verbrugge, 1982).

Gender differences in work–family conflict are related to both the nature of women's unique gender roles and differences in perceptions of their roles. Unlike men, who report that their single most important responsibility is providing financially for their families, women report that caring for children and managing household responsibilities are equal in importance to contributing to the family's financial resources (Perry-Jenkins, 1993; Perry-Jenkins & Crouter, 1990). When examining the health of women, the perceived quality of women's social roles has been found to be more important than the number of roles *per se* (Barnett & Baruch, 1985; Baruch & Barnett, 1986; Baruch *et al.*, 1987). Barnett and Hyde (2001) suggest that quality of social roles may be influenced by many variables related to increased financial, social and personal opportunities for women, expanded worldview, increased sense of self-complexity and greater similarities between self and husband, and individual differences in gender-role ideology. Additionally, it is not only the woman's appraisal of the quality of her social roles that is significant; the perception of others has an impact as well. Grandey, Cordeiro and Crouter (2005) explored the association between gender roles and job satisfaction through the use of spousal ratings wherein each couple reported the extent to which their spouse's work interfered with family time and energy. A significant negative association was detected between wives' job satisfaction and their husband's ratings of how the wife's work interfered with family. This finding suggests that assumptions regarding gender-prescribed roles such as taking care of the family can become problematic for a woman if her husband perceives that she is in violation of that role. The woman then may reason that the inability to fulfil that role is due to her job, which leads to low job satisfaction. On the other hand, wives also rated their husbands' work as affecting family life, but this acknowledgment did not result in husbands experiencing lower job satisfaction. This type of attribution related to gender roles is an experience that primarily affects women; therefore, it is essential when addressing coping orientation to look not only at the job-related stressors common among men and women, but also at the home and workplace stressors that are unique to working women. This provides information about how women assess the quality of their roles, and can give clues to the special support needs of employed women.

16.4   JOB-RELATED STRESSORS UNIQUE TO WOMEN

Management typically portrays the workplace as gender neutral, but there is ample evidence that gender bias exists on both overt and more subtle levels. This bias contributes to the special stressors facing working women. First, there is limited appreciable promotion of women to higher organizational ranks (Cowan, 1989; Grant, 1988; Kim, 1994). Hence, regardless of the fact that the opportunities for and acceptance of women in the workplace have improved, the glass ceiling effect remains, and women still are not well integrated in many organizational systems. Even where women work in traditional female professions, such as nursing, teaching, housekeeping and food service, the management is male dominated (Powell, 1988). In some instances, a 'men's club' mentality has resulted in outright discrimination and sexual harassment. The tendency is for managers to underrate and underreward women compared to men with identical credentials (Bhatnagar, 1988; Lott, 1985; Rosenfield & Stephan, 1978). Even with the same job, in the same occupation, women's earnings are typically lower than those of men (Kim, 1994; Kim, 1989; Powell, 1988). Indeed, this compensation gap *increases* as women ascend the corporate ladder into the executive ranks (Kim, 1994).

16.5   WORKPLACE SUPPORT

Research has shown that employees with strong social support are healthier and more resistant to workplace stress and its effects. Employment conditions should promote, rather than undermine, workplace support in order to preserve the resources and resiliency of the employees (Gorgievski & Hobfoll, in press). However, the existence of discrimination, sexual harassment and the glass ceiling are factors that indicate an underlying lack of institutional support for women. An absence of support for women is further evidenced by the paucity of family-friendly initiatives, ranging from childcare assistance and leave for the caretaking of sick family members, to job relocation for both members of dual-income families (Cowan, 1989). Provisions that have been developed such as flexi-time and flexi-place programmes are not widespread and do not appear to ease the burden of work–family conflict for women with major family responsibilities (Beutell & Greenhaus, 1986).

In terms of access to workplace support on an interpersonal level, women have an apparent disadvantage when compared to men. Several studies have demonstrated that workplace support has been more effective in limiting work-related stress for men than for women (Baruch *et al.*, 1987; Etzion, 1984; House, 1981). Geller and Hobfoll (1994) examined gender differences in the amount and effectiveness of interpersonal work support. Despite the fact that the men and women in this study reported receiving similar amounts of support from their coworkers and supervisors, men benefited more from these support sources. It is possible that men benefit more from their work relationships because they may interact with their colleagues on a more informal level, which House (1981) suggests may be most effective in the prevention of work stress and its negative consequences. Because individualistic characteristics are so highly valued in the workplace, and because men are inclined toward this individualistic orientation, support may be provided more genuinely among men and may be more effective since it can involve mutual exchange and spontaneous acts, rather than role-required behaviour. Some of the negative sequelae of women's limited access to effective, interpersonal work support include social isolation, difficulty finding mentors and decreased status in the workplace (Bhatnagar, 1988).

16.6   EMPHASIS ON INDIVIDUALISTIC ORIENTATION IN THE WORKPLACE

The emphasis on individualistic characteristics as opposed to communal qualities may present a key obstacle to women obtaining necessary institutional, as well as interpersonal, workplace social support. Gupta *et al.* (1983) have argued that social problems such as women's social isolation and difficulty finding mentors may be tied to women's inability to gain access to the 'old boys' network' of advancement, which involves off-the-job social and extracurricular activities essential for recognition, acceptance and promotion in most organizations. In large part, this may stem from expectations for employees to act according to the individualistic-male model of managerial success, which includes agenic characteristics such as self-reliance and dominance. Simultaneously, there are covert messages punishing women for exhibiting these male gender role traits. At the same time, however, communal characteristics, such as nurturance and interdependence, are not coping traits that are valued in most organizations (Grant, 1988). Put another way, women are paradoxically excluded from the one communal element of work – the 'old boys' network' – because their behaviour is deemed too communal and not individualistic enough, but punished for exhibiting the esteemed traits more commonly exhibited by their male colleagues.

According to some authors, conflicting expectations at work place women in an irresolvable dilemma. If they want to retain people's approval, they must demonstrate such qualities of female gender role as warmth and expressiveness. If they want to succeed professionally, however, they must act according to the individualistic, power-centred model by being assertive, competitive and firm (Bhatnagar, 1988; Grant, 1988).

Investigators assessing factors contributing to the provision of support found that assertive coping may attract support (Dunkel-Schetter & Skokan, 1990). Individuals who cope more actively and are less passive are given greater support in response to their efforts. This might suggest that assertive women demonstrating characteristics of agency would be best able to access workplace support. However, both men and women have been socialized to expect the gentle and empathic, communal role in women (Martin et al., 1983). In addition, if women's assertiveness is misread as aggressive, they may alienate and anger potential supporters.

Despite the fact that people prefer to interact with and support individuals whom they perceive to possess similar characteristics, women seem to be less positively evaluated by males, even when they exhibit traits of an individualistic orientation deemed necessary for business success (Eagly et al., 1992). Mathison (1986) found that *women* were actually more negative toward an assertive woman than were men. This phenomenon may be attributed to the different goals that people believe are achieved by association with men and women in the work domain. In the interpersonal domain, both men and women prefer supportive relationships with women (Reis et al., 1985). If women are perceived as compassionate and sensitive, they can best provide interpersonal support. If men are perceived as competent and powerful, they are best able to provide work support (Bhatnagar, 1988), so their assertive orientation may be evaluated more positively in work settings.

In one of the few experimental investigations of how assertive men and women are evaluated in the workplace, Geller and Hobfoll (1993) found evidence of a double bias, with each gender preferring to mentor and offer support to their own gender. They suggest that this may represent a historical change in women's socialization. Due to increased awareness and sensitivity to problems such as the glass ceiling and lack of mentors, women may be recognizing a need for increased camaraderie. Women also may be developing increased understanding and acceptance of women adopting a more individualistic orientation. As men do not share women's plight, they either may not be experiencing this change, or may be experiencing it more slowly. However, since males hold the majority of key supervisory positions at this time, these findings support the fact that women are at a disadvantage in terms of organizational advancement. More research in this area seems warranted.

16.7 STRESS AT HOME

The focus on stress in working women's home lives has been on inadequate household assistance from their partners. Women with families often have additional home burden because: (i) women's traditional core role has involved household responsibilities (Barnett & Baruch, 1987); and (ii) working men have been slow to pick up the slack at home. Typically, women take responsibility for much more of the family's home labour even when both members of a dual-career couple have full-time jobs (Cowan, 1989; Pleck, 1985; Powell, 1988). The most striking finding is that women spend more than twice as much time on housework and childcare than men. Although the husbands of employed wives are increasing their proportion of total family labour, the increase is due to wives' decreased participation, rather than to husbands' greater time commitments. Also, although men are increasing their number of child contact hours, women still perform the vast majority of childcare and household tasks. This unequal division of household labour contributes an average of 10 additional work hours each week to the schedules of employed women.

In addition to the roles of spouse and parent, it is women who typically take on additional family-related roles and responsibilities. For example, women's communal orientation makes them more likely than men (e.g., their husbands, partners or brothers) to become the primary caretaker for an elderly or sick family member, even when the family member is more closely related to the woman's partner or spouse (e.g., mother-in-law). With the increasing number of ageing Americans, more women are becoming primary caretakers for their children and their ageing parents, in addition to holding a full-time job.

16.8 WORK–FAMILY ROLE CONFLICT

For both men and women, family life is usually the most important aspect (Barnett & Baruch, 1987), and, along with job satisfaction, is a significant predictor of general life satisfaction (Gutek *et al.*, 1988). Yet, working women often feel conflicted about the combination of these roles. Kinnunen, Geurts and Mauno (2004) noted that a major source of conflict for women in terms of work–family balance was the combination of having a family and also a highly demanding job. This conflict emerged primarily with regard to women, as it was found that for men, issues with work–family balance are not as challenging. Because women have stronger personal, social and societal pressure to adhere to the roles focusing on family and household tasks, it is working women more so than working men who experience the strains of competing work and family demands (Barnett & Baruch, 1987; Beutell & Greenhaus, 1986).

Three different types of conflict that relate to the work–family role dilemma have been described (Beutell & Greenhaus, 1986; Gutek *et al.*, 1988). The first, *time-based conflict*, involves the distribution of time, energy and opportunities between the occupational and family roles. Here, scheduling is difficult and time is restricted because the demands and the behaviours required to enact them are incompatible. Women often experience fatigue since the two roles compete for personal resources. The second conflict has been termed *strain-based conflict*, referring to the spillover of strain, or an emotional state that is generated in one role, into the performance of another role. *Behaviour-based conflict*, the third type of work–family conflict, refers to the incompatible sets of behaviours an individual has for work and for family. Because of these separate set of behaviours, women often find it difficult to shift gears from one role to another.

For some women, their career commitment has resulted in changed priorities, in which equal priority for home and work roles replaces the traditional preference for the home role (Pines & Aronson, 1981). Some less traditionally minded women resolve the dilemma by giving the career precedence over their family whenever the two conflict. Other women, and they are increasing in number, are choosing to deal with this work–family conflict by not having a family at all (Gutek *et al.*, 1988; Powell, 1988).

Most common, however, are women who cope with their conflict at the work–family interface by over-adhering to gender-role stereotypes at home. Due to their communal orientation, many women do not view their jobs as justification for attending less to their families and household work. Therefore, they feel personal pressure that causes them to feel guilt and anxiety when they cannot fulfil all of their responsibilities. 'These women believe that in addition to being "super-professionals", they have to be "super-mothers" and "superhomemakers" (Pines & Aronson, 1981). Because childcare is hard to find, expensive and often fails, working women who are single parents or have children with a disability are likely to experience greater stress resulting from the work–family conflict (Goldberg *et al.*, 1992).

16.9 HOME-BASED SUPPORT

Researchers have concluded that employment is associated with improved mental health for women only if partner support is received, as reflected by a favourable attitude toward women working and as demonstrated by an equitable division of household labour (Kessler & McRae, 1982; Ross *et al.*, 1983). In addition, several studies have demonstrated that family support has been most effective in reducing work stress for women, while work-related sources of support have been most effective in the attenuation of these effects among men (Baruch *et al.*, 1987; Etzion, 1984; House, 1981). Help-seeking coping used at home has been associated with less interference of family with work in a mixed-gender sample, though help-seeking coping is not associated with less interference of work with family (Rotondo, Carlson & Kincaid, 2003).

Geller and Hobfoll (1994) found that household assistance from partners was related to women reporting greater tedium and work-related stress – a counterintuitive finding that also has been noted in research by Baruch and Barnett (1986) and Hochschild and Machung (1989). There are several possibilities that may account for this finding. First, the support that is provided to women by their partners must correspond to their needs (Cohen & McKay, 1985; Cutrona, 1990). It may be that the household assistance women receive is too low to meet their needs, or that another aspect of support, such as emotional support, is needed and expected, but not provided. The stress experienced by many women may also be so great that the household support may come too late to be effective. When resources are overtaxed, social support reserves may be less effective. If partner assistance does not fit the needs of women adequately, this may actually result in greater strain. According to Parry (1986), employment can reduce the risk of psychological symptoms caused by stressful life events when support is sufficient, but results in increased symptoms when adequate support is unavailable. Another possibility is that women who report receiving the greatest amounts of household assistance may be receiving 'high hassle support' (Geller & Hobfoll, 1994). Although women may be receiving assistance, the positive aspects may be associated with stress, and may overshadow the perceived helpfulness of the support. For example, if a woman must consistently remind her partner to complete household chores, or if he does them inadequately, frustration may develop and the woman may need to redo the task. Additionally, women may have difficulty accepting household assistance from their partners due to their communal orientation. Receiving a great deal of assistance may be interpreted by working women to mean they are failing at their 'real' role as wife and mother. Feelings of guilt and failure may contribute to the experience of greater strain.

16.10 COMMUNAL ORIENTATION: DEVELOPING A COLLECTIVIST PERSPECTIVE

Despite the fact that the existing literature is filled with references to women being more communally oriented as opposed to men, who tend to be more individualistic, few attempts have been made to study coping behaviour in a way that considers both perspectives. The existing literature has persisted in portraying individualistic coping as the most desirable and most effective approach. Furthermore, despite the fact that investigators have repeatedly found that men and women cope in similar ways and report equal use of problem-focused coping (e.g., Folkman & Lazarus, 1980, 1985; Folkman *et al.*, 1986a,b; Forsythe & Compas, 1987), the literature has persisted in portraying men as effective, individualistic copers and women as ineffective, emotional copers.

Women's active, direct coping has been ignored, as well as any results suggesting that men use ineffective means of coping. For instance, Parkes (1990) found that men reported more use of suppression coping than did women; in other words, men reported more use of withdrawal, restraint, compromise and ignoring the problem. Carver *et al.* (1989) found that men were more likely than women to use alcohol and drug disengagement, and Hobfoll *et al.* (1994) found that men reported more aggressive rather than assertive coping. Despite these findings, men have been consistently portrayed as being good copers.

This bias is seen even more clearly in the workplace coping literature. The majority of this research has focused on Caucasian, middle-class males to the almost total exclusion of women (Long, 1990; Long *et al.*, 1992). Even studies investigating the impact of unemployment have centred on men, despite the fact that women are more likely to lose their jobs. The impact of this has not been investigated because women are assumed to be less affected (Leana & Feldman, 1991).

Hobfoll and colleagues have addressed this issue in a line of research presenting a new model of coping, and a companion coping instrument, developed to investigate coping from both individualistic and communal viewpoints, rather than emphasizing either approach. This work has allowed investigation of how well the traditional male-biased, individualistic assumptions regarding coping actually represent the realm of coping behaviour.

16.11   THE MULTIAXIAL MODEL OF COPING

To study coping in a context that allows for both individualistic and communal orientations, we developed the multiaxial model of coping and a companion test instrument, the Strategic Approach to Coping Scale (SACS). We began with a dual-axis model (Hobfoll *et al.*, 1994), with the two axes representing active–passive and prosocial–antisocial dimensions. A communal orientation would suggest that the active–prosocial orientation would be the most effective.

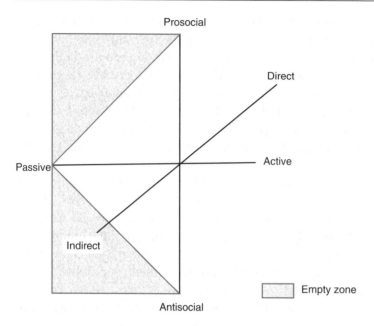

Figure 16.1   The multiaxial model of coping.

Active–antisocial action might be personally productive, but might also alienate others, be destructive to social networks, and eventually backfire on the individual. Passive–prosocial orientations could support others, but might not lead to goal-directed behaviour for the individual. Passive–antisocial behaviour could be the most destructive, both personally and socially, but might be adopted in a defensive strategy.

Expanding this model, we added another dimension, that of directness. The multiaxial model is depicted in Figure 16.1. A communal perspective suggests that, even when being active, behaviour may be either direct or indirect. For example, in Japanese culture it is socially inappropriate to embarrass your business opponent. Hence, it is common practice to manipulate the environment indirectly so that your company gains an advantage without the other company losing face (Weisz *et al.*, 1984). Such environmental manipulations demand great activity and a goal-directed posture, but they are performed indirectly and behind the scenes. Similarly, in African-American culture, people's actions may be aimed at altering settings to enhance others' well-being, rather than directly aiming actions at the people themselves (Dressler, 1985).

As depicted in Figure 16.1, not all octants of the model are believed to fully occur. Prior research did not find appreciable evidence for people who are extremely passive to be either prosocial or antisocial, but relatively passive behaviour was at times linked to prosocial or passive–antisocial coping

(Hobfoll *et al.*, 1994). This may be because when people become passive they become *a*social, rather than prosocial or antisocial. By being passive, one simply does not act towards others. We had expected a passive–aggressive kind of coping to occur, but this may be depicted better in our current model by being indirect and antisocial, rather than by seeing someone as passive and antisocial. As people become more active, their demeanour with regard to the social environment becomes more relevant according to the model. Hence, people can be active and either prosocial or antisocial in carrying out those actions.

16.12   HOW THE MULTIAXIAL MODEL OF COPING CHANGES COMMON COPING ASSUMPTIONS

Applying the multiaxial model of coping challenges certain assumptions that have been inherent in the basis of coping research to date.

> *Assumption 1:* Perhaps one of the more commonly held assumptions is that it is best to approach goals through active problem solving.

Particularly in Western cultures, attacking the problem is the valued approach to dealing with almost any situation. Any other approach would most likely be considered weak coping at best. This assumption is likely responsible for the existing literature's focus on problem-focused and emotion-focused coping. Folkman and Lazarus (1980) defined problem-focused coping as managing the stressor, while they defined emotion-focused coping as dealing with the emotional consequences of the stress. Although it was initially assumed that men were more likely to use problem-focused coping and women were more likely to use emotion-focused coping, subsequent research has failed to consistently support this (e.g., Folkman & Lazarus, 1980; Folkman *et al.*, 1986a; Vitaliano *et al.*, 1987).

Despite these findings to the contrary, the perception that men cope in problem-focused manners and women cope in emotion-focused manners has persisted. This perception has often been interpreted as suggesting that men cope actively and directly with whatever stressors they meet, while women cope passively, through only worrying about their feelings and thereby failing to cope. Thus, this focus on an individualistic perspective has lent support to positive attitudes towards the ways in which men cope and negative attitudes towards the ways in which women cope.

Approaching the same issue, that of how actively people cope, from a less individualistic perspective results in a less pejorative view of coping for women, while continuing to present men's coping in a positive way.

A more communal view of active coping would involve approaching goals through shared problem solving. Shared problem solving, as it implies, involves people addressing the stressor together, either through joint action or through joint planning. Turning to others for support, either primarily instrumental or primarily emotional, would be included in such efforts. In addition, offering support to others is part of shared problem solving.

Hobfoll (1988) found that perceived social support reinforces one's own personal resources for dealing with stress. In addition, having the support of others provides the opportunity to benefit from their strengths and resources. Although social support has often been considered a strategy for coping only with problems outside the workplace, several investigators have found that it is an important component of dealing with workplace stress as well. For instance, Long *et al.* (1992) found that individuals who perceived high emotional support from coworkers reported lower levels of occupational stress, along with better physical and mental health. Social support in the workplace has also been found to be negatively associated with work–family conflict (Carlson & Perrewé, 1999). Lack of workplace social support, when coupled with high work demands, was found to be associated with high work-related stress (Parkes, 1990), while presence of workplace social support was found to enhance active coping strategies (Long, 1990). Similarly, Dunahoo *et al.* (1998) found that social joining acted as a buffer against depression in situations of high stress, thus leaving those who used social joining strategies to cope with high-stress situations less depressed than those who did not.

Research has supported the assertion that shared problem solving can be an effective means of coping. Stone and Neale (1984) found that seeking social support was positively correlated with direct action. Hobfoll (1988) reported that perception of social support reinforces personal resources. Sarason *et al.* (1983) found that use of social support as a means of coping was associated with positive self-concepts, low anxiety and higher perceived mastery. Thus, it is likely that social support allows those who utilize it to be better able to draw upon their own resources as well as relying on the assistance of others.

Further support for the effectiveness of shared problem solving is offered by other studies as well. Vitaliano and colleagues (1990) found that individuals with psychopathology tend to cope in maladaptive ways, which included less support seeking. McLaughlin *et al.* (1988) found that for women who hold dual roles (having both a career and a marriage), good marital adjustment was associated with more overall coping and less psychological distress. They suggested that one explanation for this finding may be that shared problem solving in a marriage leads to better outcomes. Additionally, Dunahoo *et al.* (1998) found that social joining as a means of coping was associated with less anxiety and depression.

Another alternative to the assumption that individualistic action aimed at problem solving is always best is the concept that it is better to be sensitive to the environmental constraints and choose one's responses according to the situation. The assumption that problem-focused forms of coping are always effective and emotion-focused forms of coping are always ineffective has been shown to be inaccurate. Although direct, individualistic approaches to problem solving may often be valued in a business setting, such approaches would be considered inappropriate in dealing with the types of stressors that typically occur in childrearing, educational and interpersonal settings. If team play is actually valued in work settings, these same behaviours may be equally counterproductive in the work domain.

Pearlin and Schooler (1978) suggest that some problems may not even be responsive to individualistic approaches and may in fact require communal approaches. Lazarus and Folkman have repeatedly asserted that stress and coping need to be considered with a transactional approach where the interaction between the person and the environment is recognized (e.g., Dunkel-Schetter *et al.*, 1987; Lazarus, 1966). Researchers have found that, not only does coping differ by the situation in which the stressful event occurs (Folkman *et al.*, 1986a; Hobfoll *et al.*, 1994), but that the effectiveness of different means of coping differs by situation as well (Forsythe & Compas, 1987; Pearlin & Schooler, 1978). For example, problem-focused coping has been shown to be a particularly effective approach only in situations in which people have control or can change the situation (Compas *et al.*, 1988; Folkman & Lazarus, 1980; Forsythe & Compas, 1987; Miller & Kirsch, 1987; Roth & Cohen, 1986). Thus, it appears to be more adaptive and effective for individuals to be flexible in the ways in which they cope (Parkes, 1990). Ginter *et al.* (1989) investigated this issue and found that resourceful individuals varied their coping efforts according, to some degree at least, to situational characteristics. These individuals also reported fewer behavioural, cognitive and physical symptoms of stress.

> *Assumption 2:* An assumption that often goes along with the assumption that direct problem solving is always the best approach is that it is best to be aggressive.

We contend that it is better to be assertive. Assertiveness is defined as behaviour that shows confidence and firmness, without being unnecessarily forceful or belligerent. Aggressiveness, in contrast, is typified by behaviour that is both strong and hostile to others. Assertive responses to stressors allow effective coping while still considering the effects one's behaviour has on others. Dunahoo *et al.* (1998) found that whereas use of assertive action was associated with lower levels of reported depression and anxiety, aggressive and antisocial action were associated with greater anger. In another study, confrontive coping was positively associated with the existence of psychological symptoms (Folkman *et al.*, 1986b). Lending additional support to the need to consider coping from a communal perspective, Long (1990) found that active coping in the workplace was enhanced when accompanied by assertive action and the perception of interpersonal support in the workplace.

Substituting assertive coping strategies for aggressive ones allows people to cope with their own stressors without harming others in the process. In fact, assertive responding allows one to cope and still be supportive of others. This leads to better interpersonal relations with coworkers, possibly resulting in more opportunities for shared problem solving in the future. In addition, better relations with coworkers are likely to result in more shared resources, both instrumental and emotional, being available to everyone in the future.

> *Assumption 3:* Directness is another quality that is valued in individualistic, Western cultures, thus leading to the assumption that it is always best to be direct. Indirectness is often seen as synonymous with inaction.

However, as discussed earlier, in more communal cultures and subcultures, directness is often considered a negative quality. A more acceptable and valued approach to some problems would involve indirect approaches. Direct action is likely to dishonour or anger others. Indirectness would, on the other hand, allow others to 'save face' or maintain feelings of independence and self-sufficiency. The perception that indirectness is synonymous with inaction is inaccurate. Indirect approaches can, and often do, involve active coping. For instance, Dunahoo *et al.* (1998) found that indirectness was positively associated with active forms of coping.

In addition to approaching stressors indirectly because of differing social values, it is also important to recognize that, even in Western cultures, there are situations where direct action is either inappropriate or impossible. When subordinate employees disagree with their supervisors regarding the best approach for dealing with a workplace problem, it would be self-defeating for the employees to contradict their supervisors' wishes directly. However, there are indirect approaches that could lead to more successful resolution of the problems while still recognizing the supervisors' authority. In one study, coping with workplace stress through use of strategies such as withdrawal, restraint, compromise and ignoring the problem was found to be associated with lower levels of somatic and affective symptomatology (Parkes, 1990). The author interpreted this as suggesting that these suppression strategies were adaptive in low-control situations. Although withdrawal and ignoring the problem would be considered avoidant or passive types of coping, it is possible that restraint and compromise represent indirect means.

There are also situations in which a supervisor may accomplish a lot by approaching a problem indirectly. If the problem is approached in a way that reinforces or increases self-esteem and mastery in the subordinate, while also illustrating appropriate responses, the supervisor can accomplish his or her goals and improve the chances of future problems being solved appropriately by the subordinate.

Assumption 4: It is assumed that being bold and quick to respond is best. Cautious action is seen as weak.

However, a bold, quick response could also be considered impulsive. In a complicated social setting, cautious action is often the best course. Organizations often allude to sports teams as their model, and to the extent that the spontaneous, instinctive play that is necessary in football is carried to the workplace, this myth is perpetuated. Impulsive responses in situations for which all avenues of action have not been fully considered show poor judgement and may result in ineffective and possibly negative consequences.

On the other hand, cautiously considering one's options and proceeding only after weighing the alternatives is likely to result in more control over subsequent events and more efficient coping. Planful problem solving has been found to be negatively correlated with psychological symptomatology (Folkman *et al.*, 1986b). Similarly, while cautious coping was positively associated with social joining and support seeking, making it a prosocial active coping strategy, it was negatively associated with avoidance, illustrating that being cautious is not the same thing as failing to act (Dunahoo *et al.*, 1998). Furthermore, the same authors found that use of instinctive action as a means of coping was associated with higher levels of depression, while use of cautious action guarded against depression and anxiety at higher stress levels.

Assumption 5: The final assumption that will be addressed here is that people should not be too emotional. An implied component of this assumption is that women are too emotional.

Emotionality is typically assumed to interfere with rational responses. Thus, it follows that, if women are assumed to be too emotional, women are also irrational. However, we would contend that emotions are not always a handicap. Being aware of and comfortable with one's own emotions, as well as with the emotions of others, may allow one to cope more effectively with one's own problems. In addition, this awareness and comfort may permit one to better empathize and support others who are in distress, thus allowing everyone involved to participate more effectively in all types of interpersonal interactions, be they professional or social. In addition, consideration of the emotional side of an issue allows a broader conceptualization. Rather than limiting attention to only the cognitive and behavioural aspects of the situation, all three dimensions of people's lives receive consideration. This broader evaluation of stressful events may allow a more accurate assessment of the situational constraints, and thus result in more flexible, adaptive coping. Both of these issues have been addressed previously.

Although only a few assumptions regarding coping behaviour have been presented here, it is hoped that the process of presenting alternative concepts to each of these assumptions has been illustrative. The assumptions in our society are often mirrored in scientific research. These assumptions are often as Eurocentrically-biased as they are male-biased, thus leading to pejorative portrayals of Afrocentric, Hispanic and Asian cultures as well as women. Consideration of coping from both a communal as well as an individualistic perspective should allow the positive aspects of both perspectives to be valued, rather than valuing one perspective over the other.

16.13   IMPLICATIONS FOR INTERVENTION

A more communal perspective has indeed already entered the workplace, albeit in ways that have not been obviously attributed to this approach. These workplace changes are communal in that they recognize that individuals are not isolated from families, but rather are integral members of their family. They also tie the workplace and family into a common set of goals, recognizing that satisfaction and well-being in one sphere spread to the other sphere. Specifically, if a job interferes with or threatens an individual's other spheres and valued roles, the work is considered in a negative light because it affects the individual's sense of self-identity (Grandey, Cordeiro & Crouter, 2005). Therefore, if individuals feel that their job is congruent with those roles that make up their self-identity, then they may be more satisfied and this is likely to impact all aspects of their lives.

Among the most important workplace changes that promote the concept of self-identity and employee well-being are flexi-time and flexi-place. Flexi-time allows workers to alter their schedules, usually ensuring that the maximum number of employees is available at central times of the day in order to aid communication and meetings. Employees can come to work later and stay later, or come to work earlier and leave earlier. Flexi-place has been afforded increased interest by employers with the significant advances in technology and use of computers and because many employees can work out of their homes or satellite offices. This reduces commuter time and workplace expenses for utilities (e.g., energy costs), square footage and furnishings. The press for these changes has increased as women enter the workplace, but is advantageous for both men and women, especially given the high percentage of dual-career families. A study by Winett *et al.* (1982) indicated that employees derived increased satisfaction from such changes, and this can easily translate to less burnout and greater loyalty to their employers. Given expected ongoing shortage of skilled workers, employers should take heed of these changes, as maintaining a satisfied workforce is critical if employers take the term *human resources* seriously.

Changes in laws in the USA allowing individuals to take leave time for care of an ill family member is another communally based policy. It allows employees to maintain their connections with the family and the workplace, rather than placing borders between them. It is instructive how aggressively businesses fought this change and lobbied against it. Increased attention to maternity leave, extending paternity leave options and protection of females who are pregnant from losing their positions are other policy changes that have been instituted successfully. This said, our experience with workers suggests that although such policies are allowed, employers often place those who take them (women or men) on a 'mommy track' in which they are less seriously regarded for promotion and opportunities or responsibilities that might increase the chances of promotion. It has been shown that policies and arrangements endorsing a balance between work and family are essential for employees; however, simply making the options available for individuals is not enough. It is critical to increase employees' rights and entitlement to take advantage of those options without unspoken repercussions (Kinnunen *et al.*, 2006).

What has not changed in the workplace is the individualistic attitude that accompanies the 'survival of the fittest' mentality. In this regard, there continues to be an emphasis placed on individualistic styles of coping related to aggressiveness and even antisocial action. Many Western companies, particularly in the USA, seem to subscribe to a policy of team play. However, it is unclear how they apply this. Rewards are almost uniformly given for individualistic effort and goal attainment, rather than goal attainment by the group. There appears to be very little 'team play' in the team concept.

In basketball terms, it is clear how points for making baskets are tallied, but not how 'assists' are recorded and rewarded. But it is assists that result in wins (Melnick, 2001).

In workshops, one of us (S.E.H.) often asks business executives to recall what caused the basketball team, the Chicago Bulls, to win. Respondents, believing themselves knowledgeable about sports, uniformly answer, 'When Michael Jordan scored points'. The answer is incorrect, as the Bulls tended to lose when Jordan scored big. Rather, they won when he had a balance of points scored and assists made. Assists are when you set up another player to score. It is a critical statistic because it reflects not only points scored, but increasing team motivation. In discussions about how their business scores assists, executives usually state that this is done informally, or not at all. They want to play as a team, but do not apply the metaphor to practice. Yet, it is clear that supportive work climates which emphasize teamwork produce a less stressed and more involved workforce (Shadur *et al.*, 1999).

Communal intervention implies teaching the use of 'cautious action', where the feelings and honour of others is considered paramount. It implies the need to train workers in social joining. This form of coping encourages people to aid others and willingly seek aid of others.

To the extent that individualistic models prevail, this will be viewed as a sign of weakness, rather than strength. The change from one way of coping to the other is fundamental to the cultural milieu of the workplace, and is not easily achieved without directed, thoughtful intervention.

Readers will note that some of these differences are already characteristic of the workplace in some European countries. In that regard, the more socialist leanings of the workplace in Europe have been feared in the USA, with its tradition of rugged individualism. The legal protections afforded workers in such countries as the Netherlands and Sweden are much more communally oriented than what is afforded in the US workplace. Comparing to Japan, these protections may be more cultural, and do not even require laws to uphold them (Fukuyama, 1995).

16.14 CONCLUSIONS

Future research on stress and coping among women in the workplace will need to change along with the changing roles that women are adopting. Just as the workplace inevitably will be altered by the increased representation of women, so too will psychological investigation have to adopt new perspectives that change the basic assumptions of our approach to the study of workplace stress. Just as inevitably, this will also influence men's workplace coping and the way we look at men, as they will also need to adjust and adapt to new cultural imperatives.

Our principal thesis is that work will become more communal, and the communal aspects of work that have always existed will become more evident. Instead of viewing successful coping with the challenges of work as dependent on individualistic problem solving, we must gain a perspective that includes both individual and collectivist effort. Masquerading as an action orientation, there has been an accompanying set of behaviours that include aggressive and antisocial action, instinctive 'shoot from the hip' responses and indirect, antisocial strategies. Whereas the action aspects of this orientation have been well regarded, the negative companion array of behaviours has been ignored. At the same time, communal action, sensitivity to emotions of the self and others, cautious planning and reasoned action that takes the needs of others into consideration have been demeaned. Even where past research evidence has been available to challenge the 'men's club' climate in our literature review, it is apparent that this evidence has hardly influenced the way in which researchers construe coping in the workplace.

It appears that psychology has adopted similar agenic, male models of seeing the world as has the field of business. This has influenced not only our results and our interpretations, but also the very questions that we ask. When conducting workshops on these topics in business settings, we found that participants uniformly saw team play as integral to work success and productivity. However, when asked how their companies scored 'assists' of others in meeting their objectives no one noted their company as evaluating this aspect of behaviour. Similarly, when asked if supervisees were allowed to rate and give feedback to their supervisors (translate to team captains) on their supportive behaviour (or lack thereof), a similar silence was experienced. Given this climate, it is no wonder that limited collectivist styles of coping are chanced by employees. Indeed, many participants reported that when they acted communally by covering for each other's absences or *faux pas*, it was done covertly, because such behaviour was officially discouraged or even punished.

Finally, we raise an ethical, value-laden question. In studying the workplace, who is our client and what are our responsibilities? If we discover that communal aspects of coping are palliative for individuals and even lead to workplace productivity and satisfaction, are we bound to advocate these models and confront the male-dominated culture that is omnipresent? Is there a place for our role as social change agents? We cannot attempt to remain safely outside of the fray; failing to make a choice on this issue is not a value-free alternative, because it supports a certain set of values that exists in the status quo. Many psychological consultants have learned that to be invited back to the workplace we must please the purchaser of our services, i.e., senior management – most typically composed of males of a certain social class, ethnicity and culture. This potentially leads to our serving their value system. Because the senior echelons of our universities resemble the workplaces in which we study and consult in terms of their individualistic, male predominance, this is an especially sensitive issue. We must be introspective enough to realize that it has only been with the rise of women in academia that these questions have been posed.

REFERENCES

Akabas, S.A. (1988). Women, work and mental health: room for improvement. *Journal of Primary Prevention*, **9**, 130–40.

Barnett, R.C. & Baruch, G.K. (1985). Women's involvement in multiple roles, and psychological distress. *Journal of Personality and Social Psychology*, **49**, 135–45.

Barnett, R.C. & Baruch, G.K. (1987). Social roles, gender, and psychological distress. In R.C. Barnett, L. Biener & G.K. Baruch (Eds), *Gender and Stress* (pp. 122–43). New York: Free Press.

Barnett, R.C. & Hyde, J.S. (2001). Women, men, work, and family: an expansionist theory. *American Psychologist*, **56**, 781–96.

Barnett, R.C., Marshal, N.C., Raudenbush, S.W. & Brennan, R.T. (1993). Gender and the relationship between job experiences and psychological distress: a study of dual-earner couples. *Journal of Personality and Social Psychology*, **64**, 794–806.

Baruch, G.K. & Barnett, R.C. (1986). Role quality, multiple role involvement and psychological well-being in midlife women. *Journal of Personality and Social Psychology*, **5**, 578–85.

Baruch, G.K., Biener, L. & Barnett, R.C. (1987). Women and gender research on work and family stress. *American Psychologist*, **42**, 130–6.

Beutell, N. & Greenhaus, J. (1986). Balancing acts: work–family conflict and the dual career couple. In L.L. Moore (Ed.), *Not As Far As You Think: The Realities of Working Women* (pp. 149–62). Lexington, MA: Lexington Books.

Bhatnagar, D. (1988). Professional women in organizations: new paradigms for research and action. *Sex Roles: A Journal of Research*, **18**, 343–55.

Biener, L., Abrams, D.B., Follick, M.J. & Hitti, J.R. (1986). Gender differences in smoking and quitting. Paper presented at the Society for Behavioral Research Meetings, San Francisco, CA.

Billings, A.G. & Moos, R.H. (1982). Work stress and the stress-buffering roles of work and family resources. *Journal of Occupational Behavior*, **3**, 215–32.

Billings, A.G. & Moos, R.H. (1984). Coping, stress and social resources among adults with unipolar depression. *Journal of Personality and Social Psychology*, **46**, 877–91.

Blumberg, R.L. (Ed.) (1991). *Gender, Family, and Economy: The Triple Overlap.* Newbury Park, CA: Sage.

Carlson, D.S. & Perrewé, P.L. (1999). The role of social support in the stressor-strain relationship: an examination of work–family conflict. *Journal of Management*, **25**, 513–40.

Carver, C.S., Scheier, M.F. & Weintraub, J.K. (1989). Assessing coping strategies: a theoretically based approach. *Journal of Personality and Social Psychology*, **56**, 267–83.

Cheng, Y., Kawachi, I., Coakley, E.H., Schwartz, J. & Colditz, G. (2000). Association between psychosocial work characteristics and health functioning in American women: prospective study. *British Medical Journal*, **320**, 1432–6.

Cohen, S. & McKay, G. (1985). Social support, stress and the buffering hypothesis: a theoretical analysis. In A. Baum, S.E. Taylor & J. Singer (Eds), *Handbook of Psychology and Health* (pp. 253–67). Hillsdale, NJ: Lawrence Erlbaum.

Compas, B.E., Malcarne, V.L. & Fondacaro, K.M. (1988). Coping with stressful events in older children and young adolescents. *Journal of Consulting and Clinical Psychology*, **56**, 405–11.

Cowan, A.L. (1989). Poll finds women's gains have been taking a personal toll. *New York Times*, August 21, pp. 1, 8.

Cutrona, C.E. (1990). Stress and social support – in search of optimal matching. *Journal of Social and Clinical Psychology*, **9**, 3–14.

Dressler, W.W. (1985). Extended family relationships, social support and mental health in a southern black community. *Journal of Health and Social Behavior*, **26**, 39–48.

Dunahoo, C.L., Monnier, J., Hobfoll, S.E., Hulszier, M.R. & Johnson, R. (1998). There's more than rugged individualism in coping. Part 1: even the Lone Ranger had Tonto. *Anxiety Stress and Coping*, **11**, 137–65.

Dunkell-Schetter, C. & Skokan, L.A. (1990). Determinants of social support provision in personal relationships. *Journal of Social and Personal Relationships*, **7**, 437–50.

Dunkel-Schetter, C., Folkman, S. & Lazarus, R.S. (1987). Correlates of social support receipt. *Journal of Personality and Social Psychology*, **53**, 71–80.

Eagly, A.H., Makhijani, M.G. & Klonsky, B.G. (1992). Gender and the evaluations of leaders: a meta-analysis. *Psychological Bulletin*, **111**, 3–22.

Endler, N.S. & Parker, J.D.A. (1990). Multidimensional assessment of coping: a critical evaluation. *Journal of Personality and Social Psychology*, **58**, 844–54.

Etzion, D. (1984). Moderating effect of social support on the stress–burnout relationship. *Journal of Applied Psychology*, **69**, 615–22.

Folkman, S. & Lazarus, R.S. (1980). An analysis of coping in a middle-aged community sample. *Journal of Health and Social Behavior*, **21**, 219–39.

Folkman, S. & Lazarus, R.S. (1985). If it changes, it must be a process: study of emotion and coping during three stages of a college examination. *Journal of Personality and Social Psychology*, **48**, 150–70.

Folkman, S., Lazarus, R.S., Dunkel-Schetter, C., DeLongis, A. & Gruen, R.J. (1986a). Dynamics of a stressful encounter: cognitive appraisal, coping, and encounter outcomes. *Journal of Personality and Social Psychology*, **50**, 992–1003.

Folkman, S., Lazarus, R.S., Gruen, R.J. & DeLongis, A. (1986b). Appraisal, coping, health, status, and psychological symptoms. *Journal of Personality and Social Psychology*, **50**, 571–9.

Forsythe, C.J. & Compas, B.E. (1987). Interaction of cognitive appraisals of stressful events and coping: testing the goodness of fit hypothesis. *Cognitive Therapy and Research*, **11**, 473–85.

Freedy, J.R., Shaw, D.L., Jarrell, M.P. & Maters, C.R. (1992). Towards an understanding of the psychological impact of natural disasters: an application of the conservation of resources stress model. *Journal of Traumatic Stress*, **5**, 441–54.

Fukuyama, F. (1995). *Trust: The Social Virtues and the Creation of Prosperity*. New York: Free Press.

Geller, P.A. & Hobfoll, S.E. (1993). Gender differences in preference to offer social support to assertive men and women. *Sex Roles: A Journal of Research*, **28**, 419–32.

Geller, P.A. & Hobfoll, S.E. (1994). Gender differences in job stress, tedium, and social support in the workplace. *Journal of Personal and Social Relationships,* **11**, 555–72.

Ginter, G.G., West, J.D. & Zarski, J.J. (1989). Learned resourcefulness and situation-specific coping with stress. *Journal of Psychology,* **123**, 295–304.

Goldberg, W.A., Greenberger, W., Hamill, S. & O'Neil, R. (1992). Role demands in the lives of employed single mothers with preschoolers. *Journal of Family Issues,* **13**, 312–33.

Goode, W. (1960). A theory of strain. *American Sociological Review,* **25**, 483–96.

Gorgievski, M.J. & Hobfoll, S.E. (in press). Work can burn us out or fire us up: conservation of resources in burnout and engagement. In J.R.B. Halbesleben (Ed.), *Handbook of Stress and Burnout in Health Care.* Hauppauge, NY: Nova Science Publishers.

Gove, W.R. & Zeiss, C. (1987). Multiple roles and happiness. In F. Crosby (Ed.), *Spouse, Parent, Worker: On Gender and Multiple Roles* (pp. 87–103). New Haven, CT: Yale University Press.

Grant, J. (1988). Women as managers: what they can offer to organizations. *Organizational Dynamics,* **16**, 56–63.

Grandey, A.A., Cordeiro, B.L. & Crouter, A.C. (2005). A longitudinal and multi-source test of the work-family conflict and job satisfaction relationship. *Journal of Occupational and Organizational Psychology,* **78**, 305–23.

Grossman, H.Y. & Chester, N.L. (Eds) (1990). *The Experience and Meaning of Work in Women's Lives.* Hillsdale, NJ: Lawrence Erlbaum.

Gupta, N., Jenkins A.D., Jr & Beehr, T.A. (1983). Employee gender, gender similarity, and supervisor–subordinate cross-evaluations. *Psychology of Women Quarterly,* **8**, 174–84.

Gutek, B.A., Repetti, R.L. & Silver, D.L. (1988). Nonwork roles and stress at work. In C.L. Cooper & R. Payne (Eds), *Causes, Coping and Consequences of Stress at Work* (pp. 141–74). New York: John Wiley & Sons, Inc.

Haynes, S.G., LaCroix, A.Z. & Lippin, T. (1987). The effect of high job demands and low control on the health of employed women. In J.C. Quick, R. Rasbhagat, J. Dalton & J.D. Quick (Eds), *Work Stress and Health Care* (pp. 93–110). New York: Praeger.

Hobfoll, S. (1988). *The Ecology of Stress.* New York: Hemisphere.

Hobfoll, S.E. & Vaux, A. (1993). Social support: resources and context. In L. Goldberger & S. Breznitz (Eds), *Handbook of Stress: Theoretical and Clinical Aspects* (pp. 685–705). New York: Free Press.

Hobfoll, S.E., Dunahoo, C.L., Ben-Porath, Y. & Monnier, J. (1994). Gender and coping: the dual-axis model of coping. *American Journal of Community,* **22**, 49–82.

Hochschild, A. & Machung, A. (1989). *The Second Shift: Working Parents and the Revolution at Home.* New York: Viking.

House, J.S. (1981). *Work Stress and Social Support.* Reading, MA: Addison-Wesley.

House, J.S. & Wells, J.A. (1978). Occupational stress, social support and health. In A. McLean, G. Black & M. Colligan (Eds), *Reducing Occupational Stress:*

Proceedings of a Conference, HEW publication no. 78-140 (pp. 8–29). Washington, DC: US Government Printing Office.

Jackson, S.E. & Maslach, C. (1982). After-effects of job-related stress: families as victims. *Journal of Occupational Behavior*, **3**, 63–77.

Karasek, R., Baker, D., Marxer, F., Ahlbom, A. & Theorell, T. (1981). Job decision latitude, job demands, and cardiovascular disease: a prospective study of Swedish men. *American Journal of Public Health*, **71**, 694–705.

Karasek, R.A., Theorell, T., Schwartz, J.E., Schnall, P.L., Pieper, C. & Michela, J.L. (1987). Job characteristics in relation to the prevalence of myocardial infarction in the US Health Examination Survey and the First National Health and Nutrition Examination Survey, manuscript, Columbia University.

Kessler, R.C. & McRae, J.A., Jr (1982). The effect of wives' employment on the mental health of married men and women. *American Sociological Review*, **47**, 216–27.

Kessler, R.C., McLeod, J.D. & Wethington, E. (1985). The costs of caring: a perspective on the relationship between sex and psychological distress. In I.G. Sarason & B.R. Sarason (Eds), *Social Support: Theory Research and Application* (pp. 491–506). Dordrecht: Martinus Nijhoff.

Kim, J. (1994). The executive wage gap: where women stand. *Working Woman*, January, 31.

Kim, M. (1989). Gender bias in compensation structures: a case study of its historical basis and persistence. *Journal of Social Issues*, **45**, 39–50.

Kinnunen, U., Geurts, S. & Mauno, S. (2004). Work-to-family conflict and its relationship with satisfaction and well-being: a one-year longitudinal study on gender differences. *Work and Stress*, **18**(1), 1–22.

Kinnunen, U., Feldt, T., Geurts, S. & Pulkkinen, L. (2006). Types of work–family interface: well-being correlates of negative and positive spillover between work and family. *Scandinavian Journal of Psychology*, **47**, 149–62.

LaCroix, A.Z. & Haynes, S.G. (1984). Occupational exposure to high demand/low control work and coronary heart disease incidence in the Framingham cohort. Paper presented at the 17th Annual Meeting of the Society for epidemiologic Research, Houston, Texas. *American Journal of Epidemiology*, **120**, 481 (abstract).

Lane, C. & Hobfoll, S.E. (1992). How loss affects anger and alienates potential support. *Journal of Clinical and Consulting Psychology*, **60**, 935–42.

LaRocco, J.M. & Jones, A.P. (1978). Co-worker and leader support as moderators of stress–strain relationships in work situations. *Journal of Applied Psychology*, **63**, 629–34.

LaRocco, J.M., House, J.S. & French, J.R.P., Jr (1980). Social support, occupational stress, and health. *Journal of Health and Social Behavior*, **21**, 202–18.

Lazarus, R.S. (1966). *Psychological Stress and the Coping Process*. New York: McGraw-Hill.

Lazarus, R.S. & Folkman, S. (1984). *Stress, Appraisal and Coping*. New York: Springer-Verlag.

Leana, C.R. & Feldman, D.C. (1991). Gender differences in responses to unemployment. *Journal of Vocational Behavior*, **38**, 65–77.

Long, B.C. (1990). Relation between coping strategies, sex-typed traits, and environmental characteristics: a comparison of male and female managers. *Journal of Counseling Psychology*, **37**, 185–94.

Long, B.C., Kahn S.E. & Schutz, R.W. (1992). Causal model of stress and coping: women in management. *Journal of Counseling Psychology*, **39**, 227–39.

Lott, B. (1985). The devaluation of women's competence. *Journal of Social Issues*, **41**, 43–60.

Marks, S.R. (1977). Multiple roles and role strain: some notes on human energy, time and commitment. *American Sociological Review*, **41**, 921–36.

Martin, P.Y., Harrison, D. & Dinitto, D. (1983). Advancement for women in hierarchical organizations: a multilevel analysis of problems and prospects. *Journal of Applied Behavioral Science*, **19**, 19–23.

Maslach, C. (1982). *Burnout: The Cost of Caring*. Englewood Cliffs, NJ: Prentice Hall.

Mathison, D.L. (1986). Sex differences in the perception of assertiveness among female managers. *Journal of Social Psychology*, **126**, 559–606.

McCrae, R.R. & Costa, P.T. (1986). Personality, coping, and coping effectiveness in an adult sample. *Journal of Personality*, **54**, 385–405.

McLaughlin, M., Cormier, L.S. & Cormier, W.H. (1988). Relation between coping strategies and distress, stress, and marital adjustment of multiple-role women. *Journal of Counseling Psychology*, **35**, 187–93.

Melnick, M.J. (2001). Relationship between team assists and win–loss record in the National Basketball Association. *Perceptual and Motor Skills*, **92**, 595–602.

Miller, J. (1980). Individual and occupational determinants of job satisfaction, a focus on gender, differences. *Sociology of Work and Occupations*, **7**, 337–66.

Miller, S.M. & Kirsch, N. (1987). Sex differences in cognitive coping with stress. In R.C. Barnett, L. Biener & G.K. Baruch (Eds), *Gender and Stress* (pp. 278–307). New York: Free Press.

Parkes, K.R. (1990). Coping, negative affectivity, and the work environment: additive and interactive predictors of mental health. *Journal of Applied Psychology*, **75**, 399–409.

Parry, G. (1986). Paid employment, life events, social support, and mental health in working-class mothers. *Journal of Health and Social Behavior*, **27**, 193–208.

Pearlin, L.I. & Schooler, C. (1978). The structure of coping. *Journal of Health and Social Behavior*, **19**, 2–21.

Perry-Jenkins, M. (1993). Family roles and responsibilities: what has changed and what has remained the same. In J. Frankel (Ed.), *The Employed Mother and the Family Context* (pp. 245–59). New York: Springer.

Perry-Jenkins, M. & Crouter, A.C. (1990). Men's provider-role attitudes: Implications for household work and marital satisfaction. *Journal of Family Issues*, **11**, 136–56.

Pines, A.M. & Aronson, E. (with D. Kafry) (1981). *Burnout: From Tedium to Personal Growth*. New York: Free Press.

Pleck, J.H. (1985). *Working Wives/Working Husbands*. Newbury Park, CA: Sage.

Powell, G.N. (1988). *Women and Men in Management*. Newbury Park, CA: Sage.

Radecki, C. & Jennings J. (1980). Sex as a status variable in work settings: female and male reports of dominance behavior. *Journal of Applied Social Psychology*, **10**, 71–85.

Reis, H.T., Senchak, M. & Solomon, B. (1985). Sex differences in the intimacy of social interaction: further examination of potential explanations. *Journal of Personality and Social Psychology*, **48**, 1204–17.

Repetti, R.L., Matthews, K.A. & Waldron, I. (1989). Employment and women's health. *American Psychologist*, **44**, 1394–401.

Riger, S. (1993). What's wrong with empowerment? *American Journal of Community Psychology*, **21**, 279–92.

Rodin, J. & Ickovics, J.R. (1990). Women's health: review and research agenda as we approach the 21st century. *American Psychologist*, **45**, 1018–34.

Rosenfield, D. & Stephan, W.G. (1978). Sex differences in attributions for sex-typed tasks. *Journal of Personality*, **46**, 244–59.

Ross, C.E., Mirowsky, J. & Huber, J. (1983). Dividing work, sharing work, and in-between. *American Sociological Review*, **48**, 809–23.

Roth, S. & Cohen, L.J. (1986). Approach, avoidance, and coping with stress. *American Psychologist*, **41**, 813–19.

Rotondo, D.M., Carlson, D.S. & Kincaid, J.F. (2003). Coping with multiple dimensions of work–family conflict. *Personnel Review*, **32**, 275–96.

Sampson, E.E. (1993). *Justice and the Critique of Pure Psychology*. New York: Plenum Press.

Sarason, I.G., Levine, H.M., Basham, R.B. & Sarason, B.R. (1983). Assessing social support: the social support questionnaire. *Journal of Personality and Social Psychology*, **44**, 127–39.

Schaufeli, W.B. & Bakker, A.B. (2004). Job demands, job resources, and their relationship with burnout and engagement: a multi-sample study. *Journal of Organizational Behavior*, **25**, 293–315.

Schwarzer, R. & Schwarzer, C. (1996). Critical survey of coping instruments. In M. Zeidner & N. Endler (Eds), *Handbook of Coping* (pp. 107–32). New York: John Wiley & Sons, Inc.

Shadur, M.A., Kienzle, R. & Rodwell, J.J. (1999). The relationship between organizational climate and employee perceptions of involvement: the importance of support. *Group and Organization Management*, **24**, 479–503.

Sieber, S.D. (1974). Toward a theory of role accumulation. *American Sociological Review*, **39**, 567–78.

Simon, R. (1992). Parental role strains, salience of parental identity and gender differences in psychological distress. *Journal of Health and Social Behavior*, **33**, 25–35.

Stone, A.A. & Neale, J.M. (1984). New measure of daily coping: development and preliminary results. *Journal of Personality and Social Psychology*, **46**, 892–906.

Thoits, P.A. (1983). Multiple identities and psychological well-being. *American Sociological Review*, **48**, 174–87.

Thoits, P.A. (1992). Identity structures and psychological well-being: gender and mental status comparisons. Sociology Department, Vanderbilt University, Nashville, TN.

Triandis, H.C., McCusker, C. & Hui, C.H. (1990). Multimethod probes of individualism and collectivism. *Journal of Personality and Social Psychology*, **59**, 1006–20.

Verbrugge, L.M. (1982). Women's social roles and health. In P. Berman & E. Ramey (Eds), *Women: A Developmental Perspective*, publication no. 82-2298. Washington, DC: US Government Printing Office.

Vitaliano, P.P., Maiuro, R.D., Russo, J. & Becker, J. (1987). Raw versus relative scores in the assessment of coping strategies. *Journal of Behavioral Medicine*, **10**, 1–18.

Vitaliano, P.P., Maiuro, R.D., Russo, J., Katon, W., DeWolfe, D. & Hall, G. (1990). Coping profiles associated with psychiatric, physical health, work, and family problems. *Health Psychology*, **9**, 348–76.

Weisz, J.R., Rothbaum, F.M. & Blackburn, T.C. (1984). Swapping recipes of control. *American Psychologist*, **39**, 974–5.

Wethington, E. & Kessler, R.C. (1989). Employment, parental responsibility and psychological distress: a longitudinal study of married women. *Journal of Family Issues*, **10**, 527–46.

Winett, R.A., Neale, M.S. & Williams, K.R. (1982). The effects of flexible work schedules on urban families with young children: quasi-experimental, ecological studies. *American Journal of Community Psychology*, **10**, 49–64.

CHAPTER 17

Employee Assistance Programs: A Research-Based Primer

Mark Attridge

Attridge Studios, Minneapolis, USA

17.1   INTRODUCTION

Employee Assistance Programs (EAPs) are an important part of many organizations. This chapter features a review of the literature to provide a research-based overview of EAPs and their role in supporting the mental health and work performance of employees. Many aspects of EAPs are presented in this chapter, including what defines an EAP, the history of the field, the scope of EAP services, what makes EAPs unique, the market prevalence of EAPs, utilization, outcomes, the return on investment (ROI) for EAPs, and future trends. But first the business need for EAPs is examined to understand why these programs were initially developed and why they continue to flourish.

17.2   WORKPLACE MENTAL HEALTH AND ADDICTIONS

17.2.1   Why are EAPs Needed?

Comprehensive reviews of the research literature on workplace mental health abound, including reports by researchers (Brun *et al.*, 2003; Kahn & Langlieb, 2003), business groups and consultants (American Psychiatric Association, 2006; National Business Group on Health/Finch & Phillips, 2005; Watson Wyatt Worldwide, 2007), the Canadian government (Larson *et al.*, 2007), the

International Handbook of Work and Health Psychology, Third Edition. Edited by Cary L. Cooper, James Campbell Quick, and Marc J. Schabracq.

United States government (DHSS, 1999; Masi *et al.*, 2004), the European Union (McDaid, 2008), and the World Health Organization (WHO; Hyman *et al.*, 2006). There are a number of conclusions from these reviews that support the need for more employer attention to workplace mental health and addiction issues and thus also to the need for EAP services:

- Mental health disorders and addictions are widely experienced among working-age populations. An estimated one in four adults have a diagnosable mental disorder, one in five adults have an alcohol use problem, and one in eight adults have a drug or other kind of addiction.
- Many people with mental health disorders and addictions suffer from chronic medical conditions (such as heart disease, asthma, diabetes and hypertension).
- Over a third of people with alcohol and drug addictions have a high rate of also having another kind of addiction or mental disorder.
- Untreated mental health disorders and addictions can damage the individual in many ways, such as an increased risk of illness, personal problems, incidents at work or school and even family breakdown.
- Employees with untreated mental health and substance abuse disorders can lead to problems for their employers, such as poor customer relations, absenteeism, diminished work quality and performance, on-the-job accidents and disability claims, work-group morale issues and turnover.
- Society also bears the burden of consequences related to mental health, alcohol and drugs, all of which add up to hundreds of billions of dollars in economic costs in terms of lost work productivity, health care services use, law enforcement and other areas.
- Many kinds of treatments have been proven to be both clinically effective and cost-effective, but sadly most people with mental health or addiction disorders never see a professional care provider for treatment.

> The majority of adults with mental health disorders and addictions in the United States and Canada are under-diagnosed, under-treated or get no treatment at all (Green-Hennessy, 2002; Statistics Canada, 2003).

The implications of this alarming evidence are not lost on some employers. Savvy business leaders recognize the critical role that mental health factors play in the overall success of their company. This understanding has guided the development of a new approach to the design of employee health benefits called *Health and Productivity Management* (Kramer & Rickert, 2006; Loeppke *et al.*, 2007). For example, a recent survey of senior human resources (HR) executives found that mental health is now considered the number one driver of indirect business costs, such as lost productivity and absence (Employee Benefit News, 2007). This is important because these indirect kinds of costs are typically far greater than the direct costs that most employers are naively so concerned about, like health care costs and insurance claims (Goetzel, 2007; Kessler *et al.*, 2003, 2004).

17.3 PROFILE OF EMPLOYEE ASSISTANCE PROGRAMS

Many employers have responded to mental health and addictions in the workplace by implementing Employee Assistance Programs. Let us now examine the nature of EAPs.

17.3.1 Definition: What are EAPs?

EAPs are employer-sponsored programs designed to alleviate and assist in eliminating a variety of workplace problems. Employee Assistance Programs typically provide screening, assessments, brief interventions and outpatient counselling for mental health and addictions problems as part of their basic services offered to client organizations. The source of these employee problems can be either personal (legal, financial, marital or family-related, mental health problems and illnesses, including addiction) or work-related (conflict on the job, harassment, violence, stress, etc.). EAPs are a field of practice composed of multidisciplinary professionals including social workers, psychologists, professional counsellors, substance abuse counsellors and nurses.

> An EAP is a worksite-based program designed to assist organizations in addressing productivity issues and employee clients in identifying and resolving personal concerns, including health, marital, family, financial, alcohol, drug, legal, emotional, stress, or other personal issues that may affect job performance (Employee Assistance Professionals Association, 2003).

17.3.2 History: Where Did EAPs Come From?

EAPs were originally established in the 1940s to address alcohol abuse and its impact on the workplace. These early EAPs, or Occupational Alcohol Programs (OAPs) as they were originally called, helped companies to identify troubled employees and support them through the process of recovery and return to work (Trice & Schonbrunn, 2003). The US federal government promoted OAPs through legislation such as the Hughes Act of 1970, which required all federal agencies and military installations to have an OAP and its amendment in 1972 to include drug abuse (Jacobson & Kominoth, 2009). In the 1970s, OAPs realized their services had to address more than just alcohol and drug abuse. During this period many OAP professionals belonged to the *Association of Labor/Management Administrators and Consultants on Alcoholism* (ALMACA).

During the 1980s, EAPs became more popular in the United States and Canada. At this point the mix of services offered expanded to build on the focus of OAPs to feature more comprehensive elements. The field also grew through the activity of two major professional organizations: the *Employee Assistance Professionals Association* (EAPA; which evolved from ALMACA) and the *Employee Assistance Society of North America* (EASNA; which has a strong Canadian influence). When the drug-free workplace legislation was passed in 1988 in the United States, EAPs continued to grow in importance as they became vital to businesses by providing expertise and guidance to employers regarding the management of employees with addictions.

In the 1990s, EAPs became a standard component of employee benefits at the majority of large companies. EAPs responded to this growth in market penetration and the greater demands of new clients by broadening their menu of services to address issues such as work/life balance, elder care, workplace violence, drug testing and supporting company-wide changes such as mergers and downsizing. In the 2000s, EAPs continue to evolve with the rapidly changing American workplace (see final section of this chapter on trends for EAPs). Today, the number of members in the two major professional associations exceeds 5000 and is growing worldwide.

17.3.3   Scope of Services: What do EAPs do?

The primary job of an EAP professional is to meet privately with employees or their family members to identify and resolve workplace, mental health, physical health, marital, family, personal addictions or alcohol, or emotional issues that affect a worker's job performance. These kinds of cases typically comprise about two-thirds of all cases at an EAP. The most common initial reason for seeking help from an EAP is for personal relationships/marital issues. Most EAPs also offer consultative and educational services around legal and financial issues that affect employees (Wilburn, 2007). Other aspects of an EAP include services that support individual supervisors with their management and work team problems – these are called 'management consultations' – as well as more strategic consulting around organizational change and workforce development issues (Hyde, 2008). EAPs offer preventative and immediate response services for crisis and workplace critical incidents (Everly & Mitchell, 2008).

Program type

In the beginning, almost all EAPs were 'internal programs', in which EAP professionals worked for the same company that they supported. These kinds of EAPs are still common within large companies, universities and the public sector. However, the more prevalent type of EAP today is the 'external program', which has a staff of EAP professionals who are employed by an independent company and supply contracted EAP services to other companies. External EAPs hire counsellor affiliates (part-time or full-time licensed mental health professionals within the community) to provide the majority of telephonic or face-to-face clinical services. External types of EAPs are cost-effective for companies with employees at worksites in different geographical areas. There is a third type, called Blended EAPs, in which the company has a few key EAP managerial staff and this group works with an external EAP vendor to provide the counsellors and other services (Turner, Weiner & Keegan, 2005).

17.3.4   The Core Technology: What makes EAPs Unique?

There are several aspects of EAPs that contribute to their unique role in employee benefits and the larger health care system. Such attributes include how the EAP is accessed, the focus of the EAP on restoring employee work performance, specialization in alcohol and drug addiction problems and being responsive to difficult issues or incidents that affect the workplace.

Confidential, free, and immediate access

Arguably, the most essential function of a successful EAP is its ability to provide confidential services, free of charge, when needed to employees and, oftentimes, their family members. Additionally, EAP services are voluntary, and most employees who use EAP services do so through self-referrals. Virtually all EAPs feature some form of 24-hour assistance every day of the year. This is accomplished through advanced telephone and web-based technologies. Knowing that this help is always available can be reassuring to employees and supervisors.

Core technology

The EAP core technology, developed by Paul Roman and Terry Blum over 20 years ago, represents the essential components of employee assistance

Table 17.1   EAP core technology components

Core technology component

1   The identification of employees' behavioural problems includes assessment of job performance issues (tardiness, absence, productivity, work relationships, safety, etc.)
2   The evaluation of employees' success with use of EAP service is judged primarily on the basis of improvement in job performance issues
3   Provision of expert consultation to supervisors, managers and union stewards on how to use EAP policy and procedures for both employee problems and for management issues
4   Availability and appropriate use of constructive confrontation techniques by EAP for employees with alcohol or substance abuse problems
5   The creation and maintenance of micro-linkages with counselling, treatment and other community resources (for successful referral of individual EAP cases)
6   The creation and maintenance of macro-linkages between the work organization and counselling, treatment and other community resources (for appropriate role and use of EAP)
7   A focus on employees' alcohol and other substance abuse problems

(Roman & Blum, 1985, 1988; Roman, 1990). There are seven components (See Table 17.1). The key is for the EAP counsellor to assess how an employee's concern – or presenting problem – is affecting the workplace and his or her ability to function at work. The EAP counsellor is trained to help the employee to identify the stressors that impact work and determine how the person can better cope with the situation. This 'work-function' perspective, while central for EAPs, may or may not be shared by other mental health providers in the community or outpatient network who may elect not to focus on work issues when treating a client. Another core component is to have the EAP staff work closely with the company in order to train managers and supervisors on how to successfully engage the EAP and to understand the larger issues of importance to the organization. It is critical for the EAP staff to know the range of resources available to assist employees from within the company and from the surrounding local community. Even though it was first introduced more than 20 years ago, a recent survey conducted this year found that the vast majority of professionals active in the EA field today (85%) were familiar with the EAP core technology (Bennett & Attridge, 2008).

Alcohol and drug issues

In 1990, the seventh component of the EAP core technology was added (Roman, 1990). This component harkens back to the days of OAPs and places a strong emphasis on screening and assessments for alcohol and drug issues. The workplace offers a useful context for the identification and referral for individuals with drinking and drug abuse problems (Roman & Blum, 2002). The EAP can provide confidential services to management and staff workers with substance use disorders and associated mental health disorders. This typically means being directly involved in providing screening, referring employees for treatment and offering follow-up care and support during recovery. In such cases, sometimes the political leverage that comes from the EAP counsellor being affiliated with the employer can help employees with substance troubles to get into treatment in order to keep their job. This process can also use what has been called 'constructive confrontation', in which the EAP professional leads others at the company in a coordinated intervention with the person in trouble from alcohol or drug abuse. Thus, by offering access to an EAP, an employer can be more successful in reducing harm from the misuse of alcohol and other drugs by having a dedicated and experienced resource available and ready to support the company's alcohol and drug policy.

Crisis

EAPs can also deliver unique value in their ability to increase awareness of, and preparedness for, traumatic incidents and the kinds of serious workplace problems to which managers are not comfortable in responding on their own, such as natural disasters, workplace bullying and violence, domestic abuse, fatal on-the-job accidents and suicide (Paul & Thompson, 2006). Avoiding a lawsuit from a critical incident or effectively dealing with sensitive human resources issues can be a value trump card for an EAP.

17.3.5 Market Penetration: How Many Companies have an EAP?

Due in part to this unique mission and their relatively low cost, EAPs are now widely adopted across North America. EAPs have become the primary channel for many workers to get their first access to mental health care and addiction treatment services, particularly in unionized environments and medium to larger size organizations (Csiernik, 2002). For example, in the regional province of Ontario, Canada during the period of 1989 to 2003, the number of employer organizations with an EAP doubled – going from 28% to 67% (Macdonald et al., 2007). A more recent 2006 national survey of Canadians found that half of workers (50%) had access to an EAP where they worked (Desjardins Financial Security, 2006).

The figures on EAP market penetration are similar in the United States. In 1985, about 31% of companies in the United States had an EAP and this had risen to 33% in 1995 (Hartwell *et al.*, 1996). In the next seven years, this figure had almost doubled. A 2002–3 national survey in the United States revealed that 60% of full-time workers were employed in settings with an EAP (Roman & Blum, 2004). In 2007, about three-quarters of all businesses in the United States had an EAP (Employee Benefit News, 2007). Similar findings come from the most recent Society for Human Resources Management Survey of Employer Benefits [SHRM] (2008). It found that in 2008 three- quarters of businesses in the United States (75%) offered EAP services to their employees. This figure is up slightly from five years earlier, when it was 70% in the 2004 SHRM survey. However, in 2008 as in past years, having an EAP varied substantially based on company size, ranging from 52% for small employers (1–99 staff), 76% for medium employers (100–499 staff), and 89% for large employers (500+ staff)(SHRM, 2008). Today, well over 100 million American workers have access to an EAP (Masi *et al.*, 2004).

17.3.6   Utilization: How often are EAPs used?

Utilization rates for an EAP are commonly measured by a metric that compares the total number of people who use the EAP for a clinical issue (which is primarily employees but also includes some spouses and dependants) to the total number of employees active at the company the EAP supports. For many years the typical EAP clinical case utilization rate has been between 5% and 10% of the number of total employees at the company (Amaral, 2005). The amount of contact with the EAP service is actually much higher that the clinical case utilization rate would suggest, as each individual case can have multiple sessions (or calls) with an EAP counsellor. The average number of counselling sessions used by an employee with access to a six-session maximum model is about four sessions (Jacobson & Hosford-Lamb, 2008). EAPs with a telephonic-based external program model tend to have an average number of contacts per case that is even lower.

Although 5% use among all employees may not seem that significant, keep in the mind that the relevant group for clinical use of an EAP is really not the entire employee population, but rather it is more appropriately the 10 to 20% or so with mental health disorders, addictions or personal life events in a given 12-month period that merit clinical assistance and direction into community services or professional treatment. Indeed, one would hope that the vast majority of employees at a given company should be healthy and functioning well enough *not* to need the EAP. Depending on the rate of turnover at a company, the cumulative use rate for an EAP over a number of years is even higher, as an employee may use it one year and not need to do so again for several years. For example, a 2006 survey found that about one in 10 workers (11%) with access to an EAP had used ever it (Desjardins Financial Security, 2006).

In addition, about 10 to 20% of the total caseload of all EAP users is of a much different nature than those who need assistance for their own personal or family issues. These other kinds of EAP users are supervisors who need help to better manage a worksite issue or other staff needing support after a workplace critical incident. Some EAPs also can have a large slice of their total mix of EAP services devoted to supporting organizational development and more strategic issues at the company (Hyde, 2008). Still others use the EAP in a more preventative mode and seek information and educational materials from the EAP office or website or onsite training workshops. This kind of non-clinical contact can double or triple the total contact use rate for an EAP over just the clinical case rate.

17.4   EAP OUTCOMES AND BUSINESS VALUE

17.4.1   Effectiveness and Outcomes: Do EAPs Help?

All EAPs measure the level of client satisfaction with program services and most find it to be very high (Dersch *et al.*, 2002; Phillips, 2004). For example, one study used an independent survey firm and random sampling techniques to conduct follow-up interviews with over 1,300 cases nationally from an external model EAP. The results revealed that 95% of users reported being satisfied with the EAP service (Attridge, 2003c). But having high levels of client satisfaction is not enough to show the full value of an EAP. Also needed is evidence of clinical symptom relief and work performance improvement among EAP clients (Csiernik, 2004; Roman, 2007). These outcome areas produce immediate returns to the company as well as create additional long-term cost savings in related areas later on (reduced health care claims, disability insurance claims, less turnover, etc.).

EAP outcomes

Studies show that, when appropriately administered to emphasize the core technology components, EAP services produce positive clinical change, improvements in employee absenteeism, productivity and turnover, and savings in medical, disability or workers' compensation claims (Attridge & Amaral, 2002; Kirk, 2006; McLeod & McLeod, 2001; Yandrick, 1992).

Table 17.2 EAP impact on employee work performance: results from six studies

Improved work performance	Sample size	EAP model	Source
61% of all cases had improved work performance	1,190 cases	Internal programs at many universities with mostly in-person model	Phillips (2004)
50% of all cases had improved absence and productivity at work	882 cases	Internal program with in-person model	Kirk (2006)
64% of cases with work issues as primary problem had improvement after EAP use; Average of 46% improved productivity rating on 1–10 scale for EAP cases	Not specified – 10,000+	National data warehouse with dozens of EAPs; mostly internal programs with in-person model	Amaral (2008a)
Reduction from 15% to 5% of all clients who 'could not' do their daily work or who experienced 'quite a bit' of difficulty doing their daily work in past four weeks	59,685 cases	Blended program with mostly in-person model	Selvik et al. (2004)
57% of cases had improvement in ability to work productivity, with average gain in productivity of 43% on 1–10 scale	11,909 cases	National EAP provider – external program with mostly telephonic model	Attridge (2003a)
Number of work cut-back in past 30 days was reduced from 8.0 days to 3.4 days (58% gain in productivity)	3353 cases	National EAP provider – external program with mostly telephonic model	Baker (2007)

Examples of results from six major contemporary studies illustrate the kinds of improvements obtained after EAP use in the primary outcome area of work productivity for individual employees. These findings consistently show improvement of presenteeism problems, both from EAPs with a traditional in-person model or from those with an external model with telephonic contact between employee and counsellor (see Table 17.2).

EAP referrals

A necessary part of the EAP service is to appropriately refer some of the clinical cases – particularly those cases requiring more extensive psychotherapy, pharmacological treatment or alcohol/drug treatment – to providers of mental health care outside of the EAP. Such referrals are usually to outpatient clinical settings staffed by licensed psychologists, psychiatrists, social workers or other professionals. At this point the referral client must pay for these services however the benefit is arranged. In these cases, the effectiveness of the EAP thus ultimately rests with these other providers.

Fortunately, the success rates for the treatment for some of the most common mental health disorders are quite high. According to a landmark study that examined over 300 meta-analysis papers (each paper itself a review of many other original studies), outpatient mental health treatment is largely effective at improving patient functioning (Lipsey & Wilson, 1993). A recent randomized control experimental design study demonstrated the effectiveness of mental health treatments on reducing clinical symptoms for depression and improving work absence and presenteeism outcomes (Wang et al., 2007). Consumer opinion research has also found generally positive results from the perspective of clients who used mental health services (Seligman, 1995). Thus, the evidence strongly indicates that once people with mental health disorders can get to a treatment provider – perhaps after referral from the EAP – the treatments are generally effective at restoring better mental health and work functioning.

Some studies indicate that EAPs are particularly effective at helping employees with substance abuse issues to navigate successfully through the many treatment options available and with providing follow-up support and case-management assistance after treatment to reduce relapse issues and improve the return-to-work process (Blum & Roman, 1995; Cook & Schlenger, 2002). A survey of over 800 EA professionals experienced in this area found that almost nine in 10 referral cases from the EAP were believed to be successful in completing their recommended specialized treatment for alcohol or drug issues (Attridge, 2003b). As with mental health, literature reviews of the hundreds of outcome studies on alcohol and drug abuse treatment have agreed upon the general effectiveness that professional treatment can provide to those suffering from alcohol and drug abuse problems (Canadian Centre on Substance Abuse, 2005; Miller et al., 2003; NIDA, 1999). In particular, the combination of cognitive behavioural therapy, pharmacological therapy and self-help peer support groups has been the most helpful in getting addicts to reduce and better manage their alcohol or drug use for long periods of time.

17.4.2 EAP and ROI: Dollars and (Business) Sense

Employers purchase EAPs to provide services to the individual employees, members of their family, and the organization as a whole. A fundamental management question then becomes whether or not their EAP is providing enough value to cover the cost of sponsoring the service. In other words, is the financial return on investment (ROI) a positive ratio? For perspective, fees for EAPs in the last decade have been in the range of $15 to $25 dollars per employee per year (Hartwell *et al.*, 1996; Sharar & Hertenstein, 2006). The average annual cost to employers for single coverage in the United States in 2007 was $4,479 (Kaiser, 2007). Thus, this level of cost for an EAP represents about one-half of 1% of total health care costs at most companies. Thus, EAPs are one of the least costly of all benefits services for most companies.

To help answer the ROI question, the 'EAP Business Value Model' was created to better conceptualize the components of total business value that mental health workplace services can offer employers (Attridge & Amaral, 2002; Attridge, Amaral & Hyde, 2003; Amaral & Attridge 2004, 2005; Attridge, 2005). This model organizes the business value that results from positive employee mental health into three classes of outcomes that are important to employers: health care outcomes; human capital outcomes; and organizational outcomes.

- The *health care value component* includes the impact of the program on medical, mental health, disability and workers' compensation claims. These are the direct costs paid by most employers that can be routinely measured and tracked.
- The *human capital value component* comprises indirect costs. It represents the savings that an employer can expect when effective prevention and intervention services result in avoided employee absenteeism, reduced presenteeism and turnover and enhanced employee engagement, retention and recruitment.
- The *organizational value component* includes costs associated with workplace safety risk management, legal liability risk prevention, organizational culture change, improved worker morale, and secondary impacts on health costs and human capital costs. Ultimately, these costs affect the bottom line of company net profitability.

This triadic model is a useful heuristic for understanding what an EAP can do for a company. Most researchers and industry experts now believe that there is enough solid evidence in each of these value component areas to 'make the business case' for providing greater access to mental health services in general and to workplace-based services in particular (American Psychiatric Association, 2006; Attridge, 2005, 2008a; Finch & Phillips, 2005; Goetzel *et al.*, 2002; Kessler & Stang, 2006a; Langlieb & Kahn, 2005). This conclusion is supported by many case studies of EAP outcome value at companies such as Abbott Laboratories, America On Line (AOL), Campbell Soup, Chevron, Crestar Bank, Detroit Edison, DuPont, Los Angeles

City Department of Water & Power, Marsh & McLennan, McDonnell Douglas, NCR Corp, New York Telephone, Orange County (Florida), Southern California Edison, the U.S. Postal Service, and the U.S. Federal Government (Blum & Roman, 1995; Yandrick, 1992).

The typical analysis produces an ROI between $5 and $10 in return for every $1 invested in the EA program (Attridge, 2007; Hargrave *et al.*, 2008; Jorgensen, 2007). In fact, as in most other cost-benefit studies of health care services, the financial benefits from the area of improved employee productivity (presenteeism) comprises the largest and most immediate part of the overall cost savings to the employer from employees' use of EAP services (Goetzel, 2007; Hargrave *et al.*, 2008). Several ROI calculator tools are available that offer rough estimates of illness burden costs and potential savings from prevention and intervention programs for mental health and alcohol problems in the workplace (Attridge, 2008b; see the following websites: www.alcoholcostcalculator.org, www.bipolarsolutions.com, www.depressioncalculator.com, and www.intelliprev.com).

17.5 FUTURE TRENDS IN EAP

Before closing this chapter, a number of advances in the field must be acknowledged. These trends include integration of EAP with other areas of employee benefits, Internet-based EAP, measurement and interventions for employee engagement and presenteeism, research on EAP and expansion of EAP around the world.

17.5.1 EAP Trend 1: Integration with Other Employee Benefits

In the last decade, EA professionals have begun to collaborate with other business groups in the areas of work/life, health and wellness, and disability management to address the mental and physical needs of employees and develop prevention and early intervention programs that try to improve overall health and well-being. The number of EAPs with integration activity has increased from about one in four in 1994 to over one in three in 2002 and is now expected to be the majority of EAPs (Herlihy & Attridge, 2005). Part of the reason for this growth is a natural business development response to the rise in the popularity of work/life (W/L) programs and the benefits of collaboration between EAP and W/L. Another reason is that EAPs are well suited to offer prevention services that target employee behavioural risks and workplace culture issues (Caggianelli & Carruthers, 2007; Goetzel & Ozminkowski, 2006). There are many examples of how EAPs are increasingly delivering their services in greater integration and collaboration with work/life and wellness kinds of services (Attridge, Herlihy & Maiden, 2005; Csiernik, 2005).

There is also a conceptual and empirical rational for greater collaboration among health and workplace service providers towards delivery of comprehensive organizational wellness (Bennett, Cook & Pelletier, 2003; Grawitch, Gottschalk & Munz, 2006). In addition, there is now a strong scientific evidence base for the effectiveness of potential EAP partners in the areas of worksite wellness and stress management intervention programs that have been shown to improve employee health and work performance (see meta-analysis by Parks & Steelman, 2008).

Also important are the findings from a new survey that the majority of EAP professionals consider prevention to be a core component of their professional identity and that about a third of EAPs already deliver prevention-oriented services to employees and organizations (Bennett & Attridge, 2008). The prevention services provided most often by EAPs to their client organizations (on at least a quarterly basis) were alcohol or other drug screening/training (40%), team building (32%) and depression screening (25%). Given the increasing prevalence of delivering prevention services and the positive attitudes towards them among providers, some have even argued that preventive services should be added to the core technology of EAP (Bennett & Attridge, 2008).

17.5.2   EAP Trend 2: Internet Services and e-Counselling

Related to the greater integration of EAP with other health and wellness services is an increasing use of the Internet in the promotion and delivery of EAP (Richard, 2003, 2009). Web-based services have allowed many employees to become more familiar with the purpose of EAPs. Websites for EAPs are becoming more elaborate, offering access to provider lists, tip sheets, Webinars and self-assessment tools. Many of these sites are even embedded within the larger company intranet or human resources website. One advantage of this common portal approach is a lessening of the reluctance some people have to seek out counselling. At Ernst & Young, when they combined the EAP, work-life and HR/benefits website functions, the result was a big increase in the use of the EAP and of the work-life services – from 8% and 12%, respectively to a combined 25% annually (Turner, Weiner & Keegan, 2005). There is less stigma associated with addressing addictions and delivering prevention programs through the Internet, where it can be accessed at anytime, with relative anonymity. Although still a small fraction of all client contact, the use of online or web-based counselling between EAP clinicians and employees is advancing as a new practice model (Parnass *et al.*, 2008).

17.5.3   EAP Trend 3: Measuring Employee Work Performance

Given that one of the unique features of employee assistance is a focus on the work productivity of employee clients, it has been surprisingly difficult for EAPs to accurately measure productivity in order to assess clinical symptom severity and to gauge improvement. This scenario has dramatically changed in the last decade due to recent advances in the validity and reliability of self-report tools for measuring employee productivity, absence and health factors (Attridge *et al.*, 2009). There are now several brief assessment tools that can reliably and validly measure employee productivity/presenteeism and absence. One of most widely tested tools is the *Health and Work Performance Questionnaire* (HPQ), developed by the World Health Organization and Harvard University (Kessler *et al.*, 2003, 2004). The HPQ has subscales of a seven-item Presenteeism Scale and a four-item Absenteeism Scale and norms from more than 200,000 workers worldwide. A short form of the HPQ is being adopted by leading employers in the United States for use as an annual all-company benchmarking practice (see website for the Integrated Benefits Institute). This HPQ measure has also been incorporated into standard use among dozens of EAP providers who combine their operational experiences in a large international reporting database (Amaral, 2008b).

The opportunities that better measurement of worker performance provides for EAPs (and other health service providers) is enormous as it allows the comparison of EAP cases over time before and after use of the EAP and the comparison of the EAP cases to the rest of the employees on work absence and productivity metrics (Attridge, 2004). Even more significant is the trend among leading companies to switch their focus from reducing 'negative' outcomes (such as absence and presenteeism) to encouraging the development and maintenance of 'positive' outcomes such as employee engagement. Indeed, major studies by the Gallup organization, Watson Wyatt and others on employee engagement have linked it to overall company profitability and customer loyalty (Grawitch *et al.*, 2006; Harter *et al.*, 2003; Watson Wyatt Worldwide, 2002).

17.5.4   EAP Trend 4: Revitalizing Research

Although there are several key research-based books and texts on EAP (Oher, 1999; Attridge, Herlihy & Maiden, 2005; Richard, Emener & Hutchinson, 2009), the empirical research on EAPs is a relatively small literature. For example, one review found almost 200 reports on the business value of EAPs, but few works were from peer-reviewed research journals and almost all of these EAP studies use non-experimental research methods (Attridge &

Fletcher, 2000). Instead, most of the reports in this review were conference presentations, trade journal articles or industry white papers. However, these weaknesses in research rigour are largely due to the applied nature of the service delivery context and are not unique to EAPs as they are common to much of the research conducted on workplace health issues (Attridge, 2001; Kasl & Jones, 2003; Kessler & Stang, 2006b). Nonetheless, much has already been learned from this past research and operational practices have been established well enough to allow for EAP industry accreditation of provider companies and certification of individual professionals. Yet, more basic research is needed on the factors that determine just which kinds of operational practices drive service quality, user satisfaction and important outcomes (Roman, 2007; Sharar, Amaral & Chalk, 2007). Higher quality research on the effectiveness and value of EAPs can also be used to argue for general fee increases, which have tended to stagnate or even go down in the past decade due to pressures of 'commoditization' of the industry (Sharar & Hertenstein, 2006).

The good news is that there is robust political support for research and opportunities for disseminating it through the two major industry organizations. Each association has research committees and work groups, conferences and publication outlets for research work (the peer-reviewed *Journal of Workplace Behavioral Health: EAP Practice and Research,* published by Haworth Press and affiliated with EASNA; and the *Journal of Employee Assistance*, published by EAPA).

A practical limitation to more and better research on EAPs is that there are so few people trained in how to do quality research who specialize in the area of EAP and only a handful of university-level programs that focus on EAP exist to produce new scholars (Pompe & Sharar, 2008). In addition, compared to the heyday era of abundant government funding for alcohol-related services, hardly any financial support exists today for EAP research from the industry or from government (Roman, 2007). Most of the research that is done is paid for by larger EAP providers, conducted by external consultants, or contributed by university students and professors. A promising new development, however, is the creation of a foundation dedicated exclusively to funding basic and applied research in the employee assistance field (Tisone, 2008).

17.5.5   EAP Trend 5: Going Global

The employee assistance concept began in the United States and remains very popular with over 75 local chapters of EAPA. However, there has also been significant expansion and adaptation of employee assistance services more recently in other countries. For example, there are EAPA member chapters located in Australia, Canada, Greece, Ireland, Japan, South Africa and the United Kingdom as well as some start-up activity in Chile and China. The EASNA organization hosts its annual institute on an alternating basis between cities in Canada and the United States. There also has been some qualitative research on the progress of EAP development in Australia (Kirk & Brown, 2005; Smith, 2006), Europe (Hoskinson & Beer, 2005; Nowlan, 2006; Malhomme, 2008), Germany (Barth, 2006; Gehlenborg, 2001), India (Siddiqui & Sukhramani, 2001), Ireland (Powell, 2001; Quinlan, 2005), Israel (Katan, 2001) and South Africa (Maiden, 1992, 2001). With all of this global interest in EAP, the profession has a strong future and many opportunities for positive change and evolution (Burke, 2008).

17.6 CONCLUSION

Employee Assistance Programs have a long history of supporting employees and organizations in a variety of ways. They bring a unique focus on how to maintain or restore employee work performance through troubles with mental health, addiction and workplace events. The role of employee assistance in supporting worker mental health and job performance is already a key component to the overall success of thousands of organizations. This chapter has used a research literature review to provide an overview of why companies need an EAP, what defines EAP, what are its roots, what services are commonly provided, what makes EAPs unique, how many employers have an EAP, how often employees use the EAP, outcomes from EAP use, and their business value to employers. Also examined were five trends in the EAP field, focusing on service integration, the Internet, measurement, research and globalization.

REFERENCES

Amaral, T.M. (2005, October). *How does your EAP measure up? A review of national benchmarking data drawn from the EAP Data Warehouse.* Paper presented at the annual conference of the Employee Assistance Professionals Association, Philadelphia, PA.

Amaral, T.M. (2008a, April). *Getting noticed: practical outcome evaluations to show EAP value.* Paper presented at the annual institute of the Employee Assistance Society of North America, Vancouver, BC, Canada.

Amaral, T.M. (2008b, April). *Global benchmarking: implications of research data for EAP best practices.* Paper presented at annual institute of the Employee Assistance Society of North America, Vancouver, BC, Canada.

Amaral, T.M. & Attridge, M. (2004, November). *Communicating EAP business value: successful strategies for measurement, reporting, and presentations.* Presented at the annual conference of the Employee Assistance Professionals Association, San Francisco, CA.

Amaral, T.M. & Attridge, M. (2005, May). *Expanding business value through EAP partnerships: a review of research and best practices.* Paper presented at annual institute of the Employee Assistance Society of North America, Chicago.

American Psychiatric Association – Partnership for Workplace Mental Health. (2006). *A Mentally Healthy Workforce: It's Good for Business.* Washington, DC: American Psychiatric Association.

Attridge, M. (2001). Can EAPs experiment in the real world? *EAPA Exchange*, **31**(2), 26–7.

Attridge, M. (2003a, March). *EAP impact on work, stress and health: national data 1999–2002.* Paper presented at the bi-annual Work, Stress and Health Conference – American Psychological Association/National Institutes of Occupational Safety and Health, Toronto, ON, Canada.

Attridge, M. (2003b, November). *EAPs and the delivery of alcohol and drug services: results of the EAPA/Join Together 2003 survey of EAPA members.* Paper presented at annual conference of the Employee Assistance Professionals Association, New Orleans, LA.

Attridge, M. (2003c, November). *Optum EAP client satisfaction and outcomes survey study 2002.* Paper presented at the annual conference of the Employee Assistance Professionals Association, New Orleans, LA.

Attridge, M. (2004, November). *Measuring employee productivity, presenteeism and absenteeism: implications for EAP outcomes research.* Paper presented at the annual conference of the Employee Assistance Professionals Association, San Francisco.

Attridge, M. (2005). The business case for the integration of employee assistance, work/life and wellness services: a literature review. *Journal of Workplace Behavioral Health*, **20**(1), 31–55.

Attridge, M. (2007, August). *Customer-Driven ROI for EAPs.* Audio-conference Workshop. Yreka, CA: Advanced Training Institute – EAP Technology Systems, Inc.

Attridge, M. (2008a). *A Quiet Crisis: The Business Case for Managing Employee Mental Health.* Vancouver, BC: Human Solutions.

Attridge, M. (2008b, March). *Return-On-Investment calculations for behavioral health: development and application.* Paper presented at the bi-annual Work, Stress and Health Conference, American Psychological Association/National Institutes of Occupational Safety and Health, Washington, DC.

Attridge, M., & Amaral, T.M. (2002, October). *Making the business case for EAPs with the Core Technology.* Paper presented at the annual conference of the Employee Assistance Professionals Association, Boston, MA.

Attridge, M., Amaral, T.M. & Hyde, M. (2003). Completing the business case for EAPs. *Journal of Employee Assistance*, **33**(3), 23–5.

Attridge, M., Bennett, J.B., Frame, M.C. & Quick, J.C. (2009). *Corporate health profile: measuring engagement and presenteeism.* In M.A. Richard, W.G.

Emener & W.S. Hutchison, Jr. (Eds), *Employee Assistance Programs: Wellness/Enhancement Programming* (4th edn, pp. 228–36). Springfield, IL: Charles C. Thomas.

Attridge, M. & Fletcher, L. (2000, November). *Annotated bibliography of research on EAP outcomes and cost-benefit.* Paper presented at annual conference of the Employee Assistance Professionals Association, New York, NY.

Attridge, M., Herlihy, P. & Maiden, P. (Eds) (2005). *The Integration of Employee Assistance, Work/Life and Wellness Services.* Binghamton, NY: Haworth Press.

Baker, E. (2007, October). *Measuring the impact of EAP on absenteeism and presenteeism.* Paper presented at the annual conference of the Employee Assistance Professionals Association, San Diego, CA.

Barth, J. (2006). Germany: A difficult market for EAPs. *Journal of Employee Assistance*, **36**(1), 26.

Bennett, J.B. & Attridge, M. (2008). Adding prevention to the EAP core technology. *Journal of Employee Assistance*, **38**(4), 3–6.

Bennett, J.B., Cook, R.F. & Pelletier, K. R. (2003). Toward an integrated framework for comprehensive organizational wellness: concepts, practices, and research in workplace health promotion. In J.C. Quick & L.E. Tetrick. (Eds), *Handbook of Occupational Health Psychology* (pp. 69–95). Washington, DC: American Psychological Association.

Blum, T. & Roman, P. (1995). *Cost-Effectiveness and Preventive Implications of Employee Assistance Programs.* Rockville, MD: U.S. Department of Health and Human Services, Substance Abuse and Mental Health Services Administration, Center for Mental Health Services.

Brun, J-P., Biron, C., Martel, J. & Ivers, H. (2003). *Analysis of Workplace Mental Health Programs in Organizations. IRSST Report A-342.* Montreal, Quebec: Institut de Recherche Robert-Sauvé en Santé et en Sécurité du Travail.

Burke, J. (2008, April). *The current global view of EAPs and the opportunity for tomorrow.* Paper presented at the annual institute of the Employee Assistance Society of North America, Vancouver, BC, Canada.

Caggianelli, P. & Carruthers, M. (2007). An integrated approach to behavioral health. *Journal of Employee Assistance*, **37**(3), 16–18.

Canadian Centre on Substance Abuse. (2005). *National Framework for Action to Reduce the Harms Associated with Alcohol and Other Drugs and Substances in Canada: Answering the Call.* Ottawa, ON: Health Canada and Canadian Centre on Substance Abuse.

Cook, R.F. & Schlenger, W. (2002). Prevention of substance abuse in the workplace: review of research on the delivery of services. *Journal of Primary Prevention*, **23**, 115–42.

Csiernik, R. (2002). An overview of employee and family assistance programming in Canada. *Employee Assistance Quarterly*, **18**(1), 17–34.

Csiernik, R. (2004). A review of EAP evaluation in the 1990s. *Employee Assistance Quarterly*, **19**(4), 21–37.

Csiernik, R. (2005). What we are doing in the Employee Assistance Program: meeting the challenge of an integrated model of practice. *Journal of Workplace Behavioral Health*, **21**(1), 11–22.

Department of Health and Human Services (DHHS). (1999). *Mental Health: A Report of the Surgeon General*. Rockville, MD: U.S. Department of Health and Human Services, Substance Abuse and Mental Health Services Administration, Center for Mental Health Services.

Dersch, C.A., Shumway, S.T., Harris, S.M. & Arredondo, R. (2002). A new comprehensive measure of EAP satisfaction: a factor analysis. *Employee Assistance Quarterly*, **17**(3), 55–60.

Desjardins Financial Security. (2006). *Desjardins Financial Security Survey on Health and the Desjardins National Financial Security Index 2006 edition*. Montreal, Quebec: Desjardins Financial Security.

Employee Assistance Professionals Association (EAPA) (2003). *EAPA Standards and Professional Guidelines for Employee Assistance Programs* (2003 edition). Washington, DC: EAPA.

Employee Benefit News. (2007). *Innerworkings: A Report on Mental Health in Today's Workplace*. Washington, DC: Partnership for Workplace Mental Health and Employee Benefit News.

Everly, G.S., Jr. & Mitchell, J.T. (2008). *Integrative Crisis Intervention and Disaster Mental Health*. Elliott City, MD: Chevron.

Finch, R.A. & Phillips, K. (2005). *An Employer's Guide to Behavioral Health Services*. Center for Prevention and Health Services. Washington, DC: National Business Group on Health.

Gehlenborg, H. (2001). Occupational social work in Germany: a continuously developing field of practice. *Employee Assistance Quarterly*, **17**(1–2), 17–41.

Goetzel, R.Z. (2007, May). *What's the ROI for workplace health and productivity management programs?* Paper presented at the annual institute of the Employee Assistance Society of North America, Atlanta, GA.

Goetzel, R. & Ozminkowski, R. (2006). Integrating to improve productivity. *Journal of Employee Assistance*, **36**(4): 25–8.

Goetzel, R.Z., Ozminkowski, R.J., Sederer, L.I. & Mark, T.L. (2002). The business case for mental health services: Why employers should care about the mental health and well-being of their employees. *Journal of Occupational and Environmental Medicine*, **44**(4), 320–30.

Grawitch, M.J., Gottschalk, M. & Munz, D.C. (2006). The path to a healthy workplace: a critical review linking healthy workplace practices, employee well-being, and organizational improvements. *Consulting Psychology Journal: Practice and Research*, **58**(3), 129–47.

Green-Hennessy, S. (2002). Factors associated with receipt of behavioral health services among persons with substance dependence. *Psychiatric Services*, **53**(12), 1592–8.

Hargrave, G.E., Hiatt, D., Alexander, R. & Shaffer, I.A. (2008). EAP treatment impact on presenteeism and absenteeism: Implications for return on investment. *Journal of Workplace Behavioral Health*, **23**(3), 283–93.

Harter, J.K., Schmidt, F.L. & Keyes, C.L.M. (2003). Well-being in the workplace and its relationship to business outcomes: A review of the Gallup studies. In C.L.M. Keyes & J. Haidt (Eds), *Flourishing: Positive Psychology and the Life Well-Lived* (pp. 205–24). Washington, DC: American Psychological Association.

Hartwell, T., Steele, P., French, M., Potter, F., Rodman, N. & Zarkin, G. (1996). Aiding troubled employees: the prevalence, cost, and characteristics of employee assistance programs in the United States. *American Journal of Public Health*, **86**(6), 804–8.

Herlihy, P. & Attridge, M. (2005). Research on the integration of Employee Assistance, Work/Life and Wellness services: past, present and future. *Journal of Workplace Behavioral Health*, **20**(1–2), 67–93.

Hoskinson, L. & Beer, S. (2005). Work-life and EAPs in the United Kingdom and Europe: a qualitative study of integration. *Journal of Workplace Behavioral Health*, **20**(3–4), 367–79.

Hyde, M. (2008, April). *EAPs as workplace behavior experts: do you share the dream?* Paper presented at annual institute of the Employee Assistance Society of North America, Vancouver, BC, Canada.

Hyman, S., Chisholm, D., Kessler, R.C., Patel, V. & Whiteford, H. (2006). Mental disorders. In *WHO Report: Disease Control Priorities Related to Mental, Neurological, Developmental and Substance Abuse Disorders* (pp. 1–20). Geneva, Switzerland: World Health Organization.

Jacobson, J.M. & Hosford-Lamb, J. (2008). Working it out – social workers in Employee Assistance. *Social Work Today*, **8**(2), 18.

Jacobson, J.M. & Kominoth, C. (2009). Impaired professionals: unique challenges for employee assistance programs. In W. Emener, W. Hutchison, Jr. & M. Richard. (Eds), *Employee Assistance Programs: Wellness/Enhancement Programming* (4th edition, pp. 319–27). Springfield, IL: Charles C. Thomas.

Jorgensen, D.G. (2007). Demonstrating EAP value. *Journal of Employee Assistance*, **37**(3), 24–6.

Kahn, J.P. & Langlieb, A.M. (Eds) (2003). *Mental Health and Productivity in the Workplace: A Handbook for Organizations and Clinicians*. San Francisco: Jossey-Bass.

Kaiser Family Foundation and Health Research and Educational Trust (2007). *Employer Health Benefits – 2007 Annual Survey*. Washington, DC: Kaiser Family Foundation and Health Research and Educational Trust.

Kasl, S.V. & Jones, B.A. (2003). An epidemiological perspective on research design, measurement, and surveillance strategies. In J. Campbell Quick & L.E. Tetlock. (Eds), (*Handbook of Occupational Health Psychology* (pp. 379–98). Washington, DC: American Psychological Association Press.

Katan, J. (2001). Occupational social work in Israel. *Employee Assistance Quarterly*, **17**(1–2), 81–95.

Kessler, R.C., Barber, C., Beck, A., Berglund, P., Cleary, P.D., McKenas, D. *et al.* (2003). The World Health Organization Health and Work Performance Questionnaire (HPQ). *Journal of Occupational and Environmental Medicine*, **45**(2), 156–74.

Kessler, R.C., Ames, M., Hymel, P.A., Loeppke, R., McKenas, D.K., Richling, D. *et al.* (2004). Using the World Health Organization Health and Work Performance Questionnaire (HPQ) to evaluate the indirect workplace costs of illness. *Journal of Occupational and Environmental Medicine*, **46**(6), 523–37.

Kessler, R.C. & Stang, P.E.. (Eds) (2006a). *Health and Work Productivity: Making the Business Case for Quality Health Care*. Chicago: University of Chicago Press.

Kessler, R.C. & Stang, P.E. (2006b). Intersecting issues in the evaluation of health and work productivity. In R.C. Kessler & P.E. Stang. (Eds), *Health and Work Productivity: Making the Business Case for Quality Health Care* (pp. 1–26). Chicago: University of Chicago Press.

Kirk, C.H. (2006). The effectiveness of a problem resolution and brief counseling EAP intervention. *Journal of Workplace Behavioral Health*, **22**(1), 1–12.

Kirk, A.K. & Brown, D. F. (2005). Australian perspectives on the organizational integration of employee assistance services. *Journal of Workplace Behavioral Health*, **20**(3–4), 351–66.

Kramer, R.M. & Rickert, S. (2006). Health and productivity management: market opportunities for EAPs. *Journal of Employee Assistance*, **36**(1), 23–33.

Langlieb, A.M. & Kahn, J.P. (2005). How much does quality mental health care profit employers? *Journal of Occupational and Environmental Medicine*, **47**(11), 1099–109.

Larson, S.L., Eyerman, J., Foster, M. S. & Gfroerer, J.C. (2007). *Worker Substance Use and Workplace Policies and Programs (DHHS Publication No. SMA 07-4273, Analytic Series A-29)*. Rockville, MD: Substance Abuse and Mental Health Services Administration (SAMHSA), Office of Applied Studies.

Lipsey, M.W. & Wilson, D.B. (1993). The efficacy of psychological, educational, and behavioral treatment confirmation from meta-analysis. *American Psychologist*, **48**(12), 1181–209.

Loeppke, R., Taitel, M., Richling, D., Parry, T., Kessler, R.C., Hymel, P. & Konicki, D. (2007). Health and productivity as a business strategy. *Journal of Occupational and Environmental Medicine*, **49**(7), 712–21.

Macdonald, S., Csiernik, R., Durand, P., Wild, T.C., Dooley, S., Rylett, M., Wells, S. & Sturge, J. (2007). Changes in the prevalence and characteristics of Ontario workplace health programs. *Journal of Workplace Behavioral Health*, **22**(1), 53–64.

Maiden, R.P. (Ed.) (1992). *Employee Assistance Programs in South Africa*. Binghamton, NY: Haworth.

Maiden, R.P. (Ed.) (2001). *Global Perspectives of Occupational Social Work*. Binghamton, NY: Haworth.

Malhomme, N. (2008, April). *The global workforce: EAP risk and reward in Europe*. Paper presented at the annual institute of the Employee Assistance Society of North America, Vancouver, BC, Canada.

Masi, D., Altman, L., Benayon, C. *et al.* (2004). EAPs in the year 2002. In R.W. Manderscheid & M.J. Henderson. (Eds), *Mental Health, United States, 2002*. Rockville, MD: Substance Abuse Mental Health Services Administration, Center for Mental Health Services, DHHS Pub. No. SMA-3938.

McDaid, D. (Ed) (2008). *Mental Health in Workplace Settings: Consensus Paper*. Luxembourg: European Communities. Available at: http://www.ec-mental-health-process.net.

McLeod, J. & McLeod, J. (2001). How effective is workplace counseling? A review of the research literature. *Counseling Psychotherapy Research*, **1**(3), 184–91.

Miller, W.R., Wilbourne, P.D. & Hetema, J.E. (2003). What works? A summary of alcohol treatment outcome research. In R.K. Hester & W.R. Miller. (Eds), *Handbook of Alcoholism Treatment Approaches: Effective Alternatives* (3rd edn, pp. 13–63). Boston, MA: Allyn and Bacon.

National Institute on Drug Abuse (NIDA). (1999). *Principles of Drug Addiction Treatment: A Research-Based Guide, FAQ11*. Bethesda, MD: NIDA.

Nowlan, K. (2006). The United Kingdom: practical support and expert assessment. *Journal of Employee Assistance*, **36**(2), 25.

Oher, J.M. (Ed.) (1999). *The Employee Assistance Handbook*. New York: John Wiley & Sons, Inc.

Parks, K.M. & Steelman, L.A. (2008). Organizational wellness programs: a meta-analysis. *Journal of Occupational Health Psychology*, **13**(1), 58–68.

Parnass, P., Mitchell, D., Seagram, S., Wittes, P., Speyer, C. & Fournier, R. (2008, April). *Delivering employee eCounseling programs: issues and experiences.* Paper presented at the annual institute of the Employee Assistance Society of North America, Vancouver, BC, Canada.

Paul, R. & Thompson, C. (2006). Employee Assistance Program responses to large-scale traumatic events: lessons learned and future opportunities. *Journal of Workplace Behavioral Health*, **21**(3–4), 1–19.

Phillips, S.B. (2004). Client satisfaction with university employee assistance program. *Journal of Workplace Behavioral Health*, **19**(4), 59–70.

Pompe, J.C. & Sharar, D. 2008. Preparing for the challenges of research. *Journal of Employee Assistance*, **38**(2), 7–9.

Powell, M.A.G. (2001). Occupational social work in Ireland. *Employee Assistance Quarterly*, **17**(1–2), 65–79.

Quinlan, M. (2005). A social partnership approach to work-life balance in the European Union. *Journal of Workplace Behavioral Health*, **20**(3–4), 381–94.

Richard, M.A. (2003). Cyberspace: issues and challenges for EAP providers. *Employee Assistance Quarterly*, **19**(2), 51–60.

Richard, M.A. (2009). Cyberspace: the new frontier for Employee Assistance Programs. In M.A. Richard, W.G. Emener & W.S. Hutchison, Jr. (Eds), *Employee Assistance Programs: Wellness/Enhancement Programming* (4th edition, pp. 288–92). Springfield, IL: Charles C. Thomas.

Richard, M.A., Emener, W.G. & Hutchison, W.S., Jr. (Eds) (2009). *Employee Assistance Programs: Wellness/Enhancement Programming*, 4th edition. Springfield, IL: Charles C. Thomas.

Roman, P.M. (1990). Seventh dimension: a new component is added to the EAP 'core technology.' *Employee Assistance*, February, 8–9.

Roman, P.M. (2007, May). *Underdeveloped workplace opportunities for Employee Assistance Programs*. Paper presented at the annual institute of the Employee Assistance Society of North America, Atlanta, GA.

Roman, P.M. & Blum, T.C. (1985). The core technology of employee assistance programs. *The ALMACAN*, **15**(3), 8–9, 16–19.

Roman, P.M. & Blum, T.C. (1988). Reaffirmation of the core technology of employee assistance programs. *The ALMACAN*, **19**(8), 17–22.

Roman, P.M. & Blum, T.C. (2002). The workplace and alcohol problem prevention. *Alcohol Research and Health*, **26**(1), 49–57.

Roman, P.M. & Blum, T.C. (2004). Employee assistance programs and other work-place preventive strategies. In M. Galanter & H.D. Kleber. (Eds), *The Textbook of Substance Abuse Treatment* (3rd edn, pp. 423–35). Washington, DC: American Psychiatric Association Press.

Seligman, M.P. (1995). The effectiveness of psychotherapy. *American Psychologist*, **50**(12), 965–74.

Selvik, R., Stephenson, D., Plaza, C. & Sugden, B. (2004). EAP impact on work, relationship, and health outcomes. *Journal of Employee Assistance*, **34**(2), 18–22.

Sharar, D.A., Amaral, T.M. & Chalk, M.B. (2007, May). *The need for employer-driven EAP performance outcomes*. Paper presented at the annual institute of the Employee Assistance Society of North America, Atlanta, GA.

Sharar, D.A. & Hertenstein, E. (2006). Perspectives on commodity pricing in Employee Assistance Programs (EAPs): a survey of the EAP field. *WorldatWork Journal*, First Quarter, 32–41.

Siddiqui, H.Y. & Sukhramani, N. (2001). Occupational social work in India. *Employee Assistance Quarterly*, **17**(1–2), 43–63.

Smith, R. (2006). Australia: rethinking the strict CISM model. *Journal of Employee Assistance*, **36**(2), 26.

Society for Human Resources Management. (2008). *Employee Benefits*. Washington, DC: Society for Human Resources Management.

Statistics Canada. (2003). *Canadian Community Health Survey, Mental Health and Well-Being 2002*. Ottawa, ON: Statistics Canada.

Tisone, C.R. (2008). Employee Assistance Research Foundation: A call to action. *Journal of Workplace Behavioral Health*, **23**(3), 205–15.

Trice, H.M. & Schonbrunn, M. (2003). A history of job-based alcoholism programs 1900–1955. In W.G. Emener, W.S. Hutchison, Jr. & M.A. Richard (Eds), *Employee Assistance Programs: Wellness/Enhancement Programming* (3rd edn, pp. 5–27). Springfield, IL: Charles C. Thomas.

Turner, S., Weiner, M. & Keegan, K. (2005). Ernst & Young's Assist: how internal and external service integration created a 'Single Source Solution'. *Journal of Workplace Behavioral Health*, **20**(3–4), 243–62.

Wang, P.S., Simon, G.E., Avorn, J., Azocar, F., Ludman, E.J., McCulloch, J., Petukhova, M.Z. & Kessler, R.C. (2007). Telephone screening, outreach, and management for depressed workers and impact on clinical and work productivity outcomes. *Journal of the American Medical Association*, **298**(12), 1401–11.

Watson Wyatt Worldwide. (2002). *Human Capital Index: Human Capital as a Lead Indicator of Shareholder Value*. Washington, DC: Watson Wyatt Worldwide.

Watson Wyatt Worldwide. (2007). *Mental Health in the North American Labour Force: Literature Review and Research Gap Analysis*. Authors: Ricciuti,

J., Attridge, M., Steacy, R., Durant, G., Ausqui, J., DeBartolli, K. & Clarkson, A. Toronto, ON, Canada: Watson Wyatt Worldwide. Available from http://www.mentalhealthroundtable.ca/documents.html.

Wilburn, C. (2007). Helping employees with financial problems. *Journal of Employee Assistance*, **37**(2), 12–13.

Yandrick, R.M. (1992). Taking inventory: process and outcome studies. *EAPA Exchange*, July, 22–35.

PART V

Organizational Approaches to Health and Well-Being

CHAPTER 18

Organizational Culture, Leadership, Change and Stress

Manfred Kets de Vries and Laura Guillén Ramo

INSEAD, France

and

Konstantin Korotov

European School of Management and Technology, Germany

Like all weak men he laid an exaggerated stress on not changing his mind
(W. Somerset Maugham, *Of Human Bondage*)

'Any company can become a great place to work'. This is an appealing statement, but how are 'great places to work' characterized? At the heart of the definition of a great place to work are trust and mutual respect between senior executives and their employees, and value-driven leadership – performance with purpose. Great places to work show a strong commitment from CEO and senior management (who walk the talk), a genuine belief that people are indispensable for the business, active communication among the entire organization, the perception of a unique culture and identity, a well-articulated vision, and values that are lived and experienced at all levels of the organization (Schrage, 1999; Kets de Vries, 2001a, 2006).

But even if many executives know what characterizes a great place to work, they fail in their attempts at creating one. Why are these organizational characteristics – in theory quite clear – so difficult to attain? How do organizations become and remain great places to work? What can leadership do to motivate people to create a better organization? And how do high

International Handbook of Work and Health Psychology, Third Edition. Edited by Cary L. Cooper, James Campbell Quick, and Marc J. Schabracq.

performance organizations keep stress among their employees at acceptable levels? In this chapter, our aim is to increase our understanding of organizational change processes and the relationships between change, organizational culture, leadership and stress.

Organizations have to adapt their behaviour on a continuous basis in order to sustain their competitive advantage. The need for change usually induces a high degree of stress (Kets de Vries & Balazs, 1998; Lichtenstein, 2000). The good news is that it is precisely this that constitutes a major catalyst for organizational change. As the saying goes, 'no gain without pain'. Stress at individual and organizational levels can help get change on its way. Stress is an acknowledgement of the serious consequences if the organization carries on ignoring changes in the environment. Negative emotions are potential triggers of change.

Changing mindsets is never easy. Usually, a strong jolt is needed before people realize that the traditional way of doing things is no longer adequate. Awareness of the need for change is achieved most effectively when the employees in an organization come under internal and external pressure. Organizational stress from both directions, and the associated discomfort, may trigger organizational change processes.

Kets de Vries refers to a four-stage process to illustrate how leaders accept the need for change (Kets de Vries & Miller, 1984; Kets de Vries, 2001a 2006). First, pain in the organizational system makes people aware of the serious consequences of perpetuating existing patterns. Second, key power holders react to this awareness with shock and disbelief. Third, these reactions can activate defensive routines that block further movement – fear of the unknown may contribute to a reluctance to introduce the kind of change that is needed. Some executives will be concerned that any form of change will threaten their professional identity and financial security (Kets de Vries, Carlock & Florent-Treacy, 2007). Consequently, the organization may continue to act as if nothing is happening. Finally, there is the recognition that the status quo cannot be maintained and that change has to be faced. There comes a point when clinging on to the status quo only creates greater problems and a higher level of stress. At that point, diving into the unknown is the lesser of two evils and the organization is ready to enter the change process. Figuring out how to deal with this may seem an insurmountable obstacle for the key power holders in an organization, especially if cultural norms have broken down in a changing environment.

What are the factors that cause stress in organizations? How can organizational change be conceptualized? And what can be done to transform the mindset of people within the organization?

In the first part of this chapter, we discuss the internal and external pressures that may trigger organizational change – or conversely hinder it and add to levels of personal and organizational stress. The second section explores how we can conceptualize change management. In the third section, we comment on the process of individual and organizational transformation and describe how to create the psychological space that can help it to take place (Korotov, 2005; Kets de Vries & Korotov, 2007).

18.1 LEADERSHIP AND STRESS

Some of the external factors that can cause pain in organizations are threats from competitors, declining profits, decreasing market share, scarcity of resources, deregulation, technological demands, and problems with suppliers and groups of customers. Examples of internal pressures are ineffective leadership, morale problems, a high turnover of capable people, absenteeism, labour problems, increased political behaviour in the company and turf fights (Kets de Vries, 2001a).

Because of the importance of leadership to organizational functioning, we are going to focus on the relationship between leadership and stress and look at it from two different perspectives. First, we will talk about stress associated with playing a leadership role in an organization and then examine how the level of stress experienced by employees in an organization may be related to the way leadership executes its role. Stress at the individual level may transform into stress at the organizational level; dysfunctional leadership may convert into free-floating paranoid and depressive anxiety within the organization as a whole (Jaques, 1974). We start by looking at the psychological costs of ineffective leadership at the individual level and go on to explore how this translates into organizational stress.

Kets de Vries, Korotov and Florent-Treacy (2007) argue that recent changes in society and the world of work have contributed to a significant rise in the psychological pressures of leadership. For example, Coyne and Coyne (2007) suggest that "the mere arrival of a new organizational leader represents a high level of stress for the various constituencies in the organization including the new boss." There are a number of factors that contribute to this:

1. *Loneliness at the top.* With an executive's progression along the career and responsibility ladder, there is an inevitable change in the composition of his or her network. Old relationships become difficult to maintain, as the pressure of the position demands the establishment of many new connections without the luxury of time. The development of trust between people doesn't happen overnight; it takes time.
2. *Feeling envied.* Inevitably, people at the top become objects of envy in organizations and societies. Recent discussions about the need to curb the

earnings of the people at the top of organizations in Europe initiated by leaders and government members in a number of countries are welcomed by many, despite the fact that the pay gaps between the highest and lowest paid in Western European companies are among the smallest in the world (Thornhill, Milne & Steen, 2008). Some leaders may find being an object of envy highly disturbing and stress inducing.

3. *'Now what?'* The race to the top requires a lot of effort and energy. However, when an executive reaches a position of significance, identifying the next goal can become a major headache. How much further do they want to go? How much more responsibility, fame, challenge, money, etc., do they want? Wondering whether enough is enough or whether they should go for more can be a major source of stress.

   To the person in the executive corner office, the 'now what?' crisis is particularly acute, given trends in executive turnover at the top. A recent Booz Allen Hamilton study by Lucier, Wheeler and Habbel (2007) suggests that in the period from 1995 to 2006 there was a 59% growth in annual CEO turnover. Within the same period there was a dramatic 318% increase in performance-related involuntary turnover. In 2006 almost one in every three departing CEOs left involuntarily, a surge from only one to eight in 1995. The tension of high expectations and an unstable future is contributing to the stress levels of senior executives.

4. *Being watched.* Various social constituencies pay significant attention to the lives of people who run organizations. From paparazzi to government officials, from investment analysts to business school professors, and from journalists to stand-up comedians, lots of people make a living out of observing leaders of organizations. They are all very good at pointing out the mistakes these executives make and their and their organizations' misfortunes. With every action under such severe scrutiny, leaders often find themselves having to check every word with their lawyers and public relations professionals before they open their mouth. Authentic behaviour and actions become a luxury. Corporate scandals, and the dubious behaviour of some of the world's business elite, will only lead to increased attention being paid to people at the top in both the public and private domain.

5. *Fear of losing power.* High-level positions bring a lot of power and unprecedented opportunities. However, power soon becomes very addictive (Kets de Vries, 2006) and the fear of losing something that might have been difficult to obtain can be deeply stressful. In some cases, people threatened with potential loss of power engage in malevolent acts to hang on to it.

6. *Guilt.* At certain times in their career, many executives become aware that the important people around them – including close family members and friends – have made great sacrifices to get them where they are. Some of

these sacrifices are often irreversible. The executive may feel guilty about the cost of his or her success. It may have alienated the family.

7. *An ever-steeper learning curve.* In a knowledge-driven society, many learned competencies become obsolete at the speed of light. Executives often find it difficult to accept the need to learn new things, and, more importantly, to unlearn some of the things that brought them success in the first place. The challenge of unlearning old things and learning new ones is exacerbated by the fact that executives have less and less discretionary time as they progress along the leadership ladder. There are few structured learning opportunities for people at the top that simultaneously challenge the individual and create a safe environment for growth and development (Korotov, 2005).

All members of an organization are intimately affected by the actions or inactions of those at the top. Many senior executives are genuinely unaware of how their behaviour may impede healthy functioning in the organization. Not only do they fail to realize how stress inducing their behaviour can be, they often have no idea how to manage their own stress level. This lack of self-awareness can seriously affect performance throughout the organization (Kets de Vries *et al.*, 2007).

Kets de Vries (Kets de Vries & Miller, 1984; Kets de Vries, 2006) has identified a number of constellations of neurotic executive behaviours contributing to elevated stress among followers:

1. *The dramatic leader* constantly seeks attention and craves excitement, activity and stimulation. Such a person is often touched by a sense of entitlement and tends toward extremes.
2. *The suspicious leader* is extremely vigilant, constantly on the watch for possible attacks and personal threats, and always prepared to counter a personal attack or an attack on the organization. Hypersensitive and distrustful, such leaders attempt to obtain the full control over what is going on in the organization and become overinvolved in analysis and decision-making processes.
3. *The detached leader* is withdrawn and uninvolved in the organization's present and future. He or she reduces interaction with organizational members and the outside world to a minimum. Decisions are often vacillating and inconsistent.
4. *The depressive leader* often lacks self-confidence and is plagued with serious self-esteem issues. Self-involved, a depressive leader may be ignorant of the needs of followers, clients and suppliers. Lacking energy, force and drive, he or she may tolerate mediocrity and scare away dynamic and hopeful followers.

5. *The compulsive leader* dominates the organization from top to bottom, insisting that everyone conforms to strict rules developed at the top. Dogmatic or obstinate, a compulsive leader is obsessed with perfectionism, detail, routine and rituals.

Because organizational culture is highly susceptible to the influence of leadership behaviour, neurotic leadership patterns lead to toxic organizational cultures – and vice versa. Neurotic leadership patterns trigger social defences in followers, diverting energy away from attaining organizational goals.

Stress in the organization makes employees question the fundamental purpose of the organization. Existential anxiety of this kind accelerates all sorts of dysfunctional organizational processes, such as unrealistic ideals, toxic corporate cultures, neurotic organizations, or problems with motivation. Within such a work environment, people experience negative emotions, become alienated, and drift with no sense of direction. A dysfunctional culture like this can impede any remedial action on the part of senior executives. Even if they sincerely want to improve organizational health, they don't know how to go about it. This kind of vicious circle can only be broken by creating a culture of purposeful performance – a concerted effort towards organizational renewal.

But even if most organizations accept that they must either change or die, a remarkable number of change initiatives fail (Beer & Nohria, 2000). The first critical step is to develop the leader's awareness of the kind of leadership behaviour that has a negative impact on the organization's membership. But many leaders are sadly reluctant to seek and receive honest feedback about the impact their behaviour has on their subordinates. What measures can be taken, in spite of people's resistance to change, to manage organizational renewal? How can leaders take advantage of their adaptive capacity to turn their organizations into great places to work?

18.2   ORGANIZATIONAL CHANGE MANAGEMENT

Various authors (e.g. Beer & Nohria 2000; Palmer & Dunford, 2002) have suggested two approaches to organizational change. The 'hard' approach is where shareholder value is the only legitimate measure of corporate success; the 'soft' approach is to develop a corporate culture that enhances human capability through individual and organizational learning. According to Beer and Nohria (2000), change can be managed through engagement in controlling activities and shaping capabilities.

Drawing on this polarity, organizational change processes may be induced by transformations in the 'real' (external) world, such as modifying existing technology, or changing organizational structure and policies, as well as in the inner world of the individuals (Amado & Ambrose, 2001; Kets de Vries, 2001a, 2006). There is an identifiable continuum in this process, ranging from intended to unintended change outcomes (Palmer & Dunford, 2002). Intended change presupposes rational modifications. In this case, change agents assume that by introducing planned (and rational) changes, the entire organization will change in the intended direction. Unfortunately, changing organizational structure, policies or making rational decisions may generate only the illusion of order and control. Usually, the CEO and other influential executives assume that employees will internalize the new rules and regulations they prescribe and the organization will change. However, employees are not necessarily rational human beings but subject to a considerable amount of out-of-awareness behaviour.

Organizational defensive patterns cannot be changed merely by making structural changes (Argyris, 1993; Kets de Vries, 2001a, 2006). The introduction of structural changes only scratches the surface of any transformation effort, because as we have already intimated, there are changes that cannot be easily and obviously manipulated by the power holders in an organization. These are changes in the employees' inner world – the way they perceive reality. Considerable social interaction is needed among organizational participants to bring about mindset change. Because a large amount of behaviour takes place at an unconscious level, mindset changes are not easily accomplished. If organizational leaders want to be effective, however, they have to pay heed to these processes.

The organizational change process that we are going to illustrate is based on a model (Kets de Vries, 2001a) that recognizes the interplay of a number of variables:

- Change implies intended outcomes, characterized by the introduction of directed actions in the 'real' world, such as introducing new technologies (including web-based ones), activities or structures.
- Change requires a new interpretation of events and the construction of shared meanings among participants at all levels of the organization, a process that can be facilitated through group coaching experiences.
- To make organizational change effective, we need to explore the unconscious in daily work events. We need to understand what is really happening in the organization.

All too often, senior executives ignore the inherent tensions between the 'hard' and the 'soft' issues. Beer and Nohria (2000) and Kets de Vries (2001a) maintain that there are ways to resolve these tensions, and that they require goals that embrace the paradox between controlling activities and shaping capabilities. To enable organizational change, leaders must set directions from the top that engage all the people in the organization, and simultaneously address the 'hard' issues (structures, technology and systems) and 'soft' issues (corporate culture and values). In the next section we illustrate how such a transformation process can be implemented within an organization.

18.3   TRANSFORMATIONAL PROCESSES

The role of senior executives in leading organizational change processes is to provide supportive leadership that fosters a shared mindset and new behaviours. They must also ensure that changes are institutionalized in the daily social practices of the organization. Kets de Vries's (2001a, 2006) model of change provides a roadmap that helps management overcome organizational resistance by using a participative approach to engage the entire organization in the change process. Referring to the model, we will examine the four stages of the organizational change processes – creating a shared mindset, changing behaviour, institutionalizing change, and transforming the organization.

18.3.1   Creating a Shared Mindset

The first leadership task is recognizing the need for change. To get the process of change into motion requires a strong inducement in the form of pain or distress. At this point, leaders may face the unknown with multiple stress-inducing fears: am I doing the right thing? Will my team support my decisions? Am I able to make unpopular decisions? Am I able to lead the change process? How am I going to 'sell' my project? Even when the need for change has been acknowledged, people may still need a push that converts their fears into something actionable.

Bennis and Thomas (2002) use the term 'crucibles' to describe the often traumatic negative events (life-threatening episodes, periods of self-doubt) that leaders experience and which force them to confront change. Crucible experiences unleash deep self-reflection and a process of trial and error that helps them examine their distinctive leadership abilities. Astute senior executives will take advantage of the learning potential of 'crucibles' by making appropriate developmental interventions within the organization. But they cannot do it alone. Key power players need to build strong alliances and obtain social support with other power players in the organization.

Social support has been identified as the single most important factor in helping an individual overcome barriers to change (Kets de Vries & Balazs, 1998). To provide social support, organizations may need to create safe environments for managing personal and organizational change. But before someone can change direction, he or she has to stop.

Executive coaching or transformational executive development programmes provide safe environments for structured feedback. Such feedback tools, particularly 360-degree instruments that touch on psychodynamic processes, allow a leader to observe and reflect, to identify behavioural patterns that contribute to personal and organizational stress, and to start thinking about change. These transformational programmes, which frequently take the form of in-company workshops, may foster behavioural change that helps executives become more effective in organizational and personal settings. A significantly higher level of self-awareness is one of the usual outcomes of such programmes (Kets de Vries *et al.*, 2008). Change facilitators in these transformational programmes are some social practices (such as group coaching, networking and 360-degree feedback processes), the elaboration of action plans, the exploration of new selves through a test-and-learn process and the creation of a learning community that supports results over the long term (Kets de Vries *et al.*, 2008).

Members of the senior executive team should take the lead in participating in these transformational group interventions. They will have the opportunity to deal with otherwise 'undiscussable' issues and establish a shared leadership focus. In addition, these interventions may build a richer, deeper understanding of the leaders as individuals and the real reasons for their behaviour. The main objective of participating in transformational workshops is to develop a shared mindset characterized by collective ambition, commitment and motivation. Participation by a group of senior executives may help them recognize the need for action and acquire an external focus, critical at this stage of the transformation process (Kets de Vries & Balazs, 1998). The programme can elucidate the organizational change agenda at several different levels:

1. A discussion of the core values and desired culture of the organization. In addition, a gap analysis will be needed, comparing what is desired and what is really practised in the organization. Effective organizational cultures are strategically appropriate, guide day-to-day employee behaviour in a tangible way, and promote adaptability and change.
2. The development of a distinctive leadership brand. A leadership brand provides focused leadership through a combination of innovative skills, executives' team dynamics and excellence in execution. It maintains and promotes the distinctive competencies of the organization.
3. Clarification of the developmental leadership work that needs to be done to make executives fit the corporate culture and to enhance and maintain the distinctive, competitive advantages of the organization.

Transformational programmes must take place within a holding environment that helps lower defensive reactions, build mutual respect, foster transparency and establish trust. The interventions facilitate insights that illuminate hidden areas of the organization that need to be taken care of as a precondition for change. At the same time, they help build agreements about what needs to be changed and how the change process will be enacted. These transformational experiences have the following characteristics:

- Change agents create *learning* (Wenger, 1998) or *transitional* spaces (Winnicott, 1989; Korotov, 2005; Kets de Vries & Korotov, 2007) where executives have the opportunity to reinvent themselves, helping them to pick up the threads of stagnated development.
- Through *reflection*, change agents can bring to the surface and criticize the tacit understandings that have grown up around the repetitive experiences of a specialized practice and can make new sense of uncertain situations (Schön, 1983). A process of learning is promoted by the creation of meaning from past or current events, which serves as a guide for future behaviour (Daudelin, 1996).
- The creation of transitional space (Kets de Vries & Korotov, 2007) allows executives the opportunity to *play* (Schrage, 1999). Innovative, creative thinking is not a rational or logical process; it is much more like playing, exploring and trying new possibilities.
- In a transitional space, executives *feel free and safe* to express ideas and feelings. Public commitments consolidate the process of internalization and increase their motivation towards action.

Transformational group experiences of this sort bolster trust, collaboration and commitment among the organizational participants. There are three types of transitional experiences involved in the process: (i) relinquishing earlier, dysfunctional, but still valued roles, ideas and practices; (ii) creating, finding and discovering new, more adaptive ways of thinking and acting; and (iii) coping with the stress that accompanies the changing conditions derived from both outside and within the organizational system. These transitional experiences can help set directions through focused leadership and a new, more coaching-oriented mindset.

Effective leaders recognize that employees need support when they are in the process of reinventing the organization. Creating a coaching culture is the ideal way to align management behaviour with business objectives and develop people's emotional intelligence, encouraging continuous learning and recognizing achievements by providing constructive feedback. The major turning point comes when the organization's leadership moves from being autocratic to authoritative. The role of the leader changes to that of being a more autocratic figure to that of a coach – a person who works with employees to help them discover the answers (Daudelin, 1996).

18.3.2 Changing Behaviour

Employees' participation and involvement are the key success factors for organizational commitment. People at all levels of the organization need to be involved in the change effort (Kets de Vries & Balazs, 1998). The next leadership task is to make sure that people at all levels of the organization have internalized the change.

Leaders recognize that the will to change is not enough; they have to work to promote the appropriate skills that will adjust the repertoire of behaviours of all organizational members. Changing behaviour starts with consolidating new ways of doing things to gain competitive advantage.

A sense of direction will have been achieved through the reflection process described earlier. With this focus in place, the time has come to align the important players in the organization behind the leadership's new vision for the future. Leaders need to engage and empower their subordinates by transmitting that vision, the core values and desirable new behaviour patterns. Repetition of the change message and implementation of systems, structure and activities will aid the process of internalization. For a change process to be effective, executives have to be convinced both cognitively and emotionally of the advantages that the change effort will bring (Kets de Vries & Korotov, 2007).

Change will be accompanied by many fears. Some executives may be fearful of uncertainty (what do I need to do now?), obsolescence (everything I know is useless), self-doubt (am I capable of change?) and lack of significance (do I like these changes?). In the same way that the transformational workshop created a safe space for the transition process, the leadership of the organization needs to manage stress levels by making the organization a safe holding environment. The most salient role of leaders at this point is that of coach, enhancing the individual change process through trust and support (Kets de Vries, Korotov & Florent-Treacy, 2007).

Ambivalence is a key obstacle to change at this stage: people both want and don't want change. Miller and Rollnick (2004) suggest motivational interviewing as a tool for helping people resolve their ambivalent feelings and move on. Leaders can help employees to explore the underlying cognitive and affective processes that trigger commitment and effective change. Worst-case scenarios have to be explored. Confronting and resolving ambivalence may create a tipping point to bring the executive on board (Kegan & Lahey, 2001).

Informal networks and symbolic actions are inseparable from social support. Leaders must make sure that people at all levels of the organization are committed to the new way of doing things and that everyone is working in the same direction. Outputs at this stage are a focused/coaching corporate culture, and setting up appropriate systems, technology and structure for its long-term sustainability. Symbolic actions, which integrate learning with sense-making (Schwandt, 2005), provide a framework for articulating the change initiative.

18.3.3 Institutionalizing Change: Building Competencies, Practices and Attitudes

Leaders need to institutionalize change by building new competencies and practices. Training and development are facilitated through skill-building exercises and other on-the-job practices (e.g. mentoring, job shadowing, job rotations or job assignments).

Practice is crucial at this point and leaders need to recognize the immense learning potential hidden in everyday experience. To what extent has change been actionable? What is actually happening in the organization? Leaders must keep abreast of the day-to-day effects results of the change effort. They have constantly to evaluate the desirability of outcomes and introduce corrective action if necessary. Desired outcomes must be rewarded in bite-size portions, making the overall task more palatable. Sanctions have to be put into place for undesirable behaviour.

18.3.4 Transforming the Organization

At this point, the successful functioning of new behaviours and ideas should be apparent to all organizational participants. Obvious indicators of this are high levels of job satisfaction and productivity. But the good/bad news is that the change process is never-ending. Organizations need to build an innovation-driven culture that confronts change in a natural and incremental way: a coaching culture will facilitate the adaptability this implies. Leaders will need periodically to revise their assumptions and gather data from the organization to identify new requirements for change.

Having transcended the leadership crisis and established a focused, inspirational and coaching organization, participants will be bound in a compelling connective tissue of vision, mission, culture and structure. There will be clear leadership focus and the organization will be in the mood for change. At this point, organizations become authentizotic (coined from the Greek words for authenticity and vital to life) entities, a key quality of which is continuous self-renewal (Kets de Vries, 2001b). The action-reflection processes permit individuals and organizations to adapt continuously to the demands of change.

Reflective approaches require a coaching executive role (Daudelin, 1996). This supposes that the safe transitional space will, in the long run, be expanded to become a permanent feature of the system, part of its culture (Amado & Ambrose, 2001). The authentizotic organization finds meaning in work and invests trust in its people. It takes pride in what it is doing and the people who are doing it. It is this that makes the difference and makes an organization a great place to work.

18.4   CONCLUSIONS

Whether we like it or not, organizations are systems that change continuously. And facing change cannot be the result of a last minute wake-up call or a sudden eureka experience. It has to be a continuous process so that organizations can adapt seamlessly to the environment through an innovation-driven culture.

Summing up the observations made in this chapter, we've looked at how to address the journey of change and identified a number of challenges:

- Challenge 1: executives have to recognize that the status quo can no longer be maintained and that change is inevitable.
- Challenge 2: to make the change process effective, we need to control strategic activities and to become involved in shaping the inner world of employees. To manage this duality, the organization needs participative leadership, a focus on the 'hard' and the 'soft,' a process that leaves space for spontaneity, and a reward system that reinforces the strategic behaviours that sustain competitive advantage.
- Challenge 3: to create adaptive organizations, a shared change mindset that provides focused/coaching leadership and a clear sense of direction through a well-articulated vision are needed.
- Challenge 4: it is important to make sure that people at all levels of the organization are committed to change. This may mean the introduction of sanctions if people are resistant.
- Challenge 5: an effort has to be made to build strategic attitudes, competencies and practices within the organization. A reward structure should be put in place to support desirable behaviour.
- Challenge 6: organizational results have to be achieved and maintained over time by enforcing the organization's adaptive capability and the creation of an innovation-driven culture through continuous coaching practices.

The impact of these change processes may be tremendous and they may extend their influence to the whole organization. Coaching-focused leadership can provide a platform for sustainable organizational effectiveness and be an appropriate approach to engaging and developing others. Workplaces will be *healthier* in the sense that there will be plenty of fun, cooperation, trust and meaning.

Change initiatives usually include shifts in strategy, structure, systems and technology, but they also need a permanent and lasting transformation of the internal world of the employees. But, as we have emphasized, attention has to be given to external social (symbolic) practices. Symbolic actions serve to build the capabilities of the members at all levels by constructing new shared meanings of daily experiences. In this environment, the salient role of leaders turns into the role of coach to their teams to promote trust and social support.

More than ever before, leaders need to lead from a different place (Pascale, Lillemann & Gioja, 1997), placing themselves in a zone of discomfort, learning to tolerate ambiguity and coaching their teams appropriately. Only then will organizations have the adaptive capability of self-renewal that characterizes authentizotic organizations. If that is the case, a result orientation and a coaching corporate culture are entwined. This ability for continuous self-renewal will make all the difference. It creates the vitality that characterizes authentizotic organizations. As the Swiss writer, Henri Frederic Amiel once said, 'So as long as a person is capable of self-renewal, they are a living being'.

REFERENCES

Amado, G. & Ambrose, A. (Eds) (2001). *The Transitional Approach to Change.* London: Karnac Books.

Argyris, C. (1993). Education for Leading-Learning. *Organizational Dynamics,* **21**(3), 5–17.

Beer, M. & Nohria, N. (2000). Cracking the code of change. *Harvard Business Review,* **78**(3), 133–141.

Bennis, W.G. & Thomas, R.J. (2002). Crucibles of leadership. *Harvard Business Review,* **80**(9), 39–45.

Coyne, K.P. & Coyne, E.J., Sr. (2007). Surviving your new CEO. *Harvard Business Review,* **85**, May, 62–9.

Daudelin, M.W. (1996). Learning from experience through reflection. *Organizational Dynamics,* **24**(3), 36–48.

Jaques, E. (1974). Social systems as defense against persecutory and depressive anxiety. In G.S. Gibbard, J.J. Hartmann & R.D. Mann (Eds), *Analysis of Groups.* San Francisco: Jossey-Bass.

Kegan, R. & Lahey, L. (2001). *How the Way We Talk Can Change the Way We Work: Seven Languages for Transformation.* San Francisco: Jossey-Bass.

Kets de Vries, M.F.R. (2001a). *The Leadership Mystique: Leading Behavior in the Human Enterprise*. London: FT/ Prentice Hall.

Kets de Vries, M.F.R. (2001b). Creating authentizotic organizations: well functioning individuals in vibrant companies. *Human Relations*, **54**(1), 101–11.

Kets de Vries, M.F.R. (2006). *The Leader on the Couch: A Clinical Approach to Changing People and Organizations*. San Francisco: Jossey-Bass.

Kets de Vries, M.F.R. & Balazs, K. (1998). Beyond the quick fix: the psychodynamics of organizational transformation and change. *European Management Journal*, **16**(5), 611–22.

Kets de Vries, M.F.R., Carlock, R.S. & Florent-Treacy, E. (2007). *Family Business on the Couch: A Psychological Perspective*. Chichester: John Wiley & Sons, Ltd.

Kets de Vries, M.F.R., Hellwig, T., Guillen Ramo, L., Florent-Treacy, E. & Korotov, K. (2008). Long-term effectiveness of a transitional leadership development program: an exploratory study. *INSEAD Working Paper 2008/24EFE*.

Kets de Vries, M.F.R. & Korotov, K. (2007). Creating transformational executive education programs. *Academy of Management Learning and Education*, **6**(3), 375–87.

Kets de Vries, M.F.R., Korotov, K., & Florent-Treacy, E. (2007). Introduction: a psychodynamic approach to leadership development. In: M. Kets de Vries, K. Korotov & E. Florent-Treacy, Coach and Couch. Hampshire: Palgrave Macmillan.

Kets de Vries, M.F.R. & Miller, D. (1984). *The Neurotic Organization*. San Francisco: Jossey-Bass.

Kets de Vries, M.F.R., Vrignaud, P., Florent-Treacy, E. & Korotov, K. (2007). INSEAD Global Leadership Centre – 360-degree feedback instruments. An Overview. *INSEAD Working Paper 2007/01/EFE*.

Korotov, K. (2005). Identity Laboratories. *INSEAD PhD Dissertation*. INSEAD, Fontainebleau, France, and Singapore.

Lichtenstein, B.B. (2000). Self-organized transitions: a pattern amid the chaos of transformative change. *Academy of Management Executive*, **14**(4), 128–41.

Lucier, C., Wheeler, S. & Habbel, R. (2007). The era of the inclusive leader. *Strategy+Business*, **47**, 1–14.

Miller, W.R. & Rollnick, S. (2004). Taking oneself into change: motivational interviewing, stages of change, and therapeutic process. *Journal of Cognitive Psychotherapy: An International Quarterly*, **18**(4), 299–308.

Palmer, I. & Dunford, R. (2002). Who says change can be managed? Positions, perspectives and problematic. *Strategic Change*, (11), 243–51.

Pascale, R., Lillemann, M. & Gioja, L. (1997). Changing the way we change. *Harvard Business Review*, **75**, November/ December.

Schön, D.A. (1983). *The Reflective Practitioner*. New York: Basic Books.

Schrage, M. (1999). *Serious Play: How the World's Best Companies Simulate to Innovate*. Boston, MA: Harvard Business School Press.

Schwandt, D.R. (2005). When managers become philosophers: integrating learning with sense-making. *Academy of Management Learning and Education*, **4**(2), 176–92.

Thornhill, J., Milne, R. & Steen, M. (2008). Accent on egalite: Europe loses patience with its wealthy elite. *Financial Times*, 9 June. www.ft.com, accessed on 9 June 2008.

Wenger, E. (1998). *Communities of Practice: Learning, Meaning and Identity.* Cambridge: Cambridge University Press.

Winnicott, D.W. (1989). *Psychoanalytic Explorations.* London: Karnac Books.

CHAPTER 19

Building Interventions to Improve Staff Well-Being

Gordon Tinline and Ben Moss

Robertson Cooper Ltd, UK

The research-based case for improving staff well-being in organizations is very robust (e.g. Donald *et al.*, 2005; Cropanzano & Wright, 1999). This chapter takes that as a given and provides our perspective as experienced practitioners on the critical issues that need to be addressed to improve staff well-being, and practical advice for doing so. There are three main stages to this:

1. Building the business case.
2. Measuring well-being and engagement levels.
3. Taking action to improve working lives.

19.1 BUILDING THE BUSINESS CASE

Without a business case there is little hope of engaging business leaders with the idea of investing in well-being. There will almost certainly be those in your organization who equate well-being with providing free massages and doing yoga in the workplace, rather than seeing it as a tangible and valuable process of improving levels of psychological well-being every working day. This means that it's often difficult to present a solid business case for investing in the well-being of the workforce. However, the proof is available and when you pull it together it should be powerful enough to convince even the most hard-headed director.

A critical role of the business case is to help focus on the stakeholders of well-being in the organization and then to connect this with the

International Handbook of Work and Health Psychology, Third Edition. Edited by Cary L. Cooper, James Campbell Quick, and Marc J. Schabracq.

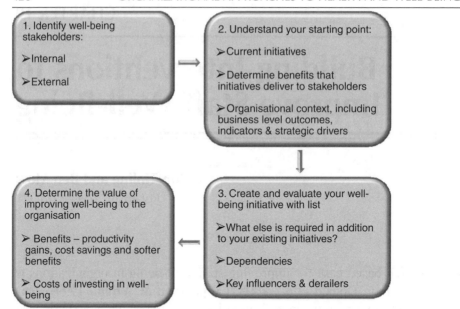

Figure 19.1 Process for Structuring the Well-being Business Case

business-level outcomes that are to be influenced by improving well-being. It's a process that brings together the research evidence and integrates it with your organizational objectives for well-being. The research and case studies give the board confidence that well-being interventions really work, while the organization-specific information makes the vision and benefits of an engaged workforce feel real for their business.

When we, at Robertson Cooper, are asked to advise clients on how to build a business case for well-being we use the model shown in Figure 19.1 to structure the process.

19.1.1 Stage 1: Identify well-being stakeholders

Starting with well-being stakeholders helps to ensure that there is a clear focus on the needs of staff groups who will be affected by, and can affect, the levels of well-being in the organization. It usually helps to include at least one group of senior managers or leaders.

19.1.2 Stage 2: Understand your starting point

Once the stakeholders are identified, it's important to focus on current organizational activity around well-being. At this point, it's useful to list all

Table 19.1   Stakeholder Analysis Matrix

Initiatives	Stakeholder group A	Stakeholder group B	Stakeholder group C
1	Benefits of initiative 1 to stakeholder group A	Benefits of initiative 1 to stakeholder group B	Benefits of initiative 1 to stakeholder group C
2	Benefits of initiative 2 to stakeholder group A	Benefits of initiative 2 to stakeholder group B	Benefits of initiative 2 to stakeholder group C
3	Benefits of initiative 3 to stakeholder group A	Benefits of initiative 3 to stakeholder group B	Benefits of initiative 3 to stakeholder group C

current well-being initiatives and note the benefits that each delivers to the stakeholders that have already been identified. Using the matrix shown in Table 19.1 can help to do this and may reveal that either some stakeholders currently receive no benefits or that some initiatives do not deliver any benefits to stakeholder groups.

It is also important to consider the organizational context at this stage. This includes considering the business-level outcomes that are important to the organization when it comes to improving well-being and employee engagement (e.g. sickness-absence rates, turnover, patient satisfaction etc.). Which outcomes would get key stakeholders' attention in terms of buying into the well-being improvement effort? What indicators are likely to be most effective to measure progress in relation to achieving these outcomes? This is also the right time to consider strategic drivers that are relevant to well-being initiatives. How do the business-level outcomes that you want to influence link to the organization's mission/strategy/business objectives?

19.1.3   Stage 3: Creating and evaluating your well-being initiative wish list

Creating a wish list is all about considering what else is required in terms of well-being initiatives. It's where you examine the matrix and identify the gaps – for example, are there outcomes that are not influenced by any of the existing initiatives?

It's also an opportunity to feed in the thinking that has been done about current strategic drivers: what additional initiatives are suggested by them? How can they support existing well-being initiatives? It's also a good time to think about well-being initiatives that have been considered desirable for a while, but have not yet been implemented: how can they fill the gaps in the matrix?

The aim is to end up with a wish list that combines new and existing initiatives. Review this list in the light of the target outcomes identified earlier in the process and evaluate the extent to which the initiatives deliver benefits to key stakeholder groups.

When you have a final list it's important to evaluate it thoroughly to take into account the current organizational context. This includes thinking about dependencies in terms of whether the success of a particular initiative is dependent on something else that is happening, for example, a funding decision or critical timescales. Also, consider the people/groups who are likely to affect the success of intended interventions. Are there key groups or individuals who can play a significant influencing role in ensuring the success of an initiative – or who could possibly completely 'derail' it? It is essential to identify these people/groups at this point and make plans to involve them in your efforts.

19.1.4   Stage 4: Determine the value of improving well-being to the organization

The final stage of building the business case for investing in well-being and employee engagement involves generating a clear picture of how the costs and benefits balance out. This enables the organization to take a robust view on the extent to which it is 'worth' gearing up to make the investment.

The benefits The first aspect of this stage concerns the benefits. Where possible it's always useful to generate cash-based figures to express the value that improving well-being will deliver to the organization. It is possible to do this using research-based information about the improvements that are possible and combining them with industry standard figures (e.g. Robertson, 2007). It is also important to try to envisage how things will be qualitatively different and improved when working life in your organization is characterized by high levels of well-being, e.g. better leadership, a stronger sense of purpose for all staff, a more supportive and healthy environment. It is often harder to generate cash figures for such outcomes, but these are not required or possible for every aspect of improvement.

The costs The second part of this stage involves identifying and quantifying the costs of the investment to the organization. Clearly, it's almost impossible to significantly change quality of working life, leadership/management style and fundamental aspects of the prevailing corporate culture without investing in it. There are usually external costs involved in this type of work, as organizations rarely have all of the expertise they need to make a real difference internally. It is therefore important to revisit your final list of initiatives and make an estimate of the external costs required to implement them. Finally, don't forget to take the internal resources required to successfully implement the initiatives into account and wherever possible quantify them. External consultants can play a valuable role in helping to design and implement integrated approaches to well-being, but these projects are seldom successful unless the organization in question is fully involved and committed. A good place to start is revisiting the key stakeholder groups that you identified and estimating the time required from each. After that, consider who else will need to be involved – e.g. the internal communications department.

19.2   MEASURING WELL-BEING AND ENGAGEMENT LEVELS

Once senior management is convinced of the need to invest in well-being, the first step is to measure how the workforce currently sees the well-being situation. In order to be in a position to effectively direct your investment it's important to generate an understanding of the blockers and enablers of well-being. This usually means an organizational-level survey that is specifically designed to measure these things, because it is almost impossible to make good decisions based on a few questions about well-being in the annual staff survey. The area of well-being and engagement is far too rich and cross-cutting to be tapped adequately in this way.

The best results come from an in-depth assessment of the current well-being situation. Other tools are available, but in this section we will mention two specific approaches to measurement, both of which are well suited to this stage of well-being initiatives.

The first, unsurprisingly, comes from the Health and Safety Executive (HSE 2005) in the form of their management standards for work-related stress. They have produced an assessment known as the Indicator Tool which is specifically designed to measure whether common sources of workplace stress exist. The tool measures perceptions about the work environment related to six areas:

• Demands – workload, work environment.
• Control – how much say a person has in how they do their work.

- Support – the encouragement and resources provided by the organization/line manager.
- Relationships – promoting positive working relationships and avoiding conflict.
- Role – whether employees have clear roles that they understand.
- Change – how well organizational change is managed and communicated.

Straight away it should be clear how understanding perceptions of these different areas across the organization can inform your decisions about where to focus improvement efforts. Think back to the initiatives that you identified earlier – consider the extent to which they may impact employees' perceptions of these areas.

One word of warning on a technical aspect of measuring well-being: It's important not to over-interpret the HSE Indicator Tool assessment – it provides a good indication of how staff view their working environment in important areas relating to stress and well-being, but it does not assess the impact of these on staff. To illustrate the difference, consider an example: if a member of staff indicates that they often have to work very intensively (an Indicator Tool item) it does not follow automatically that this damages their well-being. Some people enjoy and are motivated by intense work activity, particularly if they have a clear purpose for engaging in it. Once the Indicator Tool is completed and analysed it may well be important to investigate further the impact of the perceptions it reveals on staff health, commitment and well-being.

The HSE, as is consistent with their role as a risk regulator, provide some useful guidance around their tool, but the organization will usually need to work hard at using the results to effect real change. Further information on this approach is available at http://www.hse.gov.uk/stress/index.htm.

The other approach is ASSET, a tool originally developed by Cary Cooper and the product development team at Robertson Cooper in 2002. It measures the presence of similar barriers and enablers to well-being as the HSE indicator tool, but goes further to ask employees about whether these things actually trouble them. ASSET also measures health outcomes and self-reported productivity so that it's possible to link the sources of stress that are experienced in the organization with reported psychological and physical outcomes. Finally, ASSET includes measures of more positive aspects of working life, such as levels of motivation and commitment to (and from) the organization.

When a whole organization completes the tool it is possible to see where the hotspots of stress are, but also where pockets of best practice lie. ASSET has an extensive norm base so it enables an objective comparison

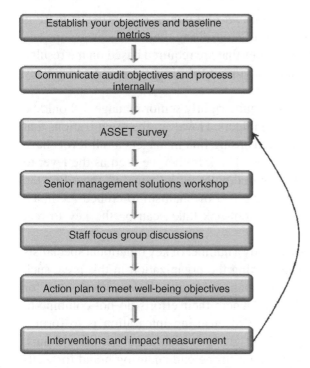

Figure 19.2   The ASSET process

to be made with other similar organizations. This analysis can be conducted inside the client organization using online software that enables well-being professionals to compare the results from different departments, job levels, geographical locations etc. Again, the purpose of this stage is to enable you to make more informed decisions about where to invest in improving well-being. Figure 19.2 shows a standard ASSET process, but in general this is adapted to the needs of the organization in question.

To put this process in context, there are a number of additional considerations that need to be worked through successfully if a well-being audit is to prove fully effective. Key examples of these are:

- *Staff communication*: many organizations regularly survey staff without fully engaging them in the process. A successful audit will have a coherent identity and be promoted effectively to differentiate it from previous surveys that may have taken place. It will be connected with existing activity and positive messages around promoting well-being. In addition, there will be a clear plan for communicating the results with staff in a meaningful dialogue.

- *Seeing the audit as a means to an end and not an end in itself*: there is little to be gained by surveying staff, consulting them in focus groups and then failing to implement the actions that are required based on the results. All this does is raise expectations without fulfilling them and adds to any existing cynicism.

- *Engaging managers at all levels*: quite rightly senior managers should be involved in the audit as key stakeholders. However, the organizations that get most value from audits tend to ensure line managers at all levels have access to results for their areas too. This can then be used as the lever to encourage them to enter ongoing dialogues with their staff regarding the issues that emerge. Using the audit as a mechanism to embed a climate of shop-floor communication, or tool-box talks, can be the key to real engagement.

- *Integrating support*: there are usually a number of key functional specialists who have a role to play in supporting the organization in this area, such as HR, health and safety and occupational health. However, it's easy for them to end up operating in silos where their efforts do not combine to deliver maximum value. One way of ensuring integration is to form a cross-functional well-being support group, which, amongst other things, is tasked with building and owning a strong and enduring brand for well-being improvement.

19.3   A PRACTICAL GUIDE TO TAKING ACTION TO IMPROVE WORKING LIVES

One of the biggest pitfalls for well-being initiatives is 'consultation without action' – staff show a lot of goodwill when they complete these surveys and they are entitled to see a clear plan of action when the results are in. But once the organization understands the well-being situation, it's not just action plans that staff are looking for – they want to see improvement too, so it's important to budget beyond the initial survey and include enough time and funds to actually make a difference.

Clearly, the actual actions that are taken post-survey depend on what the workforce is telling the organization and on the business-level outcomes that were identified as being important earlier in the process. In fact, many organizations we have worked with have seen this as the start of a much broader change process. The work done on the business case helps enormously at this stage because, while it doesn't predetermine post-survey actions, it means there is a shared understanding about the starting point and goals, as well as a set of ideas for new initiatives. The results of the survey can now be put into the mix and can be used to modify plans based on the views of the workforce.

Whether the organization has conducted a well-being audit or not there is a need to produce an integrated action plan to improve well-being and engagement with clear and measurable outcomes. This should have senior management endorsement with a commitment to providing the resources to support its successful implementation.

The gradual adoption of the HSE stress management standards by many organizations is indicative of the evolving agenda in the area of well-being. As discussed earlier in this report, the starting point for this has often been a compliance mindset with the perceived need being to implement the approach recommended by the regulator. Typically, this might lead an organization to rush into issuing the HSE's Indicator Tool survey to a sample of staff, followed perhaps by a few focus groups. However, there are risks to this approach if organizations have not properly thought through how to position the approach and how to use the results to inform a sustainable improvement plan. A compliance mindset, normally linked to stress risk management, can become a barrier to addressing well-being and engagement fully and is likely to lead to a defensive management approach of just controlling risk rather than going beyond this to realize positive benefits.

Thinking a bit more broadly and proactively about taking action to improve well-being and employee engagement, all initiatives and interventions designed to improve organizational outcomes via the workforce can be classified into one of three categories:

- **Composition** (the procedures used to recruit, select and place people into specific roles in the organization).
- **Training and development** (processes for learning and development).
- **Situational engineering** (e.g. the design of the work that people do, the structure and processes that operate in the organization and the work environment – including less tangible factors such as culture and climate).

This view can help you to get to grips with myriad options for intervening to improve well-being. Many organizations work hard on all of these categories – designing recruitment and selection processes to recruit the best talent; taking a strategic approach to identify training and development needs; aligning these with the strategic goals of the organization; bringing expertise to bear on issues of work design, organizational structure, change management and more besides.

We will look shortly at these different layers of intervention more closely, but before we do it's important to highlight some more general considerations when taking action to improve well-being:

- Wherever possible design an integrated set of interventions targeting specific areas and outcomes for improvement, employing different categories or 'layers' of intervention.
- Ensure clear success metrics are in place to evaluate the success of each intervention.
- Carefully consider a broad range of possible consequences that may flow from a particular intervention, in particular think carefully about any unintended consequences that may develop and adopt risk management strategies where appropriate.
- Avoid launching interventions as new change initiatives where there is a climate of change weariness. Consider how new interventions might be woven into existing programmes of activity rather than launched as a new one. Aim to achieve measurable benefits before declaring the success of any intervention.
- Involve all legitimate stakeholders in designing interventions, recognizing that their needs can only be met if there are clear operational and business benefits to be achieved by doing so.
- Build well-being improvement into the fabric of the organization as a continuous improvement journey and avoid short-term 'magic bullet' thinking. Build a brand that defines the long-term identity and essence of well-being in the organization.

Table 19.2 illustrates how the three different categories or layers of intervention – composition, development and situational engineering – can be used to identify practical actions when applied to some of the key enablers of psychological well-being.

Going through the process of populating this kind of matrix – particularly guided by results of a well-being survey or audit – can simplify the sometimes daunting process of action planning well-being interventions. It provides a structure for considering where it is possible to leverage well-being for the benefit of the organization.

Ultimately many action plans employing multi-layered interventions will have an overriding objective of reducing sickness absence, particularly in the public sector where it tends to be significantly higher than in the private sector. One organization that adopted a multi-layered approach with a demonstrable impact on sickness absence is Kent Police (see Box 19.1).

Table 13.2 Layers of intervention

Well-being influence	Layered intervention options (examples)		
	Composition	Development	Situational engineering
Balanced workload	Recruit staff with skills and work styles better suited to the required work Increase staff numbers	Develop managers to balance staff challenge and support more effectively Train staff in work-smarter/ time management techniques	Review and improve work planning and distribution mechanisms Reduce workload Improve technology and resources
Collaborative relationships	Construct work teams with a better balance of team role preferences Change promotion criteria to increase emphasis on team-working skills	Train managers and customer facing staff in conflict management techniques Coach managers who over-use a command and control leadership approach	Increase cross-functional team working Redesign office layout to increase space for informal collaboration
Enhanced control	Select staff with high internal locus of control Redeploy people who feel they cannot exert sufficient control in their current role Select managers who are happy to delegate control	Train staff using cognitive behavioural approaches to learn to control their thinking and reactions for positive outcomes Assertiveness training to develop staff to take control	Redesign jobs to maximize perceptions of control Reduce layers of management
Sense of purpose	Introduce realistic job previews to improve fit between candidate goals/ aspirations and organizational goals Promote managers based on their track record in inspiring teams to perform well above their previous level	Introduce training in goal-setting techniques for all new managers and supervisors Coach senior managers with the objective of improving their skills in articulating a compelling vision Board development to create shared vision	Design and implement a strong well-being brand Reduce bureaucracy Reduce levels of the organization so mission and vision is more visible

---

Box 19.1 Kent Police improve well-being to reduce absenteeism

Kent Police used ASSET to measure well-being and then implemented a programme of interventions to drive organizational development and improvement. The initiatives that were launched following the survey included:

- Introducing psychological screening for staff entering vulnerable units (e.g. Child Protection).
- Introducing the W8wise@work campaign, including staff MOTS, plus diet and exercise programmes.
- Introducing 'Well Person' checks and offering them to all staff.
- Rolling out a new Attendance Management programme.

In just two years, these and other initiatives led to a **25% reduction in sickness absence** (that's 18,600 sick days saved per year across a workforce of around 6000 people), as well as improvements in ASSET scores when a second survey was administered. The CIPD estimate that the average cost of a day's absence is £78, so that would equate to a saving of nearly £1.5 million per annum for Kent Police. More details of this project are available at http://www.robertsoncooper.com/Pages/Resources/Case-Studies.aspx.

19.3.1   Senior Management Ownership – Take Responsibility but Share Power

Another frequent barrier to success is to see the well-being improvement action plan as being owned by HR, health and safety or occupational health. It is not unusual for senior managers to delegate action planning and ownership of the plan to one of, or a combination of, these specialist functions. At best this approach is misguided, and at worst it is an abdication of a key leadership role. Leaders are responsible for creating and developing organizational culture – as the management thinker Max De Pree put it they 'define reality' for the workforce. In this sense, well-being and the interventions that are required to maintain and improve it are matters of strategic relevance and importance.

There is a difficult balance for leaders to strike here between having a vision that encourages employees to be highly engaged and giving away enough control to enable that to happen. In this sense, traditional command and control style leadership and management is usually the enemy of employee engagement. In organizations characterized by this style of leadership employees are 'sold to' as if they were an external customer. In such organizations, relentless internal marketing about the next change or type of behaviour required tends to switch employees off. This is in marked contrast to more modern conceptions of leadership as an exercise in 'co-creation' and 'involvement' that aims to proactively create situations where employees are part of the solution design process – and not just in the sense of completing a staff survey. The message to staff inherent in such approaches to leadership is simple: 'You're involved and our job as leaders is to provide the right conditions for you to contribute your best work' (Smythe, 2007). Clearly, many UK organizations have a long way to go to get to this situation, but the drive to get there can only come from those at the top. Once the conditions are created employees also have to accept their responsibility for behaving as productive partners in the process.

In his excellent book, *Chief Engagement Officer*, John Smythe provides some powerful insights into the role that leaders need to play if well-being and engagement are to thrive in organizations. He makes the point that 'engagement' can be defined narrowly – it's simply an integral part of organizational and local decision making. So, what becomes key is the leader's capacity to engage with staff in ways that add value to everyday decision making and change. But what is also critical to adding value is the way that the organization's design opens up large-scale change to the right groups. The idea is that if the right groups are engaged they will add value to day-to day decisions and larger processes of change – but, of course, senior leaders have to learn to give some of the control away to get this reward and that can require a major mindset change for some. The author also notes that positive engagement practices such as those described above and in the case study below could pre-empt reliance on more bureaucratic consultation processes imposed by regulation and tradition. For example, you only have to look at the rise of social networking and sharing websites to see that what once was thought of as 'chaos' or 'anarchy' is now an accepted part of 'how we do things'. Imagine a world without YouTube, MySpace or FaceBook! These revolutionary concepts were all based on a positive ethos of sharing for the good of the community – whether that be programmers, musicians, film-makers or society at large. Organizations are no different – they are just communities of people who are gathered together for a common purpose – and as with the online communities mentioned above, ways of communicating, sharing and generating knowledge have changed forever. This has profound implications for the way that businesses are organized, led and managed. To reset the bar, John Smythe introduces a good ground rule for all leaders to adhere to:

Decisions are not complete until leaders have planned the engagement of their people.

Figure 19.3   Well-being drivers that leaders influence and the HSE Management Standards

Another point that the book from which the above case study makes is that the style of leaders will either turn people on or off – both one-to-one and en masse. The idea that leaders and managers have a major role to play in defining the experience of employees is not a new one, but there is now a much better understanding of the leadership behaviours that influence well-being levels across the workforce. With this understanding comes a greater willingness to invest in ensuring that these behaviours are part of the prevailing corporate culture. Figure 19.3 shows the areas where leadership style through well-being enablers has a direct impact on staff well-being and stress perceptions (using the HSE Management Standards structure).

So leaders and leadership behaviour is important, but equally pivotal is the role of line managers and the relationships they develop and maintain with their direct reports. There are two main reasons for the importance of the line manager role:

- They play a central role in building and sustaining an engaged and enthusiastic workforce.
- Management processes, intended to ensure that employees' behaviour is aligned with the goals of the organization, are limited by the reactions that they produce from the workforce.

The second point reinforces the central issue in this report – that organisations need an engaged and positive approach from their people, otherwise change and other interventions, whatever they are intended to achieve, will not produce a positive reaction from the workforce and will therefore be less effective. Line manager behaviour is critical for enhancing and sustaining high levels of psychological well-being in any organization. This relationship is the most important one for all employees. The line manager is the link between the goals and mission of the organization and the day-to-day behaviour of the employee. As far as psychological well-being is concerned, the key to the success of this relationship is the extent to which the manager strikes the balance between challenge and support for the employee. Feeling suitably challenged and being able to strive to reach goals is a critical factor in building psychological well-being and self-confidence, both within the workplace and elsewhere. However, when challenge levels are too great or the goals are really unachievable people need support. Balancing these two types of behaviour is perhaps the most important managerial skill for developing a high well-being, high resilience workforce.

This highlights what is often a central development need for managers that needs to be addressed, increasing their capacity and skills to balance challenge and support effectively. This is often best achieved through one-to-one coaching, but at the very least should be the subject of training. The impetus for this may be to enable managers to be more supportive to improve collaboration, as indicated in Table 19.2. Alternatively, it may stem from a need to up-skill middle managers in challenging more effectively upwards and at their peer level, as well as with their direct reports.

At Robertson Cooper we have developed the Leadership Impact approach that seeks to help managers to fully understand the impact of their leadership behaviour on the well-being and engagement of their staff. The well-being enablers in Figure 19.3 can and should be influenced by leaders. To do so effectively they need to understand their own behavioural preferences in these critical areas – and these are linked to their personality or natural style. For example, some managers will find it difficult to delegate due to a strong perfectionist streak and as a result their staff may feel they are given limited opportunity to exert influence over areas of work they feel should be within their span of control. Or, a senior manager's desire for change and achievement may cause him or her to push people too hard on occasion. The key point is that self-awareness in critical areas is the starting point for developmental change. On its own it does not guarantee development, but it is an essential precursor.

19.3.2   Influencing Senior Managers

Probably the ultimate barrier to success in improving well-being and engagement are the attitudes and beliefs that some senior managers and directors appear to hold about these areas. There is still a tendency for some senior leaders to see them as soft issues that HR should tackle to allow them to concentrate on the performance of the business. Ultimately, well-being and engagement will take root in an organization only when the people leading it truly believe these are strategic and performance issues. The business case approach we have described earlier in this report is part of making this connection, but another important ingredient is making a personal connection with senior people, focusing on their well-being. It's important to win their buy-in and develop open and strong relationships with the key stakeholders at the top of the organization. For example, a major global pharmaceutical company had a coach spend a year talking to all of its senior executives one to one about their well-being and work–life balance. This was originally intended as a one-off initiative, but created such a demand from the senior executives that it became a permanent role for the coach! Crucially the company also sees this as part of a climate change process which has led to a strong belief that good health and well-being is good business, and has opened the door for an ongoing programme of activity throughout the organization. When you get it right at the top level it's possible to make big changes to how things are done in the organization.

19.4   SUMMARY

Practical benefits are clearly achievable from building and implementing well-being improvements. However, they should be entered into with a realistic time frame in mind and with maximum staff involvement and ownership at their heart.

This chapter has highlighted that there are three essential stages organizations should work through to improve well-being and engagement in a way that is sustainable:

1. Build a compelling business case.
2. Measure levels of well-being and engagement.
3. Take action to improve working lives.

Inevitably this should be an ongoing cycle of activity, where the impact of actions taken is reviewed against the expected business benefits, as well as being checked with the workforce to ensure that value is being added. There is no doubt that there are significant challenges associated with taking meaningful action to improve the working lives of staff – from getting funding and senior management buy-in to overcoming initial cynicism among the workforce. However, organizations are starting to design and define processes for reaping the benefits available by investing thoughtfully in the area of well-being and engagement. The result is a range of exciting new ways of working that benefit both organizations and staff alike. And ultimately, that's what the next phase of developing well-being in the workplace will be about in the UK: creating new ways of working that benefit everybody.

REFERENCES

Cropanzano, R. & Wright, T.A. (1999). A 5-year study of change in the relationship between well-being and performance. *Consulting Psychology Journal: Practice and Research*, **51**, 252–65.

Donald, I., Taylor, P., Johnson, S., Cooper, C., Cartwright, S. & Robertson, S. (2005). Work environments, stress and productivity: an examination using ASSET. *International Journal of Stress Management*, **12**, 409–23.

HSE (2005). *The Management Standards for Work-related Stress*. http://www.hse.gov.uk/stress/standards/standards.htm.

Robertson, S. (2007). Using business psychology to close the well-being gap. *Selection and Development Review*, **23**(4).

Smythe, J. (2007). The CEO: *Chief Engagement Officer: Turning Hierarchy Upside Down to Drive Performance*. London: Gower.

CHAPTER 20

Stress and Effectiveness: An Approach for Changing Organizational Culture[1]

Marc J. Schabracq[2]
Human Factor Development, The Netherlands
and
Iva Smit[3]
E&E Consultants, The Netherlands

The chapter gives an overview of sources of stress and ineffectiveness in work and the work environment. Several underlying factors are discussed. Apart from change in itself, these factors involve a surplus or a shortage of the following characteristics: degree of task challenge, as well as orderliness, social embedding, and compatibility of values and goals. We then describe an approach of organizational culture change, which uses the occurrence of stress reactions as signals to indicate where the organizational culture is less than effective. Once employees have identified the main problems in this way, workshops can be set up to enhance the effectiveness of their work as well as their well-being.

[1] For a much more elaborated treatment of this subject, we refer to Schabracq (2007).

[2] Marc J. Schabracq PhD (Schabracq@humanfactor.nl) has published some 25 books, as well as more than 100 articles and book chapters. He works as an independent organizational consultant in the fields of stress management, organizational and personal change, elderly personnel and forensic psychiatry.

[3] Iva Smit PhD (E&E Consult, ismit@efp.nl) is Director of the Expertise Centre for Forensic Psychiatry (EFP, Utrecht NL). She has published several books and a great number of articles and book chapters. As a consultant, she also works in the fields of organizational culture and health. In addition, she is an expert in the operational analysis of fraud, as well as the design and application of AI-based systems for simulation and decision support.

International Handbook of Work and Health Psychology, Third Edition. Edited by Cary L. Cooper, James Campbell Quick, and Marc J. Schabracq.
© 2009 John Wiley & Sons, Ltd. Published 2015 by John Wiley & Sons, Ltd.

20.1 INTRODUCTION: ORGANIZATIONAL CULTURE, EVERYDAY REALITY AND STRESS

The concept of organizational culture is hard to define. This difficulty stems from the wide and diverse use of the term organizational culture, as well as from the fact that most of organizational culture does not meet the eye. However, following the logic of the biblical saying that a tree is known by its fruits, one can say that organizational culture produces the everyday reality of an organization. This everyday reality, at least in principle, is open for inspection. Everyday reality refers to how things are in the organization, and what its stakeholders do and experience. Everyday reality not only entails the recurring forms of the organizational members' routines, but also includes matters such as the housing and lay-out of the organization and the common reality stemming from that housing and lay-out, with its blueprints for behaviour, perception, thought and feeling. When employees are unable and/or unwilling to fit their behaviour into the relevant formats provided by the culture, their behaviour becomes less effective, while they also experience stress and alienation. This makes everyday reality a logical point of application for interventions aiming at the optimization of organizational well-being.

Though the actual forms of everyday reality may have come about in somewhat coincidental ways, the result is a highly predictable way of doing. Everyday reality turns out to be a solid reality, which one shares with all involved and in which the organization's members can firmly belief (Schabracq, 1991, 2007). Other possible approaches don't develop, simply because the original approaches were good enough – at least, they apparently did not generate insurmountable difficulties – and, as it is, something can take only one form at a time. The organization's members just keep on enacting the everyday reality's forms, as if their routines represent the only possible way to do things, making the everyday reality even more solid in the process. Such a developmental process is called 'autopoiesis' (Maturana & Varela, 1980), its result a self-organizing system (De Bono, 1990).

The forms that make out everyday reality are open to inspection, even though usually nobody inspects them extensively. As long as these forms are properly displayed, the organizational members hardly pay conscious attention to them. Though the forms are experienced as self-evident parts of reality, they provide all involved with a multitude of cues, signalling:

- which 'piece' or 'play' they are playing;
- the roles in the play which all players are enacting;
- where they are in the play, i.e. the relevant scene and lines.

These cues enable others to display the appropriate complementary behaviour, which in its turn provides cues for the next lines of the other actors. In this way one's posture and movements serve as proposals to enact a certain situation and its inherent relations (Schabracq, 1991), even though the posture and movements are hardly perceived as such. They are just automatically being acted upon.

Everyday reality essentially consists of non-problematic routines, habitual ways to respond to the permanent or recurrent demands resulting from fulfilling the functions of organizational culture. So, organizational culture is about recurrent solutions for recurrent problems (Schabracq, 2007). People continuously re-enact, reconstruct, recognize, represent and recite the forms and meanings of culture (Moscovici, 1984), and abstain from other possibilities. Most of the endless repetition of all this activity stays out of awareness. Though essentially a never-ending Sisyphus labour, we just do it with a calm fanaticism: we sustain the discipline to not pay attention to other possibilities and ignore our not paying attention to these other possibilities. In this way we create a reality that provides stability and continuity, as well as normality and perceived safety. To the degree that enacting this everyday reality is effective at our work, we can lose ourselves in our tasks, without being needlessly distracted and disturbed, blissfully ignoring all the effort involved. As a result, everybody knows what to do, what to attend to and whom to involve in it. If this self-evident everyday reality is not realized, the functionality of the organization and the effectiveness of its members break down, and stress and alienation ensue. This breakdown, which results in stress and alienation, can be a matter of the characteristics inherent in that reality, but it can also be a consequence of changes in the organization and the work.

Of course, stress and alienation are undesirable, but they also have an important positive function: they serve as signals, as they clearly indicate that something is wrong (Schabracq & Cooper, 2001): the organizational culture apparently does not provide a proper solution here anymore and chances are that the effects of this go beyond the mere stress and alienation phenomena.

The everyday reality can be divided in four domains:

- the challenge inherent in the work itself;
- the orderliness of the work environment;
- the social embedding of the work; and
- the fit between the values and goals of individual employees and those of the organization.

In each of these domains, disturbances can arise, which can be described as a surplus or shortage of what in itself is a good thing. These disturbances result in a situation in which the individual must do something that he cannot do, or does not want to do. This then results in a loss of control and effectiveness, as well as in stress and alienation (Schabracq & Cooper, 2003). The middle regions on the other hand go together with a feeling of safety and self-evidence, the feeling of living in a manageable, comprehensible and meaningful reality (Antonovsky, 1987). In organizations and work, the 'middle regions' – the exact nature of which of course varies per individual – allow for functionality. We return later to the sources of stress brought about by the surpluses and shortages of these domains, but first we examine the impact of change in organizations.

20.2   EVERYDAY WORK: STABILITY AND CHANGE

Everyday work, like every form of reality, depends on the attention we pay to that work. When we focus our attention on something else, the reality of the work dissolves and no longer determines our actions, which diminishes the effectiveness of our work. The easiest and best way to keep on focusing our attention on our work is to let the work engage us as if by itself, so that we do not need to force ourselves. To engage us in such a way, the work needs certain characteristics, while at the same time the work environment should not provide too much in the way of diversion that will needlessly demand our attention. As far as these conditions are met, the working reality is effective. We experience functioning in an effective work reality as self-evident, accompanied by a sense of trust and control. Though maybe we hardly experience these feelings as such, we usually do experience their absence, though we can adapt to their absence in the second stage of stress (Schabracq, 2003).

The reality of our everyday work life provides us with important outcomes, which turn that reality into quite an addictive comfort zone. We have also invested a lot in bringing about and keeping up this reality: it took much effort to acquire the necessary skills; it demanded, and still demands, a lot of highly repetitive work, and a strict discipline of our attention. As a result, we tend to perceive this comfort zone as a self-evident part of our identity. Consequentially, we perceive outside pressure to change these adaptations as an infraction, which may cause all kinds of stress reactions. Such pressure may for instance evoke all sorts of unpleasant emotions, which we prefer not to feel. Moreover, we know our present outcomes, but have no idea what the future will bring us. So we tend to fight off such infractions, which is often denominated by the antagonists of the change as 'resistance to change', which by its association with the psychoanalytical concept of 'resistance' actually implies a disqualification of the response as being unconscious and irrational.

Though we experience this comfort zone as a part of ourselves, it is a part of organizational culture as well: we share the concerns evoked by impending change with many of our colleagues. These shared concerns, and the emotions they trigger, tend to turn our attempts to hold on to our comfort zones into a collective enterprise: it feels only logical to support each other in this respect. The mutual support can make the collective resistance to fight off change surprisingly effective and well coordinated. This resistance can also arise when it concerns changes for the better, that is, as seen from an outside perspective. This collectively fighting off change is far from surprising. When we define culture as a repertory of standard solutions to standard problems, it is only logical that it strives for stability and continuity. Only as far as an organizational culture accomplishes this objective, can it provide reality and normality to its members.

Though it is only natural for organizational cultures, and their members, to fight change, this resistance can become a deadly course when it interferes with their adaptation to changes in the outside environment. As it is, the change in the environment has increased in an unprecedented way and is still increasing at an accelerating pace. As a result, many companies must adapt to their changing environment as well as they can, which often boils down to radical changes in employees' everyday reality. Adapting to these changes requires new skills and knowledge from them. Though this kind of change does not occur in the same degree in all organizations, everywhere more employees than ever are confronted with changes that they did not ask for.

All these changes must be integrated in our everyday reality in a manageable way. One can – with some right – state that such an adaptation is a sheer perversion of our organizational cultures, as it is the main objective of an organizational culture to provide standard solutions to standard problems. Though such a statement may feel justified, it is not particularly helpful in adapting to these changes. Still, if adapting implies changes in our work, it will diminish the effectiveness of our functioning for some time and may lead to stress and alienation. Too much change in too little time then does threaten the effectiveness of our functioning. Examples of such changes are all kinds of reorganizations, new policies, changes in tasks and task demands, mergers and new managers, as well as new technology, computer systems and software. All of these changes can give rise to severe stress reactions and disturbances of effectiveness.

20.3 THE WORK ITSELF

Effective work is a matter of the challenge demanded by the work: the challenge should be neither too little nor too much, as effective functioning only takes place in the 'middle region'.[4] Something similar applies to an effective work environment. Here such 'right' middle regions play a role as well, though now several variables are involved. Here too, 'too much' or 'too little' of such a variable implies a lower level of effectiveness.

Taking 'task challenge' as an example, it is obvious that we can't perform a task that is too challenging, i.e. too difficult, too extensive, etc. On the other hand, a task that challenges us too little causes problems in the longer run also: we get bored, our attention is diverted, etc. However, the right degree of challenge, the 'middle region' – the nature of which of course varies per individual – enables us to function effectively. We can consider this middle region as an illustration of a very old and widespread ethical concept, namely 'the narrow path of virtue' or 'the golden mean', a central concept in the thinking of Aristotle and Christian medieval philosophy, as well as in classical Chinese philosophy.

The work is organized functionally and effectively to the degree that we can keep our attention on the work. Put differently: the work must be challenging enough, while at the same time we must be able to handle the challenge.

20.3.1 Work that Implies Insufficient Challenge

When work does not challenge us sufficiently to hold our attention while we still must do that work, we must turn to another kind of attention: we force ourselves to keep our mind on our work. Such a forced form of attention soon becomes very tiring. We can only go on in such a way for a limited period of time. Then attention is diverted, we can become strangely sleepy, and it becomes difficult to do the work. Social contacts often play a crucial part here in keeping us somewhat focused and effective anyhow. Moreover, unchallenging tasks often have to be done in large quantities, and at a fast pace. As a result, these tasks also can be too challenging at the same time as well. Several causes of insufficient challenge are discussed here.

- *Too few activities to fill the time and lack of demands.* Having insufficient activities to fill the time in a work situation, while not being

---

[4] Checklists for surpluses and shortages of challenge inherent in the work, as well of the following domains, are to be found in Schabracq (2007).

allowed to leave either, is for many people very unpleasant. Too little to do is the stuff where imprisonment is made of. The same goes for too slow a work pace and a lack of demands. In the longer run, we become drowsy, get bored and have difficulty concentrating on the little work we must do. We become less effective, and chances are that we make more mistakes.

- *Work with insufficient meaning.* Work without much meaning appeals insufficiently to our talents and motives. As a result, it is hard to keep our mind on the tasks' execution, which makes us ineffective. Insufficient meaning can be a matter of very little variation, and much short-cycled repetition. A good example is working at a conveyor belt. Often such tasks are quite easy, which is not good for concentration either. The lack of meaning can also stem from the remoteness of the task's contribution to the final product.
- *Too little decision latitude.* Some tasks are so overly regulated that every-thing – breaks, the sequence of partial tasks, work pace, and so on – is fixed. This lack of freedom occurs for example at counters or call centers, or when our work links us up to some machine or assembly line we cannot influence. Often such work is strictly supervised as well, with or without the help of electronic devices. Strict supervision can also interfere with the social contact during the work.
- *Very formalized work.* In some organizations, the way tasks are performed is more important than the results and outcomes. The task then turns into painstakingly sticking to time-consuming formal procedures, checks and double checks, a ritual way of working, without paying attention to, or even disdaining, outcomes and results. The task itself may even become empty and devoid of meaning. More of this is described in Section 20.4.2.

20.3.2 Tasks that Imply too Much Challenge

Work can also demand a level of challenge that is too far beyond our compe-tence. We then start to make mistakes, and are unable to deal with the task in a systematic way, or to survey things properly. We experience mental chaos, and task performance breaks down. The following issues can play a part:

- *Too many things to do in too little time.* Doing things at high speed can be pleasurable, as long as everything goes well. We can surprise ourselves, be proud of ourselves, and enjoy relaxing afterwards. It becomes a different story when things do not go well, for example when we cannot concentrate, are angry about the way in which the work was allocated to us, are tired, or feel that we are not doing well. In general, deadlines should not be too limiting, nor too numerous.

- *Tasks that are too difficult*. Difficult tasks can have similar effects as too little time. A different scenario ensues, however, when the work is much too difficult, for example due to a lack of necessary experience or training. We then block ourselves completely or task performance becomes chaotic. Attempts to repair mistakes take a lot of time, and are not always successful. We can try to work around the problems, to get some of the work done anyhow, if that is at all possible.

- *Serious consequences*. The challenge presented by a task becomes greater to the degree that the consequences of doing it wrong become more serious, for example when we must take a decision that has serious consequences for different parties. Sometimes we do not even have all the necessary information to make the best decision. Still, we do not want others to suffer needlessly from this, and want to do everything correctly, which is impossible. Because organizations have become flatter, and more responsibility has been pushed down to the work floor, people who were used to doing what the boss said, now have to take such decisions themselves. For these people, having to take such decisions can make their work more challenging than they like it to be.

- *Ambiguities*. In many jobs, we must do well, without knowing what exactly is expected of us. When we are bothered by this, it is much harder to carry out the task effectively. Ambiguity can take many forms. Sometimes the goals of the task are unclear: 'I more or less manage things around here'. Sometimes, it is the way in which the goals must be attained: 'How you do it, doesn't interest me much. I don't even want to know, as long as you do it'. Sometimes also, it is a matter of insufficient feedback: 'Did it work out?' 'We'll know more in five years'. Other issues that can affect our effectiveness are a lack of clarity of responsibilities ('I think you should take this up with Peterson'. 'No, I must have you'.), appointments ('I told you it would be soon'), criteria for performances and quality ('You meant something like this?'), and so on.

- *Too many divergent responsibilities*. When a job implies too many divergent responsibilities, the result may be a decrease in effectiveness too. Such a job demands from us that we mentally change gear a lot, concerning both problems and people, do very different things, and keep many loose ends in our heads. Moreover, we never are ready, as each time, as if by itself, the next responsibility emerges, so that we cannot really relax and recover. Furthermore, the different responsibilities may interfere with each other from time to time, for example when the timely completion of the one makes the timely completion of the other impossible, and vice versa (a familiar problem for many secretaries).

- *Incompatible responsibilities*. A special case of divergent responsibilities is role conflict, or incompatible responsibilities. A familiar example is the position of the lower manager. Pleasing his superior by increasing production may evoke a conflict with his employees. This conflict is not only a matter of his employees not wanting to work harder, but they also may see him as the advocate of their interests. However, when our poor lower manager takes on that role, he risks a conflict with his management. Though a performance that is fully satisfactory to both parties will remain problematic, he has still been hired to do as good a job as he can.

20.4   THE WORK ENVIRONMENT: ORDERLINESS

Orderliness of the work environment has a physical component, as well as a behavioural or procedural one. Both components have to be 'in order', that is, both should be arranged in a way that makes them effective, i.e. contributing to the goal attainment inherent in our work. To that end, the environment should be relatively free of irrelevant elements that demand attention, and interfere with task performance. Being 'in order' implies also that the work environment should be relatively constant and stable, so that we can become fully familiar with it, and optimally attune to it. Of course, the individual differences in what comprises optimal orderliness are big.

The physical component of orderliness of our work environment involves its architecture and interior design, as well as the furniture, machinery and other equipment. Preferably, all gear is accessible and in the right places, ideally in a way that meets the priorities inherent in the task, so that at all times we can easily do what needs to be done, also when something goes wrong. When something breaks down, it should be repaired or replaced, so that all equipment is in a working condition. In addition, all gear must be well maintained and clean. Maintenance and cleaning imply that we actively and habitually have to reinstitute the order of the work environment: this order has to be 'reconstructed' and tidied, time after time.

Physical orderliness is often accentuated by emphasizing and marking distinctions and relations (Ashcraft & Scheflen, 1976; Kaplan & Kaplan, 1982). An example is grouping objects that belong together. Moreover, we can mark objects that belong together by giving them a common background, colour or label, or by enclosing them in some frame that functions as a visual border. We can also provide kindred objects with another marker such as a text, lines, thresholds, arrows, pictograms, special materials, special lettering and so on. With the help of these artefacts, we can highlight borders and points that need our special attention.

This kind of orderliness provides us with clear 'set points' of what is normal (Frijda, 1986), and facilitates the automatic intermittent scanning of the task environment for possible intrusions and disturbances. Intrusions and disturbances simply stand out more in this way. This effect is probably also one of the reasons why tidying and cleaning can have a pleasant centring effect: once finished, we have apparently tamed all irregularities and disturbances.

Such a stylized display of orderliness suggests that our environment is ruled by a plan that takes care of everything: apparently, everything goes as it is meant to go, for things are not in this kind of order by themselves. Such a display suggests the kind of control that excludes surprises. Some organizations even go further, and have designed everything in their own specific company style, in their 'own' colours, and with their own logo on all kinds of objects. Here too the message is clear: everything goes as it is meant to go, and we are on top of things.

As an orderly work environment draws no special attention, we hardly notice it. We can thus 'blindly' proceed with our tasks. Though every working environment needs some orderliness, it is logical to assume that especially difficult and complex tasks, as well as tasks with many unpredictable elements, profit most from an orderly and stable environment, because these tasks need more of our undivided attention.

Also, the physical lay-out must provide good physical work conditions, in the sense of lighting, sound, temperature, sitting comfort, effort in using the equipment, air quality and so on.

The relation between the physical environment and our habitual behaviour is of a dialectical nature: how we design our environment and how we behave mutually determine each other. So the way our workplace is designed very much determines how we walk, where we sit, as well as what we see, hear and feel there. The other way around, we design and furniture our workplace in a way that accommodates our preferred routines. We manufacture normality and everydayness in our life by continuously repeating ourselves, and by a strict discipline of attention (Schabracq, 2007). As we repeat ourselves in a remarkably strict, more or less ritualized way, our habitual behaviour becomes an all-important source of orderliness to ourselves, as well as to others.

20.4.1 Too Little Orderliness

Too little orderliness may seriously hamper our effectiveness, for example when several issues fight for our attention, making it impossible to attend to a single issue long enough to deal with it properly. Also too little orderliness can lead to all kinds of loose ends in our head, lines of action that just stop somewhere, and ambiguous, inconsistent and even downright conflicting cues for action, while things around us go wrong, are changed, still do not work and are changed again. Some people just love such a chaos, and are very good at it. To others, work degenerates into an endless succession of daily hassles (Kanner *et al.*, 1981), which destroy their effectiveness.

Too little orderliness can be found in all kinds of professional firms, stock exchanges, dealer rooms of merchant banks and in the media (TV studios and editorial offices of journals). Too little orderliness is often caused by change, for example in times of (successive) reorganizations and mergers, when the old rules are no longer applicable, while new ones still have to be developed. Moreover, in such cases there are all kinds of rumours about changes of jobs and departments, early retirements and lay-off, which easily usurp our attention. Too little orderliness may have diverse causes, which can reinforce each other also. We discuss some examples:

- *Dysfunctional work conditions.* If a work environment does not have appropriate lighting, temperature, auditory and olfactory conditions, as well as proper furniture and gear to do the job properly, it interferes with the proper division of attention for the tasks, which can disturb effective functioning. Such an environment signals that the organization is not 'in order', and does not care much for its employees. Something similar happens when we are annoyed by the dirtiness or disarray of our work environment.
- *Broken or ill-functioning tools and apparatus.* When a tool or apparatus that we need for our work does not function well, we can't go on with our task as planned, as long as it is not mended. This cannot only ruin our mood, but it obviously disrupts the effectiveness of our functioning as well.
- *Flexible workplace.* In order to make optimal use of the available workstations in offices where employees are only part-time present, some organizations use flexible workplaces. Apart from the fact that working at different workstations in itself can interfere with orderliness, not all places are equally appealing to everybody Also it happens sometimes that all stations are occupied. All of this may interfere with effective functioning.
- *Flexible working hours.* Flexible working hours can interfere with orderliness and effectiveness of our work in several ways. Apart from the interference with our daily rhythm, which influences our activation and alertness, flexible working hours can make it impossible to reach colleagues and staff we need to speak to do our job properly. Moreover, flexible working hours interfere with family life, and periodic leisure activities and pastimes. All of this becomes worse when the daily work is divided in parts with 'free' periods in between.

- *Being a member of a 'pool'.* Some organizations place support staff, such as secretaries, in a 'pool', to let them work for different people in different departments. This arrangement prevents them from acquiring any thorough knowledge about the tasks of each of these employees and departments. Installing such a pool leads to an undesirable annihilation of useful knowledge as well. Working in a pool can even mean that secretaries work every day for somebody else, without much possibility to properly finish a somewhat extended assignment. Working in a pool also prevents support staff from building appropriate relations with the people they work for. As a result, they only do the simplest of tasks for different employees, time after time, not using and developing their skills.
- A *starting or fast-growing organization.* In a starting organization, it is not unusual that everybody does everything. The same occurs in rapidly growing organizations. In both cases there is a lack of structure, standard procedures and specialized well-trained employees. As a result, everybody is terribly busy reinventing the wheel, while the speed at which the work is done is far from impressive.
- *High sick leave, turnover, or many temporary employees.* In an organization with high levels of sick leave, turnover or a high proportion of employees on temporary contracts, the employees with longer tenure are often exclusively busy filling holes, and putting out the most acute fires. In addition they have to break in new people, and hardly have time left to do their own work. Moreover, many of the newly trained employees leave after a short time, which makes the efforts of breaking them in rather meaningless. All these activities can have a cumulative adverse effect. Moreover, in an organization with high sick leave and turnover, more things tend to go wrong, as high sick leave and turnover can be considered as a case of choosing with one's feet.

20.4.2 Too Much Emphasis on Orderliness

When maintaining orderliness demands too much attention and turns into a goal in itself, it obscures the original goal, namely getting the actual task done. Sticking to time-consuming orderly procedures, with their checks and double checks, leads also to a severe limitation of what we are allowed to do. As a result, it interferes with the work effectiveness and efficiency, which manifests itself, for example, in problems of internal and external communication, 'political' relationships, slow decision making and stagnation of projects. These problems present themselves as unchangeable data, ruled by relentless and indifferent natural laws. To actually get something done can become next to impossible: too many rules, too many people who have to approve first, too long communication lines. This formalization may make it very hard to keep our attention focused on the task. This kind of orderliness occurs frequently in bureaucratic organizations, such as ministries and other public and semi-public organizations, but also in multinational companies and other organizations with a rigid hierarchy, such as military and paramilitary organizations, and some churches. The causes are obvious: too many rules and too strict a hierarchy with very precisely delineated communication lines and responsibilities.

People working in such organizations develop a good eye for rank, status symbols, movements up and down, and their possibilities and dangers. There is much political jargon, of a somewhat legalistic nature, some difficult words and little concrete content. This is also the language use of a permanent conspiracy, with its inherent suspicion and fear of outsiders. When outsiders ask an employee of such a bureaucratic organization – with whom they further relate quite well – a factual question about his work, the outsider often experiences a kind of 'praecox Gefühl', the feeling that it suddenly is impossible to make contact. This pre-war term was used as indication that the other person was suffering from 'dementia praecox', or schizophrenia, as it is now called (Grube, 2006).

At the individual level, too much orderliness leads to hiding of emotions and denial of problems. Too much orderliness is characterized by a ritual way of working, just going through the moves, following conventions, disapproving ostentatiously of deviations, without paying much attention to – or even disdaining – outcomes and results. Moreover, many colleagues are bored, and will not take any risks, afraid as they are to make a bad impression. Still they want everything to go their way, and such a system offers definite possibilities for this. Many people, however, eventually cannot stand such a way of working. They complain about high work load, and many suffer from alienation and aversive emotions. Because deviant moods and activation states are contagious (Schabracq, 1991), this may have a serious paralyzing effect.

20.5 THE WORK ENVIRONMENT: SOCIAL EMBEDDING

Work implies social relationships, that is, the relatively stable ways in which specific persons relate to each other. The forms of relations are of course determined by their history, but standardized cultural units and formats are used for their construction, while their development follows culturally determined scenarios. Within a relation we know more or less what the other party expects us to do, and to attend to, as well as what we may expect from him. As a result, relations are important in bringing about repetitiveness and stability into our work environment, which in its turn contributes to the work environment's orderliness.

First, there are the relations with the people with whom we relate regularly. These people form our social network. A good network is big enough, extends over different organizational levels and departments, and includes people from outside the organization, such as clients, suppliers, government representatives and fellow professionals. The network consists mostly of persons we more or less trust and like. The main outcome of a network consists of making everyday business manageable. As the interactions in most relations are often highly repetitive in character, such relations give us an opportunity to display a familiar repertoire of activity in those relations, in principle to make them as effective and pleasurable as possible. The development of and care for a network takes time and effort: to be optimally effective, relations need history.

As working together means sharing experiences, an important outcome of a social network is the opportunity for pleasant and meaningful contacts. Moreover, because we are in the same line of work, chances are that we have similar interests and hobbies, and even that we are of a likeminded nature, both conditions for getting along well. As a result, some relations grow into personal and even intimate ones (Hall, 1969). We find protectors, as well as favourite subordinates, colleagues and people elsewhere, with whom it is pleasurable to interact. No wonder that, when we lose or quit our job, the loss of these relations and their outcomes is often felt to be the most unpleasant consequence. The need for such relations also turns out to be one of the primary reasons to take on a job again at a later age (Krijnen, 1993).

The pleasant contacts inherent in such relations result in emotional support and a general sense of belonging, and can help to reduce tension and aversive emotions. This effect is brought about by entering the different kind of reality of just socializing, a time-out from the more stern and impersonal reality of work. Emotional support and sense of belonging probably are also a matter of exposing ourselves to emotional contagion (Schabracq, 1991), i.e. letting ourselves be 'infected' by the other's pleasant mood and livelihood, a phenomenon that Montaigne (1580/1981) had already described in the sixteenth century.

Apart from the pleasurable contacts, belonging to a team or group can be rewarding in itself. Doing things together and being part of a greater social system, forming a 'we', can be gratifying in itself. The fact that the others are there as well, and do their work too, also suggests that there is some meaning and logic to our presence and activities at the work site. Moreover, these other people usually are familiar to us, which adds to the predictability of our work environment, and by that to its orderliness. As it is, unfamiliar persons are habitually introduced, in a way that their presence becomes understandable and normal (Goffman, 1971, 1972).

Another outcome of a good network is that it enables us to get and give strategic information, warnings, advice, factual help, protection and feedback about our own performance and position. A good network also allows us to team up with other employees to fight our battles. All these outcomes make a well-developed social network important in controlling our work environment: our network determines – and is determined by, for that matter – our informal power position in the organization and its politics. This power position, its direct outcomes and the sense of control resulting from it are of considerable importance in keeping our functioning effective.

All in all, a well-developed social network helps us to develop an optimal freedom of acting, which enables us to focus on our work. Here too, however, when the social network becomes too important, and takes too much time, this interferes with the effectiveness of our work.

Being embedded in the organization as a whole in itself can also bring us important outcomes. The embedding gives us for example a consistent and continuous background that enables us to experience our presence in the organization as normal and real, and also adds to the orderliness of the work environment. The embedding too is a matter of continuous repetition, in this case of displaying 'normal' patterns of behaviour, and keeping up normal appearances, to show that nothing special is going on. Most of the time, this display entails conduct and appearance that is considered to be normal in the external environment of the organization too, though the display often is almost imperceptibly styled by the specific organization. By this conduct and appearance, we show how well socialized we are: we belong there and are true members, who can be trusted not to do anything irresponsible or unexpected. We actually can use the word 'we'.

By styling our behaviour and appearance, we also point tacitly to our place and function in the organization, as well as to the kind of relation we are in at the moment (Vrugt & Schabracq, 1991). This styling involves our body language, linguistic usage, clothing, hairdo and the use of accessories such as glasses, bags and jewellery. Though this styling usually is not explicitly worded, a transgression (wrong conduct, wrong clothes, wrong shoes) usually is obvious at once to all parties. By enacting prescribed conduct, we continuously supply each other, in a completely self-evident way, with the right cues to act in a self-evident way as well (Schabracq, 1991).

When something goes wrong, in the production process or in the social realm, we also have a standard repertoire to repair the normal state of affairs, and to restore orderliness. For example, when we are slipping, we may act as if everything is under control 'really', for example by smiling and pulling a funny face. Other examples are reassuring each other verbally that nothing serious has happened, or by explaining that these things do happen, are nobody's fault, and do not undermine the reality of our projects. Goffman (1971, 1972) presents a goldmine of other examples. In this way, our relations provide us with a continuous, highly redundant, but tacit series of situational or relational propositions about what is expected of us, and what we can expect from others (Watzlawick, Beavin & Jackson, 1968). This bombardment with situational proposals is so redundant and omnipresent that it suggests a solid reality, where everything is under control and nasty surprises are excluded. Harré (1979) speaks of 'social musak' ('musak' being the music in elevators and supermarkets that is supposed to soothe us into feeling at ease).

Another outcome of being embedded in organizational social relationships is that it serves us as a stage. Being embedded in an organization allows us to use our work to show off highly valued work-related qualities, such as professional skills, diligence, collegiality, persistence, sense of humour, courage and creativity. We can even use the organization as a theatre to be good in general. The terms 'stage' and 'theatre' are not accidental here. An organization offers more distance and privacy than a family, a bigger audience, as well as more off-stage opportunities and time for preparation. We can use our work in this way to develop and demonstrate a beautiful 'public' character of a more general kind. This 'self-expression' also may have offshoots in wider circles. At least it is good exercise material.

20.5.1   Too Little Social Embedding

Too little social embedding implies that we must work without some or all outcomes of that embedding, such as pleasurable contacts, belonging to a group, a comfortable, informal power position, a solid social reality and a stage to perform. Without these outcomes, many people find it hard to focus on their work, and they become less effective, especially when that task is not interesting in itself, or doesn't have other outcomes they highly value. Many people, moreover, experience isolation, and the anonymity resulting from it as unpleasant. As it is, the social relations at work are to many people the main reason to come to work every day.

The sudden loss of a part of this embedding often is very painful and is experienced as a life event, that is, an event that unsettles our fixed ways of doing things and paying attention, and demands a new adaptation from us. As a result, such a loss of social embedding may interfere with our effectiveness. This may be a matter of our own departure from our department or organization, as well as of the disappearance of other people. Such a loss may evoke grief and alienation, just as in the case of the loss of a loved one. A lack or loss of social embedding can have very diverse causes. We give the following examples:

- *Lack of feedback, appreciation and support.* Many employees get little feedback, appreciation and support from their manager. This may be a matter of their manager's poor social skills and being busy with other things. In many organization, however, such a lack is part of the organizational culture. There feedback is only given about things that go wrong. This lack of feedback, appreciation and support may be of negative influence on our motivation, and by that on our effectiveness.
- *Role transitions.* Examples of role transitions in an organization are entry, job change, dismissal, retirement and work disability. Of course, these various transitions greatly differ, also in the degree in which they go together with impairment of functioning. However, in all cases we have to part from a certain position, its activities and its social relations. How this parting is experienced varies, depending on the specific nature of the transition, the degree to which it is voluntary, and the person involved. It can be experienced as a serious loss, with all inherent emotions (e.g. Allen & Van der Vliert, 1984), which interfere with the effectiveness, but it can also be felt as a relief. In general, impending transitions interfere with the effectiveness of functioning in the last stage of the old job. In the case of retirement, this last stage may take many years, the phenomenon of 'getting in lane' (Henkens & Van Solinge, 2003), characterized by rejecting training programmes, and letting go.
- *Decay of social networks.* The social networks of elderly employees tend to decay. The people who hired them, their patrons and sponsors have left. Gradually, almost all their favourite, familiar colleagues, superiors, assistants and outside contacts also disappear from sight too. Moreover, older employees often are not inclined to actively fill up the empty spaces, as they tend to be more reserved than the younger ones in this respect (Winnubst & Schabracq, 1996). This implies that elderly employees must abandon an important part of the outcomes of such a network, which can seriously interfere with their effectiveness.
- *Massive layoff.* When an organization slims down – which happens a lot lately – and lays off or outsources many employees, those who stay behind experience the problems mentioned above to an intensified degree. Moreover, such a course of affairs can lead to feelings of unpleasantness and guilt ('What have we done to be still working here?'). Also, the people who stay are likely to lose their trust in the organization's intentions. This so-called survivors' sickness (Kets de Vries & Balazs, 1997) diminishes employees' commitment and motivation, and, by that, their effectiveness.

- *Physical barriers that impede social contact.* Physical barriers can cause social isolation. An example is the lonely position of a crane driver high above his mates. Noise, or the protection against noise, which makes it impossible to have a conversation, is another example. A third one is the work cubicle, the crude partitioning device to subdivide a larger room, which has become widely known from the *Dilbert* strips. Especially in simple work – in which personal contacts are all important for work satisfaction – such physical hindrances can needlessly impair work satisfaction and motivation.

- *Communication problems between the top and the work floor.* Social isolation at the top of the organization is a serious problem. Apart from interfering with the effectiveness of the manager in question, it harms the quality of the organizational communication in general, both bottom-up ('The management hasn't a clue about what we are doing here, and it seems a good idea to keep it that way') and top-down ('Some things you cannot explain to them; they just don't get it'). The causes differ. On the one hand, some managers think it unwise to interact openly with employees because of their possible hidden agendas. Often this is a manager's defence against the greater attention that employees pay to their manager (see Section 20.5.2). On the other hand, employees tend to feel fearful and unwelcome. Moreover, groups that have incompatible interests often perceive each other in a distorted way, and entertain prejudices and stereotypes about each other. Lastly, both parties can usually improve their social skills considerably. This kind of poor communication and the resulting poor management negatively affect the effectiveness of everyday working life.

- *A climate of distrust and conflicts.* A climate of distrust and conflicts results in contacts remaining limited to the few people we trust, so that we can become rather isolated. A similar outcome may occur in an organization with too much orderliness.

20.5.2   Too Much Social Embedding

Here, we focus on forms of social embedding that demand too much conscious attention from us, which goes at the expense of doing our actual work properly.

- *Lack of privacy.* A good example of lack of privacy is to be found in so-called office gardens. Apart from being aggravating and distracting in its own right, this lack of privacy may lead to self-consciousness, embarrassment and even anxiety of failure. A special case of lack of privacy involves being exposed to stressed and highly emotional colleagues, which can be highly contagious and disturb the effectiveness of our functioning (Schabracq, 1991).

- *A too person-oriented organizational culture.* In some organizational cultures, it is usual to share all life's joys and sorrows with each other, both work-related and private ones. This mutual self-disclosure may easily interfere with the appropriate division of attention needed for work, and hamper our effectiveness. This interference especially occurs when people are very busy, or when failing to pay attention to our colleagues is interpreted as being unkind.

- *Unbalanced social exchange – getting more than we give.* Getting much more attention and feeling than we give is part of the fate of 'stars'. As a result, their everyday reality has become much larger than life, while, as human beings, they are able to cope only with a normally sized life. For many 'stars', this dilemma interferes with the manageability of their everyday work situations, especially when they believe in their extraordinary status, which is more likely to happen to somebody with poor self-esteem. This variant of unbalance is by the way an important theme in literature (the Greek dramas, Shakespeare, etc.), as well as in the popular media.

- *Continuously changing social settings.* Having to work all the time in different and changing teams or projects, with different managers and diverse people, with divergent priorities and competencies, can interfere with our effectiveness. This interference occurs for example a lot in matrix organizations or consulting firms. In a multinational organization, this may also be a matter of working in different countries, with people from diverse cultural and linguistic backgrounds. A seemingly simpler variant of this in a relatively stable work environment is getting a new manager.

20.6 THE WORK ENVIRONMENT: COMPATIBILITY OF CONVICTIONS, VALUES AND GOALS

Employees and organizations both have their convictions, values and goals, and, in a sense, the same applies to our organizations. As long as our personal convictions, values and goals are compatible with the organizational ones, which usually is the case, they jointly determine and shape our everyday work and relationships. Sometimes, however, they are not compatible, and this then interferes with our effectiveness. To give some idea of the issues that may give rise to incompatibilities of organizational convictions and our own ones, we give the following (not fully mutually exclusive) examples:

- What the organization is about, its reason for being there, its goals.
- How the organization should relate to its environment.

- What the constituent parts of the organization are, and how these parts should relate to each other.
- What we talk about and attend to in the organization, or more simply: what 'really' exists, and what 'does not exist'. This has all kinds of implications for what we can and may do, think and say.
- What is good and what is bad in the organization: the organizational virtues and sins, and their relative importance.
- How power is divided and exercised.
- How the organization sees, values and treats its employees, and the relevant categories and criteria here.
- How the members of the organization are expected to relate to each other.
- The commitment, effort and productivity that are expected.

Generally speaking, a good fit on the above issues is an important factor in the effectiveness of a work environment, as it allows us to do our work in a self-evident way. From our individual perspective, a good fit means also that we can to a sufficient degree accomplish our personal goals in and by our work. The compatibility of personal and organizational convictions, values and goals usually comes about rather organically. First, organizations and potential employees select each other. Then the employees who have been selected are socialized, that is, they learn about and accept the organizational convictions and values. In the longer run, acceptation turns into identification, and the organizational convictions and values become their own. The people who don't fit in often go away by themselves, or are dismissed (Schneider, 1987), which, of course, doesn't exclude all individual problems.

20.6.1   Too Little Compatibility of Convictions, Values and Goals

It has become clear that too little compatibility between our own and the organizational convictions and values leads to poor effectiveness. Here, some descriptions of specific causes of too little compatibility are described:

- *Organizational change.* Often incompatibility of convictions, values and goals arises when organizations change radically, for example by a reorganization, merger, privatization or the appointment of a new manager. Goals as greater quantity of production, more flexibility and being more client-directed can become prominent, while values such as technical perfection and professional freedom can lose their dominant role. However, the latter two may have been for us the very reason to work there. The change then leaves us with work that has been stripped of many of its challenges and meaning. Some of these changes are especially relevant for employees over 50.

The most important problem with many organizational changes, especially for employees over 50, is that many of these changes go against what the organizations expected of these employees previously. During their working life, many older employees have effectively unlearned to act in the way the organization now asks from them. Organizations nowadays have to become flatter, as well as more flexible, transparent, less product- and more market-oriented, etc. The principal consequence is that employees have to become more autonomous, decisive and creative: they have to act as if they were 'internal entrepreneurs', who work for themselves, and not for an organization owned by other people. To some people – especially some older employees –however, the formula 'be free and make us rich' is absurd. Moreover, older employees often have learned, mostly the hard way, to mistrust management intentions. Stories about employability and the disappearance of lifetime employment do not improve things.

- *Discrepancy between 'espoused theory' and 'theory in use'.* Another issue of incompatible convictions and values is usually more problematic to younger employees than to older ones, namely the problems that may arise when the organization is ambiguous about its own convictions and values. This ambiguity is mostly a matter of depicting a much nicer image of its own convictions and values – the 'espoused theory' – than the convictions and values that determine the actual everyday reality – the 'theory in use' (Schon, 1983). When newcomers innocently identify with the nicer image, which even can be the reason why they come to work there, they are bound for trouble.

20.6.2   Too Much Compatibility of Values and Goals

- *Giving more than we get.* When we embrace organizational or job values and goals too intensely, we cannot say no to requests that appeal to these values or goals. When we for example fully identify with the values and goals of nursing or social work, it becomes very difficult to turn down a request for help from a client. Instead, we see responding to the request as our calling, and tend to take on more and more. Being unable to say no to our work can also be a matter of liking that work very much, and being very good at it. As a result, people bite off more than they can chew, even to the extent that they do little else, and their effectiveness diminishes. All these forms of imbalance can be characterized as 'giving more than we get', the mirror image of 'getting more than we give', or stardom. Younger employees, who have not yet learned to develop and guard their own limits, are, on average, more susceptible to this imbalance than older employees.

In the long run, giving more than we get can result in burnout (Schaufeli & Buunk, 2003), and all kinds of physical complaints such as ME and RSI. These complaints can be characterized as functional, that is, these complaints incapacitate us so much that they effectively take us out of the situation that caused them. The impersonal, and sometimes even antisocial, demeanour characteristic of burnout can be seen as an awkward form of self-protection against the tendency to give much more than we get.

20.7   INTERVENTIONS

Reading the text of this chapter[5] is a good preparation for workshops to improve the effectiveness of teams and departments. Such a workshop is facilitated by one or, preferably, two change agents. The participants of a workshop are members of a team, or department, including the team or department manager. The maximum group size lies somewhere around 16 persons. For bigger groups a system of representation is used, in which each workshop participant represents one or two colleagues. Representing others then implies that the person who represents one or two other persons goes through step 7 (to be described later in this section) with the people he represents.

The everyday reality of the work floor here is the point of departure. The approach consists of mapping the main sources of ineffectiveness within the team and department, finding out about the causes of these sources and their mutual relations, devising as many solutions as possible, determining the best solutions, implementing these solutions, and monitoring and improving these solutions. This approach encompasses the following steps.

1. The members of the organization individually read the text of this chapter, about the sources of ineffectiveness.
2. Each member then composes a top five of sources of ineffectiveness in his own team or department.
3. If possible, all the data can be assembled and then analysed with the help of some basic statistics and data-mining techniques. This can give the change agents some insights in the most relevant causes of ineffectiveness. This step can be very helpful, but is not strictly necessary.

---

[5] In Schabracq (2007) checklists are to be found that correspond with the abovementioned factors of ineffectiveness, which can be used as an appropriate tool in this respect.

4. The change agents interview key representatives of the team or department. The information generated by step 3 can be used as point of departure. If this information is not available, the personal top five of the key representative in question serves as point of departure. The interviewer tries to surface underlying causes of the sources of ineffectiveness, as well as relevant assumptions and goals. Steps 3 and 4 are meant as a preparation for the change agents, which may also help them to custom-tailor the workshop.

5. The workshop will take one day part to two whole days. Separate day parts can be used to work out particular issues. The workshop takes place in a place outside the organization, with good catering and, if needed, sleeping facilities, where the members are not disturbed by other stakeholders.

6. The workshop starts with a short discussion of the text by the change agent(s), and answering all possible questions about the text.

7. The members of the workshop divide themselves in groups of three or four, and discuss their top fives for 45 to 60 minutes, to find a common top five of sources of ineffectiveness.

8. The subgroups reassemble, and their top fives are pooled on a whiteboard or flip-over. A number one gets five points, a number two four, and so on. The points of similar or the same sources of ineffectiveness are added. The intention is to pool sources, to come to as small as possible number of sources of ineffectiveness arranged in order of importance.

9. The causes of the different sources of ineffectiveness and their relations are examined by the whole group. A good rule of thumb here is the Pareto principle, i.e.: 20% of the causes accounts for 80% of the effects.

10. The workshop first examines what can be done about the most important source of ineffectiveness and its causes. Then the next important one is discussed, and so on. The intention is to find as many interventions per source of ineffectiveness, and their causes.

11. The next step consists of combining solutions, looking for better, more pleasant and more intelligent solutions and testing their feasibility and practical value. Team members can implement some of these solutions themselves. Other solutions demand actions of a manager, an HR officer or an external consultant.

12. The team or department divides the responsibilities for each of the actions over the different members. This is primarily a matter of voluntarily taking responsibility for a certain activity.

13. For each action, a time path is developed with sub-goals and deadlines. Essentially this involves each time the who, what and when.

14. A date is set for the next meeting. Each of the members agrees to keep track of everything that goes wrong, or not completely right, and

promises to think of solutions for these issues. These problems and solutions subsequently are the input for the next session.

15. During the next sessions the change agents are doing the facilitating as well, but remain more in the background, while the manager is now the facilitator.

16. The next step can then consist of the change agents coaching the manager.

The essence of this approach is inciting the team and department members to solve their own problems, creating support and a platform for their solutions in the process. In practice, the main problems to be solved here usually are communicational and planning problems. Important underlying causes often lie in the area of ethics. Important issues are responsibility, honesty, courage, fairness and justice.

REFERENCES

Allen, V.L. & Vliert, E. Van Der (Eds) (1984). *Role Transitions*. New York: Plenum Press.

Antonovsky, A. (1987). *Unraveling the Mystery of Health. How People Manage Stress and Stay Well*. San Francisco: Jossey-Bass.

Ashcraft, N. & Scheflen, A.E. (1976). *People Space*. Garden City, NY: Anchor Press/Doubleday.

De Bono, E. (1990). *I am Right, You are Wrong*. London: Mica Management Resources.

Frijda, N.H. (1986). *The Emotions*. Cambridge: Cambridge University Press.

Goffman, E. (1971). *Relations in Public*. New York: Harper & Row.

Goffman, E. (1972). *Interaction Ritual*. Harmondsworth: Penguin.

Grube, M. (2006). Towards an empirically based validation of intuitive diagnostic: Rumke's 'praecox feeling' across the schizophrenia spectrum: preliminary results. *Psychopathology*, **39**, 209–17.

Hall, E.T. (1969). *The Hidden Dimension*. Garden City, NY: Doubleday.

Harré, R. (1979). *Social Being*. Oxford: Blackwell.

Henkens, K. & van Solinge, H. (2003). *Het eindspel [The Endgame]*. Assen/Den Haag: Van Gorcum/SMS.

Kanner, A.D., Coyne, J.C., Schaefer, C. & Lazarus, R.S. (1981). Comparison of two modes of stress management: daily hassles and uplifts versus major life events. *Journal of Behavioral Medicine*, **4**, 1–39.

Kaplan, S. & Kaplan, R. (1982). *Cognition and Environment*. New York: Praeger.

Kets de Vries, M.F.R. & Balazs, K. (1997). The downside of downsizing. *Human Relations*, **50**, 11–50.

Krijnen, M.A. (1993). *Onderzoek WAO-Instroom 1991, AH-Operations [Study Influx Disablement Insurance Act 1991, AH-Operations]*. Amsterdam: UvA.

Maturana, H.R. & Varela, F.J. (1980). *Autopoiesis and Cognition.* Dordrecht: D. Reidel.

Montaigne, M. (1580/1981). *Essays.* Harmondsworth: Penguin.

Moscovici, S. (1984). The phenomenon of social representation. In R.M. Farr & S. Moscovici (Eds), *Social Representations* (pp. 3–69). Cambridge: Cambridge University Press.

Schabracq, M.J. (1991). *De inrichting van de werkelijkheid* [*The Design of Reality*]. Amsterdam/Assen: Boom.

Schabracq, M.J. (2003). Everyday well-being and stress in work and organizations. In M.J. Schabracq, J.A.M. Winnubst & C.L. Cooper (Eds), *Handbook of Work and Health Psychology* (2nd edn, pp. 9–36). Chichester: John Wiley & Sons, Ltd.

Schabracq, M.J. (2007). *Changing Organizational Culture. The Change Agents' Guidebook.* Chichester: John Wiley & Sons, Ltd.

Schabracq, M.J. & Cooper, C.L. (2001). *Stress als keuze [Stress as a Choice].* Schiedam NL: Scriptum.

Schabracq, M.J. & Cooper, C.L. (2003). To be me or not to be me. About alienation. *Counselling Psychology Quarterly,* **16**, 53–79.

Schaufeli, W.B. & Buunk, A.P. (2003). Burnout. In M.J. Schabracq, J.A.M. Winnubst & C.L. Cooper (Eds), *Handbook of Work and Health Psychology* (2nd edn, pp. 383–425). Chichester: John Wiley & Sons, Ltd.

Schneider, B. (1987). The people make the place. *Personnel Psychology,* **40**, 437–53.

Schon, D. (1983). *The Reflective Practitioner.* New York: Basic Books.

Vrugt, A. & Schabracq, M.J. (1991). *Vanzelfsprekend gedrag [Behavior that Speaks for Itself].* Amsterdam/Assen: Boom.

Watzlawick, P., Beavin, J.H. & Jackson, D.D. (1968). *Pragmatics of Human Communication.* London: Faber & Faber.

Winnubst, J.A.M. & Schabracq, M.J. (1996) Social support, stress, and organization. In M.J. Schabracq, J.A.M. Winnubst & C.L. Cooper (Eds), *Handbook of Work and Health Psychology* (2nd edn, pp. 87–102). Chichester: John Wiley & Sons, Ltd.

CHAPTER 21

Epilogue

Cary L. Cooper
Lancaster University, UK
James Campbell Quick
The University of Texas at Arlington, USA
and
Marc J. Schabracq
Human Factor Development, The Netherlands

21.1 A MORE POSITIVE FUTURE

While there are concerns and issues in the domain of work and health psychology as we expressed in the opening chapter for this third edition of the *Handbook*, there are positive advances emerging as well. Hence, we see a more positive future (Cartwright & Cooper, 2008). Along this line, Macik-Frey, Quick and Nelson (2007) identify four of these positive advances in the broad domain of occupational health. These are: positive health, leadership, mood and emotion, and intervention. Here we touch on the first three of these issues, reserving the issue of interventions for Section 21.3 as the conclusion of the chapter.

21.1.1 Positive Health

Seligman and Csikszentmihalyi (2000) have led psychology towards a more positive future with their call for positive psychology as the science of positive subjective experience. Included in positive psychology's mission is the need to focus on both human strengths and positive institutions. This mission of positive psychology compliments the other two missions of psychology, which are to prevent problems and to repair damage. The latter mission is manifest in therapy and therapeutic intervention. Nelson and Cooper (2007)

International Handbook of Work and Health Psychology, Third Edition. Edited by Cary L. Cooper, James Campbell Quick, and Marc J. Schabracq.

extend this new science of positive psychology with their inclusive view of positive organizational behaviour (POB), a concept first framed by Luthans and set forth by him in their collected volume (Luthans, Youssef & Avolio 2007). Their view includes states, traits and processes. Positive health and positive psychology are making their way into work environments through their extensions in positive organizational behaviour, thus reshaping work and health psychology.

21.1.2 Positive Leadership

Leadership itself can be a positive and constructive force in work environments, with health leaders serving as primary prevention agents for tens, hundreds and thousands of employees in organizations. These positive leaders display integrity and courage while making a positive impact on the work done within their domains of influence (Quick, Macik-Frey & Cooper, 2007). This is authentic and emotionally competent leadership that lifts and leads rather than driving and abusing. Authentic leaders express their true selves while displaying hope, optimism and confidence. Great leaders move us and they devote themselves in compassionate ways to the well-being, development and advancement of their followers. This stands in contrast to the Neanderthal leaders who exploit workers, are ultimately self-centred and focus only on self-serving personal gain and blind ambition.

21.1.3 Positive Emotions

Nelson and Cooper (2007) include several chapters that address emotions and psychological well-being in their work. It is not possible to come to work without bringing one's hopes, dreams, aspirations and deep emotions as well. Positively healthy work environments harness human emotion in ways to fulfil the individual and move the organization forward for productive gain. Even emotions that are sometimes identified as negative, such as anger, can be turned to positive gain at work. There are times and places when justifiable anger and outrage warrant appropriate and targeted action to right wrongs and correct injustices. The failure to act in those times and places is a failure of integrity, a failure of courage and a failure of heart. However, anger is one of those emotions that may alternatively be harmful and do damage in the workplace. Therefore, it is most appropriate to experience compassion, have the ability to seek and offer forgiveness when wrongs have been done, and aim to bring out the very best in the persons with whom we work. Rather than focusing exclusively on their actions and behaviours, our call should be to seek to know their intentions and what is truly in their hearts. Only when we truly know the person can we act in constructive and positive ways that bring out the best in them, and in ourselves.

21.2 PSYCHOLOGICALLY HEALTHY WORKPLACES

Macik-Frey, Quick and Nelson (2007) suggest that occupational health psychology emerged from preventive medicine, psychology and engineering with the aim of either preventing health problems in organizations or helping to repair the damage, some of which inevitably occurs. As we have noted above, prevention and treatment (i.e., repairing damage) are only two of the missions of psychology. The emergent third mission of psychology is to build upon strength factors, which is the domain of positive psychology as we have traced it in the positive advances noted in Section 21.1. In this vein the psychologically healthy workplace initiatives in the United States emerged from the cooperative agreement between the National Institute for Occupational Safety and Health and the American Psychological Association. Macik-Frey *et al.* (2009) present a framework for psychologically healthy workplaces based on a critical review of the research literature. The key issues within this framework are health workplace practices, employee well-being and organizational improvements. Underpinning this framework is a set of four guiding principles of organizational health that were originally set forth by Adkins, Quick and Moe (2000). These principles are:

1. Health exists on a continuum of mortality to vibrant well-being.
2. Organizational health is a continuous process, not an obtainable state.
3. Health is systemic in nature and results from interconnections of multiple factors.
4. Organizational health relies on fulfilling relationships that are achieved through communication, collaboration and relationship-building actions.

The PATH (Practices for Achievement of Total Health) model is briefly summarized below. The PATH model originates in healthy workplace practices, which are proposed to positively impact both employee well-being and organizational improvements. Please see Macik-Frey *et al.* (2009) for a full set of original references and details on the development and presentation of the model. The model provides for the interaction of employee well-being and organizational improvements, the two outcome variables.

21.2.1   Healthy Workplace Practices

The PATH model identifies five categories of healthy workplace practices: work–life balance, employee growth and development, health and safety, recognition, and employee involvement. The authors briefly explore each of these categories of practices, which are designed to have specific and varied positive impacts upon employee well-being and organizational improvement.

21.2.2   Employee Well-Being

Employee well-being represents the physical, mental and emotional facets of employee health, though there is no general agreement on the best indicators of it. The authors provide an array of indicators in their PATH model, which are: physical health, mental health, stress, motivation, commitment, job satisfaction, morale and climate.

21.2.3   Organizational Improvements

The PATH model proposes specific organizational improvement outcomes that result from healthy organizations. The authors note eight illustrative organizational improvements in this statement of the model. They are: competitive advantage, performance and productivity, reduced absenteeism and turnover, reduced accident and injury rates, increased cost savings, hiring selectivity, improved service and product quality, and better customer service and satisfaction.

21.3   INTERVENTIONS

Lest we paint an overly positive picture of work and health psychology, a caveat is in order. Over the years, the editors of the *Journal of Occupational Health Psychology* and others have called for intervention studies to validate the theories and practices in our disciplinary domain. We continue to be concerned with the relatively few research studies that have emerged despite these calls for well-designed intervention studies. The narrower field of health psychology alone does have a set of individual intervention studies that cover a range of specific and individual therapeutic interventions. However, we need more and different studies. The notion of organizational therapy which Edgar Schein and Manfred Ketz de Vries talked about in the late 1990s never caught on. So, maybe we need to create more of a bridge between the domains of work and health psychology with that of organizational development.

True, there has been considerable knowledge accumulated concerning risk factors in organizations, along with their connections to occupational illnesses and injuries, but comparably less is known about effective interventions for reducing the risk factors. Reviews of the intervention literature have produced disappointing results. Health promotion programmes, along with other occupational health and safety interventions as a whole, have not demonstrated sustained changes in employee behaviours. It should be recognized that researchers face challenges in studying interventions, and that control group designs and randomization are not often possible. And, interventions are often guided by practical considerations, rather than being informed by theory.

Additionally, it is true that interventions evolve and change once they are implemented. Consider, for example, the history of health circles used in Germany which were adapted from quality circles and other employee participation approaches. Health circles operate on the assumption that employees are in the best position to improve their own job conditions (Macik-Frey, Quick & Nelson, 2007). They evolved from simple research projects focused on changing work conditions (risk factors) to comprehensive programmes that are now commonly used to enhance employees' health. A typical health circle process takes 15 months to complete, including a health report and survey, multiple health circle meetings and evaluation. Originally health circles only included employees, but some companies now use separate health circles for managers.

To end on a positive note, we do need to build on the emergence of the positive science of strength factors and well-being. There is now an accumulating body of research evidence about such individual strength factors as self-reliance, resilience, vigour, engagement and hope. These strength factors have been linked to individual health outcomes. The natural next step is to go into workplaces and design and then test and examine ways to enhance these strengths for collective health and well-being. These interventions should then be evaluated, well-designed, scientific studies. We need both great practical science and great scientific practice – they go together like a hand in a glove. Care should be taken to address the level of change intended (individual and/or organizational). As just mentioned, many studies have focused on the individual as the target of change, and have shown that individual-level interventions alone may not enhance health if the organization does not change too. The concept of healthy organizations means that along with profits and productivity, the collective well-being of employees is an important outcome.

REFERENCES

Adkins, J.A., Quick, J.C. & Moe, K.O. 2000. Building world class performance in changing times. In L.R. Murphy & C.L. Cooper (Eds), *Healthy and Productive Work: An International Perspective* (pp. 107–32). Philadelphia: Taylor & Francis.

Cartwright, S. & Cooper, C.L. (2008). *The Oxford Handbook of Organizational Well-Being*. Oxford: Oxford University Press.

Luthans, F., Youssef, C. & Avolio, B.J. (2007). Psychological capital: investing and developing positive organizational behavior. In D.L. Nelson & C.L. Cooper (2007). *Positive Organizational Behavior*. Thousand Oaks, CA: Sage.

Macik-Frey, M., Quick, J.C. & Nelson, D.L. (2007). Advances in occupational health: from a stressful beginning to a positive future. *Journal of Management*, **33**, 809–40.

Macik-Frey, M., Quick, J.D., Quick, J.C. & Nelson, D.L. (2009). Occupational health psychology: from preventive medicine to psychologically healthy workplaces. In A-S.G. Antoniou, C.L. Cooper, G.P. Chrousos, C.D. Spielberger & M.W. Eysenck (Eds), *Handbook of Managerial Behavior and Occupational Health* (pp. 3–19). Edward Elgar Publishers.

Nelson, D.L. & Cooper, C.L. (2007). *Positive Organizational Behavior*. Thousand Oaks, CA: Sage.

Quick, J.C., Macik-Frey, M. & Cooper, C.L. (2007). Managerial dimensions of organizational health: the healthy leader at work. *Journal of Management Studies*, **44**, 189–205.

Seligman, M.E.P. & Csikszentmihalyi, M. (2000). Positive psychology. *American Psychologist*, **55**, 5–14.

Index

International Handbook of Work and Health Psychology, Third Edition. Edited by Cary L. Cooper, James Campbell Quick, and
Marc J. Schabracq.
© 2009 John Wiley & Sons, Ltd. Published 2015 by John Wiley & Sons, Ltd.